Mathematical Models in the
Social and Behavioral Sciences

MATHEMATICAL MODELS IN THE SOCIAL AND BEHAVIORAL SCIENCES

ANATOL RAPOPORT

Institute for Advanced Studies
Vienna, Austria

A Wiley-Interscience Publication

JOHN WILEY & SONS

New York   Chichester   Brisbane   Toronto   Singapore

Library of Congress Cataloging in Publication Data

Rapoport, Anatol, 1911–
  Mathematical models in the social and behavioral
sciences.

  Translation: Mathematische Methoden in den
Sozialwissenschaften.
  "A Wiley-Interscience publication."
  Includes index.
  1. Social sciences—Mathematical models. I. Title.
H61.25.R3613 1983   300′.724   82-20114
ISBN 0-471-86449-8 (pbk.)

Printed in the United States of America

10 9 8 7 6 5 4 3 2 1

Preface

This book, first published in German (*Mathematische Methoden in den Sozial-wissenschaften*, Würzburg: Physica-Verlag, 1980), grew out of courses I gave as guest professor at the Institute for Advanced Studies in Vienna. Quantitative and mathematical approaches to the social sciences are incorporated both in the teaching curriculum and in the research approaches of that institution. However, the very fact that these approaches are specifically mentioned in the description of the Institute's program attests to the circumstance that these methods are still not generally regarded as indispensable in the development of the social sciences as they obviously are regarded in the development of the physical sciences. For this reason, a deliberate orientation of the social sciences toward quantification and mathematization still requires justification.

The most widely accepted justifications of any approach are those based on pragmatic expectations. So it has been with the natural sciences, which enjoy social support in proportion to their contributions to control over the natural environment, affluence, power, and so on. Can the social sciences aspire to a similar status on similar grounds? If so, can this status be achieved by transplanting the spectacularly successful mathematical methods of theory construction from their natural habitat in the physical sciences to the soil of social science? If, on the other hand, the triumphal unfolding of mathematized theory cannot be duplicated in the social sciences, is there some other justification for infusing mathematical ways of thinking into the social sciences?

While teaching courses with the explicit goal of inculcating mathematical concepts and reasoning into thinking about social phenomena, I was constantly confronted with such questions. Quality and effectiveness of teaching depend in large measure on the motivation of the students. The courses on which this book is based were given in the late 1960s and in the 1970s, mostly to young Austrians seeking postgraduate training in sociology or political science and to students already equipped with some mathematical skills and seeking to apply them outside the conventional fields such as the physical sciences or technology. Of these students, only about 15% continued their careers in academic pursuits, where they could apply what they learned by simply teaching it to *their* students. The majority sought (and usually found) positions in public or private sectors of the Austrian economy or as "professional" sociologists, political scientists, or statisticians in public administration bodies. For this reason, whatever purely intellectual interest these young people had in the input or impact of mathematics in the social sciences stemmed from already existing personal predilections. The maintenance of the interest depended on the strength of these predilections, not on reinforcements of specific career requirements. Such leanings toward and appreciation of mathematical ways of thinking were frequently manifested in students in the Mathematics and Computer Science Department of the Institute but seldom by those in the two social science departments (sociology and political science). For most of these young people, the raison d'être of the social sciences was the betterment of society, and "relevance" was an instantaneous litmus test for taking an idea seriously or dismissing it. A strong "antipositivist" bias was coupled with this attitude. To the extent that it found articulate expression, it was embodied in a conviction that the "methods of natural science," in particular, the primacy of "objective" data, quantification of observations, mathematical deduction, and so on, are in principle inapplicable in the social sciences, and attempts to force the latter into the mold of the natural sciences would serve to sterilize them or, worse, put them at the service of ossified privilege or antihuman forces. Thus since acquaintance with quantitative and mathematical methods in the social sciences was required of all social science students at the Institute, some answers to these misgivings had to be incorporated in any purposeful teaching of these approaches.

In America, the problem of justification is different, almost an opposite one, as it were. There the "positivistic" approaches to the behavioral sciences proliferated luxuriantly and found wide acceptance, and with them mathematical modeling came into its own. Questions of "relevance" are raised more often in the technocratic vein. Will mathematization of the social sciences, following the path blazed by the physical sciences, render social events more controllable and so help close the gap between our mastery of the physical environment and our helplessness in the face of social forces? Since this English version of the book is addressed also to American readers, some answers to questions of this sort have to be given.

In deciding to face these questions (as has been said, for pedagogical reasons), I clearly did not intend to "sell" mathematization of the behavioral sciences to either ideologically or technocratically oriented students on their own terms. For that matter, no convincing case can be made on the basis of contemporary contributions of mathematical approaches to the social sciences that anything resembling the magnificent edifice of the physical sciences is being constructed. The emancipation of humans from the blind forces of history is not in the making. From the numerous examples in this book (a fairly representative sample reflecting the state of the art), it should be clear that mathematical modeling in the social sciences is a highly opportunistic venture. Not what seems especially important for the solution of pressing social problems but rather what seems to fit into a mathematical model is usually chosen for "applying" mathematical methods worked out previously in an abstract context.

This book is offered as an attempt to demonstrate the *integrative* function of the mathematical mode of cognition. It was my hope that once this integrative function is appreciated, the questions posed by ideological or pragmatic demands will be seen in a different light. Thus the goal pursued in this book is that of restructuring habits of thinking about social phenomena. The advantages of this restructuring cannot be seen clearly in advance; they can be appreciated only after the restructuring has taken place. Here I can state only the grounds for my own faith in the beneficial effects of mathematical thinking. Mathematics is the lingua franca of all science because it is contentless. Whenever a scientific theory can be represented and developed in mathematical language, it is thereby related to all other theories formulated and developed in that language. If the ideal of the "unity of science" bridging both diverse contents and cultural differences can be achieved at all, this will be done via mathematization.

This book is structured to emphasize this integrative function of mathematics. The principal theme of each part is a class of mathematical tools (models or methods) rather than a content area. In this way, the different areas of social science encompassed by mathematical analogies come into unified focus. Models based on differential equations deal with changes in the sex composition of human populations (Chapter 1), with contagion processes (Chapter 2), or with arms races (Chapter 3). Essentially the same stochastic model represents certain aspects of social mobility (Chapter 10), certain demographic dynamics (Chapter 11), and suggests forecasts of the recruitment needs of an organization (Chapter 9). Set theoretic language provides the conceptual framework for a rigorous analysis of certain types of conflict resolution—for example, those modeled by cooperative games (Chapter 19)—and also for the principles underlying democratic collective decisions (Chapter 18).

The content areas represented here range over psychology, sociology, political science, and anthropology. Mathematical economics is not represented (except tangentially through utility theory and the theory of games), first because this area was not included in the courses on which the book is based; second, because there is no dearth of textbooks and treatises on that subject.

Restrictions of space have limited presentations of applications to a few chosen examples to illustrate each method. Topics of importance regretfully omitted from the final version include cluster analysis (see Tryon and Bailey, 1970), latent structure analysis (see Lazarsfeld and Henry, 1968), and spectral analysis (see Mayer and Arney, 1973–1974). An extensive treatment of the mathematical methods discussed in Parts II and III can be found in Kemeny and Snell (1962) and in Fararo (1973). Throughout the book, the interested reader is repeatedly referred to more detailed treatments of topics discussed. "Classical" methods (e.g., differential equations) are, of course, explained in textbooks available everywhere.

One further word is in order about the selection of examples of mathematical models. Among these, not only apparently interesting and fruitful ones will be found, but also questionable and even clearly sterile ones. These were included to show the development of mathematical models in the social sciences in historical perspective and at times to provide leverage for instructive criticism. Learning from the mistakes of others is less painful than learning from one's own.

I am grateful to John Wiley & Sons for providing the opportunity to write another version of this book and so to incorporate some revisions, which I felt were needed. Some chapters of the German version were combined, others separated, some substantially rewritten or expanded to accommodate recently published material. Chapter 6 of the present version has been added.

I take further pleasure in expressing heart-felt thanks to Ilse Reichel and Ingrid Schmidbauer, who typed the manuscript in a language foreign to them, and to Regina-Cernavskis and Gerda Suppanz for preparing the figures.

ANATOL RAPOPORT
Vienna, Austria
October 1982

Contents

PART III. STRUCTURAL MODELS   259

PART IV. PROBLEMS OF QUANTIFICATION   393

PART V. CONCLUDING REMARKS   465

A Note on Notation

Letters

Sets are usually designated by capital italic letters, elements of sets by lower case letters. Random variables are denoted by capital letters, specific values assumed by them by lower case letters. For example, $\Pr[X \leqslant x]$ designates the probability that a random variable X assumes a value no larger than x.

Vectors are denoted by lower case letters; for example, $x = (x_1, x_2, \ldots, x_n)$. Matrices are denoted by capital letters, their scalar elements by lower case letters; for example, $M = (m_{ij})$ designates a matrix with elements m_{ij} in ith row, jth column.

Parentheses

Sets represented by their elements are usually indicated by braces; for example, $\{x, y, z\}$. Accordingly, $U(\{x, y, z\})$ designates the value of a function U whose argument is the set $\{x, y, z\}$ (see Chapter 12). Sets consisting of single elements are also designated in order to adhere to the logic of operations on sets. For example, $Y - \{x\}$ designates the set resulting when the element x is deleted from the set Y (since "subtraction" is a binary operation on sets, not on sets and elements). Where there is no danger of confusion, braces are omitted in functions on sets. For instance, $v(abc)$ instead of $v(\{a, b, c\})$ denotes the value of an n-person cooperative game to a set of players $\{a, b, c\}$ acting as a coalition (see Chapter 19).

Round parentheses are used for *ordered* n-tuples. For instance, $(abcd)$ may indicate that objects a, b, c, d are preferred in that order (see Chapter 12).

Open intervals are set in parentheses, closed intervals in brackets. For example, (a, b) denotes the sets of all real numbers larger than a and smaller than b; $[a, b]$ the set of all real numbers equal to or larger than a and equal to or smaller than b. The meaning of a half-open (half-closed) interval, $[a, b)$ or $(a, b]$, is clear.

Angular parentheses are used to enclose the elements defining mathematical objects. For example, $G = \langle N, V \rangle$ designates a graph G defined by a set of vertices N and a binary relation V (see Chapter 14). $\langle N, v \rangle$ designates a cooperative game defined by a set of players N and a characteristic function v (see Chapter 19).

Summations

In addition to the usual symbol of summation over consecutively indexed quantities—for example, $\sum_{i=1}^{n}$—the following special summation symbols are used. $\sum_{y}'$ designates summation over all y distinct from a specific x. $\sum_{i \in S} x_i$ designates summation over x_i, whose indices i are elements of a given set S. When the numbers x belong to a set fixed in a given context, summation over these numbers is denoted by $\sum_{x}$.

Some Special Symbols Used in This Book

$x \succ_S y$:	Imputation x dominates imputation y via a given set of players S (see Chapter 19).
$x \succ y$:	Imputation x dominates imputation y via unspecified set or sets of players.
$x \succ y$:	x is preferred to y (see Chapter 12).
$x \precsim y$ or $y \succsim x$:	x is not preferred to y.
$x \sim y$:	x is not preferred to y, and y is not preferred to x (also, "x is indifferent to y").
$x \cong y$:	x is approximately equal to y.
$x \sim y$:	x is proportional to y.
$\Rightarrow$:	implies.
$\Leftrightarrow$:	implies and is implied by.
$\exists$:	there exists. For instance, "$y \notin I_0 \Rightarrow \exists x \in I_0,\ x \succ y$" is read, "for every imputation y not an element of the set I_0, there exists an imputation x in I_0 which dominates y."

Introduction: Goals and Means

Scientific knowledge, as distinguished from other modes of cognition (poetic, introspective, religious, tradition-preserving), is characterized by objectivity, generality, and precision. Of these criteria, generality and precision are matters of degree. Objectivity is more nearly an all-or-none criterion: it enters the definition of a *fact*, a state of affairs reported in equivalent ways by *independent* observers.

That generality of scientific knowledge is a matter of degree is reflected in the paradigm of a scientific assertion: "If..., then...." The "if" part specifies conditions under which observations are to be made, the "then" part specifies what will be observed. The range of conditions under which a given state of affairs is expected to be observed serves as a measure of generality of a scientific assertion.

All scientific knowledge is shared by means of language. Linguistic utterances carry both denotative and connotative meanings. The former relate words and combinations of words to *referents* (things, events, and so on), which are assumed to constitute knowable reality. The latter evoke associations, which may or may not be relevant to the denotative meanings. Scientific knowledge is coded and communicated in ways that tend to reduce the connotative components of meaning. Words purged of connotative meaning are called *terms*. Terms are more precise than words of common usage, because their ranges of meaning are narrower. The Latin names of plants and animals are common examples. They denote species, which are usually narrower and hence more precise designations than common names of plants and creatures. The meanings of terms used in physics (for example, force, energy, power, and so on) are further examples of terms, that is, words from which all the usual connotations (related to, say, traits of human character) have been removed.

Mathematics is a language in which the ideals of objectivity, generality, and precision are realized in the highest degree. Typically (though not exclusively), assertions in this language refer to quantities. Terms referring to quantities are obviously both more objective and more precise than common usage words with quantitative denotations. The statement "This table is large" leaves much to be desired with regard to objectivity and precision; it may reflect the speaker's experience with tables or the intended use for the table. "This table is 250 cm long and 120 cm wide, hence 3 m² in area" is more objective and more precise. The connotations of "large" (which may depend on both the speaker's and the listener's experiences and attitudes) have been eliminated from the original statement, and its meaning has been thereby substantially narrowed.

Furthermore, the statement "The area of a rectangular table equals the product of length and width" *generalizes* the idea conveyed. Stated as a *formula, A* (area) = *L* (length) × *W* (width), the assertion becomes a compact representation of a potential *infinity* of assertions, since any numbers can be substituted for *L* and for *W*, whereupon *A* becomes known. Here the "If..., then..." format is realized: If the length of a table is *L* and its width *W*, then its area is *A*.

In attempting to systematize modalities of cognition, philosophers (and, in fact, most people) distinguish between *quantities* and *qualities*. Unlike the former, the latter appear to be impervious to counting or measurement. However, advances in the physical sciences have revealed quantitative aspects of many categories perceived by our senses as "qualities." Color, pitch, and tone timbre are notable examples. The pitch of a pure tone is completely determined by the frequency of air waves it produces. Analogously, the colors of the rainbow are manifestations of frequencies of electromagnetic radiation. The timbre of a tone is determined by the relative amplitudes of its overtones. In view of the objectivity and greater precision of quantitative descriptions and because these descriptions lend themselves more easily to generalizing summarization, it is easy to see why mathematics was incorporated into the language of science in the late Renaissance, from the very inception of what we now call "modern" science.

The cognitive fruits of mathematical language became fully apparent when the power of mathematical *deduction* was tapped. Scientific knowledge is accumulated by two modes of reasoning, induction and deduction. Induction proceeds from particular observations to generalized inferences. Thus by observing that every human eventually dies, we are moved to infer that all humans are mortal—an inductive inference. Deduction proceeds from general principles to conclusions about particular cases. If all humans are mortal and Socrates is a human, we conclude that Socrates is mortal—a deductive conclusion. There is a crucial destinction between inductive and deductive modes of cognition. Induction depends on observations; deduction does not. Deduction amounts only to manipulations of symbols; in its most elementary form, of words. For instance, from the assertion "John is the husband of Mary" we can deduce the assertion "Mary is the wife of John." We need not observe John and Mary to establish that the deduction is valid. Its validity depends solely on the rules of English, according to which both assertions say the same thing.

Every deductive conclusion is, in the last analysis, a tautology. It says the same thing as the premises from which it was deduced. "Mary is the wife of

John" is deduced from the premis "John is the husband of Mary" and asserts the same thing. "Socrates is mortal" is deduced from two premises, "All men are mortal" and "Socrates is a man," and says the same thing as these premises. If the premises are "true" (in the sense to be discussed below), the conclusion *must* be "true," provided the deduction was made in accordance with certain specified rules (also to be discussed below). But the *validity* of the deduction does not depend on the "truth" of the premises. Deduction fits the "If..., then..." paradigm. The "if" part refers to the premises; the "then" part to the conclusion.

Premises from which mathematical deductions are made are called *axioms* or *postulates*. A set of such axioms or postulates serves as the foundation of a mathematical system or discipline. For example, Euclidean geometry rests on a number of axioms referring to quantities (for example, "quantities equal to the same quantity are equal to each other") and on a number of postulates referring to idealized spatial concepts (for example, "a straight line is the shortest distance between two points"). Conclusions derived from these axioms and postulates are called *theorems*. For example, the statement "In a right triangle, the square of the hypotenuse has the same area as the sum of the areas of the squares of the other two sides" is a theorem. Ordinary arithmetic rests on axioms that establish rules of addition and multiplication; for example, the distributive rule: $a(b + c) = ab + ac$. That the product of the sum and the difference of two numbers equals the difference of their squares is a theorem derived from these axioms.

The ancient Greeks, who laid the foundations of deductive geometry, regarded the axioms and postulates as "self-evident truths." The theorems derived from them may be anything but self-evident. However, since conclusions arrived at by deduction seem to be compelling, it appeared to some philosophers that absolutely certain truths about the world could be attained by this method. Plato was most insistent in asserting that observations, necessarily perturbed by error and limited to specific instances, were far inferior to instrospective reasoning as a method of discovering truth. There is a scene in *Meno* where Socrates leads a young slave through a proof of a special case of the Pythagorean Theorem in order to demonstrate that truth arrived at by reasoning can be grasped even by a lowly untrained mind.

In modern philosophy of mathematics, the axioms and postulates underlying a mathematical discipline are regarded as no more than conventions, "rules of the game" as it were, rather than "self-evident truths." This view reflects a concept of mathematics as a purely deductive procedure—manipulation of symbols according to prescribed rules. Whatever relations can or ought to be established between the symbols and assertions on the one hand, and things or events in the observable world on the other, raises problems of crucial importance in science but is entirely outside the scope of mathematics as such.

A major impetus to the abandonment of the notion of self-evident truth, as it applies to the postulates of mathematics, was given by the resolution of a problem with which mathematicians wrestled in the eighteenth and early nineteenth centuries. Of the postulates of Euclidean geometry, one in particular made some mathematicians uneasy, namely, the so-called parallel postulate. The postulate asserts that through a point external to a given line, one and only one line can be drawn in the same plane which fails to meet the given line however far it is produced. Somehow the postulate did not seem as self-evident as the others; for example, that between two distinct points one and only one straight line can be drawn. Accordingly, attempts were made to prove this postulate, that is, to derive it as a theorem from the other more compellingly acceptable postulates. All such attempts failed. The resolution of the difficulty came when J. Bolyai in Hungary and N.I. Lobachevsky in Russia each proved independently that the parallel postulate was independent of the others. That is to say, it could be replaced by another postulate incompatible with it without introducing a contradiction into geometry. In consequence, many *non-Euclidean* geometries were constructed. In so-called hyperbolic geometries, an infinity of lines can be passed through a point external to a line in the same plane which fail to meet it ever. In so-called elliptic geometries, there are no parallel lines at all. Consequences of postulates contradicting Euclid's parallel postulate introduce no internal contradictions into the resulting geometries. However, some of these consequences are, of course, incompatible with some theorems of Euclidean geometry. In a hyperbolic geometry, the sum of the angles of a triangle is less than $180°$; in an elliptic geometry, greater. In both, the sum of the angles depends on the area of the triangle.

If one adheres to the view that geometry is a mathematical description of "actual" space, one must face the question as to which geometry is the "true" geometry. Since none of them can be invalidated by an internal contradiction, it follows that the answer to this question cannot be found by pure deduction. If the question can be decided at all, the answer can come only through observation, that is, by comparing the conclusions of the different geometries about spatial relations with measurements. In principle, one could measure the sums of angles of triangles to see whether they are equal to, less than, or greater than $180°$. Such procedures, however, are beset with difficulties. The excess or deficiency in the sum of the angles of a non-Euclidean triangle becomes very small, hence undetectable by physical measurements, as the area of the triangle becomes small. Triangles accessible to our measurements are "small" in terms of cosmic dimensions, so that "locally" the geometry of physical space may appear Euclidean, even though space "as a whole" may not be. Moreover, a triangle is supposed to be bounded by "straight lines," and the question arises as to what should be taken as a *physical* "straight line." We may identify the path taken by a beam of light with a "straight line," but since 1919 it is known that light beams are "bent" in the neighborhood of large masses.

However we approach the problem of determining the nature of physical space, we see that this involves more than pure deduction. For the sake of clarity, therefore, it seems advisable to define mathematics (and geometry in particular) as a purely deductive discipline, concerned only with the *validity* of propositions, not with their empirically established *truth*. This view severs the link between mathematical concepts and observable referents. Mathematicians become free to construct a rich variety of mathematical systems, each restricted only by the requirement of internal consistency.

Some elementary systems of this sort are familiar to the layperson. Consider the "arithmetic" associated with a 24-hour clock. Six hours after 19:00 on this clock the time is 01:00. We can express this by writing $19 + 6 = 1$, which of course is false in "ordinary" arithmetic. Nevertheless, cyclic addition, based on identifying 24 with zero, works very well in telling time and in computing the time any number of hours ahead or ago.

A somewhat more complex example is an "arithmetic" that reflects the results of rotating a cube through multiples of $90°$ around any of its three axes. The cube can be in any of 24 positions. Starting with an arbitrarily selected position labeled zero, we can reach any other position by a combination of rotations, in fact, in several different ways. Let the elements (analogous to numbers) of our rotation arithmetic be combinations of rotations, each corresponding to the resulting position of the cube. Our arithmetic will contain 24 distinct elements. An "addition" of two such elements will be interpreted as the element that corresponds to the resulting position of the cube starting from zero when the rotations are performed consecutively. Thus the "sum" of two rotations is again a rotation, just as in ordinary arithmetic the sum of two numbers is again a number. Moreover, it turns out that this addition is associative: $a + (b + c) = (a + b) + c$. But this addition is not in general commutative; $a + b$ does not always result in the same position of the cube as $b + a$. (The reader is invited to try it with a die.) Thus rotation arithmetic is different from clock arithmetic. Both have 24 elements and associative additions, but addition in clock arithmetic is commutative, whereas addition in rotation arithmetic is not.

The readings of the clock are *representations* of the clock arithmetic; the positions of the cube are a representation of rotation arithmetic. These representations serve a *heuristic* purpose. They help us visualize the operations. In principle, however, a mathematical system is independent of its possible representations. As pointed out, its validity depends only on its internal consistency. Conversely, the 24-element arithmetic with commutative addition is a *model* of the 24-hour clock, and a particular 24-element arithmetic with noncommutative addition (there are several such arithmetics) is a model of the system of $90°$ rotations of a cube. The results of operations in these mathematical models can be regarded as predictions of clock readings and of positions of the cube, respectively. A mathematical model *fits* its referent system to the extent that the predictions deduced from its postulates are verified by observations.

Now in the case of the two models just described, we expect the correspondence between model and referent to be perfect, because the physical events involved (namely, the passage of time and the rotations of the cube) are *defined* by the readings of the clock and the resulting positions of the cube, respectively. No events external to those embodied in the models are allowed to interfere. The situation is different when physical events independent of our operations are involved. For instance, if we used another clock to measure the passage of time, our predictions about the readings on our clock might not be confirmed. Models of phenomena that are not tautological are never perfectly confirmed. Inevitably, errors of measurement or events not accounted for in the model introduce discrepancies.

As illustration, consider a simple model of a physical phenomenon embodied in the assumption "The elongation of the spring in a spring balance is proportional to the weight impinging on it." This assumption translated into the language of mathematics reads

$$L = L_0 + kW, \tag{1}$$

where L_0 is the length of the spring unemcumbered by a weight, W the weight impinging, k a constant of proportionality, and L the length of the elongated spring. By measuring the length of the spring with $W = 0$, we determine L_0. By measuring the length L with $W = 1$, we determine $k = L - L_0$. Now the model *predicts* the length of the spring corresponding to *any* weight W. We can now *test* the model (determine the goodness of its fit to observations) by comparing the predicted values of L with observed values as we vary W. The predictions may or may not turn out to be accurate within the precision of our measurements. To the extent that they are accurate (which is, in the last analysis, a matter of degree), our model fits physical reality. Discrepancies between predictions and observations can be ascribed either to accidental errors (for example, in reading the elongations or in determining the weights on another scale) or to the failure of the model as an accurate description of the way the spring responds to stresses impinging on it.

Note that in testing this model, the weights must be determined independently; for instance, on a beam balance. We cannot use our spring balance to determine the weights, for if we did, the weights would be determined by the elongation of the spring, and the model would become *unfalsifiable* (tautological). In other words, to reflect knowledge about the external world, a model must be *falsifiable*: Its predictions must not be *logically* compelling; we must be able to imagine violations of our predictions that are free of internal contradictions.

To summarize, the predictions of a mathematical model of some aspect of reality are derived by mathematical deduction. The test of a mathematical model is accomplished by induction, that is, by a generalization of repeated observations. Mathematical deductions are logically compelling, but, being tautological, they say nothing about the external world. Induction does generate assertions about the external world, but these assertions are not logically compelling. The two procedures complement each other. They are the two pillars of scientific cognition.

The requirements of objectivity, generality, and precision, which, as we said at the outset, characterize scientific cognition, can be encapsulated in two questions to be constantly kept in the foreground of consciousness: "What do you mean?" and "How do you know?" The first question is a demand for defining words. The criterion of objectivity requires that definitions be purged of connotative meanings, since denotative meanings are more firmly linked to common experiences of independent observers. Furthermore, the criterion of precision enhances the role of quantitative definitions, which prevail in the so-called exact (mathematicized) sciences. The second question is a demand for evidence for the truth or the validity of the assertion. Validity is established by rigorous deduction, which again enhances the role of mathematics. Truth is established by experiences of independent observers (to satisfy the requirement of objectivity). The requirement of generality is satisfied via induction from observations. Again quantification enhances the precision of assertions.

The complementarity of inductive and deductive reasoning solves the age-old problem of attaining "certain" knowledge. The certainty of deductive reasoning is bought at the price of severing the premises and even the terms in which assertions are cast from referents in the external world. The connection between assertions and observations is kept at the price of giving up certainty. The mathematization of the exact sciences does not confer certainty as long as these sciences are imbued with empirical content. But the quantified concept of probability permits estimates of the *degree* of certainty of scientific assertions. Thus while the quest for absolute certainty about the external world must be acknowledged to be futile, the scientific mode of cognition can confer a progressively greater degree of certainty on our knowledge about the external world.

Ordinarily, degree of certainty is associated with frequency of confirmation of an assertion. However, the amount of credence conferred on a scientific assertion depends also on how *improbably* the assertion would be deemed to be true *before* it was confirmed by observation. By way of example, consider the claim of a water dowser that the sudden deflection of a forked stick indicates the presence of underground water at the site. To test the truth of the implied claim that dowsing is effective in the search for underground water, it is not sufficient to record the relative frequency of successes and failures. It is also necessary to compare the frequency of successes with the frequency of finding water at *arbitrarily* selected sites. If the difference between the two frequencies is not statistically significant, the dowser's "theory" deserves no credence.

In contrast, the *a priori* probability that an eclipse of the sun will take place in a specified locality at a specified time several years or even decades hence is extremely small. The confirmation of this event lends extremely strong credence to the underlying mathematical theory of the motion of heavenly bodies.

The "classical" formulation of the so-called scientific method focuses on the predictive aspects of scientific assertions. According to the descriptions of the method frequently given in textbooks, a scientific investigation begins with observations, preferably under controlled or at least constant conditions. The specific conditions are embodied in the "if" part of the "If . . . , then . . . " paradigm; the results of observations, in the "then" part. The next step is an inductive inference, which extends the paradigm to "If . . . , then always . . . " An assertion of this sort constitutes a *hypothesis*. A *test* of the hypothesis follows, whereby the specified conditions are arranged or a situation is selected where they are satisfied. The *generalization* representing the inductive inference becomes a *prediction* of what will be observed. Corroboration of the prediction constitutes a *confirmation* of the hypothesis, conferring a greater degree of confidence in its "truth". Noncorroboration constitutes a *refutation* of the hypothesis. An unconfirmed hypothesis is discarded in favor of another. The new hypothesis may be a *modification* of the original one, incorporating additional features of the conditions which had not been taken into account, so as to remove the discrepancy between prediction and observation. The new hypothesis is then tested, closing the cycle of observation–generalization–test–new generalization–test, and so on.

Aside from the fact that actual scientific investigations seldom follow this routine, the scheme omits some of the most important features of scientific cognition. It says nothing about the relation between verbal assertions and their referents in the external world, nothing about the principle of parsimony, and it ascribes a trivial role to deduction.

The semantic problem (the relation between words and referents) will be treated later. To see the role of parsimony, imagine how the method might be applied to the investigation of the action of pumps before the principles of hydrostatics were understood. In antiquity, the action of pumps was explained by the maxim "Nature dreads vacuum." Stated as an "If . . . , then always . . . " inference, the maxim becomes "If a vacuum is created above a body of water, then water always rises to fill it." This prediction is corroborated as long as the column of water is not required to rise more than about 10 meters above the surface. Beyond this limit, the pump will not work. The hypothesis can easily be modified to incorporate the exception, whereupon the underlying maxim or "law of nature" would read "Nature dreads vacuum but not beyond 10 vertical meters."

Modifications of this sort can be piled up *ad infinitum*, but the resulting theory would become heavily encumbered by ifs and buts. It would not reflect the basic simplicity of nature, which has been an article of faith and a major impetus to the scientific enterprise. Hypotheses elaborately tailored to fit observed facts violate the principle of parsimony.

A fruitful hypothesis is one that predicts observations outside the category of observations already made. Instead of "Nature dreads vacuums," consider the hydrostatic principle, according to which the greatest height of a column of water in a vacuum is one that exerts a pressure on the surface over which it stands equal to the pressure of the atmosphere on that surface. We cannot estimate the maximum height of the column from that hypothesis alone, but we can observe it to be about 10.3 meters. In addition, we can observe that mercury is about 13.6 times heavier than water. We can therefore deduce that 7.6 cm of mercury will be supported in an evacuated tube standing over a dish of mercury—a new prediction, involving another substance.

Formulation of the hydrostatic principle requires more than observation. It requires the acquisition of *concepts* lacking in antique and medieval natural philosophy; for instance, the concept of *pressure* mathematically defined. It requires a quantitative orientation—the habit of undertaking measurements—to supplement the taxonomic orientation (thinking in terms of categories and their "properties"), which governed philosophic thought before the advent of modern science.

In the observation–hypothesis–test paradigm, deduction enters in generating a prediction of a particular observation on the basis of a general principle arrived at by induction, as in a syllogism: "Water will fill a vacant space; the space above the piston of this pump is vacant; therefore water will fill it." The hydrostatic hypothesis introduces more sophisticated deduction, involving *calculations* of the heights of columns of various liquids supported by a given atmospheric pressure.

A mathematical model of some natural phenomenon is essentially a hypothesis generated by mathematical deductive techniques. Since these techniques can be extremely involved, the predictions embodied in a mathematical model serving as a hypothesis can be logically far removed from the premises underlying the model. It is in this regard that mathematical models acquire their great theoretical leverage.

To illustrate, we will examine two approaches to the investigation of the pendulum, one predominantly inductive, the other deductive and guided by a mathematical model.

According to legend, Galileo's systematic study of the pendulum was instigated by his observations of a lamp hanging from the ceiling of the Pisa Cathedral and swinging in the wind. Being quantitatively oriented, Galileo measured the period of its oscillation (by comparing it with his pulse). He noted that the period did not depend on the amplitude of the swing. Being also experimentally oriented, Galileo undertook to verify this observation under controlled conditions. By comparing the periods of two pendulums, one with a bob made of lead, the other of cork, he found that the period was also independent of the weight of the bob. By counting the numbers of swings of two pendulums swinging with different amplitudes, he was able to verify (as it seemed to him) that the period is indeed independent of amplitude. Finally, Galileo found that increasing the length of the string increased the period. (This relation was utilized in measuring the pulse of medical patients by a pendulum with adjustable lengths.)

I could find no evidence that the specific mathematical relation between the length and the period of the pendulum (the latter proportional to the square root of the former) was known to Galileo. But he could have established this relation by a procedure similar to the way he established the relation between the distance traversed by a falling body and the time elapsed. Had he done this, Galileo could have formulated three "laws" of the pendulum:

1. The period is independent of the mass of the bob.
2. The period is independent of amplitude.
3. The period is proportional to the square root of the length.

The inductive procedure reveals no logically compelling connection between the three "laws." Moreover, it obscures a vital discrepancy between the second "law" and observations. The discrepancy was pointed out by another investigator, who noticed that the period increases with amplitude when the amplitude becomes sufficiently large. Galileo chose to disregard this report. Or he might have attributed the discrepancy to experimental error.

Let us now derive the theory of the pendulum from a mathematical model. In a mathematical model, the situation examined must necessarily be idealized.

Only what is thought to be essential in the situation is incorporated in the model; other features are ignored. The simplest mathematical model of a pendulum pictures the bob as a *point mass* suspended from a perfectly rigid ceiling by a perfectly rigid weightless rod and constrained to move in a plane. Effects of friction and air resistance are ignored. Underlying the model is a "law of motion," according to which the *acceleration* of a moving body is proportional to the ratio of the component of the force acting upon it in the same direction and its mass. In symbols,

$$F = ma, \tag{2}$$

where F is the component of force in the direction of acceleration, a the acceleration, m the mass of the bob, and the units are chosen to make the constant of proportionality 1. We will also need the following symbols:

$\theta = $ the angle between the rod and the plumb line.[1]

$x = $ the horizontal deviation of the bob from the equilibrium position (when the rod is vertical).

$t = $ time.

$d\theta/dt = $ the rate of change of θ (the first derivative of θ with respect to time).

$d^2\theta/dt^2 = $ the rate of change of the rate of change of θ (the second derivative with respect to time).

$s = $ the distance of the bob from equilibrium position along the arc of swing.

$L = $ the length of the rod.

$g = $ the acceleration of a freely falling body.

By geometry, $s = \theta L$. Since the rod is perfectly rigid, L is constant, so that $ds/dt = L(d\theta/dt)$; and $d^2s/dt^2 = L(d^2\theta/dt^2)$. Furthermore, by trigonometry, $F = -mg \sin \theta$, and Equation 2 becomes

$$mg \sin \theta = -mL\frac{d^2\theta}{dt^2}$$

or

$$\frac{d^2\theta}{dt^2} = -\frac{g}{L} \sin \theta. \tag{3}$$

Equation 3 is a *differential equation*, in which a derivative of a dependent variable (θ) with respect to an independent variable (t) is expressed as a function of the dependent variable. The general solution of this equation would express θ as a function of t, g, L, and certain constants that can be determined by specifying the initial position and velocity of the bob. Assuming g, L, and the initial conditions known, the solution would predict θ, that is, the position of the bob at any specified time.

The general solution of Equation 3 cannot be expressed in so-called elementary functions.[2] But it can be considerably simplified by an approximation, adequate for small values of θ. Namely, when θ is only a few degrees (a small fraction of a radian), the distance along the arc, s, can be approximated by x, the horizontal deviation of the bob. Substituting x for s on the left and x/L for $\sin \theta$ on the right of Equation 3, we obtain the approximate differential equation

$$\frac{d^2 x}{dt^2} = -\frac{gx}{L}, \tag{4}$$

whose solution is

$$x(t) = A \sin\left(\sqrt{\frac{g}{L}}\, t\right) + B \cos\left(\sqrt{\frac{g}{L}}\, t\right). \tag{5}$$

If the pendulum starts with initial deviation $x(0) = x_0$ and initial velocity $ds/dt = 0$, we must have $A = 0$, $B = x_0$, and Equation 5 becomes

$$x(t) = x_0 \cos\left(\sqrt{\frac{g}{L}}\, t\right), \tag{6}$$

which specifies the position of the bob at any time t.

To calculate the period, we solve for t when the bob returns for the first time to its initial position x_0. When this occurs, we have

$$\cos\left(\sqrt{\frac{g}{L}}\, t\right) = 1$$

$$t = 2\pi \sqrt{\frac{L}{g}} = P \tag{7}$$

From this equation, we read that P (the period) is independent of both the mass m and of the initial displacement x_0, hence of the amplitude, and also that the period is proportional to the square root of L, the length of the rod.

Note that the independence of P from m (the mass of the bob) is also implied by the "exact" Equation 3. So one of Galileo's inductive inferences is also a deduced consequence of our model. That the period is proportional directly to the square root of the length and inversely to the acceleration of gravity can also be deduced from Equation 3. However, the independence of the period from the amplitude is deducible only from our approximate Equation 4. The solution of the exact Equation 3 would exhibit the period as a function also of x_0, hence of the amplitude. For very small amplitudes, however, the period would be very nearly independent of it. In his experiments, Galileo either failed to detect the increase of the period with amplitude or attributed it to extraneous disturbances like friction or air resistance.[3]

We see that the approximate mathematical model reveals the interconnection among all the three principles governing the simple pendulum. The "exact" model reveals that only Equation 3 is exact, but that Equation 4 is only an approximation. Moreover, the exact model predicts that discrepancies between Equation 4 and observations become larger as the amplitude becomes larger. Finally, the mathematical models (both the exact and the approximate) reveal the dependence of the period not only on L but also on g, the acceleration of gravity, and so predict changes in the behavior of the pendulum at various altitudes and latitudes on the earth's surface and on other planets.

The same unifying and predictive power of a mathematical model is demonstrated on a vaster scale of planetary motion. In the seventeenth century, J. Kepler discovered three "laws" of planetary motion:

1. Every planet in the solar system moves in an ellipse in which the sun is at one of the foci.
2. The radius vector from each planet to the sun sweeps over equal areas in equal intervals of time.
3. The square of the period of revolution is proportional to the cube of the planet's mean distance from the sun.

These "laws" were inductive inferences made by Kepler on the basis of Tycho Brahe's astronomical observations. Later all three were mathematically deduced by Isaac Newton from a single model, the law of universal gravitation,

$$F = \frac{Km_1m_2}{r^2},\qquad(8)$$

where F is the force of attraction between two point masses, m_1 and m_2, separated by distance r, and K is a constant of proportionality.

Given an initial configuration (positions and velocities) of planets, all future configurations can be deduced from the model. They can also be deduced from Kepler's laws but not accurately, because the gravitational interaction among the planets is not taken into account in those laws.

The predictive power of Newton's model was dramatically demonstrated when it led to the discovery of Neptune. Uranus was discovered by observation in 1781. Its orbit was deduced theoretically by taking into account not only the gravitational attraction by the sun but also perturbations due to the gravitational forces exerted by the other planets. However, the orbit of Uranus showed discrepancies that could not be explained by these perturbations. From a purely *empirical* point of view, therefore, Newton's model appeared to be disconfirmed. The mathematical model, however, suggested a way out; namely, a bold hypothesis—that another, yet unknown planet was responsible for the perturbations in Uranus' orbit. The immense task of calculating the position of this hypothetical planet was undertaken independently by U.J.J. Leverrier in France and J.C. Adams in England. Adams communicated his results to the Berlin observatory in September 1846, and Neptune was found almost immediately within one degree of the predicted position.

The amalgamation of induction and deduction, as illustrated in the above examples, made possible the construction of the colossal intellectual-technological edifice which we know as science. Within two centuries, natural science has radically changed both the conditions of and the outlook on human life. It seemed in the course of the nineteenth century that humans could become masters of their own destiny by shaping the forces of nature to satisfy their needs, for science conferred not only the power of prediction but also the power of control as embodied in technology—devices for harnessing and directing the forces of nature.

However, faith in enduring "progress," which marked the prevailing outlook of the Western world during the nineteenth century, floundered in the wake of the disasters of the twentieth century: the horrendous destruction unleashed by military uses of advanced technology, the social trauma engendered by worldwide depression, by the brutalities of totalitarian regimes, and, more recently, by the shattering of the image of a better future in the face of threats of a nuclear holocaust, of the exhaustion of resources, and of the degradation of the environment.

As a consequence of these traumas and these fears, attitudes toward science in the Western world have changed in two different ways. On the one hand, a deep distrust of science has spread through many sectors of the public, aggravated by the customary identification of science with technology, previously regarded as a source of affluence and an instrument of liberation from disease and drudgery, now seen as the breeding ground of means of total destruction, a threat to individual autonomy, and the chief agent of environmental degradation. On the other hand, the miseries of our century have been attributed to a gap between human beings' rapidly growing mastery over nature and their failure to equip themselves with a comparable ability to control their own behavior, especially behavior channeled by social forces and institutional imperatives. According to this view, our troubles stem not from "too much science" but, on the contrary, from "not enough science." If only the mode of cognition developed in natural science could be made to govern social and institutional arrangements, so the argument goes, man could get back on the road to progress toward continued betterment of life on earth.

The idea is not new. A century and a half ago, A. Comte (1830–1842) projected the transplantation of the scientific method into the social realm. However, apart from recommending the extension of the scientific mode of cognition to the study of social phenomena and applying the knowledge so gained to the design of policies, Comte had little to say about what was to be done.

Modern proponents of social science modeled after the natural sciences have been more explicit. They introduced statistical methods in evaluating data related to human behavior and social events, thus paving the way for quantification and inductive inferences based on relative frequencies of observed categories of events. The huge volumes of data accumulated in censuses and surveys created a pressing need for some sort of integration. Mathematical approaches to the behavioral sciences were partly instigated by this need.

This book is a survey of mathematical methods adapted to investigations in psychology, sociology, anthropology, decision theory, and political science. Mathematical economics, where the most extensive applications of these methods are found, will be touched upon only tangentially because there is no dearth of textbooks and monographs in that established discipline. The aim here is to present more "controversial" and also more diversified techniques and applications.

In many instances, exposition will be supplemented by critical comments. These are necessary because the history of mathematization in the behavioral sciences is quite unlike the triumphant unfolding of mathematical physics. It reflects, for the most part, disconnected attempts. Successes are spotty. Furthermore, the criteria for "success" of a mathematical model or theory in the behavioral sciences are less clear cut than in the physical sciences. In the latter, the adequacy of a model or theory is almost universally judged by its predictive power. If the same criterion were applied to mathematical models in the behavioral sciences, unqualified successes would turn up only rarely. As we shall see, however, the value of mathematization in the behavioral sciences depends on aspects other than predictive power and the concomittant potentiality of exercising control over events.

The goal of mathematization in the behavioral sciences will be classified roughly into prediction, optimization, and insight. The models emphasizing each of these goals will be called, respectively, predictive, normative, and analytic-descriptive. Furthermore, models will be categorized with regard to the mathematical tools used in their construction: "classical," stochastic, and structural.

The predictive model was exemplified by the model of the pendulum and by the Newtonian model of the solar system. Normative models involve, as a rule, an optimization problem. Therefore, in addition to assumptions underlying relations among variables and/or their derivatives, normative models involve explicitly or implicitly postulated values or else some highly idealized state of affairs. For instance, the Carnot cycle is a model of a heat engine operating under ideal conditions. It is shown that even under these conditions, only a fraction of the heat supplied to the engine can be converted into work. In this way the theoretically optimal efficiency of the engine is determined.

Actually, all models of physical phenomena involve idealization. We have seen this in our model of the pendulum represented by a point mass, a weightless rod, and so on. In a way, therefore, all models are normative in this respect. In the behavioral sciences, however, normative models usually involve an *actor*, who attempts to realize some state of affairs that is optimal from his point of view. Such a model may prescribe a decision or a course of action to this actor. In addition to the variables describing a "state of the system," a normative model often also involves variables which the actor can *control*. Models involving the exercise of control or selection of *strategies* are predominant in *decision theory*, which will be subsumed under behavioral sciences in this book.

We have seen that predictive models, in view of idealizations contained in them, involve a normative component. Conversely, normative models of decision theory involve a predictive component—conclusions regarding how a "perfectly rational actor" would behave in a given situation. There is, however, an important difference between the way normative and predictive components of models are related in natural and in behavioral sciences. In the former, the postulated idealized conditions can often be closely approximated. To the extent that they are realized, the deduced predictions of the model become increasingly accurate. This is seldom the case in the behavioral sciences. For instance, a "perfectly rational actor" is often so far removed from flesh and blood actors that this fictitious concept cannot serve as a reasonable approximation.

The most formidable obstacle confronting the behavioral scientist attempting to follow the path blazed by natural science is the absence of any analogous to firmly established "laws of nature," such as conservation of mass and energy, universal gravitation, wave mechanics governing the propagation of electromagnetic radiation, and so on. Principles sometimes assumed to govern social processes have no comparable foundation. Models of these processes are usually postulated *ad hoc* with the view of testing them in each particular instance. Confirmations are often no more than "statistically significant differences" between observations under different conditions, seldom reinforcements of generally valid principles analogous to the "laws of nature."

For these reasons, mathematically oriented behavioral scientists, especially in recent decades, have turned their attention to models that are neither predictive nor normative, to so-called analytic-descriptive models. The goal is to gain a clearer understanding of the structural frameworks in which events involving human actions take place.

Ever since the idea of extending the "scientific method" to the behavioral sciences gained aherents, the criterion of predictive power, as it applies to theories in the behavioral sciences, has been challenged frequently. In psychology and in the social sciences, so the argument goes, "understanding" rather than prediction is the proper goal. The criteria for understanding, however, vary along the subjective-objective spectrum. "Understanding" is subjective if it is confined to a single individual or to individuals with a specific cultural background. In everyday life, one person "understands" the actions of another if she can imagine analogous motivations, aspirations, or anxieties in herself. A psychoanalyst may feel she "understands" the psychic dynamics of a patient if she can formulate it in words and phrases current in a psychoanalytic conceptual system. Different ideologies "understand" the nature of humans, history, and society in different ways. Understanding imparted by a mathematical analytic-descriptive model is of a different sort. It is generated by a compact, mathematically rigorous description abstracted from a real system or embodied in a conceptual scheme. The descriptions do not generate predictions and do not provide means of control, but the words used in the descriptions are purged of all subjective connotations. They are confined to mathematically defined terms. "Understanding" in the context of an analytic-descriptive model means understanding a network of interconnected relations.

Along with the three goals of mathematization in the behavioral sciences, this book will be concerned with three types of mathematical tools: "classical," stochastic, and structural. Classical mathematics revolves around quantitative relations expressible as analytic functions of variables. These functions have regions of *continuity*, where arbitrarily small changes in independent variables produce arbitrarily small changes in dependent variables. For instance, the equation describing the fall of a body along an inclined plane,

$$s = \tfrac{1}{2}g \sin(\theta)t^2 \tag{9}$$

stems from a classical model. Here s is the distance traversed, t the time elapsed, θ the angle of inclination of the plane, and g the acceleration of gravity. The variables s, θ, and t are all defined in a *continuum*, and the equation expresses s as an analytic function of θ and t.

The concept of the continuum underlies the fundamental tool of mathematical physics—the calculus. The differential calculus introduces the concept of the rate of change (derivative) and the rate of change of the rate of change (*its* derivative). If the rate of change of position represents velocity, the rate of change of velocity represents acceleration. We have seen that a fundamental "law of motion" relates force to acceleration and serves as a foundation of classical mechanics. The fundamental concepts of mechanics stem from the concept of continuously changing quantities.

Equations involving both variables and their derivatives are called differential equations, of which Equations 3 and 4 are examples. If the independent variable with respect to which derivatives are taken is time, their solutions represent the dependent variables as functions of time and of the initial conditions, which makes models based on such equations predictive models. Other models (normative or descriptive) where time does not enter as a variable will also be subsumed under classical models so long as analytic functions are central in their formulation.

The tremendous deductive power of classical mathematics has made possible the construction of the imposing edifice of mathematical physics. Early proponents of mathematical methods extended to the behavioral sciences attempted to utilize the machinery of differential equations in models of social phenomena. Examples of these attempts are found in Chapters 2 and 3.

Today, these attempts are only of historical interest. The direct transplantation of the classical apparatus into the behavioral sciences did not succeed in the sense of unifying these sciences under the aegis of deductive mathematics, as was the case in physics. In retrospect, the dimming of the prospect can be attributed to two reasons. First, as already stated, behavioral theories do not rest on fundamental "laws of nature," confirmed without known exceptions and regarded as reflections of universal realities. To be sure, *regularities* have frequently been observed in human behavior and in social events. But these empirically established regularities are only weakly, if at all, connected with each other. This precludes the establishment of an ever more comprehensive theory by mathematical deduction. Second, quantification in the behavioral sciences is beset by problems that are obviated in the physical sciences. Measurement of fundamental physical quantities—time, mass, extension—presents no conceptual difficulties. Moreover, quantities so obtained can be subjected to arithmetic operations. Two units of length laid end to end make a stretch two units long. The weight of two stones is the sum of their weights. Multiplication and division of different physical quantities generate new quantities—meters per second (velocity), foot-pounds (work), and so on. Quantification of concepts current in the behavioral sciences, such as political power, cohesion of a group, subjective perception of light intensity, cannot be carried out in the same straightforward manner. And even if some measurement procedure is adopted for quantifying these concepts, questions arise about the sorts of operations than can be performed on the quantities. We will return to this problem. At present, we will turn our attention to quantification based on counting.

Countable quantities are prominent in the behavioral sciences and present no methodological problems, as long as the entities or events counted are clearly recognizable as belonging to established categories. Such are numbers of right and wrong answers in a learning task, numbers of people belonging to a given category or living in a given locale, frequencies of births, deaths, marriages, divorces, and so on. Mathematical models involving these frequencies are rooted in probability theory. These *stochastic* models play a prominent part in mathematicized behavioral sciences and have more successes to their credit than classical models because they circumvent the difficult problem of measuring intangible or poorly defined "quantities." They also circumvent the task of definitive prediction imposed on the "exact" sciences. Predictions deduced from stochastic models are probabilistic. They become increasingly deterministic when the number of countable entities or events becomes very large, but this determinism is a consequence of statistical laws, not of "natural laws." In this way, stochastic models compensate to a certain extent for the absence of firmly established natural laws in the behavioral sciences.

Of central interest in stochastic models are probability distributions of *random variables*. Values assumed by these variables may be continuous or discrete. Classical mathematics, supplemented with some special techniques developed in probability theory and in mathematical statistics, is an appropriate tool in models based on continuous random variables. Special tools developed in so-called *finite mathematics* serve stochastic models based on discrete or nonquantifiable variables representing distinct categories. Prominent among these tools is the *calculus of matrices*. For this reason, models that make use of matrix calculus will be subsumed under stochastic models, even if probabilistic concepts are not involved in them explicitly.

The prevailing conception of mathematics is that of a science that deals exclusively with quantities. The idea of extending mathematical methods to the study of behavior is often dismissed on the grounds that the most important determinants of human behavior cannot be quantified and therefore cannot be incorporated into a mathematical scheme. A similar argument was advanced by W. Hamilton,[4] who dismissed G. Boole's mathematization of logic on the grounds that logic deals with qualitative, not quantitative, aspects of human thought processes (Boule, 1854). In view of the prominent role played by quantities in mathematics, this view is understandable. Nevertheless, it is misguided. The essence of mathematics is rigorous deduction. In fact, logic, also concerned with rigorous deduction, can be regarded as a branch of mathematics. With equal justification, mathematics, characterized by special techniques of deduction, can be regarded as a branch of logic. It is in this sense that B. Russell defined mathematics as the totality of propositions in the form "p implies q." Thus the elements that enter a mathematical model need not be quantities. They can be *relations*. For instance, the assertion "If A is the father of B, and C is the sister of A, then C is an aunt of B" can be viewed as a mathematical assertion in the same way as the assertion "If $x = 2y$, and $z = 3x$, then $z = 6y$."

Mathematical models in which relations play a central role will be called structural models. Networks of relations describing a kinship system, a sociogram, or the structure of an organization depicted by its channels of communication, lines of authority, or the apportionment and schedules of tasks are examples of structural models. Among structural models, we shall also include models predominant in contemporary developments of mathematical psychology, where the establishment of appropriate methods of quantification of measurement is a central problem.

Mathematical tools predominant in structural models are set theory, the theory of graphs, and its generalizations. In the same way that differential equations are best suited for predictive models and probability theory is best suited for normative models involving optimization of decisions in risky situations, structural mathematics is best suited for nonquantiative analytic-descriptive models—models of structure. However, examples can be found of every combination of goals and means. The whole scheme can be represented by a matrix with rows designating the tools and columns designating the goals, as shown in Table 1.

The entries of this matrix represent areas of investigation where particular goals and tools are central. Most of these areas will be discussed in this book.

Simulation of behavioral phenomena with the aid of computer technology can also be regarded as a "tool" in mathematicized behavioral science. It is not listed as a separate tool in our scheme because simulation techniques can be used in all three types of models. Properties of classical models, formulated as large systems of nonlinear differential equations impervious to solution by

Table 1. Areas of Research Where Various Types of Mathematical Models and Various Research Goals Predominate

	Predictive	Normative	Analytic-Descriptive
Classical	Contagion processes Arms races Dynamic macroprocesses	Models with control	Equilibrium distributions Demographic statics
Stochastic	Rote learning models Concept formation Social mobility	Statistical decision theory	Distribution of sizes of groups
Structural	Evolution of sociograms	Normative organization models	Sociometry Theory of social choice

analytic methods, can be investigated by computer simulation. The so-called Monte Carlo technique essentially embodies simulations of stochastically modeled phenomena. Properties of large networks (structural models) have also been studied by computer simulation.

The obvious advantage of simulation is the opportunity it provides for studying properties of very large complex models. Its limitations stem from the fact that these properties are revealed only when specific numerical values are assigned to the parameters of the models (or specific relationships are embodied in structural models). Thus knowledge gained about how the behavior of a simulated system depends on the parameters can only be fragmentary—related to specific cases. Simulation can therefore be conceived as a quasi-experimental approach to mathematicized behavioral science, where postulated instead of actually observed conditions serve as the "if" component in the "If . . . , then . . . " paradigm.

Physical measurement essentially involves comparing magnitudes with a "unit" magnitude, the length of a certain rod, the weight of a certain object, the interval between two regularly occurring events, and so on. It is fortunate for science that philosophical problems related to measurement arose only after this simple conception had laid firm foundations for mathematical physics. For instance, in the light of the law of universal gravitation, mass and weight must be distinguished; in the light of relativity theory, space and time intervals appear to depend on the motion of the observer; questions have been raised about the operational meaning of a "regularly occurring event," and so on. These questions, however, led to refinements of the fundamental concepts without invalidating the physicist's mathematical operations on measured quantities. He could still define velocity as the ratio of distance traversed to the time interval elapsed; instantaneous velocity as a limit of this ratio, that is, as the derivative of distance with respect to time; acceleration as the derivative of velocity; force as the product of mass and acceleration, and so on. The fundamental concepts of mathematical physics are defined in terms of such operations.

Measurements of "nonphysical" magnitudes present problems of a different sort, generated by the absence of a concrete unit. The psychologist, for example, may want to quantify, that is, measure, a subject's preference among a set of objects. He can get information by asking the subject to order the objects from most preferred to least preferred or by eliciting comparisons between pairs of objects. But these procedures will establish a "preference scale" only if the subject's answers are "consistent." For instance, if in paired comparisons a subject prefers x to y and y to z, we may expect her to prefer x to z. If she does, so that the preference order $x \succ y \succ z$ is established, we may expect the subject to arrange all three objects in the same order of preference. Moreover, if the subject is indifferent between x and y and between y and z, we may expect her to be indifferent between x and z. In other words, we may expect her "indifference relation" as well as her "preference relation" to be *transitive*.

But will it? We can readily imagine a situation where it is not. Presented with two cups of coffee with different amounts of sugar, suppose the subject prefers one to the other. But if the difference between the amounts of sugar is minute, the subject may be indifferent between them because she cannot detect the difference. Now if we present the subject with three cups of coffee with s, $s + d$, and $s + 2d$ grams of sugar, respectively, she may be indifferent between the first and the second and between the second and the third, but not between the first and the third, if she can distinguish the difference $2d$ but not d.

Measurement is essentially assigning numbers to magnitudes. In measuring preferences among objects, we want to assign a number of each object (call it a *utility*) which reflects the subject's degree of preference for the object. Thus we want to assign larger numbers to more preferred objects and equal utilities to objects between which the subject is indifferent. But if the subject's indifference relation is not transitive, we cannot do so because "equality" *is* a transitive relation in a number system. Let us, however, bypass problems of this sort, which arise in mathematical psychology, and consider the simpler situation, where both the preference relation and the indifference relation are transitive. In assigning larger numbers to more preferred objects and equal numbers to objects between which the subject is indifferent, we establish an *ordinal utility scale* for the particular subject with respect to a particular set of objects.

The ordinal scale reflects both the subject's preference and his indifference between any two objects, but it does not reflect the magnitudes of the preference *differences*. That is, from utilities assigned to x, y, and z we can infer that the subject prefers x to y and y to z. But we cannot infer that his preference of x to y is greater (or smaller) than his preference of y to z. The particular numbers we have assigned to x, y, and z do not give us this information because we could have used other numbers with equal justification as long as their magnitudes correspond to the subject's preferences. For instance, to reflect the preference ordering $x \succ y \succ z$, we could have assigned 3, 2, and 1 respectively to x, y, and z, but also 7, 0, and -1 or 100, 99, and $\sqrt{2}$.

The question arises whether we can elicit more information from the subject which would enable us to compare utility differences. We might try asking the subject whether his preference for x over y is stronger or weaker than his preference for y over z. Usually, however, people find it difficult to answer questions of this sort. A more promising approach was proposed by J. Von Neumann and O. Morgenstern (1947).

Suppose x represents an orange, y an apple, and z a banana, and the subject prefers them in that order. We offer the subject a choice between

(i) An apple
(ii) A lottery ticket that entitles her to an orange with probability p or a banana with probability $(1-p)$. Such a lottery ticket will be denoted by $(p, 1-p)$.

If the subject chooses (i), we adjust the probabilities of the lottery so that "orange" becomes more probable (hence "banana" less probable). If she chooses (ii), we adjust the probabilities in the opposite direction.

Now if the lottery represented the orange with probability 1, the subject would, according to her stated preference, prefer the lottery to the apple. Likewise, if the lottery represented the banana with probability 1, she would prefer the apple. It is reasonable to assume that when the probability of orange is some p_a $(0 < p_a < 1)$ and of banana $(1-p_a)$, the subject will be indifferent between this lottery and the apple.

Now let us assign utilities 1, $u_a = p_a$, and 0 to orange, apple, and banana, respectively. The choice of 1 and 0 for the "best" and "worst" prizes is arbitrary. The choice of u_a is justified by the fact that once utility 1 has been assigned to orange and 0 to banana, the *statistically expected* utility of the lottery $(p_a, 1-p_a)$ is $(p_a)(1) + (1-p_a)(0) = p_a$. Because of the subject's indifference between the lottery and the apple, $u_a = p_a$ is also the utility of the apple.

Our three numbers, 0, u_a, and 1 now reflect not only the relative magnitudes of the utilities of these objects but also the relative magnitudes of the differences between these utilities; in fact, the ratio of these differences. We have now established an *interval* scale of utility.

The distinction between an ordinal and an interval scale can be brought out by noting how much "freedom" we have in assigning utilities to objects. In the case of the ordinal scale, our freedom of choice was restricted only by the relative (algebraic) magnitudes of the utilities. In mathematical terms, the ordinal scale *admits* all order-preserving transformations. That is, any transformation of the numbers representing utilities on an ordinal scale is permissible, as long as it preserves the order of magnitudes of the numbers. In the case of the interval scale, our freedom is more limited because the class of transformations admitted by that scale is narrower. Only *positive linear* transformations will preserve the property of the interval scale reflected in the concept of expected utility. These transformations are of the form

$$u' = au + b \qquad (a > 0) \tag{12}$$

To show that all positive linear transformations have the required property, let us apply any such transformation to our utilities, 0, u_a, and 1. We have

$$u'(1) = a + b; \quad u'(u_a) = au_a + b; \quad u'(0) = b. \tag{13}$$

On the new utility scale, $u'(L_p)$, the expected utility of any lottery $L_p = (p, 1 - p)$ is

$$(a + b)p + b(1 - p) = ap + b. \tag{14}$$

Since we set $u_a = p_a$ on the old scale, and u_a is transformed to $au_a + b$ on the new scale, we see that the utility of the apple is still represented by the utility of the lottery $(p_a, 1 - p_a)$.

Conversely, it can be shown that *only* a positive linear transformation preserves the required property of the utility scale.

Now that we have a method for establishing an interval utility scale for any three objects, we can attempt to apply it to any number of objects. As before, we will assign 1 to the most preferred object and 0 to the least preferred. We present the subject with choices between a lottery ticket $(p, 1 - p)$ involving these two objects and each of the others and calibrate p until the subject is indifferent in each case. We then assign utilities to the objects to correspond to those values of p and obtain the set of utilities $u_1 = 1, u_2, u_3, \ldots, u_{n-1}, u_n = 0$ for the set of n objects.

But now new questions arise. Our utility scale was based on expected utilities of lotteries involving only the most preferred and the least preferred prizes. Will the required property of utility be manifested in lotteries involving other prizes; in particular, in lotteries involving more than two objects from the set? Specifically, suppose we present to our subject lotteries $L = (p_1, p_2, \ldots, p_n)$. The utility of a lottery is defined in our scheme as the associated expected utility

$$u(L) = u_1 p_1 + u_2 p_2 + \cdots + u_n p_n. \tag{15}$$

Will the subject prefer lottery L_1 to lottery L_2 if and only if $u(L_1) > u(L_2)$? This is indeed the condition that we require our utility model to satisfy.

Again, in view of the frequent unpredictability of individual human behavior, we must be prepared to witness violations of this condition. And again, rather than give up the idea of constructing an interval scale of utility, the mathematical psychologist makes explicit the conditions that his observations must satisfy to guarantee the *existence* of such a scale. These conditions are embodied in axioms (see Luce and Raiffa, 1957, Chapter 2).

Some of these axioms are in obvious accord with "common sense." Suppose, for example, the subject prefers x to y. Then presented with two lotteries involving x and y, $L_1 = (p_1, 1 - p_1)$ and $L_2 = (p_2, 1 - p_2)$, where $p_1 > p_2$, we can certainly expect our subject to prefer L_1 to L_2 because the former offers a greater chance of getting the more preferred prize. This expectation is embodied in one of the axioms.

Another axiom states that if the subject is indifferent between a lottery L_1 and a prize x involved in another lottery L_2, then if lottery ticket L_1 is substituted for x in L_2, the subject should still be indifferent between L_2 and the resulting lottery.

Still another axiom states that "two-stage" lotteries should have the same utilities as simple lotteries, provided the net probabilities of the prizes are the same in both. To illustrate, let a simple lottery L offer a prize x with probability p and nothing with probability $(1 - p)$. A two-stage lottery L' offers a ticket to lottery L with probability q or nothing with probability $(1 - q)$. Consider a simple lottery L'' that offers x with probability r or nothing with probability $(1 - r)$. If $r = pq$, then according to the axiom the subject should be indifferent between L' and L''.

Observation of gambling behavior suggests that this expectation may or may not be corroborated. Some people prefer two-stage lotteries to simple ones, others simple ones to two-stage ones, even if the net probabilities associated with the prizes are the same. Clearly, "emotional" rather than "rational" factors are involved in these preferences. In an empirically oriented predictive model of choice behavior, such factors may have to be taken into account. Here, however, we are concerned not with a predictive model but only with problems arising in constructing a measurement scale of preferences.

The above discussion served to bring out two important aspects of the mathematical approach to the behavioral sciences; namely, the special problems that arise in constructing scales of measurement and the use of axiomatic formulation *preparatory* to constructing a model, whether in a predictive, normative, or analytic-descriptive mode.

As we have seen, serious problems of measurement arise where there is no concrete unit to serve as a standard of comparison. This situation arose in physics in connection with the measurement of temperature. The uniform gradation of a thermometer reflects the assumption that an alcohol thermometer will give the same readings as a mercury thermometer. It is fortunate that it does; otherwise the problem of establishing a scale of temperature would be much more difficult. The relatively uniform expansion of heated bodies permits the establishment of an interval scale of temperature in degrees Fahrenheit, Celsius, and so on. Hence these scales must be related by a positive linear transformation:

$$F = \tfrac{9}{5}C + 32; \qquad C = \tfrac{5}{9}F - \tfrac{160}{9} \tag{16}$$

where F is degrees Fahrenheit and C is degrees Celsius.

When these scales are used, *ratios* of temperatures make no sense. For instance, if the temperature was $10°C$ on Monday and $20°C$ on Tuesday, we cannot say that Tuesday was twice as warm as Monday because the same temperatures on the Fahrenheit scale are $50°F$ and $68°F$, which, of course, are not in the same ratio. In many branches of physics, ratios of temperatures enter in a theoretically significant way. These ratios have acquired meaning only in consequence of establishing a *ratio* scale for temperature. On this scale, only the *unit* is chosen arbitrarily. On conventional scales (for example, Celsius or Fahrenheit) the point of origin, that is, $0°$, was also chosen by convention. But on the absolute (Kelvin) scale, this point of origin is fixed in nature, the so-called absolute zero.

The ratio scale admits only the *similarity transformation*:

$$u' = au \qquad (a > 0). \tag{17}$$

It is easily seen that the similarity transformation is a special case of the positive linear transformation obtained by setting $b = 0$ in Equation 12. The positive linear transformation is, in turn, a special case of the order-preserving transformation (because it is also order-preserving).

In general, the scale that admits a narrower class of transformations is called a *stronger* scale. The strongest scale of all is the *absolute* scale, which admits only the trivial identity transformation, $u' = u$. For example, probability is given on an absolute scale because both the origin and the unit of that scale are fixed as the probability of the impossible event and the probability of the certain event, respectively.

The strength of a scale of measurement is of utmost importance in mathematical models because the legitimacy of mathematical operations on measurable quantities depends on it. As we have seen, ratios of quantities measurable only on an interval scale have no meaning because they do not remain invariant when linear transformations (admissible for that scale) are applied to these quantities. Only ratios of differences remain invariant on that scale and thus are meaningful. For example, if the temperature drops to 59° F on Wednesday, we can say that the drop was one half the rise of temperature from Monday to Tuesday. This statement remains true if we record the temperatures in degrees Celsius.

Multiplication and division are both meaningful when applied to quantities on a ratio scale, but exponentiation is not; x^y has no meaning if x and y are given on ratio scales. Exponentiation and its inverse (taking logarithms) can be applied only to dimensionless numbers given on an absolute scale.

Behavioral scientists who become quantitatively oriented but who are unaware of these restrictions sometimes write meaningless mathematical-*looking* formulas to express some intuitive relationship. I once saw the expression $E = MC^2$ intended to represent the relationship of efficiency (E) of a work group to its morale (M) and its competence (C). To give meaning to this relationship, it is not enough to indicate how "efficiency," "morale," and "competence" are to be measured. It is also necessary to show that these measurements can be obtained on scales strong enough to permit the indicated operations. Thus a theory of scale construction is a vital component in the development of mathematical models of behavior.[5]

Another important aspect of model building in the behavioral sciences is the prominence of the *axiomatic approach*. The physicist also constructs theories on axiomatic foundations. For instance, the basic physical laws (conservation of mass and energy, laws of motion, and so on) can be regarded as axioms. As we have seen, however, the axioms underlying systems of measurement are of another kind. They are not statements about "reality" (as physical laws are) but rather about conditions to be satisfied if quantification is to make sense. In fact, the behavioral scientist has no axioms analogous to the highly reliable physical laws. The assumptions that underlie models of behavior remain hypotheses, not established "facts." usually, these hypotheses are fitted *ad hoc* to various contexts, which precludes the construction of a grandoise edifice of behavioral science analogous to that of mathematical physics.

The axioms (as distinguished from hypotheses) underlying analytic-descriptive models in the behavioral sciences relate to the internal consistencies of such models. For instance, the axioms underlying the construction of an interval utility scale relate to certain consistencies in choice behavior that guarantee the mere existence of such a scale for a given subject in a given situation. In terms of this scale (if it exists), the preferences of the subject can be compactly described. Once such a scale is established, it can perhaps be used to construct a predictive theory; for instance, one that relates subjects' preferences to their personalities or the preferences of a given subject under different conditions.

The axiomatic approach is not limited to problems of quantification. As we shall see, it reaches its peaks of prominence in nonquantitative analytic-descriptive models. For example, in the theory of social choice (see Chapter 18), it was precisely the discovery of an internal inconsistency among the axioms proposed for a "democratic" rule of social decision that instigated far-reaching investigations based on analytic-desciptive models of social choice.

The axiomatic approach embodies the clearest expression of the spirit of mathematics and of its role as a language of *complete clarity*. The axioms lay bare the skeleton of our thinking process and thus subject us to the strictest intellectual discipline. At the same time, the axiomatic approach endows the mathematical model builder with freedom because the only restriction on a system of axioms is its internal consistency. This almost paradoxical blend of freedom and discipline (which in human affairs are often regarded as "opposites") is, perhaps, the most valuable asset of mathematical thinking.

The topics discussed in this book will be grouped in accordance with the predominant mathematical tools used in the investigations rather than by their content areas. This arrangement reflects the view that a mathematical method can serve as a unifying principle for behavioral sciences better than a content area. In the natural sciences, content areas do provide natural foci of conceptual organization. Physics treats of general properties of matter, regardless of its chemical composition; chemistry distinguishes between different kinds of matter; physiology examines events that constitute living processes of individual organisms; population genetics provides explanations of biological evolution, and so on. It would seem that similar foci of conceptualization could be identified in the behavioral sciences. Psychology is concerned with the perception, motivations, and behavior of individuals; sociology, with structures of large human aggregates, and so on.

However, this systematization of the behavioral sciences by disciplines has not led to clear and potent unifying concepts analogous, say, to temperature in physics, valence in chemistry, respiration in physiology, or selection pressure in population genetics. Mathematical methods do suggest pervasive unifying principles. They do so in physics. Consider the following differential equations.

$$m \frac{d^2 x}{dt^2} + r \frac{dx}{dt} + kx = f(t) \tag{18}$$

$$L \frac{d^2 q}{dt^2} + R \frac{dq}{dt} + \frac{q}{C} = F(t) \tag{19}$$

In Equation 18, x is the displacement of a harmonic oscillator from its equilibrium position, m is the mass of the oscillator, r is friction or air resistance, k the restoring force per unit of displacement, and $f(t)$ the imposed force as a function of time (t). In Equation 19, an equation of an electrical system with alternating current, q is electric charge, L is inductance, R the resistance, and C the capacitance of the system, while $F(t)$ is the imposed voltage as a function of time.

The two equations have exactly the same mathematical form but represent two widely different contents. Thus a type of mathematical model unifies two different theories—the theory of sinusoidal oscillators and the theory of the alternating current.

We will find that similar mathematical models can represent widely different contents in the behavioral sciences. A differential equation or a system of such equations can serve as a model in any context where it is reasonable to assume relations between measurable quantities and their rates of change. A graph can describe any structure based on a network of binary relations. Probabilistic assumptions about a subject's responses can generate models both of choices based on preference and discriminations of stimulus intensities. Similar stochastic processes underlie models of social mobility, some dynamic demographic models, and simple learning models. In this way, mathematical models provide a rigorous foundation for theories based on analogy by removing subjective, connotative aspects of analogical thinking, leaving only demonstrable structural bases of analogy. It is in this sense that the mathematical approach imparts understanding and insights.

A word is in order on the selection of topics in this book. Both relatively fruitful and relatively sterile mathematical treatments of various content areas have been included. The inclusion of the latter was motivated by three aims: to present the mode of thinking that guided the early, for the most part unsuccesful attempts to mathematicize behavioral science; to provide leverage for a critical evaluation of the use of mathematical models outside the natural sciences; and to illustrate the social pressures that stimulated the development of these models. These aspects will be discussed more fully in the last chapter.

NOTES

[1] The angle is measured in radians. One radian subtends an arc of a circle, whose length equals the radius of the circle. Thus $360° = 2\pi$ radians.

[2] The general solution of Equation 3 can be expressed as an elliptic function.

[3] It is remarkable that Galileo ignored the observation, called to his attention by another experimenter, that the period of a pendulum swinging through large arcs does depend on the amplitude. Although Galileo was an enthusiastic experimenter, his ideas were influenced by Plato's idealistic conceptions. Perhaps for this reason he attributed the observed nonisochronic properties of the pendulum to extraneous factors, that is, violations of ideal conditions.

[4] A philosopher; not to be confused with the mathematician, W. Hamilton.

[5] For a thorough discussion of this problem, see Luce (1959b).

PART I

CLASSICAL MODELS

CHAPTER ONE

Mathematical Demography

One of the earliest mathematical models of relevance to social science is the Malthusian model of population growth. T.M. Malthus (1798), it will be recalled, argued that a human population tends to outstrip available food supply because the population grows in geometric progression while available arable land grows only in arithmetic progression. That is to say, the population tends to increase by a multiplicative factor in equal intervals of time, whereas arable land can be increased only by constant amounts in equal intervals of time. Thus population tends to be an exponential function of time, whereas the amount of arable land can be only a linear function of time. No matter how steeply the linear function increases, an exponential function will eventually exceed it. The mathematical model from which the population is derived as an exponential function of time can be formulated as a differential equation:

$$\frac{dp}{dt} = kp, \tag{1.1}$$

where p is the size of the population, dp/dt its rate of growth, and k is a constant. The equation reflects the assumption that the increase per individual per unit time is constant.

Equation 1.1 can be written

$$\frac{dp}{p} = k \, dt. \tag{1.2}$$

Integrating both sides, we have

$$\log_e p = kt + K, \tag{1.3}$$

where K is a constant of integration. Taking exponentials and imposing the condition $p(0) = p_0$, we have

$$p(t) = p_0 e^{kt}. \tag{1.4}$$

If k, the (constant) rate of growth per individual, is negative, Equation 1.4 represents *exponential decay*, whereby the population tends to zero. If k is zero, the population remains constant. If k is positive, the population must exceed any given size.

Since unlimited growth is never actually observed, other factors must be acting to stem population growth. Malthus supposed that these factors would be catastrophic; for example, mass starvation. It is, however, possible to conceive a constraint on population growth that acts gradually, dependent, say, on the size of the population already attained. Specifically, suppose k is not a constant but a linearly decreasing function of population size:

$$k(p) = a - bp, \tag{1.5}$$

where now a and b are constants. Substituting Equation 1.5 into Equation 1.1, we obtain

$$dp/dt = ap - bp^2. \tag{1.6}$$

Proceeding as above, we rewrite Equation 1.6 as

$$\frac{dp}{ap - bp^2} = \frac{(1/a)dp}{p} + \frac{(b/a)dp}{a - bp} = dt. \tag{1.7}$$

Integrating, rearranging, and imposing the initial condition $p(0) = p_0'$, we obtain the population size as a function of time:

$$p(t) = \frac{ap_0 e^{at}}{a - bp_0(1 - e^{at})}. \tag{1.8}$$

The function of time represented by Equation 1.8 is called a *logistic* function, and a population that grows in this way is called a logistic population. During the nineteenth and the first decades of the twentieth century, several countries in Western Europe and the United States exhibited population growth curves of this type. The curves are S-shaped, showing initial increase and later decrease in the rate of growth (that is, the first derivative) and tending to a constant value. Indeed, if we let t go to infinity in Equation 1.8, $p(t)$ approaches a/b asymptotically. Thus a logistic population does not "explode," as does a Malthusian population. The dependence of the rate of increase (that is, the excess of the birth rate over the death rate) per individual on the size of the population acts as a "brake" and leads to a "zero-growth" steady state. A typical "logistic" population is shown in Figure 1.1.

The logistic is not the only function characterized by an S-shaped graph. Any such graph can be "fitted" (in a finite time span) by a polynomial of sufficiently high degree; indeed, to any desired degree of approximation. There is, however, a fundamental difference between fitting a set of data by a curve defined

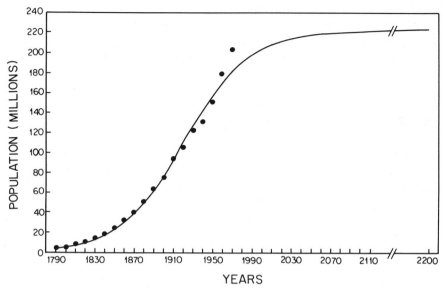

Figure 1.1. U.S. population growth fitted by a logistic curve Equation (1.8) with $a = 0.03067$ per capita per year (estimated from increase between 1790 and 1800) and $b = 1.363 \times 10^{-10}$ (projecting to asymptotically constant population of 225 million). Note the "slump" in the Depression decade 1930–1940 and the "spurt" in the decades following.

by some mathematical formula and constructing a mathematical model from which a mathematical formula is derived. In the former case, the constants (that is, the coefficients of a polynomial) are not in general readily interpretable. They are introduced *ad hoc* to fit the data, so that the formula is no more than a mathematical description of the observed data. In contrast, the constants that enter a mathematical model (the *parameters* of the model) usually reflect some assumptions about the underlying dynamics. For example, in Equation 1.6, the parameter a can be interpreted as the rate of growth per individual per unit time of a population of very low density, whereas b can be interpreted as the effect of crowdedness, inasmuch as in a high-density population, the rate of contact between individuals moving randomly in their environment is proportional to the square of the density and so, in a fixed area, to the square of population size. According to this model, the growth rate is negatively affected by frequency of contact. In nonhuman populations, such contacts may involve competition for available food supplies; in human populations, an awareness of "crowdedness." Interpretation of parameters confers upon a mathematical model a degree of theoretical leverage, which curve-fitting ordinarily does not do.

The Malthusian and the logistic models of population growth represent the simplest use of classical mathematical methods in demography, the branch of sociology concerned with the size and composition of human populations. Two sorts of problem are central in demography. One concerns the composition of a population; that is, its components identified by sex, ethnic origin, or some other characteristic. Dynamic models designed to account for changes in the sizes of such components are called *change-of-components models.* The other is concerned, among other things, with the age distribution of a given population. The corresponding models are called *cohort-survival models.* We shall examine examples of each type of model in turn.

MODELS OF SEX COMPOSITION

Let the two components of a population be males and females. According to the Malthusian hypothesis, the rate of growth per unit time per individual remains constant. However, the overall rate of growth depends on the size of the population, more precisely on both the number of males and the number of females, whereby the coefficients representing this dependence may be different for males and for females. The simplest generalization of the Malthusian model for two components leads to a pair of differential equations:

$$\frac{dm}{dt} = am + bf \tag{1.9}$$

$$\frac{df}{dt} = gf + km, \tag{1.10}$$

where m and f are the numbers of men and women, respectively, and a, b, g, and k are constants.

The model is based on the assumption that men and women are approximately equally represented in the population and that matings are random. Neglected is the biological fact that a man can impregnate several women in rapid succession but a woman can be impregnated only once in one or two years. If u and v are birth rates of males and females, respectively, *per couple*, $u/2$ and $v/2$ are the respective birth rates per capita. Let μ and v be the respective death rates per capita of men and women. Then if we write $a = u/2 - \mu$, $g = v/2 - v$, $b = u/2$, and $k = v/2$, we obtain Equations 1.9 and 1.10.

To solve the system, we differentiate Equation 1.9 with respect to t:

$$\frac{d^2m}{dt^2} = a \frac{dm}{dt} + b \frac{df}{dt}. \tag{1.11}$$

Substituting Equation 1.10 for df/dt, we get

$$\frac{d^2m}{dt^2} = a \frac{dm}{dt} + bgf + bkm. \tag{1.12}$$

Solving for bf in Equation 1.9 and substituting into Equation 1.12, we obtain

$$\frac{d^2m}{dt^2} = a \frac{dm}{dt} + g \frac{dm}{dt} + (bk - ag)m. \tag{1.13}$$

Equation 1.13 is in the form

$$\frac{d^2m}{dt^2} + p \frac{dm}{dt} + qm = 0, \tag{1.14}$$

where p and q are constants. The general solution of equations of this type is

$$m(t) = Ae^{r_1 t} + Be^{r_2 t},\qquad(1.15)$$

where r_1 and r_2 are the roots of the polynomial

$$x^2 + px + q = 0,\qquad(1.16)$$

while the constants A and B are determined by the initial conditions. Here $r_1 = \frac{1}{2}(a+g+h)$; $r_2 = \frac{1}{2}(a+g-h)$ with $h = \sqrt{(a-g)^2 + 4bk}$. Consequently, we have $m(t)$ as a function of time, which also determines $f(t)$ as a function of time. Specifically,

$$m(t) = A \exp\left\{\frac{(a+g+h)t}{2}\right\} + B \exp\left\{\frac{(a+g-h)t}{2}\right\}\qquad(1.17)$$

$$f(t) = \frac{A(-a+g+h)}{2b}\exp\{(a+g+h)t/2\} + \frac{B(-a+g-h)}{2b}\exp\{(a+g-h)t/2\}\quad(1.18)$$

The constants A and B are determined by the initial conditions; namely, $A+B = m(0)$; $A(-a+g+h) + B(-a+g-h) = 2bf(0)$. A variable of interest is the sex ratio:

$$s(t) = \frac{m(t)}{f(t)} = \frac{1 + Be^{-ht}/A}{(g-a+h)/2b + Be^{-ht}(g-a-h)/2Ab}.\qquad(1.19)$$

As t tends to infinity, the sex ratio tends to

$$s(\infty) = \frac{2b}{(g-a+h)}.\qquad(1.20)$$

Or, in terms of birth and death rates,

$$s(\infty) = \frac{2u}{(v-u) + 2(\mu - v) + \sqrt{(u+v)^2 + 4(\mu - v)^2 - 4(u-v)(\mu - v)}}\qquad(1.21)$$

If the birth rates and/or the death rates are disparate, the sex ratio can become considerably larger or smaller than unity. When this happens, men or women may become *marriage dominant*. For example, women are marriage dominant if they are strongly outnumbered by men, so that almost every woman can find a husband, but men can find wives. In that case, the overall birth rate will depend predominantly on the number of women. If men are marriage dominant, the birth rate will depend predominantly on the number of men. To reflect such situations, Equations 1.9 and 1.10 are modified accordingly. The interested reader is referred to Goodman (1952).

Another interesting feature is the threshold between a dying-out and an "exploding" population. From Equations 1.17 and 1.18, we see that this threshold is given by the condition $(a+g) = -h$, or by definition of h as

$$(a+g)^2 = (a-g)^2 + 4kb,\qquad(1.22)$$

which simplifies to $ag = kb$, or, in terms of birth and death rates,

$$(u - 2\mu)(v - 2v) = uv. \tag{1.23}$$

If u and v are both positive, the two factors on the left of Equation 1.23 must have the same sign. But μ and v must both be positive (since people are mortal). Therefore the equality cannot be satisfied if $(u - 2\mu) > 0$ and $(v - 2v) > 0$. It could be satisfied if $(u - 2\mu) < -u$ and $0 > (v - 2v) > -v$, or if $0 > (u - 2\mu) > -u$ and $(v - 2v) < -v$. In the former case, $u < \mu$ and $v > v$; in the latter, $u > \mu$ and $v < v$. In either case, at least one sex would be dying out. Eventually, the number of males and females would become widely disparate, so that Equations 1.9 and 1.10 could no longer apply. Consequently, the only way a population represented by Equations 1.9 and 1.10 could become stabilized is if the birth and death rates of both sexes were equal.

FERTILITY, MORTALITY, AND AGE DISTRIBUTION

We turn to the cohort-survival model. A characteristic of central interest in mathematical demography is the age distribution of a population. Clearly this distribution is a crucial factor not only in the rate of growth or decline of the population, which depends essentially on the proportion of women of child-bearing age, but also in other important respects; for instance, the available labor force, the need for educational and medical facilities, the extent of demand for old age pensions, and so on. Thus projections of future age distribution of a population can play an important part in social planning.

How is the age distribution of a population determined, and how does it affect population growth? What factors contribute to changes in this distribution? Under what conditions will the distribution become stabilized?

We will first consider a population in which fertility and mortality schedules (to be defined below) are constant in time. Moreover, immigration and emigration will be ignored, so that only births and deaths effect changes in population size. The problem to be solved first is that of determining the age distribution that has already been stabilized. The problem of how the age distribution becomes stabilized will be considered later.

Although disparate proportions of men and women in a population have a bearing on the rate of growth (see p. 35), approximately equal proportions, typical in human populations, make it possible to confine attention to women. In the models to be presently discussed, the population will be assumed to consist of females.

A population with a constant age distribution is called *stable*. Note that stability in this context does not imply a constant population size. In fact, a population with a constant birth rate and a constant death rate (which, as we shall see, are implied by a constant age distribution) grows (or declines) exponentially; that is, it is a *Malthusian* population.

We need the following notation.

$m(a)$: rate of bearing female children at age a (fertility schedule). That is, $m(a)$ represents the probability that a female of age a will give birth to a daughter in a given year.

$\mu(a)$: death rate at age a (mortality schedule). That is, $\mu(a)$ represents the probability that a female of age a will die in a given year.

$c(a)$: proportion of women of age a. That is, $c(a)da$ is the fraction of the females between ages a and $a + da$. Note that by definition $\int_0^\infty c(a)\, da = 1$.

The birth rate b and the death rate d (number of females per female per year born or dying, respectively) can be calculated from the above quantities. Namely,

$$b = \int_0^\infty c(a)m(a)\, da \text{ is the female birth rate.}$$

$$d = \int_0^\infty c(a)\mu(a)\, da \text{ is the female death rate.}$$

Thus

$r = b - d$ is the rate of growth of the population, the yearly increase of females per female.

$N(t)$: the total number of females in the population at time (that is, year) t. If $N(0)$ is the size of the female population at time 0, its size at time t will be $N(0)e^{rt}$, and its size a years ago was $N(0)e^{-ra}$.

Similarly, if $B(t)$ and $D(t)$ respectively are the total numbers of births and deaths per year, we have

$$B(t) = B(0)e^{rt},$$
$$D(t) = D(0)e^{rt}.$$

Finally, we introduce

$p(a)$: the probability that an arbitrarily selected female *survives* to age a.

A cohort of women born in some year will be depleted by the mortality schedule $\mu(x)$, where x ranges from 0 to a. If $\mu(x)$ were independent of age x, the fraction of this cohort surviving to age a would be $e^{-\mu a}$. Since, however, μ is a function of age x, the fraction that survives to age a will be

$$p(a) = e^{-\int_0^a \mu(x)dx}, \tag{1.24}$$

which can be regarded as the probability that an arbitrarily selected female will survive to age a.

Differentiating both sides of Equation 1.24 with respect to a, we obtain the relationship between the mortality schedule and the survival probability $p(a)$:

$$\mu(a) = -\frac{dp}{da}\frac{1}{p(a)} \tag{1.25}$$

The age distribution $c(a)$ can now be calculated as follows.

Given birth rate b, the number of females born a years ago was bNe^{-ra} and the number that has survived to age a is $bNe^{-ra}p(a)$. Dividing by the total number N, we have

$$c(a) = \frac{bNe^{-ra}p(a)}{N} = be^{-ra}p(a). \tag{1.26}$$

Since $\int_0^\infty c(a)\,da = 1$, we also have

$$b = \int_0^\infty e^{-ra}p(a)\,da \tag{1.27}$$

Further, since $\int_0^\infty c(a)m(a)da = b$, we have

$$\int_0^\infty e^{-ra}p(a)m(a)\,da = \frac{1}{b}\int_0^\infty c(a)m(a)\,da = 1 \tag{1.28}$$

If $p(a)$ and $m(a)$ are known, the rate of growth of the population, r, can be determined as the value that satisfies Equation 1.28.

Given $m(a)$ and $\mu(a)$, hence also $p(a)$ (determined by Equation 1.24), the growth rate r of a stable population can be determined by numerical procedures. Starting with an arbitrary value of r, we calculate the integral (Equation 1.28). Clearly, the value of this integral must decrease as r increases. Consequently, if the value of the integral is less than 1, r should be decreased; if greater than 1, increased until the value of the integral becomes 1.

It is, of course, desirable to derive r analytically; that is, as an explicit function of the population parameters. For this purpose, additional characteristics of the population are required.

$GRR = \int_0^\infty m(a)\,da$, the *gross reproduction rate*, defined as the expected number of daughters per woman, assuming that she lives through her age of reproduction.

$NRR = \int_0^\infty m(a)p(a)\,da$, the *net reproduction rate*, defined as the expected number of daughters per female in the population (clearly smaller than GRR, since some females do not survive through their reproductive age).

$\bar{m} = \dfrac{\int_0^\infty am(a)\,da}{\int_0^\infty m(a)\,da}$, the *mean age of reproduction*.

$\sigma^2 = \dfrac{\int_0^\infty a^2 m(a)\,da}{\int_0^\infty m(a)\,da}$, $-\bar{m}^2$, the *age variance* of the fertility schedule.

$T = \dfrac{\log(NRR)}{r}$, the *mean length of generation* in a stable population.

An approximate formula for $r = \log(\mathrm{NRR}/T)$ is given by

$$r = \frac{\log(\mathrm{GRR})p(\bar{m})}{\bar{m} - \sigma^2\mu(\bar{m}) + \log(\mathrm{GRR})p(\bar{m})/2\bar{m}} \qquad (1.29)$$

Note that all the population parameters on which the rate of growth of a stable population depends can be calculated from just two characteristics of the population, the fertility schedule, $m(a)$, and the mortality schedule, $\mu(a)$. Partial derivatives of r with respect to any of these parameters represent the corresponding sensitivities of the rate of growth to changes in these parameters. These partial derivatives, being themselves functions of the same parameters, depend on their magnitudes, which vary, sometimes widely, in different populations. For instance, GRR depends on the frequency of early marriages, on birth control practices, and, to some extent, on longevity (if a substantial proportion of women do not survive through their fertile period). The mortality parameter $\mu(\bar{m})$, hence also $p(\bar{m})$, depend on the state of health, hygiene, and so on. Values of GRR as low as 0.30 (that is, an average of only 0.30 daughters per female) and as high as 4.20 have been recorded. In some populations, almost all women survive through their age of fertility; in others, less than one third. Values of $\bar{m}$ have been observed to vary between 26 and 33 years.

By way of illustration, Table 1.1 shows differences in r (per thousand) resulting from 10% changes in the various parameters, coupled with different values of GRR. In all cases, $\bar{m}$ was taken as 28, $p(30)$ as 0.85, and σ^2 as 45.

The mean age of fertility, $\bar{m}$, is usually observed to be close to 30, and mortality at that age, $\mu(m)$, close to $\log[2\bar{m}/p(\bar{m})]$. On the basis of these observations, another approximate formula for r can be written, which will be used below:

$$r = \frac{[(\bar{m}+30)/60]\log p(30) + \log \mathrm{GRR}}{\bar{m} - \sigma^2(\log \mathrm{GRR})/2\bar{m}} \qquad (1.30)$$

We see from the table that r is more sensitive to changes in GRR and in $p(30)$ than to changes in σ^2. We see also that the sensitivity of r to GRR and to $p(30)$ varies only slightly at different values of GRR, but its sensitivity to $\bar{m}$ depends considerably on the value of this parameter.

Table 1.1 *Differences in r (per 1,000) Resulting from 10% Changes in the Various Parameters When the Levels of GRR are as Indicated*

Parameter Subject to 10% Change	Level of GRR			
	0.80	1.00	2.00	4.00
GRR	3.35	3.40	3.53	3.68
$p(30)$	3.28	3.30	3.56	3.43
$\bar{m}$	1.53	0.79	−1.68	−4.46
σ^2	0.01	0.00	0.04	0.18

Source: Adapted from Coale, 1972.

The last observation brings out a feature of population dynamics that may not be intuitively evident. Namely, when the gross reproduction rate is large, an increase of the mean reproduction age (that is, later childbearing) has a negative effect on the rate of growth, as one would expect; but if GRR is small, later childbearing seems to have a positive effect on population growth, contrary to common sense expectations. On closer examination, however, this result is paradoxical only if it is interpreted to mean that postponing births will by itself increase the rate of growth. The point is that postponing births will (other things being equal) reduce GRR and through it will reduce r, as can be seen from Equation 1.29. The increase of r with $\bar{m}$ for low values of GRR is derived by differentiating r *partially* with respect to $\bar{m}$; that is, by assuming that GRR remains constant while $\bar{m}$ increases. But GRR can remain constant while $\bar{m}$ increases only if some other changes occur; for example, if infant mortality decreases. It turns out that such other changes more than offset the "braking" effect of postponed births on r if GRR remains constant.

The theoretical significance of the stable population model derives from the fact that the age distribution and the rate of growth of any population with fixed fertility and mortality schedules must eventually (that is, asymptotically) become stable. This is a mathematical result. In actual populations, of course, fertility and mortality schedules undergo changes which have not been considered in the model, not to speak of changes induced by immigration and emigration. Nevertheless, the theoretical result is important because it points to the different sources of change in the population parameters. Given a population which because of its history has an age distribution different from that of a stable population, but in which fertility and mortality schedules have become stabilized, we can expect the age distribution of this population to approach that of the *same* stable population, regardless of its age distribution at the time when this stabilization occurred.

This trend toward a steady state, independent of the initial state, characterizes many dynamic models. As a simplest example, consider the logistic model represented by the differential Equation 1.6 and its solution (Equation 1.8). As t tends to infinity, the size of this population tends to a/b, which is independent of p_0, the initial population size. As we shall see in later chapters, many dynamic stochastic models also have this property of "equifinality."

Observations of "equifinality" have led some philosophers (and some biologists of the "vitalist" persuasion) to postulate the principle of "teleological causality" (related to Aristotle's "final cause"), according to which events are guided by "purposefulness," a striving to attain some definite future state. That this concept may reflect a naive anthropomorphic view is suggested by the fact that "equifinality" can be derived from a dynamic mathematical model without reference to a future state toward which the system represented by the model presumably "strives."

Consider the "equifinality" exhibited by the growth of some organisms. It can be experimentally demonstrated that if the growth of such an organism is temporarily arrested (for example, by restricting its food supply), then after the constraint has been removed, the organism "catches up"; that is, attains a final size not significantly different from that attained by controls not subjected to the constraint. It may appear that the organism "strives" to attain a certain final size and will do so even if it is temporarily "frustrated."

This sort of "equifinality" can be derived from a simple mathematical model of growth suggested by L. von Bertalanffy (1951) without recourse to teleological notions. Assume that the growth of an organism depends on two processes: anabolism and catabolism. Anabolism is the transformation of ingested food into the organism's biomass. Catabolism is the breakdown of biomass into waste products eventually excreted. If we assume that the rate of ingestion of nutrients is proportional to the surface area of the organism (say, because nutrients enter the body by diffusing through the surface as in some simple organisms) while the rate of breakdown of biomass is proportional to the volume (because catabolism occurs throughout the body of the organism), the rate of growth of the biomass, m, can be represented by the following differential equation:

$$\frac{dm}{dt} = am^{2/3} - bm \qquad (a, b \text{ constants}). \tag{1.31}$$

Since in a body of a given shape, m can be taken to be proportional to the volume and $m^{2/3}$ to the surface, the first term on the right of Equation 1.31 represents anabolism; the second catabolism.

Setting $dm/dt = 0$, we obtain the "final" (asymptotically approached) biomass as

$$m = \left(\frac{a}{b}\right)^3, \tag{1.32}$$

which is independent of the initial mass.

Let us return to population dynamics. The proof that a population with fixed fertility and mortality schedules must tend to a stable population was given by A.J. Lotka (1939). The proof consists of two parts. First it is shown that a population in which the number of births grows exponentially (that is, $B(t) = B(0)e^{rt}$) while the mortality schedule remains constant tends toward a constant age distribution, a constant birth rate, a constant death rate, and consequently a constant rate of growth. Next it is shown that once the fertility and mortality schedules are fixed, the births, $B(t)$, tend toward an exponential function. It follows that once the fertility and mortality schedules are fixed, the population tends toward a stable population. The reader interested in the mathematical details is referred to Lopez (1961), Lotka (1939), and Coale (1972).

We have mentioned a model of a population with a declining rate of growth; namely, the logistic model (see p. 32). We have seen, however, that in order to determine the principal features of a population, more information is required than is contained in the simple Malthusian or logistic models. In particular, the fertility and mortality "profiles" (schedules) of a population must be known. In the case of a stable (Malthusian) population, these schedules determine the overall birth and death rates, the (constant) rate of growth, and the (steady-state) age distribution. In the case of a nonstable population, all these characteristics are functions of time, and their determination (as functions of time) is considerably more involved. The interested reader is referred to the pioneering work of A.J. Lotka (1939), aimed appropriately at determining the "true" rate of growth of a population, which cannot be determined on the basis of current birth and death rates alone.

Here we will present, following A.J. Coale (1972), an analysis of population dynamics where mortality is constant but fertility declines at a constant rate; that is, is reduced by the same factor each year in all ages. As before, we consider only the female population.

The first task is to determine the number of births per year in such a population as a function of time. The fundamental integral equation is

$$B(t) = \int_0^\infty B(t-a)m(a, t)p(a)\, da. \tag{1.33}$$

On the right, $B(t-a)$ represents the number of female births a years before the time (t) in question; $p(a)$ is the fraction of these females that have survived to age a, that is, are alive at time t; $m(a, t)$ is the number of births per female of age a in year t; and the integral sums all these births over a to give the total number of births in year t.

Denoting the net reproduction rate (NRR, see p. 38) by $R(t)$, we can write Equations 2.33, in view of $\text{NRR}(t) = R(t) = \int_0^\infty m(a, t)p(a)\, da$, as

$$B(t) = R(t) \int_0^\infty B(t-a)f(a, t)\, da, \tag{1.34}$$

where

$$f(a, t) = \frac{m(a, t)p(a)}{\int_0^\infty m(a, t)p(a)da}. \tag{1.35}$$

Since $m(a, t)$ declines at a constant rate, we have

$$m(a, t) = m(a, 0)e^{kt} \qquad (k < 0). \tag{1.36}$$

Hence equation 1.33 can be written as

$$B(t) = R(0)e^{kt} \int_0^\infty B(t-a)f(a, 0)\, da. \tag{1.37}$$

Note that the limits of the integral (Equation 1.34) and hence Equation 1.37 can be taken as α and β, which denote respectively the lowest and the highest age of reproduction because $m(a, t)$ vanishes outside these limits. By the Mean Value Theorem of Integral Calculus, there exists a value of a, $T(t)$ $(a \leqslant t \leqslant \beta)$ such that

$$\int_\alpha^\beta B(t-a)f(a, 0)\, da = B(t - T(t)).[1] \tag{1.38}$$

With declining fertility, $R(t)$ will eventually equal 1, beginning with some value greater than 1. If we fix the origin of time at that year, we can write $R(0)=1$. Then Equation 1.37 can be written as

$$B(t) = e^{kt}B(t - T(t)).$$ (1.39)

In general, $T(t)$ will vary with t. As a first approximation to the solution of Equation 1.39, Coale assumes that $T(t)$ is independent of t: $T(t) = T_0$, the mean length of a generation approached as the net reproduction rate approaches unity. The origin of time being fixed at that moment, we have

$$T_0 = \frac{\int_0^\infty ap(a)m(a)\,da}{\int_0^\infty p(a)m(a)\,da}.$$ (1.40)

When T_0 replaces $T(t)$ in Equation 1.39, the solution of this difference equation is easily found to be

$$B(t) = B(0)\exp\left(\frac{k}{2}t + \frac{k}{2T_0}t^2\right).$$ (1.41)

If, as assumed, $k < 0$, $B(t)$ will continually decline from $t = 0$ on, as expected. If, however, we project $B(t)$ to the past ($t < 0$), we see that the expression in the braces on the right of Equation 1.41 is positive for $t > -T_0$ and negative for $t < -T_0$. To see this intuitively, assume that a "short time ago" ($t > -T_0$), the population was smaller, and, although fertility was greater, it was not sufficiently greater to compensate for the smaller population. A "long time ago" ($t < -T_0$), fertility was sufficiently greater to overcompensate for the smaller rate of growth.

To project $B(t)$ from an arbitrary year, we must drop the assumption that $R(0) = 1$. However, the first approximation represented by Equation 1.41 has been shown to be sufficiently accurate in projecting a simulated population over several decades.

A second approximation gives an almost exact solution of Equation 1.37:

$$B(t) = B(0)\exp\left[\frac{k}{2} + \frac{\sigma^2 k}{2T_0}\left(\frac{1}{T_0} - \frac{k}{12}\right)t + \frac{k}{2T_0}\left(1 + \frac{\sigma^2 k}{4T_0}\right)t^2 + \frac{\sigma^2 k^2}{6T_0^3}t^3\right].$$ (1.42)

To calculate the age distribution, we observe that

$$N(a, t) = B(t - a)p(a).$$ (1.43)

Using the approximate formula (Equation 1.41) for $B(t)$, we have

$$N(a, t) = B(t)\exp\left(-\frac{k}{2}a + \frac{k}{2T_0}a^2\right)\exp\left(-\frac{kt}{T_0}\right)p(a).$$ (1.44)

Now at a particular time t, we have $r(t) = \log R(t)/T(t)$ (see p. 38). If we use the approximation used in deriving Equation 1.41, namely $T(t) = T_0$, Equation 1.44 can be written as

$$N(a, t) = B(t)\exp\left[-\frac{k}{2}a + \frac{k}{2T_0}a^2 - r(t)a\right]p(a).$$ (1.45)

Thus

$$c(a, t) = \frac{N(a, t)}{N(t)} b(t) \exp\left[-\frac{k}{2} a + \frac{k}{2T_0} a^2 - r(t)a \right] p(a). \qquad (1.46)$$

We can now examine the ratio of age distribution associated respectively with a population with constantly declining fertility and a stable population characterized by the same values of parameters at time t. Recall that for a fixed t, the age distribution of a stable population is given by

$$c_s(a, t) = b_s(t)e^{-r(t)a}p(a). \qquad (1.47)$$

Then the ratio of the age distribution is given by

$$\frac{c(a, t)}{c_s(a, t)} = \frac{b(t)}{b_s(t)} \exp\left(-\frac{k}{2} a + \frac{k}{2T_0} a^2 \right). \qquad (1.48)$$

The exponent on the right of Equation 1.48 vanishes for $a = T_0$, is positive for $a < T_0$, negative for $a > T_0$. This implies that the population with a history of declining fertility is "younger" than a stable population characterized by the same parameters at a given time t. This should be intuitively evident because during its history (that is, at times $t' < t$) the former population had a higher fertility, and we have already seen that of two populations with the same mortality, the population with higher fertility is "younger."

To illustrate the test of the model, we examine the age distribution in the United States in 1930. The fertility of that population had been declining since 1910 at an average rate of 1.64% per year. Figure 1.2 shows a comparison between the age distribution of a population with this history of declining fertility and a stable population with the same parameters in 1930 (dotted curves). The actual 1930 age distribution is shown by the solid curve. We see that the agreement between observed and theoretical age distributions is almost perfect in middle and old age. The deviations in younger ages can be ascribed to factors not incorporated into the model.

Similar methods lead to derivation of population parameters of a population with changing mortality. The interested reader is referred to Coale (1972), Chapter 5.

We have seen that all the parameters of a stable population are determined by its fertility and mortality schedules. We can therefore assess the effects of changes in these schedules on the parameters of the population after it has become stabilized (see Coale, 1956). The ratio of the age distributions of two populations is given by

$$\frac{c_2(a)}{c_1(a)} = \frac{b_2 p_2(a)e^{-r_2 a}}{b_1 p_1(a)e^{-r_1 a}} \qquad (1.49)$$

Let us first assume that the mortality schedules and hence the survival probabilities of the two populations are equal. Then Equation 1.49 reduces to

$$\frac{c_2(a)}{c_1(a)} = \frac{b_2}{b_1} e^{-\Delta r a} \qquad (1.50)$$

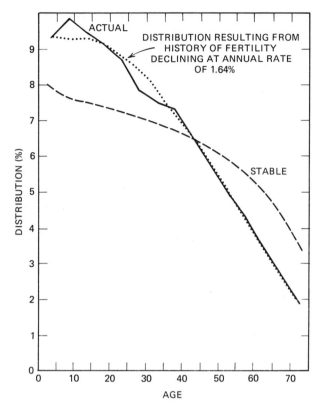

Figure 1.2. (Adapted from Coale, 1972). Age distribution for the white female population in the United States; 1930 actual, stable, and distribution resulting from a history of fertility declining at an average rate observed in the United States from 1910 to 1930.

where $\Delta r = r_2 - r_1$. We have labeled the populations so that $r_2 > r_1$, hence $\Delta r > 0$. From Equation 1.50, we see that the ratio of the age distribution decreases with age. Moreover, since $\int_0^\infty c_1(a)\,da = \int_0^\infty c_2(a)\,da = 1$, neither age distribution curve can lie entirely above the other. Unless the two curves are identical, they must cross at some age $\hat{a}$. This means that the population with the higher growth rate will be "younger" than the other: it will have a higher proportion of females below age $\hat{a}$ and a lower proportion above that age. The age $\hat{a}$ at which the curves cross is approximately equal to the average of the two mean ages of the populations.

Next we seek a relation between the fertility schedules and the birth rates of the two populations and between the birth rates and the rates of growth. These relations will, in general, depend on the specific "shapes" of the fertility schedules. However, given two populations with fertility schedules that differ only by a constant, so that $m_2(a) = km_1(a)$, these relations can be determined rather simply (by our assumption that $k > 1$).

Recall the population parameter T and the mean length of a generation defined by $e^{rT} = NRR$ (see p. 38). If $m_2(a) = km_1(a)$ and $p_2(a) = p_1(a)$, we must have $T_2 = T_1 = T$.

Assuming the two populations equal in size at $t = 0$, we have

$$N_1(T) = N(0)e^{r_1 T}; \qquad N_2(T) = N(0)e^{r_2 T}. \qquad (1.51)$$

Since $m_2(a)/m_1(a) = k$, on the average, k times as many daughters are born per year to the faster growing population. Hence

$$k = e^{\Delta r T}; \qquad \Delta r = \log_e \frac{k}{T} \qquad (1.52)$$

Thus the effect on the rate of growth of multiplying the fertility schedule by a constant is established. The effect on the birth rate and on the age distribution can be obtained from the following considerations.

Since $\hat{a}$ was defined as the age at which $c_2(a) = c_1(a)$, it follows that

$$1 = \frac{c_2(\hat{a})}{c_1(\hat{a})} = \frac{b_2}{b_1} e^{-\Delta r \hat{a}} \qquad (1.53)$$

$$\frac{b_2}{b_1} = e^{+\Delta r \hat{a}}. \qquad (1.54)$$

Combining Equations 1.52 and 1.54, we obtain

$$\log_e \frac{b_2}{b_1} = \frac{\hat{a}}{T} \log_e \frac{m_2(\hat{a})}{m_1(\hat{a})} \qquad (1.55)$$

$$\log_e \frac{c_2(a)}{c_1(a)} = \frac{\hat{a} - a}{T} \log_e \frac{m_2(\hat{a})}{m_1(\hat{a})}. \qquad (1.56)$$

Equation 1.55 says that the quotient of the birth rates is larger or smaller than the quotient of the fertility schedules according to whether $\hat{a}$ is larger or smaller than T. When $\hat{a} > T$, the quotient of birth rates is larger than that of fertility schedules. Intuitively, this is the result of the following consideration. When $\hat{a} > T$, the higher fertility is associated with a "more favorable" age distribution (shorter generation span) and produces a more than proportionately higher birth rate. Equation 1.56 establishes the effect of the higher fertility schedule on the age distribution.

We have seen that the assumption $m_1(a) = km_2(a)$ reveals a simple effect of varying fertility schedules on the age distribution of a population. The age distribution curve "rotates" about a point $\hat{a}$. This effect holds whenever one population is characterized by a higher *effective fertility* than another. "Effective higher fertility" of a stable population is one that produces a greater rate of growth when coupled with the same mortality schedule. In our simplified model, our two populations clearly differed in their effective fertilities.

The effect of differential mortality schedules is not so simple. To see this, consider Equation 1.26. The slope of the age distribution curve depends on the population characteristics $p(a)$ and r. Suppose one population has a "more favorable" mortality schedule than another; specifically, a higher survival rate at all ages. If the fertility schedules are equal, the population with the higher survival rates can be expected to have a higher rate of growth. Now a larger r will tend to make the decrease of $c(a)$ steeper, but a larger $p(a)$ will tend to make the age distribution curve flatter. Which of these tendencies will prevail depends significantly on the difference between the "shapes" of the survival rates.

Suppose, for example, two stable populations are characterized by the same fertility schedule, but their mortality schedules differ by a constant: $\mu_2(a) = \mu_1(a) - k$. Then although the population with a lower mortality schedule will grow more rapidly, the age distributions of the two populations must be the same. To see this, observe that in view of Equation 1.24,

$$p_2(a) = e^{-\int_0^a \mu_2(x)dx} = e^{-\int_0^a [\mu_1(x) - k]dx} = p_1(a)e^{ka} \tag{1.57}$$

Since

$$\int_0^\infty e^{-r_1 a} p_1(a)m(a)da = \int_0^\infty c_1(a)da = 1 = \int_0^\infty c_2(a)da = \int_0^\infty e^{-r_2(a)} p_2(a)m(a)da,$$

we must have

$$\frac{c_2(a)}{c_1(a)} = \frac{b_2}{b_1} e^{-ka} \cdot e^{ka} = \frac{b_2}{b_1}. \tag{1.58}$$

But the two populations have the same fertility schedule and hence equal birth rates. Therefore $b_2/b_1 = 1$, and the age distributions are identical.

In comparing hypothetical populations with different fertility schedules, we have assumed that these schedules differ by a multiplicative constant. Although this assumption may be not too unrealistic, the corresponding assumption of proportional survival schedules $p(a)$ is not. Mortality of human populations has been drastically reduced during the past century or two in both industrialized and nonindustrialized countries, but the drops in mortality have been very different for different ages. By far the largest drop has been in infant mortality. Substantial drops in the mortality of the aged have also been observed. In contrast, the reduction of mortality from childhood to middle age has been much less pronounced. Figure 1.3 shows two typical comparisons.

The ordinates of the curves are values of $\mu_1(a) - \mu_2(a)$ for the pairs of populations compared at various ages from birth to old age. The solid line represents these differences between two populations characterized by so-called West Model Life Tables[2] where $\mu_1(a)$ is the mortality of a population with life expectancy of 30 years; $\mu_2(a)$, of a population with life expectancy of 65 years. The dotted curve shows the corresponding differences for the Swedish female population in the years 1901–1910 and in the years 1955–1960. We see that in both cases, the largest differences are at birth (age 0), and that this difference drops sharply to about age 10, remains approximately constant or rises very slightly to just past middle age, then rises again in old age, substantially in the "West Model" but only slightly in Sweden.

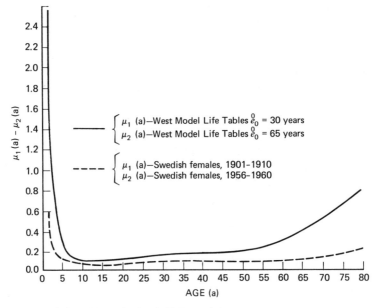

Figure 1.3 (Adapted from Coale, 1972). Typical differences in age-specific mortality.

Thus unlike the effects of changes in the fertility schedule, the effects of changes in the mortality schedule cannot be as easily determined analytically and suggest recourse to numerical methods.

For values of x near 1, $\log_e x$ can be approximated by $(x - 1)$. Therefore, if the survival probabilities and the rates of growth of the two populations are not too disparate, we can write

$$\log_e \frac{p_2(a)e^{-r_2 a}}{p_1(a)e^{-r_1 a}} = \frac{e^{-r_2 a}p_2(a) - e^{-r_1 a}p_1(a)}{e^{-r_1 a}}. \tag{1.59}$$

Thus

$$\int_0^\infty \log_e \left[\frac{p_2(a)}{p_1(a)} e^{-\Delta r a}\right] e^{-r_1 a}p(a)m(a)da = \int_0^\infty \left[\frac{e^{-ra}p_2(a)}{p_1(a)} - 1\right] e^{-ra}p_1(a)m(a)da \tag{1.60}$$

$$= \int_0^\infty [e^{-r_2 a}p_2(a)m(a) - e^{-r_1 a}p_1(a)m(a)]da. \tag{1.61}$$

On the other hand, in view of

$$b = \int_0^\infty c(a)m(a)da = \int_0^\infty be^{-ra}p(a)m(a)da, \quad \int_0^\infty e^{-ra}p(a)m(a)da = 1, \tag{1.62}$$

which holds for both terms of Equation 1.61. Hence

$$\int_0^\infty \log_e \left[\frac{p_2(a)}{p_1(a)} e^{-\Delta r a}\right] e^{-r_1 a}p_1(a)m(a)da = 0. \tag{1.63}$$

Substituting $c_1(a)/b_1$ for $e^{-r_1 a} p_1(a)$ in Equation 1.63 and multiplying by b_1, we obtain

$$\int_0^\infty \left[\log_e \frac{p_2(a)}{p_1(a)} - \Delta r a \right] c_1(a) m(a) da = 0. \tag{1.64}$$

We have assumed that $p_2(a)$, $p_1(a)$, $c_1(a)$, and $m(a) = m_1(a) = m_2(a)$ are all known. We want to determine Δr. We begin by substituting small values of Δr into Equation 1.64, whereby we obtain positive values of the integral. (We note that the integral can be taken between the lowest and the highest childbearing ages, that is, between about 15 and 45 years, since outside of this range $m(a)$ vanishes.) As we increase Δr, the value of the integral decreases until it becomes zero. The corresponding value of Δr is the value sought.

Next we determine b_2/b_1. Assuming that the age distributions are not too disparate, we again introduce the approximation

$$\log_e \frac{c_2(a)}{c_1(a)} \cong \left[\frac{c_2'(a)}{c_1(a)} - 1 \right]. \tag{1.65}$$

Then within the range of our approximation, we get

$$\int_0^\infty \log_e \left[\frac{c_2(a)}{c_1(a)} \right] c_1(a) da = 0, \tag{1.66}$$

or

$$\int_0^\infty \left[\log_e \frac{p_2(a)}{p_1(a)} - \left(\Delta r a - \log_e \frac{b_2}{b_1} \right) \right] c_1(a) da = 0. \tag{1.67}$$

Since we have already determined Δr, all quantities in the integrand of equation 1.67 are known except $\log_e(b_2/b_1)$.

We then proceed as before. We begin by substituting an arbitrary value for b_2/b_1. If the integral (Equation 1.67) turns out to be positive, we decrease this value; if negative, we increase it until the integral vanishes.

As we have seen, a constant difference between mortalities produces no difference in age distribution. Intuitively, a sharp drop in infant mortality would be expected to make a population "younger" (by letting more children survive), and increased longevity in old age would be expected to make it "older."

Comparison of age distributions in Sweden in the first and middle decades of this century reveals a marked "aging" of the population (see Figure 1.4).

This aging has at times been attributed to reduced mortality. However, comparing the much sharper drop of infant and child mortality in Sweden with the slight rise in old age longevity, we would intuit that the former would have a greater effect than the latter. If this is so, then the aging of the Swedish population should be attributed entirely to the drop in *fertility* between the early and the middle years of this century. This conclusion is corroborated by the hypothetical comparisons shown in Figures 1.5 and 1.6.

In Figure 1.5, the earlier age distribution is compared with a hypothetical age distribution which would have resulted if the fertility of 1896–1900 were combined with the mortality of 1946–1950. We see that the greater life expec-

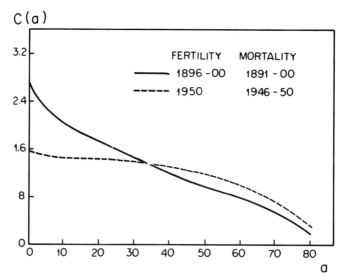

Figure 1.4. (Adapted from Coale, 1956). Age distribution for females in Sweden. Solid curve: fertility and mortality at the turn of the century; dotted curve: fertility and mortality in the mid-twentieth century.

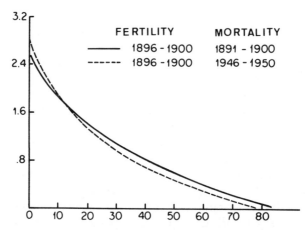

Figure 1.5. (Adapted from Coale, 1956). Solid curve: fertility and mortality at the turn of the century; dotted curve: hypothetical age distribution with fertility as at the turn of the century and mortality as in the mid-twentieth.

tancy of 1946–1950 would have had practically no effect (alone) on the age distribution. If anything, it would have made the population somewhat *younger*. This result contradicts a widespread opinion that greater life expectancy leads to an "older" population.

The reason for the actual result is easy to see: the main cause of increased longevity is the reduction in infant mortality. The surviving children contribute

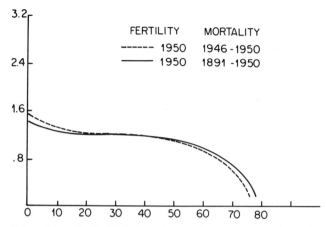

Figure 1.6. (Adapted from Coale, 1956). Dotted curve: fertility and mortality in the mid-twentieth century; solid curve: hypothetical age distribution with mortality as at the turn of the century and fertility as in the mid-twentieth century.

to the proportion of younger persons, compensating the increase in the proportion of older persons.

Figure 1.6 shows a comparison between the 1950 age distribution and the distribution which would have resulted if the mortality of 1896 were combined with the fertility of 1950. Again the difference is very slight. The hypothetical population is not "younger" than the actual one. Death carries away more old people but also more children.

A.J. Coale summarizes the changes in the Swedish population profile as follows.

1. The reduction in fertility has a greater effect on the rate of growth than the reduction in mortality. Fertility alone would have reduced r by 1.7%, while mortality alone would have increased it by only 0.82%.

2. The increase in the growth rate effected by the linear component of mortality reduction effects a 0.47% change in Δr. The infant mortality component increases r by about 0.36%. Thus the reduction in mortality (although its effect is almost one half that of fertility on the rate of growth) has a small effect on the age distribution.

3. The effect of reduced child mortality on the age distribution is equivalent to an increase of about 12% in fertility (excluding the effect of reduced mortality in the first five years of life.)

4. The effect of the same reduction in child mortality on the age distribution is larger if fertility remains the same (and is low).

5. In spite of reduced old age mortality, the proportion of old persons in the population is reduced.

   Consequently, the "aging" of the Swedish population in the first half of this century is to be ascribed entirely to reduced fertility, which has "overcompensated" for the reduced mortality of older people.

NOTES

[1] The mean value theorem of integral calculus states that if f and g are continuous functions in the interval (a_1, a_2) and f does not change sign in this interval, there exists a point $\bar{a}$ $(a_1 \leqslant a \leqslant a_2)$ such that $\int_{a_1}^{a_2} g(a) f(a) da = g(\bar{a}) \int_{a_1}^{a_2} f(a) da$. Here $g(\bar{a}) = B(t - a)$, $T(t) = \bar{a}$, $\int_{\alpha}^{\beta} f(a, 0) da = 1$, and t is a parameter.

[2] A.J. Coale (1972, p. 9) mentions four characteristic sets of age patterns of mortality, where within each set if the mortality rate is known at one age, it can be accurately predicted at another age. "West Model Life Tables" represent one of these four patterns. The symbol $\overset{\circ}{e}_0$ in Figure 1.3 refers to life expectancy at birth.

CHAPTER TWO

Contagion and Diffusion

A contagious disease spreads in consequence of contacts between infected and uninfected individuals. Thus the rate of spread depends on the frequency of such contacts and on the probability that an infection occurs on contact. The latter can be regarded as the "contagiousness" of the disease. Clearly several other factors may be involved; for example, the extent of immunity to the disease in the population, the rate with which infected individuals are removed from the population by isolation, recovery, or death, and so on. In developing mathematical models of contagion, it is convenient to begin with the simplest assumptions, adding complications as they become necessary.

In the simplest case, it is assumed that (1) the probability of contact between any two individuals during a given short interval of time is the same for all, (2) contagiousness remains constant, and (3) an individual once infected remains infected and contagious during the entire process. Let $z(t)$ represent the fraction of the population infected at time t and Δz the expected increment of this fraction in an interval of time Δt. Then $\Delta z/\Delta t$ is proportional to the probability of contact between an infected and an uninfected individual. If the population is large, we can write for the rate of spread at time t:

$$\frac{dz}{dt} = az(1 - z). \tag{2.1}$$

That is, the rate of spread is proportional to the product of the fractions of infected and uninfected individuals in the population.

The general solution of Equation 2.1 is

$$z(t) = \frac{z(0)e^{at}}{1 - z(0)(1 - e^{at})}. \tag{2.2}$$

If we set $t = \infty$ in Equation 2.2, we obtain $z(\infty) = 1$. That is, every one must eventually become infected. Since this hardly ever happens in real epidemics, a modification of the model is called for.

Generalizations of the model suggested by the rare occurrences of 100% infection come readily to mind. Models that lead to less than total infection can be constructed in several ways. We might assume that only a fraction of the population is susceptible to the disease. Or we might assume that the contagiousness decreases with time. We might also assume that the infectivity of an infected individual depends on the time elapsed since he became infected, or that infected individuals are removed from the population in some way, say by recovery or quarantine or by death.

Each of these assumptions or combinations of them leads to another model.

Assuming that only a fraction θ of the individuals are susceptible, instead of Equation 2.1 we write

$$\frac{dz}{dt} = az(\theta - z) \tag{2.3}$$

Then Equation 2.3 becomes

$$z(t) = \frac{\theta z(0)e^{\theta at}}{\theta - z(0)(1 - e^{\theta at})} \tag{2.4}$$

with $z(\infty) = \theta$. That is to say, only the susceptible become ultimately infected.

To introduce the dependence of contagiousness on time, we let $a = a(t)$. Note that the parameter a in Equation 2.3 incorporates the probability (or the frequency) of contacts as well as the probability of infection upon contact. Thus a change in this parameter over time may represent either a decrease of contagiousness, say through built-up immunity in the population, or a decrease in mobility in the population. The general solution of Equation 2.2 with $a = a(t)$ is

$$z(t) = \frac{z(0)\exp[\int_0^t a(\tau)d\tau]}{1 - z(0)\{1 - \exp[\int_0^t a(\tau)d\tau]\}} \tag{2.5}$$

We note that $z(\infty)$ depends on $\int_0^\infty a(t)dt$. In particular, if the integral converges, say to A, then the total fraction of infected will be

$$z(\infty) = \frac{z(0)e^A}{1 - z(0)(1 - e^A)} \; . \tag{2.6}$$

If, however, the integral diverges, everyone will become infected.

Assume now that the infectivity of an individual depends both on the duration of the process t and on the time τ elapsed since the infectious individual became infected. Thus $a = a(t, \tau)$. This model has a bearing on some structural models to be discussed later, so we will consider it in some detail.

We introduce the following notation.

N: the total number of individuals in the pupulation.

$x(t)$:   the total number of infected at time t.

$x_0 = x(0)$:   initial number of infected.

α: frequency of contacts per unit time.

$p(t, \tau)$:   the probability that contact results in transmission of infection if it occurs at time t and if time τ has elapsed since the infectious individual became infected.

Note that we have split the contagiousness parameter in two: α, a constant representing only frequency of contacts, and $p(t, \tau)$, a function of both the "clock time" t (the duration of the process) and of the "private time" τ, the time since the infection of a particular individual.

Choose a fixed t and let $\lambda = t - \tau$ so that an individual infected at time λ has been infected for time $\tau = t - \lambda$. Consider now the number of individuals infected in the interval $(t, t + \Delta t)$ by only those individuals who had become infected in the interval $(\lambda, \lambda + \Delta \lambda)$. We denote this number by $\Delta x(t, \Delta \lambda)$. The expected total number of individuals infected in the interval $(t, t + \Delta t)$ will be denoted by $\Delta x(t)$ and, accordingly, the expected number infected in the interval $(\lambda, \lambda + \Delta \lambda)$ by $\Delta x(\lambda)$. Since $p(t, \tau) = p(t, t - \lambda)$, we have

$$\Delta x(t, \Delta \lambda) = \alpha[N - x(t)]\Delta x(\lambda)p(t, t - \lambda)\Delta t. \qquad (2.7)$$

On the right side of Equation 2.7, $\alpha[N - x(t)]\Delta t$ represents the expected number of contacts in the interval $(t, t + \Delta t)$ between the uninfected an an arbitrarily chosen individual. Multiplying this quantity by $\Delta x(\lambda)$, we obtain the expected number of contacts in the interval $(t, t + \Delta t)$ between the uninfected and those who had been infected in the interval $(\lambda, \lambda + \Delta \lambda)$. Multiplying this quantity by $p(t, t - \lambda)$, we obtain the expected number of new infections in the interval $(t, t + \Delta t)$ due to those infected in the interval $(\lambda, \lambda + \Delta \lambda)$, which is the left side of Equation 2.7.

For $\Delta x(\lambda)$ we can write $[\Delta x(\lambda)/\Delta \lambda]\Delta \lambda$ or, passing to the limit as $\Delta \lambda$ tends to zero, $(dx/d\lambda)d\lambda$. Then the number of infections in the interval $(t, t + \Delta t)$ due to *all* the individuals who became infected in the open interval $(0, t)$ is given by $\alpha[N - x(t)]\int_0^t (dx/d\lambda)p(t, t - \lambda)d\lambda$.

Further, the number of infections in the interval $(t, t + \Delta t)$ due to those who were already infected at time 0 is given by $\alpha[N - x(t)]x_0p(t, t)\Delta t$ where $x_0 = x(0)$. Altogether, then, we have for the expected number of new infections in the interval $(t, t + \Delta t)$:

$$\Delta x(t) = \alpha[N - x(t)]\left[x_0p(t, t) + \int_0^t \frac{dx}{d\lambda} p(t, t - \lambda)d\lambda \right]\Delta t. \qquad (2.8)$$

Dividing by Δt and letting Δt tend to zero, we obtain for the rate of growth of the number infected:

$$\frac{dx}{dt} = \alpha[N - x(t)]\left[x_0p(t, t) + \int_0^t \frac{dx}{d\lambda} p(t, t - \lambda)d\lambda \right]. \qquad (2.9)$$

For the fraction of infected, we have

$$z(t) = \frac{x(t)}{N}.$$

Let $A = \alpha N$, $z_0 = x_0/N$. Dividing both sides of Equation 2.9 by N, we obtain

$$\frac{dz}{dt} = A(1-z)\left[z_0 p(t, t) + \int_0^t \frac{dz}{d\lambda} p(t, t-\lambda)d\lambda \right]. \tag{2.10}$$

This is the integro-differential equation of the dynamics of an epidemic represented by the above model.

It can be shown that if p is independent of both t and τ, the solution of Equation 2.10 reduces to Equation 2.2. If p depends on t alone, it reduces to Equation 2.5.

A special case of this model was treated by Kermak and McKendrick (1927). The probability $p(t, \tau)$ is assumed to depend on τ (the "private time") alone, specifically $p = e^{-k\tau}$, k constant. Then

$$\int_0^\infty Ap(\tau)d\tau = \int_0^\infty Ae^{-k\tau}d\tau = \frac{A}{k}, \tag{2.11}$$

the total number of infectious contacts per infected individual during the course of the process. Equation 2.10 now reduces to

$$\frac{dz}{dt} = (1-z)\left(Az_0 e^{-kt} + Ae^{-kt} \int_0^t \frac{dz}{d\lambda} e^{k\lambda}d\lambda \right). \tag{2.12}$$

Or, since

$$-(1-z)^{-1} = \frac{d}{dz} \log_e(1-z),$$

Equation 2.12 can be written

$$-e^{kt} \frac{d}{dt} \log_e(1-z) = Az_0 + A \int_0^t \frac{dz}{d\lambda} e^{k\lambda}d\lambda. \tag{2.13}$$

Put $\log_e(1-z) = y$; $z = 1 - e^y$; $dz/dt = -e^y\, dy/dt$. Then Equation 2.13 becomes

$$\ddot{y} + k\dot{y} = Ae^y\dot{y}, \tag{2.14}$$

where the dots over the variables designate, as usual, derivatives with respect to time. The first integral of Equation 2.14 is

$$\dot{y} + ky = Ae^y + K, \tag{2.15}$$

where K is determined by the initial conditions:

$$y(0) = \log_e(1-z_0); \qquad \dot{y}(0) = -Az_0, \tag{2.16}$$

which imply

$$K = k \log_e(1-z_0) - A. \tag{2.17}$$

Thus

$$\dot{y} + ky = A(e^y - 1) + k \log_e(1-z_0). \tag{2.18}$$

Restoring the original notation and separating the variables, we have

$$\frac{dz}{(1-z)\{k \log_e[(1-z)/(1-z_0)] + Az\}} = dt, \tag{2.19}$$

from which we obtain t in terms of a quadrature as a function of z:

$$t = \int_{z_0}^{z} \frac{d\zeta}{(1-\zeta)\{A\zeta + k \log_e[(1-\zeta)/(1-\zeta_0)]\}}, \tag{2.20}$$

and so z as a function of t and the parameters z_0, A, and k.

To get $z(\infty)$, the ultimate fraction of infected, we put $t = \infty$. Now the right side of Equation 2.20 becomes infinite when the denominator of the integrand becomes zero. This certainly occurs when $\zeta = 1$. But $\zeta = 1$ implies that everyone is infected. If the denominator in Equation 2.20 becomes zero when ζ is less than 1, we can determine the corresponding value of z by setting the expression in the brace equal to zero:

$$Az + k \log_e \frac{1-z}{1-z_0} = 0. \tag{2.21}$$

From Equation 2.21, we obtain

$$z(\infty) = z^* = 1 - (1-z_0)e^{-az^*}, \tag{2.22}$$

where $a = A/k$, which is a transcendental equation determining z as a function of a.[1]

Equation 2.22 can be solved for a:

$$a = \frac{1}{z^*} \log_e \frac{1-z_0}{1-z^*}, \tag{2.23}$$

from which values of z^* can be obtained by plotting a against z^* for different values of z_0, the initial fraction of infected.

When z_0 is very small (say when contagion starts with a single individual in a very large population), it turns out that if each individual infects on the average two individuals (throughout the entire process), the total fraction of infected will be very nearly 0.8. For three infections per individual, the total fraction will be about 0.94. Already four infections per individual ultimately result in 99% of the population being infected. On the other hand, if the average number of infections transmitted by an infected individual is less than one, then the total fraction of infected will remain infinitesimal; that is, the number infected will be negligible compared with the total population, assumed to be infinitely large. This can be interpreted as nonoccurrence of an epidemic. The result can be seen from the plot of $z(\infty)$ against a with $z_0 = 0$ (see Figure 2.1).

Note that $z(\infty) \equiv 0$ is a solution of Equation 2.22 when $z_0 = 0$. Another solution is represented in Figure 2.1 by the solid curve extrapolated to a dotted curve below the axis. Since negative values of $z(\infty)$ are meaningless in the present context, the plot of $z(\infty)$ is represented by $z(\infty) = 0$ for $0 \leqslant a \leqslant 1$ and by the solid

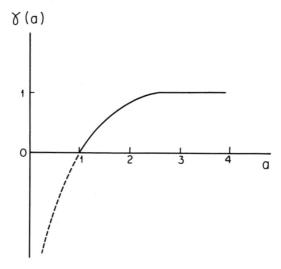

Figure 2.1. Asymptotic fraction of infected $[z(\infty) = \gamma)]$ plotted against a, the average total number of contacts per individual, assuming the initial fraction of infected to be infinitesimal ($z_0 = 0$).

curve for $a > 1$. This curve enables us to see at a glance the sensitivity of $z(\infty)$ to the average number of infections transmitted by an individual. Hence, assuming the validity of the model, the effectiveness of prophylactic measures, such as quarantine, in controlling an epidemic can be assessed.

It remains to interpret the underlying assumptions of the above model; namely, $p(\tau) = e^{-k\tau}$. This can be interpreted to mean that the infectivity of each individual decreases exponentially from the time of infection. It can also be interpreted to mean that a certain number of infected individuals selected at random are removed from the population per unit time. Such a process may reflect the quarantining of randomly selected infected individuals or their recovery or their death. Specifically, the assumption implies that the probability of such removal for any infected individual at any given moment is independent of how long he has been infected. On this ground, the model is probably unrealistic. However, although the time course of the process depends on the specific form of $p(\tau)$, the ultimate fraction of infected depends only on the integral $\int_0^\infty Ap(\tau)d\tau$. Thus the asymptotic prognoses of the model do not depend on the above simplification.

A mathematical model of some phenomenon is essentially a rigorous formulation of some assumptions about the factors governing the phenomenon. The consequences of the assumptions are derived mathematically. If the model is predictive, these consequences amount to predictions about observations, whereby a connection is established between the model and its empirical content. However, the derivation itself involves only mathematical reasoning, which is independent of the empirical content of the model. This means that if the same assumptions are made about any other phenomenon, the derivation would proceed in exactly the same way.

The phenomena modeled by the above contagion models were presented as epidemics. This was done "to fix ideas," as it were. Similar assumptions could have been made about any other process where transmission by contact is involved, for example, information can also be assumed to be transmitted by contacts whereby "nonknowers" become "knowers" by coming into contact with the latter.

In our age, mass media are the most important source of public information. The spread of some kinds of information may depend on contacts between individuals. We will now examine a model of "contagion" which incorporates both forms of transmission.

Let μ represent the "intensity" of the mass media source; specifically, μ is proportional to the probability that in a given short interval of time, a non-knower is reached by the source and thereby becomes a knower. We assume that a knower is also a spreader; that is, is "infectious." However, a spreader can forget the information or lose interest in spreading it further. In either case, he ceases to be "infectious." In the present model the variable of interest is the number of *spreaders* in a population as a function of time, when the rate of depletion of spreaders, either through forgetting or through loss of interest, is proportional to their number. In such cases, the spreader becomes a nonknower. He can, however, again become a knower (and spreader) by coming into contact with a knower. This model was treated by D.J. Bartholomew (1967).

Let N be the size of the total population, $n(t)$ the number of spreaders at time t, α the coefficient of contagion (referring both to individual contacts and contacts with mass media), and β the constant of proportionality relating the rate of removal of spreaders to their number. Then our model is expressed by the differential equation

$$\frac{dn}{dt} = \alpha(N - n)(n + \mu) - \beta n. \tag{2.24}$$

In some respects, this model resembles the contagion model with exponentially decreasing infectiousness of infected individuals (see p. 54ff). In other respects, however, it is different. In the previous model, decreasing infectiousness was regarded as equivalent to removing infected individuals from the population as "spreaders" only. They remained *infected* individuals. Whether the removal was interpreted as recovery or death, the number of infected at any time was interpreted as the number that *had had* the disease. Thus the asymptotic number of infected was a count of all those that had had the disease after infinite time. In the present model, $n(\infty)$ is interpreted as the ultimate number of spreaders; that is, their number when a steady state is established between the depletion and the accretion of spreaders.

We introduce additional notation.

$$\rho = \frac{\beta}{\alpha}$$

$$a = \frac{N\alpha}{\beta} = \frac{N}{\rho}$$

$$h = \sqrt{N\mu + \frac{(N-\rho-\mu)^2}{4}}$$

$$b = \frac{h + n(0) - (N-\rho-\mu)/2}{h - n(0) + (N-\rho-\mu)/2}.$$

The general solution of Equation 2.24 is

$$n(t) = \frac{N-\rho-\mu}{2} + h\left(\frac{be^{2hat}-1}{be^{2hat}+1}\right). \tag{2.25}$$

As t tends to infinity, we have

$$n(\infty) = \frac{n-\rho-\mu}{2} + h, \tag{2.26}$$

which can be obtained directly by setting dn/dt equal to 0. For the ultimate fraction of spreaders, we have

$$\frac{n(\infty)}{N} = \frac{1-\rho/N-\mu/N}{2} + \sqrt{\frac{\mu}{N} + \frac{(1-\rho/N-\mu/N)^2}{4}}. \tag{2.27}$$

Thus the ultimate number of spreaders depends on two ratios, ρ/N and μ/N.

In the Kermack-McKendrick model, where contagion occurs only through individual contacts, the contribution of the mass media is not included. Comparison with Bartholomew's model can be made by setting $\mu = 0$. Then the ultimate fraction of knowers (spreaders) becomes

$$\frac{1}{2}\left(1 - \frac{\rho}{N}\right) + \frac{1}{2}\left[1 - \frac{\rho}{N}\right]. \tag{2.28}$$

This quantity equals either $1 - \rho/N$ or zero, depending on whether $\rho/N < 1$ or $\rho/N > 1$. Now $N/\rho = N\alpha/\beta = a$. Further, $N\alpha$ is the expected number of contacts by an individual per unit time, and $1/\beta$ is the expected length of time during which a spreader remains a spreader. Therefore N/ρ is the expected total number of contacts made by a spreader throughout the duration of the process (note that $N/\rho = a$ corresponds to a in the Kermack-McKendrick model). Therefore the Bartholomew model exhibits a "threshold effect" identical to that derived from the Kermack-McKendrick model.

Observe also that with $\mu = 0$, Equation 2.24 reduces to a logistic differential equation where $(N - \rho)$ instead of N represents the total population (assuming $\rho < N$). Thus Bartholomew's model from which diffusion of information through the mass media is eliminated is formally equivalent to the model represented by Equation 2.3, with ρ/N playing the role of θ, the fraction of the population that is "immune".

The rate of growth of z^* as a function of a (total number of contacts per spreader) is considerably slower in Bartholomew's model than in Kermack and McKendrick's. There, it will be recalled (see p. 57), $z^*(2) = 0.80$, $z^*(3) = 0.94$. In Bartholomew's model, $z^*(2) = \frac{1}{2}$, $z^*(3) = \frac{2}{3}$. At first sight, this may seem surprising, inasmuch as in the Kermack–McKendrick model, a spreader once removed no longer functions as a spreader ever, whereas in the Bartholomew model, when a spreader ceases to be a spreader (by forgetting or by losing interest in spreading), he remains in the population as an nonknower and may again become a spreader by "remembering" or by having his interest rekindled. The reason for the slower spread in Bartholomew's model is that z^* represents the ultimate fraction of active spreaders, whereas in the Kermack-McKendrick model, z^* represents the fraction of the population who *have been* spreaders (or who have had the disease) regardless of whether they have been removed or not.

Another direction in which the simplest contagion model can be generalized leads to a model with several states in which an individual may find himself. This generalization can be relevant to the general theory of epidemics, since it is possible to distinguish between the state of being both infected and infectious, being infected but noninfectious, recovered with immunity, recovered without immunity, dead, and so on.

In a social context, the states can represent several patterns of behavior; for example, ideological or political commitments, and so on. To the extent that contacts among individuals stimulate transitions from one state to another, the general format of contagion models applies. This format can be represented by the following system of differential equations of the first order and second degree:

$$\frac{dx_1}{dt} = a_1 x_1 + \sum_{j=1}^{n} b_{1j} x_1 x_j + c_1$$

$$\frac{dx_2}{dt} = a_2 x_2 + \sum_{j=1}^{n} b_{2j} x_2 x_j + c_2 \qquad (2.29)$$

$$\vdots$$

$$\frac{dx_n}{dt} = a_n x_n + \sum_{j=1}^{n} b_{nj} x_n x_j + c_n, \qquad b_{ii} = 0 \quad (i = 1, 2, \ldots, n).$$

This model represents a system with n states. The x_i $(i = 1, 2, \ldots, n)$ are numbers (or fractions) of individuals in state i at time t. The first terms on the right represent the "self-induced" rates of change in x_i; for instance, the spontaneous generation or spontaneous depletion of those in state i. In the former case, $a_i > 0$; in the latter, $a_i < 0$. The summation terms represent contagion. If an individual in state i comes in contact with one in state j, conversion in either direction may take place, depending on whether b_{ij} is positive or negative. The c_i represents influx or outflow of individuals into or out of the system at constant rates.

The general solution of Equation 2.29 would exhibit $x_i(t)$ as functions of time. Note, however, that besides the parameters determined by initial conditions, the general model involves $2n + n^2$ system parameters. These are generally not directly observable and therefore free parameters to be estimated. For $n = 6$, the model contains 48 such free parameters (including initial conditions), which essentially precludes a meaningful test of the model. So the model cannot be conceived as a deterministic-predictive one.

An example of a model of this sort, which, for reasons just stated, must be regarded as sterile, is Richardson's mathematical model of war moods. Nevertheless, in spite of its sterility, the model has a historical interest. Moreover, classical dynamic models of large systems have been a point of departure for another approach to mathematical theories of social systems, namely, computer simulation, to be discussed below. We will therefore examine Richardson's model of war moods in some detail.

Richardson's attempt to construct a mathematical theory of war represents a departure from traditional methods of political science and political history. Historical accounts of wars center around pressures generated by ambitions of rulers or, from a more sophisticated point of view, around pressures generated by economic rivalries, nationalism, militarism, colonial expansion, and the like. In each of these conceptualizations, a degree of voluntarism is involved. War is pictured as a means used to attain specific ends. Richardson, being a pacifist, was not interested in goal-directed determinants of war. He regarded war as a phenomenon determined by "blind forces." Being also a physicist, Richardson attempted to describe these forces in terms of system dynamics. In the next chapter, we will examine a Richardsonian model of an arms race. Here we will examine Richardson's formulation of a contagion model, which he believed to be relevant to a theory of war.

Richardson (1948) conceived of a "state" of a nation in terms of a distribution of certain affects in the population. These affects appear as attitudes toward the inhabitants of another nation or towards war in the course of its progress. These are the war moods.

Specifically, an individual belonging to one nation may be either "friendly" or "hostile" towards the inhabitants of another, regarded not as specific individuals but in the abstract. An attitude of this sort may also be ambivalent. An individual may be overtly friendly but covertly (that is subconsciously) hostile. Or, on the contrary, he may be overtly hostile, as demanded by the imperatives of "patriotism," but covertly friendly. Such an attitude may be instigated by war-weariness, a phenomenon clearly observed in the late phase of World War I. War-weariness can also be a covert state or an overt one, as in anti-war demonstrations or in other manifestations. (Richardson cites a by-election in Britain in 1917, in which an opponent of the war was victorious.)

Thus a large number of states are defined, and the state of the system representing a nation can be defined as a vector whose components are proportions of persons in each of the attitude states. Next the dynamics of war moods is represented as a system of differential equations comprising a generalized contagion model. The underlying assumption is that war moods are contagious: changes of state occur in individuals who come in contact with individuals in other states or even in the same state. For instance, when overtly hostile individuals from two warring nations come in contact on the battle field, with a certain probability one or the other or both pass into an irreversible state: dead.[2]

As we have seen, the large number of free parameters and the virtual impossibility of assessing even the overt states on a mass scale preclude any remotely conceivable application of the model. However, Richardson, being a pioneer in mathematicized social science, was primarily interested in showing how certain well-known effects observed in mass behavior could be *conceived* as consequences of system dynamics; in particular, the spread of war hysteria, especially in Britain, France, and Germany in the summer of 1914, and the onset of war weariness in the waning years of the war. In Chapter 24, we will examine a quantitative empirical approach to war moods, as reflected in diplomatic exchanges and other actions of governments.

IMITATIVE BEHAVIOR

A much less ambitious model of social contagion was proposed by N. Rashevsky (1951). Although it, too, is difficult or, perhaps, impossible to subject to empirical tests, at least it exhibits features that may be responsible for some dramatic aspects of mass behavior. The model, therefore, has at least some conceptual leverage.

Rashevsky's approach to the mathematization of social phenomena contains remnants of reductionism.[3] Having begun his career as a physicist, Rashevsky blazed the first paths of mathematical biology along the lines of biophysics. First he attempted to construct a theory of cell division on the basis of diffusion forces generated within the cell by the viscosity of protoplasm. In the light of subsequent findings of molecular biology, this model is now of only historical interest. More successful was Rashevsky's mathematical theory of nerve excitation, based on biophysical considerations. Fundamental in this theory was an equation that expresses the rate of accumulation of an excitatory potential in the vicinity of the nerve membrane as a function of the intensity of an externally applied stimulus and of the level of excitation itself. If ε is the level of excitatory potential, Rashevsky writes:

$$\frac{d\varepsilon}{dt} = AI - a\varepsilon. \tag{2.30}$$

Here I is the intensity of the impressed stimulus (for example, an electric current). The second term on the right expresses the spontaneous dissipation of the excitatory "substance" (for example, by diffusion).

This model, applicable to some extent in neurophysiology, was transferred by Rashevsky bodily into behavioral theory. Here the "level of excitation" refers to the propensity of an individual to perform a given action at a given moment. This propensity is identified in a reductionist manner with the degree of excitation of appropriate nerve fibers.

Whatever its philosophical justification, the assumption of continuity between neurophysiological and behavioral formulations is neither demonstrable nor necessary. Nevertheless, there is no a priori reason to reject Equation 2.30 out of hand as the foundation of a behavioral model. It could conceivably serve as a purely formal assumption in a behavioral theory, provided the propensity of an individual to perform a given action were operationally defined in a given context. As will be seen, such operational definitions are implicit in Rashevsky's treatment. Propensities to act in a given manner are defined in terms of probabilities, while intensities of stimuli are defined in terms of numbers of individuals acting in that manner. Thus we are dealing with a contagion model or with a model of imitative behavior, as Rashevsky called it.

Let each individual in a population have a choice between actions R_1 and R_2. For example, R_1 may be giving assent to some government policy and R_2 opposition to it. Or R_1 may be going along with a fashion and R_2 not going along with it, or something of this sort. Whether at a particular time R_1 or R_2 will be preferred by the individual is supposed to depend on a quantity ϕ, which is itself a difference between two quantities, ε_1 and ε_2. These two quantities can be interpreted as levels of excitation of appropriate nerve pathways or, dropping the reductionist mode of speaking, simply as pressures on the individual to perform R_1 or R_2 respectively.

Next it is assumed that each individual in the population is psychologically characterized by a certain ϕ. If the individual's ϕ is very large, he is almost certain to perform R_1; that is, with probability close to one. If ϕ is very large *negatively*, that is, if ε_2 is much larger than ε_1, the individual has a strong predisposition in the opposite direction.

The quantity ϕ is distributed in the population with some frequency $N(\phi)$. That is, $N(\phi)$ is the number of individuals with values of ϕ between ϕ and $\phi + \Delta\phi$. Thus $\int_{-\infty}^{\infty} N(\phi)d\phi = N$, the number of individuals comprising the population. If at a given time $P_1(\phi)$ is the probability that an individual characterized by ϕ will perform R_1, then the number of individuals characterized by ϕ and performing R_1 at that time will be given by

$$x(\phi) = P_1(\phi)N(\phi). \tag{2.31}$$

Similarly,

$$y(\phi) = P_2(\phi)N(\phi) \tag{2.32}$$

represents the number of individuals characterized by ϕ who perform R_2. We have, of course, $P_1 + P_2 = 1$.

Imitation is introduced as follows. Each individual who performs R_1 acts as a stimulus which adds to each individual's ε_1 an additional amount ε_1'. The total intensity of the stimulus enhancing the probability of performing R_1 by the given individual is proportional to X, the total number of individuals performing R_1. An analogous assumption is made with respect to R_2. Thus using the fundamental Equation 2.30, we have

$$\frac{d\varepsilon'_1}{dt} = AX - a\varepsilon'_1$$

$$\frac{d\varepsilon'_2}{dt} = AY - a\varepsilon'_2. \tag{2.33}$$

Here $X = \int_{-\infty}^{\infty} x(\phi)d\phi$ and $Y = \int_{-\infty}^{\infty} y(\phi)d\phi$ denote the total number of individuals performing R_1 and R_2, respectively. The constants A and a are assumed to be the same for all individuals. Of course, one can also assume that these parameters are distributed in the population. In view of the overall crudeness of the model, however, such a "refinement" would hardly be worth the mathematical complexities introduced by it. The purpose of constructing a mathematical model of this sort is not to lay a foundation for a predictive theory but rather to see whether some interesting aspect of mass behavior can be captured by it.

Putting $\psi = \varepsilon'_1 - \varepsilon'_2$ and subtracting the second of equations 2.33 from the first, we obtain

$$\frac{d\psi}{dt} = A(X - Y) - a\psi. \tag{2.34}$$

If the distribution $N(\phi)$ is symmetric with respect to $\phi = 0$, then in the absence of external stimuli $X = Y$, and consequently the equality will persist. However, let an accidental fluctuation occur. Then the quantity that determines whether a given individual performs R_1 or R_2 is no longer ϕ but $\phi + \psi$. As $\phi + \psi$ increases, the probability P_1 that R_1 will be performed increases, which further increases ψ and with it P_1. Similar considerations apply to Y and through it to the frequency of R_2. Thus the situation may be unstable. To determine conditions of stability. We must make specific assumptions concerning the distribution $N(\phi)$. For want of empirical evidence concerning this distribution, Rashevsky chooses the mathematically convenient Laplacian distribution:

$$N(\phi) = \tfrac{1}{2}N\sigma e^{-\sigma|\phi|} \tag{2.35}$$

Next the quantity ϕ, which characterizes a given individual at a given moment, is assumed to be subject to fluctuations taking place within each individual. The corresponding density function was taken by Rashevsky to be also Laplacian:

$$p(\phi) = \tfrac{1}{2}ke^{-k|\phi|}. \tag{2.36}$$

In view of Equation 2.36, in the absence of external stimulation, an individual characterized by ϕ at a given moment performs R_1 at that moment with probability P_1 given by

$$P_1(\phi) = \begin{cases} 1 - \tfrac{1}{2}e^{-k\phi} & \text{when } \phi \geq 0 \\ \tfrac{1}{2}e^{k\phi} & \text{when } \phi < 0 \end{cases} \tag{2.37}$$

When an external stimulus in the form of $\psi = \varepsilon'_1 - \varepsilon'_2$ is present, this probability is given by

$$P_1(\phi, \psi) = \begin{cases} 1 - \frac{1}{2}e^{-k(\phi + \psi)} & \text{when } \phi \geq -\psi \\ \frac{1}{2}e^{-k(\phi + \psi)} & \text{when } \phi < -\psi \end{cases} \tag{2.38}$$

Now in view of Equations 2.31 and 2.32, we can write Equation 2.29 as

$$\frac{d\psi}{dt} = A \int_{-\infty}^{\infty} [x(\phi) - y(\phi)]d\phi - a\psi. \tag{2.39}$$

In the presence of the external stimulus ψ, we have

$$x(\phi) = N(\phi)P_1(\phi, \psi); \qquad y(\phi) = N(\phi)[1 - P_1(\phi, \psi)]. \tag{2.40}$$

In this way, the parameter ψ is incorporated in $x(\phi)$ and $y(\phi)$; thus the integral in Equation 2.39 becomes a function of ψ. Since $P_2 = 1 - P_1$, we have

$$\int_{-\infty}^{\infty} [x(\phi) - y(\phi)]d\phi = \int_{-\infty}^{\infty} N(\phi)[2P_1(\phi, \psi) - 1]d\phi. \tag{2.41}$$

We first calculate the integral equation 2.41 for $\psi > 0$. Substituting Equation 2.35 for $N(\phi)$ and Equation 2.38 for $P_1(\phi, \psi)$, we obtain

$$\int_{-\infty}^{\infty} [x(\phi) - y(\phi)]d\phi = \frac{N\sigma}{2} \left\{ \int_{-\infty}^{-\psi} e^{\sigma}[e^{k(\phi + \psi)} - 1]d\phi + \int_{-\psi}^{0} e^{\sigma\phi}[1 - e^{-k(\phi + \psi)}]d\phi \right.$$
$$\left. + \int_{0}^{\infty} e^{-\sigma\phi}[1 - e^{-k(\phi + \psi)}]d\phi \right\}. \tag{2.42}$$

Evaluating the first integral on the right of Equation 2.42, we have

$$\int_{-\infty}^{-\psi} e^{\sigma\phi}[e^{k(\phi + \psi)} - 1]d\phi = e^{-\sigma\psi}[(k + \sigma)^{-1} - \sigma^{-1}]. \tag{2.43}$$

Evaluating the second, we have

$$\int_{-\psi}^{0} e^{\sigma\psi}[1 - e^{-k(\phi + \psi)}]d\phi = \frac{1}{\sigma} + \frac{ke^{-\sigma\psi} - \sigma e^{-k\psi}}{\sigma(\sigma - k)}. \tag{2.44}$$

Evaluating the third integral, we have

$$\int_{0}^{\infty} e^{-\sigma\psi}(1 - e^{-k(\phi + \psi)})d\phi = \frac{1}{\sigma} - \frac{e^{-k\psi}}{\sigma + k}. \tag{2.45}$$

Adding the right sides of Equations 2.43, 2.44 and 2.45 and multiplying by $\sigma AN/2$, we obtain, after simplification, the following differential equation for $\psi > 0$:

$$\frac{d\psi}{dt} = AN\left[1 + \frac{k^2 e^{-\sigma\psi}}{\sigma^2 - k^2} - \frac{\sigma^2 e^{-k\psi}}{\sigma^2 - k^2}\right] - a\psi \tag{2.46}$$

or, writing $F(\psi)$ for the expression in the bracket,

$$\frac{d\psi}{dt} = AN\left[F(\psi) - \frac{a\psi}{AN} \right].$$ (2.47)

We now plot $F(\psi)$ against ψ and, on the same graph, $a\psi/AN$ against ψ. Figure 2.2 (symmetrically extended for $\psi < 0$) shows two cases: (1) when the slope of $a\psi/AN$ is larger than $F'(0) = dF/d\psi$ at $\psi = 0$ and (2) when it is smaller.

We observe that if $F'(0) < a/AN$, then whenever $\psi < 0$, $d\psi/dt > 0$, and whenever $\psi > 0$, $d\psi/dt < 0$. This means that a deviation from the equilibrium state at $X = Y$ will tend to be "corrected" and, accordingly, equilibrium will tend to be restored. If, on the other hand, $F'(\psi) > a/AN$ at $\psi = 0$, then whenever $\psi > 0$, $d\psi/dt > 0$ and vice versa. Clearly, in that situation, deviation in either direction from the equilibrium at $X = Y$ will tend to be magnified. In this case, the equilibrium at $X = Y$ will be untenable. The slightest deviation from it will make ψ increase (if the deviation is positive) or decrease (if it is negative) until one or the other of the other intersections of the curve representing $F(\psi)$ and the line representing $a\psi/AN$ is reached. Similar analysis shows that these two equilibria are stable.

To derive the condition of stability at $X = Y$, we calculate $F'(0)$. This turns out to be

$$F'(0) = \frac{k\sigma}{k + \sigma} = \left(\frac{1}{k} + \frac{1}{\sigma} \right)^{-1}.$$ (2.48)

In view of the meanings of the parameters k and σ implicit in Equations 2.35 and 2.36, we see that $1/k$ is a measure of how "erratic" each individual is with respect to his parameter ϕ, and $1/\sigma$ is a measure of the heterogeneity of the population with respect to the same parameter. Consequently, if $1/k + 1/\sigma$ is large, the members of the population oscillate considerably in their degree of preference between R_1 and R_2 and/or the population shows a wide range of

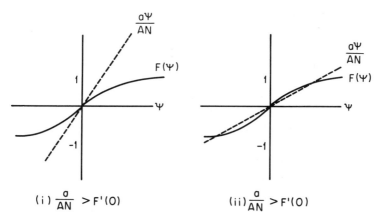

Figure 2.2. Functions $F(\psi)$ and $a\psi/AN$ plotted against ψ. (i): equilibrium at $\psi = 0$ stable; (ii): equilibrium at $\psi = 0$ unstable.

degrees of preference. The system is stable if the *inverse* of this quantity (the right side of Equation 2.49) is small. Hence the system is stable if the individuals "oscillate" a great deal in their preferences and/or vary a great deal in their individual preferences for either action. To put it another way, the system is unstable if most of the individuals are indifferent between R_1 and R_2 most of the time. In this situation, the effect of imitation is maximized. To use the term coined by David Riesman, the population consists largely of "other-directed" individuals. On the contrary, the system is stable if most individuals fluctuate in their preferences and if the mean values around which these fluctuations occur are widely dispersed.

Let us now see what the variability of individuals' preferences and the heterogeneity of the population are to be compared to. The condition of stability, as we have seen, is

$$\left(\frac{1}{k} + \frac{1}{\sigma}\right)^{-1} < \frac{a}{AN}. \tag{2.49}$$

Consider first the factor a/A. The system is stable if this factor is large; that is, if a is large relative to A. Referring to Equation 2.34, we see that stability is enhanced if the dissipation rate of outside influence (a) is large relative to the "responsiveness" of $d\psi/dt$ to $(X - Y)$, A; that is, if this influence is short-lived, as we would expect.

So far, the results are intuitively expected: stability is enhanced if the "internal influence" (fluctuations independent of the influence of others) are larger than external influences and if many individuals have strong preferences for one or the other form of behavior.

There is, however, another factor; namely, N, the size of the population. Since stability is enhanced if the right side of Equation 2.49 is large, we see that stability is enhanced (other things being equal) if the population is small. Consequently, instability is enhanced if the population is large. It is intriguing to note that we have derived something resembling the "mob effect"—the tendency of large masses of people to swing one way or another, depending on which way the "wind blows."

Conditions of stability (or instability) are a principal concern in the so-called systems approach to social phenomena. Economic crises, runaway inflation, escalating arms races, and, in more trivial contexts, rapidly developing fads and crazes are all pictured as consequences of disturbances of unstable equilibria. The concept of stability becomes especially important in social-scientific investivations aimed at deriving methods of effective control of these phenomena.[4] We will examine this problem in somewhat greater detail in Chapter 5.

In the models of epidemics presented above, distances between individuals were not taken into account. Stated otherwise, the probability that two individuals come in contact in a given time interval was assumed to be the same for all pairs of individuals. In Rashevsky's model of imitative behavior, only the total number of individuals acting in one manner or another influenced the probability that a given individual will behave one way or another. Both of these assumptions amount to the assumption that the population is always "instantaneously" mixed; that is, the density of individuals behaving in a given manner is always uniform throughout the population. In real contagion processes, this is not the case. Mixing is not instantaneous because individuals move about with finite speed. Thus in addition to the contagion process a diffusion process is involved.

Classical models of diffusion processes involve partial derivatives of density, which represent the gradients of density along the various dimensions of the space in which the diffusion takes place. Thus the diffusion of a solute through a solvent, the spread of heat through a body, or of a pollutant through the atmosphere can be modeled by partial differential equations with boundary conditions determined by the geometry of the underlying space. A contagion process does not enter such models unless chemical reactions are involved. As we have seen, a differential equation of a contagion process involves nonlinearity because contact probabilities depend on products of densities of infected and uninfected individuals.

A contagion process coupled with a diffusion process would have to be represented by a nonlinear partial differential equation. General solutions of such equations usually entail formidable difficulties. Even if general solutions could be found in some special cases, their relevance to contagion processes involving human behavior could be questioned because in such processes "distances" between individuals (which underlie density gradients) do not necessarily correspond to geographical distances. Rather, some notion of "social distance" as a determinant of contact probabilities would have to be introduced, and this would involve assumptions concerning the topology and metric of "social space," matters about which very little is known. We will discuss some attempts to introduce some characteristics of social space into contagion models in a later chapter.

NOTES

[1] Note the analogy with the random net model discussed in Chapter 15 [See Equations 15.00).

[2] Actually, Richardson's model of war moods should be represented by a system of equations more general than Equation 2.29:

$$\frac{dx_i}{dt} = \sum_{j=1}^{n} a_{ij}x_j + \sum_{j=1}^{n}\sum_{k=1}^{n} b_{ijk}x_jx_k + c_i \qquad (i=1,2,\ldots,n)$$

The first term on the right represents spontaneous transitions from or to a state; the second, transitions to any state resulting from contacts between individuals in any states; the third, sources or sinks. Such a model with n states would be characterized by $n^3 + n^2 + 2n$ parameters (including initial conditions). Richardson's model of war moods contains six states. Its general representation would contain 264 parameters!

[3] Reductionism is an attempt to relate social events to psychological ones, these to biological, and the latter to physico-chemical. This outlook is reflected in Rashevsky's formulation of behavioral tendencies in terms of presumed processes in the nervous system.

[4]In the 1960s, neighborhoods inhabited by whites and blacks were generally sharply separated in large American cities. As forced segregation was relaxed, blacks moved into white neighborhoods. The result was not racially mixed neighborhoods, as integrationists hoped, but a replacement of white neighborhoods by black ones. This effect was called "tipping." T. C. Schelling (1971) proposed simulation models of this phenomenon. The degree of "tolerance" for living in proximity of the other race enters as a parameter. An interesting result is that "tipping" occurs even if the tolerance parameter is by no means small, even when the population *prefers* a mixed neighborhood. Tipping is explained by the circumstance that the system possesses stability thresholds, which are eventually transcended. In this respect, Schelling's models have some resemblance to Rashevsky's. An essential difference is that Schelling's models of neighborhoods, unlike Rashevsky's imitation model and all elementary contagion models, do not depend on complete mixing of the population. For this reason, they are considerably more complex, and their treatment requires the aid of computers.

CHAPTER THREE

Arms Races

The models of contagion discussed in Chapter 3 were formulated as single ordinary differential equations involving one independent variable and one dependent variable. We mentioned in passing systems of differential equations involving one independent and several dependent variables as models of a contagion process in which individuals could be in one of several states (see p. 61). Analytical solutions of such systems, that is, explicit expressions for the variables as functions of time, can be found only in special cases. In particular, if all the differential equations of the system are *linear*, that is, involve the dependent variables in at most the first degree, general methods of obtaining solutions are known. Such a linear system has the form

$$\frac{dx_i}{dt} = \sum_{j=1}^{n} \alpha_{ij} x_j + c_i \qquad (i = 1, 2, \ldots, n), \tag{3.1}$$

where α_{ij} and c_i are functions of time satisfying certain conditions.

In the simplest case, α_{ij} and c_i are all constants. By proper translations of the dependent variables $(x_i' = x_i + \delta_i)$, where δ_i are constants determined by α_{ij} and the c_i, the system can be transformed into a *homogeneous* system involving no constant terms c_i. In what follows, we shall suppose that these translations have been performed. The system will be solved in terms of the new variables. The solution of the original system can then be obtained by simply performing the inverse translations, $x_i = x_i' - \delta_i$.

A homogeneous system of linear differential equations with constant coefficients α_{ij} $(i, j = 1, 2, \ldots, n)$ can be rewritten as a single differential equation of the nth order:

$$\frac{d^n s}{dt^n} = \beta_{n-1} \frac{d^{n-1} x}{dt^{n-1}} + \cdots + \beta_0 x, \tag{3.2}$$

where β_i are constants determined by α_{ij}. The general solution of Equation 3.2 will then also be the general solution of the linear system. It is found by the following procedure. An nth degree polynomial is formed in which the kth power of the variable corresponds to the kth derivative of the variable in Equation 3.2, the "zeroth" derivative being understood as the variable itself. Call the n roots of this polynomial $r_1, r_2, \ldots, r_n$. If the roots are all distinct, the general solution will be given by

$$x_i(t) = A_{i1}e^{r_1 t} + A_{i2}e^{r_2 t} + \cdots + A_{in}e^{r_n t}, \tag{3.3}$$

where A_{ij} are constants determined by the initial conditions and the coefficients α_{ij} of the system.

To illustrate, let us solve the system

$$\frac{dx_1}{dt} = ax_1 + bx_2 \tag{3.4}$$

$$\frac{dx_2}{dt} = cx_1 + fx_2. \tag{3.5}$$

Differentiating Equation 3.4, we obtain

$$\frac{d^2x_1}{dt^2} = a\frac{dx_1}{dt} + b\frac{dx_2}{dt}. \tag{3.6}$$

Substituting the right side of Equation 3.5 for dx_2/dt in Equation 3.6, we obtain

$$\frac{d^2x_1}{dt^2} = a\frac{dx_1}{dt} + b(cx_1 + fx_2). \tag{3.7}$$

Solving for x_2 in Equation 3.4 and substituting into Equation 3.7 gives

$$\frac{d^2x_1}{dt} = (a+f)\frac{dx_1}{dt} + (bc - af)x_1, \tag{3.8}$$

which is of the form of Equation 3.2 with $\beta_1 = (a+f)$, $\beta_0 = (bc - af)$. The roots of the polynomial

$$m^2 - (a+f)m + (af - bc) \tag{3.9}$$

are

$$r_1 = \tfrac{1}{2}[(a+f) + \sqrt{(a-f)^2 + 4bc}];$$
$$r_2 = \tfrac{1}{2}[(a+f) - \sqrt{(a-f)^2 + 4bc}].$$

Accordingly,

$$x_1(t) = A_{11}e^{r_1 t} + A_{12}e^{r_2 t} \tag{3.10}$$
$$x_2(t) = A_{21}e^{r_1 t} + A_{22}e^{r_2 t}. \tag{3.11}$$

To determine A_{ij}, we must impose the initial conditions. These may be initial values of the variables or their derivatives. In our case, the system is of the second order, so two independent conditions must be imposed. Suppose these conditions determine $A_{11} = A_{12} = 1$. Then A_{21} and A_{12} are determined by

a, b, c, and f. The reader can verify that Equation 3.4 and 3.5 will be satisfied if

$$A_{21} = \frac{r_1 - a}{b} \; ;$$

$$A_{22} = \frac{r_2 - a}{b} , \qquad (3.12)$$

where r_1 and r_2 are given as functions of a, b, c, and f as shown above.

To complete the picture, the nature of the general solution of a system of linear differential equations in more general contexts will be briefly described.

If equations of higher order than the first are contained in the system, these can be replaced by a corresponding number of first order equations. For instance, a differential equation of the form of Equation 3.2 can be rewritten as follows. Let $x = x_1$. Further,

$$\frac{dx_1}{dt} = x_2$$

$$\frac{dx_2}{dt} = x_3$$

$$\vdots$$

$$\frac{dx_n}{dt} = \beta_{n-1} \frac{dx_{n-1}}{dt} + \beta_{n-2} \frac{dx_{n-2}}{dt} + \cdots + \beta_0 x, \qquad (3.13)$$

which is of the form of Equation 3.1.

If the roots are complex, that is, $r = \alpha + \gamma i$, where $i = \sqrt{-1}$, the exponential $e^{(\alpha + \gamma i)t} = e^{\alpha} \cdot e^{\gamma i t}$ is a product of a real exponential and a periodic function of t in virtue of the relation $e^{\gamma i t} = \cos(\gamma t) + i \sin(\gamma t)$. If the conditions imposed on A_{ij} determine real values of the variables, the imaginary terms vanish.

If some roots are multiple, the corresponding exponentials are replaced by products of polynomials in t and exponentials. Suppose, for example, $r_i = r_j = \cdots$ $r_k = r$. Then the corresponding term of the general solution will be $P(t)e^{rt}$, where $P(t)$ is a polynomial of one less degree than the number of coincident roots. Note that the number of arbitrary constants thus is not reduced.

Depending, therefore, on the nature of the roots, the functions $x_i(t)$ may or may not contain oscillations. If they do, the oscillations may be with constant or constantly increasing or constantly decreasing amplitudes. Functions without oscillations may tend to zero or may become positively or negatively infinite as t tends to infinity.

General methods of solving systems of linear differential equations are also known for the case where the coefficients α_{ij} are functions of t, but we shall have no occasion in this book to discuss them.

For the purpose of the discussion to follow, two cases will be distinguished: (1) where the functions $x(t)$ of the homogeneous system all tend to zero, and (2) where at least one of them becomes positively or negatively infinite. Systems of the former kind will be called *stable*: the variables tend toward steady states, and their derivatives tend to zero. Systems of the latter kind will be called *unstable*. In a linear system with constant coefficients, the necessary and sufficient condition of stability is that the real parts of the roots r_i are all negative.

A pair of linear differential equations with constant coefficients was proposed by Lewis F. Richardson (1960b) as a model of an arms race between two rival nations. We turn our attention to that model.

Richardson regarded mutually reinforcing fears as a major cause of international wars. He found support for this idea in the writings of Thucydides, who pointed out that the Peloponesian War (431–404 B.C.) could have been the result of reciprocal suspicions between Athens and Sparta: each assumed that the other's preparations for war were evidence of aggressive intentions.

Thucydides' argument was, perhaps, the earliest appeal to what is now called the *self-fulfilling prophesy*. If X assumes that Y is hostile toward him, X is likely to engage in behavior that will make Y hostile in fact, even though initially Y's hostility may have been only in X's mind. *Mutatis mutandis*, the argument applies to Y.

Mathematically, mutually reinforcing hostility can be expressed as a pair of differential equations. Let x represent the "amount of hostility" expressed by X toward Y. (For the moment, we by-pass the question of how this "amount of hostility" can be measured.) Y's level of hostility, y, will now be assumed to be proportional to the rate of change of X's hostility, and vice versa. We write

$$\frac{dx}{dt} = ay \qquad (a > 0) \tag{3.14}$$

$$\frac{dy}{dy} = bx \qquad (b > 0). \tag{3.15}$$

Differentiating Equation 3.14 with respect to t, we have

$$\frac{d^2x}{dt^2} = a\frac{dy}{dt}. \tag{3.16}$$

Substituting into the right side of Equation 3.15, we obtain

$$\frac{d^2x}{dt^2} = abx. \tag{3.17}$$

The general solution of Equation 3.17 is

$$x(t) = Ae^{\beta t} + Be^{-\beta t}, \tag{3.18}$$

where $\beta = \sqrt{ab}$ and A and B are determined by the initial conditions $x(0)$ and $y(0)$, whereby $y(t)$ is also determined. Since $\beta = \sqrt{ab} > 0$, $x(t)$ increases without bound as t tends to infinity, and so does $y(t)$. Thus the model loses its physical significance. As in the case of population growth, it is necessary to introduce constraints. These enter the differential equations as negative terms on the right side.

$$\frac{dx}{dt} = ay - mx \tag{3.19}$$

$$\frac{dy}{dt} = bx - ny. \tag{3.20}$$

To make use of these equations in a predictive theory, the variables must designate some observable quantities. Thus we need a concrete index of the "amount of hostility." Richardson chose the armament budgets of nation states as an index of perceived hostility in line with his argument that the level of armaments of a state (or a bloc of states) is perceived as evidence of hostile intentions by another state or bloc that feels threatened by the other's war preparations.

If we further suppose that the stimulus to increasing one's own armament level is essentially a weighted *difference* between one's own and the other's war potential (in military parlance, the so-called gap), we arrive at Equations 3.19 and 3.20.

One more pair of terms is needed to complete the description of Richardson's fundamental model. Some reject the notion that the growth of armament budgets is only the result of mutual fears and suspicions, maintaining that there are more "objective" stimulants to increasing armaments in the modern international system; namely, standing grievances that nations have against each other. Specifically, the argument implies that even if nation Y disarmed, X would still increase its armaments and vice versa to deal with the eventuality of war precipitated by *basic* hostilities between the nations stemming from incompatible goals, ideological commitments, and the like. This assumption is not reflected in Equations 3.19 and 3.20 since setting $x = y = 0$ also makes dx/dt and dy/dt vanish and so ensures the continuation of the disarmed state.

To meet this argument, Richardson adds constants to both equations. We now write

$$\frac{dx}{dt} = ay - mx + g \tag{3.21}$$

$$\frac{dy}{dt} = bx - ny + h. \tag{3.22}$$

If g and h are both positive, dx/dt and dy/dt are positive, even if $x = y = 0$. Once the underlying attitudes of our two nations toward each other have been introduced as constants into the model, we can imagine that they could be negative. In that case, g and h serve to attenuate the rates of armament increase and can be interpreted as "reservoirs of good will." Such an interpretation raises the problem of providing an index for "good will' to represent not only the underlying attitudes but also negative armament levels, which become possible when g and h are negative.

Richardson supposed that the flow of trade between the nations represents an index of "negative hostility." Note that this interpretation ensures dimensional balance. If armament budgets are expressed in money units, the left sides of Equation 3.21 and 3.22 are expressed in money units per unit time. The constants a, b, m, and n must then be expressed in inverse time units, while g and h must be in money units per unit time, which is the way trade flow is represented.

Next, Richardson undertakes to "test" the model. As an example of an arms race, he took the war preparations of the Allies and the Central Powers in the years 1909–1913. Accordingly, X represents the bloc consisting of Russia and France; Y, Germany and Austro-Hungary. At this point questions might be raised as to why England was not included on one side and Turkey on the other, not to speak of other belligerents at the very start of the war. We shall return to these questions. For the moment, let us follow Richardson's development of the model.

Seeing no way of estimating the six system parameters of his model, Richardson introduced a drastic simplification by assuming $a = b$, $m = n$. In a way, this simplification increased the theoretical leverage of the model since the number of free parameters was thereby reduced from six to two. Adding Equations 3.21 and 3.22, we obtain

$$\frac{d(x+y)}{dt} = (a-m)(x+y) + (g+h). \tag{3.23}$$

Letting $(x+y) = z$, $(a-m) = k$, $(g+h) = f$, we get

$$\frac{dz}{dt} = kz + f, \tag{3.24}$$

where now k and f are the only free parameters. The general solution of Equation 3.24 is

$$z(t) = \left(z_0 + \frac{f}{k}\right)e^{kt} - \frac{f}{k}. \tag{3.25}$$

Recall that $z(t)$ represents the combined armament levels of the two blocs. Equating the response coefficients a and b and the constraint coefficients m and n precludes the separation of $x(t)$ and $y(t)$.

The most conspicuous feature of the solution is the very different behavior of the system depending on whether k is positive or negative; that is, on whether a is larger or smaller than m. If $a < m$, $k < 0$, and, consequently, the first term on the right of Equation 3.25 approaches zero as t tends to infinity. The asymptotic value of z in this case is $-f/k$, which is positive or negative, depending on whether $f = (g+h)$ is positive or negative. In the former case, the "sum of the grievances" is positive and the system approaches a steady state of "hostility." In the latter case, the system approaches a "friendly" steady state. (In this model, $z = (x+y)$ is interpreted as the algebraic sum of combined armament budgets and combined trade flows; thus in the former case, armament budgets exceed trade; in the latter case, vice versa.)

The situation is quite different if $a > m$. In that case, $k > 0$, and the absolute magnitude of the first term increases without bound, which means that the absolute magnitude of z also increases without bound. The *direction* of this increase depends on the sign of the coefficient, $z_0 + (g + h)/(a - m)$. Here $(a - m)$ represents the inherent dynamics of the system and, as such, should be assumed to be independent of the initial conditions. On the other hand, $(g + h)$ may be interpreted as reflecting a particular historical situation embodying the attitudes of the blocs toward each other (say, in view of the alliances concluded). Thus $(g + h)$ may be regarded as reflecting initial conditions. As for z_0, since it represents the state of the system at the beginning of the process, it certainly reflects specific initial conditions. Thus the direction of the "escalation," whether toward every-increasing hostility interpreted as a runaway arms race, or toward every-increasing friendliness, which could be interpreted as disarmament and/or increasing trade volumes, depends crucially on where the process starts.

This interpretation provides an interpretation which Richardson derived from the test to which he subjected his model. An exponential growth of the combined armament budgets would be symptomatic of an unstable system $(a > m)$. Moreover, Equation 3.23 implies that the rate of increase of the combined armament budgets is a linear function of their level. The plot of the successive increments in the combined armament budgets of the two blocs against the combined budgets is shown in Figure 3.1.

The good fit of this plot impressed Richardson. He went on to derive further theoretical consequences of his model. Since the growth of armaments in the years preceding World War I was positively exponential, the system must have been inherently unstable. As we have seen, however, the direction of the trajectory of an unstable system depends on the conditions at the start of the process, which in our case was in the year 1909. Had the conditions of that time been different, the process might have gone the other way, to disarmament,

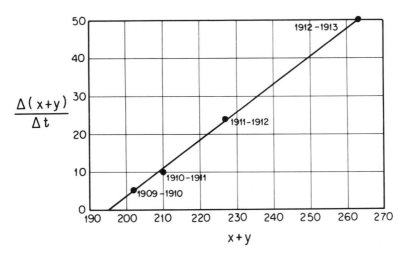

Figure 3.1. Abcissae: combined armament budgets of France, Russia, Germany, and Austro–Hungary in years preceding World War I. Ordinates: increases in combined armament budgets.

increased trade, perhaps a united Europe. The levels of armament budgets and of trade flow between the blocs in 1909 led Richardson to conjecture that if the trade flow were larger (or, equivalently, the armament budgets smaller) by about £5 million, the direction of the process would have been toward disarmament and cooperation.

I say "conjecture" rather than "conclude" because it is unlikely that even Richardson would consider this formally derived result as a conclusion to be taken seriously. It is not the content of the result that matters, but what the result suggests. It sharpens our awareness of instabilities that may be inherent in many aspects of social dynamics and points up the possibility of social processes "tipping" in one or another direction, often in consequence of rather small differences in initial, at times controllable, conditions. In fact, the concepts of "stability" and "instability" of armament programs, particularly those of superpowers, are now firmly entrenched in the conceptual repertoires of people professionally or politically concerned with those processes.

In sum, Richardson's first attempt should be regarded as a point of departure rather than a predictive theory. He himself introduced numerous modifications of the basic model, examined different sources of data, and went on to construct models of the next prominent arms race, that between Germany and Russia in 1933–1939. Here he was confronted with new problems. The gold standard, prevalent in Europe before World War I, had disappeared, and it became necessary to find indices of armament levels and trade levels other than money units freely convertible to gold.

The problem of what nations to include in a particular arms race was never satisfactorily solved. We have mentioned Richardson's exclusion of England, Turkey, and other belligerents from the first arms race. Possibly their inclusion would have spoiled the almost perfect fit obtained by Richardson, and so would have necessitated the introduction of additional free parameters. On the other hand, if including particular belligerents while excluding others happens to give a good fit, one does not know whether the "success" of the theory is an accident or whether it suggests some rationale. For instance, it might be argued that England and Turkey were not the "principals" in the arms race; they entered the war only in consequence of their treaty commitments, not as a result of perceived immediate threats.

Discussions and speculations of this sort can go on endlessly. In light of them, Richardson's model indeed appears simplistic. On the other hand, attempts of this sort can be credited with *instigating* theoretical discussions along certain lines; namely, along the lines of systems dynamics. This must be regarded as the impact of Richardson's contribution.

Among the many Richardsonian models of arms races proposed since his time, one in particular deserves closer scrutiny; namely, that proposed by Taagepera and collaborators (1975). Before we consider that model, let us return to the more general form of Richardson's model where the response parameters of the two blocs are not necessarily equal. The deduced results are a straightforward generalization of the results obtained from the simplified version. They can be best represented graphically.

Setting dx/dt and dy/dt equal to zero in Equations 3.21 and 3.22 and solving for x and y, we obtain two straight lines in $X-Y$ space:

$$y = \frac{m}{a} x - \frac{q}{a} \tag{3.26}$$

$$y = \frac{b}{n} x + \frac{h}{n} \tag{3.27}$$

Barring the special case where the slopes of the two lines are equal, the lines will intersect at some point in the $X-Y$ plane. At that point both derivatives vanish. In principle, therefore, the system could be stabilized at that point. For the equilibrium to be stable, however, we must have $ab < mn$ or, equivalently,

$$\frac{m}{a} > \frac{b}{n}. \tag{3.28}$$

This can be easily seen in Figures 3.2 and 3.3.

In Figure 3.2 the inequality (Equation 3.28) is satisfied: the slope of the line represented by Equation 3.26 is larger than the slope of the line represented by Equation 3.27. In Figure 3.3 the inequality is violated.

The dynamics of the system is determined by the time courses of dx/dt and dy/dt. Whenever $dx/dt > 0$, x tends to move to the right in the $X-Y$ plane; it tends to move to the left whenever $dx/dt < 0$. Similarly, whenever $dy/dt > 0$, y tends to move up in the $X-Y$ plane; it tends to move down whenever $dy/dt < 0$. The two intersecting lines divide the entire plane into four regions, each corresponding to a pair of signs of dx/dt and dy/dt. These are indicated in the figures. The general directions of motion of the point (x, y) is deduced from these signs. We see that in Figure 3.2 the motion is always toward the equilibrium point (stability), whereas in Figure 3.3 it is always away from that point (instability).

The condition of stability represented by Equation 3.28 shows that each actor's response parameters contribute to stability or instability of the entire

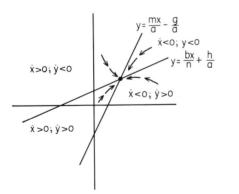

Figure 3.2. The Richardsonian arms race in $(x-y)$-space. The stable case.

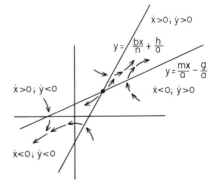

Figure 3.3. The Richardsonian arms race in $(x-y)$-space. The unstable case.

system. We cannot have one of the actors increasing his armaments indefinitely while the other stabilizes his armament level. Nor can one disarm while the other stabilizes. In sum, the dynamics of the two subsystems are *linked*, which, of course, was the starting assumption in Richardson's model.

Now, exponential growth of armament levels can be observed (within a finite time span) even if the two systems are not linked. For instance, let the system be described by the following equations:

$$\frac{dx}{st} = ax \tag{3.29}$$

$$\frac{dy}{dt} = by \qquad (a, b > 0). \tag{3.30}$$

The general solution of this system is

$$x = x_0 e^{at} \tag{3.31}$$

$$y = y_0 e^{bt}. \tag{3.32}$$

Each variable grows exponentially and their sum also exhibits the principal feature of exponential growth. Note, however, that this system is very different from Richardson's. The armament level of each nation stimulates (instead of inhibits) the rate of armaments growth of *that* nation, while the armament level of the other nation has no effect. We are dealing here not with mutual interactive stimulation but entirely with *self-stimulation*.

It is this model that Taagepera and his collaborators (1975) "pitted" against the Richardsonian model in the context of the arms race between Israel and the Arab countries. The comparison suggested that the self-stimulation model fits the data better than the mutual stimulation model.

Again the deduced result cannot be taken seriously as a definitive conclusion. It is, however, richly suggestive and thought provoking. The well-known rationale for increasing armament budgets is the danger of "falling behind" the potential enemy. Although the concrete significance of the so-called gaps in military capacity from the standpoint of "security" has been repeatedly questioned, nevertheless the impact of *mutual* stimulation as the driving force behind an arms race has usually been taken for granted. The implications of Taagepera's result challenge even this assumption. The driving force behind the burdgeoning of the technology of destruction may not even be the perceived external threat, but merely the self-stimulating demands of the technology itself. The fundamental mechanism of *any* exponential growth of any "population" is a constant average reproduction rate per unit per unit time, whether the "population" is composed of organisms or objects or actions or published scientific papers. The mechanism of reproduction is, of course, different in each context. Organisms reproduce by built-in biological mechanisms. Scientific papers, when read by scientists, stimulate investigations that result in more papers. Sectors of technology, as they become progressively more complex, "give birth" to other sectors that support their continued development. Witness the stimulus provided by aviation technology to communication technology and to the technology associated with weather prediction. The same can be said of weapons systems.

Thus the conjecture that armaments increase by self-stimulation rather than by reciprocal stimulation has considerable intuitive appeal. There is no reason, however, to ignore the possibility that both self-stimulation and reciprocal stimulation (along with constraints) are operating on the global military machine; and this raises the problem of assessing the relative importance of each factor and the sensitivity of the system to changes in each of the relevant parameters.

If this problem is approached "seriously," that is, with the view of gaining substantive knowledge and not merely as an exercise in heuristics, model building must be supplemented and at times replaced by detailed empirical investigations. In pursuing these, however, theoretical and methodological considerations cannot be laid aside, since in order to conduct systematic empirical studies, one must know what to observe. If the studies are quantitative, as they are almost of necessity if the findings are to be objective, the important problem of index construction presents itself. Already Richardson faced the problem of standardizing armament expenditures by a common unit in the absence of the gold standard. Contemporary studies of armament races, especially of the nuclear arms race, center on the destructive potential of weapons systems rather than on their cost. In fact, discontinuous changes (so-called breakthroughs, as technocrats like to call them) in military technology may obscure the relation between destructive potential and cost.

For this reason, the construction of "reality-oriented" models of arms races is beset by formidable difficulties. Nevertheless, arms races represent a context in which classical mathematical models may have an important application potential. This is suggested by the conjecture that the large war-waging systems may be governed at least in part by their own internal dynamics. Realization that this is so may itself contribute to changes in presently prevailing conceptions of "national interest," "national security," and so on. Developed with this aim in view, mathematical models of arms races appear not so much as steps toward exercise of control on the basis of reliable predictions (that is, as predictive or normative models) but rather in an analytic-descriptive capacity. By conveying a deeper understanding of the general nature of this phenomenon, a mathematical theory of arms races, if widely understood, can contribute to an ideological shift, which could produce a change in the "social reality." It should be constantly borne in mind that the prevailing ideologically grounded conceptions of social reality are an integral part of that reality.

CHAPTER FOUR

Global Modeling

The models of arms races examined in Chapter 3 represent an elementary attempt to formulate a *systemic* approach to a large-scale social phenomenon. Any definition of a system involves a specification of a portion of the world, some entities of interest contained in it, and interactions among these entities. In some physical systems, the constituent elements can be clearly identified and the interactions among them can be formulated in terms of known physical laws. For example, the elements of the solar system are the sun and the planets; the interactions are the gravitational forces that these elements exert on each other.

Constructing a mathematical model of a system involves singling out variables of interest and stating the mathematical relations among these variables or, in the case of dynamic models, among the variables and their rates of change. For instance, in the case of the solar system, the variables of interest are the positions of the heavenly bodies, their rates of change (velocities), and the rates of change of the rates of change (accelerations). The entire system of interactions is formulated as a system of differential equations whose solution is an expression of the positions of the planets as functions of time.

In the case of arms races, the variables of interest were the armament levels of the rivals. The system was formulated as a pair of differential equations relating the rates of change of the armament levels to these levels.

Extension of this approach to models of social phenomena is beset by two sorts of difficulty. First, whereas in physical systems the variables of interest are usually obvious and few, those involved in social phenomena are often extremely numerous, and criteria for distinguishing crucial variables from incidental ones are not clear. Second, data on which measurements of the variables could be based are frequently lacking or are unreliable.

There is a third difficulty, common to both natural and social contexts; namely, the frequently formidable complexity of the equations needed to represent some models. This difficulty, however, can sometimes be overcome by the use of computer technology. In fact, the availability of this technology has stimulated the formulation of some enormously complex models of social phenomena.

In what follows, we examine some recent applications of the systemic approach to what is called "global modeling."

First, however, it behooves us to point out the methodological and motivational continuity between the pioneering work of the early, heuristically oriented classical models and the recently developed methods of "futuristics."

Mathematical theories of arms races proliferated in the 1960s. The posthumous publication of Richardson's work in 1960 was doubtless a major stimulus in this development. Equally important was the intellectual climate of that decade. The fear of a nuclear holocaust became acute, especially in the aftermath of the Cuban missile crisis in 1962, when the world appeared to have been brought to the "brink" by an eyeball-to-eyeball confrontation between the two nuclear superpowers. Moreover, the "systemic" nature of the factors precipitating the outbreak of the war came into focus against the background of nuclear weapons. Traditionally, wars were conceived, at least in political circles, as results of clashing "interests" or incompatible goals of nation states—the "continuation of politics by other means." With the advent of weapons of total destruction, at least lip service was paid to the idea that no victors could emerge from a war involving the superpowers. Thus traditional political and economic goals of war lost their significance; and the "rationale" for waging war with well-defined political, economic, or even military goals evaporated.

Nevertheless, the expectations of war were not attenuated. Only the focus shifted—from external determining factors (economic, political, ideological) to internal systemic factors of the global war machine itself. While Richardson deliberately ignored the traditional "rationale" of war because of his pacifist convictions, his followers had a more pragmatic reason for doing this. Even in the minds of policy makers, the traditional rationales receded into the background. "Security" measured by destructive power became the only publicly defensible goal of maintaining and expanding military might. All ministries of war became ministries of defense. Although in justification of the continued "balance of terror" the outbreak of a major war was still attributed to a presumed "act of aggression" by the other side, the very "act of aggression" was frequently pictured as aimed at incapacitating one's own strategic position; that is, a purely "defensive" goal. In this way, a rationale was provided for one's own option to commit an act of aggression, which in this context was called a "preemptive strike." In the framework of military thinking, which focuses on the capabilities of the opponent rather than on his actual intentions, a decision to launch a preemptive strike may appear "rational." If, however, both sides act "rationally," both may suffer irreparable losses. So much is clear even to many military strategists. Further, the complexity of nuclear weapons systems and the necessity of making decisions within minutes, raises the specter of an "accidental war" triggered by some failure of the system rather than by anyone's intentions. These dangers directed even military strategists to "systemic" thinking, that is, to the analysis of the war machine as a system driven by its own dynamics instead of by exogenous decisions. For instance, the arguments for a "second strike" (retaliatory) capacity and against a "first strike" (preemptive) capacity are based on the presumed greater stability of the global war machine resulting from the former as compared with the latter.

Since the late 1960s, impending catastrophes other than war have come to the forefront of attention at least in the industrially developed countries. The most publicized of these are the population explosion, the depletion of non-renewable resources, and the physical degradation of the environment (air, water, and soil pollution). The exhaustion of the food supply by exponential population growth was, of course, already foretold by Malthus (1798). In the generally optimistic view of the future that prevailed in Europe during the nineteenth century, Malthus' warning tended to be disregarded. His predictions seemed to be refuted by the apparently unlimited potential of science and technology in providing solutions to problems of survival via ever-increasing knowledge on exploiting natural resources and sources of energy.

There are several reasons why Malthusian ideas are now taken more seriously. First, exponential growth is notoriously deceptive. Consider the following simple problem in arithmetic. An organism, grown in a jar, divides every minute. The process starts with a single organism at 11:00 a.m. At 11:59, the jar is half full. When will it be full? Answer: at 12:00 noon. The answer is, of course, mathematically obvious, but to many it may appear unexpected and to some dramatic. Even more dramatic is the conclusion that if the organisms continue to increase at the same rate, then in two more hours they will fill a volume that includes the sun.

Clearly, this model of an "exploding population" is unrealizable, but a lesson can be drawn from it. Namely, extrapolations from initial observations can be seriously misleading. If the dividing organisms are microscopic, the volume they fill in the first quarter hour may still be microscopic, giving no indication of what might come. The human population of this planet may have been increasing at nearly the same rate for centuries, but it is only now that the "population explosion" has become a household word.

The human population of this planet passed the billion mark in the early nineteenth century, that is, after hundreds of thousands of years of man's existence. It passed the second billion mark a little over a century later, the third billion in a few decades. By all indications, the fourth billion mark has just been passed (written in 1980).

There is no question that the capacity of the terrestrial environment to produce food has a physical limit: *all* observable quantities are bounded. Granted that this absolute limit is still unknown and that presently apparent limits may be extended by techniques still to be discovered, nevertheless the fact that the *doubling* of the world's population is now visible within an individual life span *forces* the Malthusian prophesy into public consciousness.

Another factor contributing to the revival of Malthusian ideas is the social "shrinkage" of the planet. In Malthus' time, Europe and the areas colonized by

Europeans were the only "known" world. Of course we mean "known" in the social, not in the geographical, sense. Somewhere in India or China there were famines in which millions perished. But these catastrophes did not have nearly the impact on the European mind as the Irish potato famine of the 1840s. In our day, a famine occurring anywhere in the world cannot be ignored since the entire planet is "socially known." A cynic may disregard the impact of humanitarian concerns, but no one can disregard the political impact of such catastrophies. Thus not only the explosive growth of the world population but also the Malthusian constraint has left the realm of abstract mathematics and has moved within the horizon of perceived reality; that is, mass starvation has become highly visible and interlinked with other global concerns and with global politics.

Finally, a most important component of neo-Malthusianism is the ascendancy of the systemic approach to social phenomena. Malthus postulated an exponential (geometric) growth of population and a linear (arithmetic) growth of available arable land and showed that the former must under all circumstances outstrip the latter. His conclusion was that unless the growth of population was curbed, "nature" would impose its own constraint, namely, hunger. This conclusion was largely dismissed on the grounds that Malthus' model failed to take into account scientific and technological developments. In fact, it is still dismissed by technocratic optimists on those grounds. What became highly visible in recent decades is that technological developments have their *own* by-products and side effects which may have catastrophic consequences. These effects come into prominence in several contexts. The Oklahoma dust bowl was seen as the result of deforestation—a process intended to *increase* the area of arable land. The toxic effects of insecticides became apparent only a few years after they were hailed as a major breakthrough in agricultural technology. The effectiveness of antibiotics has been damped by adaptive mutations in pathogenic microorganisms. The spread of television, which may have been envisioned by nineteenth century technocratic Utopians as a powerful medium of universal education, has contributed to the rise of functional illiteracy, at least in North America. And, of course, industrial pollution is the most dramatic deleterious side effect of burgeoning technology. Some futurologists maintain that the lethal dangers of uncontrolled pollution exceed those of uncontrolled arms races.

The systemic view stems from a recognition that everything has an influence on everything else. Of course more than this recognition is required to construct a usable theory of the future. One thing, however, is clear: simple extrapolation of observed trends will not do. It is a simple matter to observe the time course of some variable, be it population, trade flow, or whatever, to fit the plotted curve by an equation, and on the basis of this equation to predict future values of the variable. One could repeat this process with any number of variables, but the results may be worthless since the interactions among the variables have been left out. The main task of the system theorist is to take these interactions into account. Decline of infant mortality contributes positively to population growth; population growth exerts pressures on the food supply; these pressures may stimulate technological developments; but these developments may change patterns of land use, which decreases the area of arable land, which aggravates the problem of food supply, which increases the death rate or creates global political pressures that increase the probability of wars, and so on, and so on.

We will examine a "world model" proposed by J.W. Forrester in 1971 which has instigated much discussion, some productive, some less so. It has also served as a stimulus for the development of futuristics along system-theoretic paths.

Forrester considers five basic variables as the cornerstone of his world model: population, capital investment, natural resources, fraction of capital devoted to agriculture, and pollution.

The book *World Dynamics* was evidently written for the general reader as it contains no mathematical notation except the description of the computer program used in the simulation. Nevertheless, the model is essentially a classical one based on a system of differential equations. This is evident from the verbal descriptions of the model. Two kinds of variables are distinguished—levels and rates. The levels are the values of the basic variables (or of their components), which are functions of time, the independent variable. The rates are the time derivatives of the basic variables. These derivatives are functions of one or more of the system variables, not of their rates. To cite Forrester (1971, p. 18), "The two kinds of variables are necessary but at the same time sufficient for representing the system."

In mathematical language, this means that the systems considered can all be represented by ordinary differential equations.

The program proceeds by step-wise numerical integration of the underlying differential (more precisely, difference) equations. This means that the ratio of finite increments $\Delta x/\Delta t$ is substituted for the derivative dx/dt of each variable x. Further, if the increment Δt is taken as the unit of time, we need to consider only the increment of the variable x, that is, Δx. For example, the differential equation of exponential population growth is rewritten as a difference equation:

$$\Delta p = p(i) - p(i-1) = ap(i-1) \tag{4.1}$$

or

$$p(i) = (a+1)p(i-1) \text{ for } i = 1, 2, \ldots \tag{4.2}$$

If a were a constant, the integrated (summed) function $p(i)$ would be represented essentially by an exponentially rising curve. But a as a component of the system is not constant. It is influenced by the values of several variables of the system through "paths of influence," which may be quite complex. A citation from *World Dynamics* (p. 26) will serve as an illustration of the reasoning: "If population rises, capital investment ratio decreases, capital investment ratio in agriculture decreases, food potential (per person) from capital investment decreases, food ratio decreases, birth-rate-from-food-multiplier decreases, birth rate decreases, and population decreases. The chain of influence through the death rate works in the same direction. Here we have a negative feedback loop, which tends to stabilize the population."

With regard to other variables, however, we may have a sudden transition from a negative (stabilizing) feedback to a positive (destabilizing) feedback loop. Such may be the case with pollution. Ordinarily, the rate of dissipation of pollution increases with the concentration of pollutants in the medium. The simplest model of this situation is represented by the differential equation:

$$\frac{dP}{dt} = I - aP. \tag{4.3}$$

Here P represents the concentration of pollutants, I the rate of input of pollutants into the medium. The parameter a involves the time constant of dissipation. If this parameter is constant, pollution dissipates at a rate proportional to its own concentration. (Recall Rashevsky's formally identical equation representing nerve excitation and its analogues in mass behavior.) With constant a, dP/dt vanishes when $P = I/a$, and the situation is stabilized. However, the parameter a may itself be a decreasing function of P; for example, $a = a_0 e^{-kP}$. Now Equation 4.3 becomes

$$\frac{dP}{dt} = I - a_0 P e^{-kP}. \tag{4.4}$$

In Figure 4.1, the constant I and the function $a_0 e^{-kP}$ are both plotted against P with the values of I, a_0 and k chosen to illustrate the failure of the system to stabilize. The rate of increase of pollution is represented by the difference between the value of I and the lower curve. At first this difference decreases and it appears as if the system tends toward stabilization. However, the two curves fail to cross, so that after the concentration of pollutants passes a certain level P^*, the difference $I - a_0 P e^{-kP}$ begins to increase, tending to a constant value I. But this constant value represents not the *level* of pollution but the *rate of increase* of pollution. Under these circumstances, the level of pollution increases without bound.

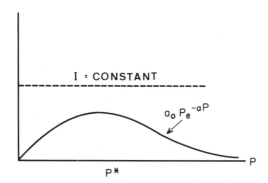

Figure 4.1.   Constant input of a pollutant (I) and a dissipation rate dependent on the concentration plotted against concentration P.

Again we must remember that no physical variable can increase without bound. Nevertheless, whether this particular one does so or not becomes an academic question if its magnitude exceeds certain limits critical for the continuation of life on this planet.

If we were to represent the complex postulated relationships among all the variables and their rates of change included in the above model, our system would be highly nonlinear, as has been shown by elementary examples. The task of obtaining analytic solutions of the system must therefore be forgone. The computer program provides *illustrative* solutions for some chosen values of the parameters.

In Forrester's program, wherever possible, numerical values of the system variables were estimated from data. As for the dependence of some of the parameters on others, these had to be guessed (that is, simply assumed). This sort of guesswork is not as damaging to the method as it might seem since the model represents a framework of what *might* happen if the values of the parameters and the nature of their interdependence were guessed correctly. Once the framework exists, any one who wishes to challenge the author's guesses can supply his own and examine *their* consequences.

We will illustrate the work of this program by exhibiting some "pictures" of the future which it generated in response to different inputs of parameter values. These pictures can be regarded as results of conceptual experiments. The paradigm "If so, . . . then so" manifests itself in the formulation of the model, which embodies not only the assumed values of the parameters but also the assumed chains of influence. This is the "If so, . . . " part. The resulting picture, produced by the computer which performs the task of mathematical deduction too difficult for man, is the "then so" part.

One such picture is shown in Figure 4.2. Population, natural resources, capital investment, and pollution are observables. "Quality of life" is an index compounded of production of food and other material goods (positive contributions), crowding, and pollution (negative contributions). The choice of this index is, of course, arbitrary. It is introduced simply to permit a summary overview of the time course of what may be taken as a normative measure of the global condition.

We note that according to the model, quality of life steadily rose after 1900. The extrapolation of this trend represented by the tangent to the curve reflects the assumption common in the first decades of the century that quality of life would keep on rising. It did rise as long as the rate of depletion of natural resources and the increase in pollution were small. After 1940, however, the rate of depletion of resources becomes considerable and the rate of increase in pollution perceptible, with the result that the quality of life curve levels off and begins to decline after about 1950. In the meantime, capital investment still keeps rising, indeed at an increasing rate, and so does the population, while quality of life keeps declining. Finally, around 2025 the depletion of resources and pollution arrests and reverses the growth of population (by increasing the death rate or by reducing the birth rate or both.) Eventually, the growth of

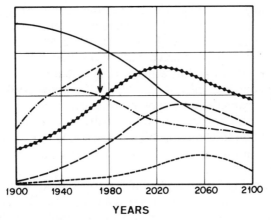

Figure 4.2. (Adapted from Forrester, 1971). Time courses of various indices in Forrester's global model extrapolated to year 2100. ———— Mineral resources, – • – • – • – Population, – · – · – · – Quality of life, — — — — Capital investment, – – – – – – – Pollution.

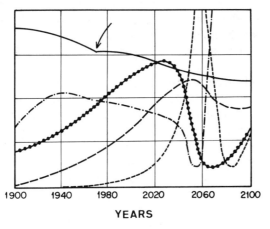

Figure 4.3. (Adapted from Forrester, 1971). Same indices as in Figure 4.2 extrapolated on the hypothesis of reduced exploitation of mineral resources after 1970 (as shown by the arrow).

capital investment is also reversed, but quality of life keeps declining at the beginning of the twenty-third century.

Forrester's model was much criticized for failing to take into account the adjustments that human societies can make in response to changing conditions. However, the purpose of models of this sort is never to predict what *will* happen but rather to see what *might* happen if the model is a reasonable representation of system dynamics and if the system is "left to itself." As for interventions, these can easily be incorporated into the computer programs.

Figure 4.3 shows an overview of global conditions following an intervention represented by an abrupt change of a controllable parameter. Imagine that in 1970 some global authority reduced the rate of use of natural resources (with the view of conserving them) to 25% of the rate at that time. This change is shown in the change of the negative slope of the natural resources variable in 1970. It is assumed that aside from this change, all the other relations postulated in the model remained the same. As a result of the reduction, the decline in quality of life is somewhat attenuated, but not reversed. On the other hand, the effect of the change on capital investment is such that the rise in this variable continues until about 2050 instead of leveling off at about 2030 as before. This, in turn, has a catastrophic effect on pollution, which "explodes" out of the range of the picture. Death rate increases dramatically and world population drops from about six billion to about one billion within a half century. If the drop is due to a huge death rate, it reflects a global disaster (in terms of our present values) unprecedented in history.

Now the principal utility of models of this sort should be clear. The picture that emerges in Figure 4.3 is certainly a striking one and, I believe, for the most part unexpected. It is not an actual prognosis. It merely describes what could happen (assuming always that the model is sufficiently close to reality) if people *did* try to exercise control in a way suggested by "common sense." Certainly the decision to conserve global resources sounds reasonable. It could conceivably be made if attention were concentrated on the impending exhaustion of natural resources as the principal danger inherent in global trends. The model demonstrates the inadequacy of "common sense" in attempting to guide complex systems.

An inexperienced driver starting to skid on an icy road instinctively steps on the brake and turns the wheel in the direction opposite to the direction of the skid. Both actions are wrong. To get out of the skid, he should not step on the brake and he should turn the wheel in the direction of skidding. A simple analysis of the forces involved will demonstrate the validity of this prescription. But of course the skidding driver has neither the time nor the inclination to perform this analysis. For this reason, it is necessary for him to *know* what to do and to resist his natural inclination to do the wrong thing.

Forrester's global model was not the first of its kind, but it was the first that attracted wide attention, probably because in the 1970s awareness of the problems generated by overpopulation and other dangers on a global scale became acute. Today the number of proposed models is several dozen. Most of them involve an economic component and a demographic component. There are also several models dealing specifically with pollution. These, however, include only physical (chemical, meteorological) processes and so fall outside the scope of this book.

The economic component of a global model typically involves output of production as a function of labor force, capital, land, and level of technology. The demographic component relates demographic variables—for example, GRR, $m(a, t)$, and so on (see Chapter 1)—to economic factors. These models can be categorized as "classical" to the extent that a system of differential equations is their underlying paradigm. However, because almost all of them require recourse to computer simulation and because digital computers are predominantly used, the differential equations are formulated as difference equations in the way shown in the above discussion of Forrester's model.

There is one notable exception, the so-called logistic substitution model, describing technological change. It is a global model in the sense that it depicts a social process on a large scale, but it is simple enough to be treated analytically, being concerned with only one type of variable, namely, shares of a market accruing to several competing technologies. We will present it as an illustration of how even the simplest contagion model adequately describes a process in a context not usually associated with contagion.

COMPETITION AMONG PRIMARY ENERGY SOURCES

Consider a primary energy source, such as wood. At some time, coal is introduced as another primary source. With time, the use of coal increases while the use of wood decreases. The process can be conceived as a competition between wood and coal for the energy market. Suppose the competition is represented by the following model. Whenever an "encounter" occurs in the energy market between a wood-burning device and a coal-burning device, the advantage is on the side of the latter, so that with a certain probability the wood-burning device is converted to a coal-burning device. This process is representable by the simplest contagion equation (see p. 53):

$$\frac{dz}{dt} = az(1 - z) \tag{4.5}$$

where $z(t)$ is the fraction of the energy market commanded by the coal-burning device.

As we have seen, the solution of Equation 4.5 is given by

$$z(t) = \frac{z(0)e^{at}}{1 - z(0)(1 - e^{at})}. \tag{4.6}$$

If we replace the parameter $z(0)$ by another parameter, b, where $e^b = z(0)/[1 - z(0)]$, we can rewrite Equation 4.6 as

$$z(t) = 1 + \exp(-at - b), \qquad a, b > 0 \tag{4.7}$$

or

$$\log_e \frac{z}{1 - z} = at + b. \tag{4.8}$$

Thus if the logistic substitution model is correct, the plot of $\log_e z/(1 - z)$ against time ought to be a straight line. In testing the model, the two parameters of this line, a and b, can be estimated from the data. Figure 4.4 shows a test of the model for four different technological changes on the world scale.

Figure 4.5 suggests that the model is also well corroborated for a particular technological change in four different industrialized countries.

According to the logistic substitution model applied to two competing technologies, the new technology ought to eventually replace the old one completely. If, however, additional technologies enter the market, the erstwhile

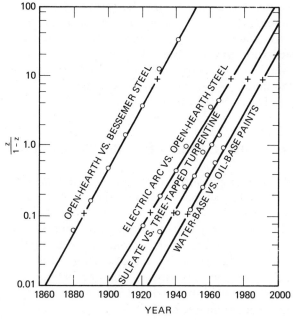

Figure 4.4. (Adapted from Marchetti and Nakicenovic). Technological substitution in the production of steel, turpentine, and paints. Ordinates: $z/(1-z)$ on a logarithmic scale.

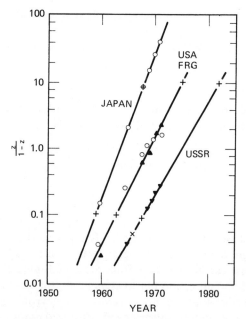

Figure 4.5. (Adapted from Marchetti and Nakicenovic). Substitution of the basic oxygen furnace for open-hearth and Bessemer steel production in four countries. On the line in the middle, the triangles represent West Germany and the circles represent the United States.

new technology becomes an older technology and loses some share of the market to the newer ones. For instance, coal was constantly increasing its share of the market when it was competing against wood. Eventually, however, petroleum entered the market, encroaching upon coal's share. It is reasonable to suppose that eventually nuclear fission will encroach upon oil, and possibly nuclear fusion or solar energy or both will encroach upon nuclear fission. C. Marchetti and N. Nakicenovic (1979) have generalized the logistic competition model as follows. Let the potentially competing energy technologies be labeled $1, 2, \ldots,$ n in the order of their entering the market. It is assumed that each technology goes through three stages: growth, saturation, and decline. Further, only one technology is in the saturation stage at any given time. In its declining stage, a technology declines logistically, that is, the plot of $\log_e z/(1 - z)$ is a straight line with negative slope. In other words, the decline of a technology is not influenced by the competition among the other technologies. In its saturation stage, a technology commands what is left of the market from the shares commanded by the technologies that are still growing (logistically). After the current saturating technology has entered its declining stage, the next oldest technology enters is saturation stage, and so on.

This means that when a technology is in its growth stage and in its declining stage, $\log_e z/(1 - z)$ is represented respectively by two straight lines, one with a positive slope ($a > 0$), one with a negative slope ($a < 0$). These two lines are joined by a curve (representing the saturation stage) determined by the residual share of the market accruing to the saturating technology. Formally, the model is represented by the following equations representing each technology in its growth phase:

$$z_i(t) = 1 + \exp(-a_i t - b_i) \qquad (i = 1, 2, \ldots, n) \tag{4.9}$$

Clearly, these equations cannot apply to all n technologies simultaneously, for if one technology competes with another for the same market and if this competition is represented by the contagion Equation 4.5, the other must decline logistically.

The share of the market of a logistically declining technology k competing with a growing technology i is represented by

$$z_k = 1 - z_i = \frac{1 - z_i(0)}{1 - z_i(0)(1 - e^{a_i t})}. \tag{4.10}$$

Hence

$$1 - z_k = \frac{z_i(0) e^{a_i t}}{1 - z_i(0)(1 - e^{a_i t})}. \tag{4.11}$$

Writing, as before, $z_i(0)/[1 - z_i(0)] = e^{b_i}$, we have

$$\log_e \frac{z_k}{(1 - z_k)} = \log_e e^{-b_i - a_i t} = -a_i t - b_i \tag{4.12}$$

which is of the same form as Equation 4.8 with the signs of the parameters

reversed. Therefore Equation 4.5 represents all the technologies except the one
(j) that is in the saturation stage. The share of this technology's market is given
by

$$z_j(t) = 1 - \sum_{i \neq j} z_i(t). \tag{4.13}$$

These assumptions are quite strong and rather artificial, but the model appears
to be well corroborated historically.

Figure 4.6 shows plots of $\log_e z/(1-z)$ against time for wood, coal, oil, natural
gas, atomic energy (fission), and combined solar-fusion energy from 1850 to the
present and extrapolated on the basis of parameters a and b estimated from
historical data for each except the last. The prognosis for solar-fusion is purely
hypothetical since only scanty data are available on solar energy and none on
fusion.

The plot in Figure 4.6 was obtained by using all available historical data. To
test the predictive power of the model, it is necessary to use only part of these
data to estimate the parameters in order to see how the data not used are fitted
by the same equations with values of the parameters already fixed. The results
are shown in Figure 4.7.

The data for wood, coal, and oil were used only for the period 1900–1920.
For coal and oil, both the predictions (from 1920 to the present) and the "postdictions" (for the period before 1900) are still very well corroborated. There is,
however, a marked deviation in the data on natural gas, which penetrates the
market after 1920 at a rate faster than predicted. It should be borne in mind,
however, that the predictions on the basis of 20 years were made for a half
century ahead, with a world depression and a world war in between.

The example illustrates a case of successful predictions of a global social
process deduced from a simple classical model. The success can be attributed to

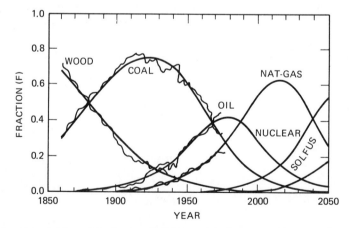

Figure 4.6. (Adapted from Marchetti and Nakicenovic). Comparison between theoretical and
observed fraction of energy market for wood, coal, oil, and natural gas. Use of nuclear (fission) and
combined solar-fusion energy is shown only as projection.

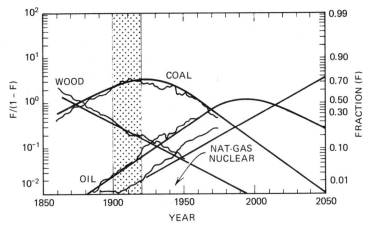

Figure 4.7. (Adapted from Marchetti and Nakicenovic). Same comparison as in Figure 4.6 but based only on data from 1900 to 1920 in estimating the parameters.

the massive aggregation of data (which reduces the "noise" in the system) and to the circumstance that the interactions among the variables apparently have been weak. The only interactions entering the model were those of competition between technologies taken one pair at a time, but these apparently were sufficient for an accurate description of the process. Comparable successes cannot be expected from more general models involving large numbers of variables with unknown parameters and strong interactions, the nature of which can only be hypothesized. For this reason, global models ought not to be regarded as predictive models on which policies can safely be based. On the other hand, they can be of value in "hypothetical sensitivity analyses" on the supposition that the structure of the model (that is, the *form* of the equations) has some resemblance to the system represented. That is, information can be obtained about the relative importance of the various parameters—the degrees of change in the overall behavior of the system when different parameters undergo changes of given magnitudes. We have already seen an application of this sort in Chapter 1 (see Table 1.1), where changes in various variables of interest were deduced as consequences of a 10% change in a given parameter.

A vital difference between that application and analogous applications of global models is that in the former the interactions between the variables are *mathematically* (that is, tautologically) valid because these interactions reside in the definitions of the variables, which is not true of the interactions between variables involved in economic or economic–demographic models. These interactions cannot be deduced mathematically. They can be established only empirically. Here the social scientist is stymied because he has no "global laboratory" at his disposal. Computer simulation serves as a *surrogate* of a global laboratory. The social scientist can make many alternative hypotheses about the situation and can change the postulated parameters as he pleases. He can also make alternative hypotheses about the real world, but he cannot change the parameters of the real world as he pleases. Computer simulation provides a partial solution to this problem.

In the 1950's, when the use of computers was becoming widespread, some engineers in Ann Arbor, Michigan, concerned with traffic problems asked the city for financial support for a computer simulation project to aid in the design of an optimal timing and synchronization of traffic signals to facilitate the flow of traffic. In refusing this application, the city fathers made a counterproposal: "Take the keys to all the traffic lights in the city," they said, "and experiment with them to your heart's content. We will implement any synchronization plan you recommend."

The good will was apparently there, but an understanding of what was involved was not. Experimenting with the real traffic lights system would have created a mess and would probably have been stopped before any usable results could be obtained. It is hard to imagine the magnitude of the mess that would be created if it were possible to tamper with the real global system just to see how it works or breaks down.

Computer simulation can be regarded as an extension of man's capacity to think. Thinking is what enables man to envisage possible consequences of actions without trying them out in reality. Computer simulation is thinking on a very large and complex scale.

CHAPTER FIVE

Models of Control

A particular textbook exercise requires the student to maximize the area of a rectangular field enclosed by a fence on three sides and bordering a river on the fourth, the length of the fence being given.

Let x be the length of the field along the river. Then if f is the given length of the fence, the width of the field will be $y = (f - x)/2$. Accordingly, the area will be given by

$$A = \frac{x(f-x)}{2} . \tag{5.1}$$

A is a continuous function of x and equals zero when $x = 0$ and when $x = f$. Therefore A attains a maximum at some intermediate value of x. The problem is to find this maximizing value. Differentiating Equation 5.1 with respect to x, we obtain

$$\frac{dA}{dx} = -\frac{x}{2} + \frac{f-x}{2} . \tag{5.2}$$

A is maximized when this derivative vanishes. Setting the right side of Equation 5.2 equal to zero, we obtain $x = f/2$. That is, one half of the fence should run parallel to the river.

The problem is an elementary special case of a class of problems where the goal is to maximize or minimize some given function of two sets of variables. One set comprises the so-called *control* variables. These can be manipulated by the problem solver. The other set comprises *state* variables. These reflect some "law," which may be a law of nature or some relations that are incorporated in the model of the situation. A typical control problem of this sort also involves *constraints*, that is, relations among the state and/or control variables that must be satisfied.

For example, in the above problem we can regard y as a control variable (since we are free to choose the width of our rectangle) and x as a state variable because by geometry xy is the area of the rectangle. The constraint was $f - x - 2y = 0$. In what follows, we shall replace y by u, the usual designation of a control variable, and f by P to avoid confusion with the notation used for constraints.

In the general case, the control variables are depicted by a vector $u = (u_1, u_2, \ldots, u_m)$; the state variables by a vector $x = (x_1, x_2, \ldots, x_n)$; and the constraints by a vector $f = (f_1, f_2, \ldots, f_n)$ set equal to zero, that is, by a set of equations $f_i = 0$ $(i = 1, 2, \ldots, n)$. When u_i have been determined, the constraints are in the form of n equations in n variables x_i. It is assumed that this system of equations has a solution. In particular, if they are linear nonhomogeneous equations in x_i, the matrix of coefficients must be nonsingular.

In our problem, the constraint comprised just one equation: $f(x, u) = P - x - 2u = 0$.

The more general problem can be represented in the following form:

Maximize (or minimize) $J(x, u)$, a function of $n + m$ variables
Subject to $f(x, u) = 0$ (n equations).

Problems of this sort can be solved with the aid of the so-called Hamiltonian:

$$H(x, u, \lambda) = J(x, u) + \sum_{i=1}^{n} \lambda_i f_i(x, u)$$

$$= J(x, u) + \lambda^T \cdot f. \tag{5.3}$$

Remark: H is a scalar function of $n + m + 1$ variables. J is a scalar function of $n + m$ variables. λ^T is a row vector (transposition of a column vector λ) with components $(\lambda_1, \lambda_2, \ldots, \lambda_n)$, and f is a column vector with n components. Thus $\lambda^T \cdot f$ is the inner product of two vectors, and is a scalar.

The term $\lambda^T \cdot f$ is adjoined to guarantee the satisfaction of the constraints $f = 0$, as H varies in consequence of manipulating u. Note that when $f = 0$, $H = J$. The constants $\lambda_1, \ldots, \lambda_n$ are determined in the course of the solution of the problem.

If a vector u maximizes or minimizes J and, in view of the constraints $f = 0$, also H, we must have $dJ = 0$ for arbitrary infinitesimal variations du, while $f = 0$. Thus *necessary* conditions for a maximising or minimising j are

$$\frac{\partial H}{\partial \lambda} = f(x, u) = 0; \quad \frac{\partial H}{\partial x} = 0; \quad \frac{\partial H}{\partial u} = 0. \tag{5.4}$$

Remark: The derivative of a scalar H with respect to any vector $v = (v_1, v_2, \ldots, v_r)$ is the vector $(\partial H/\partial v_1, \partial H/\partial v_2, \ldots, \partial H/\partial v_r)$.

In our area-maximizing problem, we have

$$H = xu + \lambda(P - x - 2u). \tag{5.5}$$

Thus the necessary conditions for a maximum (or a minimum) are

$$\frac{\partial H}{\partial x} = u - \lambda = 0; \quad \frac{\partial H}{\partial u} = x - 2\lambda = 0; \quad \frac{\partial H}{\partial \lambda} = P - x - 2u = 0. \tag{5.6}$$

These conditions ensure that J is stationary at the point (x, u, λ) so determined. An actual maximum (or a minimum) is ensured in the general case if a certain *sufficient* condition involving the second derivative of J with respect to u is satisfied.

Remark: The second derivative of a scalar with respect to a vector is a first derivative of a vector with respect to a vector, which is a matrix. For instance, $f_x = \partial f / \partial x$, the derivative of the vector f with respect to the vector x, is the $n \times n$ matrix

$$\begin{pmatrix} \partial f_1 / \partial x_1, \partial f_1 / \partial x_2, \ldots, \partial f_1 / \partial x_n \\ \partial f_2 / \partial x_1, \partial f_2 / \partial x_2, \ldots, \partial f_2 / \partial x_n \\ \vdots \\ \partial f_n / \partial x_n, \ldots, \partial f_n / \partial x_n \end{pmatrix}$$

Similarly, $\partial^2 H / \partial u^2 = H_{uu}$ is an $m \times m$ matrix, $f_u = \partial f / \partial u$ is an $n \times m$ matrix, and so on.

The sufficient condition for maximizing (or minimizing) J involves the following $m \times m$ matrix:

$$\left(\frac{\partial^2 J}{\partial u^2} \right)_{f=0} = H_{uu} - H_{ux} f_x^{-1} f_u - f_u^T (f_x^T)^{-1} H_{xu} + f_u^T (f_x^T)^{-1} H_{xx} f_x^{-1} f_u. \quad (5.7)$$

If this matrix is positive definite, J is minimized; if negative definite, J is maximized.

In our elementary problem, $H_{xx} = H_{uu} = 0$, $H_{xu} = H_{ux} = 1$, $f_x^{-1} = -1$, $f_u = -2$. Thus

$$\left(\frac{\partial^2 J}{\partial u^2} \right)_{f=0} = -(1)(-1)(-2) + 2(-1)(1) = -4 < 0. \quad (5.8)$$

This is a 1×1 matrix with eigen-value -4, hence negative definite, and we now know that $x = P/2$, $u = P/4$ actually maximize the area of the rectangle. Note that $\lambda = P/4$ was determined in the course of the solution.

ALLOCATION OF RESOURCES

This method of solving a control problem will now be illustrated by the problem of allocating resources in providing health services. We follow the presentation of D. Hughes and A. Wierzbicki (1980).

Let categories of patients (for example, by age, diagnosis, and so on) be indexed by j ($j = 1, 2, \ldots, J$); modes of care (for example, outpatient, inpatient) by k ($k = 1, 2, \ldots, K$); levels of care (for example, length of stay in hospital) by L ($l = 1, 2, \ldots, L$). Let x_{jk} be the number of patients in category j who receive care k (per head per population per year); y_{jkl}, the supply of resources of type l received by each patient in category j receiving mode k. Further, let X_{jk} and

Y_{jkl} represent the maximum demands, respectively, of x_{jk} and y_{jkl}; R_l, the total available resources for services of type; and C_l, the cost per patient of level of care of type l.

Assume that the aggregate behavior of agencies constituting the health care system reflects an effort to maximize the number of patients served and the amount of resources received by the patients. This objective can be expressed by the objective function:

$$U(x, y) = \sum_{jk} g_{jk}(x_{jk}) + \sum_{jkl} x_{jk} h_{jkl}(y_{jkl}) \qquad (5.9)$$

Here g_{jk} and h_{jkl} are functions of their arguments defined as follows:

$$g_{jk}(x) = \frac{\sum C_l X_{jk} Y_{jk}}{a_j} \left[1 - \left(\frac{x}{X_{jk}} \right)^{-\alpha_j} \right] \qquad (5.10)$$

$$h_{jkl}(y) = \frac{C_l Y_{jkl}}{\beta_{jkl}} \left[1 - \left(\frac{y}{Y_{jkl}} \right)^{-\beta_{jkl}} \right], \qquad (5.11)$$

$\alpha_j, \beta_{jkl} > 0$.

Note that g_{jk} and h_{jkl} are negative for values of x and y smaller than X_{jk} and Y_{jk} respectively. They are monotone increasing, tending to zero as x and y tend to X_{jk} and Y_{jk} respectively. The objective function $U(x, y)$ can be interpreted as deficiency in health services provided. In striving to maximize $U(x, y)$, that is, to bring it as close as possible to zero, the health agencies are striving to minimize this deficiency. Further, the derivatives of g_{jk} and h_{jkl} with respect to their arguments decrease. This reflects "diminishing returns" of $U(x, y)$: as x and y get closer to their maximum values, the effort to increase them further should become less intense. The costs C_l of resources are introduced so that marginal increases in U when ideal levels are achieved ($x = X$, $y = Y$) equal marginal costs.

The model is characterized by parameters C, X, Y, α, and β appropriately indexed. More will be said about these parameters below.

The constraints are represented by the inequalities

$$0 \leqslant x_{jk} \leqslant X_{jk}; \qquad 0 \leqslant y_{jkl} \leqslant Y_{jkl} \qquad (5.12)$$

and by

$$F_l(x, y) = R_l - \sum_{jk} x_{jk} y_{jkl} = 0 \qquad \forall l \qquad (5.13)$$

Inequalities 5.12 specify that the number of patients and the resources provided are not to exceed the total demands. Equation 5.13 specifies that the total services of type l are not to exceed the available resources of that type and that all available resources R_l ($l = 1, 2, \ldots, L$) are to be utilized.

The problem is to determine x and y (that is, all x_{jk} and y_{jkl}) so as to maximize $U(x, y)$ under the given constraints.

The Hamiltonian is now

$$H(x, y, \lambda) = U(x, y) + \lambda^T \cdot f(x, y) \qquad (5.14)$$

where $U(x, y)$ is given by Equation 5.9 and $F(x, y)$ by Equation 5.13. Note that

x and y are now vectors with components x_{jk} and y_{jkl} respectively. $F(x, y)$ is also a vector (of functions) with components F_l ($l = 1, 2, \ldots, L$), and λ is the vector ($\lambda_1, \lambda_2, \ldots, \lambda_L$).

The solution of the problem involves the following steps.

1. Set $\partial H/\partial x = \partial H/\partial y = 0$ to determine $\hat{x}(\lambda)$ and $\hat{y}(\lambda)$.
2. Substitute $\hat{x}(\lambda)$ and $\hat{y}(\lambda)$ into the Hamiltonian to determine $\hat{H}(\lambda)$.
3. Set $\partial \hat{H}/\partial \lambda = 0$ to determine $\hat{\lambda}$.
4. Verify that $\hat{\lambda}$ minimizes $\hat{H}(\lambda)$ with respect to λ. A sufficient condition for a unique minimum is that the so-called Hessian matrix $\hat{H}_{\lambda\lambda}$ with elements $\partial^2 \hat{H}/\partial \lambda_i \partial \lambda_j$ ($i, j = 1, 2, \ldots, L$) be positive definite.
5. Verify that $\hat{x}$ and $\hat{y}$ maximize $H(\hat{x}, \hat{y}, \lambda)$ with respect to x and y. A sufficient condition for a unique maximum is that the Hessian matrix H_{zz}, where z is the concatenation (x, y) of vectors x and y, be negative definite.

If the unique minimum and the unique maximum are established, $\hat{x}(\hat{\lambda})$, $\hat{y}(\hat{\lambda})$, and $\hat{\lambda}$ constitute the solution of the problem.

We will illustrate the method by solving the allocation problem in its simplest form for $J = K = L = 1$.

We are interested primarily in the optimal fractions of the total demands, that is, in $p = x/X$ and $q = y/Y$. Since the maximum and the minimum of the Hamiltonian remain invariant if the Hamiltonian is multiplied by a constant, we substitute pX for x, qY for Y, and divide by XY to form the Hamiltonian:

$$H = \frac{C}{\alpha}[1 - p^{-\alpha}] + \frac{pC}{\beta}[1 - q^{-\beta}] + \frac{\lambda R}{XY} - \lambda pq. \tag{5.15}$$

To obtain $\hat{H}(\lambda)$, we set the partial derivative of H with respect to p and q equal to zero.

$$\frac{\partial H}{\partial p} = Cp^{-\alpha-1} + \frac{C(1 - q^{-\beta})}{\beta} - \lambda q = 0; \tag{5.16}$$

$$\frac{\partial H}{\partial q} = pCq^{-\beta-1} - \lambda p = 0. \tag{5.17}$$

Solving Equations 5.16 and 5.17 for p and q (as functions of λ), we obtain

$$\hat{p} = \left[\frac{(\beta + 1)(\lambda/C)^{\beta/(\beta+1)} - 1}{\beta}\right]^{-1/(\alpha+1)} \tag{5.18}$$

$$\hat{q} = \left(\frac{\lambda}{C}\right)^{-1/(\beta+1)}. \tag{5.19}$$

Substituting Equations 5.18 and 5.19 into Equation 5.15, we obtain

$$\hat{H} = \frac{C}{\alpha}\left\{1 - \left[\frac{(\beta+1)\mu - 1}{\beta}\right]^{\alpha/(\alpha+1)}\right\} + \frac{C}{\beta}\left[\frac{(\beta+1)\mu - 1}{\beta}\right]^{-1/(\alpha+1)}(1 - \mu)$$

$$+ \frac{C\mu^{(\beta+1)/\beta}R}{XY} - C\mu\left[\frac{(\beta+1)\mu - 1}{\beta}\right]^{-1/(\alpha+1)}, \tag{5.20}$$

where we have written μ for $(\lambda/C)^{\beta/(\beta+1)}$. Thus $\lambda = C\mu^{(\beta+1)/\beta}$, $d\mu/d\lambda = \beta/C(\beta+1)\mu^{-1/\beta}$. To minimize $\hat{H}$, we calculate $d\hat{H}/d\lambda = (dH/d\mu)(d\mu/d\lambda)$. The calculation is tedious but straightforward and yields, after simplification,

$$\frac{d\hat{H}}{d\lambda} = \frac{R}{XY} - \frac{1}{\mu}\left[\frac{\beta}{(\beta+1)\mu-1}\right]^{1/(\alpha+1)}. \tag{5.21}$$

If a minimum exists, it must be where $dH/d\mu = 0$. For arbitrary rational values of α and β, finding a minimum involves finding a real root of a polynomial of arbitrary degree. At this point, however, we only want to establish that a unique minimum exists. To show this, we note that the expression in the brackets on the right side of Equation 5.21 must be positive, hence μ is restricted to the interval $(\beta/(\beta+1), \infty)$. When μ is near $\beta/(\beta+1)$, $dH/d\lambda < 0$. On the other hand, as μ tends to ∞, $dH/d\lambda$ tends to $R/XY > 0$. Therefore a minimum must exist. To show that it is unique, note that $d\hat{H}/d\lambda$ is an increasing function of μ and therefore of λ.

Next we examine the second derivative of $H(x, y, \lambda)$ with respect to the vector (x, y); that is, the Hessian matrix:

$$H_{zz} = \begin{pmatrix} d^2H/dp^2 & d^2H/dp\,dq \\ d^2H/dq\,dp & d^2H/dq^2 \end{pmatrix} \tag{5.22}$$

In view of Equations 5.16 and 5.17,

$$H_{zz} = \begin{pmatrix} -(\alpha+1)p^{-\alpha-1} & 0 \\ 0 & -C(\beta+1)q^{-\beta-1} \end{pmatrix}, \tag{5.23}$$

which is readily seen to be negative definite. It remains to find the value of λ which minimizes $\hat{H}(\lambda)$. If the values of the parameters X, Y, C, R, α, and β are given, this can be done by numerical methods.

So posed, the problem of control appears as a normative (prescriptive) model. To use it as such (that is, to prescribe an allocation policy), we must know the values of all the parameters. Of these, R (the available resources) and C (the costs) could be determined independently of the model. As for the total demands, X (maximum number of persons requiring resources) could be estimated from experience, and Y (the "ideal" level of services) could be set by medical experts. But an estimation of α and β, which relate to the "diminishing returns" of $U(x, y)$, regarded as a "utility function" (see p. 21ff), would present difficulties.

However, the problem could also be formulated as a descriptive (or predictive) model. Namely, *assuming* that the aggregate efforts of the health care allocation agencies are represented by $U(x, y)$, the solution of the problem would be a deduced prediction of how health care resources would be distributed depending on the values of the parameters. If R and C are given, the problem is to estimate X, Y, α, and β by fitting the deductions of the model to the observations of actual resource distributions. If the model is corroborated, that is, if reasonably good fits can be obtained, we can with some justification regard the parameters so estimated as a reflection of social reality. Then we are in a position to predict changes in the allocation pattern as these parameters change. We can also determine the sensitivity of the allocation pattern to changes in the parameters. For example, available resources and costs are certainly subject to change. So are estimates of the maximum number of persons requiring services and the experts' opinions about the "ideal" levels of the various services. We could, of course, also change the assumptions of the model. For instance, subtracting the total cost from the objective function would reflect an effort to economize in addition to an effort to maximize services. We could also drop the requirement that all resources be used up, keeping only the requirement that the amounts of each resource used does not exceed what is available.

Hughes and Wierzbicki solved the simplest allocation problem ($J = K = L = 1$) with cost subtracted from the objective function. The dependence of the variables x and y on the parameters is clearly seen in the deduced relationships

$$\frac{R}{XY} = p \left[\frac{(\beta p^{-(\alpha+1)} + 1)}{\beta + 1} \right]^{-1/\beta} \tag{5.26}$$

$$\frac{R}{XY} = q \left[\frac{(\beta + 1)(q^{-\beta} - 1)}{\beta} \right]^{-1/(\alpha+1)} \tag{5.27}$$

which permit a simple graphical illustration of how the number of patients (x) and the level of service (y) relative to the demands depend on the total resources relative to the total demand.

The example illustrates a "duality" between descriptive and normative models.[1] If an objective function is known, a model with control can generate a prescription of a policy under the given (or assumed) constraints. If the objective function is not known, the model with control can generate predictions of behavior of an actor who is guided by an *assumed* objective function. If the predictions are corroborated, so is the assumed objective function.

This duality is also apparent in the theory of games. Originally, game-theoretic models of conflicting interests were conceived as normative models. The objective of each of two or more actors (players) was assumed to be the maximization of his *payoff* (utility of the outcome of the game) under the constraint that other players have the same respective objectives. The "solution" of the game in this conception is a prescription of a *strategy* (see p. 326) for each player; or, in the context of an *n*-person cooperative game (see p. 328), a prescription of an apportionment among the players of their joint payoff, assuming that the players are collectively rational and maximize their joint payoff by appropriate coordination of strategies.

Alternatively, the solution of a game can be compared with the actual strategies used by the players or with observed distributions of the joint payoffs. The comparison constitutes a test of the assumption underlying the model.

MODELS OF DYNAMIC CONTROL

The models examined so far were static. That is, the problem was to find values of variables optimizing an objective function without reference to time. A dynamic model of control involves the problem of finding functions of time that optimize an objective function. Such a model is exemplified in the following control problem.

We are given a system of differential equations:

$$\dot{x} = f[x(t), u(t), t]. \tag{5.28}$$

The left side is the vector $(dx_1/dt, dx_2/dt, \ldots, dx_n/dt)$, where $x_1(t), x_2(t), \ldots, x_n(t)$ are called the *state variables*. Thus f is also a vector with n components: $f = (f_1, f_2, \ldots, f_n)$, where f_i are specified functions of $x(t)$, $u(t)$, and t. Also $u(t)$ is a vector with m components: $u(t) = (u_1, u_2, \ldots, u_m)$, where u_i are functions of t to be determined. The functions $u_i(t)$ are the *control variables*. Once these functions are determined, the system (Equation 5.28) becomes a system of ordinary differential equations of the first order with t as the independent variable and the $x_i(t)$ as dependent variables. Thus given a sufficient set of boundary conditions, the $x_i(t)$ are determined. They comprise the *trajectory* of the system.

There is an actor who can choose a particular form of $u(t)$ and thus determine the trajectory of the system. His problem is to do this in an "optimal way." Criteria for optimization are specified, as usual, in terms of maximizing or minimizing some objective function. In control problems, this objective function is typically a functional of $u(t)$ and of the trajectory $x(t)$. For example, the objective function may be given by the definite integral

$$J = \int_0^T \phi[x(t), u(t), t]\, dt \tag{5.29}$$

where ϕ is a specified function of x, u, and t.

By choosing $u(t)$ [thereby also determining $x(t)$], the actor determines the value of J. His task is to choose $u(t)$, the control vector, so as to maximize (or minimize) J. Thus the problem is formulated as follows:

Minimize (or maximize) $J = \displaystyle\int_0^T \phi[x(t), u(t), t]\, dt$

Subject to $\dot{x} = f[x(t), u(t), t]$

and prescribed initial conditions, say $x(0) = x_0$.

Two general methods for solving control problems have been developed. One, called the maximum principle, was developed initially by L. Pontriagin in the Soviet Union; the other, called dynamic programming, was developed by R. Bellman in the United States. The first method gives a clearer picture of the problem in classical terms, the latter is more adapted to computer technology. We will outline the principal steps of the first method.

STEP 1. Construct the *Hamiltonian*:

$$H = \phi(x, u, t) + \lambda \cdot f(x, u, t) \tag{5.30}$$

Here λ is a vector (called the adjoint vector) whose n components are as yet undetermined functions of t: $\lambda = (\lambda_1(t), \lambda_2(t), \ldots, \lambda_n(t))$. Note that on the right of

Equation 5.9 $\phi(x, u, t)$ is a scalar, and so is the inner product

$$\lambda \cdot f = \lambda_1 f_1 + \lambda_2 f_2 + \cdots \lambda_n f_n \qquad (5.31)$$

Hence H is a scalar. It is, of course, formally a functional, since its value depends on the "shapes" of $u(t)$, $x(t)$, and $\lambda(t)$. However, once the problem is solved, these functions are determined, and H behaves as an ordinary function of t.

STEP 2.   Set $\partial H/\partial u = 0$ and solve for u in terms of λ, x, and t.

Since the derivative of a scalar with respect to a vector is a vector, (see p. 104), $\partial H/\partial u = 0$ represents m equations, to be solved for m unknowns, the components of u in terms of the components of λ, the components of x, and of t. Once u has been expressed in terms of λ, x, and t, the vector f can be expressed as another vector g with components $g_1, g_2, \ldots, g_n$, all functions of λ, x, and t.

STEP 3.   Construct the system of differential equations

$$\dot{\lambda} = -\frac{\partial H}{\partial x} \qquad (5.32)$$

$$\dot{x} = g(\lambda, x, t) \qquad (5.33)$$

with boundary conditions $x(0) = x_0$, $\lambda(T) = 0$.[2]

Since x and λ are both vectors with n components, each of the vector Equations 5.32 and 5.33 comprises n scalar equations. We thus have a system of $2n$ ordinary differential equations of the first order. These, together with the $2n$ boundary conditions, n on the components of x and n on the components of λ, determine trajectory of the system.

STEP 4.   Solve the above system of $2n$ differential equations.

If the system is linear, it yields to the general analytic methods of solution. The boundary conditions introduce a complication in that n of them apply to the initial moment of the trajectory, while n apply to the final moment T. Special techniques have been developed to deal with problems of this sort.

STEP 5.   After the system is solved, λ and x are determined as functions of t. Since u was already expressed in terms of λ, x, and t (see Step 2), it is also determined as a function of t in the interval $(0, T)$. It is shown that under proper conditions the function $u^*(t)$ so determined is the desired optimal control, thus the "optimal" trajectory of the system is also determined.

In applications it is often useful to express u as a function of both x and t. In this formulation it is possible to control the system by observing its current state (provided the current state is observable).

A MODEL OF ARMS CONTROL

This method has been used to construct an idealized model of arms control (Gillespie and Zinnes, 1975). Arms control means different things to different people. The general public and people concerned with the economic burdens and dangers associated with an uncontrolled arms race may think of arms control as an agreement between rival powers to limit the size of their respective war machines to alleviate the burdens and attenuate the dangers while preserving "security" as it is conventionally understood. An agreement of this sort might be instigated by a realization by both sides that the war machine "if left to itself" might be governed by a Richardsonian process and might lead to disaster if the system is inherently unstable. On the other hand, the problem of arms control may appear to the policy makers *of one side* as a classical control problem. In this formulation, the other side is not assumed to exercise control. It is assumed to behave "reactively" in accordance with a specified model. Gillespie and Zinnes assume this model to be represented by Richardson's equations (see Chapter 3) applied to the *other* side.

Call the actor exercising control U and his level of armaments $u(t)$. In this model $x(t)$ is the only state variable and $u(t)$ is the only control variable. In these terms, Richardson's equation applied to the armament level $x(t)$ of the other side (X) is

$$\dot{x} = au(t) - mx(t) + g. \tag{5.34}$$

The interpretation of the constants is as in Richardson's model except that the situation is viewed entirely from U's point of view. Namely, a represents U's perception of his threat to X; m is U's perception of X's fatigue and expense constraint; g is U's perception of X's grievance against U. Now we posit U's objective function:

$$J = \int_0^T \{[u(t) - qx(t)]^2 + c[u(t) + x(t)]\} \, dt. \tag{5.35}$$

This objective function was constructed with the following considerations in mind. U wishes to keep his armament level $u(t)$ as close as possible to a certain *proportion* of $x(t)$. For instance, U may suppose that he is secure against X if his armament level is twice X's, in which case $q = 2$, U may feel himself secure if his armament level is half of X's, in which case $q = \frac{1}{2}$. Thus q is a parameter determined by U's conception of "security." Further, U admits that in principle, high levels of the combined armaments $u(t) + x(t)$ are undesirable. The parameter c represents the weight he gives to the burden of total armaments. Thus the integrand in Equation 5.35 represents a "cost" of sorts. This cost increases monotonically with the total armament level and also increases with the discrepancy between $u(t)$ and $qx(t)$ in *either* direction. Falling behind X represents a cost in U's estimation; but being ahead of X also represents a cost since U's goals consist in maintaining armaments purely for defensive purposes. In his estimation, armaments in excess of the "security level" do not add to security and constitute only an unnecessary burden, besides instigating armament increases on the part of X.

So *J* is an objective function to be minimized, subject to the constraints represented by Equation 5.34, the state equation, which reflects the *inherent* dynamics of the system. Note further that the integrand in Equation 5.35 represents cost per unit time at each moment of time t, so that minimizing *the integral* over a given time period $(0, T)$ amounts to minimizing total cost over that interval. The final time T denotes U's "horizon."

We proceed to solve the arms control problem as formulated by U.

STEP 1.

$$H = [u(t) - gx(t)]^2 + c[u(t) + x(t)] + \lambda(au - mx + g). \tag{5.36}$$

Note that since the system is described by a single differential equation, $x(t)$ and $\lambda(t)$ are both scalars.

STEP 2.

$$\frac{\partial H}{\partial u} = 2(u - qx) + c + \lambda a$$

$$= 2u - 2qx + c + \lambda a = 0. \tag{5.37}$$

Thus

$$u = qx - \frac{a\lambda}{2} - \frac{c}{2}. \tag{5.38}$$

STEP 3.

$$\dot{\lambda} = -\frac{\partial H}{\partial x} = 2q(u - qx) - c + m\lambda. \tag{5.39}$$

Substituting Equation 5.38 into Equations 5.39 and 5.34, we obtain

$$\dot{\lambda} = \lambda(m - qa) - c(q + 1) \tag{5.40}$$

$$\dot{x} = x(qa - m) + g - \frac{a^2\lambda}{2} - \frac{ac}{2}. \tag{5.41}$$

This is the system of differential equations to be solved with boundary conditions $x(0) = x_0$, $\lambda(T) = 0$.

STEP 4.   Examining the system, we find that Equation 5.40 does not contain x and so can be solved directly for $\lambda(t)$. With imposed boundary condition $\lambda(T) = 0$, the solution of Equation 5.40 is

$$\lambda(t) = \frac{c(q + 1)}{m - aq} \{1 - \exp[(T - t)(aq - m)]\} \tag{5.42}$$

STEP 5.   Assuming that U can observe $x(t)$, the level of armaments of his opponent, we choose to express u as a function of x and t. Accordingly, substituting Equation 5.42 into Equation 5.38), we obtain the formula for "optimal" control:

$$u(t) = qx(t) + \frac{ac(q + 1)}{2(aq - m)} [1 - \exp\{(T - t)(aq - m)\}] - \frac{c}{2}. \tag{5.43}$$

It is interesting to note that if U were not concerned with the total level of armaments, that is, if c were equal to zero, the second and third terms on the right side of Equation 5.58 would both vanish. "Optimal control" would then consist of keeping $u(t) = qx(t)$. Whether the armament levels would stabilize would depend entirely on the sign of $(aq - m)$. Substituting $u(t) = qx(t)$ into Equation 5.34, we obtain the differential equation

$$\dot{x} = (aq - m)x + g. \tag{5.44}$$

If $aq < m$, $x(t)$ will tend asymptotically to an equilibrium at $g/(m - aq)$. If, however, $aq > m$, the system is unstable and the absolute value of x will increase without bound.

If $c > 0$, the situation is more complex. Since we are primarily interested in $u(t)$, we turn our attention to Equation 5.43. In particular, we want to know the initial value of $u(t)$. The quantity of interest is the second term on the right. Setting $t = 0$, we obtain

$$u(0) = qx_0 + \frac{ac(q + 1)}{2(aq - m)} \{1 - \exp[T(aq - m)]\} - \frac{c}{2}. \tag{5.45}$$

Consider first the stable case, when $m > aq$. The exponent in the braces is negative, hence the expression in the brackets is positive. On the other hand, the coefficient before the bracketed expression is negative; consequently, the second term is negative, and so is the third term if $c > 0$. We see that in this case U must begin his control with $u(0) < qx_0$, that is, he must set his armament level below his "security" level. When t becomes equal to T, the second term will vanish. Nevertheless, the third term (constant) remains negative, so that u will still remain below the "security level."

We turn to the unstable case, where $m < aq$. The exponent in the braces is now positive. The expression in the brackets is negative, but the coefficient is now positive. Thus the middle term is again negative and $u(t)$ remains below the "security level."

The unstable case differs from the stable case in one important respect. If T is sufficiently large, that is, when U's "horizon" is large, or putting it in another way, if he is concerned with *long-term* minimization of costs, the absolute value of the middle term becomes very large. This means that a "far-sighted" actor will begin his control with a very low armament level. In particular, if T and c are sufficiently large, he should disarm *unilaterally*. According to the model, X will (presumably) respond to this by reducing his armament level in turn. In this case the direction of the arms race can be reversed.

The assumption that only one actor controls the system is, of course, highly unrealistic. If we assume that both actors exercise control and that their objective functions are different, we can model the situation by a *differential game*.

Now the system is represented by a pair of differential equations:

$$\dot{x} = f[x(t), y(t), u(t), v(t)] \tag{5.46}$$

$$\dot{y} = g[y(t), x(t), v(t), u(t)]. \tag{5.47}$$

Here $x(t)$ and $y(t)$ are the state variables, $u(t)$ and $v(t)$ are control variables. X controls $u(t)$, Y controls $v(t)$.

The objective functions of X and Y, respectively, are

$$J_1(u, v) = \int_0^T \phi[x(t), y(t), u(t), v(t)]dt \tag{5.48}$$

$$J_2(v, u) = \int_0^T \psi[y(t), x(t), v(t), u(t)]dt, \tag{5.49}$$

where X wishes to minimize J_1 while Y wishes to minimize J_2.

Problems of this sort with "dual control" are special cases of differential games.

The solution of the game determines the optimal control functions which bring the system to equilibrium, if it exists.

A differential game model involving both armament levels and foreign military assistance by two rival powers was worked out by Gillespie, Zinnes, and Tahim (1973). In that model, the control functions $u(t)$ and $v(t)$ refer to amounts of foreign military assistance given by the two powers, respectively. It is not assumed that the armament levels $x(t)$ and $y(t)$ are *directly* controlled by the powers. However, because these variables represent the dynamics of the system, they are determined once $u(t)$ and $v(t)$ are chosen.

The objective functions postulated by Gillespie and Zinnes reflect the following components of "cost":

1. The discrepancy between one's own and other's foreign military aid grants—a sort of concern about a disturbance in the "balance of power."
2. The discrepancy between one's own and other's armament level—also a balance of power concern.
3. The absolute levels of one's own and other's armaments and volumes of foreign military assistance (appropriately weighted) reflecting a concern with economic burden, dangers of escalation, perhaps proliferation of nuclear weapons, and so on.

As in the previous model, the stability of the system is of central interest. If the system is stable, the solution of the differential game is analogous to a solution of a noncooperative two-person game. However, equilibrium solutions of such games present problems of their own, which will be discussed below. In general these equilibrium solutions are not Pareto-optimal. *Both* players can do better in other outcomes that are not in equilibrium, if instead of striving to minimize their objective functions independently, they cooperated in bringing about a mutually more satisfactory result. To illustrate a situation of this sort, we will consider a much simpler (static) model.

PARASITISM AND SYMBIOSIS

Consider two actors, X and Y, who produce a certain commodity in the amounts x and y, respectively, under the following condition: X keeps the fraction p of the amount he produces and surrenders $q = 1 - p$ to Y. Similarly, Y keeps the fraction p of y and surrenders the amount $(1 - p)y$ to X. The respective objective functions of the two actors are represented by

$$J_1 = \log_e(1 + px + qy) - bx \tag{5.50}$$

$$J_2 = \log_e(1 + qx + py) - by. \tag{5.51}$$

These functions can be interpreted as follows. The quantities $(px + qy)$ and $(py + qx)$ represent respectively the amounts of the substance received by X and Y. The logarithms represent "diminishing returns" in the utilities of these amounts to the actors. The unit has been added to the arguments of the logarithms to make the utilities vanish when $x = y = 0$. The coefficient b represents the cost per unit of substance in producing it. Thus J_1 and J_2 represent the net utilities to X and Y respectively when X produces x and Y produces y.

We will also assume that only nonnegative values of x and y are meaningful. Each actor controls the amount he produces. Let us see what happens when each actor attempts independently to maximize his objective function.

Since X controls only x, he will try to maximize J_1 by setting the partial derivative of J_1 with respect to x equal to zero. Similarly, Y will attempt to maximize J_2 by setting $\partial J_2/\partial y = 0$. Differentiating J_1 and J_2 with respect to x and y, respectively, we have

$$\frac{\partial J_1}{\partial x} = \frac{p}{1 + px + qy} - b = 0 \tag{5.52}$$

$$\frac{\partial J_2}{\partial y} = \frac{p}{1 + py + qx} - b = 0. \tag{5.53}$$

Solving Equations 5.52 and 5.53 simultaneously for x and y, we obtain

$$\hat{x} = \hat{y} = \frac{p}{b} - 1 \tag{5.54}$$

as the apparently "optimal" values of x and y respectively. Note that $\hat{x} > 0$ and $\hat{y} > 0$ if and only if $p > b$, which we henceforth assume.

Suppose now that X and Y agree to produce x and y in equal amounts. Putting $x = y$ in Equations 5.50 and 5.51, we obtain

$$J_1 = \log_e(1 + x) - bx \tag{5.55}$$

$$J_2 = \log_e(1 + y) - by. \tag{5.56}$$

Instead of partial derivatives, we now have total derivatives.

$$\frac{dJ_1}{dx} = \frac{1}{1 + x} - b = 0 \tag{5.57}$$

$$\frac{dJ_2}{dy} = \frac{1}{1+y} - b = 0,$$ (5.58)

whence the optimal values of x and y are now

$$x^0 = y^0 = \frac{1}{b} - 1.$$ (5.59)

Comparing Equation 5.59 with Equation 5.54, we see that when X and Y are bound by the "contract" $x = y$, they each produce more when they try to maximize their objective functions. To see whether they do *better* in this circumstance, we must compare the values of their objective functions with those attained when the two are acting independently.

Substituting $x = y = p/b - 1$ into Equations 5.50 and 5.51, we obtain

$$\hat{J}_1 = \hat{J}_2 = \log_e\left(\frac{p}{b}\right) - p + b.$$ (5.60)

On the other hand, substituting $x = y = 1/b$ we obtain

$$J^0 = J_1^0 = J_2^0 = \log_e\left(\frac{1}{b}\right) - 1 + b.$$ (5.61)

Thus for each actor

$$J^0 - \hat{J} = \log_e\left(\frac{1}{p}\right) - 1 + p.$$ (5.62)

This difference is positive for all values of p ($0 < p < 1$).

Let us return to the situation where the two actors strive to maximize their objective functions independently. In x–y space, the point $\hat{x} = \hat{y} = p/b - 1$ represents an equilibrium since both partial derivatives $\partial J_1/\partial x$ and $\partial J_2/\partial y$ vanish at that point. The stability of this equilibrium, however, depends on whether $p > q$ or $p < q$. The two straight lines representing Equations 5.52 and 5.53 intersect at that point.

As shown in Figure 5.1, the pair of lines divide the x–y plane into four regions. The signs of $\partial J_1/\partial x$ and $\partial J_2/\partial y$ are shown in the figure in parentheses in each of the regions. As the actors attempt to maximize their respective objective functions, the point (x, y) moves as shown by the arrows. We see that the system shown in Figure 5.1(a) is stable, the points (x, y) always moves toward the equilibrium. In contrast, the system shown in Figure 5.1(b) is unstable; the point (x, y) moves away from the equilibrium. Figure 5.1(a) represents the situation where $p > q$; Figure 5.1(b) where $p < q$. We see that in the unstable situation, either x or y will eventually vanish, depending on the initial position of the point (x, y). When this happens, one or the other will produce nothing, but will get a fraction q of what the other produces.

It is interesting to inquire whether the "parasite" does better than he could if he "cooperated" with the other, that is, whether parasitism is more advantageous

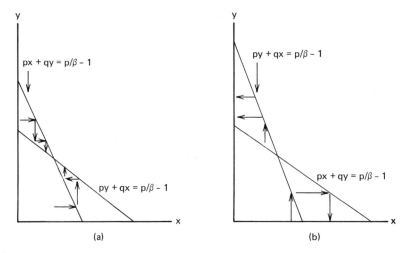

Figure 5.1.   Equations 5.52 and 5.53 in $(x-y)$-space. (a): the stable case; (b): the unstable case leading to parasitism.

than symbiosis. This depends on the magnitudes of the parameters of the system, p and b. For parasitism to occur at all, we must have $p < q$, that is, $p < \frac{1}{2}$. It can be shown that parasitism "pays" for some values of $p < \frac{1}{2}$ and b, but for other values it does not.

LINEAR PROGRAMMING

Applications of the differential calculus in control problems crucially depends on the possibility of obtaining maxima or minima by differentiation. Optimization problems frequently encountered in economics or in management science often preclude the use of these techniques. This happens when both the objective function and the constraints are linear functions of their arguments. Geometrically such problems are represented by regions bounded by straight lines, planes, or hyperplanes. These configurations have "corners," at which derivatives do not exist. For this reason, another technique for solving problems of this sort has been developed, called *linear programming*. It is illustrated by the following example.

We have at our disposal two foods, X and Y. X contains n_1 units of nutrient N and m_1 units of nutrient M per unit weight. Y contains n_2 and m_2 units of N and M per unit weight respectively. X costs c_1 money units per unit weight; Y, c_2 money units. We wish to compose a diet consisting of X and Y which contains minimum prescribed amounts of N and M and is cheapest. Thus the problem has the following format.

$$\text{Minimize } U(x, y) = c_1 x + c_2 y \qquad (5.63)$$

$$\text{Subject to } n_1 x + n_2 y \geqq n \qquad (5.64)$$

$$m_1 x + m_2 y \geqq m \qquad (5.65)$$

$$x \geqq 0; \quad y \geqq 0.$$

To fix ideas, assume that the two straight lines representing the constraints intersect in the first quadrant of the $X - Y$ plane and that the slope of the line representing the objective function is intermediate between the slopes of the constraint lines. Then the problem can be geometrically represented as in Figure 5.2.

The shaded regions above and to the right of the constraint lines represent points (x, y) that satisfy each of the two linear constraints. (Of course all the points in the first quadrant satisfy the constraints $x = 0$, $y = 0$.) The intersection of these two regions is called the *admissible* region (since in it both linear constraints are satisfied).

The family of dotted lines represents the equation $c_1 x + c_2 y = c$ for different values of c, that is, the cost of the diet. As the dotted line shifts to the left, $U(x, y)$ decreases, that is, the cost is reduced. The requirement of minimizing cost is fulfilled when this line is as far to the left as possible and still contains a point (or points) within the admissible region. In our example, this happens when the line goes through the "corner," that is, through the intersection of the constraint lines. Thus the optimal values of x and y and the corresponding cost of the cheapest diet are determined.

Imagine now that the nutrients M and N can be provided in "pure form," that is, by pills containing units of N and pills containing units of M. A manufacturer of these pills can offer a diet satisfying the requirements expressed by Equations 5.64 and 5.65. Being interested in profit, she wants to get the highest possible prices p and q for her pills, but she is subject to the constraints of competition: her "pure" diet should not cost more than the "natural" diet. Her problem can also be formulated as a linear programming problem, namely:

$$\text{Maximize } V(p, q) = pn + qm \qquad (5.66)$$

$$\text{Subject to } pn_1 + qm_1 \leqq c_1 \qquad (5.67)$$

$$pn_2 + qm_2 \leqq c_2. \qquad (5.68)$$

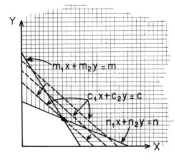

Figure 5.2. A graphical representation of a linear programming problem.

The objective function represents the price of the "pure" diet. The constraints represent the requirement that the price of the synthetic food substituted for a unit of each natural food shall not exceed the unit cost of the natural food.

This problem is called the *dual* of the original problem, which is called the *primal*. All linear programming problems come in pairs, each being the dual of the other.

It is shown in the theory of linear programming that each has a solution if and only if the other has a solution. Moreover, when the values of the variables determined by each solution are substituted in the objective function, the value of the objective function is the same in both problems.

To illustrate, let us solve the primal and dual of the diet problem under the assumptions made above; namely, that the lines representing the constraints intersect in the first quadrant and that the slope of the family of lines representing the constraints is intermediate between the slopes of the constraint lines. Then the solution of each problem will be represented by the intersection of the constraint lines.

The solution of the primal problem is represented by the intersection of the lines $n_1 x + n_2 y = n$ and $m_1 x + m_2 y = m$; that is:

$$\hat{x} = \frac{mn_2 - m_2 n}{\Delta} \tag{5.69}$$

$$\hat{y} = \frac{n_1 m - m_1 n}{\Delta} \tag{5.70}$$

where $\Delta = n_1 m_2 - m_1 n_2$. The solution of the dual problem, represented by the intersection of the lines $pn_1 + qm_1 = c_1$ and $pn_2 + qm_2 = c_2$, is

$$\hat{p} = \frac{c_1 m_2 - c_2 m_1}{\Delta} \tag{5.71}$$

$$\hat{q} = \frac{n_1 c_2 - n_2 c_1}{\Delta}. \tag{5.72}$$

Substituting Equations 5.71 and 5.72 into Equations 5.66 and Equations 5.69 and 5.70 into Equation 5.63, we obtain

$$U(\hat{x}, \hat{y}) = V(\hat{p}, \hat{q}) = \frac{c_1 nm_2 - c_1 mn_2 + c_2 mn_1 - c_2 nm_1}{\Delta}. \tag{5.73}$$

The connection between linear programming problems and the theory of games can be seen in the "opposite interests" of the actors faced with the primal and the dual problems respectively. In the diet problem, one actor strives to minimize cost, the other to maximize price. Both problems can be represented simultaneously as a *two-person constant-sum game* (see p. 326) where each player strives to maximize his gain, which, in the context of such a game, means that he strives to minimize the gain of his opponent under the constraint that the opponent strives to do the same. Assuming that each "does his best," the outcome of such a game is a *maximin* outcome for each player, that is, the maximum of the minimal gains guaranteed by each of his available *strategies* (courses of action). What is a maximin for one player is a *minimax* (the minimum of the maxima) for the other. The game has a "solution" if the maximin and the minimax are equal. The fundamental theorem of game theory states that every two-person constant-sum game, in which each player has a finite number of available strategies, has a solution. In contrast, not every linear programming problem has a solution, but if it has, the solution can also be represented by a maximin (or minimax). The equality of the two corresponds to the equality of the solution of the primal and the dual problems.

If a linear programming problem has a solution, it can always be represented as a conflict of interest between two actors, i.e., as a two-person zero-sum game. In that case, the duality of the linear programming problem corresponds to the two views of the game, as it is seen by the one or the other player. One attempts to maximize: he chooses the maximum of all possible minima (maximin). The other attempts to minimize: he chooses the minimum of all the possible maxima (minimax). As we shall see, various meanings of "duality" all express the idea of seeing a problem from two different perspectives.

GLOBAL MODELS WITH CONTROL

In global modeling, the idea of control was introduced in response to the much criticized results derived from Forrester's model (see Chapter 4). To be sure, control is not entirely eliminated from that model. In one version of it, exploitation of renewable resources is decreased; say, in response to awareness of impending crisis caused by depletion of the resources (see p. 89). Such control, however, is applied not with the aim of optimizing some well-defined objective function, as is done with the aid of control theory. Criticism of Forrester's model centered on this point. It has been argued that societies can be guided to "adjust" to situations and that these adjustments can be guided by better justified prognoses than adjustments that appear to be reasonable in the light of verbal arguments. A model referred to in futuristics as the Bariloche Model (see Mallman, 1977) was developed as an attempt to apply continual control to the world system with a definite objective function in mind.

In contrast to the definition of "quality of life" in terms of indices of production, crowdedness, and pollution, as it appears in Forrester's model, "quality of life" is now understood in terms of average life expectancy of human beings. It can be argued, of course, that life expectancy is no better index of "quality of life" than productivity and so on, if only because it is not obvious that a long miserable life is preferable to a short "happier" one. However, life expectancy already contains certain variables related to productivity, certainly to food production. How life expectancy depends on other factors is, of course, not known with any impressive precision, but the relation can be estimated by comparing life expectancies in various regions of the globe with other indices characteristic of these regions. Life expectancy, then, to be maximized in the Bariloche model is taken as the objective function.

The model starts in 1980. It is assumed that several indices of the world system can be controlled. Thereafter, controls are introduced in a way that permits a maximum increase in global life expectancy from year to year under the postulated constraints of the system. These constraints involve, in addition to the postulated dynamics of the system, the requirement that the amount of calories and proteins available to every individual on the planet shall not sink below a specified minimum, as well as the requirement that each person shall have a minimum of 10 square meters of urban-type living space.

Needless to say, the prognoses derived from the Bariloche model were quite different from those derived from Forrester's model because the underlying assumptions of the two models differ radically. For instance, one of the assumptions in the Bariloche model is that as conditions of life improve, birth rate *falls*. There is some empirical evidence for this relation, but it is far from conclusive. Next, the depletion of natural resources and the pollution explosion, factors that are crucial in Forrester's model, do not enter the Bariloche model. These two differences are, perhaps, sufficient to account for the very different trajectories of the world system derived from the two models. Over and above these, there is still a third fundamental difference; namely, the introduction of *continual* control in the Bariloche model. The assumption of on-going control amounts to an assumption of a world authority empowered to distribute resources, assign labor forces, and so on. At present, no such authority exists; nor is any envisaged in the foreseeable future. For this reason, the "optimistic" Bariloche model cannot in any way be regarded as a predictive model. It merely shows what could happen if people could think effectively (which in this context means mathematically) and could act in accordance with values suggested by considerations of human welfare as it is conceived by the authors of the model, *provided* the assumed dynamics of the system represents reality reasonably well. The last proviso is questionable in view of the omissions mentioned above.

Nor can the "pessimistic" model of Forrester be regarded as a predictive model, even though it improves on simple extrapolation of trends without consideration of interactive system dynamics, for *any* on-going control is absent from that model. It may be utopian to postulate on-going rational control as in the Bariloche model; still, some social adaptation to changing conditions may occur from time to time. The danger is that for such adjustments to occur, the changes must be sufficiently visible, and when this happens it may be too late, as in the case of malignancies, which usually "announce" themselves when it is too late to do anything about them. This analogy is, perhaps, the strongest justification for constructing world models. They may indicate "symptoms" that must be watched when they are still incipient and in themselves suggest no cause for alarm. The problem of exercising control remains unsolved, of course, at least in our time. Perhaps another justification for world models is that they lift the issue of control from the level of rhetoric to the level of analysis. The tools of analysis are still extremely crude, and for this reason the conclusions drawn from various world models must compete with "common sense" imperatives often rooted in prejudices, tribal loyalties, and simple unwillingness to follow involved reasoning without any solid guarantees that the chains of reasoning are based on solid foundations of knowledge. Refined tools, however, can be fashioned if there are crude tools to refine.

Another source of theoretical leverage of control models resides in the above-mentioned duality between prescriptive and descriptive models. In the case of global models with control, this leverage cannot be utilized. As we have seen, in a predictive model, estimation of parameters is made on the basis of available data, but no data are available because there is no history of a "global policy." On the other hand, armament policies may have been pursued during arms races, which Richardsonian models (see Chapter 3) do not take into account. Thus the duality between prescriptive and descriptive models may be utilized in this context.

The simple arms control model of Gillespie and Zinnes is practically inapplicable as a prescriptive model, not only because of the drastic simplifications, but also because of the extreme difficulty of estimating the parameters. With regard to the parameters embodied in the objective function (q and c), the builder of the arms control model can get around the difficulty by pointing out that his task is to prescribe a policy based on the *actor's* personal estimates of these parameters, which reflect only the actor's values, not "objective reality". Not so with regard to the parameters of the state equation (a, m, and g). These must reflect "objective reality." In fact, the stability of the system depends on the relative magnitudes of a and m (see p. 108). Consider, however, what these parameters represent: a reflects U's perception of X's perception of the threat of U's armament level; m reflects U's perception of X's "fatigue" or else of X's perception of how this threat is alleviated by his own armament level! Not many decision makers would venture to guess the magnitudes of a and m, let alone place much confidence in their guesses. More likely, they would have considerable difficulty trying to understand what these parameters represent "in the real world."

The situation is different if the model is conceived as a descriptive model. If we assume that U exercises optimal control and X reacts to it in accordance with Richardson's equation, we can fit the deduced trajectories $u(t)$ and $x(t)$ to observations, since u and x are, in principle, observable. If the fit is reasonably good, we can estimate q, c, a, and m, and g from historical data, thus getting some idea about U's values (from q and c) and about X's "actual" perceptions (from a, m, and g). It is not to be expected, of course, that this drastically simplified model will be adequately corroborated, but it can serve as a point of departure for extending Richardson's purely reactive models of arms races to models where attempts are made to exercise control.

NOTES

[1] This "duality" is not to be confused with the duality associated with linear programming problems and with two-person constant-sum games (see p. 115).

[2] When the state of the system is prescribed for $t = 0$ but not for $t = T$, the boundary condition on $\lambda(t)$ is $\lambda(T) = 0$.

CHAPTER SIX

The Weber-Fechner Law Reexamined

One of the earliest mathematical models pertaining to psychological phenomena is known as the Weber-Fechner law. Weber (1846) investigated the ability of human subjects to distinguish intensities of stimuli, such as the loudness of tones or the brightness of lights. For each intensity, he sought to establish a "just distinguishable difference" (JND). Later we will discuss some difficulties associated with this problem. At any rate, Weber did determine (with a margin of error, naturally) a JND associated with each intensity of a stimulus and found that in general this quantity increased with the intensity of the stimulus. It appeared that when the intensity x of a stimulus exceeds a certain value s_0, below which the stimulus is not perceived at all, JND is proportional to the intensity. Denoting JND by $\Delta(s)$ (an increment of intensity), we can write "Weber's Law" as

$$\Delta(s) = Ks \qquad \text{for } s > s_0, \tag{6.1}$$

where K is independent of s.

Fechner (1860) derived this relation from a mathematical model that relates the physical intensity of a stimulus to its psychologically perceived intensity. "Fechner's law" states that the subjectively perceived intensity $\psi(s)$ is proportional to the logarithm of the physical intensity:

$$\psi(s) = k \log s \qquad \text{for } s > s_0. \tag{6.2}$$

Differentiating both sides, we have

$$\frac{d\psi(s)}{ds} = \frac{k}{s} \tag{6.3}$$

or, since we are dealing with finite quantities,

$$\Delta(s) = \frac{s\Delta(\psi)}{k}. \tag{6.4}$$

Now $\Delta(\psi)$ can represent the smallest distinguishable difference as it is *subjectively* perceived. It can therefore be assumed to be subjectively perceived as a constant (independent of s). Denoting $\Delta(\psi)/k$ by K, we obtain Weber's law.[1]

Before we undertake a detailed critical analysis of Fechner's model, let us examine a situation where it appears to be eminently appropriate. So far, no operational definition has been offered for "physical intensity." For some modalities, interpretations of "intensity" immediately suggest themselves; for example, the loudness of a tone or the brightness of a light mentioned above. The "intensity" of a weight can be naturally defined as the weight itself. All of these definitions relate to the energy carried by the stimulus. In the case of weight, energy is reflected in the work required to lift the weight through a given distance. In the case of a tone, with loudness (that is, amplitude) held constant, energy is proportional to frequency. Hence associating intensity with the frequency of a tone is consistent with these definitions.

Now a reasonably musical person recognizes intervals between pairs of tones; for example, thirds, fifths, and so on. Moreover, a succession of such intervals (a melody) is recognized independently of the key in which it is played or sung. An interval between two tones is defined as the ratio of their frequencies. For instance, the octave corresponds to the ratio 1:2, a major third to 4:5, and so on. On the other hand, subjectively intervals are perceived as "distances" between tones, that is, as the difference of their positions in a scale (difference in their pitches). This relation between physical and subjectively perceived intensity can be deduced, if we assume that subjective perception of pitch is proportional to the logarithm of the frequency:

$$\psi(s_1) = k \log s_1$$
$$\psi(s_2) = k \log s_2$$
$$\psi(s_1) - \psi(s_2) = k(\log s_1 - \log s_2) = k \log\left(\frac{s_1}{s_2}\right) \tag{6.5}$$

That is, ratios of frequencies are perceived as differences of pitch.

In the case of tone frequencies, subjective perception of frequency ratios is directly interpretable in terms of recognition of intervals, which in turn is related to well-established and well-nigh universal cultural practice (music). In the case of other modalities, an analogous interpretation would present some difficulties. Consider the perception of differences in weight. Given three fixed weights, w_1, w_2, w_3, and a variable weight, x, a subject might be asked to calibrate x (by small increments or decrements) until the difference $w_3 - x$ appears to him equal to $w_1 - w_2$. But this procedure cannot be expected to yield as "clean" and consistent results as the simple observation that a person who can "carry a tune" recognizes a melody in any key. Specifically, once an experimental subject has fixed x in the manner indicated, he must also perceive the differences $(w_1 - w_3)$ and $(w_2 - x)$ as equal if the model $\psi(w) = k \log w$ is to be corroborated, which he may or may not do. In the case of other modalities, the calibration procedure might be quite difficult. For example, given three fixed saline solutions, s_1, s_2, s_3, and a variable solution, x, the subject may find it extremely difficult to adjust the concentration of x so that the differences in salinity are perceived as "equal." In calibration procedures, errors must be expected and accounted for in a mathematical model purporting to relate physical intensities to perceived intensities.

In a probabilistic model of "just distinguishable difference" this is done. In fact, the experimental procedure designed to test the model *makes use of* the subject's errors instead of treating them as a nuisance. The subject is presented with pairs of stimuli. Usually one of these, s, is fixed, while the other, x, varies. To fix ideas, suppose s is always presented first, followed by x. The subject is asked to say which stimulus is "larger" (louder, heavier, sweeter, and so on). In a forced choice situation, the answer, "I don't know," is not permitted. The answers are labeled "1" and "2." In repeated presentations of the same pair (s, x), $p_i(s, x)$ denotes the relative frequency and hence an estimate of the probability of the answer "i" ($i = 1, 2$) for that pair.

It is expected and generally confirmed that when x is much "smaller" than s, the subject always answers "1," that is $p_1(s, x) = 1$, $p_2(s, x) = 0$; and when x is much larger than s, $p_2(s, x) = 1$. When x is close to s, the subject makes errors, that is, $0 < p_2(s, x) < 1$. Moreover, in the range of x where $p_2(s, x) \neq 0, 1$, $p_2(s, x)$ increases with x, which is also expected on intuitive grounds. If each pair (s, x) is presented very many times, the plot of $p_2(s, x)$ against x is fitted by a smooth S-shaped curve. The mathematical expression describing this curve is called the *psychophysical function*. In what follows, we will write $p(s, x)$ for $p_2(s, x)$. A curve of this sort is shown in Figure 6.1.

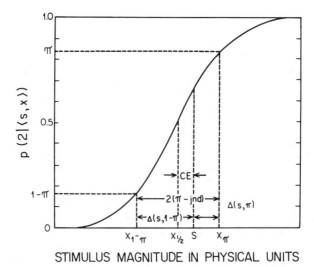

Figure 6.1. (Adapted from Luce and Galanter, 1963). Graphical representation of a psychophysical function.

Now if JND characterizing a given subject and related to a given $s > s_0$ were a fixed quantity, $p(s, x)$ might be represented by a step function, taking on values $0, \frac{1}{2}$, and 1. That is, for values of x sufficiently smaller or larger than s, the subject would always answer correctly. For values of x where $|s - x| <$ JND, since "I don't know" is not permitted, in the absence of bias toward one response or the other, the subject could be expected to answer at random with equal probabilities, that is, $p(s, x) = \frac{1}{2}$.

In paired comparison experiments, however, what is typically observed is not a step function but an S-shaped curve of the sort described above. Thus JND does not turn out to be a fixed quantity. To define it as a quantity, some range of x must be *chosen* where the subject makes "sufficiently many" errors. This is done by choosing a number π $(0 < \pi < \frac{1}{2})$ and defining JND as $x_{1-\pi} - x_\pi$ corresponding to $p(s, x) = \pi$. The value $\frac{1}{4}$ for π is most commonly chosen, but of course this choice is no more than a convention.

Since π is now included in the operational definition of JND, the JND associated with a given value of s must be regarded as a function of both s and π. It is denoted by $\Delta(s, \pi)$ and called Weber's function. Accordingly, Weber's law can be formulated as

$$\Delta(s, \pi) = K(\pi)s \qquad \text{for } s > s_0. \tag{6.6}$$

That is, the coefficient of proportionality, K, although assumed to be independent of s, should be expected to vary with π. The necessity to take the arbitrary choice of π into account suggests a reformulation of Fechner's model. R.D. Luce and E. Galanter (1963) called this reformulation *Fechner's problem*: For a fixed π $(0 < \pi < 1)$, find the "smooth," strictly monotonic functions ψ such that for all $s > s_0$

$$\psi[s + \Delta(s, \pi)] - \psi(s) = g(\pi), \tag{6.7}$$

where g, although it may depend on π, is independent of s.

Let us see how the solution of Fechner's problem (if it exists) is related to Fechner's model.

If the necessity of including the parameter π in the operational definition of JND is ignored, Equation 6.7 reduces to

$$\psi[s + \Delta(s)] - \psi(s) = g \quad \text{(a constant)}. \tag{6.8}$$

Fechner's model is $\psi(s) = k \log s$. Now the left side of Equation 6.8 is $\Delta\psi(s) = k\Delta \log s = k\Delta(s)/s$ for small values of $\Delta(s)$. But according to Weber's law, $\Delta(s)/s =$ constant, Thus if π is left out of consideration, Fechner's model is in accord with Weber's law and is corroborated if Weber's law is empirically corroborated. In this way, Fechner's model can be regarded as a solution of Equation 6.8 "for all values of π," since π is not contained in $\Delta(s)$.

We have seen, however, that in an empirical determination of JND, π *must* be included in the definition of JND. Luce's formulation of Fechner's problem takes this fact into account.

Equation 6.7 is a functional equation. The existence of solutions to such equations is by no means guaranteed in general. To continue with our analysis, however, let us assume that a solution exists. If one exists, we face another problem: there are too many solutions. In fact, it is shown (see Luce and Galanter (1963)) that if $u^*(x)$ is a monotone function satisfying Equation 6.7, then $u(s) = u^*(s) + F[u^*(s)]$ also satisfies Equation 6.7 if and only if F is a periodic function with period g, that is, $F(x + g) = F(x)$ for all x.

Thus a solution of Fechner's problem as formulated above would give us not a "law" relating physical intensities of stimuli to subjectively perceived intensities but a nondenumerable infinity of such "laws." Figure 6.2 shows two possible solutions of Equation 6.7, a "simple" one represented by the solid curve, and an embarassingly complicated one represented by the dotted curve, obtained by adding some periodic function of g to the simple solution. For any given value of π, the sum of the simple solution and any periodic solution with the same period and with any amplitude that still leaves $u(s)$ monotonic would also be a solution. Moreover, for each value of π the period of the added periodic function would be different. Clearly, then, the set of solutions to Equations 6.7 would not represent a satisfactory mathematical model.

A restriction imposed on $g(\pi)$ suggests a reformulation of Fechner's Problem that removes this difficulty. We will now demand that $g(\pi)$ be a *strictly monotonic increasing* function of π. In view of our operational definition of JND, this condition is appropriate, as can be seen from Figure 6.1. Let us see what this restriction implies. In stating Fechner's Problem, we have demanded that $u(s)$ be a "smooth" function of s. Continuity can be taken as part of the definition of "smoothness." We have seen that if $u^*(s)$ is a solution to Equation 6.7, $u(s)$ is also a solution if and only if $u(s) = u^*(s) + F[u^*(x)]$, and F is periodic with period g. It turns out that if $u(s)$ and $u^*(s)$ are both continuous, and if $g(\pi)$ is strictly monotone increasing in π, then F has a nondenumerable infinity of

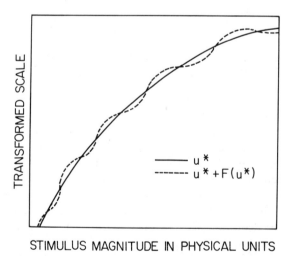

STIMULUS MAGNITUDE IN PHYSICAL UNITS

Figure 6.2. (Adapted from Luce and Galanter). The functions represented by the solid and the dotted curve both satisfy the functional Equation 6.7.

periods. It is also known from analysis that together with the continuity of $u(s)$ and $u^*(s)$, this implies that F is a constant. Thus if $u^*(s)$ is a solution to the reformulated Fechner's problem, then every other solution must be of the form $u(s) = u^*(s) + c$, a constant. We now still have a nondenumerable infinity of solution, but this multitude is no longer embarassing, for if subjective intensities can be determined on a scale no stronger than an interval scale (see p. 21f), the origin of this scale can be chosen arbitrarily, so that an arbitrary additive constant entering the determination of this scale is inevitable.

So far, we have assumed that the functional Equation 6.7 has a solution. As has been said, a functional equation does not necessarily have a solution. We are, however, particularly interested in the question of whether a solution to Equation 6.7 exists (given the above-mentioned restriction on $g(\pi)$) when some particular relationship between JND and stimulus intensity has been empirically established. We have assumed that Equation 6.6 represents such a relationship. Actually, however, the relationship found in many experiments is a more general one. It has been called the generalized Weber's law:

$$\Delta(s, \pi) = K(\pi)s + C(\pi) \tag{6.9}$$

where K and C are independent of s.

The final result on the reformulated Fechner's Problem states that a solution of it exists, provided $C(\pi)/K(\pi) = \gamma$, a constant (independent of π). Specifically, the general solution is of the form

$$u(s) = A \log(s + \gamma) + B, \tag{6.11}$$

where $A > 0$ and B is a constant.

Note that condition $C(\pi) = \gamma K(\pi)$ is quite strong. It implies that the logarithmic transformation of physical into subjective intensities is an adequate model only if the ratio of the slope and the intercept of the straight line representing $\Delta(s, \pi)$ as a linear function of s is independent of π.

In the formulation of Fechner's problem as a functional equation (see Equation 6.7), no mention was made of the Weber-Fechner law. Perhaps for this reason, Luce and Galanter (1963) state that Weber's Law and Fechner's Law are independent of each other. However, because Fechner's law is usually associated with perceived magnitudes as logarithmic transformations of physical magnitudes, which turns out to be the solution of the reformulated Fechner's problem, a connection between Fechner's law and Weber's law does exist. It would perhaps be more accurate to say that Fechner's *problem*, in which the form of Weber's function $\Delta(s, \pi)$ is not prejudged, is independent of Weber's law, which does prescribe the form of the function.

Fechner's problem can be formulated in another way. Suppose it is established empirically that $p(s, x)$ is a function of only the perceived difference between intensities:

$$p(s, x) = h[\psi(x) - \psi(s)]. \tag{6.12}$$

Can monotone increasing functions ψ and h be found that satisfy the functional Equation 6.12? In other words, can we find an appropriate transformation of objective intensity and an appropriate transformation of the differences between perceived intensities to satisfy Equation 6.12 when the psychophysical function is given? This is called the Equally-Often-Noticed Difference Problem. Luce and Galanter (1963) have shown that this problem has a solution if and only if the reformulated Fechner's problem has a solution. Suppose ψ is a solution of that problem. Then by definition of $\Delta(s, \pi)$, $x = s + \Delta(s, \pi)$ if $p(s, x) \neq 0$ or 1, and

$$\psi(x) - \psi(s) = g(\pi) \tag{6.13}$$

where $g(\pi)$ is strictly monotonically increasing with π and consequently has an inverse. Call the inverse function h. Then

$$h[\psi(x) - \psi(s)] = h[g(\pi)] = \pi = p(s, x). \tag{6.14}$$

Conversely, if ψ and h solve Equation 6.12, then

$$p[s, s + \Delta(s, \pi)] = \pi = h\{\psi[s + (s, \pi)] - \psi(s)\}. \tag{6.15}$$

Since h is strictly monotone increasing, it has an inverse. Call it g. Then

$$g(\pi) = \psi[s + \Delta(s, \pi)] - \psi(s), \tag{6.16}$$

and ψ is also a solution of the reformulated Fechner's problem. In this proof, no mention is made of Weber's law, that is, of the specific form of Weber's function $\Delta(s, \pi)$.

Any transformation of the measure of physical intensity into a measure of perceived intensity is called a psychophysical law. Clearly, any such a "law" must be empirically corroborated in several experiments. So far, we have discussed experiments where the determination of JND is involved. The perception of musical intervals was an exception; it appears to provide a "direct" corroboration of this transformation. There are other experiments where a transformation is tested without recourse to JNDs. Suppose intensity is identified with weight. The subject is presented with a large number of weights and is asked to select those that appear to him to be "equally spaced." These then serve as equally spaced points on the abscissa of a graph, and the objective magnitudes of the weights are plotted against them.

The plot represents the objective intensity s as a function of the perceived intensity. If s is strictly monotonic, it has an inverse ψ. Then $\psi = \psi(s)$ is the required transformation.

S.S. Stevens (1961) gathered impressive masses of data which suggest that the psychophysical law in most experiments has the form of a power function rather than a logarithmic one:

$$\psi(s) = \alpha s^\beta, \tag{6.17}$$

where α and β are positive constants $0 > \beta > 1$.

If $\psi(s)$ is monotone increasing with decreasing first derivative. The logarithmic function also has this property. With two free parameters, good fits can usually be obtained using either function, and since data and measurements are always subject to errors, it may be difficult to choose between the two transformations.

Stevens (1959) resorted to further tests of the power function model. He presented stimuli of two different modalities and asked subjects to calibrate the intensity of one modality until it was perceived "equal" to the intensity of the other. At first thought, this would seem very difficult to do, but it turned out that the subject could do this with fair consistency.

Now let the psychophysical law referring to one modality be $\psi(s) = \alpha s^\beta$, and the law referring to the other modality be $\psi'(t) = \alpha' t^{\beta'}$. When $\psi(s)$ and $\psi'(t)$ appear as "equal," we have

$$\alpha s^\beta = \alpha' t^{\beta'}; \qquad s = \left[\frac{\alpha'}{\alpha}\right]^{1/\beta} t^{\beta'/\beta}. \tag{6.18}$$

That is to say, as s and t vary, although they are perceived equal to each other, the relation between them is also represented by a power function. Since α, α', β, and β' have been independently estimated, Equation 6.18 *predicts* a relation between these variables.

Now it has been argued that on the basis of a logarithmic psychophysical law, the relation between equally perceived intensities of different modalities also turns out to be a power function. Indeed, if $\psi(s) = a \log(s/b) = \psi'(t) = a' \log(t/b')$, then

$$s = b(b')^{-a'/a} t^{a'/a}. \tag{6.19}$$

There is, however, an important difference between the predictions based on Equation 6.18 and those based on Equation 6.18. The parameters a' and a depend on the units in which the physical intensities are expressed and therefore can be chosen arbitrarily. Consequently, their ratio can also be chosen arbitrarily and represents a *free* parameter. On the other hand, the parameters β and β' are parameters that have been determined on the absolute scale (being dimensionless). Thus Equation 6.19 depends on two free parameters, whereas Equation 6.18 depends on only one and for this reason has greater theoretical leverage. Thus the somewhat challenging title of Stevens' paper, "To honor Fechner and to repeat his law" (1961a), is to a certain extent appropriate.

NOTE

[1] Thus the representation of a subjectively perceived intensity as a logarithmic function of objective intensity has been called the Weber-Fechner law (see Weber, 1846, Fechner, 1860). D. Bernoulli (1738) proposed the same relationship for the "utility of money" to solve the so-called St. Petersburg Paradox. If the utility of money were a linear function of the amount of money, the expected utility of a gamble which pays 2^k units of money when tosses of a fair coin result in k successive heads would be infinite. The "diminishing returns" of a logarithmic utility function ensure a finite expected utility.

CHAPTER SEVEN

Application of Catastrophe Theory to Models of International Conflict

Consider a Richardsonian system depicted by Equations 3.21 and 3.22 with $mn > ab$, that is, with the condition of stability satisfied. Setting $dx/dt = dy/dt = 0$ and solving for x and y, we obtain

$$x^* = \frac{ah + gn}{mn - ab}; \qquad y^* = \frac{bg + mh}{mn - ab}. \tag{7.1}$$

To the outside observer, who perceives only the state of the system, the system appears to be at equilibrium at that point in x–y space because its state does not change.

Suppose now that the parameters of the system a, b, m, n, g, and h undergo changes without, however, disturbing the position of the equilibrium state. For example, we may have the parameters change so that the two intersecting lines represented by the right sides of Equations 3.21 and 3.22 are set equal to zero and rotate about this equilibrium point, their point of intersection.

The parameters are not directly observable; only the equilibrium state (x^*, y^*) is. So if the position of the equilibrium remains constant, our observer will not be aware of the changes in the parameters. We have seen, however, that the *stability* of the system depends on a relation among the parameters a, b, m, and n. If as a result of the changes in these parameters, inequality $mn > ab$ is reversed, the system will become unstable. It will suddenly "take off" either toward ever-increasing armament levels or toward disarmament, depending on the direction of the initial disturbance. The observer, ignorant of the relationship that determines the stability of the system, will be unable to ascribe the sudden change in the system's behavior to any "cause."

More generally, suppose that the changes in the parameters are reflected in the changes of the equilibrium (x^*, y^*). Now the observer will be aware that the system is undergoing changes. As long as the inequality $mn > ab$ is satisfied, small changes in the parameters will produce small changes in the state of the system. As soon as the inequality is reversed, however, this will no longer be true. Again, the behavior of the system will be radically different.

Conditions of stability and their prime importance are well known to system engineers. The assumption that social macrosystems also crucially depend on the stability or instability of certain states deserves serious consideration. In what follows, we will examine an approach to social macrosystems based on this assumption. The mathematical tool used in this approach is derived from classical analysis and is called catastrophe theory.

Catastrophe theory has attracted the attention of mathematically oriented social scientists precisely because it provides a perspective for explaining sudden transitions or "explosions" in massive human behavior which remain unexplainable in terms of models that by their nature associate small changes in "effects" with small changes in "causes." At times, social scientists posit "thresholds" to account for observed discontinuities between "causes" and "effects." It is postulated that when the "causes" (that is, the independent variables of a mathematical model) remain within a certain range, the system behaves according to one set of "laws"; but as soon as some variable exceeds a posited threshold value, the system comes to be governed by another set of "laws."[1] Clearly, assumptions of this sort are *ad hoc*; they may describe behavior but do not get at the underlying mechanisms. Catastrophe theory provides tools for *deriving* sudden changes in the behavior of a system without resorting to *ad hoc* assumptions.

We have seen that Richardson's model of the arms race also provides an explanation of this sort. Rashevsky's model of imitative mass behavior is another example. As we have seen, Rashevsky's "mob" can be either in a single stable equilibrium state or in one of the two stable equilibrium states, depending on the direction of a certain inequality among the parameters. Figure 2.2 depicts this inequality geometrically. As long as the slope of the straight line through the origin remains large, the equilibrium at $\psi = 0$, that is, $X = Y$, remains stable. As the slope of the line decreases, the equilibrium will remain stable until the slope becomes sufficiently small for the straight line to intersect the curve at three points instead of one. Then the equilibrium at the origin will become unstable. A slight perturbation in either direction will "throw" the mob into one or the other of the two new equilibria represented by the other two intersections of the straight line with the curve. Without knowing the direction of the disturbance, we do not know which way the mob will be swayed, but the model does provide an explanation for the sudden shift.

The point of departure in Richardson's and Rashevsky's model was one or two differential equations. In principle, the solutions of these equations in the form of dependent variables as functions of time provide the complete dynamics of the systems. Equilibrium states and their stability characteristics are by-products of the analysis. Catastrophe theory does not treat the detailed dynamic aspects of macrosystems. Instead it focuses on equilibrium states as functions of system parameters.

Typically, a system possesses several equilibrium states. These are depicted on the so-called *critical manifold* (to be explained below). The parameters are called *control parameters*. They move in the *control space.* as They move, the dependent variable representing a possible observed equilibrium (state of the system) moves on the critical manifold. In a moment, we shall see how the nature of the motion of the control variables determines the nature of the motion of the observed state. In particular, we shall see how the "jumps" of the state variable are explained in terms of the geometry of the critical manifold.

THE MATHEMATICAL MODEL UNDERLYING ELEMENTARY CATASTROPHE THEORY

Consider a polynomial in x of degree r $(r \geqq 3)$:

$$f(x; a_1, a_2, \ldots, a_{r-2}) = x^r - a_{r-2}x^{r-2} - a_{r-1}x^{r-1} - \cdots a_1 x. \qquad (7.2)$$

Note that the term involving x^{r-1} and the constant term are missing. This involves no loss of generality because the constant term can be eliminated by translating the origin of f, and the term involving x^{r-1} can be eliminated by translating the origin of x. The choice of 1 for the leading coefficient amounts to a choice of unit for x. These transformations do not affect the *qualitative* aspects of the system to be investigated. Thus a polynomial of the third degree will have a single parameter a_1, and generally a polynomial of the rth degree will involve $r - 2$ parameters, $a_1, a_2, \ldots, a_{r-2}$. These are the control parameters.

A *critical point* of the function represented by Equation 7.2 is a value of x where the derivative df/dx vanishes. Thus a polynomial of degree three may have two, one, or no critical points. This is easily seen from the fact that the derivative of a polynomial of degree three is a quadratic polynomial, which may have two real roots, in which case f has two critical points; two coincident roots, in which case f has one critical point; or two imaginary roots, in which case f has no critical point. The situation is pictured in Figure 7.1.

A fundamental assumption of catastrophe theory is that the state of the system is always the value of the variable x that determines the *minimum* of f. The ration-

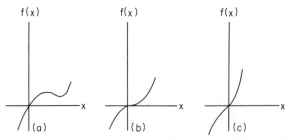

Figure 7.1. Plots of cubic polynomials. (a): with two critical points; (b): with one critical point; (c): with no critical point.

ale for this assumption stems from the behavior of physical systems. For example, mechanical systems tend toward a state in which the potential energy of the system is a minimum; closed thermodynamic systems tend toward a state of maximum entropy, that is, minimum free energy. A light beam passing through different media at different speeds minimizes the time of passage between two given points, and so on. In welfare economics, a theory prescribes an equilibrium state in which the welfare function is maximized (that is, its negative, the "illfare" function, is minimized). We see that whether we fix our attention on the maximum or the minimum is not important, so the minimum is chosen by convention.

The next assumption of catastrophe theory is that the changes in the value of the control parameters are governed by "slow" macrodynamics, while the trend of the system variable toward the equilibrium state is governed by "fast" microdynamics. Again, examples of this sort can be found in physics. Consider the pressure of a gas in a cylinder with a movable end. It is assumed that as the volume of the cylinder increases, the pressure decreases in accordance with Boyle's Law. Actually, this relationship holds only when uniform pressure has been reestablished in the cylinder following the disturbance created by the expansion. Strictly speaking, then, the law holds only if the volume changes "infinitely slowly" (slow macrodynamics) or, equivalently, if equilibrium is reestablished "infinitely quickly" (fast microdynamics).

In a social context, slow macrodynamics can be thought to represent gradual historical change of a system's parameters, while fast microdynamics represents the adjustment of the system to these changes, generated, for example, by deliberate social actions or decisions. Thus at all times, the system is essentially in an equilibrium determined by the values of the parameters at a particular time.

From Figure 7.1 it can be seen that the third degree polynomial $x^3 - a_1 x$ has a (single) local minimum only if it has two critical points, one of which is a local maximum. The location of the minimum and whether it exists is determined by the control parameter a_1. Figure 7.2 represents a plot of both the maxima and the minima of the third degree polynomial against a_1. Imagine that a_1 moves from right to left. As long as $a_1 > 0$ the system is observed to be in the corresponding minimum state x^*. When a_1 reaches 0, x^* reaches 0. When a_1 become negative, the equilibrium state at x^* "disappears." It is important to note that x^* disappears not because it has reached 0. The origin of the state variable x is defined arbitrarily. The "reason" for the disappearance of x^* is that when $a_1 < 0$, there exists no equilibrium state in that system. The system itself may exist, but now it can "find" no equilibrium to "settle" in, as it were. The situation is analogous to that represented in the Richardsonian arms race. However, because catastrophe theory considers only observable stable equilibrium states, the system is no longer "observable" if there is no such state. The fast microdynamics carries it immediately "out of sight," as it were.

Consider now a system represented by the fourth degree polynomial

$$x^4 - a_2 x^2 - a_1 x. \tag{7.3}$$

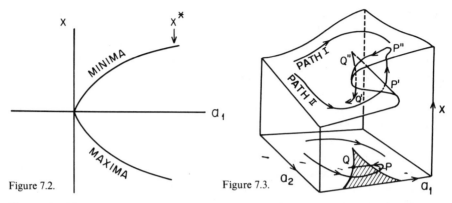

Figure 7.2.   Figure 7.3.

Figure 7.2. The upper branch of the parabola is the locus of points x^* at which the cubic poly-nomial is minimized as a_1 takes on different positive values. The lower branch is the locus of maxima. When $a_1 = 0$, the two critical points coincide and represent neither a minimum nor a maximum. When $a_1 < 0$, the cubic polynomial has no critical point.

Figure 7.3. The Cusp Catastrophe. Graphical representation of the minima and maxima of a fourth degree polynomial as functions of the control parameters a_1 and a_2.

Since the derivative of f with respect to x is a cubic polynomial, it has at least one real root, and it may have three distinct real roots or two coincident and one distinct real root or three coincident real roots. Because the leading coefficient is positive and the polynomial is of even degree, there must be at least one minimum.

The behavior of this system will depend on how the control parameters move in the control space, which in this case is a plane with coordinates (a_1, a_2). This model is depicted in Figure 7.3. The "floor" of the space pictured in the figure is the control space. The origin is the corner at the extreme left. The "roof" of the space is the curved surface partly folded, so that in some places a vertical line from the floor will intersect this surface at only one point and in other places at three points. This surface is the critical manifold. The x (vertical) coordinate of any point (on the upper or lower sheet or on the single sheet, where the roof has only one sheet) represents a possible observable state of the system corresponding to the point (a_1, a_2), the projection of the point onto the floor. Points on the middle sheet (where there are three) are maxima of f and hence do not represent stable equilibria.

Where a vertical line intersects the critical manifold at only one point, the system has a single minimum; where there are three intersection points, there are two minima, one on the uppermost sheet, the other on the lowest.

On the floor of the figure, we see a "shadow" (that is, projection) of the region in the space where the critical manifold has three sheets. The pointed end of that shadow is called a *cusp*. The contour of the shadow is called the *locus of bifurca-tion*. It encloses the *bifurcation region*.

Let us now follow the path of x^* as the point $a = (a_1, a_2)$ moves along the control space. Assume first that the path is the one shown by the arc with the arrow pointing to the right. Here a_1 and a_2 are initially small, and at first only

a_1 increases until the path turns to the right, at which time a_1 remains essentially constant and a_2 increases. The movement of x^* induced by this path of the point a is shown on the critical manifold as Path I: x^* first "climbs uphill," then turns to the right along the high part of the roof. The change in x^* caused by continuous change in a_1 and a_2 is continuous.

Let us now see what happens if the point moves along the arc with the arrow pointing toward us. The corresponding motion of x^* on the critical manifold is shown as Path II. When the point enters the region of bifurcation, x^* is still on the lower level of the critical manifold surface. However, when a reaches P, x^* reaches the "fold" at P'. It cannot go off the surface. The only thing for x^* to do after a passes out of the bifurcation region near P is to jump to the upper sheet, namely to P''.

We see that shortly thereafter, point a turns around and reenters the region of bifurcation. Now x^* moves on the upper sheet toward Q''. It reaches Q'' when a reaches Q. But at Q'' the minimum again disappears, and x^* must jump down to Q' on the lower sheet.

The catastrophe model, besides providing an explanation of how continuous changes in the independent variables (control parameters) of a system result in sudden changes in the dependent variable (observed state), has another property of interest to the social scientist. To illustrate it, we will assume that the point a is in the bifurcation region of the above model, which is called the Cusp Catastrophe. Knowing this fact alone does not tell us where x^* is located on the critical manifold. It may be either on the upper or on the lower sheet. To know where it is, we must know how a got to its position. If it entered the bifurcation region from the left (see Figure 7.3) while x^* was moving along Path II, then x^* will find itself on the lower sheet. But if it entered the bifurcation region from the right while x^* was moving "downhill" on the upper sheet, x^* will find itself still on the upper sheet. In this way, the catastrophe model depicts a situation in which knowing the value of the parameters alone is not enough to know the state of the system; it is also necessary to know the history of the system.

CATASTROPHE MODELS OF INTERNATIONAL VIOLENCE

We will now examine some aspects of international violence in light of a catastrophe model. The metaphorical connotations of many mathematical terms are sometimes deceptive. From the connotations of the word "catastrophe" it might be surmised that catastrophe theory could be applied to the study of war because "catastrophe" is often synonymous with "misfortune," and wars are also often regarded as misfortunes. Actually, "catastrophe" in its mathematical sense has nothing to do with misfortune. It does have a great deal to do with discontinuities in the course of events. So it is the suddenness of the onset of a war that might be the feature on which catastrophe theory might shed some light. It turns out that the theory can suggest explanations not only for the discontinuous features of war but also for the relative continuity of changes in the level of conflict associated with the onset of war and its termination.

An interesting difference has been pointed out between the courses of World War I and World War II. The former was characterized by sudden transitions from relative peace to intense violence and from intense violence to cessation of hostilities. World War II did not exhibit these sudden transitions. Let us look at the two situations more closely.

In retrospect, pre-1914 Europe seems to have been relatively peaceful. To be sure, it was an armed camp, and the occurrence of war among the major powers was expected. But there was no acute hostility presaging the explosion until a very short time before it occurred. Even the assassination of the Austrian Crown Prince on June 28, 1914, did not immediately create a war atmosphere. Relations among the powers continued within the limits of diplomatic courtesy. Above all, divisive ideologies did not pervade international politics. Only the Austrian ultimatum to Servia on July 28 brought the realization that Europe was on the brink of war, and war did come in a few days. Moreover, the fury of World War I exploded immediately. Casualties in August and September were enormous. Nor did the level of violence abate on the Western Front. It was still at its height during the German offensives in the spring and summer of 1918. Then, in the fall of 1918, hostilities ceased almost as suddenly as they had begun.

The course of World War II was quite different. The buildup of tensions went on for years, ever since Hitler came to power in 1933. Moreover, after the short Polish campaign, the war remained quiescent for several months. The intensity of violence began to rise in the spring of 1940 and rose continuously thereafter, reaching its peak in 1942 and 1943 in Russia and in the Pacific. Then it seems as if the intensity of war gradually diminished. Victory came to the Allies in phases, first over Italy, then over Germany's East European satellites, then over Germany, and finally over Japan.

Can the difference between the two courses of the two world wars be accounted for by a single mathematical model? Perhaps it can.

Let x^* represent the "level of violence" of an international system. Since we shall be dealing here with an analytic-descriptive model rather than a predictive one, operational definitions of variables are not immediately called for. To fix ideas, we might conceive x^* as the rate of casualties. In the absence of war, the rate of casualties is zero. Negative values of x^* are more difficult to interpret. As we have seen, Richardson attempted to identify "negative hostility" with international trade volumes. Other interpretations can be suggested. At any rate, in deriving the purely qualitative consequences of the catastrophe model (as we will do), concrete referents of variables need not be specified.

We will assume that the "level of hostility" (however interpreted) depends on two variables: a_1, the "degree of incompatibility" of aspirations of states or of demands they make on each other, and a_2, the "tightness" of the alliance structure.

Note that a_1 measures not so much the level of aspiration (to power, prestige, trade advantages, and so on) of nations as the degree to which these aspirations encroach upon one another. Thus during the eighteenth and nineteenth centuries, the imperial powers of Europe had enormous appetites. However, to the extent that there were still peoples to conquer and to subject to colonial rule,

Britain, France, Belgium, the Netherlands, and so on could still carve out their empires at the expense of the peoples of Asia and Africa without serious clashes among themselves. On the other hand, France's aspiration to regain Alsace-Lorraine after 1871 and Germany's equal determination to keep it exemplifies incompatible aspirations. The parameter a_1 is a *global* measure. It refers to some sort of aggregation of these incompatible aspirations, not the aspirations of particular states.

As for a_2, it is low when the existing alliance structure is "loose," that is, when there are many opportunities to choose between different alliance partners. It is high when the alliance structure is rigid.

At the beginning of the twentieth century, the European Great Powers were conceived as constituting the "international system." Referring to Figure 7.3, assume that the system started at the "peaceful" corner with a_1 and a_2 both small. Since the vertical coordinate represents the level of international violence, the state of war is represented by the highest part of the "roof."

Eventually, the system wound up in the diagonally opposite corner, that is, in the state of war with rigidly solidified alliances.

Now the system can go from its initial position to the diagonally opposite corner in two different ways (among others). It can first increase a_1 to a maximum, then increase a_2 while a_1 remains large; or it can first increase a_2, then a_1. If it follows the former course, x^* will "climb uphill," sticking to the upper sheet of the critical manifold as it passes the surface above the region of bifurcation. If it follows the latter course, it has to pass the region of bifurcation and, as we have seen, it will find itself on the lower sheet as its projection enters the region, and will jump to the upper sheet as the projection leaves the region. Thus if "incompatibility of aspirations" increases first and the firming of alliances follows, there will be a gradual buildup from a low value of x^* to a high value. If alliances are firmed first and increase of incompatibility follows, there will be a sudden jump of x^* from a low to a high value.

In this way, the catastrophe model suggests a hypothesis. On the basis of the observation that the transition from no violence to high violence was sudden at the onset of World War I, we can hypothesize that alliances among the European powers were firmed first, after which the aspirations became increasingly more incompatible. Below we will examine some historical evidence for this hypothesis.

The sudden transition from high violence to cessation of war requires that the system again passes through the bifurcation region. This means that a_1 has to decrease while a_2 remains high. Thus another hypothesis is suggested relating to the end of World War I; namely, that incompatibility of demands decreased, while the alliance structure remained tight. We will examine historical evidence for this hypothesis also.

The genesis of World War II, with its gradual rise in the level of violence and a gradual decline, suggests that in that situation, a_1 increased first, then a_2; and then toward the waning phase of the war, a_2 decreased first, then a_1. Evidence for this hypothesis will also be examined.

So far we have examined the very simplest catastrophe models involving one and two control parameters. The one-parameter model has been called the *Fold*, after the appearance of the critical manifold in Figure 7.2, which looks like a bent wire. The two-parameter catastrophe has been called the *Cusp*, after the appearance of the bifurcation region (see Figure 7.3). Progressively more complex catastrophies involve more control parameters. The next in order with three parameters is called the *Swallowtail*. The control space of this catastrophe is three-dimensional, and the state variable, being a function of the three parameters, must be represented by a coordinate in the fourth dimension. So this model cannot be visually represented, but mathematical analysis does not depend on a visual representation. Projections of the multidimensional bifurcation regions onto the (a_1-a_2) plane can be represented visually, and it is from the shapes of these projections on that plane that the fanciful names of the catastrophe types derive. The four-parameter catastrophe has been called the *Butterfly*, and the five-parameter the *Wigwam*.[2]

The Butterfly has been proposed by Holt et al. (1978) as a model of the international system with the intensity of violence as the dependent variable. We turn to this model.

The first two parameters of the Butterfly are identical with those of the Cusp model: a_1 represents the perceived degree of incompatibility of aspirations, a_2 the rigidity of the alliance structure. In addition, it will be useful to introduce more general designations of the control parameters independent of social context to emphasize their topological significance. a_1 is called the *normal* factor because when the other control parameters are kept constant, x^* is a monotone increasing function of a_1. a_2 is called the *splitting* factor. (We have seen how a single minimum of f splits into two minima when a_2 is large.)

The control parameter a_3 is called the *bias* factor. It alters the position and the shape of the bifurcation locus, thus emphasizing the aspects of a_1. It also moves the critical manifold up and down. The control parameter a_4 is called the *butterfly* factor. As Holt et al. explain, the butterfly factor "creates three cusps as it increases at the vertex of the main cusp and these form a triangular pocket giving rise to the pictorial image of a butterfly. On the manifold above this pocket there is a triangular portion of a sheet between the upper and lower sheets, which in the colorful language of catastrophe theory is called the 'pocket of compromise'" (Holt et al., 1978, p. 189).

The appropriateness of this designation in the context of international conflict stems from the following properties of the Butterfly. In a certain region of control space, the function f has three minima. Thus when the control point $a = (a_1, a_2, a_3, a_4)$ is in that region, x^* can be on any of the three sheets of the critical manifold. Since x^* is a measure of the degree of violence, the positions on the upper sheet can be interpreted as "war," those on the lower surface can be referred to as "peace," and those on the middle sheet something in between, for instance, "cold war" or "detente." The region in the control space where this is possible is the "pocket of compromise."

It remains to interpret the events leading up to the outbreak of international violence and to its eventual attenuation, recorded in history as World War I and World War II, in light of the Butterfly model. We follow the interpretation of historical events suggested by Holt et al.

Assuming that at the turn of the century, Europe was a "relatively peaceful place," the first changes in the international weather are attributed to the tightening of the alliance structure (increase of a_2). Although the Triple Alliance (Germany, Austro-Hungary, Italy) was in force, Italy was not entirely committed to it, as her neutrality at the start of World War I and subsequent entry on the side of the Allies suggests. On the other hand, the formation of the anti-German bloc progressed steadily with the Anglo-French accord of 1904 and the Anglo-Russian agreement of 1907. With the emergence of the Triple Entente, Europe became clearly polarized. Following the Bosnian Crisis of 1908–1909, shifts in the alliance structure (except for Italy) became highly improbable.

The bias factor (violence potential) also kept increasing. The machine gun came on the scene in the Russo-Japanese war. The inter-bloc arms race (studied by Richardson) began in earnest around 1909.

The butterfly factor (response time) of the system during the Bosnian Crisis of 1909 and again during the Balkan Wars of 1912–1913 was, one might suppose, quite short. Still, the "pocket of compromise" apparently still existed in 1913, as reflected in the conference on Balkan issues held from December 1912 to August 1913. In the crisis preceding the outbreak of World War I, the butterfly factor apparently shrank and in July disappeared altogether. The choice was now between peace and war, and the impetus of the crisis ignited the war.

The genesis of World War II seemed to have been different. In the early 1930s, the normal factor (incompatibility of demands) began to rise quickly, as reflected in France's demands on Germany for reparations. The splitting factor, however, remained small (rigid alliances were not formed). For instance, as late as 1939, both Western powers and Germany sought a pact with the Soviet Union. The bias factor started to rise sharply only in the late 1930s with the rapid rearmament of Germany. The butterfly factor was high (slow decisions) up until 1938 (the Munich Pact), then declined. In sum, the normal factor led the other control parameters and so produced the gradual instead of precipitous rise of conflict intensity.

The different courses of dissipation in violence toward the ends of the two wars can also be related to different schedules of changes in the control parameters. In World War I, after the spring and summer offensives launched by the Germans on the Western Front failed, Germany actively sought a negotiated peace (decline of a_1). However, the alliance structure (except for Russian defection) remained rigid. Thus the control parameter had to pass through the bifurcation region, which according to the model generated a sudden transition from high violence to no overt violence.

The events of 1944–1945 were quite different. Unconditional surrender remained the rigid objective of the Allies (a_1 remained high). The alliance structure, on the other hand, loosened in the waning months of the war as the issues of the Cold War began to overshadow the common aims of military victory. As we have seen, when a_2 leads a_1 in a decline, the bifurcation region is avoided and the dependent variable declines gradually.

To what extent these explanations are to be taken seriously is a matter of judgment. Certainly they go farther than Richardson's conjecture that World War I was a consequence of the fact that inter-bloc trade in the years preceding the war was £5 million too low or, equivalently, the combined armament budget was £5 million too high. Nevertheless, the Richardsonian model already contains the germ of the idea embodied and developed in catastrophe theory: that the stability or instability of a dynamic system as the determinant of its "fate." Catastrophe theory, unlike Richardson's model, does not treat system dynamics. It is concerned exclusively with statics. Bypassing the difficulties of complex nonlinear dynamic models, catastrophe theory concentrates on the intricacies of statics (more precisely, comparative statics) of such models. Note that all the dynamic models that can be regarded as underlying catastrophe theory must be nonlinear. For instance, the polynomial f could be regarded as the time derivative of the dependent variable, in which case we are dealing with a differential equation of at least the third degree. The richness of catastrophe theory models stems from the complexity of nonlinear dynamics. The multiplicity of parameters permits the inclusion of several factors as determinants of violence.

Incompatibility of demands or aspirations, the rigidity of alliance structures, the level of violence potential (war technology) and the impetuousness of decisions, especially in crisis, have all been discussed in the literature with different distributions of emphasis. For example, singling out incompatibility of demands reflects the traditional "Clausewitzian" view of international politics as a perpetual struggle for power; or else the more recent concept of "aggressor nations" bent on conquest. The venerable "balance of power" theory implies that a "loose" alliance structure is an inhibitor of war since it permits a reinstatement of balance by a "pivot nation" changing sides. Britain played that role throughout the nineteenth century. The role of armament races has been recognized already by Thucydides and was central in Richardson's approach. Decision time is a concept inherent in the emphasis on personal factors in the management of conflicts and crises. A large butterfly factor is associated with deliberation; a small one with snap judgments and impetuous decisions. It is noteworthy that this factor governs the existence of a "compromise region"— equilibrium states intermediate between "war" and "peace." Decision time can also be regarded as the speed of activation of the war machine. The importance of this factor looms large in push-button warfare (nuclear exchanges), where minutes are perceived to be of the essence.

Aside from this possibility of accommodating a multiplicity of determinants of a dependent variable (in these models, the level of international violence), catastrophe theory does three things. First, it binds the factors into a tight system of interdependence, thus transcending the severe limitations of linear models with their emphasis on essentially independent, additive effects of multiple causes. Second, it reveals systemic features hitherto neglected; for instance, the order in which the determinants of observed states change their values. In doing so, catastrophe theory suggests hypotheses that are quite unlikely to have occurred to any one in the light of hitherto predominant models. Finally, catastrophe theory displays the much discussed "states" of the international system as positions in a space. Although the multidimensionality of this space (except in the two simplest cases) precludes its full diagrammatic representation, projections of the space onto three-dimensional subspaces can be made visualizable an important aid to "holistic" understanding of complex processes.

A projection of the Butterfly model depicting intuitively perceived or imagined states of the international system is shown in Figure 7.4.

The origin of the $(a_1 - a_2)$-plane is the upper left corner. The corresponding position on the critical manifold is labeled "classical balance of power"; that is, spheres of influence have been clearly delineated and excessive demands are not made, since no state has sufficient power to force others to concede to them. Note that in this context, "balance of power" does *not* mean a polarized world. The alliance structure is loose, not tight; there are opportunities to switch alliances in order to preserve the "balance of power." The level of international violence (hostility) is comparatively low.

At the lower left corner, a_1 is low, but a_2 is high. There are few, if any, incompatible demands, and everyone is permanently allied with everyone else—a world federation. At this point, hostility is lowest.

The upper right corner represents high incompatibility of demands and a loose (or nonexistent) alliance system—a Hobbesian "war of all against all." Perhaps the perpetual tripartite war in Orwell's *1984* can be subsumed under this condition. Recall that the "two-against-one" alliance is constantly shifting in that war; a gruesome caricature of the "balance of power" ideal in which the object of restoring balance is not to keep peace, but on the contrary to perpetuate the war.

The lower right corner of the control space (high a_1 and high a_2) represents war between two rigorously organized blocks, such as was expected in the 1950s

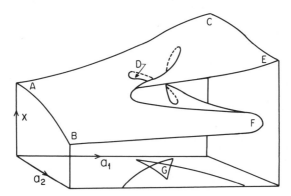

Figure 7.4. The Butterfly Catastrophe model of an international system projected on a three-dimensional space.

and 1960s before the emergence of a potential third superpower created opportunities for shifting alliances.

The region above the tail of the butterfly has three sheets. The lowest sheet is labeled "Detente." It should be visualized as passing underneath the sheet labeled "Cold War." It represents a relatively low level of international hostility. "Cold War" is the middle sheet. As long as the "pocket of compromise" exists (that is, when the butterfly factor is sufficiently large), an increase of a_1 on the Cold War surface need not erupt in war. However, if the butterfly factor shrinks or disappears altogether, the situation becomes explosive. As we have seen, the position and the extent of the "pocket of compromise" depends both on the bias factor (violence potential) and on the decision-reaction time.

A development of predictive theories based on catastrophe models is difficult to envisage because for the most part convincing operational definitions, let alone procedures for measuring or estimating the control parameters, are lacking. How would one quantify, for example, "the degree of incompatibility of goals" or "the rigidity of the alliance structure" in the Cusp model depicting the onset and the termination of the two world wars? The control parameters of the Butterfly model, "destructive potential" and "decision time," could perhaps be quantitatively defined, but certainly not with the precision required for a theory that would purport to predict the discontinuities in the behavior of the system. For this reason the relevance of catastrophe theory to the behavioral sciences has been questioned.

It seems, however, that catastrophe theory has served the analytic-descriptive function of mathematicized behavioral science. The phenomena that the theory purports to "explain" are primarily sudden transitions coupled with a hysteresis effect.

Interesting examples of such explanations can be found in the context of changes of perception engendered by ambivalent drawings, an effect long known to psychologists (see Necker, 1832). One such drawing is shown in Figure 7.5. The drawing is perceived either as a male face or as a female figure. Usually, a subject perceives only one of these, and only after intensely looking at the drawing, the other. (Some subjects can see the other image only after much prompting, some not at all.)

Figure 7.5.   (Adapted from Fisher, 1967). An ambiguous drawing.

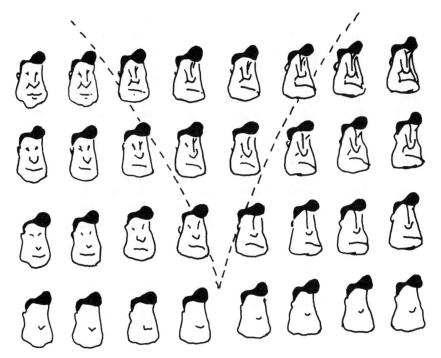

Figure 7.6. (Adapted from Poston and Stewart, 1978). A Cusp Catastrophe model of an ambiguous drawing.

Figure 7.6 shows gradual modifications of the drawing in two dimensions. The drawings in the left column predispose perception toward the face, those in the right column toward the figure. The top row contains much detail, the bottom row very little. The plane of the paper is the control space of a Cusp Catastrophe model. If we start at top left, proceed down to the bottom row, then to the right, to lower right, then up, we experience a gradual change from face to figure. Note that this path avoids the bifurcation region indicated by the dotted cusp curve. If, on the other hand, we proceed along the top row, passing through the bifurcation region, we are likely to experience an abrupt change of gestalt. Moreover, if we proceed in the top row from right to left, the figure will persist through the bifurcation region and will shift to the face as we emerge from it. If we proceed from top left to top right, the face will persist through the bifurcation region, shifting to the figure as we emerge from it. This is the hysteresis effect.

If the reader does not feel this hysteresis effect, this can be attributed to the fact that he/she already is aware of the two gestalts. Positive results are likely to be obtained from a subject unfamiliar with the drawing.

Many situations observed by social psychologists can be "explained" in a similar manner.[3] Suppose a certain form of behavior is influenced by two factors; for instance, internal predisposition (attitude) and external social pressure. (Recall Rashevsky's parameters ϕ, related to predisposition, and ψ, related to imitation of others.) The upper surface of the critical manifold of a Cusp Catastrophe can represent one pattern of behavior, R_1, the lower surface the other pattern, R_2. If social pressure to perform R_2 is low and the predisposition to R_1 initially high, R_1 will be performed. If social pressure to perform R_2 continues to be low while the predisposition to perform R_1 gradually decreases, eventually shifting to a predisposition to perform R_2, behavior will change gradually; the frequency of R_1 will gradually decrease, eventually becoming smaller than the frequency of R_2. Behavior follows a path on the critical manifold that avoids the bifurcation region. If, on the other hand, the predisposition to R_1 remains high while social pressure to perform R_2 increases, there may initially be a strong resistance against performing R_2, until social pressure passes a threshold. When this happens the shift toward R_2 will be sudden. In this situation, the bifurcation region has been traversed. It has frequently been observed that "converts" tend to be more fervent partisans of a view that they previously abhorred than its adherents.

Faced with a threatening antagonist, an animal may be motivated both by fear and rage. Fear predisposes to flight, rage to fight. But if fear and rage are "equally strong," intermediate behavior, that is, standing still (which was expected by a medieval philosopher of an ass between two equally attractive bales of hay) is not frequently observed. The animal will either flee or attack. If fear is initially low while rage increases, the animal may exhibit symptoms of rage of gradually increasing intensity; for instance, a dog may at first growl, then bare his teeth, and finally attack. If, however, fear is initially high while rage increases, the shift from cowering to attack may be sudden.

In interpersonal attraction, affect and information can be regarded as the two control parameters. In the absence of information, initial ardor in a romantic attachment may cool gradually, eventually passing to dislike. If, while ardor remains high, deleterious information is received about the object of affection, it may at first be disbelieved (resistance), but once believed may change love into hatred.

In these interpretations, catastrophe models clearly cannot be used predictively for want of precise quantitative measurements. However, they do serve as analytic descriptive models in that they provide a structurally analogous explanation for phenomena with widely different contents.

NOTES

[1] In computer simulation of such processes, thresholds of this sort are frequently built into the programs.

[2] The names of the various catastrophes, like that of the Cusp, were suggested by the shapes of the bifurcation regions projected on the (a_1-a_2)-space.

[3] The interested reader is referred to the special issue of *Behavioral Science* (1978, Vol. 23, No. 5) and to Zeeman (1976).

PART II

STOCHASTIC MODELS

CHAPTER EIGHT

Uses of the Poisson Distribution and Its Generalizations

Stochastic processes are used in mathematical theories of behavioral phenomena in two ways. A model may be formulated as a stochastic process governing the behavior of some system, and from it deductions can be made about the probabilities that the system will be in any of its possible states at some future time. Or else, some frequency distribution is observed (for instance, of numbers of people or events in different categories) which one assumes to be an *equilibrium distribution* of an underlying stochastic process. Then one seeks a stochastic process that may have given rise to this observed distribution.

The first approach aims primarily at a predictive theory, except that the deduced predictions are made probabilistically instead of categorically. The second approach aims at an explanatory theory. It deduces an observed distribution from a postulated "genesis" of probabilistically determined events.

We restate some fundamental concepts underlying the theory of stochastic processes.

For the purpose of this discussion, a *random variable* will be regarded as a real variable that obeys a specified *probability law* expressed as follows:

$$\Pr[X \leqslant x] = F(x). \tag{8.1}$$

The right side of Equation 8.1 is a real function of x which specifies the probability that the random variable X assumes a value not greater than some specified real number x.

We will consider only two classes of such functions.

(i) $F(x)$ is a continuous function of x with a derivative everywhere except possibly at a finite number of points.

(ii) $F(x)$ has discontinuities at a countable number of points and is constant between these points. Such functions are called *step functions*. They undergo sudden increments ("jumps") at specified values of x.

If $F(x)$ is continuous, X will be called a *continuous random variable*. If $F(x)$ is a step function, X will be called a *discrete random variable*.

By definition of probability, we must have $0 \leqslant F(x) \leqslant 1$ for all x. Moreover, because the event $X \leqslant x_1$ *implies* the event $X \leqslant x_2$ whenever $x_1 \leqslant x_2$, we must have $F(x_1) \leqslant F(x_2)$ for $x_1 \leqslant x_2$. That is to say, $F(x)$ is a *nondecreasing* function of x. Finally, by definition of a real number and of $F(x)$, we must have $F(-\infty) = 0$ and $F(+\infty) = 1$. In other words, $F(x)$ "starts" with value 0 at $-\infty$ and eventually increases either continuously or by "jumps" toward 1. If $F(x)$ is continuous, it may or may not actually reach 1 before x becomes infinite. Once $F(x)$ becomes 1, it retains that value.

If $F(x)$ has a derivative everywhere, this derivative $f(x) = F'(x)$ will be called the *density function* of X. In view of this definition, we see that

$$F(x) = \int_{-\infty}^{x} f(t)dt. \tag{8.2}$$

If X is a discrete random variable, it assumes specified values with finite (positive) probabilities. In that case, we can define the *probability distribution* $p(x)$ of X, where

$$p(x_i) = \Pr[X = x_i] \qquad (i = 1, 2, \ldots) \tag{8.3}$$

and x_i are the points of discontinuity of $F(x)$. It is easy to see that when X is discrete,

$$F(x) = \sum_{x_i \leqslant x} p(x_i), \tag{8.4}$$

where the summation is taken over all the points of discontinuity of $F(x)$ equal or less than x. Also, if x_{i-1} and x_i are two consecutive points of discontinuity,

$$p(x_i) = \Pr[X = x_i] = F(x_i) - F(x_{i-1}). \tag{8.5}$$

The connection between the density function of a continuous random variable $f(x)$ and the probability distribution of a discrete random variable $p(x)$ can be seen from the following relation which applies to a continuous random variable X:

$$\Pr[x \leqslant X \leqslant x + dx] = \int_{x}^{x+dx} f(t)dt = f(x)dx + o(dx) \tag{8.6}$$

where dx is an infinitesimal increment of x.[1] Thus $f(x)dx$ is a probability like $p(x_i)$. It is important to keep in mind, however, that unlike $f(x)dx$, $f(x)$ is not a probability. Rather, the probability that X lies within a small interval $(x, x + dx)$ is approximately *proportional* to $f(x)$, with dx as the factor of proportionality.

From definitions of $f(x)$, $p(x)$, and $F(x)$, it follows that

$$\int_{-\infty}^{\infty} f(x)dx = \sum_{x_i} p(x_i) = 1. \tag{8.7}$$

STOCHASTIC PROCESSES

A stochastic process is formally defined as a *family* of random variables indexed by either a continuous parameter t or a discrete index n. A particular stochastic process is specified when its probability law is given. The probability law for a stochastic process with a continuous parameter has the form

$$F_{X(t_1), X(t_2), \ldots, X(t_m)}(x_1, x_2, \ldots, x_m) = \Pr[X(t_1) \leqq x_1, X(t_2) \leqq x_2, \ldots, X(t_m) \leqq x_m].$$
$$(8.8)$$

This notation is interpreted as follows. Select m values of the (continuous) parameter t, $(t_1, t_2, \ldots, t_m)$. These will determine m random variables from the family $X(t)$; namely, $X(t_1)$, $X(t_2)$, ..., $X(t_m)$. The right side of Equation 8.8 denotes the *joint* probability that these m variables fall within the ranges indicated. This probability is a function of the m values $x_1, x_2, \ldots, x_m$. The set of subscripts on F on the left side of Equation 8.8 *specifies* this function. In other words, once $t_1, t_2, \ldots, t_m$ have been chosen and thus the m random variables from the family $X(t)$ have been selected, a particular function of m real variables $x_1, x_2, \ldots, x_m$ (a probability law) has been *specified*. And this must be the case for every choice of m ($m = 1, 2, \ldots$) and every choice of $t_1, t_2, \ldots, t_m$.

In particular, let $m = 1$. Then Equation 8.8 reduces to

$$F_{X(t)}(x) = \Pr[X(t) \leqq x].$$
$$(8.9)$$

That is, once t has been chosen and a particular random variable $X(t)$ thus selected, the probability law of this random variable as given by Equation 8.1 must be specified. But this is not yet enough to specify the stochastic process. The joint probability law for any pair of random variables from the family must also be specified; likewise for any triple, quadruple, and so on.

The specification of a stochastic process with a discrete index is analogous. The probability law must be specified for any set of m random variables ($m = 1, 2, \ldots$) selected from the family $X(n)$.

A specification of this sort in the general case is clearly out of the question because it involves an infinite number of probability laws. However, just as many mathematical functions can be incorporated into single formulas which specify an infinite number of values of a dependent variable corresponding to an infinite number of values of an independent variable, so some stochastic processes can be specified by a finite number of functional expressions, at times by a single expression. These are the stochastic processes in applications.

In the simplest case, we may have all the random variables of a family identical (that is, characterized by the same probability law) and all statistically independent. In this case, we are dealing with a single random variable X. We need to specify only its probability law, $\Pr[X \leqq x] = F(x)$, in order to specify the entire stochastic process, for in that case, the left side of Equation 8.8 is equal to $[F(x)]^m$ for every m-tuple of the family. The stochastic processes we shall be dealing with will be only somewhat more complex.

A useful tool in the study of stochastic processes is the *characteristic function* of the process. Given m random variables from the family $X(t)$, $X(t_1)$, $X(t_2)$, ..., $X(t_m)$, the characteristic function of the process $X(t)$ is defined as

$$\phi_{X(t_1), X(t_2), \ldots, X(t_m)}(u_1, u_2, \ldots, u_m) = E[\exp\{i(u_1 X_1 + u_2 X_2 + \cdots + u_m X_m)\}],$$

(8.10)

where we have written X_j for $X(t_j)$, $j = 1, 2, \ldots, m$ and $i = \sqrt{-1}$. The right side of Equation 8.10 denotes the statistical expectation (the mean) of the random variable denoted by the expression in the brackets.

Under very general conditions, specification of the probability law of a stochastic process specifies its characteristic function, and vice versa. One reason for introducing the characteristic function is that it greatly facilitates the derivation of stochastic processes that are composed of other stochastic processes.

Note that the concepts of discreteness and continuity are involved in the theory of stochastic processes in two ways. We may have a discrete or continuous parameter that designates the members of a family of random variables, and these random variables may themselves be either discrete or continuous. All combinations are possible. We may have a discrete family of discrete variables, a continuous family of discrete variables, a discrete family of continuous variables, or a continuous family of continuous variables.

THE POISSON PROCESS

We will now examine a stochastic process of great importance in applications—the Poisson process. It is important in its own right because it underlies many stochastic models, and it also serves as a "building block" in constructing more complex stochastic processes.

The Poisson process $\langle N(t), t \geq 0 \rangle$ is defined by a family of discrete random variables indexed by a continuous parameter. This notation indicates that the continuous parameter t ranges from 0 to infinity. Once the probability law has been defined for each random variable $N(t)$ of the family, the probability law for the entire process can be determined in consequence of the special properties of the Poisson process. Namely, the Poisson process is a *stationary process with independent increments.*

Stationarity and independent increments are reflected in the following relations. Consider two values of the parameter s and t with $t > s$. Because $N(t)$ and $N(s)$ are particular random variables for fixed s and t, so is $[N(t) - N(s)]$. That the process is stationary means that the probability law of $[N(t) - N(s)]$ depends only on $(t - s)$, not on particular values of t and s separately. That the process has independent increments means that given two nonoverlapping intervals, (s, t) and (u, v), the random variables $[N(t) - N(s)]$ and $[N(v) - N(u)]$ are statistically independent.

The Poisson process can now be specified as follows:

(i) $\Pr[N(0) = 0] = 1$ (8.11)

(ii) $\Pr[N(t) - N(s) = x] = \dfrac{[v(t - s)]^x}{x!} e^{-v(t - s)}$ $(x = 0, 1, \ldots),$ (8.12)

where v is a constant parameter. Equation 8.12 represents the so-called Poisson distribution, from which the Poisson process derives its name.

As has been said, in order to specify a stochastic process, we must specify all the *joint* probability laws for all the m-tuples of random variables from the family. It is easily shown, however, that in the case of the Poisson process, once the parameter v has been specified, the joint probability law for any m-tuple of random variables $N(t)$ can be determined and so the stochastic process can be specified.[2]

If the parameter t represents time, the Poisson process can be regarded as a model of the following situation. Consider a sequence of events occurring in successive moments of time $\tau_1, \tau_2, \ldots,$ and assume that the probability that an event occurs in an infinitesimal interval $(t, t + dt)$ is $v\,dt$, where v is a constant; that is, independent of t and of the occurrence of any other events of the sequence. The parameter v is called the *intensity* of the process. It can be shown to be equal to the expected (mean) number of events occurring per unit time.[3]

Situations that can reasonably be modeled by a Poisson process are not uncommon. Consider airplane crashes. If we assume that these accidents occur independently of each other and, moreover, that a crash can occur with the same probability in any short interval of time, then the Poisson process is an appropriate model of the situation.

Since the Poisson process is derived from certain assumptions of independence and equiprobability of events, these *assumptions* can be tested by comparing observations with the predictions of the Poisson process. Since these predictions are only probabilistic, however, the observations must be made over several intervals of time. Moreover, the units of time in which to count the occurrences must be sufficiently large to be likely to contain one or more events. In our example, had we taken an hour for our unit of time for airplane crashes, the parameter v would be very small (being the average number of airplane crashes per hour), so that by far the largest number of hours would be devoid of crashes. But if we were examining the occurrences of automobile accidents in a country, we might well take an hour as the unit of time. In testing the model, we would record the number of accidents occurring in each hour over several hundred hours. Then we would count the number of hours in which no accident occurred, exactly one accident, exactly two accidents, and so on. If these numbers were proportional within tolerable error to the terms on the right side of Equation 8.12 with $(t - s) = 1$, this sequence of events could be regarded as a Poisson process; that is, the underlying assumptions of the process would be corroborated.

In general, we would *not* expect the model to be corroborated, because the frequency of accidents is known to depend on the hour of the day, on the day of the week, and on the season. The model might well be corroborated, however, if the hours chosen for observation were as "alike" as possible, say at the same time of day on a weekday. Then a Poisson distribution of the number of accidents might well emerge.

Instead of examining units of time for the number of events occurring in them, we can fix some interval of time and examine the numbers of individuals who have experienced no events, one event, two events, and so on during that interval. In the case of automobile accidents, we can take a stretch of time (for example, 10 years) during which there will be drivers who have had several accidents. If the "propensity" for accidents is the same for all drivers and if accidents are independent events, then X, the random variable representing the number of accidents experienced by an arbitrarily selected driver, should be Poisson distributed:

$$\Pr[X = x] = p(x) = \frac{\lambda^x}{x!} \, e^{-\lambda} \qquad (x = 0, 1, 2, \ldots). \tag{8.13}$$

If the observed distribution differs markedly from the Poisson distribution, we are led to reexamine the assumptions of the model. Important sources of discrepancy are (1) the heterogeneity of the population and (2) a "contagion" effect. We will consider each in turn.

HETEROGENEITY AND CONTAGION

In the context of accidents, the heterogeneity of the population may be reflected in a different propensity for accidents (what psychologists call "accident proneness") that characterizes different individuals. In a stochastic model, this heterogeneity is introduced by defining the intensity of the process as a random variable Λ. This random variable has its own distribution, which must be incorporated into the calculation of the distribution of accidents. Consequently, some assumption must be made about the distribution of Λ. Whether this assumption can be regarded as a reasonable representation of reality will depend on the test of the model. Hence the mathematician is to some extent justified in choosing this assumption by mathematical expedience: he chooses a distribution that is mathematically tractable. A class of distributions that has this property comprises the so-called *gamma distributions*.

The frequency function of a gamma-distributed random variable Λ is given by

$$f(\lambda) = \frac{m^n \lambda^{n-1} e^{-m\lambda}}{\Gamma(n)} \tag{8.14}$$

where m and n are the parameters of the distribution.[4]

Consider now the characteristic function of the random variable X, whose distribution is given by Equation 8.13:

$$\phi_X(u) = E(e^{iuX}) = \sum_{j=0}^{\infty} \exp[iuj]p(j) = \sum_{j=0}^{\infty} e^{iuj}\frac{\lambda^j}{j!}e^{-\lambda} = \exp[\lambda(e^{iu}-1)]. \quad (8.15)$$

If, as we have assumed, λ is a value assumed by a random variable Λ with distribution function $F(\lambda)$, density function $f(\lambda)$, and characteristic function $\phi_X(u)$, then we can write *for a fixed* λ:

$$E[e^{iuX}] = \exp[\lambda(e^{iu}-1)]. \quad (8.16)$$

This characteristic function is expressed as a *conditional* expectation, *given* that $\Lambda = \lambda$. Then the characteristic function of the random variable Y, *compounded* from the Poisson variable X and the random variable Λ, will be given by

$$\phi_Y(u) = \int_{-\infty}^{\infty} \exp\{\lambda(e^{iu}-1)\}f(\lambda)d\lambda = \phi_\Lambda\left(\frac{e^{iu}-1}{i}\right). \quad (8.17)$$

That is to say, this characteristic function will have the same form as the characteristic function of X (see Equation 8.15) except that $(e^{iu}-1)/i$ will take the place of u in $E(e^{iu\Lambda})$.[5]

In our case, we have assumed that Λ is gamma-distributed. The characteristic function of any gamma-distributed variable Λ is

$$\phi_\Lambda(u) = \left(1 - \frac{iu}{m}\right)^{-n}, \quad (8.18)$$

where m and n are the parameters of the distribution. Therefore, in view of Equation 8.17, we have

$$\phi_Y(u) = \left[1 - \frac{(e^{iu}-1)}{m}\right]^{-n} = \left(\frac{m}{1+m-e^{iu}}\right)^n = \left(\frac{p}{1-qe^{iu}}\right)^n, \quad (8.19)$$

where we have written $p = m/(1+m)$, $q = 1-p$.

But the right side of Equation 8.19 is the characteristic function of a negative binomial distribution. Hence Y has a negative binomial distribution:[6]

$$p(y) = \binom{y+n-1}{y}p^nq^y \quad (y=0, 1, 2, \ldots ; n=1, 2, \ldots) \quad (8.20)$$

The parameters n and p of a negative binomial distribution purporting to describe a set of data can be estimated from the relations

$$E(Y) = \frac{nq}{p}; \quad \text{Var}(Y) = \frac{nq}{p^2}. \quad (8.21)$$

Using these estimates, we can compare an observed distribution with the negative binomial distribution. Table 8.1 shows the frequency distribution of the number of accidents in a factory compared with both a Poisson distribution and a negative binomial distribution.

Table 8.1. *Distributions of Numbers of Persons Who Have Had Different Numbers of Accidents in a Specified Time Period*

Number of Accidents y	Number of Persons with y Accidents	Poisson Distribution $\lambda = 0.429$	Negative Binomial $n = 1.3, p = 0.752$
0	200	188.2	199.0
1	64	80.7	64.9
2	17	17.4	18.7
3	6	2.5	5.1
4	2	0.3	1.4

Source: Adapted from Hill and Trist (1953).

The considerably better fit of the negative binomial, compared with the Poisson distribution, suggests that the population is not homogeneous; that is, "accident proneness" differs among the workers. This inference is in accord with common sense and suggests that the safety record might be improved by screening the applicants for jobs in the factory to eliminate the more "accident prone." The effectiveness of such screening depends on two conditions: (1) applicants indeed differ with regard to accident proneness and (2) the tests can detect the difference. But it turns out that the discrepancy between the observed distribution of accidents and the Poisson distribution does not definitively establish an *inherent* heterogeneity of the population. Another effect called the *contagion* effect may also cause the discrepancy.

Suppose the population is initially homogeneous; that is, each worker has the same initial accident proneness, but the accidents are not independent of each other. A "positive" contagion effect could be manifested in an increase of proneness following an accident (for example, if having an accident makes the worker more nervous). A "negative" contagion could be manifested in a reduced proneness following an accident (for example, if having an accident would make a worker more careful).

Let the "state of a worker" at time t be represented by the number of accidents he has had up to time t. Thus if a worker has had i accidents by time t, he is said to be in state i. If this worker has an accident at time t, he passes from state i to state $(i + 1)$ at time t. If accidents occur in accordance with a Poisson process, the probability that the worker has an accident in a short time interval $(t, t + dt)$ is $v\,dt$, where v is independent of t and of the number of accidents the worker has had (that is, of his state). Let $p_i(t)$ be the probability that the worker is in state i at time t. In particular, $p_0(t)$ is the probability that he has had no accident up to time t. Then the rate of change of $p_0(t)$ will be given by

$$\frac{dp_0(t)}{dt} = -v p_0(t). \tag{8.22}$$

Thus

$$p_0(t) = p_0(0)e^{-vt}. \tag{8.23}$$

If we set $t = 0$ at the time when no accident has yet occurred, $p_0(0) = 1$, so that

$$p_0(t) = e^{-vt}. \tag{8.24}$$

Similarly, for $i = 1, 2, \ldots$, we have

$$\frac{dp_i(t)}{dt} = vp_{i-1}(t) - vp_i(t). \tag{8.25}$$

The first term on the right represents an increment due to the passage from state $(i - 1)$ into state i. The second term represents the decrement due to passage from state i to state $(i + 1)$. For $i = 1$, Equation 8.25 becomes

$$\frac{dp_1(t)}{dt} = vp_0(t) - vp_1(t). \tag{8.26}$$

Substituting Equation 8.24 into Equation 8.26, we get

$$\frac{dp_1(t)}{dt} = ve^{-vt} - vp_1(t), \tag{8.27}$$

Whose solution is

$$p_1(t) = vte^{-vt}. \tag{8.28}$$

By iteration, we obtain

$$p_i(t) = \frac{(vt)^i}{i!} e^{-vt} \qquad (i = 2, 3, \ldots), \tag{8.29}$$

that is, the terms of the Poisson distribution with parameter vt.

We now introduce the contagion process by assuming that v increases by a constant increment with the occurrence of each accident. Thus

$$v_{01} = v$$
$$v_{12} = v + \beta$$
$$v_{23} = v + 2\beta, \qquad \beta > 0,$$

and so on. The subscripts ij on the vs indicate that the successive vs are associated with the transitions from state i to state j.

Our differential equations now become

$$\frac{dp_0}{dt} = -vp_0$$

$$\frac{dp_i}{dt} = [v + (i-1)\beta]p_{i-1} - (v + i\beta)p_i \qquad (i = 1, 2, \ldots). \tag{8.30}$$

The solution of the system is

$$p_0 = e^{-vt}$$

$$p_i = \left[\frac{v(v + \beta) \ldots [v + (i-1)\beta]}{i!\beta^i} \right] [e^{-vt}(1 - e^{-\beta t})^i] \quad (i > 0). \tag{8.31}$$

Now the expression in the brackets on the right side of Equation 8.31 can be written as

$$\binom{v/\beta + i - 1}{i},$$ (8.32)

which is the binomial coefficient in the negative binomial distribution.

Next, we introduce r and γ, defined by

$$\gamma = \frac{e^{-\beta t}}{1 - e^{-\beta t}} ; \qquad r = \frac{v}{\beta}.$$ (8.33)

Then

$$1 + \gamma = \frac{1}{1 - e^{-\beta t}} ; \qquad \frac{\gamma}{1 + \gamma} = e^{-\beta t} ; \qquad \left[\frac{\gamma}{1 + \gamma}\right]^r = e^{-vt}$$ (8.34)

and

$$\frac{1}{1 + \gamma} = 1 - e^{-\beta t} ; \qquad \left[\frac{1}{1 + \gamma}\right]^i = (1 - e^{-\beta t})^i.$$ (8.35)

Therefore Equation 8.31 can be written

$$p_i = \binom{r + i - 1}{i}\left[\frac{\gamma}{1 + \gamma}\right]^r\left[\frac{1}{1 + \gamma}\right]^i,$$ (8.36)

which is a negative binomial distribution with parameter r corresponding to n in Equation 8.20 and $\gamma/(1 + \gamma)$ corresponding to p in Equation 8.20. Note that i in Equation 8.36 corresponds to y in Equation 8.20.

The discorroboration of the Poisson process model gives evidence that one or more of the assumptions of that model are not justified. But *which* of the assumptions is violated and in which way cannot, as a rule, be immediately established. For instance, the negative binomial may have been generated by either of two sorts of heterogeneity: *inherent* heterogeneity, which exists in the population at the start of the process, or *evolving* heterogeneity, which results from the fact that people's accident proneness changes during the process as a result of accidents. To what extent the observed distribution can be attributed to one or the other effect, to a mixture of both, or to neither is a question that suggests further, more detailed analysis.[7]

MODELS BASED ON RENEWAL PROCESSES

Our definition of the Poisson process was based on a discrete random variable $N(t)$ characterized by a Poisson distribution with mean vt, where v was a parameter characteristic of the process and t was a continuous parameter, the index of the corresponding family of random variables. Another definition of the Poisson process centers on *interarrival* times $T_1, T_2, \ldots$; that is, the intervals between successive events. Each interarrival time is a continuous positive random variable that has an *exponential* distribution with the same parameter:

$$F(t) = 1 - e^{-vt}, \qquad t \geq 0. \tag{8.37}$$

The two definitions are shown to be equivalent.

The Poisson process is an example of a *counting process* in the sense that $N(t)$ "counts" the number of occurrences up to time t. Thus the Poisson process can be also designated by

$$X(t) = \sum_{n=1}^{N(t)} (1), \tag{8.38}$$

where the upper limit of the summation is a Poisson-distributed random variable with mean vt.

The process represented by Equation 8.38 can be generalized in various ways by substituting functions of another random variable Y for 1 in the above summation. For example, the *compound Poisson process* is defined as

$$X(t) = \sum_{n=1}^{N(t)} Y_n, \tag{8.39}$$

where Y_n are identically distributed random variables. The *filtered Poisson process* is defined by

$$X(t) = \sum_{n=1}^{N(t)} w(t, \tau_n, Y_n), \tag{8.40}$$

where Y_n are again identically distributed random variables, τ_n are random variables denoting the arrival times of the events underlying the Poisson process $N(t)$, and w is some specified function of its three arguments.

We will consider a generalization of the Poisson process in another direction involving the interarrival times T_1, $T_2, \ldots$, where $T_i = \tau_i - \tau_{i-1}$. As in the Poisson process, the Ts will be assumed to be identically distributed positive random variables, but no longer necessarily exponentially distributed. Such processes are called *renewal processes*. Like the Poisson process, they can be regarded as counting processes and are denoted by $\langle N(t), t \geq 0 \rangle$ where, as before, $N(t)$ is a random variable denoting the number of occurrences up to time t.

The theory of renewal processes is based on an integral equation called the *renewal equation*:

$$g(t) = h(t) + \int_0^t g(t - \tau) f(\tau) d\tau. \tag{8.41}$$

Here $f(t)$ and $h(t)$ are assumed given, and $g(t)$ is an unknown function to be solved for. The equation is fundamental in renewal theory because many functions of interest in that theory satisfy that equation.

For instance, we may be interested in $m(t)$, called the *mean value function* of a counting process. That is, $m(t) = E[N(t)]$, the expectation of the random variable $N(t)$. Since $N(t)$ is a discrete random variable, it has a probability distribution

$p_{N(t)}(n)$ $(n = 0, 1, 2, \dots)$. Thus

$$m(t) = \sum_{n=0}^{\infty} n p_{N(t)}(n). \tag{8.42}$$

In a renewal process, the interarrival times $T_1, T_2, \dots$ all have a density function $f(t)$ and a distribution function $F(t)$. We will now show that in such a process, $m(t)$ satisfies the integral equation

$$m(t) = F(t) + \int_0^t m(t - \tau) f(\tau) d\tau, \tag{8.43}$$

which is formally equivalent to Equation 8.41 with $m(t)$ playing the role of $g(t)$, and $F(t)$ of $h(t)$.

Let us first show that this is the case for a Poisson process. Here $m(t) = vt$, $F(t) = 1 - e^{-vt}$, and $f(\tau) = ve^{-v\tau}$. Substituting into Equation 8.43, we have

$$vt = 1 - e^{-vt} + \int_0^t (vt - v\tau) v e^{-v\tau} d\tau. \tag{8.44}$$

Differentiating both sides of Equation 8.44 with respect to t, we have

$$v = ve^{-vt} + ve^{-vt}\big|_{\tau=0}^{\tau=t} = e^{-vt} - e^{-vt} + v = v. \tag{8.45}$$

Thus $m(t)$ satisfies the renewal equation in this case.

In the general case, we can write

$$m(t) = \int_0^{\infty} \{E[N(t)] \mid T_1 = \tau\} f_{T_1}(\tau) d\tau. \tag{8.46}$$

The first factor of the integrand represents the conditional expectation of $N(t)$ when the first interarrival time has some specified value τ. This conditional expectation multiplied by the density function of T_1 and integrated over the range of T_1 gives the overall (unconditional) expectation of $N(t)$.

Now if the *first* event occurs at time $\tau > t$, $N(t) = 0$. If $\tau \leqslant t$, then

$$\{E[N(t)] \mid T_1 = \tau\} = 1 + m(t - \tau). \tag{8.47}$$

That is to say, we get the expected number of events at time t, given that the first event occurred at time τ, by adding this first event to the expected number of events that have occurred in the interval $(\tau, t]$. Substituting Equations 8.47 into Equation 8.46, we obtain

$$m(t) = \int_0^t f(\tau) d\tau + \int_0^t m(t - \tau) f(\tau) d\tau = F(t) + \int_0^t m(t - \tau) f(\tau) d\tau \tag{8.48}$$

because the integrand in Equation 8.46 vanishes for $\tau > t$.

Since the interarrival times of a renewal process are independent identically distributed random variables, their common distribution function $F(t)$ completely determines the process; that is, its probability law. Given the distribution function, $m(t)$ can be determined by solving the renewal equation. Conversely, if we are given the mean value function of a renewal process, we can determine the probability law of the renewal process.

The theory of renewal processes can be applied to projecting the recruitment needs of an organization in maintaining a constant size. By "organization" we will mean here simply a population of individuals who work in a given enterprise. From time to time, the individuals leave the organization. With respect to a given origin of time, the length of stay of an individual in the organization is a random variable T. Therefore the number of individuals leaving the organization in the interval of time $(0, t)$ is also a random variable. In fact, this random variable is defined by the counting process $\langle N(t), t \geqq 0 \rangle$, where the events counted are the successive departures of individuals from the organization. If the "interdeparture" times are identically distributed independent random variables, we are dealing with a renewal process. If the organization is to maintain its size, we need some information about the number of departures, say in the next interval of time $(0, t)$, in order to provide for the replacement of an approximately equal number of individuals. We cannot, of course, predict the exact number of departures since this number is a random variable. But we can base our recruitment plans on the expected number of departures. This is the mean value function $m(t)$ of the postulated renewal process. It can be determined by Equation 8.48, once the distribution function of interdeparture times is known.

Also of practical interest is the *recruitment density*; that is, the time derivative of $m(t)$. Differentiating Equation 8.48 with respect to time, we obtain

$$m'(t) = f(t) + m(0)f(t) + \int_0^t m'(t - \tau)f(\tau)d\tau$$

$$= f(t) + \int_0^t m'(t - \tau)f(\tau)d\tau, \tag{8.49}$$

because $m(0) = 0$. Thus recruitment density satisfies the same kind of integral equation as the mean value function.

To determine $m(t)$ or $m'(t)$, we need to know $F(t)$. Now $F(t)$ represents the probability that an arbitrarily selected individual in our population will leave the organization no later than t. These probabilities (that is, the propensities to leave) may be different for different individuals. Recall that we encountered the same problem in connection with the distribution of accidents—the problem of heterogeneity. For example, the distribution of T, called completed length of service (CLS), may be exponential for every individual but have different parameters. Then the probability that an arbitrarily selected individual will leave no later than t will no longer be exponential. To see this, let the parameter of the exponentially distributed CLS in the population be itself a random variable Λ with a gamma-type density function given in Equation 8.14. Then the density function of T in the entire population will be given by

$$\int_0^\infty \frac{\lambda e^{-\lambda t} m^n \lambda^{n-1} e^{-m\lambda}}{\Gamma(n)} d\lambda = \frac{m^n}{\Gamma(n)} \int_0^\infty \lambda^n e^{-\lambda(m+t)} d\lambda = \frac{nm^n}{(m+t)^{n+1}}. \tag{8.50}$$

The density function given by Equation 8.50 is more skewed than the exponential density function. That is, its values for t smaller and larger than the mean are greater than the corresponding values of an exponential density function with the same mean. The same sort of effect can result from "habituation." Recall that an exponential distribution of T means that the probability of leaving the organization in any short interval of time $(t, t + dt)$ is $\lambda\, dt$ for any given individual, where λ is independent both of t and of the time that individual has already spent in the organization. That is, roughly speaking, departure is a purely random event. In reality, the probability of leaving may well depend on the length of stay. It may increase with the length of stay if the individual becomes tired of staying in one job; or, on the contrary, it may decrease as the length of stay increases, as when the individual is concerned with retaining his or her seniority or becomes progressively attached to the job or place of residence or whatever.

Given either assumption, the individual CLS will not be exponentially distributed. Thus the collective CLS distribution may deviate from the exponential either because of heterogeneity or because the probability of departure depends on an individual's length of stay, or both. The problem of separating individual and collective determinants of the overall CLS is interesting in its own right. For the moment, however, we regard the overall CLS, hence $F(t)$, as given. We are interested in determining $m(t)$ or $m'(t)$; that is, in solving the renewal equation. To simplify notation, let us write $h(t)$ for $m'(t)$.

Integral equations of the form of Equation 8.49 can sometimes be solved with the aid of *Laplace transforms*.[8] Taking the Laplace transforms of both sides of Equation 8.49, we obtain

$$h(s) = f(s) + h(s)f(s) \qquad (8.51),$$

whence

$$h(s) = \frac{f(s)}{1 - f(s)}. \qquad (8.52)$$

Since $f(t)$ is presumed to be known, so is its Laplace transform $f(s)$. Thus the Laplace transform of $h(t)$ is a known function of s. If this function corresponds to the Laplace transform of a known function, we can determine $h(t)$ as a function of t, which was the problem to be solved. Unfortunately, the inverse of the Laplace transform cannot always be found in closed form.

As a special case of $f(t)$, we might consider

$$f(t) = p\lambda_1 e^{-\lambda_1 t} + (1 - p)\lambda_2 e^{-\lambda_2 t}. \qquad (8.53)$$

This corresponds to the situation when our population is a mixture of two subpopulations in proportions p and $(1 - p)$, each being characterized by an exponential CLS with parameter λ_1 and λ_2 respectively. Taking the Laplace transform, we have

$$f(s) = p\left(\frac{\lambda_1}{\lambda_1 + s}\right) + (1 - p)\left(\frac{\lambda_2}{\lambda_2 + s}\right). \qquad (8.54)$$

Substituting Equation 8.54 into Equation 8.52, we obtain

$$h(s) = \frac{p\lambda_1/(\lambda_1 + s) + (1 - p)\lambda_2/(\lambda_2 + s)}{1 - p\lambda_1/(\lambda_1 + s) - (1 - p)\lambda_2/(\lambda_2 + s)}. \tag{8.55}$$

This Laplace transform is "invertible," being the Laplace transform to

$$h(t) = \mu^{-1} + [p\lambda_1 + (1 - p)\lambda_2 - \mu^{-1}]\exp\{-[p\lambda_2 + (1 - p)\lambda_1]t\}, \tag{8.56}$$

where $\mu = p/\lambda_1 + (1 - p)/\lambda_2$ is the mean CLS.

Note that $p\lambda_1 + (1 - p)\lambda_2 \geqq \mu^{-1}$. Thus the second term on the right of Equation 8.56 is non-negative (in general, positive). The second term, however, decays exponentially, so that eventually $h(t)$, which is the rate of loss, approaches an asymptote equal to the inverse of the mean CLS. When this occurs, equilibrium can be maintained by setting the rate of recruitment to the overall rate of loss. Until that time, recruitment has to be in excess of the rate of loss at equilibrium. This is because as people leave, the "age" distribution (in the sense of time of service) of the population changes. The situation is entirely analogous to population dynamics. When the equilibrium distribution has not yet been established, we cannot expect the overall death rate to remain constant, even if there are no external factors affecting it. It changes because the age distribution of the population changes.

Another way of looking at the situation is by analogy with natural selection. In a heterogeneous population, the first to leave are those with a larger propensity to leave; that is, those with the larger λ. Those who remain are likely to be those with the smaller λ, and their rate of departure is smaller. At equilibrium, the mixture is "properly balanced," so that the rate of departure corresponds to the reciprocal of the overall mean of CLS.

Thus the solution of the recruitment problem depends on the particular function $f(t)$, related to the probability that an individual leaves the organization at time t. If the depletion of personnel is representable as a Poisson process, $f(t) = \lambda e^{-\lambda t}$, where λ is a parameter, the same for every individual. The simplest generalization of this model represents the population as characterized by two parameters, λ_1 and λ_2, in which case $f(t)$ is a mixed exponential given by Equation 8.53. If the parameter Λ is a random variable with a gamma-type distribution, $f(t)$ has the form of Equation 8.50.

A. K. Rice, J. M. M. Hill, and E. L. Trist (1950) compared fits of three different functions $f(t)$ to actual numbers of employees who left two firms after different periods of completed service. The results are shown in Tables 8.2 and 8.3.

As can be seen, the fit obtained from the exponential function is poor, whereas those obtained from the mixed exponential and from $f(t)$ given by Equation 8.50 are quite good. Neither of these two is significantly better than the other, but the mixed exponential has the advantage of enabling the renewal equation to be solved in closed form. That is, the Laplace transform of $h(t)$ determined by the mixed exponential is invertible (see Equation 8.56), whereas that determined by Equation 8.50 is not.

Unfortunately, the mixed exponential can be expected to give good fits only

Table 8.2.   Distribution of Numbers of Persons Who Left Glacier Metal Co. After Different Periods of Employment

CLS	Number of Persons Who Left	Exponential	Mixed Exponential	Equation 8.50
Less than				
3 months	242	160.2	242.0[a]	242.0
3 months	152	138.9	152.0[a]	150.3
6 months	104	120.4	101.4	103.8
9 months	73	104.5	72.7	76.5
12 months	52	90.6	55.8	59.2
15 months	47	78.5	45.7	47.4
18 months	49	68.1	39.1	38.8
21 months or more	487	444.8	497.1	488.0
Total	1206	1206.0	1206.0	1206.0

Source: Adapted from Bartholomew (1967).
[a]These values correspond exactly to the data, because they were used in estimating the parameters.

Table 8.3.   Distribution of Numbers of Persons Who Left J. Libby & Sons After Different Periods of Employment

CLS	Number of Persons Who Left	Exponential	Mixed Exponential	Equation 8.50
Less than				
3 months	182	103.9	182.0[a]	195.4
3 months	103	86.8	103.0[a]	87.5
6 months	60	72.4	60.7	51.8
9 months	29	60.5	38.0	35.0
12 months	31	50.5	25.5	25.6
15 months	23	42.1	18.6	19.7
18 months	10	35.2	14.7	15.8
21 months or more	191	177.6	186.5	198.2
Total	629	629.0	629.0	629.0

Source: Adapted from Bartholomew (1967).
[a]These values correspond exactly to the data, because they were used in estimating the parameters.

within comparatively short time horizons. (In the case of the two firms prognoses were made for only about two years.) For longer prognoses, other functions $f(t)$ are more suitable. Particularly, the logarithmic normal distribution of completed length of service represents the data more accurately in that it rises for small values of t, reaches a sharp peak, and then declines in agreement with the observation that the largest number of people do not leave *immediately* after being recruited as is implied by exponential functions and by Equation 8.50.

A disadvantage of the logarithmic normal distribution, such as that of $f(t)$ represented by Equation 8.50, is that it leads to a noninvertible Laplace transform. To get around this difficulty, D. J. Bartholomew (1963) proposed a method of approximating $h(t)$ by $H^0(t)$, obtained as follows:

$$h^\circ(t) = f(t) + \frac{F^2(t)}{\int_0^t G(x)dx}, \qquad (8.57)$$

where $G(t) = 1 - F(t)$. The approximate function $h^0(t)$ agrees with any exact function $h(t)$ in the following respects:

(i) It coincides with $h(t)$ at the origin:

$$h^0(0) = h(0) = f(0) \qquad (8.58)$$

(ii) It approaches the same limit as $h(t)$ as t tends to infinity:

$$\lim_{t \to \infty} h^0(t) = \lim_{t \to \infty} h(t) = \mu^{-1} \qquad (8.59)$$

(iii) The first two derivatives of $h^0(t)$ at the origin coincide with those of $h(t)$:

$$\left. \frac{d^i h^0(t)}{dt^i} \right|_{t=0} = \left. \frac{d^i h(t)}{dt^i} \right|_{t=0} \qquad (i = 1, 2) \qquad (8.60)$$

That is, $h^0(t)$ coincides very nearly with $h(t)$ for small values of t and, in view of Equation 8.59, also for large values of t.

(iv) The approximation $h^0(t)$ coincides exactly with $h(t)$ if $f(t)$ is exponential, in which case

$$h^0(t) = h(t) = \lambda. \qquad (8.61)$$

The determination of $h^0(t)$ is illustrated for the case of Equation 8.50 and of the logarithmic normal distribution.

If $f(t) = nm^n(m+t)^{-n-1}$, $G(t) = m^n(m+t)^{-n}$. Then, writing $\mu = (m/n - 1)$, we have

$$\int_0^t G(x)dx = \mu \left[1 - \left(\frac{m}{m+t} \right)^{n-1} \right] \qquad (8.62)$$

$$h^0(t) = \frac{n}{m} \left(\frac{m}{m+t} \right)^{n+1} + \frac{\{1 - [m/(m+t)]^n\}^2}{\mu\{1 - [m/(m+t)]^{n-1}\}} \qquad (8.63)$$

In fitting $f(t)$ to real data, n turns out to be mostly between 0.5 and 1, which implies that $h(t)$ would decrease quite slowly. This means that equilibrium can be expected to be established only after a long time, so that the transient solution of the renewal equation is of practical interest.

If $f(t)$ is logarithmic normal,

$$f(t) = \frac{1}{\sqrt{2\pi}\sigma t} \exp\left[-\frac{1}{2}\left(\frac{\log_e t - \omega}{\sigma}\right)^2\right] \tag{8.64}$$

$$F(t) = \Phi\left(\frac{\log_e t - \omega}{\sigma}\right), \tag{8.65}$$

where $\Phi(t) = \int_{-\infty}^{t} (1/\sqrt{2\pi})e^{-x^2/2}\,dx$, ω is the mean, and σ the standard deviation of a random variable whose logarithm is normally distributed. Thus $h^0(t)$ can be calculated using tables of the normal probability integral. As can be seen from Equation 8.57, equilibrium will not be reached until $X = (\log_e t - \omega)/\sigma$ is large enough for $F(t) = \Phi(X)$ to be nearly 1. For large values of X, $\Phi(X)$ can be approximated by

$$\Phi(X) = 1 - \frac{1}{\sqrt{2\pi}X} e^{-X^2/2}. \tag{8.66}$$

Using these approximations and reasonable values of ω and σ, Bartholomew showed that it would take about 400 times the mean value of CLS for $h^0(t)$ to get within 2% of the equilibrium value μ^{-1}. Clearly, in this case, too, the transient solution of the renewal equation rather than the equilibrium rate of recruitment is of practical interest. The reader may recall the similarity between these considerations and those related to determining the "true" rate of growth of a population in which the age distribution has not yet become stabilized (see Chapter 1).

The approximation $h^0(t)$ can be improved by an approximation of the next order given by

$$h^1(t) = f(t) + \int_0^t h^0(t - x)f(x)dx. \tag{8.67}$$

To utilize the full power of the stochastic model, one should obtain not only the expectations of $N(t)$, the number of recruits required at future times, but also the entire distribution of this number regarded as a random variable or at least its variance, which could give some idea about the uncertainty of the prognosis. It is shown that the second moment of $N(t)$, that is, $E[N^2(t)]$, is given by the following equation:

$$E[N^2(t)] = m(t) + 2 \int_0^t m(t - x)h(x)dx. \tag{8.68}$$

Having determined $m(t)$ and $h(t)$ by the methods described above, we can calculate $E[N^2(t)]$ and hence the variance of $N(t)$ in view of

$$\text{Var}[N(t)] = E[N^2(t)] - [m(t)]^2. \tag{8.69}$$

Similar methods can be used in situations when an organization is growing or shrinking in some known manner. For details, the interested reader is referred to Batholomew (1967).

NOTES

[1] $o(dx)$ is an infinitesimal of higher order than dx. Thus $f(x)dx$ is a first approximation to $\int_x^{x+dx} f(t)dt$.

[2] Let $N(t)$ and $N(s)$ be two random variables from the family of random variables defining a Poisson process. We seek the probability law for the pair $\{N(s), N(t)\}$; that is, $\Pr[N(s)=x_1, N(t)=x_2]$. Let $s \leqslant r \leqslant t$. Then $\Pr[N(s)=x_1, \ N(t)=x_2] = \sum_{k=0}^{x_2-x_1} \Pr[N(s)-N(0)=x_1, \ N(r)-N(s)=k, \ N(t)-N(r)=x_2-k-x_1]$. In view of independence of increments, this joint probability equals

$$\sum_{k=0}^{x_2-x_1} \Pr[N(s)-N(0)=x_1] \Pr[N(r)-N(s)=k] \Pr[N(t)-N(r)=x_2-k-x_1].$$

Thus if the probability law of the random variable $N(t)-N(s)$ is given for all s and t—that is, in view of stationarity for all values of $(t-s)$—the probability law for all pairs $\{N(s), N(t)\}$ can be found. Continuing in this way, we can find probability laws for all m-tuples $\{N(t_1), N(t_2), \ldots, N(t_m)\}$.

[3] This follows from the relation

$$\sum_{x=0}^{\infty} \frac{x v^x e^{-v}}{x!} = v.$$

[4] The function $\Gamma(n)$ is defined by $\int_0^{\infty} x^{n-1} e^{-x}\, dx$ for all $n > 0$. If n is a positive integer, $\Gamma(n) = (n-1)!$

[5] Let $Y = \{X, \Lambda\}$ be a composite random variable. The conditional expectation of Y, given $\Lambda = \lambda$, is expressed by "averaging" the conditional expectation over all possible values of λ. The same applies to the characteristic function of Y.

[6] Generally, the term "negative binomial" is used only when r is a positive integer. Equation 8.20 is a generalization of this distribution for the case when r is a positive real number. Thus

$$\binom{r+y+1}{y} = \frac{r(r+1)(r+2)\ldots(r+y-1)}{y!}.$$

[7] Perhaps "allergy model" is a more appropriate designation for this model than "contagion model," since it is assumed that the accident proneness of a worker increases when *this worker* has an accident. However, the model can be interpreted as a "contagion model" in the following context. The accident proneness of every worker in a factory increases by β after each accident in the factory. Our population is a population of *factories*, and the p_i are the expected proportions of fact es in which i accidents will have occurred $(i = 1, 2, \ldots)$.

Feller (1966, p. 57), in discussing the (generalized) negative binomial distribution, writes:

"The contagion model enjoyed great popularity, and ... was fitted empirically to a variety of phenomena, a good fit being taken as an *indication of contagion.*

"By coincidence, the same distribution ... had been derived previously ... by M. Greenwood and G. U. Yule with the intent that a good fit should *disprove presence of contagion* .... We have thus the curious fact that a good fit of the same distribution may be interpreted in two ways diametrically opposite in their nature as well as in their practical implications. This should serve as a warning against too hasty interpretations of statistical data."

Actually, the data in Table 8.1 were originally compared with a contagion (or allergy) model. We have intentionally interpreted them in terms of heterogeneity to emphasize the relation between the two models.

[8] The Laplace transformation of a function $f(t)$ defined for $t \geq 0$ is given by $f^*(s) = \int_0^{\infty} e^{-st} f(t)dt$.

CHAPTER NINE

Steady-State Distributions

An area of transition from deterministic to stochastic models comprises models that deal with *steady-state distributions*. Here the underlying process is probabilistic, but the deduced predictions are deterministic. Namely, the *ultimate* (steady state) distribution of *frequencies* is predicted; these may refer to classes of things, persons, or events singled out for observation. Of course, a distribution of frequencies of occurrence can also be regarded as a probability distribution. That is, the distribution indicates the probability that an arbitrarily selected thing, person, or event will be observed to belong to one of the preassigned categories.

We will illustrate this area of contact between deterministic and stochastic models by applying both a control model and a stochastic model to the derivation of the so-called *Zipf's law* in statistical linguistics. The control model will make no use of a stochastic process. The stochastic model will make use of it as the point of departure.

G. K. Zipf (1949) made extensive studies of so-called *rank-size distributions*. Consider the cities of a country ranked by population. For example, in the United States, New York has rank 1, Chicago rank 2, and so on. Let the rank of a city be the abscissa and its population the ordinate of a graphical representation of the relationship. Clearly, by definition of rank and size, the latter will be, in general, a monotone decreasing function of the former, as can be seen in Figure 9.1.

What sort of curve, defined by a mathematical function, can be fitted to this relationship? Zipf believed that the equation

$$RS = \text{constant}, \tag{9.1}$$

where R denotes rank and S size, applies to a great variety of situations of this sort. For instance, corporations as well as cities can be rank-ordered by size, say by their assets, by the number of employees, or what not. Zipf believed that the relation $RS = $ constant is valid also for corporations. He collected large

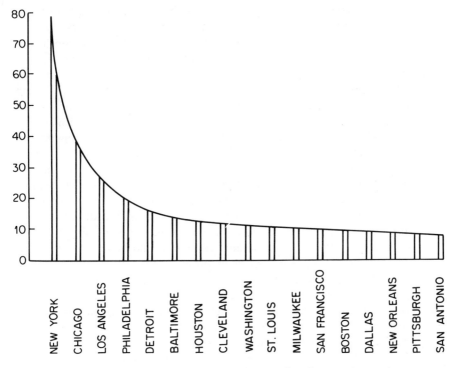

Figure 9.1. 1960 populations of largest U.S. cities plotted against their ranks.

masses of data of the most varied sort. His "law" seemed to him to be consistently confirmed.

Zipf was especially intrigued by the rank-size relation as it applies to word frequencies in a large sample of verbal output, called a *corpus*. Here the "size" of a word is interpreted as its frequency of occurrence. In English, for example, the most frequently occurring word in any large corpus (say a book or several issues of a newspaper) is "the." This word is, accordingly, assigned rank 1. It is followed by other "heavy duty" words, like "a," "that," "in," and so on. The plot of frequency of occurrence vs. rank again turns out to have the characteristic shape, approximately fitted by the hyperbola $RS = $ constant.

Zipf's explanation of this apparent regularity is vague, bordering on the fantastic; so much so that ordinary scientific standards of evaluation or criticism cannot be applied to it. I will, however, restate it because it contains a germ of an idea that was later incorporated into a rigorous mathematical model.

THE "PRINCIPLE OF LEAST EFFORT"

The so-called principle of least effort, which Zipf believed to be a law governing human behavior, was supposed by him to be the analogue in the behavioral sphere of the *principle of least action* in physics. Now "action" in physics, like all other precise concepts, is defined mathematically; namely, as the integral of work over an interval of time. It is shown that the laws of classical mechanics and of optics can be formulated in terms of an extremum (a maximum or a minimum) of this integral.

As such, the principle of least action is only a way of expressing in a compact form the assumptions underlying classical mechanics and optics. But it has a "teleological" connotation. For example, an implication of the principle of least action is that a beam of light passing through a medium of varying density from one point in space to another will follow a path that minimizes the time of passage. Since the speed of light depends on the density of the medium, this path is not necessarily a straight line. It appears as if light "chooses" the "most efficient" path somewhat as a motorist chooses a route which is not necessarily the most direct but is the "quickest" because of road or traffic conditions.

Confusing the precise physical concept of "action" with the vague, purely intuitive concept of "effort," Zipf became convinced that he had discovered a "law" of human behavior in terms of which the apparently ubiquitous rank-size relation could be explained.

The problem of communication by language can be seen as a juxtaposition of two problems, one of encoding, the other of decoding. The speaker encodes his or her ideas in words; the hearer decodes the words to reproduce their "meanings," that is, the speaker's ideas.

Now the speaker would spend the least effort if he encoded all his ideas in a single word. The hearer would spend the least effort if each word stood unequivocably for exactly one idea. Clearly, the purpose of communication would be defeated if the speaker "had his way," for then his meaning could not be deciphered at all. On the other hand, the cost of encoding would be excessive if each idea had to be coded in a separate word. Language, regarded as a "mapping" of ideas upon words, can be conceived of as a "compromise" between economy of effort by the speaker and the needs of the hearer.

In fact, we find many words in every language that have many meanings. These are usually short words that occur with the greatest frequencies. In English (aside from articles, prepositions, and conjunctions), they are words like "go," "keep," "do," and so on.

The above considerations suggest that "minimization of effort" may, after all, play some role in shaping the rank-size distributions observed in large verbal outputs. B. Mandelbrot (1953) succeeded in constructing a mathematical model built on this idea. For this he needed a precise quantitative index of "effort," and he associated the effort in producing a word with its length. Specifically, he used the number of letters in a written word as a crude measure of the "cost" of producing it. Subsequently, he generalized this measure in permitting the various constituents of a word (whether letters or phonemes or whatever units) to be characterized by different "costs."

ZIPF'S LAW DERIVED FROM A MINIMIZATION MODEL

Imagine that we undertake to construct a language. At our disposal is an alphabet of G letters. If we wish to "minimize cost," we will use up all the G letters to make G different one-letter words, these being the "cheapest." Having used up all the possibilities of making one-letter words, we go on to two-letter words, of which there are G^2 possible words, then to the G^3 three-letter words, and so on. Next, we rank-order the words, beginning with the "cheapest." According to the crude measure, all the one-letter words cost one unit, all the two-letter words cost two units, and so on. Thus words of rank 1 through G cost 1 unit, words of rank $(G+1)$ through $(G+G^2)$ cost 2 units, and in general words of rank G^n cost n units. We thus have the following approximate relation:

$$C = \log_G R, \tag{9.2}$$

where C is the cost of a word of rank R.

Let $P(R)$ be the probability with which a word of rank R appears in a large verbal sample. Then the average cost per word in a sample of N words will be

$$\sum_{R=1}^{N} P(R)\log_G R. \tag{9.3}$$

The speaker wants to minimize this average cost. She could do this by using only the cheapest words, each endowed with many meanings. In the extreme case, suppose the speaker used only one cheapest word on which all possible meanings were loaded. Then the speaker would confine her utterances to repetitions of that one word. As we have seen, this would defeat the purpose of communication. In the language of the mathematical theory of communication, the *information* transmitted per utterance would be equal to zero because one would know in advance what "signal" was going to be sent by the speaker.

Now in the mathematical theory of communication, a measure is used for the average *amount of information*, I, transmitted per signal issuing from a source that selects signals from among N available signals. Assuming statistical independence of sequential selection,

$$I = -\sum_{i=1}^{N} p_i \log p_i, \tag{9.4}$$

where p_i is the probability that the ith signal is selected. The base of the logarithms determines the units of I. The solution of the problem to be solved does not depend on the base of the logarithms.

The problem of economical coding can be stated as follows:

Minimize $\quad \sum_{R=1}^{N} P(R)\log R$

Subject to $\quad -\sum_{R=1}^{N} P(R)\log P(R) = I > 0$ (a constant) $\qquad (9.5)$

and $\quad \sum_{R=1}^{N} P(R) = 1.$ $\qquad\qquad (9.6)$

Constraint 9.5 expresses the requirement that in the process of "economizing," the average information per word in the language is not reduced to zero (as it would be if all messages were coded in the cheapest word). Constraint 9.6 simply expresses the fact that $P(R)$ are probabilities.

Applying the method described in Chapter 5, we form the Hamiltonian

$$H = \sum P(R)\log R + \lambda \sum P(R)\log P(R) + \mu \sum P(R), \tag{9.7}$$

where λ and μ are constants to be determined. Next, we set all the partial derivatives of Equation 9.7 with respect to $P(R)$ $(R = 1, 2, \ldots, N)$ equal to zero. We thus obtain the system of equations

$$\log R + \lambda \log P(R) + \lambda + \mu = 0 \qquad (R = 1, 2, \ldots, N). \tag{9.8}$$

Taking exponentials, we obtain

$$\exp[\log R + \lambda \log P(R) + \lambda + \mu] = 1 \tag{9.9}$$

$$RP(R)^{\lambda}e^{\lambda+\mu} = 1 \tag{9.10}$$

$$RP(R)^{\lambda} = e^{-\mu-\lambda} = \text{constant.} \tag{9.11}$$

Substituting $e^{-1-\mu/\lambda}R^{-1/\lambda}$ for $P(R)$ in Equations 9.5 and 9.6, we can determine the constants λ and μ. They are functions of N, the size of the vocabulary of our language, and of I, the average amount of information transmitted per word.

Formula 9.11 coincides with Zipf's law if $\lambda = 1$. Actually, λ varies slightly from sample to sample of verbal outputs. It is almost always somewhat smaller than 1, but it is generally close to 1 in corpuses with very "rich" vocabularies. Such, for example, is the sample represented by James Joyce's famous novel, *Ulysses*.

The above argument does not depend on the assumption that the constituent units of words are letters, nor that the cost of each constituent unit is the same. All that we need to assume is that the cost of a word is the sum of the costs of its constituent units. On the basis of this weaker assumption, we obtain the following expression for the number of words that cost C units:

$$N(C) = N(C - C_1) + N(C - C_2) + \cdots + N(C - C_G), \tag{9.12}$$

where C_i is the cost of the ith letter of our alphabet. This is so because the first term on the right is the number of words of cost C in which the cost of the first letter is C_1; the second term is the number of words of cost C in which the first letter is of cost C_2, and so on. Thus the sum on the right represents the total number of words of cost C.

The first approximation of the solution of Equation 9.12 gives the relation $C(R) = \log_M R$, where M is the largest root of the equation

$$\sum_{i=1}^{G} M^{-C_i} = 1. \tag{9.13}$$

If we take the next approximation to the solution of Equation 9.12, we obtain

$$C(R) = \log_M(R + m) + C_0 \qquad (9.14)$$

where m and C_0 are constants. If we use Equation 9.14 instead of log R in Equation 9.8, we obtain a further generalization of Zipf's law:

$$P(R)(R + m)^{1/\lambda} = \text{constant}, \qquad (9.15)$$

which reduces to the original form of Zipf's Law if $m = 0$, $\lambda = 1$.

It turns out that Equation 9.15 gives a better approximation of almost all observed rank-size relations involving large samples than the formula originally proposed by Zipf. This is not surprising in view of the fact that m and λ are free parameters that can be used to improve the fit. The constant on the right side of Equation 9.15 is determined by the size of the sample and so is not a free parameter. The parameters m and λ characterize the nature of the sample.

In the context of statistical linguistics, Mandelbrot's model has an interesting rationale. It is possible that languages evolve in the direction of maximizing information per word under the constraint of constant cost (that is, effort) per word; or else in the direction of minimizing effort under the constraint of constant average information per word. Thus the so-called principle of least effort vaguely formulated by Zipf may not be entirely without empirical content. How this principle can be applied to other rank-size relations remains unclear.

RANK-SIZE DISTRIBUTION DERIVED FROM A STOCHASTIC MODEL

An entirely different approach to rank-size relations was taken by H. Simon (1955); namely, via deriving the steady-state distribution of a stochastic process. Once again, we examine the model in the context of statistical linguistics. However, as we shall see, the connection between the derived rank-size relations and those derived in other contexts is somewhat easier to grasp.

Instead of a rank-size relation, we will examine the size-frequency relation defined as follows. The "size" of a word will denote, as before, its frequency of occurrence in a given corpus. Associated with this "size" is the number of words in the corpus that occur with that frequency. Note that in "size-frequency," the term "frequency" does not mean the frequency of occurrence of a word (this frequency is denoted by "size").

In discussing the size-frequency curve, we will regard the *frequency of occurrence* (that is, the "size" of a word in the sample) as the abscissa and will denote it by i. The number of different words with "size" i will be denoted by $f(i)$, the ordinate of our curve. This curve need not be monotonically decreasing like the rank-size curve, since there is no *logical* reason for the greatest number of words to occur with the smallest frequencies. To see this, consider the following imaginary sample consisting of six different words, a, b, c, d, e, and f: *aeebcebcc ddffff.* Only one word, *a*, appears only once in this corpus. Two words, *b* and *d*, appear twice. Three words, *c*, *e*, and *f*, appear three times. Hence $f(1)=1$, $f(2)=2$, and $f(3)=3$, so that $f(i)$ *increases* with *i*. In real verbal samples, however, $f(i)$ is observed to be decreasing with *i*. About one-half of all the different words in a typical sample appear only once, about one-sixth of the words appear twice, and so on.

Following Simon, let us consider a process by which a large verbal sample accumulates, say a book. Let us keep track of the different words as they appear in the process of reading (or writing) the book, and put them into classes *i* ($i=1, 2, \ldots$) where *i* is defined as above. That is to say, by the time we have reached the *k*th word of the book, $f(1)$ words have been placed in class 1, having been encountered only once, $f(2)$ words have been placed in class 2, and so on. We now ask, "What is the probability that the $(k+1)$th word will be placed in class *i*?" Simon's model is based on two assumptions regarding this probability. The first is that it is proportional to the number of *occurrences* associated with class *i* by the time we have reached the *k*th word. The other assumption is that there is a constant probability that the $(k+1)$th word has not yet appeared in the sample.

The first assumption is based on the following considerations. If the partial sample generated by the first *k* words is sufficiently large, the distribution of occurrences of words belonging to the different classes in it should be similar to the corresponding distribution in the total corpus. But the $(k+1)$th word is a sample of one taken from the total corpus. Therefore, the probability that it belongs to the *i*th class should be proportional to the number of occurrences in that class, that is, to $(i)f(i)$, since $f(i)$ represents the number of *different* words in class *i*, and each of these has occurred *i* times.

All these considerations refer to the state of affairs when we have reached the *k*th word. Therefore, both $f(i)$ and the constant of proportionality depend on *k*. The first assumption says that the probability of putting the $(k+1)$th word into class *i* will be given by $K(k)(i)f(i, k)$, where $K(k)$ is the proportionality factor, which depends on *k* but not on *i*. The dependence of *K* on *k* will be calculated below.

The second assumption is more difficult to justify. Assuming that the total vocabulary of the author of our imagined book is finite, we must conclude that the probability of encountering a word that has not yet appeared should decrease with *k* (as his vocabulary becomes progressively "used up"). This objection is ignored in the model on the assumption that the total vocabulary of the author is much larger than the total vocabulary of the corpus. At any rate, it will be instructive to examine the consequences of the model as stated. A modification in which the probability of encountering a new word decreases has actually been introduced by Simon, but we will not examine it here. In sum, the probability that the $(k+1)$th word will be new and hence that the word will be placed into $f(1)$ will be assumed to be a constant denoted by α.

The following system of difference equations constitutes Simon's model:

$$f(1, k+1)-f(1, k)=\alpha - K(k)f(1, k) \tag{9.16}$$

$$f(i, k+1) - f(i, k) = K(k)[(i-1)f(i-1, k) - if(i, k)] \qquad (i > 1). \qquad (9.17)$$

Here $f(i, k)$ represent the *expected values* of the numbers of words in the several classes rather than the actual numbers.[1] To see this, suppose the $(k+1)$th word is new. Then class 1 will be increased by one, and the probability that this happens is α. Therefore the expected increment to that class is α. On the other hand, if the $(k+1)$th word is of class 1 (has appeared just once by the kth word), class 1 will be decreased by 1 since that word will now be promoted to class 2. The probability of that event is $K(k)(1)f(1, k)$, and consequently the expected decrement of class 1 is $K(k)f(1, k)$. Thus the right side of Equation 9.16 represents the expected net increment to class 1 and corresponds to the left side, which denotes the same thing.

Equation 9.17 is interpreted analogously. Class i will suffer either an increment or a decrement, and the equation represents the expected value of the net increment, which may be positive or negative.

The requirement that the exhaustive sum of probabilities must be 1 determines the value of $K(k)$ to be $(1-\alpha)/k$. The asymptotic steady-state solution of Equations 9.16 and 9.17 then turns out to be

$$f(i) = AB(i, \gamma + 1), \qquad (9.18)$$

where A and γ are constants, and $B(i, \gamma + 1)$ is the Beta function.[2]

For large i (that is, in the "tail" of the distribution), $f(i)$ is approximately proportional to $i^{-(\gamma+1)}$. Thus if $\gamma \cong 1$, it is approximately proportional inversely to i^2. Moreover, if $\gamma = 1$ and N is the total number of words in the corpus, we have $f(1)/N = \frac{1}{2}$, $f(2)/f(1) = \frac{1}{3}$, and so on. These results correspond to observations on corpora where γ in Mandelbrot's model is close to unity.

It remains to point out the connection between the rank-size relation and the size-frequency relation. As can readily be seen, the former function can be approximated by an integral of the latter because the integral $\int_1^i f(x)dx$ represents approximately the total number of different words *up to* "size" i. But if this number is R, then R is the rank of the word of size i. Conversely, the formula relating frequency to size is approximated by the derivative of the formula relating size to rank. Moreover, since the integral was taken in the direction of *decreasing* size, the derivative must be taken with the opposite sign. Since

$$-\frac{d}{dx}\frac{1}{x} = +\frac{1}{x^2}$$

it follows that if rank is inversely proportional to size, size must be inversely proportional to the square of the frequency, which is the result obtained from Simon's model for the special case when $\gamma = 1$. It corresponds to the original formulation of Zipf's law.

In contexts other than verbal outputs, Simon's stochastic model seems to be more relevant than Mandelbrot's because the role of information-theoretic considerations is difficult to see in those contexts, whereas Simon's assumptions relating rates of growth of classes to the size already attained may apply in many diverse instances.

For example, Simon's model can be interpreted as a stochastic process governing increments or decrements in the sizes of firms (defined by assets or by numbers of employees or some other appropriate measure). If in a given situation the number of firms n remains constant, a "death process" (firms going out of business) must be introduced in addition to the "birth process" (new firms being organized). It can be shown that under appropriate assumptions, the asymptotic distribution of the sizes of firms will be a Yule distribution, which is closely related to the Beta distribution.

For large values of i, the Yule distribution is also approximated by a power function: $f(i)$ is proportional to $i^{-(\gamma+1)}$. In economic contexts, this distribution is often referred to as the *Pareto Law* because V. Pareto (1896–1897) used it to describe the distribution of wealth.

Another size-frequency distribution often observed in economic contexts is the logarithmic normal. This is the distribution of a random variable whose logarithm is normally distributed. If random variable Z with means m and variance σ^2 is normally distributed, its density function (see p. 144) is

$$f_Z(z) = \frac{1}{\sqrt{2\pi}\sigma} \exp\left[-\frac{(z-m)^2}{2\sigma^2}\right].$$ (9.19)

If $Z = \log_e X$, then the density function of X is

$$f_X(x) = \frac{1}{\sqrt{2\pi}\sigma x} \exp\left[-\frac{(\log_e x - m)^2}{2\sigma^2}\right].$$ (9.20)

The lognormal distribution can be derived as the steady-state distribution of a stochastic process as follows.

Let X_t be the size of an element at time t and let the increment of size of the element at time $(t-1)$ be proportional to X_{t-1}, where the factor of proportionality is a random variable ε_t independent of X.

Then, assuming discrete time intervals, we have

$$X_t - X_{t-1} = \varepsilon_t X_{t-1}.$$ (9.21)

By iteration,

$$X_t = X_0(1 + \varepsilon_1)(1 + \varepsilon_2)\ldots(1 + \varepsilon_t)$$ (9.22)

$$\log X_t = \log X_0 + \sum_{i=1}^{t} \log(1 + \varepsilon_i).$$ (9.23)

If the chosen time interval is small, so is ε_i. Accordingly, $\log(1 + \varepsilon_i)$ can be approximated by ε_i, and Equation 9.23 reduces to

$$\log X_t = \log X_0 + \sum_{i=1}^{t} \varepsilon_i.$$ (9.24)

Thus $\log X_t$ is a sum of $(t+1)$ independent random variables. The *Central Limit Theorem* states that if ε_i have the same distribution with mean m and variance σ^2, then as t tends to infinity, the distribution of $\log X_t$ tends to a normal distribution with mean $E[\log X_0] + mt$ and variance $\sigma^2 t$. This in turn implies that the distribution of $\log X_t$ is logarithmic normal.

Therefore, the assumption that ε_i are identically distributed implies that the variance of size increases linearly with time. This is observed in some sectors of the U.S. and West German economy.

On the other hand, increase in variance of size is sometimes not observed. A model that incorporates the assumption of constant variance has been proposed by M. Kalecki (1945) in the context of growth of industrial plants.

Let Y_t be the logarithm of size and y_t the logarithm of an increment at time t, both random variables expressed as deviations from their respective means. Then if the variance in size of n plants remains the same before and after an increment, we have

$$\frac{1}{n}\sum (Y_t + y_t)^2 = \frac{1}{n}\sum Y_t^2$$

$$2\sum Y_t y_t = -\sum y_t^2 \qquad (t = 1, 2, \ldots),$$

(9.25)

where the summations are over the population of plants. Thus a negative correlation between random increments and size must hold. Assuming the simplest relation between size and increment that yields a negative correlation, Kalecki writes

$$y = -\alpha Y + z,$$

(9.26)

where α is a constant parameter and z is a random variable independent of Y. Substituting Equation 9.26 into Equation 9.25, we get, in view of the independence of z and Y,

$$\alpha = \frac{\sum y^2}{2\sum Y^2}.$$

(9.27)

Assuming that the second moment of y is small relative to the second moment of Y, we have $0 < 1 - \alpha < 1$. Thus

$$Y_0 + y_1 = Y_0(1 - \alpha_1) + z_1,$$

(9.28)

and by iteration (see Steindl, 1965, p. 33),

$$Y_t = Y_0 + \sum_{i=1}^{t} y_i = Y_0 \prod_{i=1}^{t} (1 - \alpha_i) + \sum_{i=1}^{t-1} z_i \prod_{j=i+1}^{t} (1 - \alpha_j) + z_t.$$

(9.29)

Thus Y_t is again a sum of independent random increments, and its distribution tends to normal. But Y is the logarithm of size. Therefore the distribution of size is again lognormal. The difference between this model and the previous one is that in the previous model, the increment of the logarithm of size was assumed to be independent of size (as implied by $\alpha = 0$). To see this, note that in view of Equation 9.21, $X_t = X_{t-1}(1 + \varepsilon_t)$; $\log X_t = \log X_{t-1} + \log(1 + \varepsilon_t)$; $y_t = \log X_t - \log X_{t-1} = \log(1 + \varepsilon_t)$, independent of X_t. Although this assumption of independence is replaced by an assumption of negative correlation between increment and size, Kalecki's model nevertheless also leads to the lognormal distribution.

This model of "impeded growth" (reflecting the negative correlation between increment and size) has been found to be in rather good agreement with the economy of Austria in the years 1950–1957. Qualitative evidence of this is seen in the following observations.

1. Growth rates of firms in this period are negatively correlated with initial size.
2. The variance of size remains nearly constant during the period.
3. The distribution of company sizes is not a Pareto distribution.

The theoretical leverage of stochastic models can now be discerned. All these types of distribution, the Pareto law, the logarithmic normal with identically distributed ε_i, and the "impeded growth" distribution, have the same general shape: they are "skewed"; that is, characterized by a rapid rise at small values of the random variable, followed by a slow decline in the long "tail." At times, all three may give reasonably good fits to a body of data on the size-frequency relation. Derivation of these distributions from different underlying stochastic processes, on the other hand, generates additional hypotheses concerning the *parameters* of these distributions. For instance, the stochastic process underlying the lognormal distribution with identically distributed ε_i independent of size leads to a prediction of linearly increasing variance, whereas the impeded growth model is based on the assumption of constant variance. Also, both Mandelbrot's and Simon's models of word frequency distributions lead to approximations of Zipf's law. But whereas the simplest version of the latter implies $\gamma = (1 - \alpha)^{-1} > 1$, the corresponding exponent in Mandelbrot's model (that is, λ) is not restricted. This discrepancy led to a polemic between the two authors (see Mandelbrot, 1959, 1961; Simon, 1960, 1961). In his initial paper on the derivation of Zipf's law, Mandelbrot stated that in all but a few verbal corpuses, $1/\lambda$ was observed to be larger than unity, in disagreement with the requirement of Simon's (simplest) model. Simon pointed out that the exceptions are by no means few and moreover that some variants of his model permitted λ to be smaller than unity. Discussions of this sort center on the interpretation of the parameters of the model and for this reason are usually theoretically more productive than comparisons of "goodness of fit."

DISTRIBUTIONS OF GROUP SIZES

Consider a population of human groups of various sizes (numbers of members) 1, 2, ... At any moment, a group may lose a member or gain a member. Every time this happens, the distribution of groups of various sizes will change.

Let $p = (p_1, p_2, \ldots)$ be a probability distribution, where p_i is the probability that an arbitrarily selected group in our population of groups has size i. Further, assuming that in a small interval of time dt a group can gain or lose at most one member, we define the following probabilities:

$\Pr[i + 1, i; dt]$, the probability that in any small interval of time, dt, a group of size $(i + 1)$ loses a member, that is, turns into a group of size i.

$\Pr[i - 1, i; dt]$, the probability that a group of size $(i - 1)$ gains a member, that is, turns into a group of size i.

$\Pr[i, i - 1; dt]$, the probability that a group of size i turns into a group of size $(i - 1)$.

$\Pr[i, i + 1; dt]$, the probability that a group of size i turns into a group of size $(i + 1)$.

We translate these probabilities into components of the differential dp_i:

$$dp_i = \Pr[i + 1, i; dt] + \Pr[i - 1, i; dt] - \Pr[i, i - 1; dt] - \Pr[i, i + 1; dt]. \quad (9.30)$$

The first two terms on the right represent increments in the number of groups of size i due to a loss of a member from a group of size $(i + 1)$ and due to a gain of a member by a group of size $(i - 1)$. The last two terms represent decrements in the number of groups of size i which result from either a loss or a gain of a member.

Now we must make some assumptions about the source from which individuals are recruited into the groups. We could, of course, assume that they are recruited from other groups in some interaction process. We will, however, consider another model. We will assume that a reservoir of single (unattached) individuals exists from which individuals are recruited into groups. Moreover, we will assume that when an individual leaves a group, he or she joins this pool of unattached individuals. Each of these individuals constitutes a group of size 1.

Finally, we must make some assumptions about the probabilities on the right side of Equation 9.30. The first and third of those terms refer to the event that an individual leaves a group; the second and fourth, to the event that an individual joins a group. The simplest assumption is that the probability of leaving a group in a short interval of time dt is the same for every individual, namely, $\beta \, dt$; and that the probability of joining a group is also the same for every individual, namely, $\alpha \, dt$. Thus the positive contributions to p_i (the proportions of groups of size i) will have two components: one proportional to the number of individuals in groups of size $(i + 1)$, because these groups will be reduced to size i when these individuals leave; the other proportional to the number of unattached individuals who join groups of size $(i - 1)$, thus promoting these groups to size i. The negative contributions will also have two components: one proportional to the number of individuals in groups of size i (who by leaving demote these groups to size $(i - 1)$; the other proportional to the number of unattached individuals joining groups of size i (who thereby promote these groups to size $(i + 1)$.

We thus have the following expression for the rate of change of the proportion of groups of size i:

$$\frac{dp_i}{dt} = \beta(i+1)p_{i+1} + \alpha n_1 p_{i-1} - \beta i p_i - \alpha n_1 p_i \qquad (i=2, 3, \ldots), \qquad (9.31)$$

where n_1 is the number of groups of size 1.

The corresponding equation for p_1 must be considered separately because when an individual leaves a group of size 2, *two* unattached individuals result; similarly, when one unattached individual joins another, two "groups" of size 1 disappear.

Incorporating these contributions together with those from groups of size 3 (positive due to individuals leaving and negative due to individuals joining), we arrive at the following expression for the rate of change of p_1 (see Coleman, 1964, Chapter 11):

$$\frac{dp_1}{dt} = 4\beta p_2 + \sum_{i=3}^{\infty} \beta i p_i - \alpha n_1 \sum_{i=2}^{\infty} p_i - 2\alpha n_1 p_1. \qquad (9.32)$$

Imagine now that our groups are arranged in a row of piles with singles in the first pile, pairs in the second, and so on. Our process can be regarded as two "flows," one going to the right as a group leaves the ith pile to enter the $(i+1)$th, and one going to the left as a group leaves the ith pile to enter the $(i-1)$th. Consider now the *net* rate of this flow (number of groups per unit time) to the right. This is given by

$$w_{i-1,i} = \alpha n_1 p_{i-1} - \beta i p_i \qquad (i \geqslant 2). \qquad (9.33)$$

The first term on the right represents the expected number of groups entering the ith pile from the left; the second represents the expected number exiting from the ith pile to the right. Expressing this flow in terms of expected proportions of groups, we divide through by n, the total number of groups, which is assumed to be constant. We obtain

$$\frac{w_{i-1,i}}{n} = \alpha p_1 p_{i-1} - \frac{\beta i p_i}{n}. \qquad (9.34)$$

When equilibrium is obtained, the net flow is zero. Solving for p_i, we obtain the following recursion formula:

$$p_i = \frac{\alpha n p_1 p_{i-1}}{\beta i}, \qquad (9.35)$$

and by induction,

$$p_i = \frac{p_1}{i!} \left(\frac{\alpha n p_1}{\beta} \right)^{i-1} \qquad (i \geqslant 2). \qquad (9.36)$$

But $\sum_{i=1}^{\infty} p_i = 1$, hence $\sum_{i=2}^{\infty} p_i = (1 - p_1)$. Thus

$$1 = p_1 + \sum_{i=2}^{\infty} \frac{p_1}{i!} \left(\frac{\alpha n p_1}{\beta} \right)^{i-1}, \qquad (9.37)$$

which can be written as

$$1 = \frac{\beta}{n\alpha} \sum_{i=1}^{\infty} \frac{1}{i!} \left(\frac{\alpha n p_1}{\beta}\right)^i$$

$$= \frac{\beta}{n\alpha} (e^{\alpha n p_1/\beta} - 1). \tag{9.38}$$

Solving for p_1 gives

$$p_1 = \frac{\beta}{n\alpha} \log_e\left(\frac{\alpha n}{\beta} + 1\right). \tag{9.39}$$

Substituting this value into Equation 9.35, we obtain the desired equilibrium distribution:

$$p_i = \frac{k^i}{i!(e^k - 1)}, \tag{9.40}$$

where we have written k for $\log_e(\alpha n/\beta + 1)$.

The distribution represented by Equation 9.40 is called the *truncated Poisson distribution*. Like the Poisson distribution, the truncated Poisson is characterized by a single parameter k. Before we examine applications of this model to observations, we must interpret the meaning of this parameter. It increases with n (the number of groups) and with α (the rate of recruitment) and decreases with β (the rate of detachment of individuals from groups). Therefore, for the same n, k increases as the tendency to join a group increases relative to the tendency to leave a group. However, n varies from situation to situation, so this variation must be taken into account before inferring a sociopsychological index associated with a given situation.

Consider the mean of the distribution represented by Equation 9.40; that is, the mean size of a group in our population of groups. This is given by

$$\mu = \sum_{i=1}^{\infty} ip_i = p_1 + \sum_{i=2}^{\infty} ip_i. \tag{9.41}$$

Substituting the right side of Equation 9.35 for p_i, we get

$$\mu = p_1 + \sum_{i=2}^{\infty} ip_{i-1} \frac{\alpha n p_1}{\beta i} \tag{9.42}$$

$$= p_1 + \frac{\alpha n p_1}{\beta} \sum_{i=1}^{\infty} p_i \tag{9.43}$$

$$= p_1 + \frac{\alpha n p_1}{\beta}. \tag{9.44}$$

Substituting the right side of Equation 9.39 for p_1, we have

$$\mu = p_1 + \log_e\left(\frac{\alpha n}{\beta} + 1\right). \tag{9.45}$$

Thus

$$\mu = p_1 + k; \qquad k = \mu - p_1. \tag{9.46}$$

The mean size of a group and the proportion of singles p_1 can be estimated directly from observation. Hence we have an estimate of k. Now let N be the total number of individuals in all groups. Then $N = \mu n$. Furthermore, from Equation 9.40 we obtain $p_1 = e^k/(e^k - 1)$. Therefore

$$\frac{\alpha}{\beta} N = k e^k. \tag{9.47}$$

Having estimated k, we have an estimate of $N\alpha/\beta$, the desired sociopsychological index; that is, the ratio of "affiliation" to "disaffiliation."[3]

J. James (1953) made a large number of observations of groups of people in various situations. Of the 21 situations observed, 18 were fitted very well by the truncated Poisson distribution, corroborating the hypothesis that the groups were of the so-called freely forming types where individuals join a group at random and leave by chance. The situations included children's play groups, groups of people strolling on city streets, congregating around public swimming pools, in railroad stations, and so on. Some observations were made in a small city (Eugene, Oregon, population 35,000), some in a medium city (Portland, Oregon, population 370,000), some in Seoul, Korea.

Comparisons of the model with some observations are shown in Tables 9.1 and 9.2.

On the basis of comparing the $N\alpha/\beta$ ratios, it would seem that older children have a greater tendency to "affiliate" relative to their tendency to "disaffiliate" than younger children. This is in accord with usual impressions. However, caution must be exercised in comparing these ratios because allowance must be made for the role that N, the total number of individuals, plays in the process. N is simply the total number of individuals observed. However, not the number but the density of individuals (that is, number per unit area) is the relevant factor.

Table 9.1. *Distribution of Sizes of Children's Play Groups* (School Age)

Group Size	Number Observed	Predicted by Equation 9.40
1	570	590.0
2	435	410.0
3	203	190.0
4	57	66.0
5	11	18.4
6	1	4.3

Source: Adapted from Coleman (1964).
Note: $N\alpha/\beta = 5.56$, $k = 1.39$

Table 9.2.   Distribution of Sizes of Children's Play Groups
(Kinder-garten)

Group size	Number Observed	Predicted by Equation 9.40
1	383	377.0
2	93	104.0
3	19	19.2
4	6	2.7
5	1	0.3
6	1	0.0

Source: Adapted from Coleman (1964).
Note: $N\alpha/\beta = 0.96$, $k = 0.554$

With the same propensity of individuals to join groups, the number of "joinings" may be proportional to the opportunities for interaction, hence to the density of individuals in the area observed. Without knowing the relative densities of children in playgrounds and those in nursery school, we cannot really compare their ratios of "affiliation" to "disaffiliation."

SIZES OF WAR ALLIANCES

W. J. Horvath and C. C. Foster (1963) examined the distribution of sizes of war alliances. Following their model, assume that nations are being added to the international system[4] at a constant rate r. Each nation will have a constant probability α of remaining aloof from an alliance and a probability $(1 - \alpha)$ of joining one. Next, assume that the probability that a nation joins an alliance of a given size is proportional to the number of nations already belonging to alliances of that size. Eventually, alliances break up, in which case all the members leave the system. However, each of these nations may reenter the system as a "new" yet uncommitted nation. As in the previous model, we are interested in the equilibrium distribution of alliances of various sizes. The total number of alliances will be designated by $n = \sum_{i=1} n_i$ where n_1 is the number of unaligned nations ("singlet" alliances), n_2 the number of two-nation alliances, and so on. Since we have assumed that each nation entering the system forms a "one-nation alliance" with probability α, it follows that $\sum n_i = \alpha N$, where N is the number of nations in the system.

We calculate the net change in the number of alliances of size i per unit time. The number of nations that have entered the system during unit time is r. The expected proportion of these that join already existing alliances is $(1 - \alpha)$. The fraction of the total number of nations contained in alliances of size $(i - 1)$ is $(i - 1)n_{i-1}/N$. Further, since we have assumed that the rate at which new nations join alliances of a given size is proportional to the number of nations already in alliances of that size, it follows that $r(1 - \alpha)(i - 1)n_{i-1}/N$ alliances of size $i - 1$ will be converted to alliances of size i per unit time. This is the rate of increment of alliances of size i. When new nations join alliances of size i, these are converted to alliances of size $(i + 1)$. Accordingly, we have a rate of decrement of alliances of size i; namely, $r(1 - \alpha)in_i/N$. Finally, we assume that alliances disintegrate at a constant rate q (independent of size). In sum, we are led to the following differential equation in n_i:

$$\frac{dn_i}{dt} = \frac{1}{N}\left[r(1 - \alpha)(i - 1)n_{i-1} - r(1 - \alpha)in_{i-1}\right] - qn_i \qquad (i = 2, 3, \dots) \qquad (9.48)$$

At equilibrium, the right side of Equation 9.48 is equal to zero. Further, at equilibrium, the number of nations entering the system must equal the number leaving it. By our definition of q, the expected number of alliances of size i that leave the system per unit time is qn_i. Hence the expected number of nations leaving the system per unit time is $q(\sum_{i=1} in_i) = qN$. Thus at equilibrium we must have $qN = r$. Substituting into Equation 9.48 and setting the right side equal to zero, we obtain

$$(1 - \alpha)(i - 1)n_{i-1} = n_i[i(1 - \alpha) + 1] \qquad (9.49)$$

or

$$\frac{n_i}{n_{i-1}} = \frac{(1 - \alpha)(i - 1)}{(1 - \alpha)i + 1} \qquad (i = 2, 3, \dots). \qquad (9.50)$$

Finally, we must calculate n_1. At equilibrium, we must have

$$\alpha r - \frac{(1 - \alpha)rn_1}{N} = qn_1. \qquad (9.51)$$

Substituting r/N for q, we have, solving for n_1,

$$n_1 = \frac{\alpha N}{2 - \alpha}. \qquad (9.52)$$

Equations 9.50 and 9.52 represent the equilibrium distribution sought. It turns out to be the Yule distribution.

Comparison of this model with observed alliances during the period from 1820 to 1939 is shown in Table 9.3.

The assumptions underlying the derivation of the Yule distribution are, it seems to me, much more difficult to accept as a model of alliance formation than are the assumptions underlying the truncated Poisson as a model of freely forming groups. The latter assumptions involve only chance events. In fact, the only departure of that model from the Poisson process (which serves as a null hypothesis for many observed processes) is in the inescapable assumption that an "empty" group is unobservable.

Table 9.3. Distribution of Numbers of War Alliances with Different Numbers of Participants

Number of nations in alliance	1	2	3	4	5	6	7	8+
Number of alliances observed	124	34	8	7	4	1	2	3
Predicted by Yule distribution	129	29	11	5	3	2	1	2

Source: Adapted from Howath and Foster (1963).

Unlike the model for freely forming groups, the model for alliance formation rests on several additional assumptions related to the "recruitment" of nations into the system, discrimination among alliances already existing, and the requirement that a nation does not leave an alliance *unless the entire alliance breaks up.*

As for the empirical tests of the two models, those of freely forming groups appear to be far more convincing than that of alliance formation. Observations on freely forming groups were made in situations involving hundreds or even thousands of individuals and on many different occasions in different localities. The basic similarity of the observed distributions strongly suggests the operation of the same statistical law, and since the model is based only on laws of chance, its corroboration constitutes a corroboration of a null hypothesis. That is, whatever effects besides chance account for the observed distributions of sizes of small groups in casual situations, they are too weak to be noticed.

In contrast, the test of the Yule distribution of war alliances was made in one context only, and it involved dozens instead of thousands of units. With such small populations, the use of deterministic approximations of stochastic processes is questionable. Moreover, the assumptions of the model specify a structure of the process superimposed on pure chance. From this point of view, the model is more interesting than the null hypothesis model, but it is also much more difficult to justify.

Nevertheless, the juxtaposition of the two models is not devoid of some theoretical interest when the approach is seen in historical perspective.

Lewis F. Richardson, in his studies on war and other manifestations of violence, became interested in the distribution of group sizes when he noted a similarity between observed distributions of this sort and the observed distribution of the "magnitudes of deadly quarrels" (Richardson, 1960a). For Richardson, who was a Quaker pacifist, all "fatal quarrels" were manifestations of the same sort of event. Thus he classified such "quarrels" according to sheer magnitude, defined as the logarithm to the base 10 of the number of fatalities. For instance, a murder was for Richardson a "deadly quarrel" of magnitude 0 (since $\log(1) = 0$); a riot resulting in 10 deaths was classified as a deadly quarrel of magnitude 1; a large riot with 100 victims was assigned magnitude 2, and so on through "small wars" (magnitudes 3–4) up to the two world wars, with magnitudes 7–8. A war of magnitude 9–10 would wipe out the human race.

Richardson gathered all the data he could find on murders and wars and plotted their frequencies of occurrence against magnitude. Missing from this collection were reliable data on deadly quarrels in the middle range (magnitudes 2–4). There was, however, one set of data which could fill the gap, given Richardson's assumption that all violence stems from the same sort of dynamics. These data were records of the numbers of victims of raids by bandits on villages in Manchuria during the period of Japanese occupation in the 1930s.

From the distribution of these numbers, Richardson formed a conjecture concerning the distribution of sizes of the raiding bands. Next he took police data on the estimated sizes of Chicago gangs during the Prohibition era. He found that this distribution was practically identical (including the value of the parameter) with his conjectured distribution of the sizes of Manchurian bandit groups. This led him to speculate on the underlying dynamics of "organization for violence."

Whether there is such an underlying dynamic and to what range of events it is applicable must, of course, remain an open question. There is one aspect of the Yule distribution, however, that is in accord with our intuitive notions about "organizations of violence," such as gangs, bandit detachments, and, some would say, military alliances, in all of which the Yule distribution manifests itself. Namely, it is easier to enter such a group than to leave it. It is notoriously difficult to leave a criminal gang, both for psychological reasons and in view of the penalties that often follow defections. It is also noted that nations enter military alliances one by one, but they seldom leave individually unless they are defeated in war. Such defeats are often the beginnings of the defeat of the whole coalition, after which the defeated alliance usually breaks up. It is also usual for victorious alliances to break up. Thus individual nations tend to leave coalitions only when the whole coalition breaks up, and the same can be assumed for gangs. But this is precisely the assumption that is built into the Horvath-Foster model of war alliances in contradistinction to the model for freely forming groups. In this way, some sort of rationale can be imagined for this model.

The recruitment of members can also proceed in different ways. For example, an individual may join a group because he is attracted by the group, or he can join a group because he is attracted by some member of the group. In the first

Table 9.4. Stochastic Models of Group Size Distribution Appropriate Under Various Conditions of Recruitment into and Departure from Groups

Recruitment	Random Selection of Group	Random Selection of of Partner
Departure		
Only when group is dissolved	Exponential	Yule
Individuals free to leave	Truncated Poisson	Fisher's logarithmic series

Source: Adapted from Horvath and Foster (1963).

case, the probability of joining a group could be assumed to be proportional to the number of groups of that size; in the second case, to the number of members in the group.

On the basis of the above considerations, Horvath and Foster have proposed a two-way classification of stochastic models of group size distributions, shown as entries in Table 9.4.

NOTES

[1] Strictly speaking, $f(j, k)$ is a random variable. Replacing the actual values of this variable by expected values turns the stochastic model into a "classical" one. This procedure is justified when the population is very large.

[2] The Beta function (of two variables) is defined by $B(x, y) = \int_0^1 t^{x-1}(1-t)^{y-1} dt$ $(x, y > 0)$ or, equivalently, by $B(x, y) = \Gamma(x)\Gamma(y)/\Gamma(x + y)$. Definition of $\Gamma(x)$ is given in Note 4 to Chapter 8.

[3] Following Coleman (1964), we regard $N\alpha/\beta$ rather than α/β as the sociopsychological index representing the aggregation/disaggregation ratio. An argument in favor of this interpretation is that $N\alpha/\beta$ is dimensionless, as can be seen from Equation 9.45, where $n\alpha$ must be dimensionless. On the other hand, there is good reason for the aggregation-disaggregation ratio to have dimensions "per group" since the number of groups in an individual's vicinity can be supposed to affect his tendency to join one. Here also the density (number of groups per unit area) may play a part, which is taken into account in some studies (see James, 1953). At this time many questions related to the distribution of group sizes must remain open.

[4] Here the "international system" comprises the states that waged war in the period 1820–1939.

CHAPTER TEN

Markov Chain Models of Social Mobility

In our discussion of stochastic models of group size distribution, we defined the "state" of a group as the number of individuals in it. In a given interval of time, the group can gain one or more members, lose one or more members, or suffer neither gain nor loss. Suppose, for simplicity, that a group can gain or lose only one member at a time, and we take our time interval sufficiently short so that within it the group can gain or lose at most one member. Then within that time interval, a group with i members (that is, in "state i") can either remain in that state, pass to "state $i + 1$," or pass to "state $i - 1$."

Let us now generalize this situation. Imagine a "system" that at any moment in time can be in any of a set of specified states $s_1, s_2, \ldots s_q$. Assume further that changes of state can occur only at specified moments $n = 1, 2, \ldots$ Next, assume that conditional probabilities of transition from state to state are given. That is, if the system is in state s_i at time n, the probability that it will be in state s_j at time $(n + 1)$ is given for all states i, j. These probabilities, designated by r_{ij}, are called *transition probabilities*, and the resulting stochastic model is called a *stationary Markov chain*.

A stationary Markov chain can be represented by a matrix:

$$
R = \begin{array}{c}
 \\ s_1 \\ s_2 \\ \vdots \\ s_i \\ \vdots \\ s_q
\end{array}
\begin{array}{c}
\begin{array}{cccc} s_1 & s_2 & \cdots & s_q \end{array} \\
\left(\begin{array}{ccccc}
r_{11} & r_{12} & \cdots & & r_{1q} \\
r_{21} & & \cdots & & r_{2q} \\
\vdots & & & & \vdots \\
r_{i1} & \cdots & r_{ij} & \cdots & r_{iq} \\
\vdots & & & & \vdots \\
r_{q1} & & \cdots & & r_{qq}
\end{array}\right)
\end{array}
$$

Matrix 10.1

The rows of R represent the possible states of the system at time n; the columns, the possible states of the system (the same set of states) at time $(n + 1)$. The entries are the corresponding transition probabilities. The *stationarity* of the Markov chain is reflected in the assumption that r_{ij} are independent of n.

Suppose now the system is in state s_i at time n. Is it possible for it to be in some specified state s_j at a specified future moment $(n + m)$? It is, if there is some way that the system can pass through some intervening states at times $(n + 1)$, $(n + 2), \ldots (n + m - 1)$ so as to reach s_j exactly at time $(n + m)$. In particular, if $m = 1$, the system can pass from s_i to s_j in one step if $r_{ij} > 0$. In general, it can pass from s_i to s_j in exactly m steps if there exist $(m - 1)$ states (not necessarily distinct) $s_{(k1)}, s_{(k2)}, \ldots s_{k(m-1)}$ such that $r_{i(k1)} r_{(k1)(k2)} \cdots r_{k(m-1)j} > 0$, for then the event that the system will "take this path" from s_i to s_j is not impossible.[1] (There may be several such paths, but one is sufficient to guarantee the possibility that the system *can* pass from s_i to s_j in exactly m steps.)

If the system can pass from s_i to s_j is *some* number of steps, we will say that s_j is *reachable* from s_i.

The transition probability r_{ij} may be 1. This is the case if the system always passes from s_i directly to s_j. A Markov chain may have cycles; for example, if $r_{ij} = r_{jk} = r_{ki} = 1$. If such a system comes into state s_i, it will cycle forever from s_i to s_j to s_k back to s_i. Thus if a set of states comprising a cycle is a proper subset of the entire set of states, the states outside the cycle are not reachable from those in the cycle. If the entire set of states is a cycle, all the states are reachable from any state, but in that case the behavior of the system is deterministic rather than probabilistic.

A Markov chain without cycles is called *aperiodic*. An aperiodic stationary Markov chain, in which every state s_i is reachable from any other state s_j, is called *ergodic*. In what follows, we will consider models representable by ergodic Markov chains.

Consider the matrix R^2, obtained by multiplying R by itself. According to the rules of matrix multiplication, the elements (entries) $r_{ij}^{(2)}$ of R^2 are given by $\sum_{k=1}^{q} r_{ik} r_{kj}$.

But $r_{ik} r_{kj}$ is the probability of the joint event that the system passes in one step from s_i to s_k and then passes in one step from s_k to s_j. The probabilities summed over all k give the probability that the system passes from s_i to s_j in two steps.

By induction, we obtain the elements of R^m, the mth power of R:

$$R^m = R^{m-1} R. \tag{10.1}$$

Also

$$R^{m+n} = R^m R^n \tag{10.2}$$

$$R^m = R^{m-s} R^s \qquad (1 \leqslant s \leqslant m). \tag{10.3}$$

Another useful result relates to the limit of R^n as n tends to infinity. If R is ergodic, it is shown that

$$\lim_{n \to \infty} R^n = R^*, \tag{10.4}$$

where R^* is a matrix with identical rows $r^* = (r_1^*, r_2^*, \ldots, r_q^*)$.[2]

Suppose now that initially (at $n = 0$) the system is in one of the q possible states, but we do not know in which state it is. All we know is the probability vector $r(0) = (r_1(0), r_2(0), \ldots, r_q(0))$, whose components $r_i(0)$ are the probabilities that the system is in state s_i. Given R, we can calculate the probability vector for $n = 1$; that is, the probabilities $r_i(1)$ that at $n = 1$, the system will be in state s_i. This probability vector is given by

$$r(1) = r(0)R. \tag{10.5}$$

The vector $r(0)$ is a matrix with 1 row and q columns. By the rule of matrix multiplication, we have for the entries of the right side of Equation 10.5, which, like $r(0)$, is a row vector,

$$r_j(1) = \sum_{k=1}^{q} r_k(0)r_{kj} \qquad (j = 1, 2, \ldots, q). \tag{10.6}$$

Each term of the summation represents the probability of the event that the system was in state s_k at $n = 0$ and passed from s_k to s_j. Therefore, the summation is the probability that the system will be in s_j at $n = 1$.

By iteration, we have

$$r(n) = r(0)R^n. \tag{10.7}$$

Consider now the probability vector r^*; that is, one of the (identical) rows of R^*. We have

$$r^*R^* = \left(\sum_{k=1}^{q} r_k^* r_1^*, \sum_{k=1}^{q} r_k^* r_2^*, \ldots, \sum_{k=1}^{q} r_k^* r_q^* \right). \tag{10.8}$$

But $\sum_{k=1}^{q} r_k^* = 1$ and $(r_1^*, r_2^*, \ldots, r_q^*) = r^*$. Hence $r^*R^* = r^*$; that is, r^* is left invariant when multiplied by R^*. R^* is called the *steady-state matrix* of the ergodic Markov chain defined by R. In fact, for any probability vector r, we have

$$rR^* = r^*. \tag{10.9}$$

Since $R^* = \lim_{n \to \infty} R^n$, we see that regardless of the initial probability distribution of the possible states of a system represented by an ergodic Markov chain, the probability distribution will tend toward r^*. The vector r^* is called the *steady-state distribution* of the Markov chain, or the steady vector, or the equilibrium vector. It is evidently independent of the initial distribution. It depends only on the structure of the matrix R.

A MODEL OF SOCIAL MOBILITY

Suppose a society consists of s distinguishable classes $C_1, C_2, \ldots, C_s$. To fix ideas, let us confine ourselves to the male population and let the time intervals represent successive generations. Consider a sample of men in generation 0. The proportion of men in the sample found in class C_i can be regarded as an estimate of the probability that an arbitrarily selected man in the population will be found to belong to C_i. Next, suppose we wait until all the sons of the men in our sample are men and examine their distribution through the s classes. These proportions can be regarded as estimates that an arbitrarily selected man in generation 1 will be in each of the classes. We thus have estimates of the probability vector $r(0)$ and $r(1)$.

Of primary interest is the matrix R, which transforms $r(0)$ into $r(1)$ via equation $r(1) = r(0)R$ (see Equation 10.6). The elements of R are estimates of probabilities that a son of a man in class C_i will pass to class C_j $(i, j = 1, 2, \ldots, s)$.

The matrix R can be obtained empirically as follows. Take a sample of father–son pairs. In this sample, n_{ij} will denote the number of such *pairs* in which the father belongs to C_i and the son to C_j. n_{ij} can be arranged in a matrix $N = (n_{ij})$ of which they are the elements. The row sums of this matrix will be designated by $n_{i.}$, where the dot signifies, as is usual, that the elements of row i were summed over the second index j. Thus the row sums $n_{i.}$ represent the number of father–son pairs in which the fathers are in class C_i. Analogously, the column sums $n_{.j}$ of N represent the numbers of father-son pairs in which the sons are in class C_j. It should be kept in mind that $n_{i.}$ need not represent the number of fathers in our sample who are in C_i because a father may have more than one son and so may appear more than once in a sample of distinct father-son pairs. On the other hand, $n_{.j}$ actually represents the number of sons in our sample who are in C_j because every son has only one father. We follow the exposition of R. Boudon (1973).

Let N be the total number of pairs in the sample.[3] Then $p_{ij} = n_{ij}/N$ represents the proportion of father-son pairs with fathers in C_i and sons in C_j. Like n_{ij}, p_{ij} can also be arranged in a matrix $P = (p_{ij})$. We will refer to the matrix N as the *turnover matrix* and to the matrix P as the *proportion turnover matrix*. Note that P does *not* correspond to the transition probability matrix of a Markov chain. The entries of the latter are *conditional* probabilities; namely, the probabilities that a system *being in state i* at a given step will pass to state j on the next step. The row sums of a transition probability matrix all sum to 1. The entries of the proportion turnover matrix P, on the other hand, are estimates of *joint* probabilities; namely, each entry is an estimate of the probability that an arbitrarily selected father–son pair will have the father in C_i and the son in C_j. The row sums of P are estimates of probabilities that an arbitrarily selected father-son pair will have the father in C_i $(i = 1, 2, \ldots, s)$.

It is, however, only a step from P to R, the matrix that does correspond to the transition probability matrix. The elements of R are those of P divided by the corresponding *marginals*; that is, the row sums. These entries will be denoted, as before, by r_{ij}. Thus

$$r_{ij} = \frac{p_{ij}}{p_{i.}}. \tag{10.10}$$

Once the transition probability matrix has been estimated (by R), the question arises whether it remains constant over generations; that is, whether its elements are independent of n. If they are, we can predict the probability that an arbitrarily selected man of the nth generation will be in C_i by the equation $r(n) = r(0)R^n$ (see Equation 10.7), and the predictions can be tested since these probabilities can be estimated by the corresponding proportions of men in the several classes in generation 0 and generation n. Moreover, if $r(1) = r(0)$ within acceptable sampling error, we can conclude (still assuming that the Markov chain is stationary) that the initially observed distribution will persist.

Since observation of several generations is required to test the stationarity of the Markov chain, this approach is hardly practical. The sociologist wants some measure of "social mobility" based on simultaneous observation of just two generations represented by a sample of father-son pairs. In what follows, we will examine a number of such indices. For simplicity, we will assume that every father has exactly one son.

Intuitively, we could define "perfect mobility" as a situation in which the class to which a son belongs is independent of the class to which his father belongs or belonged. Actually, more ought to be involved in the definition of "perfect mobility;" namely, that the class of a man is independent of the classes to which any of his ancestors belonged. However, since we have already assumed that the Markov chain is an adequate model of social mobility, we will assume that the class of a son depends at most on the class of his father. (In fact, this is the case even in nonstationary Markov chains, where the transition probabilities may depend on n but not on previous "history." That is to say, the crucial feature of a Markov chain is that the probabilities of states at a given step depend only on those immediately preceding and on the transition matrix associated with *that step*.)

The independence of origin condition will be satisfied if the elements of the proportion turnover matrix satisfy the following equation:

$$p_{ij} = \left(\sum_{j=1}^{s} p_{ij} \right) \left(\sum_{i=1}^{s} p_{ij} \right). \tag{10.11}$$

Note that $\sum_{j=1}^{s} p_{ij} = p_i(0)$, the proportion in C_i of men who are fathers of sons in generation 0, and $\sum_{i=1}^{s} p_{ij} = p_j(0)$ is the proportion in C_j of the sons of fathers in generation 0. Therefore, we can write for the "perfect mobility" proportion turnover matrix

$$P^{**} = (p_{ij}^{**}) = (p_i(0)p_j(0)). \tag{10.12}$$

Let $D_0 = \mathrm{diag}(p_i(0))$; that is, D_0 is a matrix whose diagonal elements are $p_i(0)$ $(i = 1, 2, \ldots, s)$ and whose other elements are all zero, and assume $p_i(0) > 0$ $(i = 1, 2, \ldots, s)$. This assumption is innocuous because the classes are defined so that none is empty. Then D_0 has an inverse, D_0^{-1}. Next, define

$$R^{**} = D_0^{-1} P^{**} = (p(1)_j). \tag{10.13}$$

That is to say, the ijth element of R^{**} is the jth component of the vector of proportions which would result from the first iteration if the turnover proportion matrix were one of perfect mobility.[4] This is so because in that case the probability of going to any class would be independent of the class of origin, and consequently the first iteration matrix would have identical rows.

The index of mobility which we will now calculate is a slight modification of one due to S. I. Prais (1955). It is based on the hypothetical expectation of the number of generations that a family would spend in a given class (or occupational stratum) if the actual estimated transition probability matrix were constant over generations.

Under this assumption, consider the families belonging to C_i. Given the transition matrix R, the proportion r_{ii} of those families will remain in C_i in the next generation and the complementary proportion $(1 - r_{ii})$ will move to other classes. This assumption ignores differential fertility and equates the number of father–son pairs to the number of fathers; that is, postulates that each family will have exactly one son, not to speak of the fact that daughters are ignored, and so on. All these simplifications are shortcomings of the model in the context of a predictive theory. However, as has already been pointed out, the theoretical leverage of a stochastic model most often resides not in its predictive power but rather in what it can suggest about the underlying structure of the system.

Inferring $R = (r_{ij})$ from $N = (n_{ij})$, we see that the proportion of families in C_i that remain in C_i for exactly one generation and then leave it is $r_{ii}(1 - r_{ii})$; the proportion that stay for exactly two generations and then leave it is $r_{ii}^2(1 - r_{ii})$, and so on. Interpreted as probabilities, these proportions generate a geometric distribution. The expected number of generations that a family in C_i will stay in C_i will be given by

$$v_i = \sum_{n=1}^{\infty} n r_{ii}^{n-1}(1 - r_{ii}) = (1 - r_{ii})^{-1}. \tag{10.14}$$

We have, accordingly, the vector $v = (v_1, v_2, \ldots, v_s)$, determined by R, which reflects a structural characteristic of the society. It expresses differentially the expectations of remaining in each of the s classes.

To obtain a measure of mobility for class C_i, we refer v_i to the corresponding component of the vector v^{**}, obtained under the assumption of perfect mobility. In view of Equation 10.13, $r_{ii}^{**} = p_i(1)$. Therefore

$$V_i^{**} = [1 - p_i(1)]^{-1}. \tag{10.15}$$

Define $w^{**} = v_i/v_i^{**}$. Thus

$$w^{**} = \frac{(1 - r_{ii})^{-1}}{[1 - p_i(1)]^{-1}} = \frac{1 - p_i(1)}{1 - r_{ii}}. \tag{10.16}$$

AD HOC INDICES OF MOBILITY

The right side of Equation 10.16 is the reciprocal of an index of social mobility proposed by D. V. Glass (1954) without reference to Markov chains. In view of the way the vector v was defined, w^{**} is, properly speaking, an index of *immobility*, so that its reciprocal can be taken as an index of mobility (which increases with greater mobility). Glass's index of immobility is complementary to his index of *mobility*. Its derivation was based on the following idea. Suppose for simplicity that there are just two classes, a "lower class," C_1, and an "upper class," C_2. The probability that an arbitrarily selected father-son pair has both father and son in C_1 is p_{11}. If this probability is simply the product of the probability of finding a pair with father in C_1 (that is, $p_{1.}$), and the probability of finding a pair with son in C_1 (that is, $p_{.1}$), then the two events are statistically independent. In that case,

$$\frac{p_{11}}{p_{1.}p_{.1}} = 1. \tag{10.17}$$

If, on the other hand, $p_{11} > p_{1.}p_{.1}$, the proportion of sons in C_1 is greater when the father is also in C_1. Thus the index I_G, expressed by the left side of Equation 10.17, is greater the less mobility there is in that society.

I_G can be written as $Nn_{11}/n_{1.}n_{.1}$. Define

$$M_G = \frac{Nn_{12}}{n_{1i}n_{i2}} = \frac{p_{12}}{p_{1.}p_{.2}} \tag{10.18}$$

and observe that M_G is complementary to I_G in the sense that its excess over unity represents the excess of pairs with fathers in C_1 and sons in C_2 over this proportion under "perfect mobility." M_G is Glass's index of social mobility. It corresponds to the reciprocal of Equation 10.16 with $i = 1$. Hence Equation 10.16 is a generalization of Equation 10.18.

The value of an index from the point of view of theory construction depends on two features. First, being essentially an "operationalization" of some intuitively perceived characteristic, it ought to reflect several facets of that characteristic. In other words, its operational meaning ought to reflect as closely as possible its intuited meaning. Second, it ought to reflect some invariance against a background of change. For instance, if a society is mobile, the proportions of people in various classes or categories may change with time, but a "good" index of mobility should be a parameter in the equations that describes the changes; that is, a quantity that remains constant under fixed conditions. Whether the several indices of mobility (to be discussed below) fulfill the second requirement is a question to be answered by data. Whether an index fulfills the first requirement can be answered by examining fictitious situations.

Consider two hypothetical societies S_1 and S_2 with structures shown in Matrices 10.2 and 10.3 (Boudon, 1973).

$$
S_1: \begin{array}{c} \\ C_1 \\ C_2 \\ \\ \end{array}
\begin{array}{cc} C_1 & C_2 \\ \left(\begin{array}{cc} 80 & 0 \\ 100 & 20 \end{array}\right) & \begin{array}{c} 80 \\ 120 \end{array} \\ 180 \quad 20 & 200 \end{array}
\qquad
S_2: \begin{array}{c} \\ C_1 \\ C_2 \\ \\ \end{array}
\begin{array}{cc} C_1 & C_2 \\ \left(\begin{array}{cc} 80 & 20 \\ 20 & 80 \end{array}\right) & \begin{array}{c} 100 \\ 100 \end{array} \\ 100 \quad 100 & 200 \end{array}
$$

Matrix 10.2   Matrix 10.3

Rows: Fathers' classes   Rows: Fathers' classes
Columns: Sons' classes   Columns: Sons' classes

Intuitively, we would regard S_1 as extremely immobile because *all* of the sons of fathers in C_1 remain in C_1. In S_2, on the other hand, some mobility is observed. Nonetheless, I_G calculated for S_1 turns out to be 1.11, whereas this index of immobility calculated for S_2 turns out to be 1.60, contrary to the direction of the intuitively perceived difference.

The source of the difficulty is easy to see by examining the marginals of the two matrices shown on the right and below the matrices. These marginals represent the social compositions of the two generations in each case. We see that in S_1, there were 80 individuals in C_1 and 120 in C_2 in the fathers' generation, but 180 in C_1 and 20 in C_2 in the sons' generation. In S_2, the social composition did not change from the first generation to the second.

The difficulty with Glass's index is that it combines two components of mobility. One component relates to the change in the distribution of the population among the classes; the other relates to the movements of people from one class to another over and above the movement that effects the redistribution. Derivation of w^{**} was guided by theoretical considerations related to the transition probabilities from class to class and led to an index from which the marginals of the transition matrix were presumably "factored out." But the procedure led to a generalization of Glass's index, which *does* depend on the marginals, as we have seen.

In light of the above illustrations, we see difficulties involved in the choice of a "good" index of social mobility. The same holds for almost any index characterizing some feature of social structure or social dynamics. Since most indices have both desirable and undesirable features, many different indices of social mobility have been proposed. For a detailed analysis of these indices, the interested reader is referred to Boudon (1973). Here we will indicate in a rather broad way the sort of problems that sociologists interested in a quantitative approach to social mobility have become aware of and how they have coped with these problems.

SEPARATING OUT STRUCTURAL MOBILITY

One class of problems has to do with separating out the so-called *structural* component of social mobility. Regarding the class composition of a society for the moment as determined by division of labor, we see that this composition may change, sometimes radically, as a result of technological advances. The occupational structures of Western societies have undergone marked changes in a few generations. For instance, the proportion of farmers has sharply declined; the proportion of blue collar workers has also declined appreciably; the proportion of white collar workers has increased, and so on.

To take the shifting composition of the population into account, we might conceptualize the total mobility of a society as the sum of two components: *structural mobility* (due to shifts in demand for different sorts of occupations) and *pure mobility* (what is left after structural mobility has been separated out). Again, for simplicity, assume two classes C_1 and C_2. Define total mobility as

$$M_T = n_{12} = n_{1.} - n_{11};$$

(10.19)

that is, the total number of pairs with fathers in C_1 and sons in C_2. Next, define

$$M_S = n_{1.} - \min(n_{1.}, n_{.1});$$

(10.20)

that is, if $n_{.1} > n_{1.}$, $M_S = 0$. In other words, if the number of pairs with sons in C_1 exceeds the number of pairs with fathers in C_1, no "new opportunities" were provided for the sons to move to C_2. In the opposite case,

$$M_S = n_{1.} - n_{.1}.$$

(10.21)

This difference reflects the "opportunities" opening up for the sons to move to C_2. According to the above conceptualization, pure mobility is given by

$$M = M_T - M_S = n_{1.} - n_{11} - n_{1.} + \min(n_{1.}, n_{.1})$$

$$= \min(n_{1.}, n_{.1}) - n_{11}.$$

(10.22)

To construct an index independent of the marginals, S. Yasuda (1964) refers M to the theoretical pure mobility which would be generated by the same marginals under conditions of perfect mobility; namely, $\min(n_{1.}, n_{.1}) - n_{1.}n_{.1}/N$. Thus Yasuda's index is

$$M_Y = \frac{\min(n_{1.}, n_{.1}) - n_{11}}{\min(n_{1.}, n_{.1}) - (n_{1.}n_{.1}/N)}.$$

(10.23)

Complementary to M_Y is the immobility index

$$I_Y = 1 - M_Y = \frac{n_{11} - (n_{1.}n_{.1}/N)}{\min(n_{1.}, n_{.1}) - (n_{1.}n_{.1}/N)}.$$

(10.24)

Returning to our hypothetical societies S_1 and S_2, we see that for S_1, $I_Y = 1$, and for S_2, $I_Y = 0.60$. In light of this index, S_2 appears to be more mobile, in accord with intuitive judgment.

For a society with s classes, Yasuda's immobility index for class C_i generalizes to

$$I_Y(s) = \frac{n_{ii} - \sum_{i=1}^{s} (n_{i.}n_{.i}/N)}{\min(n_{i.}, n_{.i}) - \sum_{i=1}^{s} (n_{i.}n_{.i}/N)}.$$

(10.25)

In view of the above discussion, it should be clear that the suitability of an index of social mobility depends on what one wishes to measure. Glass's index provides a measure of "total mobility"; Yasuda's, of "pure mobility," after the mobility due to a change of social composition (possibly generated by a change of occupational demands) has been separated out. It is not surprising, therefore, that applications of the two methods of measuring social mobility often give different results. For instance, Yasuda has shown (1964) that his index reveals a picture of mobility in various strata of Japanese society that is quite different from the picture obtained by using Glass's index. One might, perhaps, expect to see this difference because of the large shifts in occupational structure that took place in Japan since 1950. Another example of a revised picture of mobility is provided in comparing the results obtained by S. M. Lippset and R. Bendix (1960) on some Western societies with those generated by Yasuda's index. Lippset and Bendix found that their index was remarkably constant across several societies, whereas Yasuda's showed large differences.

PROBLEMS GENERATED BY HETEROGENEITY

We have seen in Chapter 8 that if the number of accidents suffered by each individual in a population is governed probabilistically by a simple Poisson process, but the intensity of the Poisson process varies from individual to individual, the number of people suffering 0, 1, 2,... accidents in a given interval of time will not be Poisson distributed. The discrepancy is a result of the heterogeneity of the population. We have also seen that a discrepancy between the observed and the Poisson distribution can be alternatively attributed to a "contagion" effect.

Similar effects are deduced in Markov chain models of social mobility. Suppose the population is composed of s classes, and each class is composed of two subclasses of families—"stayers" and "movers." The children of stayer families do not move out of their class. The children of mover families are assumed to move according to "perfect mobility."

Let m_{ij} be the number of movers from C_i to C_j, $m_i(0)$ the number of movers whose fathers belong to C_i, $m_j(0)$ the number of movers among the sons currently in C_j. Then we have

$$n_{ii} = m_{ii} + [n_i(0) - m_i(0)].\qquad(10.26)$$

The left side of Equation 10.26 is the observed number of father–son pairs with father and son in the same class C_i. The first term on the right is the number of movers in C_i who *happened* to have stayed in C_i; the second term represents the number of stayers in C_i, being the difference between the total number of sons and the number of sons who are movers.

Using the condition of perfect mobility, we have

$$m_{ij} = \frac{m_i(0)m_j(1)}{M},\qquad(10.27)$$

where the numerator on the right is the product of the marginals of the movers' turnover matrix and M is the total number of movers.

From Equations 10.26 and 10.27, we obtain the system of quadratic equations

$$n_{ii} = \frac{m_i(0)[m_i(0) - n_i(0) + n_i(1)]}{M} + n_i(0) - m_i(0),\qquad(10.28)$$

where $M = \sum_{i=1}^{s} m_i(0)$. We are interested in the composition of each class; that is, the number of movers $m_i(0)$ in each class. We determine these quantities by solving Equation 10.28 for $m_i(0)$ $(i = 1, 2, \ldots, s)$. For Equation 10.28 to have real roots, we must have the following inequalities satisfied:

$$[M + n_i(0) - n_i(1)]^2 - 4(n_i(0) - n_{ii})M \geqq 0 \qquad (i = 1, 2, \ldots, s). \quad (10.29)$$

If Equation 10.29 is not satisfied, the model obviously fails. If solution of Equation 10.28 yields acceptable values of $m_i(0)$, the question remains whether the resulting turnover matrix fits the data; that is, the off-diagonal entries of the turnover matrix. If it does (that is, if the model is to that extent corroborated), an immobility measure for each class can be obtained in the form of

$$I_W(i) = 1 - \frac{m_i(0)}{n_i(0)}, \qquad (10.30)$$

which is an index of immobility proposed by H. White (1970b). White calls this index the "inheritance fraction," referring to the accepted inherited states of the "stayer" families. White did obtain a good fit of this "stayer-mover" model using data by P. Blau and O. D. Duncan (1967). He was not, however, able to obtain a fit to British and Danish mobility tables with three classes (White, 1970a).

As we have seen in Chapter 8, the problem of heterogeneity is intimately related to that of "contagion" in accident statistics. In the context of social mobility, the problem of heterogeneity is intertwined with that of individual histories.

Instead of intergenerational social mobility, consider intragenerational job mobility. Here we can take three-month periods instead of generations for our transition steps, and so observe several distribution vectors.

The one-step transition matrix R can be obtained directly from data. Namely, r_{ij} will represent the fraction of individuals in job j in quarter 1 who had been in job i in quarter 0. If job mobility is representable by a stationary Markov chain, then by observing the vector $r(0)$, we can predict the vector $r(t)$ by the equation

$$r(t) = r(0)R^t, \qquad (10.31)$$

where R^t is the tth power of R. On the other hand, the transition matrix from quarter 0 to quarter t can be obtained directly from the data. Call this transition matrix $R^{(t)}$. Its entries $r_{ij}^{(t)}$ are proportions of individuals who were in job i in quarter 0 and are in job j in quarter t. Comparison of $R^{(t)}$ with R^t provides a test of the model based on a stationary Markov chain. In general, it is found that the diagonal elements of $R^{(t)}$ are larger than those of R^t. The discrepancy can be attributed to the heterogeneity of the population. Assume that in each job, some individuals are "stayers" and some are "movers." Then the stayers contribute positively to the diagonal entries of the *actual* two-step transition matrix, making them larger than the diagonal entries of R^2. The process continues to modify the successive multistep transition matrices $R^{(t)}$ in the same direction. In this way, the discrepancy with the stationary Markov chain can be explained. But there is an alternative explanation.

Suppose the longer a person stays in one job, the less likely she is to move, say because of accumulated seniority, attachment to community, or something of this sort. Then the probability that a person moves from job *i* to job *j* depends not only on the job in which she presently finds herself (which is the assumption embodied in the stationary Markov chain model) but also on her entire history; in particular, on how long she has *been* in her present job. Taking individual histories into account makes the calculation of successive transition probabilities quite cumbersome because the number of possible "states" increases at each step, if by a "state" we now mean a possible history of an individual. We can, however, easily surmise that the job-to-job transition matrices of two or more steps will have larger diagonal elements than the successive powers of the one-step transition matrix if the probability of staying in the same job increases with the length of stay. This effect is the same as that produced by a heterogeneous population.[5]

Actually, the "individual history" effect is also a form of heterogeneity. The difference between an individual history model and a heterogeneity model is that in the latter we assume that the population is *inherently* heterogeneous, whereas in the former we assume that it is *made* heterogeneous by the individual histories, which "branch" at each step depending on whether an individual has moved or stayed. We shall encounter a similar situation in stochastic models of learning.

An early Markovian model incorporating "individual histories" is known among builders of mathematical models of social mobility as the Cornell Model (see Blumen, Kogan, and McCarthy, 1955). We follow the presentation of McGinnis (1968).

At each step of a time-discrete stochastic process, the population under consideration is partitioned into categories d $(d = 1, 2, \ldots)$ representing the number of time intervals the members of each category have been in a given state. The transitions from state to state are represented by a different *duration-specific* probability transition matrix $_dR$.

At each step, some individuals will stay in the same state, others will move. Accordingly, the individuals are designated as "stayers" and "movers" respectively. Note, however, that these designations do not correspond to the "stayers" and "movers" in White's model (see p. 192). There the designations refer to *inherent* characteristics of families: the stayers never move; the movers may or may not move on a particular step. Here "stayers" and "movers" are individuals who *happen* to stay or *happen* to move on a particular step of the stochastic process.

Duration of stay in a state is partly analogous to the aging of a cohort (see p. 205) but with an important difference. Physiological age always increases until death, after which an individual is removed from the population. Duration of stay increases only while an individual remains in the same state. When he moves, he passes into category $d = 1$ and remains in the population. (It is as if a person were "reborn" after death.) Although this model is clearly inappropriate as a model of mobility among social classes, it seems to be appropriate as a model of job mobility (where d represents seniority) or as a model of residential mobility, where $_ds_i(t)$ represents being in state s_i and belonging to category d at time t. To fix ideas, the model refers to residential mobility, where i and j designate locations:

Residential Status Time t	Mobility Status in the Interval $(t, t+1)$			
	Stayer		Mover	
Continuing resident	$_ds_i(t)$	$_{d+1}s_i(t+1)$	$_ds_i(t)$	$_1s_j(t+1)$
Newcomer	$_1s_i(t)$	$_2s_i(t+1)$	$_1s_i(t)$	$_1s_j(t+1)$

This stochastic process could be represented by a stationary transition probability matrix with an infinite number of rows and columns, each row or column representing a "state-category" $_ds_i$ ($i = 1, 2, \ldots, m$; $d = 1, 2, \ldots$) Alternatively, it can be represented by a finite $m \times m$ matrix, which, however, is not stationary. Once the family of matrices $_dR$ is given, this (nonstationary) matrix $R(t)$ can be constructed, as will now be shown.

The expression "$x(t) \in {}_ks_j$" means "At time t, an individual is in state s_j and belongs to category $d = k$. Matrix $_dS$ is a diagonalization of $_dR$. That is, the diagonal elements of $_dS$ are those of $_dR$, and its off-diagonal elements are zeros. $_dM = {}_dR - {}_dS$. Note that the elements of $_dS$ are probabilities that an individual in category d remains in the same state; those of $_dM$ are probabilities that he moves to another state.

The assumptions of the Cornell Model can now be axiomatized.

$$C_1 : \Pr[x(t) \in {}_ks_j | x(t-1) \in {}_ds_i \text{ and } \xi]$$
$$= \Pr[x(t) \in {}_ks_j | x(t-1) \in {}_ds_i],$$

where ξ is any information about individual y prior to $(t-1)$. This is a postulate underlying all Markovian processes. It states that on a given step, transition probabilities depend only on the step and on the pair of states in question. Here the "states" are actually "state categories" $_ks_j$ and $_ds_i$. Thus the conditional probabilities are elements of the infinite state-category matrix. Since we have assumed that this matrix is stationary, the argument t can be omitted from the postulate. It is retained in the interest of generality.

$$C_2: \quad _dR(t) = {}_dR \qquad \text{for all } t.$$

This is merely a formal way of stating that the matrix $_dR$ is assumed to be stationary.

$$C_3: \quad \Pr[x(t) \in {}_ks_j | x(t-1) \in {}_ds_i] = 0, \quad \text{if } i = j \text{ and } k \neq d+1 \text{ or if } i \neq j \text{ and } k \neq 1$$

That is, a stayer must pass from category d to $d+1$ (since d designates the duration of his stay), and a mover must pass from d to 1 (since he "starts over" in the new state).

$$C_4: \quad _dS < {}_{d+1}S; \lim_{d} {}_dS = I, \text{ the identity matrix.}$$

This expresses the postulate of "cumulative inertia." The longer one stays in a state, the more probably one will continue to stay in it. Eventually, a stayer will almost certainly (or certainly) remain in that state forever.

C_5: There exists a stochastic matrix R with $r_{ii}=0$ for all i such that
$$_dM = (I - {_d}S)R.$$

That is, the matrix of movers' transition probabilities for each category is assumed to be determined once the (diagonal) matrix of stayers' transition probabilities is given.

To give the essential deductions of this model, we need some additional notation.

$A(t)$: a matrix with elements $a_{id}(t) = \Pr[x(t) \in {_d}s_i]$.

This is a matrix with m rows ($i = 1, 2, \ldots, m$) and an infinite number of columns ($d = 1, 2, \ldots$).

A_d: the dth column vector of $A(t)$ (an $m \times 1$) matrix.

$B(t) = (A(t)\zeta)^T$, that is, the transpose of $(A(t)\zeta)$,

where ζ is a column vector all of whose components are 1. Note that since $A(t)$ has an infinite number of columns, ζ has an infinite number of elements. The product is a column vector of m components (corresponding to the m rows of $A(t)$). Thus $B(t)$ is a row vector with m components.

$b_i(t)$: the ith component of $B(t)$.

Note that $b_i(t) = \sum_d a_{id}(t)$. But a_{id} represent the joint probabilities that an individual is in state s_i and category d. Thus the summation represents the probability that an individual is in state s_i at time t.

$C(t)$: a matrix with elements $c_{id}(t) = a_{id}(t)/b_i(t)$.

Thus $C(t)$ is a rectangular matrix with the same dimensions as $A(t)$.

$\bar{C}_d(t)$: a diagonal matrix whose elements are those of the dth column of $C(t)$.

Since $C(t)$ has m rows, $\bar{C}_d(t)$ is a diagonal $m \times m$ matrix. From postulates $C_1 - C_4$, the following results are deduced.

1. $A_d(t) = \sum_d {_d}M^T A_d(t-1)$ if $d = 1$
   $$= {_{d-1}}S A_{d-1}(t-1) \quad \text{if } d > 1.$$
2. $B(t) = \sum_d {_d}R^T A_d(t-1).$
3. $R(t) = \sum_d \bar{C}_d(t-1){_d}R.$
4. $R(t)$ is nonstationary in t.
5. There exists a stochastic matrix $R^* = \lim_{t \to \infty} R(t)$.
6. There exists a probability distribution vector $B^* = \lim_{t \to \infty} B(t)$.

Thus the construction of the transition probability matrix $R(t)$ and of the probability vector $B(t)$ is indicated on the basis of the state-category transition probabilities, assumed given. Although these are assumed to be independent of t, $R(t)$ is not. Its time dependence is a consequence of the time dependence of $A(t)$ and hence of $A_d(t)$, $C(t)$, and $\bar{C}_d(t)$. The time dependence of $A(t)$ stems from the fact that its elements are not transition probabilities but probabilities of *being* in a particular state-category, which are, of course, time dependent, as they also are in a stationary Markov chain. The steady-state matrix R^* of the present model differs from that of a stationary Markov chain in that its row vectors are not identical, as are those of $R^* = \lim_{t \to \infty} R^t$ in a stationary Markov chain (see p. 182).

Computation of $R(t)$ and $B(t)$ involves infinite summations. Although the convergence of these sums is established (see items 5 and 6 above), the rates of convergence are a practical consideration. An idea of these rates can be obtained by computer simulation. McGinnis (1968) reports results of such simulations using $m = 5$, a fixed $_1R$, the relation $_dS = _{d-1}S + (I - _{d-1}S)/a$ with $a = 2, 4, 10$, and 20, and R with off-diagonal elements 0.25. Limiting values of $B(t)$ (constancy of successive components within three decimal places) were obtained after 17–18 steps for $a = 2$ (rapid increase of $_dS$) and after about 300 steps with $a = 20$ (slow increase of $_dS$).

The model was applied by P. Morrison (1967) and was found to be consistent with the postulate of "cumulative inertia." His data (on residential mobility in the Netherlands) suggested, however, that in addition to duration, biological age also plays an important role in determining transition probabilities, which, of course, is not surprising since old people tend to change their domicile less frequently than young ones.

K. C. Land (1969) obtained results strikingly similar to Morrison's in a study on residential mobility in Monterey, Mexico. The large cultural difference in the cultural and ecological settings speak for the robustness of the model.

Similar models can be used in rank mobility (for example, promotion of civil servants) or in combined rank and location mobility (for example, of academics, who move from one university to another and may or may not be promoted or, at times, demoted in the process). Models depicting situations of this sort were discussed by A. P. Schinnar and S. Stewman (1978). They also extended the duration-dependent models to include inherent heterogeneity of the population.

THE PROBLEM OF IMPOSED CONSTRAINTS

Social mobility is frequently associated with democracy. This association was particularly strong in the United States when that country was a haven for immigrants predominantly from the "lower" social strata of Europe. Many of these immigrants were able to raise their social status, or at least the social status of their children, thanks to the opportunities provided by a social structure in which the accident of birth was not a decisive factor in determining that status.

Not all instances of social mobility, however, are reflections of opportunities seized by enterprising individuals. In the Ottoman Empire, the Janissaries were recruited primarily from Christian children. Assuming that the social status of Christians was lower than that of the Janissaries, being recruited represented a step upward on the social scale. Nevertheless, the dynamics of that process was quite different from that which propelled some sons of poor immigrant fathers to the business or professional class in America. Recruitment of Janissaries was an act of the authorities and was governed by quota rather than by free competition in the "market of opportunities."

To a certain extent, the assignment of social status in "democratic" societies is also governed by certain quota constraints; for example, by the availability of educational opportunities, taking cost of education into account as a component of nonavailability. Even though *who* gets the opportunities may not be decided by "authorities," *how many* can avail themselves of the opportunities may be constrained by the existing institutional structure.

R. Boudon (1973) constructed a measure of mobility by taking such constraints into consideration. His model is based on the following assumptions. (As before, the point of departure is a two-class society with C_1 a lower class, and C_2 an upper class.)

1. An authority apportions available social positions.
2. A certain amount of "free" social mobility is permitted.
3. The marginals of the turnover matrix (that is, the sizes of the classes in the fathers' generation and the sons' generation) are not under the control of the authority.

To see how the authority determines the turnover matrix, imagine two hypothetical societies with the social compositions of the fathers' and sons' generations as shown in Matrices 10.4 and 10.5 (Boudon, 1973).

$$N_1: \quad \begin{array}{cc} & \begin{array}{cc} C_1 & C_2 \end{array} \\ \begin{array}{c} C_1 \\ C_2 \end{array} & \left(\begin{array}{cc} 280 & 120 \\ 20 & 80 \end{array}\right) \begin{array}{c} 400 \\ 100 \end{array} \\ & \begin{array}{ccc} 300 & 200 & 500 \end{array} \end{array} \qquad N_2: \quad \begin{array}{cc} & \begin{array}{cc} C_1 & C_2 \end{array} \\ \begin{array}{c} C_1 \\ C_2 \end{array} & \left(\begin{array}{cc} 280 & 20 \\ 120 & 80 \end{array}\right) \begin{array}{c} 300 \\ 200 \end{array} \\ & \begin{array}{ccc} 400 & 100 & 500 \end{array} \end{array}$$

Matrix 10.4   Matrix 10.5

In each case, the authority placed 80 sons of fathers in C_2 into C_2 (that is, fixed $n_{22} = 80$). Thus, the other entries of N_1 and N_2 were determined since the marginals were given. However, the situations depicted by N_1 and N_2 are different. In N_1, there are 100 fathers in C_2 whose 100 sons (still assuming one son to each father) are available for 200 C_2 positions. The authority places 80 of these 100 sons into C_2 positions. In N_2, 200 sons of fathers in C_2 are available for only 100 C_2 positions, so the authority parcels out 80 of these *positions* to sons of C_2 fathers. In either case, the authority's *policy* is determined by the fraction

$$x = \frac{n_{22}}{\min(n_1, n_{.1})}. \tag{10.32}$$

Of course, the authority could have a policy of determining n_{11} (that is, "conscripting" a certain quota of sons of lower class fathers into lower class positions). We will assume, however, that the policy amounts to reserving upper class positions for upper class sons or of recruiting upper class sons for upper class positions, that is, fixing n_{22}.

Clearly, the maximum value of x is 1. Its minimum value, however, depends on the marginals. Consider the following turnover matrix (Boudon, 1973):

$$
\begin{array}{cc}
 & C_1 \quad C_2 \\
\begin{array}{c} C_1 \\ C_2 \end{array} & \begin{pmatrix} -40 & 240 \\ 240 & 60 \end{pmatrix} \begin{array}{c} 200 \\ 300 \end{array} \\
 & \;\;200 \;\; 300 \;\; 500
\end{array}
$$

Matrix 10.6

Here the authority decided on the policy $x = 0.20$, which means that n_{22} was to be fixed at 60. But this policy cannot be carried out, for then, since the remaining entries are determined by the marginals, n_{11} would have to be negative, which is impossible.

It is easily seen that the lower bound on x in the two-class case is given by

$$x_{min} = \frac{\max[(n_{.2} - n_{1.}), 0]}{\min(n_{2.}, n_{.2})}. \tag{10.33}$$

Boudon's immobility index is defined as

$$I_B = \frac{n_{22}/\min(n_{2.}, n_{.2}) - x_{min}}{1 - x_{min}}. \tag{10.34}$$

It is easily shown (see Boudon, 1973) that Equation 10.34 reduces to

$$I_B = \frac{n_{22}}{\min(n_{2.}, n_{.2})} \quad \text{if } n_{.2} > n_{1.}$$

$$= \frac{n_{22} - (n_{.2} - n_{1.})}{\min(n_{2.}, n_{.2}) - (n_{.2} - n_{1.})} \quad \text{otherwise.} \tag{10.35}$$

Or, expressed more compactly,

$$I_B = \frac{n_{ii}}{\min(n_{1.}, n_{.i})}, \tag{10.36}$$

where $i = 1$ if $n_{1.} > n_{.2}$; $i = 2$ otherwise.

When there are several classes, the authority has more degrees of freedom. In fact, with s classes, $(s - 1)^2$ cells of the turnover matrix can be fixed (subject to the constraint that, given the marginals, no cell entry is negative). The authority may or may not utilize the degrees of freedom at its disposal. For instance, with $s = 3$, the authority may not use its four degrees of freedom but instead adopt a single policy x, manifested in the fixation of four entries according to the following rule:

$$n_{33} = x \min(n_{3.}, n_{.3}) \tag{10.37}$$

$$n_{23} = x \min[n_{2.}, (n_{.3} - n_{33})] \tag{10.38}$$

$$n_{32} = x \min[n_{.2}, (n_{3.} - n_{33})] \tag{10.39}$$

$$n_{22} = x \min[n_{2.} - n_{23}), (n_{.2} - n_{32})]. \tag{10.40}$$

In other words, the authority begins by placing a fixed fraction x of sons of fathers in C_3 into C_3 positions (or else awarding fraction x of C_3 positions to sons of C_3 fathers); then proceeds to fix n_{23} by a similar rule, taking into account the constraint of fixed n_{33}, and so on.

Using two degrees of freedom, the authority may apportion fraction x_1 to fix n_{33} and n_{23}, then apportion fraction x_2 to fix n_{32} and n_{22}. Similarly, the authority could use three or all four degrees of freedom; that is, three or four values of x.

Now given a set of xs satisfying the constraints placed on their ranges by the marginals, the matrix N can be determined. But the sociologist is more likely to be interested in the inverse problem: given a turnover matrix N (which represents the data), to deduce the set of xs that would have produced it.

Suppose, for example, the following turnover matrix is given (Boudon, 1973):

$$
\begin{array}{c c c c c}
 & C_1 & C_2 & C_3 & \\
C_1 & 172 & 88 & 40 & 300 \\
C_2 & 8 & 32 & 160 & 200 \\
C_3 & 20 & 80 & 400 & 500 \\
 & 200 & 200 & 600 & 1000
\end{array}
$$

Matrix 10.7

The policy $x = 0.80$ applied to n_{33}, n_{23}, n_{32}, and n_{22} as in Equations 10.37–10.40 reproduces this matrix. On the other hand, the matrix (Boudon, 1973)

$$
\begin{array}{c c c c c}
 & C_1 & C_2 & C_3 & \\
C_1 & 144 & 116 & 40 & 300 \\
C_2 & 16 & 24 & 160 & 200 \\
C_3 & 40 & 60 & 400 & 500 \\
 & 200 & 200 & 600 & 1000
\end{array}
$$

Matrix 10.8

cannot be reproduced by a policy with one degree of freedom. It can be reproduced by a policy with two degrees of freedom, $x_1 = 0.80$, applied to n_{33} and n_{23}, and $x_2 = 0.60$, applied to n_{32} and n_{22}.

In principle, Boudon's model may enable the sociologist to infer the *constraints* on social mobility from a given turnover matrix. The "authority" need not, of course, be explicit; it may be implicit in tradition, in the prejudices governing the allocation of occupations associated with social status, and so on. At times, explicit constraints are discernible; for instance, in quotas applied to admitting members of minority groups into certain social classes, occupations, or educational institutions.

ASSUMPTIONS EMBODIED IN THEORIES OF SOCIAL MOBILITY

In the interest of formulating a tractable problem, the mathematical model builder must confine the model to a small number of parameters related to the dynamics of a process. Sociologists who formulate theories verbally are not bound by these constraints. They can include as many factors into their theories as they can think of, thereby forestalling criticism to the effect that they have not considered this or that. Unfortunately, the more "complete" a theory is the more difficult it is to put it to a test. Boudon lists a number of assumptions about social mobility found in theoretical sociology; for example, in Sorokin's theory (1927).

1. The individuals of each cohort are in a situation of competition.
2. At each time unit, they pass through an orientation agency which eventually provides them with a new status.
3. The position they reach at the end of the time unit depends on the position they had at the beginning, since the orientation agencies are inequalitarian.
4. A cohort with age i at time t and a cohort with age i at time, say, $(t + 1)$ may not meet the same structural conditions since the distribution of the available positions at the end of the time unit may have changed.
5. A cohort with age i at time t may not meet the same conditions as a cohort with age i at time $(t + 1)$ since the distribution of these cohorts according to their status at the beginning of the period may differ.

As we have seen, assumptions 1, 2, and 3 are formalized in Boudon's model in which the authority plays the part of the "orientation agency." In other models, this orientation agency is identified with educational institutions, admissions to which are governed at least in part by the status positions of the applicants. A transition matrix which is not a matrix of perfect mobility is also a formalization of assumption 3. Assumption 4 relates to structural mobility (availability of opportunities in successive generations or, more generally, for different cohorts). Assumption 5 may relate to differential birth rates in various classes, a factor not discussed in this chapter but embodied in more complex models. The interested reader is referred to Boudon (1973, Chapter 4). Assumptions related to the role of duration are not included in Sorokin's conception of social mobility and indeed may not be relevant in the context of social classes or strata. They should, however, be included in models of mobility referring to changes of jobs or of residence.

It must be kept in mind that the trade-off between "verisimilitude" and tractability is always a limiting factor in mathematical models. The simplest models cannot aspire to predictive power. Their function is to provide a "beachhead" for the further development of a rigorous theory.

NOTES

[1] According to the multiplication rule for probabilities, the product represents the probability that the system will pass from state i to state j along the path indicated.

[2] See E. Parzen (1962, Chapter 6).

[3] Designating both the matrix (n_{ij}) and the total number of pairs by N should cause no confusion, since the meaning can be clearly inferred from the context.

[4] To see this, consider the proportion turnover matrix of perfect mobility:

$$P^{**} = \begin{pmatrix} p_{1.}p_{.1} & p_{1.}p_{.2} \\ p_{2.}p_{.1} & p_{2.}p_{.2} \end{pmatrix} = \begin{pmatrix} p_1(0)p_1(1) & p_1(0)p_2(1) \\ p_2(0)p_1(1) & p_2(0)p_2(1) \end{pmatrix}$$

Then

$$\begin{pmatrix} p_1(0)^{-1} & 0 \\ 0 & p_2(0)^{-1} \end{pmatrix} P^{**} = \begin{pmatrix} p_1(1) & p_2(1) \\ p_1(1) & p_2(1) \end{pmatrix}$$

[5] The same considerations apply to cohorts. For instance, if we follow a cohort of married couples over years, we will observe a depletion through deaths or divorces. For simplicity, consider divorces alone. If these were completely random events represented by a Poisson process, the size of a cohort of married couples would diminish exponentially. If couples have different "divorce proneness," the number of "surviving" couples would be larger than that expected on the basis of an exponential decay. This is the heterogeneity effect. If the probability of staying married increases with years of marriage, the same effect will be observed. In this context, it could be called an "addiction effect." It is equivalent to the effect of increasing reluctance to change jobs with the length of stay in a job.

CHAPTER ELEVEN

Matrix Methods in Demography

The stationary Markov chain is a type of stochastic process (see p. 145) in which the random variables of the family $X(n)$ are all discrete (assuming a finite number of values) and index n is likewise discrete, taking on values 0, 1, 2, ... That is to say, both the state space and the index space of the family are discrete.

In many applications of the Markov chain model, the "values" assumed by the random variable of the family $X(n)$ are not numbers but qualitatively distinguishable "states." This was the case in the Markov chain models of social mobility examined in Chapter 10. The random variable was depicted as a category (class, occupation, and so on) to which a randomly selected individual of a population could belong. The stochastic feature of the model manifested itself in the transformations of that probability via the transition matrix R. Thus given any initial probability distribution of categories $C_1, C_2, \ldots, C_s$ at time $n = 0$, the probability distribution at any future time n was predicted by the model.

In applying the model to data, the probabilities must be translated into frequencies, since probabilities are never directly observable: they are estimated from observed frequencies. The substitution of frequencies for probabilities was accomplished by the turnover matrix $N = (n_{ij})$, where n_{ij} were observed numbers of father–son pairs. Thus the stochastic feature of the model was lost, since the elements of N were no longer probabilities. Nevertheless, the use of matrix algebra as well as some results from the theory of Markov chains (for example, the concept of asymptotically approached steady state) still linked the method to the concept of a stochastic process, and it was for this reason that we included the models based on matrix operations among those classified under "stochastic models." The characterizing feature singled out was based not so much on hypotheses about probabilistically determined events as on the use of matrix algebra in a manner analogous to its use in Markov chain models.

In what follows, matrices will not necessarily be probability transition matrices. We will still refer to them as "transition matrices," however, if they are used to transform frequency distribution vectors. A new feature will be introduced by dropping the assumption that the total population remains constant. We shall still be interested in steady-state distributions of the population among categories. This asymptotic distribution, however, will refer not to constant numbers of units in each category but rather to proportions in the several categories, even though the population may be growing. Recall that we dealt with just this situation in deriving the equilibrium age distribution of an exponentially growing (Malthusian) population. The theory of Markov chains will enter in the derivation of equilibrium distribution and in the derivation of the so-called migratory distance.

THE GROWTH OPERATOR

In the mathematical models of population dynamics examined in Chapter 1, migration of people was left out of consideration. Since distribution of populations among geographical regions is of central interest in demography, this aspect of population dynamics should also be analyzed. As one would expect, models of migration are closely related to models of social mobility. In fact, they deal with mobility in its literal (that is, spatial) rather than sociological sense.

Let $w(t)$ denote the size of a population at time t. Then at time $(t + 1)$ the population must be

$$w(t + 1) = w(t) + b(t) - d(t) + n(t), \tag{11.1}$$

where $b(t)$ is the number of births between t and $t + 1$, $d(t)$ is the corresponding number of deaths,[1] and $n(t)$ is the net number of migrants between t and $t + 1$ into the region occupied by our population. Of course, $n(t)$ may be either positive or negative. If we designate the crude birth rate, death rate, and migration by β, δ, and η respectively, and designate $(1 + \beta - \delta + \eta)$ by g, we can write Equation 11.1 as

$$w(t + 1) = gw(t), \tag{11.2}$$

where g is a "growth multiplier." If there are m regions, we can represent the corresponding system of m equations by the matrix equation

$$w(t + 1) = (I + B - D + N)w(t) = Gw(t). \tag{11.3}$$

Here w is an m-vector; I is the identity matrix; B, D, and N are diagonal matrices whose elements denote the crude birth, death, and migration rates of the m regions; and $G = (I + B - D + N)$ is a matrix called the *growth operator*.

The effects of in- and out-migration can be separated. We introduce the transitions matrix $R = (r_{ij})$. Its elements specify the proportions of people who migrate from region i to region j per unit time. The transpose R^T of R can replace $(I + N)$

in Equation 11.3 to yield the equivalent equation

$$w(t+1) = (B - D + R^T)w(t) = Gw(t). \tag{11.4}$$

Now we introduce cohorts; that is, groups of people born in given time intervals. Returning to the single region, we redefine the vector $w(t)$ so that its components are now numbers of people in the rth age group. Next, we define a matrix of order n:

$$S = \begin{pmatrix}
0 & 0 & 0 & \cdots & b_1 & b_2 & \cdots & b_u & \cdots & 0 & \cdots & 0 \\
{}_1d_2 & 0 & 0 & & & & \cdots & & & & & 0 \\
0 & {}_2d_3 & 0 & & & & \cdots & & & & & 0 \\
0 & 0 & {}_3d_4 & & & & \cdots & & & & & 0 \\
& & & & & & \cdots & & & & & 0 \\
& & & & & & \cdots & & & & & 0 \\
0 & 0 & 0 & & & & \cdots & & & {}_{n-1}d_n & & 0
\end{pmatrix}$$

Matrix 11.1

The entries of S are defined as follows: $b_r(r = 1, \dots, u)$ is the number of births that survive to the end of the unit time interval per person in the rth childbearing group; ${}_r d_{r+1}$ is the proportion of people in the rth age group who survive to the $(r+1)$ age group after the unit time interval. Thus we can write

$$w(t+1) = Sw(t) + n(t), \tag{11.5}$$

where now $n(t)$ is a vector whose n components correspond to the n age groups and which denotes the contribution of net migration into the region during the interval $(t, t+1)$.

Finally, we define a *migration operator* M so as to satisfy

$$n(t) = Mw(t). \tag{11.6}$$

In fact,

$$M = \begin{pmatrix}
0 & 0 & 0 & \cdots & & 0 \\
m_1 & 0 & 0 & \cdots & & 0 \\
0 & m_2 & 0 & \cdots & & 0 \\
& & & \cdots & & 0 \\
& & & \cdots & & 0 \\
0 & 0 & 0 & \cdots & m_{n-1} & 0
\end{pmatrix}$$

Matrix 11.2

Combining the effects of survivorship and net migration—that is, writing $G = S + M$—we transform Equation 11.5 into

$$w(t+1) = Gw(t). \tag{11.7}$$

To incorporate the effects of migration into a cohort survival model, one must keep in mind that the effect of "aging" is superimposed on that of migration. That is, people move not only from region to region, but also progress through a sequence of age groups. For each age group we construct an *interregional transition matrix.*

$$
_rP_{r+1}=\begin{pmatrix}
_{r,1}P_{r+1,1} & _{r,1}P_{r+1,2} & \cdots & _{r,1}P_{r+1,m} \\
_{r,2}P_{r+1,1} & _{r,2}P_{r+1,2} & \cdots & _{r,2}P_{r+1,m} \\
_{r,3}P_{r+1,1} & & \cdots & _{r,3}P_{r+1,3} \\
& & \cdots & \\
& & \cdots & \\
_{r,m}P_{r+1,1} & _{r,m}P_{r+1,2} & \cdots & _{r,m}P_{r+1,m}
\end{pmatrix}
$$

Matrix 11.3

Each entry $_{r,i}P_{r+1,j}$ in this matrix specifies the proportion of people in the rth age group in region i who, during the unit time interval, move into the $(r+1)$ age group in region j. (Thus these people not only moved, but also aged.)

Having a set of such transition matrices, one for each age group, we can now construct a transition matrix M_{ij} to satisfy

$$k_{ij} = M_{ij}w_i(t). \tag{11.8}$$

Here k_{ij} is an n-vector:

$$k_{ij} = (0, \ _2k_{ij}, \ _3k_{ij} \ldots, \ _nk_{ij}). \tag{11.9}$$

The rth component of k_{ij} denotes the number of in-migrants in the rth age group into region j from region i. The first component of k_{ij} is 0 because the first age group is the newborn who arrived by being born, not by migrating. As for M_{ij}, in view of the way the entries in $_rP_{r+1}$ were defined (see Matrix 11.3), it must be given by

$$
M_{ij}=\begin{pmatrix}
0 & 0 & 0 & \cdots & & 0 \\
_{1,i}P_{2,j} & 0 & 0 & \cdots & & 0 \\
0 & _{2,i}P_{3,j} & 0 & \cdots & & 0 \\
& & & \cdots & & 0 \\
& & & \cdots & & 0 \\
0 & 0 & 0 & \cdots & _{n-1,i}P_{n,j} & 0
\end{pmatrix}
$$

Matrix 11.4

The number subscripts fore and aft of the entries in M_{ij} refer to age groups; the letter subscripts refer to regions. Thus each entry represents the proportion of people who migrate from region i to region j and survive in the next age group.

Summing the in-migrants over all origins i, we get the total immigration of age group r into region j:

$$_rk_{.j} = \sum_i {}_rk_{ij} \qquad (r = 1, 2, \ldots, n). \tag{11.10}$$

Introducing partitioned matrices (that is, matrices whose entries are sub-matrices), we get the following matrix equation:

$$
\begin{pmatrix} k_{.1} \\ k_{.2} \\ \vdots \\ k_{.m} \end{pmatrix} = \begin{pmatrix} 0 & M_{21} & M_{31} & \cdots & M_{m1} \\ M_{21} & 0 & M_{32} & \cdots & M_{m2} \\ & & & \cdots & \\ M_{1m} & M_{2m} & M_{3m} & \cdots & 0 \end{pmatrix} \begin{pmatrix} w_1(t) \\ w_2(t) \\ \vdots \\ w_m(t) \end{pmatrix} \tag{11.11}
$$

Combining the survival operator S with the total migration operator M, we have the total growth matrix

$$
G = \begin{pmatrix} S_1 & M_{21} & M_{31} & \cdots & M_{m1} \\ M_{12} & S_2 & M_{32} & \cdots & M_{m2} \\ M_{13} & M_{23} & S_3 & \cdots & M_{m3} \\ & & & \cdots & \\ & & & \cdots & \\ M_{1m} & M_{2m} & & \cdots & S_m \end{pmatrix}
$$

Matrix 11.5

which operates on the total $m \times n$-vector $w(t)$, namely

$$
w(t) = (w_1(t), w_2(t), \ldots, w_m(t)). \tag{11.12}
$$

Here the "components" of $w(t)$ are themselves n-vectors, each being an age group vector related to a region.

Example. An an illustration, let us apply the model to the population of California and the rest of the United States in the years 1955–1960 and compare it with the more detailed cohort survival model.

Tabulation of births, deaths, and migration to California from the remainder of the United States and vice versa determines the migration transition matrix in the interval 1955–1960 and the growth operator G, thus also the vector $w(t)$. The migration transition matrix is

	California	Remaining states
California	0.9373	0.0627
Remaining states	0.0127	0.9873

Matrix 11.6

The growth operator is

$$
G = \begin{pmatrix} 1.0215 & 0.0127 \\ 0.0627 & 1.0667 \end{pmatrix}
$$

Matrix 11.7

The initial population vector, $w(1955)$, in thousands is

$$\begin{array}{l} \text{California} \\ \text{Remaining states} \end{array} \begin{pmatrix} 12{,}988 \\ 152{,}082 \end{pmatrix}$$

Multiplying G by $w(1955)$, we obtain $w(1960)$:

$$\begin{array}{l} \text{California} \\ \text{Remaining states} \end{array} \begin{pmatrix} 15{,}199 \\ 163{,}040 \end{pmatrix}$$

The last result is, of course, no more than an "accounting" result, which must agree with observations if the "input" data were correct.

Next, we examine the more detailed tabulation by cohorts. In Matrix equation 11.7, the left-hand vector is now the 1960 population by 10-year age groups. Its upper half refers to California, the lower half to the remaining states; hence $w(t + 1)$ has 18 components. The vector on the right is the corresponding vector for 1950. The matrix G has four (9×9) submatrices. The upper left submatrix is S_1, the survival matrix for California; the lower right is S_2, the survival matrix for the remaining states. The upper right and lower left submatrices represent migration.

$$G_{11} = S_{\text{cal}} = \begin{pmatrix} 0 & 0.3375 & 1.1861 & 0.4789 & 0.0424 & 0 & 0 & 0 & 0 \\ 0.8731 & 0 & 0 & 0 & 0 & 0 & 0 & 0 & 0 \\ 0 & 0.9228 & 0 & 0 & 0 & 0 & 0 & 0 & 0 \\ 0 & 0 & 0.7821 & 0 & 0 & 0 & 0 & 0 & 0 \\ 0 & 0 & 0 & 0.7891 & 0 & 0 & 0 & 0 & 0 \\ 0 & 0 & 0 & 0 & 0.6905 & 0 & 0 & 0 & 0 \\ 0 & 0 & 0 & 0 & 0 & 0.7938 & 0 & 0 & 0 \\ 0 & 0 & 0 & 0 & 0 & 0 & 0.6288 & 0 & 0 \\ 0 & 0 & 0 & 0 & 0 & 0 & 0 & 0.3540 & 0 \end{pmatrix}$$

Matrix 11.8 (Rogers, 1968)

$$G_{12} = M_{\text{us,cal}} = \begin{pmatrix} 0 & 0 & 0 & 0 & 0 & 0 & 0 & 0 & 0 \\ 0.0297 & 0 & 0 & 0 & 0 & 0 & 0 & 0 & 0 \\ 0 & 0.0399 & 0 & 0 & 0 & 0 & 0 & 0 & 0 \\ 0 & 0 & 0.0450 & 0 & 0 & 0 & 0 & 0 & 0 \\ 0 & 0 & 0 & 0.0316 & 0 & 0 & 0 & 0 & 0 \\ 0 & 0 & 0 & 0 & 0.0300 & 0 & 0 & 0 & 0 \\ 0 & 0 & 0 & 0 & 0 & 0.0145 & 0 & 0 & 0 \\ 0 & 0 & 0 & 0 & 0 & 0 & 0.0137 & 0 & 0 \\ 0 & 0 & 0 & 0 & 0 & 0 & 0 & 0.0126 & 0 \end{pmatrix}$$

Matrix 11.9 (Rogers, 1968)

$$G_{21} = M_{\text{cal,us}} = \begin{pmatrix} 0 & 0 & 0 & 0 & 0 & 0 & 0 & 0 & 0 \\ 0.1682 & 0 & 0 & 0 & 0 & 0 & 0 & 0 & 0 \\ 0 & 0.1503 & 0 & 0 & 0 & 0 & 0 & 0 & 0 \\ 0 & 0 & 0.2356 & 0 & 0 & 0 & 0 & 0 & 0 \\ 0 & 0 & 0 & 0.1565 & 0 & 0 & 0 & 0 & 0 \\ 0 & 0 & 0 & 0 & 0.0988 & 0 & 0 & 0 & 0 \\ 0 & 0 & 0 & 0 & 0 & 0.0670 & 0 & 0 & 0 \\ 0 & 0 & 0 & 0 & 0 & 0 & 0.0583 & 0 & 0 \\ 0 & 0 & 0 & 0 & 0 & 0 & 0 & 0.0560 & 0 \end{pmatrix}$$

Matrix 11.10 (Rogers, 1968)

$$G_{22} = S_{\text{us}} = \begin{pmatrix} 0 & 0.2257 & 0.9746 & 0.4252 & 0.0364 & 0 & 0 & 0 & 0 \\ 0.9903 & 0 & 0 & 0 & 0 & 0 & 0 & 0 & 0 \\ 0 & 0.9523 & 0 & 0 & 0 & 0 & 0 & 0 & 0 \\ 0 & 0 & 0.9843 & 0 & 0 & 0 & 0 & 0 & 0 \\ 0 & 0 & 0 & 0.9594 & 0 & 0 & 0 & 0 & 0 \\ 0 & 0 & 0 & 0 & 0.9176 & 0 & 0 & 0 & 0 \\ 0 & 0 & 0 & 0 & 0 & 0.8499 & 0 & 0 & 0 \\ 0 & 0 & 0 & 0 & 0 & 0 & 0.7171 & 0 & 0 \\ 0 & 0 & 0 & 0 & 0 & 0 & 0 & 0.3921 & 0 \end{pmatrix}$$

Matrix 11.11 (Rogers, 1968)

If we have grounds for assuming that the trends observed in a given time period will continue (that is, that our transition matrices are stationary), we can make forecasts based on the stationary Markov chain model. Problems arise if data have been aggregated over fairly long periods and we want to make a forecast for a short period. For instance, the unit of time in our cohort survival model was 10 years. However, we need to make a forecast for the next year. Thus we must estimate a one-year transition matrix from the 10-year transition matrix. This estimation problem is called *estimation on the basis of temporal decomposition*. In other cases we may have no data on births, deaths, or migrations, but only some successive population distribution vectors for a number of regions. We want to infer birth, death, and migration data from these distributions. This estimation problem is called *estimation on the basis of distribution data*. We address ourselves first to the temporal decomposition problem.

Suppose we are given G over n unit intervals. If we assume that the underlying process is stationary, we can put $G = R^n$, where R is the transition matrix for one time unit. It is shown in the theory of matrices that we can find a nonsingular[2] matrix N such that $N^{-1}GN = D$, where D is a diagonal matrix. Having found N, we can express G^2 as $(NDN^{-1})(NDN^{-1}) = ND^2N^{-1}$. In fact, for any power or polynomial function $f(G)$ of G, we can write

$$f(G) = Nf(D)N^{-1}. \qquad (11.13)$$

In particular, we can write

$$G^{1/n} = ND^{1/n}N^{-1} = R. \qquad (11.14)$$

Thus our problem is solved once we have found N and D. The elements of D are the eigenvalues of G. If these are all distinct, the columns of N are the characteristic vectors[3] that correspond to the eigenvalues. We will illustrate the method by decomposing our matrix G, which represents the transition matrix for a five-year period, into a product of five identical one-year matrices. We have G given by Matrix 11.7. The eigenvalues of G are found by setting the determinant of the matrix $(G - Ix)$ equal to zero and solving for x:

$$(1.0215 - x)(1.0667 - x) - (0.0127)(0.0627) = 0. \qquad (11.15)$$

The two roots of this equation are $x_1 = 1.0802$; $x_2 = 1.0080$. Hence

$$D = \begin{pmatrix} 1.0802 & 0 \\ 0 & 1.0080 \end{pmatrix}$$

Matrix 11.12

The entries of the first column of N are the two cofactors of the first row of the matrix 11.13.

$$G - x_1 I = \begin{pmatrix} 1.0215 & 0.0127 \\ 0.0627 & 1.0667 \end{pmatrix} - \begin{pmatrix} 1.0802 & 0 \\ 0 & 1.0802 \end{pmatrix} = \begin{pmatrix} -0.0587 & 0.0217 \\ 0.0627 & -0.0135 \end{pmatrix}$$

Matrix 11.13

Thus $n_{11} = -0.0135$; $n_{21} = -0.0627$. The entries of the second column of N are the two cofactors of the first row of Matrix 11.14.

$$G - x_2 I = \begin{pmatrix} 1.0215 & 0.0127 \\ 0.0627 & 1.0667 \end{pmatrix} - \begin{pmatrix} 1.0080 & 0 \\ 0 & 1.0080 \end{pmatrix} = \begin{pmatrix} 0.0135 & 0.0127 \\ 0.0627 & 0.0587 \end{pmatrix}$$

Matrix 11.14

We have now obtained N, shown as Matrix 11.15, and its inverse, N^{-1}, shown as Matrix 11.16.

$$N = \begin{pmatrix} -0.0135 & 0.0587 \\ -0.0627 & -0.0627 \end{pmatrix} \qquad N^{-1} = \begin{pmatrix} -13.8504 & -12.9668 \\ 13.8504 & -2.9821 \end{pmatrix}$$

Matrix 11.15   Matrix 11.16

The entries of $D^{1/5}$ are simply the fifth roots of the entries of D. Thus

$$D^{1/5} = \begin{pmatrix} 1.0155 & 0 \\ 0 & 1.0016 \end{pmatrix}$$

Matrix 11.17

We are now in a position to calculate $P = G^{1/5}$:

$$P = G^{1/5} = ND^{1/5}N^{-1} = \begin{pmatrix} 1.0042 & 0.0024 \\ 0.0121 & 1.0129 \end{pmatrix}$$

Matrix 11.18

With the aid of P, we can estimate the interregional distribution for successive years, given data for periods separated by several years.

A different sort of estimation problem arises if we are given vectors $w(t)$, $w(t+1), \ldots, w(t+k)$ and want to estimate a growth operator G which will produce these vectors; that is, will satisfy the matrix equations

$$\begin{aligned} w(t+1) &= Gw(t) \\ w(t+2) &= Gw(t+1) \\ &\vdots \\ w(t+k) &= Gw(t+k-1). \end{aligned} \tag{11.16}$$

Now the components of each vector $w = (w_1, w_2, \ldots, w_m)$ represent populations of m regions. Thus each vector w is an $m \times 1$ matrix. G is, accordingly, an $m \times m$ matrix. Equation 11.16 can be rewritten as the following matrix equation:

$$y = Xg. \tag{11.17}$$

Here y is a column vector with mk elements $w_1(t+1), w_1(t+2), \ldots, w_1(t+k)$, $w_2(t+1), \ldots, w_2(t+k) \ldots, w_m(t+1), \ldots, w_m(t+k)$; X is a diagonal matrix whose elements are all like Matrix 11.19; g is a column vector with m^2 elements $g_{11}, g_{21}, \ldots, g_{m1}, g_{12}, \ldots, g_{m2}, \ldots, g_{mm}$.

$$W(t) = \begin{pmatrix} w_1(t) & \cdots & w_m(t) \\ w_1(t+1) & \cdots & w_m(t+1) \\ & \cdots & \\ & \cdots & \\ w_1(t+k-1) & \cdots & w_m(t+k-1) \end{pmatrix}$$

Matrix 11.19

Matrix 11.19 represents a system of mk linear equations in m^2 unknowns (the elements of the unknown growth operator G). If $k > m$ (that is, if $mk > m^2$), the system may not have a solution. Therefore, if we assume that the growth operator is constant, we must assume that the components of y have been perturbed by "errors." We accordingly write

$$y = Xg + \varepsilon, \tag{11.18}$$

where ε is an error vector with km components. We seek the vector g that will minimize ε in some sense. This is the estimation problem on the basis of distribution data. That is, we are not given any data on births, deaths, or migration. We seek to estimate these data on the basis of a given change in a population profile.

There are several methods of solving this problem, which is formally equivalent to the problem of estimating multiple regression coefficients. The most commonly used method of solving problems of this kind is that of *least squares* (see p. 213). In this context, however, the least square method may not be applicable because it may yield negative entries of G, which cannot occur. Another method avoids this difficulty, namely that of minimizing the sum of the absolute deviations (instead of the sum of squared deviations) between the "theoretical" and the observed values of y. This method leads to a linear programming problem; namely,

$$\text{Minimize } u + v$$

$$\text{Subject to: } y = Xg + (I, -I)\begin{pmatrix} u \\ v \end{pmatrix} \tag{11.19}$$

$$g, u, v \geqq 0.$$

Here u and v are mk-vectors, I is an $mk \times mk$ identity matrix, and $u - v = \varepsilon$.

STABLE DISTRIBUTIONS

In our discussion of stochastic models, we pointed out that an ergodic probability transition matrix tends to a limit when raised to the nth power ($n \to \infty$); namely, to a matrix with identical rows. (Its transpose therefore tends to a limit with identical columns.) Our growth matrix G is not a probability transition matrix since its entries are not probabilities. Nevertheless, it has an analogous property in the sense that the matrix whose elements are the *ratios* of the elements of successive powers of G tends to a limit with identical rows *and columns*. For instance, taking the growth matrix G in our example and defining L^n as the matrix whose elements are ratios of the elements of G^n to those of G^{n-1}, we calculate L^{61} to be

$$L^{61} = \begin{pmatrix} 1.0757 & 1.0814 \\ 1.0814 & 1.0800 \end{pmatrix}$$

Matrix 11.20

As can be seen, all the elements of L^{61} are equal to the second decimal. In the long run, the elements of vector w will be growing at the same rate or, in other words, each region will receive a constant share of the total population. This allocation of the population among the regions is called the *stable interregional distribution* and is denoted by a constant distribution vector $v(t + 1) = v(t)$.

We turn our attention once again to the eigenvalues of our growth matrix. Since they are the roots of a polynomial whose degree equals the order of the matrix, they may be negative or complex. However, it is shown in the theory of matrices that the characteristic root (that is, eigenvalue) of a positive matrix that is largest in absolute value is real and positive (Perron, 1907). It has also been shown that the result holds for non-negative matrices, and moreover, that the associated characteristic vector is unique and has only positive components (Frobenius, 1912). These results can be applied to the problem of the stable interregional population.

Given a non-negative $(n \times n)$ matrix G and a non-negative scalar λ such that

$$Gw = \lambda w \tag{11.20}$$

where w is a non-negative real vector, the matrix equation

$$(G - \lambda I)w = 0 \tag{11.21}$$

represents a set of homogeneous linear equations. For the system to have a solution, the determinant of the matrix of coefficients must vanish. Thus we must have

$$|G - \lambda I| = 0. \tag{11.22}$$

Equation 11.22 solved for λ produces n roots, and we know by the Perron-Frobenius theorem that at least one of them must be non-negative with the largest absolute value. The theorem also establishes the existence of an associated characteristic vector w whose components are all non-negative. This gives the components of v, the stable interregional vector:

$$v_i = \frac{w_i}{\sum_i w_i}. \tag{11.23}$$

In our example, the eigenvalue of G with the larger absolute value was $x_1 = 1.0802$. Substituting this value into the equation

$$Gw = x_1 w \tag{11.24}$$

and solving for w, we solve for v via Equation 11.23 and obtain

$$v_1 = 0.1772; \, v_2 = 0.8228. \tag{11.25}$$

This is our long-term prognosis (if we venture to make it). If the present trend continues, almost 18% of the U.S. population will live in California.

The method indicated can be applied to the extended growth matrix involving the age distribution. Here, too, it leads to the stable distribution including both regions and age groups. It should be kept in mind that a "stable distribution" does not necessarily mean a population with zero growth. Our population could be growing or declining in numbers. A "stable distribution" refers only to the constant proportions of people in the various regions and age groups. Thus the matrix method leads to results directly analogous to those obtained by the continuous variable model in Chapter 1. The method based on transition matrices follows the changes through discrete steps and categorizes the population by discrete age groups. The "classical" method follows the changes through continuous time and categorizes the population into a continuum of categories. The latter method is a limiting case of the former.[4]

CORRELATES OF MIGRATION

An area of interest in mathematical demography is the analysis of migration. One class of studies puts *migration streams* at the centre of attention; that is, the volume and direction of movements from region to region. Their object is to derive the environmental effects of these changes. Another class of studies analyzes the migration streams into their constituents by demographic characteristics, age, sex, occupation, economic level, and so on. The object here is to study the differentials in population composition as a consequence of migration.[5]

Consider m_{ij}, the number of migrants from region i to region j. It is reasonable to suppose that this number will be positively correlated with (1) u_i, the proportion of unemployed in nonagricultural labor in region i; and (2) w_j, the hourly manufacturing wage in region j. Moreover, m_{ij} can be supposed to be negatively correlated with (3) the proportion of unemployed in region j; and with (4) the hourly wages in region i. Next, since m_{ij} are numbers of people, we can suppose that these numbers are positively correlated with (5) the product of populations (here taken as numbers of persons in nonagricultural labor in regions i and j) and negatively correlated with the distance between the two regions.[6]

The simplest model that expresses all these relations is a multiple regression equation, linear in the logarithms of the quantities involved:[7]

$$\log m_{ij} = \beta_0 + \beta_1 \log u_i + \beta_2 \log u_j + \beta_3 \log w_i + \beta_4 \log w_j + \beta_5 \log p_i$$
$$+ \beta_6 \log p_j + \beta_7 \log d_{ij} + \varepsilon_{ij}. \tag{11.26}$$

Here u_i and u_j are proportions of unemployed in regions i and j, respectively, w_i and w_j are wage rates, d_{ij} are distances between i and j, p_i and p_j are populations, and ε_{ij} is an error term. β_i are the coefficients to be determined. They are expected to be positive or negative depending on whether the correlation with the corresponding independent variable is expected to be positive or negative. In matrix form, Equation 11.21 can be written as

$$y = X\beta + \varepsilon \tag{11.27}$$

where y is a column vector with $m(m-1)$ components, β is a column vector with 8 components, X is an $m(m-1) \times 8$ matrix, and ε is a column vector with $m(m-1)$ components.

In the theory of multiple regression, it is shown that the least square estimator of β is

$$\hat{b} = (X^T X)^{-1} X^T y. \tag{11.28}$$

For any set of data represented by the vector y and the matrix X, we can estimate the vector of coefficients. These coefficients are measures (within fluctuation error) of the direction and magnitude of "influence" to be attributed to the corresponding factor. Thus the signs of the coefficients are qualitative tests (of direction only) of the model. Table 11.1 presents the results of applying this regression model to migrations among various regions of California from 1955 to 1960.

Table 11.1. Estimated Coefficients in a Multiple Regression of Migration with Respect to Several Presumed Determinants

Variable	Coefficient	Partial Correlation
Constant	−11.5133	
$\log_e u_i$	−0.58726	−0.11730
$\log_e u_j$	1.16108	0.22742
$\log_e w_i$	−1.15274	−0.08949
$\log_e w_j$	5.08408[a]	0.36842
$\log_e p_i$	0.79578[b]	0.87806
$\log_e p_j$	0.73608[b]	0.86157
$\log_e d_{ij}$	−0.70688[b]	−0.78583

Source: Adapted from Rogers (1968).

Note: $R^2 = 0.90680$

[a] $p < 0.1$.

[b] $p < 0.001$.

From Table 11.1 we see that the model is at least partially qualitatively corroborated. The signs of the coefficients that are significantly different from zero are all as expected. (The signs of the coefficients associated with u_i and u_j are reversed, but these are not significantly different from zero.) Actually, over 90% of the variance (R^2) is accounted for by this regression model.

Nevertheless, the use of this model for forecasting presents problems, for we cannot expect that the independent variables, such as unemployment rates or wage rates, will remain the same in future years. Nor does demography provide any method for estimating future values of these variables; this is the realm of economics. There is little doubt, however, that conditions studied in demography and those studied in economics interact. Inflows of workers may raise unemployment,[8] depress wages, or change conditions in some other possibly complex ways. Clearly some integration of demographic and economic theories is necessary to formulate models of these dynamics. Correlations and hence the amount of variance accounted for by this model can be improved by various refinements and alternative definitions of the determining variables.

Essentially the same sort of model can be applied to the analysis of migration differentials. From a study reported by A. Rogers (1965), the following qualitative conclusions can be drawn.

1. Young adults are the most mobile segment of the population.
2. Males tend to be more migratory than females.
3. Unemployed persons are more likely to move than employed persons.
4. Whites move more than nonwhites.
5. Professionals are among the most mobile sectors of the population.

The first three of these conclusions would be guessed by anyone familiar with the American scene. The last two are less obvious, and the last is, perhaps, the most surprising, though not when the large academic population is taken into account. It has been noted that the average stay of an American faculty member at a college or university is about four years. Whether the results are revealing of something not suspected or whether they merely corroborate generally known trends, the importance of these studies is not so much in creating new knowledge as in developing models that can be continually improved. Besides, not all of the results are obvious. We have found, for example, that the relative proportions of unemployed in two regions have no discernible effect on the overall migration from one to another. Possibly such an effect could be discerned in a more refined model where categories of migrants are taken into account.

COHORT MODELS

We turn to the analysis of migration in terms of cohorts. A cohort in this context will mean a group of people who behave "in the same way" with regard to migration. This is not to say that all the people belonging to a cohort always do the same thing, but only that they do whatever they do with the same probability. This may mean, for example, that an arbitrarily selected member of a cohort will move from region i to region j with the same probability. Still, each member of the cohort is supposed to behave independently of all other members, so that the probability that he moves does not depend on whether another member has actually moved or not. Note that in certain contexts the independence assumption is not realistic. For example, members of the same nuclear family usually move together. To take this into account, a modification of the model is required and, in fact, has been made. For the time being, we will assume that individual members of a cohort behave independently.

Let $_rk_{ij}$ be the number of people in cohort r who have moved from region i to region j in a specified time period. Then $\sum_{j=1}^{m} {}_rk_{ij}$ denotes the number of people in cohort r who were in region i at the beginning of the period, and

$$_rp_{ij} = \frac{_rk_{ij}}{\sum_{j=1}^{m} {}_rk_{ij}} \tag{11.29}$$

is the proportion of the people in cohort r in region i who moved to region j

in the specified period. We have, then, for each cohort r a transition matrix $P_r = (_r p_{ij}) (i, j = 1, 2, \ldots, m)$. (Note that we have changed our notation somewhat. We had been denoting *proportion turnover matrices* by P and probability transition matrices usually by $R = (r_{ij})$. We replace R by P here to avoid confusion between the generic subscript for a cohort and an element of R).

There being n cohorts, we have n such matrices. The observed proportions will serve as estimates of the corresponding probabilities.

The transition matrix associated with a given cohort provides some immediately perceptible information about the migratory characteristics of that cohort. In particular, the diagonal elements tell us something about the mobility of that cohort because they denote the proportions of people in that cohort in each region who did *not* move. Recall that this interpretation is exactly analogous to that derived from the model of social mobility.

COHORT DIFFERENTIATION

Regression analysis can be applied to bring out differences between two or more cohorts in the way migration depends on economic and demographic factors. The model presented previously will be somewhat modified in that the number of migrants will be assumed to depend only on

w_i, w_j: wage and salary levels in regions i and j, respectively.

p_i, p_j: sizes of labor forces in the two regions.

d_{ij}: distance between i and j.

The results of multiple regression analysis are shown in Table 11.2.

Table 11.2. Comparison of White and Nonwhite Migration Streams in California by Means of Multiple Regression

Migration Streams of Whites[a]			Migration Streams of Nonwhites[b]		
Var.	Coeff.	Part. cor.	Var.	Coeff.	Part. cor.
Const.	-6.16275		Const.	-30.6021	
$\log_e p_i$	0.77124^c	0.67062	$\log_e p_i$	2.63083^c	0.29365
$\log_e p_j$	0.67496^c	0.62046	$\log_e p_j$	1.83355^c	0.20935
$\log_e d_{ij}$	-0.80346^c	-0.65721	$\log_e d_{ij}$	-2.55513^c	-0.26627
$\log_e w_i$	0.28624	0.06989	$\log_e w_i$	-1.65939	-0.04043
$\log_e w_j$	-0.28436	-0.06944	$\log_e w_j$	0.45730	0.01115

Source: Adapted from Rogers (1968).

[a] $R^2 = 0.79983$.

[b] $R^2 = 0.26841$.

[c] $p < 0.001$.

As is immediately seen from Table 11.2, the dependence of migration on economic and demographic factors is much weaker in the non-white population than in the white population in California. Regression accounts for only 27% of the variance in the non-white population, whereas it accounts for 80% of the variance in the white population. Clearly, the analysis does not reveal the reasons for this large difference. But it calls attention to it and so suggests a task for the sociologist, namely, to pose hypotheses concerning the reasons for the difference and to find ways of testing such hypotheses.

Similar analysis performed on age and sex cohorts give further information. As expected, the young are more mobile than the old. Regression analysis involving economic factors reveals that the young are also the most responsive to economic factors. It also turns out that males are more mobile than females, corroborating the intuitively held view. In addition, females are far less responsive to economic factors than males. All in all, it appears that the classes that are the more mobile are also the classes that are more responsive to economic opportunities.

It goes without saying that results that were valid in California in the middle of this century may not be valid elsewhere or at other times. Whereas this lack of generality may be disappointing for those who seek to establish "laws" in the realm of social science, it may be taken as a challenge. Namely, if conditions are widely different in different regions or different times, one can surmise that there are geographic, social, or historic reasons for the differences. Thus the analysis brings us not to a theory but rather to the starting point of theoretical investigations. Its purpose is to bring certain facts into focus. At times, this can be done only through quite subtle mathematical analysis, which can in such circumstances be compared to an instrument of observation like the microscope.

MIGRATORY DISTANCE

Of particular interest in Markov chain models is the probability that a system currently in state s_i will move *for the first time* to state s_j on the nth step. These probabilities enter the calculation of mean first passage time; that is, the expectation of the number of steps it will take for the system to reach s_j.

Let the mean first passage time from s_i to s_j be denoted by m_{ij}. Then m_{ij} satisfies the following recursion equation:

$$m_{ij} = 1 + \sum p_{ik} m_{kj}, \qquad (11.30)$$

where the summation is over $k \neq j$.

The mean first passage times m_{ij} with $j \neq i$ provide us with a measure of "migratory distance" between pairs of regions. If m_{ij} is large, this means that the average time elapsed before region j will be visited for the first time by an individual from region i is long; hence that j is "far away" from i; if m_{ij} is small, this means that j is "near" i on the migratory distance scale.

Just as ordinary geographic distance can be expressed by the time it takes to get from one place to another, so migratory distance can be expressed in time units. Note, however, that migratory distance is not necessarily symmetric. The "distance" so defined from *i* to *j* is not necessarily equal to the distance from *j* to *i*.

One might assume that migratory distance is somehow related to geographic distance. Now we can test this hypothesis by examining correlations between migratory distances as calculated from the transition matrix via Equation 11.30 and geographic distances between corresponding regions. Again we take our data from California. Interregional distances will be defined as highway miles from county seat to county seat taken from five regions. The shortest distance was 48 miles, the longest 522 miles. Each correlation is shown for two periods, for two cohorts by race, and for two cohorts by age group in Table 11.3.

The hypothesis that migratory distance is somehow related to geographic distance is evidently not borne out by these data. When a move is made in California, it is just as likely to be to a faraway place as to a nearby place. Doubtless, the mobility conferred by the automobile is strongly reflected in this finding.

As we have seen, geographical distance enters as a significant influence in determining interregional migration flows. The fact that in the situation examined, migratory distance is essentially uncorrelated with geographical distance suggests migratory distance as another measure of "attractiveness" of one locality for the population of another.

It is expected that migratory distance undergoes changes in time and that for a given pair of localities it may be different for different subpopulations. Rogers (1968) has compared migratory distances (as calculated from migration data)

Table 11.3.   R: correlation Between Geographic and Migratory Distances Between Localities in California

Period	R
1935–1940	0.024
1955–1960	−0.012

Race	R
Whites	−0.015
Nonwhites	−0.047

Age	R
20–24	−0.014
65–69	−0.005

Source: Adapted from Rogers (1968).

among five regions of California, California as a whole, and the rest of the United States for 1935–1940 and for 1955–1960 separately for white and non-white populations, and separately for a young subpopulation (20–24 years) and an old one (65–69 years). On the basis of this comparison, several interesting findings emerge.

As expected, the migratory distances calculated for the later period are on the whole substantially smaller than those calculated for the earlier period, reflecting an increase in the geographical mobility of the population over 20 years. Note-worthy are the disproportionate changes in some migratory distances. During 1935–1940, for example, the migratory distance from Los Angeles to San Jose was four times that from Los Angeles to San Francisco. By 1955–1960, this ratio declined to 2:1. Even more striking are the findings on migratory distances for the nonwhite population. Rogers writes, "The non-white migrant distance between the San Francisco and the San Jose [areas], for example, is nine times the reverse distance and thirteen times the distance between San Francisco and the Los Angeles [areas]. This may be a reflection of the racial discrimination in San Jose's housing market."

As expected, migratory distances for the old group (65–69) are substantially larger than for the young group (20–24). However, the distances are similar in relative terms, indicating that while the young are much more mobile than the old, the patterns of their movements are about the same.

In sum, matrix analysis of demographic data can be utilized in both the pre-dictive and the analytic-descriptive mode. The growth operator is a tool of prognoses of both the size and the composition of a population on the basis of both vital statistics (births and deaths) and of migration flows.

It stands to reason that these prognoses should be made with caution, since they are essentially extrapolations from observed trends whose dynamics may change with time. In the context of an analytic-descriptive theory, matrix analysis serves to construct indices that tap the underlying structure of observed population shifts. Migration volumes alone do not present a clear picture because they depend on population sizes and geographic distances as revealed by regression analysis. Migratory distance appears to tap a more basic parameter related to the "attraction" that one locality exerts on the population of another.

Finally, matrix methods can also be utilized in the context of a normative theory by pointing out how interventions imposed on migration flows can modify the ultimate equilibrium distribution of population categories. The interested reader is referred to Rogers, 1968, Chapter 6.

NOTES

[1] In this chapter, $b(t)$ and $d(t)$ correspond, respectively, to $B(t)$ and $D(t)$ in Chapter 1.

[2] A nonsingular matrix is one whose determinant is not zero.

[3] If λ is an eigenvalue of G, the corresponding characteristic vector (or eigenvector) is the vector v that satisfies $Gv = \lambda v$.

[4]In representing the classical model of age distribution in Chapter 1, dynamics were not considered since the results referred only to equilibrium distributions. A. J. Lotka (1939) worked on the dynamics of the process. His approach was further developed by A. J. Coale (see Coale, 1972, Chapter 3).

[5]In models investigated by A. Rogers (1968), independent variables such as the "nonagicultural worker population" and so on are defined explicitly. The definitions are different in different models. Sometimes salaries of white collar workers are included in "wages," sometimes not. We omit the details because we are interested only in the general form of the models.

[6]J. Q. Stewart (1948), an early proponent of mathematical models of interacting populations, proposed a formula for "intensity of interaction" which he regarded as an analogue of the Law of Gravitation: $I_{ij} = p_i p_j / d_{ij}^{\gamma}$, where I_{ij} is the intensity of interaction, p_i and p_j the sizes of two populations, d_{ij} the distance between them, and γ is a parameter, usually observed to be between 1 and 3. The formula can be applied to migration rates between two population centers.

[7]If m_{ij} is proportional to the product of powers of two variables, log m_{ij} is a linear function of their logarithms.

[8]In fact, if the correlations between m_{ij} and u_i and between m_{ij} and u_j were significant, they might indicate that migration out of a region reduces unemployment in that region, and that migration into a region increases unemployment.

CHAPTER TWELVE

Individual Choice Behavior

Many models dealing with preferences among alternatives are based on an assumption that a person's preferences remain unchanged at least during the time of the investigation. Clearly, this need not be the case. The answer to the question, "Which do you prefer, x or y?" could well change from trial to trial.

This situation also occurs in experiments on discriminating magnitudes of stimuli. Data obtained from the question, "Which is larger (brighter, heavier), x or y?" are formally identical with those obtained from "Which do you prefer, x or y?" Inconsistencies can be observed in both kinds of data if the stimuli differ only slightly from each other. These inconsistencies can be used in operationally defining a "just discriminable difference" (as we have seen in Chapter 6), and the JND can be used in constructing a subjective scale of magnitude or of preference. Thus the methods used in discrimination experiments can be used in preference experiments.

It turns out, however, that in constructing mathematical models of preference, difficulties arise which as a rule do not arise in discrimination experiments. The reason is that in discrimination experiments, the model builder has at his disposal an objective (physical) scale of stimulus magnitudes which is often lacking in preference experiments.

In a typical discrimination experiment, the subject is confronted with two stimuli, one after the other. One is a standard stimulus, the other a variable one. The subject is to compare the two. It is assumed that the larger the variable stimulus is on an objective scale, the more frequently the subject will judge it to be the larger. Thus the subjective magnitude can be expected to be positively correlated with objective magnitude.

In preference experiments, there may be no objective magnitude scale on which the stimuli can be measured. For instance, a subject may be asked which of two geometric patterns he finds more pleasing. It would be desirable to deduce a subjective scale that would reflect his preferences via the frequencies of his responses and moreover to construct the strongest possible scale of this sort.

Without an objective scale, the problem is considerably more difficult. Before we attempt to construct a subjective scale, we must see whether such a scale exists; that is, whether certain minimal requirements for its existence are fulfilled.

In an experiment designed to answer this question, it is advisable to stack the cards *against* an affirmative answer. Then, if a positive answer can nevertheless be justified, we can also expect it under more favorable conditions.

To see this, suppose we are investigating a subject's preferences among a set of facial photographs, We could ask the subject to rank-order the photographs according to their attractiveness. This procedure would establish an ordinal scale of preference. But such an ordering would tell us little since the subject could submit a different ordering on another occasion. If we then conclude that his preferences have undergone a change, we do no more than describe our observations. We make no progress in discovering the subject's "actual" preference scale. Nevertheless, there may be such a scale that determines his choices, even though the choices on a particular occasion may be perturbed by "errors" or other accidental influences.

On the other hand, if the subject orders the photographs the same way on different occasions, we still cannot be sure that the ordering reflects his "real" preference scale. He may present the same orderings in order to appear consistent. If the first ordering did not reflect his "true" preference scale, neither did the subsequent ones. The errors that distorted his preference in the first ordering may have become fixated.

A frequently used procedure in preference experiments is *pairwise comparison*. All or sufficiently many pairs of stimuli from the given set are presented to the subject, who is asked to indicate which of the pair he prefers. If the same pair is presented several times separated by presentations of other pairs, we can expect inconsistencies. Nevertheless, the frequencies with which one member of a pair is preferred to the other may show consistencies which permit the derivation of a preference scale. If so, then a positive answer to the question of whether a preference scale can be assumed to exist can be justified, even though the cards had been stacked against it (by not inhibiting inconsistent answers.)

The mathematical problem is that of formulating necessary and/or sufficient conditions on the frequencies of indicated preferences in order to justify the construction of a preference scale.

THE CHOICE AXIOM

The situation to be examined is called a *choice experiment*. The subject is presented with a set of alternatives, of which he is to select one as the most preferred. Note that paired comparison is a special case of this situation; namely, where the set presented always consists of two alternatives.

We introduce the following notation. The set of all the alternatives used in a choice experiment will be called T. In each presentation, a subset $A \subset T$ is presented to the subject. It is assumed that the subject will *not* be consistent in his choices. When a given set A is presented several times, he will select sometimes one, sometimes another alternative as the most preferred. The relative frequency with which the subject specifies alternative $x \in A$ as the most preferred constitutes an estimate of the conditional probability $p_A(x)$; that is, the probability of choosing $x \in A$ when A is presented.

Accordingly, we write $p_T(A)$ for the probability that the alternative chosen as the most preferred when the whole set T is presented is an element of A. Thus we can write

$$p_T(A) = \sum_{x \in A} p_T(x) \tag{12.1}$$

Equation 12.1 is a consequence of the addition law of probability theory. If A is an event, the probability of A is expressed as the sum of the probabilities of the elementary events of which A is composed.

Let A and B be two subsets of T and $B \cap A$ their intersection (see p. 263). Then

$$p_T(B \mid A) = \frac{p_T(B \cap A)}{p_T(A)}. \tag{12.2}$$

In our choice experiment, the left side of Equation 12.2 is the conditional probability that when T is presented, the preferred alternative is an element of B, given that it is an element of A. The Choice Axiom asserts that

$$P_T(x \mid A) = p_A(x). \tag{12.3}$$

The left side of Equation 12.3 is estimated by the number of times $x \in A$ is chosen out of the number of times any alternative in A is chosen when T is presented. The right side is estimated by the number of times x is chosen out of the number of times A is presented.

The Choice Axiom[1] implies the following relations:

(i) $p_T(x) \neq 0 \Rightarrow p_A(x) \neq 0$.

(ii) $p_T(x) = 0$, $p_T(A) \neq 0 \Rightarrow p_A(x) = 0$.

(iii) $p_T(y) = 0$, $y \neq x \Rightarrow p_T(x) = p_{T-\{y\}}(x)$.

(iv) If $p_T(y) \neq 0$ for all $y \in T$, then $p_T(x) = p_A(x) p_T(A)$.

At first glance, these relations may appear to be self-evident. However, they are not tautologies since they can be empirically falsified. For instance, (i) asserts that if x is ever chosen as the most preferred alternative when T is presented, it will be sometimes chosen when any subset of T is presented of which x is an element. However, it may happen that a subject will sometimes choose x when a specific other alternative is included in the set presented but will never choose x when that alternative is not included in the set presented.

Relation (iii) asserts that if $y \neq x$ is never chosen when the whole set T is presented, then the probability of choosing x is not affected if y is deleted from T. As is well known, this is not always the case. Suppose the alternatives are political parties in an election. Let x and y be "moderate" parties and z an "extreme" one. A voter's preference oscillates between x and y when these are the only parties on the ballot. Let $T = \{x, y, z\}$ and $A = \{x, y\}$, so that $A = T - \{z\}$. When A is presented, the voter chooses x with probability $p_A(x) < 1$. When, however, the "extreme" party z is on the ballot, he may *always* vote for x. Thus although $p_T(z) = 0$ (the voter never votes for z), we have nevertheless $p_{T-\{z\}}(x) < 1$, $p_T(x) = 1 \neq p_{T-\{z\}}(x)$, which contradicts (iii).

If A contains only two alternatives x and y, we will write $p(x, y)$ for $p_A(x)$. That is, $p(x, y)$ is the probability that x is preferred to y in a paired comparison.

An important consequence of the Choice Axiom establishes necessary and sufficient conditions for the existence of a preference scale with certain simple properties.

Let $p_T(x) \neq 0$ for all $x \in T$, and let the Choice Axiom hold for all x and for all $A \subset T$. Then

$$p(x, z) = \frac{p(x, y)p(y, z)}{p(x, y)p(y, z) + p(z, y)p(y, x)} \tag{12.4}$$

$$p_T(x) = \frac{1}{1 + \Sigma' p(y, x)/p(x, y)} \tag{12.5}$$

where the summation is over all $y \in T$, $y \neq x$.

Proof: By consequence (iv) of the Choice Axiom, we have

$$p_A(x) = \frac{p_T(x)}{p_T(A)}. \tag{12.6}$$

If $A = \{x, y\}$, $p_A(x) = p(x, y)$. Substituting into Equation 12.6, we get

$$p(x, y) = p_T(x)/p_T(A). \tag{12.7}$$

$$p(y, x) = p_T(y)/p_T(A). \tag{12.8}$$

Therefore

$$\frac{p(x, y)}{p(y, x)} = \frac{p_T(x)}{p_T(y)}. \tag{12.9}$$

Furthermore, we have the identity

$$1 = \frac{p_T(x)p_T(y)p_T(z)}{p_T(y)p_T(z)p_T(x)}, \tag{12.10}$$

which, in view of Equation 12.9, can be written as

$$1 = \frac{p(x, y)p(y, z)p(z, x)}{p(y, x)p(z, y)p(x, z)}. \tag{12.11}$$

Substituting $1 - p(x, z)$ for $p(z, x)$ in Equation 12.11 and solving for $p(x, z)$, we obtain Equation 12.4.

To prove Equation 12.5, we note that in view of Equation 12.9, we have

$$1 + \sum' \frac{p(y, x)}{p(x, y)} = \frac{p_T(x)}{p_T(x)} + \sum' \frac{p_T(y)}{p_T(x)}, \tag{12.12}$$

where the summations are over all $y \neq x$. The right side of Equation 12.12 can be written as

$$\frac{1}{p_T(x)} \sum p_T(y) = \frac{1}{p_T(x)}, \tag{12.13}$$

where the summation is over all $y \in T$ and therefore equal to 1. Substituting Equation 12.13 into the left side of Equation 12.12 and solving for $p_T(x)$, we obtain Equation 12.5.

Using Equation 12.11 we have

$$\frac{p(x, y)p(y, z)}{p(y, x)p(z, y)} = \frac{p(x, z)}{p(z, x)}. \tag{12.14}$$

If Equation 12.14 holds for all x, y, and z in T, a preference scale can be constructed on the basis of paired comparisons. Let $u(s) = k$, where s is an arbitrarily chosen alternative in T and k an arbitrary positive constant. We set

$$u(x) = \frac{kp(x, s)}{p(s, x)}. \tag{12.15}$$

Then, in view of Equations 12.14 and 12.15,

$$\frac{u(x)}{u(y)} = \frac{kp(x, s)p(s, y)}{p(s, x)kp(y, s)} = \frac{p(x, y)}{1 - p(x, y)}, \tag{12.16}$$

where we have substituted $1 - p(x, y)$ for $p(y, x)$. Solving for $p(x, y)$, we get

$$p(x, y) = \frac{u(x)}{u(x) + u(y)}. \tag{12.17}$$

In defining $u(x)$, we have essentially assigned a "utility" u to each alternative in T. For any two alternatives x and y, $u(x) > u(y)$ if and only if $p(x, y) > p(y, x)$; that is, if and only if x is preferred to y more frequently than vice versa in a paired comparison. Further, if $u(x) > u(y)$ and $u(y) > u(z)$, then $u(x) > u(z)$. That is, $u(x)$ reflects a transitive preference relation and therefore a bona fide ordering of the alternatives. Moreover, this scale is stronger than an ordinal scale. It is, in fact, a *ratio* scale, which permits only a similarity transformation $u' = au$, where a is a positive constant that determines the choice of a unit.

As soon as the preference scale $u(x)$ is established on the basis of paired comparisons, the probability of choosing an alternative x from the set T is given by

$$p_T(x) = \frac{u(x)}{\sum_{y \in T} u(y)}. \tag{12.18}$$

Now we can observe the frequency with which x is chosen and compare it with $p_T(x)$, predicted by Equation 12.18. In this way, the Choice Axiom can be tested.

Furthermore, it must be kept in mind that the Choice Axiom applies only to situations with sufficient ambiguity of choices; that is, when every alternative x is chosen with some finite probability $p(x)$ $(0 < p(x) < 1)$. In this way, inconsistencies of choices become an advantage rather than a disadvantage. To be sure, if choices are perfectly consistent, an ordinal scale of utility can be established but no stronger scale without further information, whereas on the basis of probabilistic choices, a stronger ratio scale can be established if the Choice Axiom is corroborated[2]. Below we will examine situations in which the Choice Axiom is not corroborated.

RANK ORDERING OF ALTERNATIVES

We turn to the situation where the subject orders the entire set of alternatives from most preferred to least preferred. In doing this, she gives more information than when she chooses a single alternative from the set. Her ordering can be interpreted as the designation of the "best" alternative, of the "second best" (that is, the one that would be best if the first one were unavailable), and of the third best (which would be best if the first two were unavailable), and so on.

From this ordering we can draw a probabilistic consequence. Let the ordering of the n alternatives in T be represented by $\rho = (\rho_1, \rho_2, \ldots, \rho_n)$, where ρ_i is the alternative with rank i. We assume

$$p(\rho) = p_T(\rho_1)p_{T'}(\rho_2)p_{T''}(\rho_3) \ldots p(\rho_{n-1}, \rho_n), \qquad (12.19)$$

where $T' = T - \{\rho_1\}$, $T'' = T' - \{\rho_2\}$, and so on.

The left side of Equation 12.19 is the probability that the subject will produce the ordering ρ. The first factor on the right is the probability that ρ_1 will be chosen if the entire set is presented; the second is the probability that ρ_2 will be chosen if ρ_1 is deleted from T, and so on.

Like the Choice Axiom expressed in Equation 12.3, the relation expressed in Equation 12.19 may be empirically corroborated or it may not.

Let us now examine a possible relation between probabilities of choices in paired comparisons and probabilities of producing rank orderings of alternatives. To fix ideas, suppose $T = \{x, y, z\}$. Let $p(xyz)$, $p(yzx)$, and so on denote the probabilities of producing the corresponding rank orderings. Now the probability that in a given rank ordering x precedes y is

$$p(x; y) = p(xyz) + p(xzy) + p(zxy). \qquad (12.20)$$

It is the probability that x is preferred to y in a rank ordering experiment. On the basis of repeated paired comparisons, we can obtain another estimate of the probability that x is preferred to y. It may turn out that these two estimates are significantly different from each other. This discrepancy need not reflect the subject's inconsistency. To see this, suppose the subject uses the following procedure to determine her rank ordering. First she arbitrarily chooses a pair of alternatives; that is, any of the three pairs with probability $\frac{1}{3}$. Then she orders this pair one way or the other with a certain probability which reflects the degree of her preference in this paired comparison. Next, she chooses an alternative from this pair with probability $\frac{1}{2}$ and compares it with the third alternative. The comparison may or may not lead to a rank ordering. Suppose, for example, $\{x, y\}$ is originally chosen and x on that occasion was preferred to y. If next y was chosen and was preferred to z, the ordering (xyz) was produced on that occasion. If, however, x was chosen and was preferred to z, we obtain $x > y$, $x > z$, but the preference relation between y and z has not yet been established. In that case, y and z are compared. If $y > z$, then (xyz) is established; if $z > y$, then (xzy) is the rank ordering since we already have $x > z$.

On the basis of this procedure, the probabilities of the rank orderings can be expressed in terms of the probabilities of preference in paired comparisons and vice versa. It turns out that the paired comparison preferences are given by

$$p(x, y) = \frac{p(xyz) - p(zxy)}{p(xyz) - p(zxy) + p(yxz) - p(zyx)}, \tag{12.21}$$

which does not correspond to Equation 12.20 (see Luce and Suppes, 1965). Thus we see that the relations among choice probabilities in paired comparisons and probabilities of rank orderings depend on the procedure used by the subject in determining the latter. The same holds for the relations between the probabilities of choosing single alternatives from any presented set and the probabilities of rank orderings. The following relation may seem to be "natural":

$$p_A(x) = \sum_{R(x,y)} p(\rho). \tag{12.22}$$

The left side of Equation 12.22 is the probability that $x \in A$ is chosen when $A \subset T$ is presented. The right side is the sum of the probabilities of the rank orderings of T in which x "outranks" (precedes) all the other alternatives in A. Clearly, Equation 12.22 is a generalization of the right side of Equation 12.20. Now the question arises under what conditions the "natural" relation expressed in Equation 12.22 is satisfied. In other words, what model of choice behavior implies the validity of that relation and/or is itself implied by it?

We have already discussed one model of choice behavior based on the assumption that the subject is characterized by a fixed utility function $u(x)$ on the alternatives of T. The variations in his choices when the same set is presented are attributed to accidental errors in decisions based on the utilities. This model is called the *strict utility model* because it is based on the assumption that the subject's "real" utilities are fixed.

In contrast, the *random utility model* presupposes statistical fluctuations of the utilities themselves, so that the utility of an alternative x at a given moment is a random variable $U(x)$. The ordered set $U = (U(x), U(y), \ldots, U(z))$ represents an n-dimensional random variable or a *random vector*. Changes in the components of this vector induce changes in the joint probability $\Pr[U(x) \leqslant x, U(y) \leqslant y,$

$\ldots, U(z) \leqslant z]$ in accordance with some probability law. Nothing is said in this definition about the independence or interdependence of the components of U.

Let $y \in Y \subset T$. The probability that the utility of $x \in Y$ when Y is presented is not smaller than that of any $y \in Y$ can be expressed as follows:

$$\Pr[U(x) \geqslant U(y), y \in Y] = \int_{-\infty}^{\infty} \Pr[U(x) = t, U(y) \leqslant t, y \in Y] dt. \quad (12.23)$$

If the components of U are independent random variables, the right side of Equation 12.23 reduces to

$$\int_{-\infty}^{\infty} \Pr[U(x) = t] \prod_y{}' \Pr[U(y) \leqslant t] dt, \quad (12.24)$$

where the product is taken over all $y \in Y, y \neq x$.

Does it make any difference whether inconsistent choices are attributed to accidental deviations of choice (as assumed in the fixed utility model) or to accidental fluctuations of utility (as assumed in the random utility model)? Evidently it does, because a strict utility model can always be represented by a random utility model in which the utilities are independent random variables, but a random utility model cannot in general be represented by a fixed utility model. Thus the random utility model is a more general model. It is further shown that in a strict utility model, the relations expressed in Equations 12.19 and 12.22 always hold (see Luce and Suppes, 1965, p. 338; p. 354).

Now we will deduce a "paradoxical" result which points to the necessity of carefully examining the axiomatic foundations of stochastic models of preference. Suppose we have a random utility model of choice behavior and that a subject characterized by this model produces rank ordering with probability

$$\Pr(\rho) = \Pr[U(\rho_1) > U(\rho_2) > \ldots > U(\rho_n)], \quad (12.25)$$

where ρ_i is the alternative of rank i.

Suppose further that the *same* random utility model governs the subject's choices when she is asked to rank order the alternatives from worst to best. (That is, the probability law governing the vector U is the same in both situations.) If $p^*(\rho)$ is the probability of an ordering which is a "mirror image" of ρ, we have

$$p^*(\rho) = \Pr[U(\rho_1) < U(\rho_2) < \ldots < U(\rho_n)]. \quad (12.26)$$

Next we define ρ^* as a mirror image of ρ; that is,

$$\rho_1^* = \rho_n, \rho_2^* = \rho_{n-1}, \ldots, \rho_n^* = \rho_1. \quad (12.27)$$

Equations 12.26 and 12.27 imply

$$p^*(\rho^*) = p(\rho). \quad (12.28)$$

For the special case of two alternatives, we have, accordingly,

$$p(x, y) = p^*(y, x). \quad (12.29)$$

Finally, suppose the random utility model characterizing our subject is also a fixed utility model. This is the case if Equations 12.19 and 12.22 are both satisfied. Moreover, if the same random utility model governs both rank orderings from best to worst and from worst to best, then Equation 12.19 holds both for the probabilities $p(\rho)$ and $p^*(\rho)$:

$$p(\rho) = p_T(\rho_1)p_{T'}(\rho_2) \cdots p(\rho_{n-1}, \rho_n) \tag{12.30}$$

$$p^*(\rho) = p_T^*(\rho_1)p_{T'}^*(\rho_2) \cdots p^*(\rho_{n-1}, \rho_n), \tag{12.31}$$

where T' and so on have the same meanings as in Equation 12.19.

Since we have assumed that the model is a strict utility model, we must assume the existence of a utility function $u(x)$ on the alternatives of T. Since the unit of utility can be chosen arbitrarily, we can assume without loss of generality that $\sum u(x) = 1$.

Choose any $x, y \in T$, and let ρ be the rank ordering of T, where $x = \rho_1$ and $y = \rho_2$. Let σ be the rank ordering in which $\sigma_1 = y$ and $\sigma_2 = x$, while $\sigma_i = \rho_i$ for $i = 3, \ldots, n$. That is, σ is obtained from ρ by interchanging x and y. In view of Equation 12.30, we obtain

$$\frac{p(\rho)}{p(\sigma)} = \frac{p_T(x)p_{T'}(y)p_{T''}(\rho_3) \cdots}{p_T(y)p_{T'}(x)p_{T''}(\rho_3) \cdots}, \tag{12.32}$$

where in the numerator on the right, $T' = T - \{x\}$, $T'' = T - \{x, y\}$, and so on, while in the denominator, $T' = T - \{y\}$, $T'' = T - \{x, y\}$, and so on. Canceling identical factors from the numerator and denominator on the right side of Equation 12.32, we obtain, in view of the assumption that the model is one of strict utility,

$$\frac{p(\rho)}{p(\sigma)} = \frac{u(x)u(y)/[\sum u(z)][\sum' u(x)]}{u(y)u(x)/[\sum u(z)][\sum' u(z)]}, \tag{12.33}$$

where the summations $\sum$ are over all $z \in T$, $\sum'$ in the numerator over all $z \neq x$, and in the denominator over all $z \neq y$. Since we have chosen our unit of utility so that $\sum u(z) = 1$, we can substitute $1 - u(x)$ for $\sum'(z)$ in the numerator and $1 - u(y)$ in the denominator. Thus we can write the right side of Equation 12.32 as

$$\frac{1 - u(y)}{1 - u(x)}. \tag{12.34}$$

Now let us apply this procedure to ρ^* and σ^*:

$$\frac{p^*(\rho^*)}{p^*(\sigma^*)} = \frac{p_T^*(\rho_1^*)p_{T'}^*(\rho_2^*) \cdots p^*(\rho_{n-1}^*, \rho_n^*)}{p_T^*(\sigma_1^*)p_{T'}^*(\sigma_2^*) \cdots p^*(\sigma_{n-1}^*, \sigma_n^*)} \tag{12.35}$$

where in the numerator $T' = T - \{\rho_1^*\}$ and $T'' = T - \{\rho_1^*, \rho_2^*\}$, and in the denominator, $T' = T - \{\sigma_1^*\}$, and so on. But $\rho_1^* = \rho_n$, $\rho_2^* = \rho_{n-1}$, and so on; $\sigma^* = \sigma_n$, $\sigma_2^* = \sigma_{n-1}$, and so on. Therefore the right side of Equation 12.35 can be written as

$$\frac{p_T^*(\rho_n)p_T^*\cdot(\rho_{n-1})\ldots p^*(y, x)}{p_T^*(\sigma_n)p_T^*\cdot(\sigma_{n-1})\ldots p^*(x, y)},$$
(12.36)

where now $T' = T - \{\rho_n\}$, $T'' = T - \{\rho_n, \rho_{n-1}\}$, and so on in the numerator, and $T' = T - \{\sigma_n\}$ and so on in the denominator. Again canceling identical factors, we obtain

$$\frac{p^*(y, x)}{p^*(x, y)} = \frac{p(x, y)}{p(y, x)} = \frac{u(x)}{u(y)}.$$
(12.37)

In view of Equation 12.29, we have

$$\frac{1 - u(y)}{1 - u(x)} = \frac{u(x)}{u(y)}$$
(12.38)

or

$$[1 - u(y)]u(y) = [1 - u(x)]u(x).$$
(12.39)

The left side of Equation 12.39 is independent of x; the right side, of y. Therefore $u(x)$ must be constant for all x.

Our assumptions have led to a conclusion which certainly cannot be expected to be corroborated empirically: presented with any set of alternatives, the subject must be indifferent among them. H. D. Block and J. Marschak (1960), who first deduced this result, viewed it as a strong refutation of the strict utility model. However, as R. D. Luce and P. Suppes (1965, p. 358) remark, Block and Marschak did not state explicitly that the *same* random utility model underlies both rank orderings ρ and ρ^*. Let us examine this assumption more closely.

To avoid misunderstanding, we must keep in mind that the above stochastic models do not apply to situations where the choices can be regarded as certain. For instance, if x and y are different amounts of money, we can assume that (at least in our society) almost every one will prefer the larger amount to the smaller and will rank order the alternatives accordingly. In this situation, the subject will remain consistent. But these situations were explicitly excluded from those to which the strict utility model applies. We must therefore consider only those situations where probabilities of choices and of rank orderings are all smaller than 1.

The weakest point in the above model appears to be the assumption that the same random utility model underlies both rank orderings from best to worst and from worst to best. While the ordering from best to worst can be interpreted easily, the reverse ordering cannot, at least not so as to satisfy Equation 12.19. The former rank ordering can be interpreted as follows: "If I can choose from the entire set T, I will choose ρ_1; if I cannot have ρ_1, I will choose ρ_2, and so on.

Can the rank ordering from worst to best be interpreted in the same way? In what way can the naming of the worst alternative be interpreted as a "choice"? The following interpretation comes to mind. Let the n alternatives be n possible punishments to be meted out to the subject, whereby the actual punishment to be meted out is to be chosen equiprobably from the set. The subject may eliminate one of the punishments from the set. He can be expected to choose the worst punishment to be eliminated. Now the second worst punishment must be determined. The experimenter can proceed in two different ways:

1. She can inform the subject that the worst punishment will not be applied, and now the subject can eliminate another punishment.
2. She can inform the subject that the worst punishment cannot be eliminated, so the subject must indicate another punishment to be eliminated.

We therefore have two different operationalizations of the rank ordering from worst to best, and neither is necessarily equivalent to the operationalization of the rank ordering from best to worst. Therefore the formalism based on the assumption expressed in Equations 12.30 and 12.31, which in turn stems from applying the same random utility model to both rank orderings, cannot be justified.

For the time being, therefore, the contention that the strict utility model cannot represent "reality" has been related to other tacit assumptions incorporated in the deduction, and a refutation of the strict utility model on theoretical grounds cannot be regarded as definitive. In another context, however, the shortcomings of the strict utility model will be brought out more directly.

DISTINGUISHABILITY OF ALTERNATIVES

Suppose a music lover's utility of x (a recording of Beethoven's *Eroica Symphony*) is equal to his utility of z (a recording of Debussy's *La Mer*). The strict utility model predicts that this person, given a choice between the two records, will choose either with equal probability. Suppose now he is offered a choice between three records, x and y being two copies of the same recording of *Eroica* and z a recording of *La Mer*. Then, since $u(x) = u(y) = u(z)$, he should, according to the strict utility model, choose any of the three with probability $\frac{1}{3}$. It is, however, more reasonable to expect that the person will first decide whether he wants the Beethoven or the Debussy. If he decides in favor of Debussy, he will choose it; otherwise, he will choose one of the Beethoven records with equal probability. According to this procedure, he will choose Debussy with probability $\frac{1}{2}$ or either of the Beethovens with probability $\frac{1}{4}$, in contradiction to the Choice Axiom.

To take into account situations of this sort, a new concept must be introduced into a model of choice behavior, namely, distinguishability of alternatives. Alternatives that cannot be distinguished are pooled into a single alternative, and the probability of choosing this pooled alternative is distributed among the alternatives that compose it. More generally, the degree of distinguishability enters the determination of choice probabilities.

SIMPLE SCALABILITY

An essential idea underlying the Choice Axiom is that of *simple scalability* (Krantz, 1964). As has been said, if the Choice Axiom is satisfied, a utility can be assigned to each alternative $x \in T$. The probability of choosing $x \in A$ when $A \subset T$ is presented is then given by

$$p_A(x) = \frac{u(x)}{\sum_{y \in A} u(y)}. \qquad (12.40)$$

This model is a special case of a class of models in which

$$p_A(x) = F_A[u(x), \ldots, u(z)], \qquad (12.41)$$

where $x, \ldots, z$ are elements of A, and F_A is a function strictly increasing in its first argument and strictly decreasing in the remaining arguments. That is to say, if the utility of x increases while the utilities of the other alternatives remain constant, the probability of choosing x should increase. If the utility of an alternative other than x increases while the remaining utilities remain constant, the probability of choosing x should decrease. It is easy to see that Equation 12.40 is a special case of Equation 12.41 because Equation 12.40 is in accord with the definition of F_A.

In this respect, the postulated relation between choice probabilities seems to be convincing. If no other assumptions are made regarding the function F_A, it is difficult to imagine how the relation expressed in Equation 12.41 can be refuted. Nevertheless, our expectations in the situation with the choice among the three records are incompatible with simple scalability, as we will now show.

In spite of its generality, simple scalability has rather strong consequences. For example, let x and y be any two alternatives in A. Simple scalability implies that if $p(x, y) > \frac{1}{2}$, then $p_A(x) > p_A(y)$, provided $p_A(y) \neq 0$. We note that A is an arbitrary subset of T. Therefore the preference ordering between x and y must be independent of the set presented of which both are elements. This condition is called the principle of *independence from irrelevant alternatives*. We will see below the consequences of this principle in other decision situations. In our example with the records, we have seen that this principle can be violated. When three records are presented, each Beethoven record is expected to be chosen with probability $\frac{1}{4}$, whereas it is expected to be chosen with probability $\frac{1}{2}$ when the Debussy record is the only other choice. Thus we have $p_T(z) > p_T(x)$, whereas $p(x, z) = \frac{1}{2}$, in contradiction to simple scalability.

ELIMINATION BY ASPECTS

In what follows, we will examine the so-called *Elimination by Aspects* (EBA) model, which is not a simple scalability model. It illustrates the necessity of taking distinguishability of alternatives into account (see Tversky, 1972).

Consider the following method of choosing among alternatives. Let the alternatives be candidates for a position, and assume that the candidate to be chosen must fulfill certain requirements. For instance, she should be between 30 and 40 years of age, married with at least two years of experience, and so on. One way to choose a candidate is to begin by excluding all those who do not fulfill all the requirements. This procedure can lead to any of three possible results: (1) only one candidate fulfills all the requirements; (2) several candidates fulfill all the requirements; (3) no candidate is qualified.

A decision is clear only in the first case. In the second case, the problem arises of choosing among the qualified candidates. In the third case, the position cannot be filled. If it is important to fill the position, the requirements might be relaxed in the hope of finding a candidate who fulfills the smaller list. This procedure presents the problem of ranking the criteria according to their importance, for it is clearly desirable to drop the least important criterion. If a qualified candidate still cannot be found, the next least important criterion can be dropped, and so on.

The ranking of criteria is the basic idea of the Elimination by Aspects model. The procedure involved in it is somewhat different from the one just described. Instead of criteria, candidates are eliminated. Furthermore, criteria according to which candidates are judged are chosen probabilistically, where the probability of choosing a criterion reflects its relative importance.

To illustrate the method, let x, y, and z be the candidates, and suppose the qualifications are ranked in the order of their importance as follows:

α: Experience
β: Personality
γ: Willingness to travel
δ: Formal education
ε: State of health
ζ: Appearance
θ: Family status

In a deterministic choice procedure, a candidate without the required experience would be eliminated immediately. From those remaining, a candidate with an unsatisfactory personality would be eliminated, and so on. In a stochastic procedure, each criterion to be applied is chosen by a chance device, in which the probabilities are weighted according to the rank of the criteria.

To fix ideas, suppose only x has the requisite experience, only y has the right personality, and only z will travel. Furthermore, suppose only x and y have the required education, only x and z are in good health, and only y and z are attractive. Finally, suppose that all three are married. The situation is represented as follows:

$$x' = \{\alpha, \delta, \varepsilon, \theta\}$$
$$y' = \{\beta, \delta, \zeta, \theta\} \qquad\qquad (12.42)$$
$$z' = \{\gamma, \varepsilon, \zeta, \theta\}.$$

Here x', y', and z' represent sets of criteria satisfied respectively by x, y, and z.

We note that family status (θ) plays no role in the choice of a candidate because this criterion is fulfilled (or perhaps not fulfilled) by all three. Therefore θ need not be considered in the model.

The choice of a candidate depends on the particular criterion or criteria applied. Recall that the criterion to be applied is chosen probabilistically. If α happens to be chosen, then y and z will be eliminated automatically, so that x will get the job. If β happens to be chosen, the successful candidate will be y; if γ, then z.

If the criterion to be applied first is δ, then only z will be eliminated. Now a decision must be made between x and y. The criteria that distinguish between these two are α, ε, β, and ζ. One of these is now chosen (again probabilistically, with corresponding probability). If α or ε is chosen, x wins; otherwise, y.

On the basis of the weights assigned to the criteria, we can calculate the probabilities that any of the three candidates will be chosen. These weights are represented by $u(\alpha)$, $u(\beta)$, . . . , $u(\zeta)$. Note that x can be chosen as a result of three different sequences of events: (1) if α is applied first; (2) if δ is applied first, then α; (3) if ε is applied first, then α. Thus we obtain for the probability that x is chosen

$$p_T(x) = \frac{u(\alpha) + u(\delta)p(x, y) + u(\varepsilon)p(x, z)}{K}, \qquad (12.43)$$

where $p(x, y)$ is the probability that x is chosen over y and $p(x, z)$ that x is chosen over z, and $K = u(\alpha) + u(\beta) + u(\gamma) + u(\varepsilon) + u(\zeta)$. It remains to determine $p(x, y)$ and $p(x, z)$. Since in comparing x with y, α, β, ε, and ζ are the deciding criteria, and since x is chosen over y if either α or ε is applied, we have

$$p(x, y) = \frac{u(\alpha) + u(\varepsilon)}{u(\alpha) + u(\beta) + u(\varepsilon) + u(\zeta)}. \qquad (12.44)$$

Similarly, we have

$$p(x, z) = \frac{u(\alpha) + u(\delta)}{u(\alpha) + u(\gamma) + u(\delta) + u(\zeta)}. \qquad (12.45)$$

Substituting Equations 12.44 and 12.45 into Equation 12.43, we obtain

$$p_T(x) = \frac{1}{K}\left\{ u(\alpha) + \frac{u(\delta)[u(\alpha) + u(\varepsilon)]}{u(\alpha) + u(\beta) + u(\varepsilon) + u(\zeta)} + \frac{u(\varepsilon)[u(\alpha) + u(\delta)]}{u(\alpha) + u(\gamma) + u(\delta) + u(\zeta)} \right\}. \qquad (12.46)$$

Intuitively, we judge the degree of similarity between two alternatives by the number of features they have in common. The EBA model assigns weights to these features (aspects). The weights are assumed to be additive. In this way, a total weight can be assigned to a set of alternatives which is the sum of the weights of the aspects that these alternatives have in common and which distinguish them from alternatives not in the set. In particular, let A be a subset of T and $\tilde{A}$ the set of *aspects* which characterize every alternative in A and only these. Note the different meanings of A and $\tilde{A}$. A is a set of alternatives x, y, and so on. $\tilde{A}$ is the set of aspects α_1, α_2, and so on which uniquely characterize the alternatives in A.

The sum of the weights $\sum u(\alpha_j)$ $(\alpha_j \in \tilde{A})$ will be denoted by $U(\tilde{A})$. Thus $U(\tilde{A})$ is a sort of utility. It must, however, be distinguished from the utilities of the alternatives. (The latter do not enter into the EBA model). $U(\tilde{A})$ denotes the relative weight of the set $\tilde{A}$; that is, the importance of the aspects that are the elements of $\tilde{A}$.

In our example, $U(\{\tilde{x}\}) = u(\alpha)$, $U(\{\widetilde{x, y}\}) = u(\delta)$, and so on. Now we can write Equation 12.43 as

$$p_T(x) = \frac{U(\{\tilde{x}\}) + U(\{\widetilde{x, y}\})p(x, y) + U(\{\widetilde{x, z}\})p(x, z)}{U(\{\tilde{x}\}) + U(\{\tilde{y}\}) + U(\{\widetilde{x, z}\}) + U(\{\widetilde{y, z}\})}. \qquad (12.47)$$

In view of Equation 12.44, we can write

$$p(x, y) = \frac{U(\{\tilde{x}\}) + U(\{\widetilde{x, z}\})}{U(\{\tilde{x}\}) + U(\{\tilde{y}\}) + U(\{\widetilde{x, y}\}) + U(\{\widetilde{z, y}\})} \qquad (12.48)$$

and Equation 12.45 as

$$p(x, z) = \frac{U(\{\tilde{x}\}) + U(\{\widetilde{x, y}\})}{U(\{\tilde{x}\}) + U(\{\tilde{z}\}) + U(\{\widetilde{x, y}\}) + U(\{\widetilde{z, y}\})}. \qquad (12.49)$$

Substituting Equations 12.48 and 12.49 into Equation 12.47, we obtain an expression for $p_T(x)$ in which the aspects that specify specific alternatives do not appear. The probability of choosing x is expressed only in terms of weights which represent *any aspects* that characterize the subsets of T.

In applying the EBA model to an experimental situation, these weights become the parameters of the model, which can be estimated from the data. The method can be generalized to sets with any number of alternatives.

Let us return to the example with the records. Assume now that the two recordings of *Eroica* are different. One is conducted by Ozawa, the other by Karajan. Our music lover likes the two recordings equally well and thus assigns the same utility to each. Now the two recordings are distinguishable, but clearly they are more similar to each other than either is to the Debussy recording. For simplicity, assume the two Beethoven records have some aspects in common, but neither has any aspects in common with the Debussy record.

Now let $U(\{\tilde{x}\}) = U(\{\tilde{y}\}) = a$. That is, aspects that *uniquely* characterize the Ozawa and Karajan recordings respectively are assigned the same weight. Furthermore, let $U(\{x, y\}) = b$; that is, the aspects that the two Beethoven recordings (but not the Debussy) have in common are assigned weight b. When only *one* of the Beethoven records is compared with the Debussy record, then the weight of the former must be $a + b$, since it has aspects with weights a and b (which, recall, were assumed to be additive). According to our assumption, the person is indifferent between Beethoven and Debussy in a paired comparison. Therefore, the aspect that uniquely characterizes the Debussy record must have the same weight: $U(\{\tilde{z}\}) = a + b$.

Applying the EBA model, we have

$$p(x, y) = \frac{a}{2a} = \frac{1}{2}.$$

$$p(z, x) = p(z, y) = \frac{a+b}{2(a+b)} = \frac{1}{2}. \qquad (12.50)$$

Equation 12.50 reflects the person's indifference in all paired comparisons. In view of Equation 12.47, we obtain

$$p_T(z) = \frac{a+b}{3a+2b} > \frac{a+b(a/2a)}{3a+2b} = p_T(x) = p_T(y). \qquad (12.51)$$

Thus when all three records are presented, the probability of choosing Debussy is larger than that of choosing Beethoven. Moreover, this probability depends on the degree of similarity between the two Beethoven records. If the two records are not distinguishable, $a = 0$ (since a represents the *unique* characteristics of each record compared with the other). In this case, $p_T(z) = \frac{1}{2}$, as we have concluded in our hypothetical experiment. If the two Beethoven records have no characteristics in common, $b = 0$ and $p_T(x) = p_T(y) = p_T(z) = \frac{1}{3}$, in accordance with the Choice Axiom.

AN EXPERIMENTAL TEST OF THE EBA MODEL

So far we have discussed a hypothetical experiment (Gedanken-experiment). We now turn to a real experiment designed to test the EBA model (see Tversky, 1972).

The subjects were Israeli high school students aged 16–18. Three choice experiments were performed. In one the alternatives were random patterns of dots of different areas and different densities. The task was to choose the pattern with the largest number of dots. The second experiment was in the form of a gamble (p, w), where p was the probability of winning an amount w. The third experiment involved a choice among three applicants to a college differing in intelligence and motivation. On each trial, the choice was among alternatives x, y, and z, where x and y were more similar to each other than either was to z.

Eight subjects participated in all three experiments in 12 one-hour sessions, in which each trial was repeated several times in random sequence. Thus every subject was presented with the same choice in each experiment several times. The specific parameters were varied with each presentation to reduce the effect of memory. Choices were made both in paired comparisons and among all three alternatives. In this way frequencies of choices of each kind could be compared.

Now the Choice Axiom predicts the following relations among the choice probabilities:

$$p(x, z) = \frac{p_T(x)}{p_T(x) + p_T(z)} \qquad (12.52)$$

$$p(y, z) = \frac{p_T(y)}{p_T(y) + p_T(z)}. \tag{12.53}$$

On the other hand, the EBA model implies that the left sides of Equations 12.52 and 12.53 should be larger than the right sides because adding y (similar to x) to the pair $\{x, z\}$ or x (similar to y) to the pair $\{y, z\}$ should reduce the likelihood of choosing x (or y) from the three.

The results showed that the estimated values of $p(x, z)$ and $p(y, z)$ were indeed significantly larger than those of $p_T(x)/[p_T(x) + p_T(z)]$ and of $p_T(y)/[p_T(y) + p_T(z)]$ in experiments 2 and 3, but the differences were not significant in experiment 1.

Both the positive and negative results are interesting. They suggest the conjecture that in the choice of games and of applicants some procedure involving elimination by aspects was involved, but not in the choice of dot patterns. An explanation comes to mind. In comparing games, two prominent aspects can be distinguished; namely, the amount to be won (w) and the probability of winning it (p). According to the EBA model, which of these aspects will serve as the more probable criterion of choice depends on the weights assigned to them. Greedy optimists may be more inclined to compare amounts to be won; cautious pessimists, the probabilities of winning. Similar considerations apply to the choice among applicants. Intelligence and motivation are salient aspects. In contrast, it is far less likely that an individual asked to estimate the number of dots in a random pattern will single out the two aspects—area and density. More likely, he will try to estimate the number of dots directly. Tversky conjectures that the simple scaling model is more suited to choices determined by a single aspect than those involving more than one. The reverse is true for the EBA model.

As we have seen, the results of Tversky's experiments discorroborate the Choice Axiom in two of the three experiments. Now let us see how well the EBA model fits all three. (An agreement between a Choice Axiom model and data does not preclude an agreement with an EBA model because the former is a special case of the latter.)

The simplest assumption suggested by the EBA model is that x and y have some aspects in common, but neither has any in common with z. The assumption implies $U(\{\widehat{x, z}\}) = U(\{\widehat{y, z}\}) = 0$; $U(\{\widehat{x, y}\}) = d$; $U(\{\tilde{x}\}) = a$; $U(\{\tilde{y}\}) = b$; and $U(\{\tilde{z}\}) = c$. Thus a, b, c, and d are parameters of the model. One of these, say c, can be chosen arbitrarily, while a, b, and d are to be estimated from five observations on each subject. Specifically, we have

$$p(x, y) = \frac{a}{a+b}; \quad p(y, z) = \frac{b+d}{b+d+c}; \quad p(x, z) = \frac{a+d}{a+d+c} \tag{12.54}$$

$$p_T(x) = \frac{1}{K}\left(a + \frac{ad}{a+d}\right); \quad p_T(z) = \frac{c}{K}, \tag{12.55}$$

where $K = a + b + c + d$. Note that when $p_T(x)$ and $p_T(z)$ are given, $p_T(y)$ is determined.

The goodness of fit of the model is measured by the chi-square statistic. Significantly large magnitudes of this statistic justify the rejection of the model. Of special interest is the parameter d, which is a measure of similarity between alternatives x and y in each experiment. Table 12.1 shows estimated values of d for each subject in each experiment and the corresponding magnitude of chi-square, obtained in comparing the observed choice frequencies with those predicted on the basis of the estimated values of the three parameters a, b, d.

We see from the table that the Chi-square statistic is sufficiently large to justify rejection of the model at the 0.1 level in only two of 24 cases and in none at the 0.05 level. If this is sufficient justification for accepting the model, we can draw some "psychological" conclusions. Since d (a measure of the subjective similarity between x and y) is given on a ratio scale, we can make interpersonal comparisons with reference to the different experiments and with reference to different subjects. We could, for example, conclude that applicants x and y seem more similar to Subject 3 than gambles x and y, while the opposite is true for Subject 6. Or we could conclude that while Subject 5 sees applicants x and y as rather similar ($d = 1.23$), Subject 7 sees them as quite different ($d = 0$).

These conclusions should not be regarded as definitive. They should rather be regarded as hypotheses, to be tested in other investigations designed more directly for that purpose.

In this rather roundabout way, we have come upon a method of carrying out psychological measurements. Such measurements may be more precise than more direct ones. Surely, subjects can be asked which are more similar to each other, x and y or y and z. But this procedure would have two shortcomings. First, answers of this sort usually yield scales weaker than the ratio scale. Second,

Table 12.1. Estimated Values of the "Discrimination Parameter"
d of Different Subjects in Different Tasks

	Dots		Gambles		Applicants	
Subjects	d	Chi²	d	Chi²	d	Chi²
1	0.25	0.133	0.46	0.040	0.14	2.179
2	0.29	3.025	0.58	0.001	0.92	1.624
3	0	0.849	0.14	2.022	1.18	0.159
4	0	5.551[a]	1.56	1.053	0.51	6.863[a]
5	0	0.951	0	0.887	1.23	0.428
6	0	0.401	1.18	0.157	0.42	0.405
7	0	3.748	1.00	0.304	0	0.083
8	0	4.112	1.44	1.241	0.37	0.038

Source: Adapted from Tversky (1972).

Note: Two degrees of freedom.

[a] $p = 0.1$.

direct questions may introduce irrelevant factors because words may have unexpected connotations or because subjects may be guided by what they think the experiment expects rather than by their own impressions, and so on. The procedures described above avoid these dangers. Perceptions of similarity are measured—without mentioning similarity—on the basis of what the subject does, not what he says. Actions speak louder than words.

In these experiments, we have seen the development of an analytic-descriptive model into a predictive one. The objections raised by Block and Marschak (1960) against the strict utility model were based not on discorroborating evidence but rather on a theoretical consequence of the model incompatible with common sense. A more detailed analysis of their "Impossibility Theorem" showed that it contained tacit assumptions not contained in the strict utility model. As a consequence, a "rival" model was developed and "pitted" against a strict utility model.

Finally, it should be noted that the "aspects" assumed in the EBA model need not have any empirical referents. They appear as theoretical constructs which need not correspond to the experimenter's a priori assumptions about the attributes characterizing the alternatives. In fact, the content of the aspects does not enter the EBA model as such. In the predictions deduced from the model, only the parameters related to the weights assigned to the aspects play a role. These parameters are estimated from a sample of the data, whereupon predictions based on these estimates can be made. If the predictions are corroborated, the parameters can be interpreted "psychologically."

NOTES

[1] The Choice Axiom proposed by R. D. Luce (1959a) is not to be confused with the Axiom of Choice of set theory.

[2] Recall the construction of an interval utility scale on the basis of preferences given on an ordinal scale (see p. 21), where uncertainties are introduced by the experimenter in the form of lotteries. In the present situation, the uncertainties are introduced by the subject in the form of inconsistent choices.

CHAPTER THIRTEEN

Stochastic Learning Models

Classical models deal with two kinds of quantities: variables and parameters. In testing such models with regard to their predictive aspects, variables are usually *observed*, whereas parameters are *estimated*. The latter are not necessarily observable quantities. Specific values are assigned to them in fitting the predictions deduced from the models to data. Thus to test a mathematical model of an electrical system, the magnitude of the current can be plotted against time. These are observable variables. In fitting the theoretical curve to data, the parameters of the model (for example, inductance, resistance, capacitance) are estimated. In this context questions about what to observe and how the observables are to be measured do not arise.

In constructing classical models in the behavioral sciences, such questions continually arise. In attempting to construct a mathematical model of interactions in a human group, of an international crisis, or of the formation of a concept, the behavioral scientist may want to quantify leadership ability, degree of hostility between two rival powers, or the degree of organization of perception. To do this she must "operationalize" these concepts; that is, decide what to observe and how to measure it. Thus in Richardson's model of an arms race, armament budgets and trade volumes served as indices of "hostility" and of "good will," respectively. In later models, the destruction potential of weapons appeared to be a better index of the level of armaments than defense budgets. In global models, "quality of life," surely not easy to define, has been operationalized as life expectancy in some models, as an aggregation of several indices in others. Aggregated indices raise the question of the meaningfulness of the mathematical operations involved.

The problem of quantification "solves itself," as it were, if the observed magnitudes are simply countable numbers. Thus in models of contagion, for example, the relevant quantities are numbers of infected individuals or the number of individuals performing one or the other activity at a specified time. Difficulties may arise in determining these numbers, but not in specifying what should be observed. As for measurement, this reduces to mere counting, which presents no conceptual problem. For this reason, quantification in the behavioral sciences is frequently accomplished by operationalizing concepts to be quantified as numbers to be counted.

Underlying classical mathematical models is the concept of the continuum, where variables undergo infinitesimal changes, permitting the use of the calculus. If the numbers to be counted are very large, they can be modeled as points in a continuum, for then a difference of one unit can be regarded as infinitesimal. If these numbers are small, however, continuous approximation is not satisfactory. The change of status of one individual cannot be regarded as an infinitesimal change in the aggregate. Moreover, the behavior of individuals being notoriously erratic, recourse to probabilitic assumptions becomes necessary. Here stochastic models come into their own. A stochastic model blends with a classical one when the probability of a change of status of an individual is expressed as a derivative, which in this case represents the *expected* number of individuals (which may be a fraction of an individual) passing from one state to another in a very short interval of time. If such a translation of probability into a derivative occurs right at the start, obviating references to probabilities in the development of the model, we will call the model *pseudostochastic*, to distinguish it from genuinely stochastic models, in which probabilistic considerations are carried throughout. To illustrate the two approaches, we will describe a pseudostochastic and a genuine stochastic model of simple learning.

A PSEUDOSTOCHASTIC MODEL OF LEARNING

Consider the following experiment. A rat is repeatedly presented with a stimulus to which it can respond in one of two ways. One response is "correct" and is rewarded; the other is "wrong" and is punished. In the course of a run of many trials, the rat will make errors. The plot of cumulated errors against time will therefore be a nondecreasing curve. If in the course of the repeated trials, errors become less frequent, the slope of the curve will decrease. If errors are eventually eliminated, the curve will merge with a horizontal line.

An early pseudostochastic model of this process was constructed by H. D. Landahl (1941). Following N. Rashevsky (1938), Landahl assumed that the rat's behavior is governed by differences in the level of excitation at neural synapses and, depending on the direction of these differences, leads to "correct" or "wrong" responses.

Initially, the level of excitation at the synapse leading to the correct response is ε_{oc}; at the synapse leading to the wrong response, ε_{ow}. As learning progresses, these levels are changed as follows. After a number of trials, the levels of excitation at the two synapses are ε_c and ε_w respectively. Each of these quantities depends on the number of correct (or wrong) responses accumulated in that number of trials. If c is the number of correct responses and w the number of wrong ones, $c + w = n$.

Because of statistical fluctuations in the excitation threshold at the synapses, $\varepsilon_c - \varepsilon_w$ determines only the probability of one or the other response. Specifically, Landahl assumes that when $\varepsilon_c \geq \varepsilon_w$, the probability of a wrong response is given by

$$P_w = (1/2)e^{-k(\varepsilon_c - \varepsilon_w)}, \ k \text{ constant.} \tag{13.1}$$

Thus when the excitation levels at the synapses leading to correct and to wrong responses are equal, the probability of a wrong response is $\frac{1}{2}$. When ε_c becomes larger, the probability of a wrong response decreases.

The dependence of ε_c and ε_w on c, the number of correct responses, and on w, the number of wrong responses in n trials, is given as

$$\varepsilon_c = \varepsilon_{oc} + bc$$
$$\varepsilon_w = \varepsilon_{ow} - \beta w, \tag{13.2}$$

where b and β are constants. That is, b is the increment of ε_c per correct response, and β is the decrement of ε_w per wrong response.

If the number of trials is sufficiently large, the discrete variables c, w, and n can be approximated by real variables, which will be designated by the same symbols. Then $P_w = P_w(n)$ is the expected number of wrong responses added to the accumulated wrong responses following the nth trial. If each trial is regarded as an infinitesimal increment of n, P_w can be written as dw/dn. Thus Equations 13.1 and 13.2 can be combined into the following differential equation:

$$\frac{dw}{dn} = \frac{1}{2}e^{-k\Delta}e^{-k(bc + \beta w)} = \frac{1}{2}e^{-k\Delta}e^{-k(bn - bw + \beta w)}, \tag{13.3}$$

where we have written Δ for $\varepsilon_{oc} - \varepsilon_{ow}$, or

$$e^{k(\beta - b)w}\, dw = \tfrac{1}{2}e^{-k\Delta}e^{-kbn}\, dn. \tag{13.4}$$

Integrating both sides of Equation 13.4, we obtain

$$\frac{1}{k(\beta - b)}e^{k(\beta - b)w} = \frac{-1}{2kb}e^{-k\Delta}e^{-kbn} + K, \tag{13.5}$$

where K is a constant of integration. We note that when $n = 0$, $w = 0$, since there were no errors before the first trial. With this initial condition, we have

$$K = \frac{1}{k(\beta - b)} + \frac{1}{2kb}e^{-k\Delta}. \tag{13.6}$$

Substituting Equation 13.6 into Equation 13.5, we obtain

$$wk(\beta - b) = \log_e \frac{2b - (b - \beta)e^{-k\Delta}(1 - e^{-kbn})}{2b}. \tag{13.7}$$

Reversing signs on both sides of Equation 13.7 and dividing by $k(b - \beta)$, we derive w as a function of n:

$$w = \frac{1}{k(b - \beta)} \log_e \frac{2be^{k\Delta}}{2be^{k\Delta} - (b - \beta)(1 - e^{-kbn})}.$$ (13.8)

Equation 13.18 predicts the cumulated number of errors as a function of the number of trials. Since both variables are observable, the model can be tested. However, the model contains four free parameters, b, β, k, and Δ. Given so many free parameters, a comparatively smooth curve, especially a monotonically increasing one, can usually be easily fitted to the data. Therefore even a very good fit is not very convincing evidence for the validity of Landahl's model. Two examples of good fit to data presented by H. Gulliksen (1934) are shown in Figure 13.1.

Interpretations of the parameters provide some theoretical leverage for the model. Recall that b is essentially a measure of the effectiveness of reward, β of the effectiveness of punishment. Both parameters influence the increase of the probability of the correct response after each trial but possibly in unequal degrees. Since the values of these parameters can be estimated by fitting Equation 13.8 to data, we can get an idea about the relative effectiveness of rewards and punishments as determinants of learning, assuming, of course, that we have some confidence in the validity of the model.

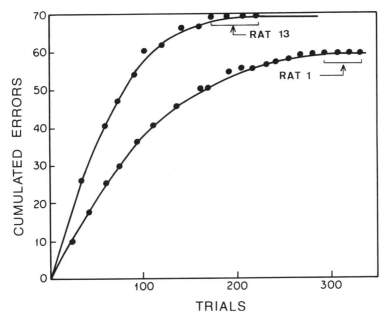

Figure 13.1. (Adapted from Gulliksen, 1934). Cumulated errors by two rats in a two-choice learning experiment.

We see from the legend to Figure 13.1 that both curves were fitted with $\beta = 0$. This could mean that the learning process of both rats was not influenced by punishments. Only rewards had a reinforcing effect on the correct response. Further, $\varepsilon_{oc} - \varepsilon_{ow}$ can be interpreted as the initial response bias. If this difference is positive, the correct response is initially favored; if negative, the wrong response. From the legend to Figure 13.1, we see that Rate 13 appears to have been "handicapped" by an initial bias toward the wrong response. This is reflected in the quicker accumulation of errors in the early trials. But Rat 13 appears to have been "smarter" than Rat 1, since his b was larger. This is reflected in the observation that Rate 13 reached the criterion of having learned the correct response (four consecutive correct responses) sooner than Rat 1.

The relation of b to "intelligence" is evident since b measures the efficiency of rewards in reinforcing the correct response (see Equation 13.2). The relation of k to intelligence is less evident. A large k means that the variance in the oscillations of excitation (or of the threshold at the synapse) around its mean value is small. This means, in turn, that a slight difference in effective excitation levels in favor of the correct response produces a large probability of this response. Thus the observation that Rate 13 reached the criterion sooner than Rat 1 could have been due either to a larger k or to a larger b. This interpretation of the parameters leads to further experimentally testable hypotheses. For instance, one can pose the question whether the estimated initial bias actually reflects an observable bias in favor of one of the stimuli (for example, a preference of white to black or left to right) which can be tested by an independent experiment. Experiments can also be designed where the contributions of b and k to the rate of learning can be assessed separately, and so on.

A LEARNING MODEL BASED ON A CONTAGION EFFECT

Now we will examine another learning model, which in the special case where $\Delta = \varepsilon_{oc} - \varepsilon_{ow} = 0$ leads to the same result (Rapoport, 1956). Let the brain be regarded as a large population of neural pathways leading to particular responses. These pathways can be conditioned to particular responses. Initially, let x_0 be the fraction of pathways conditioned (or already connected) to the correct response. During learning, the number of such pathways increases in accord with a simple contagion process. If $x(t)$ is the fraction of pathways conditioned at time t, we have, as in a contagion process,

$$\frac{dx}{dt} = ax(1 - x). \tag{13.9}$$

The solution of Equation 13.9 with $x(0) = x_0$ is

$$x(t) = \frac{x_0 e^{at}}{1 - x_0(1 - e^{at})}. \tag{13.10}$$

If a neural pathway is chosen at random at each trial, Equation 13.10 represents the probability of a correct response. Then the probability of a wrong response is

$$1 - x(t) = 1 - \frac{x_0 e^{at}}{1 - x_0 + x_0 e^{at}}. \tag{13.11}$$

This probability can be represented by dw/dt as in the previous model. Therefore the expectation of the total number of wrong responses up to time t will be given by integrating Equation 13.11 with respect to t:

$$w(t) = t - \frac{1}{a} \log_e(1 - x_0 + x_0 e^{at}). \tag{13.12}$$

Now t can be written as $\log_e(e^{at})/a$. Substituting into Equation 13.12, we have, in view of the assumption that initially correct and wrong responses are equiprobable,

$$w(t) = \frac{1}{a} \log_e \frac{2e^{at}}{1 + e^{at}} = \frac{1}{a} \log_e \frac{2}{1 + e^{-at}}, \tag{13.13}$$

which is formally identical with Equation 13.8 if $\beta = 0$, $\Delta = 0$, $kb = a$, and $n = t$.

Of course, questions regarding physiological or neurological interpretations of the underlying assumptions arise in connection with this model as well as with the previous one. There is practically no way of testing these interpretations empirically. At best, they stimulate thinking. For instance, the contagion model suggests that neural pathways conditioned to the correct response induce similar conditioning in other pathways during the learning process. The well-known phenomenon of generalization of a conditioned response may also have something to do with "induction" of this sort.

THE GENUINE STOCHASTIC MODEL

As has been emphasized, pseudostochastic models cannot be justified if the number of trials and consequently of errors is small. Another shortcoming of Landahl's model is that it can be meaningfully tested only by comparing Equation 13.8 with cumulated errors. The cumulated error curve is "smoothed out" in the sense that the random component of responses is not clearly brought out. It would be brought out in a plot of the number of wrong responses in successive blocks of trials. But this would involve a comparison between the number of errors per trial in each block and dw/dn, which would not be meaningful unless supplemented by tests of statistical significance. In short, the excellent fit of Equation 13.8 to cumulated error curves is deceptive and therefore of slight theoretical significance.

Stochastic learning models were designed to remove these shortcomings. In these models, probabilities remain as variables throughout the mathematical deductions. Eventually, these probabilities must be translated into frequencies because only frequencies are directly observable. But the aggregation of data to statistics (means, variances, and so on) takes place only after distributions of *random* variables have been specified. Because a large number of statistics can be generated by a stochastic model, severe tests can be applied to them based on data from a single experiment. Tests of comparable severity can be applied to a pseudostochastic model only by varying the conditions of an experiment.

The unit of analysis in a stochastic model is a *protocol*, a series of recorded stimuli, responses, and outcomes. For instance, let response "1" to stimuli *a* or *b* be rewarded, while response "2" to these stimuli is punished; response "2" to stimulus *c* is rewarded, and response "1" punished. A protocol will then be a series of triples; for example, $(a, 1, r)$, $(a, 2, p)$, $(b, 2, p)$, and $(c, 2, r)$, where *r* designates reward and *p* punishment.

In the simplest case, the stimulus may always be the same; for instance, a turn in a T-maze. If a turn in one direction is always correct and the other wrong, the protocol can consist of only a series of *p*s and *r*s. If, however, the same turn is sometimes rewarded, sometimes punished, the protocol will consist of a series of responses, each coupled with an outcome. Experiments of this sort are designed to study relationships between probabilities of rewards and punishments and the learning process.

It stands to reason that rewards and punishments must be perceived as such by the subject. If the subject is a rat, food may be suitable as reward and an electric shock as punishment. Or if electric shock is a punishment, the absence of shock may be the reward. If the subject is human, the experimenter's comment "Right" may serve as reward and "Wrong" as punishment.

Many stochastic models rest on the assumption that learning takes place slowly, so that at each trial the subject is characterized by a probability of responding one way or another, and that reinforcements of the correct response add small increments to the probability of its occurrence on consecutive trials. Underlying such models in an assumption that the probability of a response is determined by the proportion of a very large number of neural elements conditioned to it. Such models cannot represent learning based on deliberate information processing or rational reasoning. For instance, a person who knows that one of two keys fits a lock will know which one it is after he has tried one. In contrast, a worm in a T-maze where one turn leads to a comfortable moist chamber and the other is lined with sandpaper takes several hundred trials to learn to take the former and avoid the latter.

In some situations, human subjects also exhibit slow incremental learning. This is the case when a subject is asked to guess whether a red or a green light will go on next, and the experimenter turns on one or the other light independently of the subject's guess. If in the prearranged schedule, one light is to be turned on more frequently than the other, the subject's responses will gradually "tip" toward the light with the greater frequency of occurrence. An experiment of this sort is called a learning experiment with *experimenter-controlled* events. Experiments in which the outcomes (for example, "success" or "failure") depend entirely on the subject's responses involve *subject-controlled* events. In still other situations, outcomes depend on both what the subject does and on what the experimenter does. The distinction between the various types of experiments is methodologically important because each presents different problems associated with the estimation of parameters in a stochastic model. The estimation procedure sometimes involves advanced statistical methods. The extra work pays off in a larger amount of information that can be extracted from the data.

THE LINEAR STOCHASTIC MODEL

The model about to be discussed is called *linear* because outcomes of trials produce changes in the probability of a response that are assumed to be linear functions of the probabilities. If $p(n)$ is the probability of a particular response on trial n, the difference $p(n+1) - p(n)$ is assumed to be equal to $(\alpha - 1)p(n) + a$, where α and a lie in the interval $[0, 1]$ and are independent of p but in general depend on the outcome of the trial (for example, "success" or "failure"). Thus we can write

$$p(n+1) = Q_1 p(n) = \alpha_1 p(n) + a_1 \qquad (13.14)$$

if the outcome of the nth trial was a success, and

$$p(n+1) = Q_2 p(n) = \alpha_2 p(n) + a_2 \qquad (13.15)$$

if the outcome was a failure. Equations 13.14 and 13.15 define the transformations of $p(n)$ effected by the operators Q_1 and Q_2.

We introduce a change of notation by writing λ_i for $a_i/(1 - \alpha_i)$ where $i = 1, 2$. Equations 13.14 and 13.15 are recursive. Applying operator Q_i on $p(0)$ n times, we obtain

$$p(n) = \alpha_i^n p(0) + (1 - \alpha_i^n)\lambda_i. \qquad (13.16)$$

Hence $\lim_{n \to \infty} Q_i^n p(0) = \lambda_i$ if $\alpha < 1$. Thus λ_1 and λ_2 are the asymptotic values of $p(n)$ associated with each of the operators applied exclusively. If we assume further that the correct response is reinforced until it is fixated, we can set $\lambda_1 = \lambda_2 = 1$. Setting $q = 1 - p$, we can replace operators Q_1 and Q_2 by $\tilde{Q}_1$ and $\tilde{Q}_2$ respectively operating on q. If $\lambda_1 = \lambda_2 = 1$, Equations 13.14 and 13.15 can be written in a simpler form:

$$\tilde{Q}_1 q(n) = \alpha_1 q(n) \qquad (13.17)$$

$$\tilde{Q}_2 q(n) = \alpha_2 q(n). \qquad (13.18)$$

A TEST OF THE LINEAR MODEL

We will illustrate an application of the linear model to the analysis of an experiment conducted by R. L. Solomon and L. C. Wynne (1953).

The subjects were 30 dogs. Each dog was put in a cage consisting of two chambers separated by a partition over which the dog could easily jump. The stimulus was the turning off of a light. A few seconds afterwards an electric current was passed through the floor of the cage. The dog was to learn to jump over the partition before the current was turned on. If he did not jump in time, he was shocked. When he was shocked, he jumped over the partition to escape the shock. If he jumped before the current was passed, he avoided the shock. Thus there were two possible responses: *avoidance* (correct) and *escape* (wrong). The probability of avoidance on trial n was designated by $p(n)$, the probability of escape by $q(n) = 1 - p(n)$. Eventually all the dogs learned to avoid the shock. Thus we can set $\lambda_1 = \lambda_2 = 1$ in the linear model. Equation 13.17 represents the transformation of q from trial to trial as a result of avoidance; Equation 13.18, as a result of escape.

In general, operators Q_1 and Q_2 in Equations 13.14 and 13.15 do not commute; that is, the effect of successive applications of Q_1 and Q_2 depends on the order of application. But operators represented in the special case by Equations 13.17 and 13.18 obviously do commute. Thus if a dog responded k times with avoidance and $n - k$ times with escape in n trials, his q after n trials will be given by

$$q(n, k) = \tilde{Q}_1^k \tilde{Q}_2^{n-k} q_0 = \alpha_1^k \alpha_2^{n-k} q_0, \tag{13.19}$$

where q_0 is the initial probability of escape. Since no dog responded with avoidance on the first trial (since he "did not know" the meaning of the stimulus), we can set $q_0 = 1$.

To test the model, we must estimate the parameters α_1 and α_2. Before we describe some methods of testing these parameters, let us see how a model of this sort can be tested.

Suppose both parameters have been estimated. Then we can obtain a value of $q(n, k)$ for every pair of values n and k. However, $q(n, k)$ is a probability and therefore cannot be directly observed. If we had a sufficiently large number of "identical" dogs, this derived probability could be compared with the proportion of dogs who respond with escape on the nth trial, having responded with avoidance on k of the previous trials. With only 30 dogs at our disposal, such a comparison would not tell us much. Suppose some dogs had been shocked only once in the first 10 trials, say because they responded with avoidance on all trials after the first; some were shocked twice, and so on, and some all 10 times. If several of these categories are not empty, the number of dogs in each category will be quite small. Regardless of how many dogs will not jump on the eleventh trial, it will not be possible to establish with any reasonable certainty whether this number confirms the derived value of $q(n, k)$. Thus the translation of $q(n, k)$ into frequencies is not practical. Nevertheless, a large amount of information can be extracted from the distribution of $q(n, k)$ regarded as a random variable in the form of statistics to be compared with the data.

As has been said, every dog eventually learned to avoid the shock. Thus we can observe the trial after which each dog experienced the last shock, and on the basis of this observation determine the average number of trials to the last wrong response. This average as well as the variance of this number are statistics. The mean number of trials and its variance until the first correct response until the second correct response, and so on, are also statistics. Every statistic is a function of the estimates of the parameters of the model. Confirmation of the model can be evaluated by the degree of agreement between the observed values of these several statistics and the values of the corresponding expressions involving the estimates of parameters. In this sense the model can be subjected to a "severe" test. If it passes the test (that is, if the predicted values of several statistics agree with observations), we can regard the model as a good approximation of "reality" and can undertake a psychological interpretation of the parameters with some confidence.

ESTIMATION OF PARAMETERS

A rough and ready estimate of α_2 can be made on the basis of the proportion of dogs who did not jump over the partition on the second trial. Since all the dogs experienced shock on the first trial, we assume that $q_0 = 1$ for all dogs. This value was transformed by $\tilde{Q}_2$ as in Equation 13.18. Thus

$$q(1, 0) = \hat{\alpha}_2. \qquad (13.20)$$

Suppose three dogs responded correctly after the second trial, while 27 were shocked. Then $27/30 = 0.900$ is an estimate of α_2. By the same reasoning,

$$q(2, 0) = \hat{\alpha}_2^2. \qquad (13.21)$$

If, say, 24 dogs still have not learned to jump before being shocked after the second trial, we have $\sqrt{24/27} = 0.943$ as another estimate of α_2. Agreement between these two estimates is not impressive, but there are other estimates at our disposal.

We have mentioned the mean number of trials before the first correct response. A mathematical expression of this statistic can be derived. It can be used to derive another estimate of α_2. It turns out that this estimate gives 0.923 as a value of $\hat{\alpha}_2$. This value lies between the other two. Which is the "best" estimate?

To answer this question, we use the expression for the variance of the number of trials before the first correct response, which is also a function of α_2. We can compare this value with the observed variance of this random variable and choose for our estimate of α_2 the value that yields the closest agreement. It turns out that using 0.92 (the third of our previous estimates of α_2) yields the closest agreement.

There are still other methods of estimating α_2. By making further comparisons, we can finally arrive at what appears to be the most reliable estimate of this parameter. In our case, this happens to be 0.92. Similar procedures lead to a "best" estimate of α_1. It turns out that the best estimate of this parameter (a measure of the effectiveness of "reward"—no shock) is 0.8. On the basis of this estimate, we can assume that the reward is more effective than punishment in this learning process.

REAL DOGS AND STAT-DOGS

Our estimates of the two parameters determine the specific form of the linear stochastic model. Equations 13.14 and 13.15 now become

$$Q_1p = 0.80p + 0.20 \tag{13.22}$$

$$Q_2p = 0.92p + 0.08. \tag{13.23}$$

Now we can obtain data that would be generated by a population of "identical" dogs characterized by the above values of α_1 and α_2 and learning according to the model given by Equations 13.22 and 13.23. Namely, we can simulate the postulated learning process on a computer. Figure 13.2 shows a comparison between the "learning curve" produced by (simulated) "stat-dogs" and the observed learning curve produced by real dogs. The proportions of stat-dogs and real dogs who avoided shock are plotted against the number of the trial. The solid curve represents the expected proportion calculated from the model.

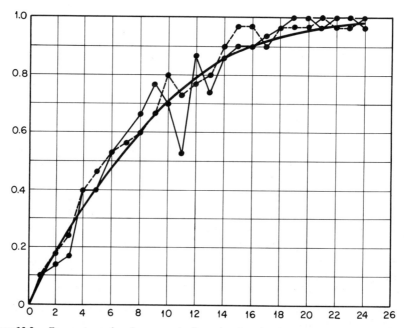

Figure 13.2. Comparison of performances by "stat-dogs" and real dogs, subjects in the Solomon-Wynne shock-avoidance experiment. Abscissae: trials, ordinates, fractions of subjects avoiding shock.

It appears that this theoretical curve fits the learning curves of the stat-dogs and of the real dogs equally well. In addition, the statistical fluctuations in both observed learning curves are similar.

Figure 13.3 shows the cumulated number of errors made by the dogs in the Solomon-Wynne experiment (circles) compared with the theoretically expected number. This curve corresponds to the cumulated error curve in Landahl's pseudostochastic model. As will be recalled, this curve also gave a good fit to data produced by Gulliksen's rats (see p. 243).

It is interesting to compare the mathematical forms of learning curves derived from the two models when $\lambda_1 = \lambda_2 = 1$. According to the linear model, the expected probability of a correct response on the nth trial is approximately given by

$$p(n) = \frac{1}{2}\left[(\lambda + \mu) + (\lambda - \mu) \frac{(p_0 - \mu)e^{\rho n} + (p_0 - \lambda)}{(p_0 - \mu)e^{\rho n} - (p_0 - \lambda)} \right], \tag{13.24}$$

where

$$\mu = \frac{1 - \alpha_2}{\alpha_1 - \alpha_2}; \qquad \rho = (1 - \alpha_2) - (\alpha_1 - \alpha_2)\lambda. \tag{13.25}$$

In our case, $\lambda = 1$ and $p_0 = 0$. Thus Equation 13.24 reduces to

$$p(n) = \frac{1}{2}\left[(1 + \mu) + (1 - \mu) \frac{-\mu e^{\rho n} - 1}{-\mu e^{\rho n} + 1} \right], \tag{13.26}$$

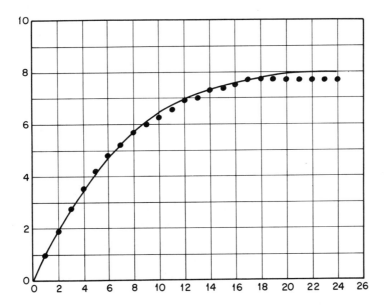

Figure 13.3. Comparison between observed and predicted cumulated errors in the Solomon-Wynne experiment. Abscissae; trials; ordinates; average cumulated errors.

or, after rearrangements, to

$$p(n) = 1 - \frac{-1 + \mu}{\mu e^{\rho n} - 1}. \tag{13.27}$$

Thus the probability of a wrong response is

$$1 - p(n) = \frac{-1 + \mu}{\mu e^{\rho n} - 1}. \tag{13.28}$$

The expected number of wrong responses is obtained by integrating Equation 13.28 with respect to n:

$$w(n) = \frac{1 - \mu}{\rho} \log_e \frac{1 - \mu}{(1 - \mu) - (1 - e^{-\rho n})}. \tag{13.29}$$

Comparing Equation 13.29 with Equation 13.8, we see that they are of the same form if we set $2be^{k\Delta} = (1 - \mu)$, $(b - \beta) = 1$, and $kb = \rho$. Taking $(b - \beta) = 1$ is justified (if $b > \beta$) since the units of b and β can be freely chosen. However, to reduce Equation 13.29 to Equation 13.8, we must also set $2be^{k\Delta} = b$; that is, $e^{k\Delta} = 1/2$.

The dimension of k is reciprocal to that of Δ. Since the units of Δ were already fixed by those of β and b, so were the units of k. Thus the numerical value of k is fixed if Equation 13.29 is to reduce to Equation 13.8. However, the two equations agree qualitatively because $k > 0$ and $e^{k\Delta} = 1/2$ imply that $\Delta < 0$; that is, an initial bias toward the *wrong* response. But in the Solomon-Wynne experiment, the wrong response was nonavoidance, and, as we have seen, none of the 30 dogs avoided shock on the first trial. Thus there really was an initial bias toward the wrong response, and we can conclude that Landahl's pseudostochastic model essentially corresponds to the linear stochastic model with respect to the *expected* values of response probabilities.

PAIRED ASSOCIATE LEARNING

So far, we have investigated learning situations in which the conditions at each trial were identical, at least from the point of view of the experimenter. For instance, a rat always had to choose between two alternatives, a correct and a wrong response. In general, in situations of this sort, a response that is correct on one trial could also be wrong on another trial (as in experimenter-controlled events). But this is not manifested when alternatives are presented.

Consider now a situation where a different stimulus is presented on each trial. The subject has to learn to associate each stimulus with one of several responses. If the stimuli and responses are in one-to-one correspondence, we have a situation called *paired associate* learning. We will discuss an experiment where whatever the subject's response to a stimulus, the correct response is always given to her by the experimenter. If the subject's memory is perfect, she will have learned the correct response to each stimulus after just one presentation of the stimulus. If, however, the number of stimuli is large, she may not always remember the correct response. In this case, we can suppose that the stimuli are conditioned probabilistically to the correct responses. The simplest assumption is that the probability of conditioning is a constant. A stochastic learning process based on this assumption was proposed by G. Bower (1961, 1962). It is called a *single element* model because each stimulus is represented by a single ("neuronal") element to be conditioned to the correct response. The formal assumptions of the model are the following:

(i)   An element can be in one of two states, conditioned or unconditioned.

(ii) The probability that an unconditioned element becomes conditioned on any trial is θ. A conditioned element remains conditioned.

(iii) On presentation of a particular stimulus, the probability of a correct response is $1/N$ if the corresponding element is unconditioned, where N is the total number of possible responses. If the element is conditioned, the probability of correct response is 1.

A conspicious difference between this model and the linear stochastic model is that according to the present model, learning does not proceed in "small steps" manifested as increments in the probability of a correct response. A correct response is either learned or not, and as soon as it is learned, it remains learned. Chance enters only in determining *whether* a correct response is learned on a particular trial. We note further that when a correct response to a stimulus has not yet been learned, all possible responses to this stimulus are equiprobable. In this way, the all-or-none nature of a learning process is represented by the model.

A MODEL OF CONCEPT FORMATION

The model of paired comparisons can be generalized in different ways. For instance, a probability of "deconditioning" (forgetting) can be introduced, or it can be assumed that guessing is systematic instead of random. We will examine a generalization that leads to a model of concept utilization, in which concept formation is part of the learning process.

Suppose the number of possible responses is smaller than the number of stimuli; that is, a particular response can be correct with reference to several stimuli. Furthermore, the stimuli associated with the same response have some properties in common that are not shared by stimuli associated with other responses. In identifying the properties that jointly distinguish a stimulus, the subject learns the correct response to a given stimulus.

Consider the following stimuli: a large red circle, a small red circle, a large green circle, a small green circle, a large red square, a small red square, a large green square, a small green square. Four of these stimuli are characterized by "largeness," four by "circularity," two are large *and* circular, and so on. The stimuli differ on three *dimensions*—size, color, and shape. Each dimension is represented by two *values*—large or small, green or red, and so on.

In this situation, a trial is called reinforced if the experimenter tells the subject whether his response was right or wrong. For instance, the experimenter can say "Right" whenever the subject's response is R_1 if the stimulus is large and R_2 if it is small; otherwise he says "Wrong." Evidently, this reinforcement rule singles out size as the *relevant* dimension and the other dimensions as *irrelevant*. The properties "large," "small," "red," and so on are called *distinctive features*. In our example, there are six distinctive features. The above reinforcement rule singles out "large" and "small" as the relevant features, and all the others as irrelevant. In general, if a particular response to a feature is either always right or always wrong, this feature is relevant. A feature is irrelevant if a particular response to it is sometimes right, sometimes wrong.

We can suppose that in learning to associate stimuli with correct responses, the subject learns to pay attention to relevant features and to ignore the irrelevant ones. In this way, the irrelevant features become *adapted*, whereas the relevant ones become *conditioned*; that is, permanently associated with correct responses.

A model of concept formation was proposed by L. W. Bourne and F. Restle (1959). It is based on the following assumptions:

(i)   On each reinforced trial, a constant fraction of nonadapted unconditioned features become conditioned. Once conditioned, a feature remains conditioned.

(ii) On each reinforced trial, a constant fraction of unadapted irrelevant features become adapted. Adapted irrelevant features remain adapted.

(iii) The probability of a response is the fraction of unadapted features conditioned to that response.

Although in our example we have identified distinctive features by specifically chosen properties of the stimuli (circularity, redness, and so on), the model does not depend on such specification. The subject may select features different from the ones the experimenter has in mind. In any case, some of the features singled out by the subject may be relevant, some irrelevant. This distinction will be formed by the experimenter's comments, "Right" and "Wrong". We can therefore assume that on each trial the entire set of features K selected by the subject will be partitioned into two classes, relevant and irrelevant.

If k is an arbitrary feature of K, then in view of (i), the probability C that this feature will be conditioned on trial $n + 1$ is given by the difference equation

$$C(k, n + 1) = C(k, n) + \theta[1 - C(k, n)], \qquad (13.30)$$

where θ is the fraction of unconditioned features that becomes conditioned on any trial. The first term on the right of Equation 13.30 expresses the assumption "once conditioned, always conditioned"; the second represents the probability that an unconditioned feature becomes conditioned on the nth trial.

Similarly, the probability A that an irrelevant feature k' will be adapted on trial $n + 1$ is given by the difference equation

$$A(k', n+1) = A(k', n) + \theta'[1 - A(k', n)], \tag{13.31}$$

where θ' is the fraction of unadapted features that becomes adapted on the nth trial. Bourne and Restle make the simplifying assumption that the same fraction of features becomes conditioned or adapted; that is, $\theta = \theta'$.

The solution of Equation 13.30 in terms of $C(k, 1)$ is

$$C(k, n) = (1 - \theta)^{n-1} C(k, 1) + [1 - (1 - \theta)^{n-1}]. \tag{13.32}$$

The solution of Equation 13.31 in terms of $A(k', 1)$ is

$$A(k', n) = (1 - \theta)^{n-1} A(k', 1) + [1 - (1 - \theta)^{n-1}]. \tag{13.33}$$

Now we can derive the probability $p(n)$ of the correct response on the nth trial. In view of (iii), we have

$$p(n) = \frac{[\text{Number of nonadapted conditioned features}]}{[\text{Number of nonadapted features}]}. \tag{13.34}$$

Since the set K was not specified, the total number of features is unknown. But whatever it is, we can express $p(n)$ as a ratio of probabilities by dividing both the numerator and the denominator in Equation 13.34 by this number. Thus

$$p(n) = \frac{\Pr[\text{A feature is nonadapted and conditioned}]}{\Pr[\text{A feature is nonadapted}]}. \tag{13.35}$$

Now on trial n, there are two kinds of unadapted features, the relevant, which cannot be adapted, and the irrelevant, which have not been adapted. Let r be the fraction of relevant features in K (K is constant throughout) and hence $(1 - r)$ the fraction of irrelevant features. Then the numerator on the right side of Equation 13.35 is given by

$$rC(k, n) + (1 - r)[1 - A(k', n)]C(k', n), \tag{13.36}$$

where $C(k', n)$ is the probability that an irrelevant feature is conditioned on trial n. The denominator is given by

$$r + (1 - r)[1 - A(k', n)]. \tag{13.37}$$

Therefore

$$p(n) = \frac{rC(k, n) + (1 - r)[1 - A(k', n)]C(k', n)}{r + (1 - r)[1 - A(k', n)]}. \tag{13.38}$$

To use Equation 13.38 for predicting observations, we must know r, θ, $C(k, 1)$, $A(k', 1)$, and $C(k', 1)$. In a situation with two possible responses, we can make some reasonable assumptions. We can assume that an irrelevant feature

k' becomes conditioned on any trial with probability $\frac{1}{2}$. In the absence of response bias, we can further assume $C(k, 1) = \frac{1}{2}$. Assuming that initially no irrelevant feature was adapted (since the subject does not know that it is irrelevant), we can set $A(k', 1) = 0$.

Substituting $C(k, 1) = \frac{1}{2}$, $A(k', 1) = 0$, and $C(k', n) = \frac{1}{2}$ into Equation 13.38, we obtain after some rearrangements

$$p(n) = 1 - \frac{\frac{1}{2}(1 - \theta)^{n-1}}{r + (1 - r)(1 - \theta)^{n-1}}. \tag{13.39}$$

If we assume that the rate of conditioning equals the fraction of relevant stimuli in the set, we can set $\theta = r$. The value of r can be increased without increasing the effective number of dimensions by adding *redundant* dimensions. For instance, in a task where R_1 is required as a response to a large stimulus, we can add a dot in the center of the corresponding figure. This feature is relevant since it is always and exclusively associated with largeness. But it is also redundant because the subject can choose either size or the dot as the relevant distinctive feature.

If R is the number of relevant redundant dimensions, then

$$r = \frac{cR}{a + bR}, \tag{13.40}$$

where cR is the number of redundant distinctive features (assumed proportional

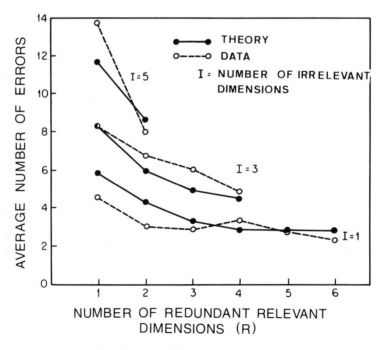

Figure 13.4.

to R), bR is the number of relevant and irrelevant distinctive features in the relevant redundant dimensions, and a is the number of distinctive features in the irrelevant dimensions.

To estimate r, we must estimate a, b, and c. Our final simplifying assumption is that the number of redundant irrelevant features equals the number of relevant redundant dimensions; that is, $b = 1$. Thus to get an estimate of r we need to estimate only a and c.

In view of Equation 13.39, we can predict the total number of errors as a function of the number of redundant dimensions R and the number of irrelevant dimensions I (both being manipulable variables).

Figure 13.4 shows a comparison between predicted and observed mean numbers of errors in a concept formation task experiment with two subjects (Bourne and Restle, 1959).

NOTE

[1] It is evident from Equations 13.17 and 13.18 that a greater rate of learning is associated with a smaller value of the parameter α.

PART III

STRUCTURAL MODELS

CHAPTER FOURTEEN

The Language of Structure

Stanislaw Andreski (1974) in his devastating critique of contemporary developments in the behavioral sciences points out that "structure" and "role" have become prestige words with which the triviality and banality of voluminous writings purporting to deal with theories of social structure and of human behavior can be camouflaged.

Builders of mathematical models cannot make use of such stratagems. If a mathematical model purports to represent a structure, it must exhibit this structure in mathematically rigorous terms. This is done by means of a specialized mathematical language called *set theory*.

SET-THEORETIC TERMINOLOGY

The fundamental categories of set theory are *elements*, *sets of elements*, and *relations on sets of elements*. Elements and sets are primitive concepts and for this reason cannot be further defined. Their meaning can only be illustrated by examples. Relations, however, can be formally defined in terms of elements and sets.

An "element" is anything that is recognized as "itself" and thus is distinguished from something else, Persons, numbers, and points in space can, in proper contexts, be regarded as elements. As a member of a particular set, an element is "atomic"; that is, not further analyzable. In other contexts, an element of a set may be itself a set and so may itself consist of elements. For instance, a person may be an element in one context of discourse, say as a member of a society, but a vast collection of elements in another context; for example, his constituent cells.

A set is a collection of elements specified with sufficient precision to make it possible to decide whether some given entity belongs or does not belong to the collection. For instance, the totality of even, nonnegative integers is a set to which "2," "28," and "0" belong, but to which "7" and "−4" do not belong.

In mathematics, elements and sets represent mental constructs whose definitions leave no room for ambiguity. If we are dealing with things and collections of things in the "real world," ambiguities can always arise, no matter how carefully the definitions are constructed. If I specify the set of "all living female human beings in Vienna on January 1, 1978," I must be prepared to deal with ambiguities associated with hermaphrodites, the exact boundaries of Vienna, persons who were "clinically" but not "physiologically" dead at the stroke of midnight, and so on. In most contexts, ambiguities of this sort create no problems, but sometimes they do, as is well known to lawyers and government officials, who must make decisions in accordance with definitions specified in regulations.

For the most part, we will designate elements by small Roman letters and sets by capital Roman letters. We will write $a \in A$ to mean "a is an element of the set A". Thus if E is the set of all nonnegative even integers, we can write $2 \in E$ and $3 \notin E$, where $\notin$ denotes "is *not* an element of."

A set can be specified in two ways: (1) by specifying the properties of its elements that distinguish it from other sets, and (2) by enumerating all its elements. Clearly, if the number of elements of a set is infinite, the second method cannot be used. Specification by enumeration, however, is often appropriate when the number of elements is not very large and where it is difficult to define the distinguishing properties of the elements precisely. This method forestalls rather fruitless arguments about what "ought" or "ought not" belong to a given set. Suppose, for example, I want to talk about "the countries of Europe." It is not *a priori* clear whether I want to include Turkey, the USSR, and Denmark (most of whose territories are not in Europe) or Monaco (since some will argue that it is not a "country"). Nor is it *a priori* clear whether I intend to regard Germany or the United Kingdom as "one country" or more than one, and so on. If I simply specify all the entities that I will regard in the discussion to follow as "countries of Europe," these ambiguities need not arise.

Specifications of sets will be set in braces, { }, within which will be given either the defining properties of the elements or an enumeration of the elements.

Examples.

1. $X = \{x : x \text{ is a nonnegative integer}\}$.
2. $[1, 2) = \{x : (1 \leqslant x < 2)\}]$ (read "the set of real numbers equal or greater than 1 and less than 2").
3. $A = \{x, y, z, w\}$ (read "the set consisting of elements x, y, z, and w").

If all the elements of a set A are also elements of a set B, we will write $A \subset B$ or $B \supset A$ (read "A is contained in B, or B contains A, or A is a subset of B"). If both $A \subset B$ and $B \supset A$, it follows that all the elements of one of these sets are also elements of the other, and we will write $A = B$; that is, A and B are one and the same set. The meanings of $A \not\subset B$, $A \not\supset B$, and so on are evident. If $A \subset B$ and $A \neq B$, A is called a *proper* subset of B.[1]

The *union* of two sets A and B, written $A \cup B$, is the set that consists of elements belonging either to A or to B (or possibly to both).

Example. If A is the set of all children and B the set of all adult males, then $A \cup B$ comprises all human males and all female children.

Remark: In view of our definition of "$\cup$," it is easy to see that $A \subset B$ implies $A \cup B = B$.

The *intersection* of two sets A and B, written $A \cap B$, is the set that comprises all the elements that are members of both A and B.

Example. If A is the set of all children and B the set of all human males, $A \cap B$ comprises all male children.

Remark: If $A \subset B$, $A \cap B = A$.

In our previous example, where A was the set of all children and B the set of all adult males, the intersection $A \cap B$ contained no elements. The set with no elements is called the *empty set* or the *null set*, and is designated by $\emptyset$. By convention $\emptyset$ is regarded as being contained in any set. Sets with all pairwise intersections empty are called *disjoint*. A specification of a set A as a union of disjoint sets is called a *partition* of A.

Union and intersection can be regarded as *binary operations* on sets in the same way as "plus" and "times" are binary operations on numbers. That is, two sets (or two numbers) connected by "$\cup$" or "$\cap$" (or by "plus" or "times") determine another set (or number). The analogy extends to several features of these operations. For example, like "plus" and "times," "$\cup$" and "$\cap$" are associative and commutative:

$A \cup (B \cup C) = (A \cup B) \cup C$, like $x + (y + z) = (x + y) + z$.
$A \cup b = B \cup A$, like $x + y = y + x$.
$A \cap (B \cap C) = (A \cap B) \cap C$, like $x(yz) = (xy)z$.
$\quad A \cap B = B \cap A$, like $xy = yx$.

Furthermore, just as "times" is distributive with respect to "plus," so is "$\cap$" distributive with respect to "$\cup$."

$$A \cap (B \cup C) = (A \cap B) \cup (A \cap C), \text{ like } x(y + z) = xy + xz.$$

Furthermore, "$\cup$" is also distributive with respect to "$\cap$."

$$A \cup (B \cap C) = (A \cup B) \cap (A \cup C).$$

Note that an analogous property does not hold in arithmetic if "$\cup$" is regarded as analogous to "plus" and "$\cap$" analogous to "times."

The analogy between $\emptyset$ and zero is apparent from the following relations, where X is any set:

$$X \cup \emptyset = X, \quad \text{like } x + 0 = x.$$
$$X \cap \emptyset = \emptyset, \quad \text{like } (x) \cdot (0) = 0.$$

In any particular context, it is convenient to define a "universal" set U which comprises all the elements that may come under consideration in that context. With respect to this U, we can now define the complement $\bar{X}$ of a set X (which is contained in U); namely, the set consisting of all the elements of U that are not elements of X. In symbols:

$$\bar{X} = \{x : x \in U \text{ and } x \notin X\}.$$

The complement of X in U can also be written as $U - X$ or U/X. The operation "minus," analogous to subtraction in arithmetic, can be extended to any pair of sets. For sets X and Y:

$$X - Y = \{x : x \in X \text{ and } x \notin Y\}.$$

Note that only those elements of Y that are also elements of X can be "subtracted" in this operation. It follows that if X and Y are disjoint, $X - Y = X$. On the other hand, if $X = Y$, $X - Y = \emptyset$, like $x - x = 0$.

The reader can verify the following relations involving complements.

$\bar{\bar{X}} = X$ (the complement of the complement of X is X). $(\overline{X \cap Y}) = \bar{X} \cup \bar{Y}$ (the complement of the intersection of two sets is the union of their complements).

$$X \cup X = X; \, X \cap X = X; \, \bar{\emptyset} = U; \, \bar{U} = \emptyset.$$

The next important concept of set theory is that of the *product set*. Consider two sets X and Y, not necessarily disjoint or even necessarily distinct. The set of all ordered pairs $\{(x, y) : x \in X \text{ and } y \in Y\}$ is called the *product* (or the *Cartesian product*) of X and Y. It is written $X \times Y$.

Examples.

1. Let M be the set of all adult males and W the set of all adult females. Then $M \times W$ is the set of all possible ordered couples (m, w) with $m \in M$ representing an adult male and $w \in W$ an adult female.

2. Let $\mathbb{R}$ be the set of all real numbers. Then $\mathbb{R} \times \mathbb{R}$ (also written $\mathbb{R}^2$) is the set of all ordered pairs of real numbers (x, y). This set can be regarded as a representation of the Cartesian plane (hence the name "Cartesian product"). The concept of product set can be extended to any finite collection of sets, whereby the elements become ordered triples, quadruples, and so on. In what now follows, we will be dealing with the Cartesian product of a set with itself.

RELATIONS

Given a set Y and the Cartesian product of Y with itself (that is, $Y \times Y$), a *relation* R on Y is defined as a subset of this Cartesian product. Thus

$$R \subset Y \times Y, \text{ where } Y \times Y = \{(y_1, y_2): y_1 \in Y, y_2 \in Y\}.$$

The connection between this definition of a "relation" and the common sense usage of "relation" can be seen as follows. Let Y be a set of adult males and consider the set of those ordered pairs of adult males belonging to Y, (y_1, y_2), in which y_1 is the father of y_2. Clearly, this set is a subset of the set of *all* ordered pairs (y_1, y_2); that is, a subset of $Y \times Y$. This subset is defined as the relation F ("is the father of"). In fact, we can write $y_1 F y_2$ (read "y_1 is the father of y_2") or, equivalently, $(y_1, y_2) \in F \subset Y \times Y$ (read, "the ordered pair (y_1, y_2) belongs to the set F of ordered pairs belonging to $Y \times Y$ whenever y_1 is the father of y_2"). This may seem like a roundabout way of saying something simple like "y_1 is the father of y_2," but it facilitates formal discussions involving relations. If we define a relation as a set, we can perform the usual set operations on it; for example, take its complement, consider its subsets, form unions and intersections, and so on. The meaning of $y_1 \bar{F} y_2$ is evident: $\bar{F}$ represents the relation that is the complement of F in $Y \times Y$.

Remark: The relation F above may be the empty set, which is the case if no one in Y is the father of anyone else in Y.

A relation R on a set Y is called *complete* if $y_1 R y_2$ holds for all y_1 and y_2 in Y (including the case when $y_1 = y_2$). In this case, it is clear that we can write $R = Y \times Y$.

Example. Let Y be a set of persons and let every person in Y know the name of every other person in Y and also his/her own name. Then the relation N on Y denoting "knows the name of" is complete.

A relation R on a set X is called *connected* if xRy or yRx holds for every x and y in X; and *weakly connected* if xRy or yRx holds for every $x \neq y$ in X.

Examples. The relation "equal or greater than" is connected on the set of real numbers. The relation "greater than" is weakly connected on the same set.

A relation is called *symmetric* if $y_1 R y_2$ implies $y_2 R y_1$.

Example. Let Y be a set of adult females, and let S be the relation "is the sister of." Then S is symmetric on Y.

Remark: If Y is a set of persons, then S is not necessarily symmetric, since we may have $y_1 S y_2$ (y_1 is a sister of y_2), but $y_2 \bar{S} y_1$ (y_2 is not a sister, being a brother of y_1). However, if S stands for "is a sibling of," then S is symmetric.

A relation is called *asymmetric* if $y_1 R y_2$ implies $y_2 \cancel{R} y_1$. In our example above, F was asymmetric. The following relations are also asymmetric: "is older than," "is heavier than," and so on.

A relation is called *reflexive* if yRy holds for every y in Y. In our example above where R denoted "knows the name of," R is a reflexive relation if we assume that everyone knows his/her own name (regardless of whether he/she knows anyone else's name).

A relation R on Y is called *transitive* if $y_1 R y_2$ and $y_2 R y_3$ imply $y_1 R y_3$.

Examples. "is older than," "is an ancestor of," "is equal to," "is divisible by." Clearly, "is the father of" is not transitive; nor is "is the brother of" (since the brother of my brother may be myself).

Consider now a relation on Y that is reflexive, symmetric, and transitive. The reader can verify that this relation *partitions* the elements of Y into subsets such that within each subset, all the elements are in that relation to each other, and no element in one subset is in that relation to any element in another subset. Such a relation is called an *equivalence relation*.

Example. Let N be the set of all integers, and let R be a subset of $N \times N$ defined as follows:

$$R = \{(y_1, y_2): y_1 \in N, y_2 \in N, \text{ and } (y_1 - y_2) \text{ is divisible by } 7\}.$$

Consider the seven subsets of N each consisting of all those integers which, upon division by 7, leave remainders $0, 1, 2, \ldots, 6$ respectively. Clearly, the union of these subsets is the entire set of integers. (This illustrates the meaning of the term "partition".) Now if $y_1 - y_2$ is divisible by 7 (that is, $y_1 R y_2$), so is $y_2 - y_1$ (that is, $y_2 R y_1$). Consequently, R is symmetric. Further, $y - y = 0$, which is divisible by any integer; hence yRy for all integers y and R is reflexive. Finally, if $y_1 R y_2$, then $y_1 - y_2 = 7k$, where k is some integer. If $y_2 R y_3$, then $y_2 - y_3 = 7m$, with m an integer; $y_1 - y_3 = y_1 - y_2 + y_2 - y_3 = 7(k + m)$, which is again a multiple of 7. Hence R is transitive. Thus R is an equivalence relation.

ORDERS

An asymmetric relation may induce an *order* on the set. Intuitively, we think of a set as "ordered" if we can decide which of any two elements "precedes" the other. For instance, we think of the alphabet as ordered, and this conception is utilized in making dictionaries and telephone books.

The alphabet is an example of a *linear order*, one which determines precedence for any pair of letters. Formally speaking, a linear order is a binary asymmetric relation P on a set X that is weakly connected (see p. 265) and transitive. The term "linear" refers to a graphical representation of a linear order. For instance, the alphabet can be represented as in Figure 14.1.

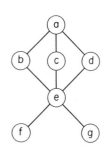

Figure 14.1. The alphabet as a linear order.　　**Figure 14.2.** A weak order.

Whenever one letter is above another in Figure 14.1, the first precedes the second in the alphabet; for example, cPq, where P denotes "precedes."

It is useful to define orders "weaker" than the linear order. This can be done by dropping the requirements of connectedness and/or transitivity. If we do not demand that our asymmetric relation P we weakly connected, we may have for some pairs of elements x, y neither xPy nor yPx ($x\bar{P}y$ and $y\bar{P}x$). For instance, let X be a set of objects and let P be the asymmetric relation "is preferred to." We assume that this relation is transitive, but it need not be weakly connected. Then if $x\bar{P}y$ and $y\bar{P}x$, we can say, "x is indifferent to y." (This is merely another way of saying that a subject who is asked to state his preference is indifferent between x and y). Call the relation "is indifferent to" I. This relation can be seen to be induced by our asymmetric relation P. Clearly, I is symmetric: if xIy, then yIx. But we have said nothing about its transitivity. We did not demand that xIy and yIz imply xIz. If we do demand this, then our asymmetric relation P determines a *weak order* on X.

Formally, a weak order is defined as follows.

(i)　There is an asymmetric transitive relation P on X.

(ii)　The symmetric relation I is defined by "xIy if and only if $x\bar{P}y$ and $y\bar{P}x$."

(iii)　I is transitive: xIy and yIz imply xIz.

A weak order is shown graphically in Figure 14.2. If an element x is on a "higher level" than y, then xPy. If x and y are on the same level, then xIy.

Figure 14.2 illustrates the weak order induced by the relation of class inclusion ("$\subset$") on the eight subsets of the set $X = \{x, y, z\}$. Subsets on a given level strictly contain all the subsets on lower levels. If two subsets are on the same level, neither contains the other. Recall that according to convention, the null set $\emptyset$ is regarded as being contained (is a subset of) every set. Accordingly, $\emptyset$ is on the lowest level.

We can "weaken" our concept of order still further by dropping the requirement that I be transitive, while retaining the requirement that P be transitive. In this case, P determines a *strict partial order*. Strict partial orders occur frequently in mathematical models of stimulus discrimination. Suppose a subject is presented with a set of musical tones of varying frequency. We will say xPy if the subject judges tone x to be "higher" than tone y. We expect this relation to be asymmetric and transitive. If the subject cannot distinguish between x and y, we can say xIy and can expect this relation to be symmetric. But we cannot expect I to be transitive, because it can certainly happen that the subject cannot distinguish between x and y because they differ only slightly in frequency, nor between y and z for the same reason, but that she can distinguish between x and z because these tones differ sufficiently to be distinguished.

A graphical representation of a strict partial order is shown in Figure 14.3. Here xPy if and only if a path along arrows exists from x to y. If no such path exists in either direction, xIy. From the figure, we see that although aIb and bIc, aPc.

Finally, we can drop the requirement that P be transitive. However, to retain a minimal property of an "order," we must keep the requirement that P produces no "cycles" in the form xPy, yPz, zPx. The property of "acyclicity" is implied by transitivity but does not imply it. To see the significance of "acyclicity," let P represent the relation "is preferred to." We would not think a set of objects to be "ordered" according to a person's preference if he preferred x to y, y to z, and z to x. Examples of such cyclic preference relations are not infrequently observed in practice and present special problems in constructing models of choice behavior. We are excluding these problems here because we are discussing asymmetric relations that induce orders on sets of elements. Acyclicity is the "least we can expect" from such a relation.

The order induced by an asymmetric relation that satisfies only the requirement of acyclicity is called a *suborder*. It is shown graphically in Figure 14.4. Here xPy if and only if an arrow goes from x to y. As can be seen in Figure 14.4, the arrows form no cyclic paths, but P is not transitive since there is an arrow from a to b and from b to c but none from a to c.

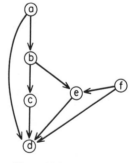

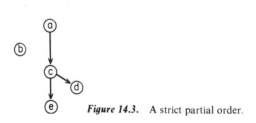

Figure 14.3. A strict partial order.

Figure 14.4. A suborder.

Remark: A linear order is also a "weak order" since it satisfies the requirements of a weak order. The terminology may be somewhat misleading because we tend to think that if something is "strong" (like a linear order), it should not be called "weak." However, such terminology, where "strength" includes "weakness," is common in mathematics. "Strong" properties are usually defined so as to include "weak" properties, which they do if they satisfy the requirements of the latter. On the other hand, "weak" properties do not, as a rule, include "strong" properties. In this sense, although strict partial orders need not be weak orders, weak orders are necessarily strict partial orders, and the latter are necessarily also suborders. When we speak of a weak order, we will mean *at least* a weak order (that is, a weak order or stronger) unless otherwise specified. Distinctions between orders of various "strengths" are made in the formal theory of social choice (see Fishburn, 1973).

FUNCTIONS

The fundamental mathematical concept of *function* can be defined as a special case of relation. Let X and Y be sets, and $X \times Y$ their product set. Consider a subset R of $X \times Y$; that is, a relation with the following properties:

(i)   For each $x \in X$, there exists an ordered pair (x, y) in R.

(ii) $(x_1, y_1), (x_1, y_2) \in R$ implies $y_1 = y_2$.

Property (i) is another way of saying that every x in X is in relation R to *some* y in Y. Properties (i) and (ii) together are another way of saying that each x in X is in relation R with *exactly one* y in Y.

A relation $R \subset X \times Y$ that satisfies (i) and (ii) is called a *function* or a *mapping* of X upon Y or from X to Y. In symbols, $R = f: X \rightarrow Y$, or $y = f(x)$.[2]
The set X is called the *domain* of f. The set Y is called the *codomain*.
If $f(x) = y$, y is called the *image* of x. The set of elements of Y that are images of elements of X is called the *range* of f.

It is important to note that the above definition does *not* imply that for every y in Y there exists an x in X related to it by R; that is, xRy. Nor does the definition imply that there is only one x in X related to a given y; that is, (x_1, y_1) and (x_2, y_1) do not necessarily imply $x_1 = x_2$. If the above two conditions *are* satisfied, the mapping $f: X \rightarrow Y$ is said to be *one-to-one*.

Example.   Let X be a set of boys and Y a set of girls. Consider a relation $R \subset X \times Y$ denoting "goes out with," such that $(x, y) \in R$ if and only if the boy x goes out with the girl y. Note that R is a relation even if some boys in X do not go out with any girls in Y. R is a function or a mapping of X upon Y if and only if every boy in X goes out with exactly one girl in Y. Next, R is a mapping of X upon Y even if some girls in Y do not go out with any of the boys in X. It is still a mapping of X upon Y if more than one boy goes out with the same girl in Y. It is not a mapping of X upon Y if some boy goes out with more than one girl. It is a one-to-one mapping if every boy goes out with exactly one girl, and every girl goes out with exactly one boy. Clearly, in this case, the number of boys in X must equal the number of girls in Y.

The connection of this definition of function and its usual meaning in mathematics can be seen as follows. Let X and Y both represent the set of all rational numbers Q. Let R denote "is the square of"; that is, $(x, y) \in R$ or xRy if and only if $y = x^2$. Then every x in X is related to some y in Y. We can write $f: Q \rightarrow Q$; $f(x) = y = x^2$. We note that not every $y \in Q$ is an image of some $x \in Q$; for instance, 3 and -4 are not. In this case Q is both the domain and the codomain of f; but the range of f is the set of rational numbers in the form m^2/n^2, where m and n are both integers and $n \neq 0$.

If $f: X \rightarrow Y$ is one-to-one and thus the corresponding relation $R \subset X \times Y$ is one-to-one, the relation $R^{-1} \subset Y \times X$, defined by $(y, x) \in R^{-1}$ if and only if xRy, is also a function called the *inverse* of f and denoted by $f^{-1}: Y \rightarrow X$; $f^{-1}(y) = x$. The element $x \in X$ is called the *inverse image* of y under f.

Example. Let X and Y both represent the set of all positive real numbers $\mathbb{R}^+$, and $f(x) = y = x^2$. Then f is one-to-one and $f^{-1}(y) = x = \sqrt{y}$.

Let X, Y, and Z be sets. Let R and S be relations; namely, $R \subset X \times Y$; $S \subset Y \times Z$. We can define a binary operation on relations called *composition*; for example, $R \circ S = T$, where $T \subset X \times Z$, $T = \{(x, z); x \in X, z \in Z,$ and there exists a $y \in Y$ such that xRy and $ySz\}$.

Example. Let X, Y, Z represent the same set of persons. Let F denote the relation "is the father of," S the relation "is a sister of," and T the relation "is a maternal aunt of." Then $T = S \circ F$, which can be interpreted as follows: xTz, or $x(S \circ F)z$, if and only if x is z's father's sister; that is, z's maternal aunt.

Clearly, $R \circ S \neq S \circ R$ in general. In the above example, $x(F \circ S)z$ if x is z's sister's father; that is, z's father (or possibly not a blood relation if "half sister" is subsumed under "sister"). In any case, x is not z's maternal aunt.

A generalization of composition to concatenation of a sequence of relations is straightforward. It should be noted that composition is not necessarily associative. Thus in concatenating several relations, the order of performing composition must be indicated.

If R and S are functions, their composition is defined as the composition of the corresponding relations.

Let $f(x) = x^2$, $g(x) = x + a$. Then $[f \circ g](x) = x^2 + a$; $[g \circ f](x) = x^2 + 2ax + a^2$.[3] We note that if f has an inverse f^{-1}, then $f \circ f^{-1} = f^{-1} \circ f = I$, the identity function defined by $I(x) = x$. Clearly, composition of functions is not generally commutative.

Composition of mappings (that is, of functions) can be conveniently illustrated in terms of permutations of finite sets of elements. Consider a finite set N of objects: $N = \{1, 2, \ldots, n\}$ and the set of all possible ordered n-tuples (that is, arrangements) of these objects. Every n-tuple is a *permutation*. A permutation can also be regarded as a one-to-one function $p_i\colon N \to N$. For instance, if $B = \{1, 2, 3, 4\}$, then the ordered quadruple $(3, 2, 4, 1)$ can be regarded as a function $p_i(1) = 3$, $p_i(2) = 2$, $p_i(3) = 4$, $p_i(4) = 1$. Since there are 24 permutations of four objects, there is a set of 24 functions $P = \{p_1, p_2, \ldots, p_{24}\}$. Note that the elements of P are permutations or ordered quadruples of the four objects or functions $p_i\colon N \to N$, *not* the elements of the original set N. When p_i is represented as an ordered quadruple, the element in the jth position of the quadruple $(j = 1, \ldots, 4)$ is the image under the mapping p_i of the element j of N.

Now we can investigate the composition of permutations. Let $p_i = (2, 3, 1, 4)$ and $p_j = (1, 2, 4, 3)$. Then $p_i \circ p_j = (2, 4, 1, 3)$ since p_i maps "1" upon "2" and p_j maps "2" upon "2"; consequently, $p_i \circ p_j$ maps "1" upon "2." Further, since p_i maps "2" upon "3," and p_j maps "3" upon "4," $p_i \circ p_j$ maps "2" upon "4," and so on.

The permutation $p_1 = (1, 2, 3, 4)$ is called the *identity permutation*. It maps each element of N into itself; that is, $p_1(x) = x$ ($x = 1, 2, 3$, or 4). Every permutation has an inverse. For instance, p_i^{-1}, the inverse of p_i above, is $(3, 1, 2, 4)$. Since p_i maps "1" upon "2," p_i^{-1} maps "2" upon "1," which is seen from the fact that "1" is in the second position of p_i^{-1}, and so on.

The reader can verify further that the composition operation "$\circ$" applied to permutation is associative; that is, $p_i \circ (p_j \circ p_k) = (p_i \circ p_j) \circ p_k$ for every p_i, p_j, p_k in P. But "$\circ$" is not in general commutative, although for some p_i, p_j, $p_i \circ p_j = p_j \circ p_i$ holds. For example, $(1, 2, 4, 3) \circ (2, 1, 3, 4) = (2, 1, 3, 4) \circ (1, 2, 4, 3) = (2, 1, 4, 3)$.

A set $G = \{x, y, \ldots\}$ together with a binary operation "$\circ$" (that is, a composition) is said to constitute a *group* if the following conditions are satisfied.

(i)   "$\circ$" is *closed*; that is, for every $x, y \in G$, $x \circ y = z \in G$.

(ii) "$\circ$" is *associative*; that is, for every x, y, z in G, $x \circ (y \circ z) = (x \circ y) \circ z$.

(iii) There is an element $e \in G$ such that $e \circ x = x \circ e = x$. This element is called the *identity element* of G.

(iv) Every element of x of G has an inverse $x^{-1} \in G$; that is, $x \circ x^{-1} = x^{-1} \circ x = e$.

It is easy to verify that the set of permutations of n objects together with the operation of composition of permutations constitute a group.

Other examples of groups are:

1. The set of integers N together with addition. The element "0" is the identity element of this group.

2. The set of positive rational numbers together with multiplication. The element "1" is the identity element of this group. The inverse of every positive rational number is its reciprocal.

3. The set of rotations of a cube around any of its three principal axes through multiples of 90°, where any two such rotations performed consecutively constitute a composition of the two rotations.

The reader can verify that the composition in each of the first two of the above example is commutative, but in the third it is not.

In the above examples, **1** and **2** are groups with infinite sets of elements, whereas the set of elements in **3** is finite since only a finite number of orientations of a cube can be generated by the rotations.

A finite group can be represented by a "multiplication table"; that is, by a matrix with rows and columns representing the elements in the same order and with the ijth entry representing the "product" of elements i and j in that order (since the binary operation of the group designated as "multiplication" need not be commutative).

If a is an element of a finite group with n elements, there is a positive integer p $(1 \leqslant p \leqslant n)$ for which a^p $(= a \circ a \circ a \circ \cdots \circ a$, p times$) = e$. p is called the *order* of a, and n is called the order of the group. A group is *generated* by some of its elements in the sense that every one of its elements can be represented as a "product" of these generating elements.

As a simple example, consider a group of order 4 generated by two elements, W and C. Its multiplication table is shown as Matrix 14.1.

$$
\begin{array}{c|cccc}
 & I & C & W & WC \\
\hline
I & I & C & W & WC \\
C & C & I & WC & W \\
W & W & WC & I & C \\
WC & WC & W & C & I
\end{array}
$$

Matrix 14.1

Clearly, the order of both W and C is 2, and the "multiplication" of this group is commutative. Matrix 14.2 represents another type of group of order 5. It is also generated by two elements, W and C.

$$
\begin{array}{c|ccccc}
 & I & C & W & W^2 & WC \\
\hline
I & I & C & W & W^2 & WC \\
C & C & W & WC & I & W^2 \\
W & W & WC & W^2 & C & I \\
W^2 & W^2 & I & C & WC & W \\
WC & WC & W^2 & I & W & C
\end{array}
$$

Matrix 14.2

In this group, both generating elements have order 5, multiplication is commutative, and $W^3 = C$, as the reader can verify from the matrix. Below we will show how this formalism can be used in representing the kinship structure of a society.

Let X and Y be two sets that can be put into one-to-one correspondence with each other; that is, a one-to-one mapping $f: X \to Y$ exists and therefore so does its inverse $f^{-1}: Y \to X$. Further, let R be a binary relation on X and S a binary relation on Y. Suppose the following condition is satisfied: for every x_1, x_2 in x and for some one-to-one $f: X \to Y$, $x_1 R x_2$ implies $y_1 S y_2$, where $y_1 = f(x_1)$, $y_2 = f(x_2)$. Then the pair or system $\langle X, R \rangle$ is said to be *isomorphic* to the pair (or system) $\langle Y, S \rangle$.

Examples. Let X be the set of all integers, Y the set of all even integers, R the relation "is greater than," S the relation "is less than," f the function $f(x) = y = -2x$. Then if $x_1 > x_2$, $-2x_1 < -2x_2$, and our conditions for isomorphism are fulfilled.

Isomorphism can also be defined with respect to a composition. Let X be a set and "$\circ$" a composition operation on its elements, Y another set in one-to-one correspondence with X, and "$*$" a composition operation on its elements. Then the system $\langle X, \circ \rangle$ is isomorphic to $\langle Y, * \rangle$ under the one-to-one mapping $f: X \to Y$ if and only if $f(x_1 \circ x_2) = y_1 * y_2$, where $f(x_1) = y_1$, $f(x_2) = y_2$.

Let X be the set of all positive real numbers and Y the set of all real numbers. Let "$\cdot$" represent multiplication and "$+$" addition. Finally, let $f(x) = y = \log(x)$. Then $\log(x_1 x_2) = \log(x_1) + \log(x_2)$, and our conditions for isomorphism are fulfilled: $\langle X, \cdot \rangle$ is isomorphic to $\langle Y, + \rangle$.

The concept of isomorphism can be applied to groups. Consider a group $G = \langle N, \circ \rangle$, where N is a set of elements and $\circ$ a binary operation on the set, and a group $G' = \langle N', * \rangle$. Assuming a one-to-one mapping $f: N \to N'$, whereby $f(a \circ b) = a' * b'$ with $f(a) = a'$, $f(b) = b'$, these two groups are isomorphic under the mapping f and under f^{-1}.

Note that the exponential function $g(x) = y = a^x$ (where a is the base to which the logarithms were taken) is the inverse of $f(x) = \log_a(x)$. Its domain is the set of all real numbers, and its range is the set of all positive real numbers.

THE STRUCTURE OF A MARRIAGE SYSTEM

We will now illustrate the use of mapping terminology in describing certain types of social structures called *prescribed marriage systems*.

Imagine a society all of those members are partitioned into a number of clans so that each individual belongs to one and only one clan. This partition is generated by an equivalence relation "belongs to the same clan as." Furthermore, each man if he marries must choose a wife from a specific clan not his own, so that two men belonging to the same clan must choose wives from the same clan not their own. Also, men from different clans may not choose wives from the same clan.

Consider the set $S = \{a, b, \dots\}$ whose elements are the clans into which that society is partitioned. The above marriage rule can be expressed as a mapping which we designate by $W: S \to S$. If a is a clan, $W(a)$ is the clan from which men belonging to a must choose their wives. Since men belonging to different clans may not choose wives from the same clan, the mapping is one-to-one and therefore has an inverse $W^{-1}: S \to S$. If a is a clan, $W^{-1}(a)$ is also a clan: namely, the clan to which men who marry women in a must belong; or, equivalently, if a woman belongs to clan a, she must choose her husband from clan $W^{-1}(a)$.

In a prescribed marriage system there are also rules which specify the clan to which the children of a marriage belong. The clan to which such children belong depends only on the clan membership of the father and of the mother, not on who these persons may be.

Now since the clan to which a husband belongs determines the clan to which his wife belongs, the rule for assigning the children of the marriage can be stated as a mapping $C: S \to S$. This mapping is also one-to-one; that is, the children of fathers belonging to different clans may not be assigned to the same clan. Thus C has an inverse C^{-1}. If a is a clan in S, then $C^{-1}(a)$ is the clan to which the fathers of persons in a belong. We see that both W and C can be regarded as permutations of S.

We summarize the above rules in four axioms that define any prescribed marriage system.

M_1: S is a partition of the society (defined by an equivalence relation "belongs to the same clan as").

M_2: W is a permutation of S.

M_3: C is a permutation of S.

M_4: $W(a) \neq a$. A husband may not choose a wife from his own clan.

M_4 can be interpreted to mean that all persons belonging to the same clan are "siblings." In practically all societies, marriages between true (that is, biological) siblings are forbidden. In a prescribed marriage system of the sort we are describing, the concept "sibling" is extended to mean "members of the same clan." Having generalized the concept "sibling," we can infer generalized concepts of other relationships. For example, "uncle" may mean a man belonging to the same clan as one's father (or one's mother); "cousins" are persons whose respective parents of either sex are "siblings," and so on.

Prescribed marriage systems observed by cultural anthropologists usually have additional rules.

M_5. Some composition of mappings W and C relate all a and $b \in S$.

In most societies, relationships are defined in terms of descent (blood relationships), (spouse), or some combinations of marriage and descent (uncle-by-marriage, in-laws, and so on). In most European societies, only some relationships by marriage are regarded as "relations." For instance, the brother of an uncle-by-marriage is not usually regarded as a "relation." It is possible, however, to regard all relationships traceable through links by blood and links by marriage as "relations." It is in this sense that M_5 prescribes that all clans be "related." This rule puts some restrictions on the permutations induced by W and C. To see this, imagine the following prescribed marriage system.

Clans

x:	a	b	c	d
$W(x)$:	b	a	d	c
$C(x)$:	a	b	c	d

Note that M_1–M_4 are all satisfied. However, M_5 is violated. Clans a and b choose their spouses from each other, and their children are again in a or b. The same is true for c and d. It follows that clans a and c are not "related" either by descent or by marriage, and the same is true for clans a and d, b and c, and b and d. M_5 prevents this situation from occurring. Presumably, the rule, perhaps coupled with some obligations associated with various kinds of "relationships," serves to hold the whole society together.

Let us now see how relationships can be expressed as compositions of blood and marriage relationships. Mappings W and C and their inverses are applied to clans. For instance, C^{-1} means "the clan to which (my) father belongs." Applying W to that clan, we get WC^{-1} as the clan from which my father must have chosen his wife; that is, the clan to which my mother belongs. Now C applied to WC^{-1} determines the clan to which the children of the *men* in my mother's clan belong. All the men in that clan are my mother's "brothers." Hence the clan CWC^{-1} contains my "cousins"; more precisely, children of my mother's "brothers," as well as the children of my mother's clan-sisters' "brothers." Such "cousins" are called matrilineal cross cousins.

In European societies, distinctions between different kinds of cousins are seldom made (although maternal and paternal grandparents, uncles, and aunts are sometimes distinguished). As we shall see below, in prescribed marriage systems, distinctions among at least four kinds of cousins become important.

M_6. Whether two persons related by marriage and descent links are in the same clan depends only on the kind of relationships and not on the clans either one belongs to.

Suppose the prescribed marriage rules imply that a given relationship defined by some combination of descent and marriage links puts two persons in the same clan (or in different clans). Then the rules must be such that any two persons biologically so related will individually be in the same (different) clans, depending only on their relationships through descent or marriage.

Given the above set of rules, it is easy to state whether a given couple may or may not marry. They may marry if the girl belongs to the clan from which the boy must choose his wife and not otherwise. However, there arises a more general question: Under what conditions may two persons related by some combination of descent and marriage links marry? This question can be answered by applying the mappings. In particular, we will show that in a prescribed marriage system governed by rules M_1-M_6, certain kinds of cousins can never marry and other kinds of cousins can marry only under certain conditions.

Four kinds of "cousinhood" can be distinguished between a boy and a girl:

Patrilineal parallel cousins (fathers are brothers)
Matrilineal parallel cousins (mothers are sisters)
Patrilineal cross cousins (boy's father is brother of girl's mother)
Matrilineal cross cousins (boy's mother is sister of girl's father)

Consider now a boy and a girl who are patrilineal parallel cousins. Their fathers, who are brothers, must be sons of either the same father or the same mother. In either case, the fathers belong to the same clan. Therefore, in view of the mapping C, the patrilineal parallel cousins belong to the same clan and are consequently "siblings" in the sense of clan membership. Thus they cannot marry. But the same reasoning, matrilineal parallel cousins cannot marry.

Let us now consider matrilineal cross cousins. The boy's mother is a sister of the girl's father. So both are in the same clan, whether they are children of the same father or the same mother. However, because they are in the same clan, the boy's mother cannot have married a man from the same clan as the girl's father (that is, from her own clan). Therefore, matrilineal cross cousins belong to different clans. They can marry *provided* the girl belongs to the clan from which the boy must choose his wife. Suppose the boy belongs to clan a. Then his father belongs to clan $C^{-1}(a)$. His mother belongs to clan $WC^{-1}(a)$, to which the girl's father (the brother of the boy's mother) also belongs. The girl, in view of mapping C, belongs to clan $CWC^{-1}(a)$. The boy can marry her if this is the clan from which he may (that is, must) choose his wife. That is to say, if the boy's clan is a and the girl's b, and they are matrilineal cross cousins, he may marry her if the following equation is satisfied:

$$b = W(a) = CWC^{-1}(a); \tag{14.1}$$

or, since the same rules apply to all clans, if

$$W = CWC^{-1}; \tag{14.2}$$

that is, if W is expressible as a composite of mappings on the right side of Equation 14.2.

By similar reasoning, it can be shown that patrilineal cross cousins may marry if and only if

$$W = CW^{-1}C^{-1}. \tag{14.3}$$

In general, given the mappings of any prescribed marriage system isomorphic to the one described with respect to relations W and C and their compositions (see p. 270), it is possible to decide whether relatives of a given type may or may not marry in any such system and, if they may, under what conditions.

Definitions of "incest" vary widely in different societies. In prerevolutionary Russia, a man was not permitted to marry the sister of his sister's husband. Recall the situation in Tolstoy's *War and Peace*, where Natasha's mother has misgivings about her daughter's engagement to Prince Bolkonsky, although it would be a brilliant match, because she would like to marry off her son Nikolai to Bolkonsky's sister Mary, which would be a highly profitable match. Also, the godparents of a child were not permitted to marry each other. Marriage rules, especially prohibitions, can become quite complex. In fact, they can conceivably become so complex that no one is permitted to marry anyone. Of course, a situation of this sort would not correspond to a prescribed marriage system as defined above. If everyone knows to which clan everyone else belongs, the set of women from which a man can (in fact, must) choose his wife is clearly defined, and so is the set of men from which a woman must choose her husband. In reality, among people in whom the concept of a social role is completely inter-woven with kinship relations, clans may not be explicitly defined or distinguished by names. There are prescriptions about who may or may not marry whom expressed in terms of kinship words used in that society. From these prescriptions, clans are *inferred* by an outside observer, usually an anthropologist. If the prescriptions are sufficiently simple, it is a relatively simple matter to describe them in compact form by *assuming* that the society is divided into clans which impose kinship relations on individuals. If the rules are complex, the task may be quite difficult. For example, H. L. White (1963, p. 107) writes about the Arunta tribe (of Australian aborigines):

> The Arunta themselves thought of their kinship system as one of eight 'subsections' . . . There was a set of classificatory kin terms. A large number of modifiers were used with the basic terms in a rather flexible way to indicate birth order and sex.

White points out, however, that an eight-clan model does not adequately account for the patterns of choosing mates. Instead, he proposes a sixteen-clan model to account for certain taboos that are not inferrable from the eight-clan model. He writes (1963, p. 117),

> " . . . only . . . the latter can explain why all persons in certain classificatory relations—whether they are 'near' or distant cases of the relation—are excluded from marriage . . . even though they belong to the same subsection of allowed spouses.

The theory of groups is a useful tool for classifying societies based on kinship systems. Consider a group generated by elements W and C. As we have seen, these elements can represent permutations on a set of clans in a prescribed marriage system. It has been shown (see White, 1963, Chapter 2) that the group of permutations representing a system that satisfies axioms M_1-M_6 must have order n, the number of clans.

Two societies with marriage systems represented by isomorphic groups are regarded as structurally identical. Thus different groups with n elements represent different types of marriage systems and suggest a taxonomy of such systems. For instance, Matrix 14.1 represents a so-called *bilateral* marriage system characterized by $W^2 = I$, $WC = CW$. In a *matrilineal* marriage system, $WC = CW$ but $W^2 \neq I$. Matrix 14.2 represents such a system. Other types are pairwise connected clans with $W^2 = I$, $WC \neq CW$. Whenever $W^2 = I$, pairs of clans exchange marriage partners.

Needless to say, marriage rules and compact representations of kinship systems are not the only contexts in which structural mathematical models of the sort described could be utilized to advantage. They could conceivably be applied to complex rules governing contracts, government regulations, conditions of inheritance, tax laws with their numerous conditional exceptions and exemptions, and so on.

A MATRIX REPRESENTATION OF A BINARY RELATION

Let $N = \{1, 2, \ldots, n\}$ and let $R \subset N \times N$ be a binary relation on N. The matrix M, whose n rows and n columns represent the elements of N, can be a representation of R if $m_{ij} = 1$ whenever $(i, j) \in R$ and $m_{ij} = 0$ otherwise. If R is reflexive, we have $m_{ii} = 1$ $(i = 1, 2, \ldots, n)$. If R is symmetric, M is a symmetric matrix. If R is asymmetric, we have $m_{ii} = 0$ and $m_{ij}m_{ji} = 0$.

Moreover, M^2 can be regarded as a representation of $R \circ R$, the composition of R with itself in the following sense: the element $m_{ij}^{(2)}$ of $M^2 > 0$ if and only if $(i, j) \in R \circ R \subset N \times N$. To see this, observe that in view of the rule for matrix multiplication,

$$m_{ij}^{(2)} = \sum_k m_{ik}m_{kj}. \tag{14.4}$$

The right side of Equation 14.4 is positive if and only if for some k, $m_{ik}m_{kj} = 1$; that is, $m_{ik} = m_{kj} = 1$. But in view of our definition of the elements of M, this means that $(i, k) \in R$ and $(k, j) \in R$, which in turn implies that $(i, j) \in R \circ R$.

This result is readily generalizable. Let $R^{(k)} = R \circ R \circ R \circ \cdots \circ R$ be a k-fold concatenation of R with itself. Then the element $m_{ij}^{(k)}$ of M^k is positive if and only if $(i, j) \in R^{(k)}$.

Some important structural aspects of communication networks can be conveniently represented by this model if the n elements of N are persons or locations and if the relation R on N is interpreted as "can communicate with."

Then $m_{ij} = 1$ denotes that i can send a message directly to j. If $m_{ij} = 0$, i cannot send a message directly to j. But if $m_{ij}^{(2)} > 0$, we know that there exists an "intermediary"; that is, at least one k, to whom i can send a message, which k can relay to j. In general, if $m_{ij}^{(r)} > 0$ for some $r > 0$, we know that i can communicate with j; for in that case, there exists at least one "path" of $(r - 1)$ direct communication links from i to j.

Now if i can communicate with j at all (directly or indirectly), he must be able to do so over at most $(n - 2)$ intermediate points since there are only $(n - 2)$ points in N besides i and j. Therefore, if i can communicate with j, he must be able to do so either directly, via one intermediate point, via two intermediates, ..., or via $(n - 2)$ intermediates. It follows that the sum of the matrices $M + M^2 + \cdots + M^{n-1}$ gives us complete information about who can communicate to whom in the communication network represented by M.

DETECTION OF CLIQUES

The matrix representation of a binary relation suggests a definition of a *social clique*. Suppose a matrix M represents the relation "names as friend." Let R be the set of rows of M and C the set of columns. Furthermore, let $R' \subset R$, $C' \subset C$. A matrix M' with R' as the set of rows and C' as the set of columns is called a *submatrix* of M if it results from deleting rows and columns of M not belonging to R' and C' respectively. A submatrix M' of M whose main diagonal entries are the main diagonal entries of M is called a *principal submatrix* of M. If M represents a binary relation on some set N, a principal submatrix $M' \subset M$ represents the same binary relation *restricted* to a subset N' of N.

Let M' be a principal submatrix of M. Following R. D. Luce and A. D. Perry (1949), we will call $N' \subset N$ a *clique* of order 1 if $m'_{ij} = 1$ for all $i \in R'$, $j \in C'$, and if no principal submatrix $M'' \supset M'$ ($M'' \neq M'$) has this property. In other words, every individual in a clique N' of order 1 names every other individual in N' as a friend, and N' represents the *maximal*; that is, the most "inclusive" superset of N' with this property.

Consider now the principal submatrices of M^2 with all positive entries. The maximal submatrices of this sort represent cliques of order 2. In a clique of order 2, everyone is either a friend or a "friend of a friend." Cliques of higher order are defined recursively.

In the analysis of social structure induced, say, by a friendship relation, "exclusive" cliques are of special interest. Members of an exclusive clique name no one outside their clique as friends. Matrix 14.3 represents a social group with 9 individuals partitioned into three mutually exclusive cliques of order 1.

The clique structure is not immediately apparent in this representation. It becomes apparent if the individuals are rearranged as shown in Matrix 14.4. In matrix 14.4, the three cliques can be seen clearly. They comprise, respectively, the subsets $\{1, 3, 6\}$, $\{2, 5\}$, and $\{4, 7, 8, 9\}$.

	1	2	3	4	5	6	7	8	9
1	1	0	1	0	0	1	0	0	0
2	0	1	0	0	1	0	0	0	0
3	1	0	1	0	0	1	0	0	0
4	0	0	0	1	0	0	1	1	1
5	0	1	0	0	1	0	0	0	0
6	1	0	1	0	0	1	0	0	0
7	0	0	0	1	0	0	1	1	1
8	0	0	0	1	0	0	1	1	1
9	0	0	0	1	0	0	1	1	1

Matrix 14.3

	1	3	6	2	5	4	7	8	9
1	1	1	1	0	0	0	0	0	0
3	1	1	1	0	0	0	0	0	0
6	1	1	1	0	0	0	0	0	0
2	0	0	0	1	1	0	0	0	0
5	0	0	0	1	1	0	0	0	0
4	0	0	0	0	0	1	1	1	1
7	0	0	0	0	0	1	1	1	1
8	0	0	0	0	0	1	1	1	1
9	0	0	0	0	0	1	1	1	1

Matrix 14.4

Cliques as defined here manifest themselves as submatrices with all positive entries; or, if the clique criteria are somewhat relaxed, as submatrices with high "densities" of positive entries. In recent developments of mathematical sociometric models, special attention has been devoted to submatrices consisting only of zeroes, or, more generally, submatrices with very low densities of positive entries. These "empty" or nearly empty submatrices are singled out in the so-called *null block models* of social structure. We will examine this approach in the next chapter.

ORGANIZATION OF WORK

Matrices have also been used in what could be called "mathematical praxiology" —a formal structural approach to the organization of work. Consider a task composed of several subtasks to be apportioned among a number of individuals. These subtasks when completed are to be "assembled" or coordinated in some manner to complete the entire task. Coordination requires channels for transmitting material or information. The totality of directed links connecting pairs of points constitute a binary relation, which in turn is representable by a matrix. The advantage of matrix representation is that it provides a simple algorithm (via matrix multiplication) for revealing composite relationships. Matrices can represent relationships not only among individuals (for example, who can communicate with whom) but also between subtasks and individuals, between items of information and individuals who possess them, between subtasks and items of information necessary to perform the subtasks, and so on.

In this way, a particular organization of a task can be formally represented by a set of matrices, and the performance by products of these matrices (which represent the flow of material and/or information). An interesting formulation of models of this sort and a discussion of experiments on group performance as a function of task organization is found in C. Flament (1963).

STRUCTURES REPRESENTED BY GRAPHS

As we have seen, a binary relation on a set can be represented by a matrix with entries "0" and "1." The representation is convenient in that it provides an algorithm for displaying compositions or concatenations of binary relations.

Another way of representing a binary relation is by a *graph*. Formally, a graph is defined as a pair $\langle N, V \rangle$, where N is a finite set and V is a binary relation on that set. A pictorial representation of a graph is shown in Figure 14.5. Represented in the figure is a set of *vertices*, some of which are connected by *arcs* (directed line segments). The set of ordered pairs of vertices (i, j) with arcs going from i to j is clearly a subset of the set of all ordered pairs (i, j) with $i \in N$, $j \in N$. This subset is the relation V.

A representation of a relation on a set by a graph is convenient in that it sometimes makes *visible* some salient features of the relation that may be important in a particular context. For instance, we might be interested in the

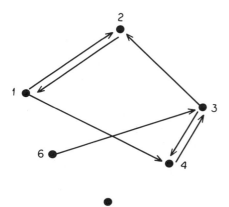

Figure 14.5. A directed graph (digraph).

existence of *cycles* (aVb, bVc, ..., kVa). These are often made apparent by the visual display.

A distinction is made between a *directed graph* (or *digraph*) and a *linear graph*. The latter is a representation of a symmetric relation. Here the arcs (now called *edges*) always go both ways, so these links between points can be drawn without arrow heads.

An important property of a graph is *connectedness*. A graph is said to be connected if it is possible to go from any point to any other point by following the arcs or edges. There are various ways of defining the *degree of connectedness* of a graph; for instance, by specifying the minimal number of points together with arcs or edges issuing from them that must be removed from a connected graph in order to make it no longer connected; or else by specifying the minimal number of arcs or edges that must be "cut" to disconnect the graph. The degree of connectedness evidently can be taken as a measure of the degree of "safety" of a communication system. This feature, too, is often made easier to perceive by the visual display presented by a graph.

In what follows, we will discuss the notion of *balance* or the *degree of balance* applied to special kinds of graphs to be presently defined, which are of interest in certain mathematical models of social structures.

A linear graph is called an *algebraic graph* if one of two real numbers is associated with each of its edges. Without loss of generality, these numbers can be taken as $+1$ and -1. A *complete algebraic graph* is one that is *completely connected*. That is, an edge labeled "plus" or "minus" connects every pair of points on the graph. Let N be a set of persons, and let either of the following statements (but not both) be true of any pair (x, y) of persons in N: "x and y are friends" or "x and y are enemies." This social structure can be represented by a complete algebraic graph.

In what follows, we will understand by a *path* in a complete algebraic graph a sequence of edges that does not pass through any vertex more than once. By a *cycle* we will understand a path that terminates on its origin and contains no other cycle.

The *sign* of a path in an algebraic graph is the sign of the "product" of the signs of its edges, in the sense that ("plus")·("plus") = ("minus")·("minus") = "plus"; ("plus")·("minus") = ("minus")·("plus") = "minus."

A complete algebraic graph is called *balanced* if all of its cycles are "positive" or, equivalently, if all of its cycles contain an even number of "negative" edges. It can be shown that a complete algebraic graph is balanced if and only if all of its three-vertex cycles are positive.

AN ANTHROPOLOGICAL OBSERVATION

In certain preindustrial societies, the so-called kinship nucleus consists of primarily four persons, father, mother, son, and maternal uncle. The latter often assumes responsibilities which in Western societies are usually assumed by a father, such as guidance and imposition of discipline on the boy.

C. Levi-Strauss (1969) has described several of these kinship nuclei in terms of "positive" or "negative" relationships that usually exist between father and mother, father and son, son and uncle, and uncle and mother. He did not mention the kinds of relationships that exist between mother and son and between father and brother-in-law. It is conjectured, however (see Flament, 1963), that the mother-son relationship is usually positive, whereas the father-uncle relationship usually tends to be negative.

Given these two relationships as fixed, it is possible to construct 16 different complete algebraic graphs with the four vertices representing the four members of the kinship nucleus. Only six of these, however, are mentioned by Levi-Strauss. They are shown in Figure 14.6. The graphs of type 1 and 2 are transformed into each other by interchanging father and uncle; those of type 3, by interchanging mother and son.

We note that all the "triangles" in the graph of type 1 are balanced (that is, positive), hence these graphs are balanced. The graphs of type 2 are not balanced, for example, the triangle mother-father-son is not balanced in either of them. These graphs could become balanced, however, if the sign of just one edge, mother-son, were changed. The graphs of type 3 are also not balanced. It is necessary to change the signs of *two* edges in order to make them balanced: either mother-son and father-uncle, or mother-uncle and father-son.

In actuality, according to Levi-Strauss, arrangements of type 1 are found quite frequently; those of type 2 are also rather frequently observed but are often "loose" (we assume this means that the relationships are not firmly fixed); whereas kinship nuclei of type 3 are quite rare. This suggests that the "degree of balance," in the sense of the minimum number of edges that must change sign to make the graph balanced, has some relationship to the "stability" of the corresponding structures.

A basic hypothesis in the theory of interpersonal relations, for which the algebraic graph serves as a model, is that an unbalanced triangle generates tensions. Consider the following simplistic but frequently observed criteria for

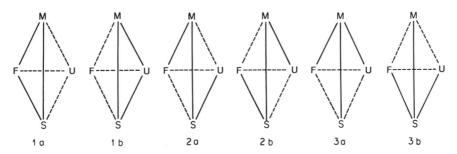

Figure 14.6. Types of kinship nuclei observed by Levi-Strauss.

categorizing others with reference to self:

> The friend of my friend is my friend.
> The enemy of my friend is my enemy.
> The friend of my enemy is my enemy.
> The enemy of my enemy is my friend.

Each of these criteria is represented by a balanced triangle. In an unbalanced triangle, a person dislikes someone whom his friend likes, he likes someone whom his friend dislikes, or he dislikes two people who dislike each other. It is assumed that in all these cases, a pressure is generated to "change the sign of an edge"—to withdraw friendship from a friend's enemy, or to offer friendship to a friend's friend, to try to reconcile two friends who are hostile to each other, or to offer friendship to one's enemy's enemy—something not infrequently observed in international relations.

It can easily be shown (see Harary, Norman, and Cartwright 1975) that a balanced complete algebraic graph can be partitioned into two subgraphs (one of which may be empty) such that within each subgraph, all the edges are positive and all the edges connecting points that are in different subgraphs are negative. That is to say, if neither of the subgraphs is empty, the "society" represented by a balanced graph is split into two camps hostile to each other.

Consider the graphs of type 1 in Figure 14.6. All its triangles are balanced. In graph 1a, mother, father, and son are an "alliance." Uncle is an "outsider," negatively related to the members of what in our society we would call the "nuclear family." In graph 1b, father is the "outsider." The situation is stable in the sense that none of the above simplistic criteria of "friend" and "enemy" is violated.

In graph 2a, mother might exert pressure on son "to be kinder to father"; or son might develop hostility against mother, who is "allied" with father. Similar tensions may be generated in the kinship nucleus represented by 2b.

Note that in graphs of type 3, *none* of the triangles are balanced. Tensions generated in that type of structure could be quite severe, which may account for the rarity of its occurrence.

As has been said, a "society" represented by a completely balanced graph is either "completely integrated" (with all edges positive) or "polarized" (split into two hostile camps). Attempts have been made to relate the degree of "polarization" of the international system to the frequency or the severity of wars occurring in such systems.

Application of models based on the degree of balance of a graph to the international system is associated with a number of difficulties. First, the complete algebraic graph model cannot be expected to describe the system because many pairs of nations cannot be classified as either "allies" or "potential enemies." Second, although an alliance between two states is usually a matter of historical record, the opposite relationship often is not, even though it may be intuitively apparent. Thus while certain aspects of the structure are based on "hard data," others are not. Finally, even though the system may be completely or almost completely polarized, the relative power (or "magnitude") of the two blocks may be equally decisive in determining the degree of tension generated by the polarization. If the blocks are approximately equal in power, we can speak of a "balance of power." If they are grossly unequal, we cannot. Thus the "balance of power" concept may be confounded with the "degree of balance" concept.

Model builders in international relations have attempted to bypass these difficulties by redefining "balance of power" and "degree of polarization" in various ways. The interested reader is referred to J. D. Singer and M. Small (1968) and to R. N. Rosencrance (1966).

NOTES

[1] Some authors reserve $\subset$ to denote a proper subset. The more general relation "is a subset of" is designated by $\subseteq$.

[2] Strictly speaking, "$f: X \to Y$" and "$f(x) = y$" have different meanings. The first expression designates the domain and the codomain of the function; the second designates the image of x in Y induced by the function.

[3] Alternately, composition of functions can be designated by $f[g(x)]$ or $g[f(x)]$. In this notation, the operations are performed from inside to outside. Here $f[g(x)] = x^2 + 2ax + a^2$; $g[f(x)] = x^2 + a$.

[4] For simplicity, we assume that each individual names himself as a friend.

CHAPTER FIFTEEN

Reduction of Structural Complexity

The definition of a binary relation as a subset of the Cartesian product of two sets (distinct or identical) suggests a straightforward generalization to subsets of two-factor, three-factor, and so on Cartesian products, which define ternary, quaternary, and so on relations. We may also have unary relations, which, in accordance with the above definition, reduce to subsets of the original set. Unary relations can, therefore, be interpreted as a singling out of a subset of elements characterized by some property. In short, the concept of relation is extremely flexible and broad.

The concept of structure can be defined with mathematical precision as a configuration consisting of a set, together with a set of relations of various orders. We shall think of a social structure in this way.

Clearly, an explicit specification of a structure by means of a simple enumeration of all the subsets of elements, pairs of elements, and so on singled out by the various relations would be neither practical nor enlightening. It becomes a task of a structural theory, therefore, to provide an "economical" description of a given structure. Such a description may involve a loss of information, but may bring out some essential features of the structure and so provide a basis for comparison between structures or for a taxonomy of structures.

As a simplest example of a social structure, consider a sociogram (that is, a set of individuals) N, and a binary relation F on this set defined by "$iFj: i$ names j as a friend." The structure is completely described by the set of pairs $\{(i, j) \in N \times N : iFj\}$. If N is not large, the digraph representing F can be perceived as a whole, and from its appearance some conclusions or conjectures can be drawn; for instance, about the cliques generated by the friendship ties, about "isolates" whom no one has named as friends, and so on. If $n = |N|$ is very large (say $n = 1,000$), the appearance of such a graph is likely to be more confusing than enlightening. Here more "economical" descriptions are certainly called for.

We note in passing that the binary relation in terms of which our structure was completely described induces relations of other orders; for example, unary relations and also ternary and higher relations. Consider, for example, the subset of N consisting of those individuals who have been named as "friend" exactly k times. This subset is entirely determined by the binary relation F. On the other hand, this subset itself constitutes a unary relation. Next, consider the set of all ordered triples of (x, y, z) of individuals in N of whom x names y, y names z, and z names x. Since this set is a subset of all triples in $N \times N \times N$, it is a particular ternary relation on N. But this relation is also completely determined once F is given.

By an "economical" description of a structure, we mean a characterization in terms of a small number of parameters. We will derive two such characterizations, one in terms of an induced set of unary relations (classes of individuals), the other induced by the totality of all the higher order relations.

To fix ideas, let n be large (for example, $n = 1,000$) and let each individual name exactly a friends. Our point of departure will be a null hypothesis; namely, that each individual names her a friends by a completely random selection from the set N.

The relation F can be represented by a digraph in which exactly a arrows issue from each vertex. The number of arrows issuing from a vertex of a digraph is called the *out-degree* of the vertex. If all vertices have the same out-degree, this number is called the out-degree of the graph. Thus we have a digraph of out-degree a. The number of arrows *converging* on a vertex is called the *in-degree* of the vertex. Clearly, the *average* of the in-degree in our graph will be a, but because of random choices, the in-degree of individual vertices will vary. In fact, it can be shown that if n is large compared to a, the random variable denoting the in-degree of a vertex in our digraph (that is, the number of choices received by an individual) will be very nearly Poisson distributed. If X is the number of choices received, then

$$\Pr[X = x] \cong \frac{a^x}{x!} e^{-a}, \tag{15.1}$$

where, it will be recalled, a is the out-degree.

Now if the choices are completely random, this means that an arbitrarily selected arrow in the graph will terminate on a particular vertex with probability $(n-1)^{-1}$. We can regard this probability "distribution" as characterizing a "degenerate" random variable Y whose distribution is concentrated entirely at one point:

$$\Pr[Y = (n-1)^{-1}] = 1.$$

Now Y represents the propensity of being chosen as a friend; that is, a measure of "popularity." In general, this propensity will not be constant throughout the population. Thus Y will have a distribution with a positive variance.

If the choices are not equiprobable but still independent events, the distribution of the number of choices received will be "flatter" than the Poisson distribution. The frequency at the extremes (very few or very many choices received) will be larger than under the null hypothesis (equiprobable choices), and the frequencies near the mean (that is, a) will be smaller. For example, if the above-mentioned "popularity" measure were gamma-distributed in the population (see p. 148), the distribution of choices received would be negative binomial, mathematically identical to the distribution of accident incidence in a heterogeneous population discussed in Chapter 8 (see p. 150).

Now the mean of the in-degree distribution is by definition fixed at a. But its variance is a free parameter and is a measure of the degree of differentiation of the individuals in the popularity dimension. This variance will be reflected in a parameter of the compound distribution, which is observable. Accordingly, we have a measure of the differentiation with regard to popularity—an index specifying a particular feature of the structure. The concrete manifestation of this feature is the number of individuals in each subset of N (unary relations) characterized by 0, 1, 2, ... choices received. The parameter or parameters of this distribution reflect the degree of individual differentiation (by "popularity") in the population.[1]

The above characterization is generated by properties inherent in the individuals as such. We will now give another characterization derived from relations *between* individuals.

Once again, consider a random digraph; that is, one constructed by randomly terminating arrows with out-degree a. We will define a *tracing procedure* as follows. Start with an arbitrarily selected vertex which represents the fraction $P_0 = 1/n$ of the n vertices. The set consisting of this single vertex will be designated by $\{P_0\}$. Next, determine the set of vertices on which the a arrows issuing from $\{P_0\}$ terminate. Call this set $\{P_1\}$. It contains at most a vertices, possibly fewer, since more than one arrow issuing from $\{P_0\}$ may terminate by chance on the same vertex. The sets $\{P_k\}$ ($k = 2, 3, \ldots$) are defined recursively. The set $\{P_{k+1}\}$ is the set of vertices on which the arrows from $\{P_k\}$ terminate and which do not belong to any of the sets $\{P_i\}$ ($i = 0, 1, 2, \ldots, k$). In other words, the set $\{P_k\}$ is the set of vertices reached *for the first time* on the kth step of the tracing. It follows that the sets $\{P_k\}$ are pairwise disjoint. The set $\{X_k\}$ is defined as $\{P_0\} \cup \{P_1\} \cup \ldots \cup \{P_k\}$.

If P_k is the fraction of vertices in $\{P_k\}$, it follows that the total fraction of vertices contacted is $X_k = \sum_{i=0}^{k} P_i$. Since P_k for $k > 0$ is a random variable, so is X_k. Moreover, if n is finite, $P_r = 0$ for some value of r, $P_k = 0$ for $k > r$, and $X_r = X_{r+1} = \cdots = X_\infty$.

We are interested in the expectation of X_∞, denoted by $E[X_\infty] = \gamma$. This quantity represents the expected fraction of vertices to which a path exists from an arbitrarily selected vertex. Clearly, this fraction depends on the out-degree of our digraph, so that $\gamma = \gamma(a)$.

If the choices are *not* independent, $\gamma(a)$ depends on some aspect of the structure of the graph. To see this, we first calculate $\gamma(a)$ under the null hypothesis that the choices are made completely independently. In particular, this means that the conditional probability that an arrow issuing from vertex x terminates on y, given that an arrow issuing from y terminates on x, is equal to $(n-1)^{-1}$; that is, the unconditional probability that an arrow issuing from x terminates on y.

Consider the kth step in our tracing procedure. The expected number of arrows issuing from the set P_{k-1} is anP_{k-1}. This expectation is a random variable because P_{k-1} is a random variable, but in the recursive formulas below it will be treated as an ordinary variable. (For justification, see Landau, 1952.)

The probability that an arbitrarily selected vertex does *not* receive one of these anP_{k-1} arrows, assuming independent choices, is $(1-1/n)^{anP_{k-1}}$, which for large values of n is approximated by $e^{-aP_{k-1}}$.

Therefore, the probability of being contacted on the kth step by at least one of the arrows issuing from P_{k-1} is $1-e^{-aP_{k-1}}$.

Consequently, the probability of being contacted *for the first time* on the kth step and thus belonging to the set P_k is given by

$$P_k = (1-X_{k-1})(1-e^{-aP_{k-1}}), \tag{15.2}$$

where $1-X_{k-1}$ is the probability of not having been contacted for the first time on any step preceding the kth.

Recalling that $X_j = \sum_{i=0}^{j} P_i$ and hence that $X_j - X_{j-1} = P_j$, we have, upon substituting into Equation 15.2,

$$X_k - X_{k-1} = (1-X_{k-1})(1-e^{-a(X_{k-1}-X_{k-2})})$$
$$= 1 - X_{k-1} - (1-X_{k-1})e^{-a(X_{k-1}-X_{k-2})}, \tag{15.3}$$

or

$$(1-X_k)e^{aX_{k-1}} = (1-X_{k-1})e^{aX_{k-2}}. \tag{15.4}$$

But the left side of Equation 15.4 is obtained from the right side by a shift of the index. Therefore,

$$(1-X_k)e^{aX_{k-1}} = \text{constant.} \tag{15.5}$$

Setting $k = \infty$, we obtain

$$(1-\gamma)e^{a\gamma} = \text{constant.} \tag{15.6}$$

To evaluate this constant, we set $k = 1$. Note that $X_0 = P_0 = 1/n$ and $X_1 \leqslant (a+1)/n$. Therefore, for n very large compared to a, the right side of Equation 15.6 is very nearly 1, and we can write with good approximation

$$\gamma = 1 - e^{-a\gamma}. \tag{15.7}$$

Note that this equation is identical with Equation 2.22 of Chapter 2 with $z_0 = 0$, where it represents the ultimate infected fraction of a population in an epidemic. The analogy between the two models is evident, since our tracing procedure is essentially a contagion process.

Nonintegral values of a can be interpreted as average out-degrees since the derivation of the equation was based only on the expectations of P_i and X_i and did not involve an assumption that the out-degree of all vertices was the same.

From the plot of γ against a (see Figure 2.1), we can read off the expectations of $\gamma(a) = X_\infty(a)$; that is, the expected total fraction of vertices contacted in a tracing that correspond to different average out-degrees of a randomly constructed graph when the number of vertices is very large. For instance, if $a = 2$, this expected fraction is 0.8.

When the choices are not independent, the above derivation is not valid. For example, the probability on the left side of Equation 15.2 can no longer be expressed as a product of the two probabilities on the right side. For some kinds of interdependence of choices, we can guess the direction in which the tracing will be modified. Suppose choices are reciprocated to a certain degree; that is, the conditional probability that y chooses x, given that x chose y, is larger than the unconditional probability. We can guess that under this condition the values of P_i and therefore of X_i will be smaller than the corresponding values under the null hypothesis. This is because when y contacts x on the ith step, reciprocating x's choice, this contact does not contribute to the increment of P_i since x has been assumed to belong to $\{P_{i-1}\}$ and so cannot belong to $\{P_i\}$.

Similar considerations apply to other choice biases that reflect the "tightness" of the relation "x chooses y." Consider the friendship relation. Suppose individual a names b and c as friends. The probability that b names c or that c names b (or both) can be expected to be larger than it would be if choices were completely independent. But b and c were already contacted by a. Therefore, if b names c or c names a, there is no contribution to the increment of individuals newly contacted on the next step.

In this way, the fraction γ depends not only on the nature of the binary relation that defines the digraph, but also on ternary and possibly higher order relations induced by the binary relation. Roughly speaking, γ depends on the amount of "structure" imposed on the graph. (We suppose that a completely random graph has "no structure" in the sense of not being "organized" in any way.)

AN EXPERIMENT

The conjecture that in real sociograms the observed value of γ will be considerably smaller than that expected under the null hypothesis was tested experimentally by Rapoport and Horvath (1961). The population consisted of about 900 junior high school pupils in Ann Arbor, Michigan. Each pupil was asked to name eight pupils of the same school as friends in order of intimacy; that is, "best friend," "second best friend," and so on. If these directions were followed exactly and if there were no absences, a digraph of out-degree 8 would have been obtained. Because of errors and absences, the actual average out-degree was about 6.

This digraph could be decomposed into digraphs of smaller out-degrees. For instance, if all but two names on each list were disregarded, a digraph of out-degree 2 would be obtained under perfect conditions. As it turned out, these two-choice digraphs had average out-degree of about 1.75.

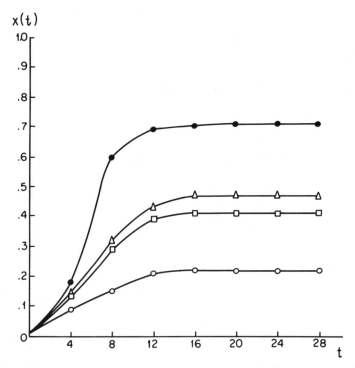

Figure 15.1. The fraction of individuals contacted in a tracing decreases monotonically as the closeness of the friendship relation increases. ○: tracing through first and second friends; □: third and fourth; △: seventh and eighth; ●: tracing through random contacts.

Several of these two-choice tracings were made, one using the first two names on each list ("best friend" and "second best friend"), one using the second and third names, and so on down to the two-choice tracing using the last two names on the lists. Figure 15.1 shows tracings through first and second, third and fourth, and seventh and eighth friends. As can be seen, the asymptotic values of X_k become larger as the friendship relation becomes more remote, approaching a tracing with independent random choices.

Given a real network, tracing through it can be made with varying values of average out-degree. The corresponding values of γ can be compared with those obtained from a random graph. The deviations of the former from the latter would reflect something about the biases generated by the overall structure of the network.

SMALL GROUPS SOCIOMETRY

American social psychologists devote considerable attention to relations arising among individuals aggregated in small groups. Families and working teams are groups of this sort. Patterns of interpersonal relations within them are clearly among the factors determining the functioning of these groups on the level of affect and attitudes on the one hand and on the level of task performance on the other. We have already mentioned studies on kinship nuclei. Similar studies were made on problem-solving groups. The latter are often artificially created to be explored under controlled conditions. "Real" work groups (for example, submarine crews) were also studied for the information they might provide about the role of interpersonal affect and attitudes as determinants of performance. Years before the launching of American space exploration missions, groups of three to five men in close contact and under various conditions of "stress" were studied, presumably to gain some knowledge of the psychological problems that might arise in such missions. Impetus to these studies was provided by C. C. Homans, whose book *The Human Group* initiated a field of research called *group dynamics.*

Sociometric methods were widely used in these studies. They were based on data supplied by the members of a group, either natural or experimental, largely in the form of binary relations: each group member names or ranks some or all members of the group according to some criterion, such as degree of "liking," desirability as a work partner, desirability as a partner in recreational activity, and so on.

A large project designed to utilize these techniques in the study of an evolving social structure (defined by affect relations) was undertaken by T. H. Newcomb (1961). Specifically, two groups were studied, each consisting of 17 young men, all enrolled as students at the University of Michigan. They were recruited as follows. A residence house was procured, and the men were invited to live in it for a year rent-free if they would cooperate in the project by providing the sociometric data required.

The two groups correspond to the two years of the project, the second experiment being essentially a replication of the first. In this way, a reasonably long period of contact was assured among group members, so that they could be regarded as a "natural" group instead of an *ad hoc* group formed for a short laboratory study; and at the same time it was possible to collect "hard data" on the interpersonal relations over a period of time by a contractual arrangement (as in an experiment).

The data were rankings by every group member of all the other 16 on a scale from "most liked" to "least liked." This set of data was gathered once a week for 16 weeks (Week 0 to Week 15) in each of the two groups. Thus all the data from the experiment could be neatly arranged in 32 17×17 matrices. In each matrix, the ijth entry denoted the ranking ("most liked" denoted by "1," "least liked" by "16") that individual i gave individual j.

The investigators faced the problem of processing these data so as to give a coherent picture of the "socioaffective" structure of that group as it appeared at each reading and, perhaps, of some trends in the evolution of this structure in time. The analysis did not seem to be guided by any unified theoretical scheme. Instead, a large variety of indices was extracted, each presumably related to some aspect of the structure.

One of the features examined was the distribution of choices of various preference ranks received. This distribution was compared with the "null hypothesis" distribution generated by random choices, and its deviation from the latter was interpreted as a measure of a "popularity bias." For instance, on the basis of random choices, the expected number of individuals receiving from 5 to 11 choices of ranks 1 through 8 is 15.70; the expected numbers receiving 0 through 4 and 12 through 16 such choices are only 0.65 each.

Table 15.1 shows the expected and the observed distributions. The surplus of individuals at the extremes (that is, those who received very few or very many choices) suggests a distribution of a "popularity" parameter in the population: some individuals have a larger than *a priori* probability of receiving one of the first eight choices than others, some smaller. One would expect this on common sense grounds. Of greater interest is the question of whether a trend exists toward greater differentiation or greater equalization of the individuals. In the former case, the extremes of the distribution would become larger in the later weeks; in the latter case, smaller.

Table 15.1 shows no convincing evidence of either trend. One might conjecture, as the investigators did, that "first impressions" were fixated in an early stage. This conjecture, however, does not take into account another trend for which evidence was found and which may have "masked" a trend toward greater differentiation. This is the trend toward greater reciprocity of choices.

Consider a particular pair of individuals. Each assigns a rank to the other from 1 to 16. The difference in the ranks that they give each other is a measure of the reciprocity of their evaluation of each other. The smaller this difference, the larger the reciprocity.

Table 15.2 shows the numbers of pairs in the high and low ranges of reciprocity.

Observe that in Week 0 these numbers do not differ significantly from numbers expected under the null hypothesis (random choices). In Week 15, however, there was a marked increase in high-reciprocity pairs at the expense of low-reciprocity pairs.

Now let us see what would happen to the distribution of choices received under perfect reciprocity. For simplicity, consider a sociogram in which each individual

Table 15.1. *No Significant Changes in the Distribution of Choices Received were Noted During Either year of the Experiment*

Expected Number of Choices Ranked 1–8	Expected Number of Persons Receiving Choices	Observed Year I			Observed Year II		
		Week			Week		
		0	1	15	0	1	15
0–4	0.65	4	3	3	2	3	5
5–11	15.70	10	12	13	11	11	8
12–16	0.65	3	2	1	4	3	4

Source: Adapted from Newcomb (1961).

Table 15.2. A Significant Increase in Reciprocity of Choices was observed During Both Years of the Experiment

	Week 0 (both years)		Week 15 (both years)	
Rank difference	Observed	Expected	Observed	Expected
0–3	110	99	149	106
4–15	144	155	123	166
	$Chi^2 = 1.82$		$Chi^2 = 27.92$	

Source: Adapted from Newcomb (1961).

makes only one choice. If every choice is reciprocated, each individual also receives exactly one choice, so that the distribution of in-degree is completely concentrated at a single vertex; namely 1, the expected number of choices received. (The variance of the distribution is zero.) Similarly, if each individual makes two choices and both are reciprocated, the distribution is again concentrated at a single point.

In general, it can be shown that as the probability of reciprocated choices increases, the variance of the distribution of choices received becomes smaller; that is, the distribution becomes more concentrated near the mean value (Rapoport, 1957). On the other hand, as we have seen, this distribution tends to become "flatter" as the variance of the popularity distribution increases; that is, as the individuals become more differentiated with regard to the probability of receiving choices. It follows that the two trends, increased differentiation and increased reciprocity, have opposite effects on the distribution of choices received. Consequently, the apparent absence of a trend toward differentiation may have been due to the fact that this trend was masked by the opposite effect of increased reciprocity.

The above analysis illustrates the interdependence of the various indices of structure. A weakness of the purely empirical approach, in which indices are examined independently one after the other, is in the failure to bring out these interdependencies.

The indices are also closely interrelated with the "topological" properties of a structure. Consider once again a sociogram with constant out-degree 2. If reciprocity is perfect, the graph representing this sociogram must fall apart into triangles.[2] And in general, under perfect reciprocity, a sociogram will tend to be "torn apart" into several components disconnected from each other. Thus an inverse relationship exists between the "degree of connectedness" and the "degree of reciprocity" in a sociogram. Indices of "connectedness" and of "reciprocity," as well as of "transitivity," "cyclicity," and many others can be defined in various ways. The mathematical relations among them are of formidable complexity. Indeed, next to nothing is known about these relations. Thus the problem of constructing an "illuminating" description of a social structure by means of indices remains unsolved, if by an "illuminating" description we mean one that captures the most essential features of the structure and also contains little redundancy in the sense of multiplicity of highly correlated indices. One of the difficulties in constructing an "efficient" set of indices is that one does not know how much additional information one gets for each additional index.

These difficulties have forced investigators using sociometric techniques to resort to intuitive analyses of social structure. Indices constructed *ad hoc* (as in the above study) are used to sketch the framework. One then attempts to describe what appear to be important features of the structure from the way the network looks on paper.

Newcomb and his coworkers defined *attractiveness* of one individual for another as the reciprocal of the rank which the latter gave the former. They defined a *high attraction unit* as one in which the pooled attractiveness of individuals for each other was at least 95% of the maximum possible for the set of that size. A sociogram for Year I, Week 15, based on high attraction units is shown in Figure 15.2.

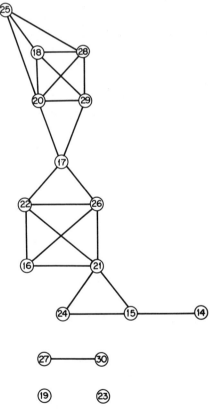

Figure 15.2. (Adapted from Newcomb, 1961). High attraction units after 15 weeks of Year I in Newcomb's communal housing experiment.

In interpreting this sociogram, it is important to keep in mind that an arbitrary subset of individuals who constitute a connected subgraph do not necessarily constitute a high attraction unit. Only subsets that constitute a *completely* connected subgraph are a high attraction unit. Thus in Figure 15.2 we see two high attraction units of four individuals each; namely, {18, 20, 28, 29} and {16, 21, 22, 26}. Two individuals connected by an edge do constitute a high attraction couple. Thus although the connected components of the sociogram are not high attraction units, they consist of high attraction units linked through "intermediaries."

The visual appearance of the sociogram so constructed suggests something about the "degree of integration" of the social group at a particular stage of the "acquaintance process." For example, in the sociogram pictured in Figure 15.2, we see one large component, one isolated high attraction pair, and two isolated individuals. Trends can also be discerned.

Figures 15.3 and 15.4 show the corresponding sociograms in Weeks 0 and 15 of Year II. The several components of the earlier sociogram appear to have merged into one large component, leaving four "isolates" suggesting a progressive "integration" of a majority, whereby some individuals have been left out.

Also of some interest are the positions of certain individuals. Observe, for example, individual 17 in Figure 15.3. He seems to be a link between two subgroups of the large integrated group. If this individual were removed, the two subgroups between which he forms a "bridge" would become disconnected. Examining the "popularity" scores of individual 17, we note that he rated highest in Weeks 0 and 1, but was not among the four highest by Week 15. One is tempted to look for a connection between this drop in popularity and the role of being a single link between two groups, which may involve a "divided loyalty" and attendant strains.

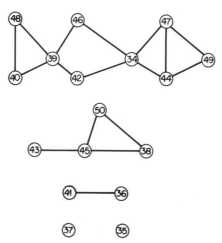

Figure 15.3. (Adapted from Newcomb, 1961). High attraction units at the start of Year II in Newcomb's experiment.

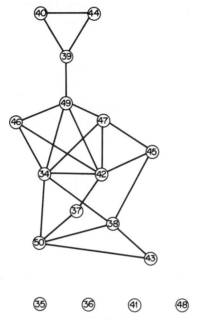

Figure 15.4. (Adapted from Newcomb, 1961). High attraction units after 15 weeks of Year II in Newcomb's experiment.

THE BLOCK MODEL APPROACH

In forming conjectures suggested by the visual appearance of sociograms, we have wandered far from methods of structural analysis based on rigorously defined parameters. The difficulty with the rigorously defined indices of structure is that these can be multiplied indefinitely without contributing in their totality to a well-integrated structural theory of social networks. A more promising direction is suggested by the so-called block model approach to social networks, to which we now turn our attention.

A social network will now be defined as a set of individuals with a *set* of binary relations on that set. For instance, "likes" and "dislikes" are two different relations. Other relations may reflect some organizational aspects of the group; for instance, "is subordinate to," "supervises," "receives information from," and so on. Still other relations may be compounded from relations; for instance, "is a friend of an enemy of," "is a brother of the wife of," and so on. The compounded relations may be of arbitrary complexity. J. P. Bennet and H. R. Alker (1977) in their model of the international system as a social group (where the individuals are states) mention the relation "is not an ally of the enemy of one's principal import source."

Such a social network can be represented by a *set* of digraphs or, equivalently, of matrices, one for each of the constituent binary relations. The basic idea of the block model approach is to partition (if possible) the set of individuals into disjoint subsets (blocks) in such a way as to exhibit the *absence* of connections between any of the individuals belonging to some block and any of the individuals belonging to another block. It should be noted that such a partition need not exhibit disjoint subsets with all the connections directed "inward" in each subset and no connections directed "outward." Such a structure would be only a special case. All that is required is a representation of the social structure which exhibits most clearly absences of connections. If a relation is represented by a matrix (see p. 278), one seeks a permutation of the rows and the corresponding columns which would bring out submatrices with adjacent rows and adjacent columns consisting entirely of zeros.

The procedure is explained most conveniently by a concrete example. Let the individuals of a social network be labeled 1–8, and let Matrix 15.1 represent one binary relation on this set, say "names as friend."

	1	2	3	4	5	6	7	8
1	0	0	0	1	0	0	0	0
2	1	0	0	1	0	1	0	0
3	0	0	0	0	0	0	1	0
4	1	0	0	0	0	1	0	0
5	1	0	0	1	0	1	0	0
6	1	0	0	1	0	0	0	0
7	0	0	1	0	0	0	0	0
8	1	0	0	0	0	1	0	0

Matrix 15.1

In Matrix 15.2, the rows and corresponding columns of Matrix 15.1 have been permuted, and the block structure thus becomes apparent. The eight individuals can be partitioned into three blocks; namely, $B_1 = \{1, 4, 6\}$, $B_2 = \{2, 5, 8\}$, and $B_3 = \{3, 7\}$.

	1	4	6	2	5	8	3	7
1	0	1	0	0	0	0	0	0
4	1	0	1	0	0	0	0	0
6	1	1	0	0	0	0	0	0
2	1	1	1	0	0	0	0	0
5	1	1	1	0	0	0	0	0
8	1	0	1	0	0	0	0	0
3	0	0	0	0	0	0	0	1
7	0	0	0	0	0	0	1	0

Matrix 15.2

We note that members of B_1 and B_3 name friends only within their own blocks.

Members of B_2, however, name as friends only members of B_1. Thus while blocks B_1 and B_3 constitute friendship cliques of sorts, block B_2 appears to consist of "hangers on" of B_1. They name individuals in B_1 as friends, but are not named in return.

Note that while the two individuals in B_3 constitute a Luce and Perry clique of order 1^3 (see p. 279), those of B_1 do not because the subgraph that represents this block is not completely connected.[4] (For this reason, we call it a friendship clique "of sorts.") In general, the blocks singled out in a block model need not have any internal connections at all, as is the case with B_2 in our example. What the block model exhibits is the *presence* or *absence* of connections among members of blocks, both with reference to intrablock and to interblock binds. Once the blocks have been established, the block model of a social structure with respect to each of the relations that define it is represented by a reduced matrix (or graph) in which the rows and columns (or the vertices) represent the *blocks*. The entry "1" in the ith row and jth column of the reduced matrix signifies the existence of *some* connections from members of the ith block to members of the jth block. In particular, a "1" on the main diagonal indicates that the corresponding block has some internal connections. The block model of our illustrative social network is shown in Matrix 15.3.

	B_1	B_2	B_3
B_1	1	0	0
B_2	1	0	0
B_3	0	0	1

Matrix 15.3

A separate block model represents each of the relations defining the social network. Simplification is achieved by reducing the order of the original matrices from the number of individuals to the number of blocks.

Consider now all possible matrices of order 2 with entries confined to "0" or "1." Clearly, there are 16 distinct matrices of this sort. However, because the labeling of the rows and of corresponding columns is arbitrary, there are only 10 distinct structures of social networks involving a single relation, where two blocks are discernible, each represented by a 2×2 matrix. The 10 types of structure are shown in Table 15.3, together with descriptive interpretations. To fix ideas, we will interpret the relation as "names as desirable sex partner."

Another interpretation of Type VIII is center-periphery. Think of a centralized transportation network as in a city with suburbs. Central portions are supplied by a transportation network and are connected with all parts of the periphery. Suburbs, however, are not connected with each other directly; to go from one suburb to another, one must go through the center. A nervous system with a brain and peripheral pathways has an analogous structure.

Type IX can be called a hierarchy. Let the relation in question be a weak order; for example, "has status no higher than." Then if the status of B_1 is higher than that of B_2, Type IX structure represents that relation.

Table 15.3.   Ten Types of Elementary Block Model

Type	Model		Interpretation
I	0	0	
	0	0	A celibate society
II	1	0	
	0	0	B_1 represents adults; B_2 children. No pederasty.
III	0	1	
	0	0	B_1: men; B_2: women. Men heterosexual; women frigid.
IV	1	0	
	0	1	B_1: men; B_2: women. All homosexual.
V	0	1	
	1	0	B_1: men; B_2: women. All heterosexual.
VI	1	1	
	0	0	B_1: men; B_2: women. Men both homo- and heterosexual; women frigid.
VII	1	0	
	1	0	B_1: men; B_2: women. Men homosexual; women heterosexual.
VIII	1	1	
	1	0	B_1: men; B_2: women. Men both homo- and heterosexual; women heterosexual.
IX	1	0	
	1	1	B_1: men; B_2: women. Men homosexual; women both homo- and heterosexual.
X	1	1	
	1	1	B_1: men; B_2: women. Homosexuals and heterosexuals in both sexes.

The number of structural types, of course, increases very rapidly with the number of blocks, and it is pointless to attempt an interpretation of each structural type for the case of three blocks. It may be the case that only a few structural types appear as actual social networks. Whether this is so is an empirical question of interest in a theory of social structure.

Analysis of network structure of the type just described is presently carried out with the aid of two algorithms used as computer programs. One, called BLOCKER, is used to test the hypothesis that a network is representable as a specific hypothesized block model. The final product of this algorithm is a listing of all partitions of the individuals (N.B.: if any) which make the reduction of a specified relation to the hypothesized block model possible. Thus BLOCKER answers the question *whether* a network can be represented by a particular block model and, if it can, lists all the ways in which this can be done. For example, if we had hypothesized a block model of Type IV for the network represented by Matrix 15.1, BLOCKER would have singled out two blocks consisting respectively of (1, 2, 4, 5, 6, 8) and (3, 7). On the other hand, if we had hypothesized a diagonal matrix of order 3 (three disjoint cliques), BLOCKER would have answered "No."

It follows that BLOCKER is applicable when the investigator already has an idea of how a social structure ought to look. Application of BLOCKER tells him whether his conjecture is correct and, if so, identifies all corresponding partitions of individuals into blocks. If the investigator has no a priori idea of the type of social structure he is dealing with, he can resort to another algorithm called CONCOR.

CONCOR answers the question, "What type of block model describes the given social structure best?" The term "best" here is related to a degree of approximation of a network by a block model. In contrast to BLOCKER, which tests a block model with respect to one relation at a time, CONCOR seeks a partition into blocks that applies simultaneously to all the relations that define a network. Each relation may be reflected in a different structure type, but the partition of the individuals into blocks is sought that applies to all the relations. In general, a trivial partition and a corresponding block model can always be exhibited; for example, one where each individual is a "block" or all the individuals form a single block. Obviously, such trivial answers are not wanted. To get a genuine reduction, one must usually sacrifice the "purity" of the block model. That is, the entry "0" in the ith row, jth column of a block model corresponding to a given relation need no longer mean that no connections go from block i to block j. It may mean that the number or fraction of positive entries in the corresponding submatrix does not exceed a certain threshold of tolerance.

The input to the CONCOR algorithm is an $n \times m$ matrix M_0 (which in a sociometric setting is usually a matrix with entries "0" and "1"). M_0 consists of m column vectors, each with n components. The correlations r_{ij} between vector i and vector j $(i, j = 1, 2, \ldots, m)$ are the elements of the $m \times m$ matrix M_1. Iterating this procedure, we determine the elements of matrix M_{k+1} as the correlations between the pairs of vectors that are the columns of M_k. Except in some rarely encountered cases, the procedure leads to the convergence of the matrices M_k to a matrix M, in which the entries are all $+1$ or -1. By a proper permutation of rows and corresponding columns, M can be displayed in the form shown in Matrix 15.4.

$$
\begin{array}{ccc}
B_1 & +1 & -1 \\
B_2 & -1 & +1
\end{array}
$$

Matrix 15.4

The entries "$+1$" and "-1" in Matrix 15.4 are matrices (not necessarily square) consisting only of $+1$s and -1s respectively. In this way, the m rows of M are partitioned into two blocks B_1 and B_2.

The input $(n \times m)$ matrix M_0 with $n = mk$ is formed by "stacking" k $(m \times m)$ matrices on top of each other. These represent k distinct binary relations on a set of m individuals. Thus CONCOR yields a partition of the m individuals into two blocks with respect to all the k relations.

In general, this partition will not exhibit pure zero blocks, but it will exhibit blocks with comparatively low density of "1" entries for each of the k relations. Roughly speaking, the algorithm maximizes the contrast between and within block and across block correlations.

Having obtained two blocks, one proceeds to apply the algorithm to each of these, obtaining a finer partition. The refinement process can be continued until the "almost zero blocks" no longer satisfy the tolerance criterion for the density of zeros in "zero blocks."

APPLICATIONS OF THE BLOCK MODEL

The data of the communal living experiment described above were analyzed with the help of both the BLOCKER and the CONCOR algorithms. Recall that BLOCKER assumes a particular block structure, then seeks to partition the population (if possible) into subsets, such that relations among individuals within and between the subsets satisfy the assumed structure. Examination of the sociogram obtained at the end of Year II suggested the hypothesis that there was a top group, members of which "disdained" others. The type IX two-block structure was chosen for the model of the "like" relation. Individual a was defined as "liking" b if a named b as either first or second choice. It turned out that the Type IX structure was corroborated if individuals 13, 9, 17, 1, 8, and 4 were assigned to the top block. That is, these individuals made their first and second choices entirely among themselves. Some of the others also named their first or second choices from among these, as indicated by the "1" in the lower left cell of the Type IX structure. The "1" entry in the lower right shows that the members of the bottom block also made "like" choices among themselves.

For the "dislike" relation, the last two choices were taken as the criterion. Type VIII (with rows and columns interchanged) was hypothesized for this relation and also corroborated by the data. That is, none of the individuals in the top block rated any of that block as last or next to last choices. But the members of the bottom block did give these low ratings among themselves, as well as to members of the top block.

The model could be further refined into a three-block model, shown in Matrices 15.5 and 15.6, representing "like" and "dislike" relations, respectively.

	B_1	B_2	B_3
B_1	1	0	0
B_2	1	1	0
B_3	1	1	1

Matrix 15.5

	B_1	B_2	B_3
B_1	0	0	1
B_2	1	0	1
B_3	1	1	1

Matrix 15.6

From Matrix 15.5, we see that the members of the bottom block are "losers": none of them receive first or second choices from outsiders. From Matrix 15.6 we see that "dislike" choices are given by members of the second block to those in the top and bottom blocks, but not within that block. As for the "losers," they receive "dislike" choices from all three blocks.

Application of the CONCOR algorithm yields the same three blocks. It will be recalled that in this algorithm no a priori assumption is made about the block structure. Thus the result provides additional evidence for the hypothesized structure.

Finally, the findings are compared with an interpretation of the sociometric data on the basis of correlations of choice ranks. P. G. Nordie (1958) identified "clusters" developing late in Year II. These consisted respectively of the following sets of individuals: $\{1, 5, 6, 8, 13\}$; $\{2, 14, 17\}$; $\{7, 11, 12\}$; $\{3, 14\}$; and $\{15, 16\}$, with individuals 9 and 10 not assigned to any cluster. It will be noted that each of these clusters is contained in one of the three blocks defined above if individuals 2 and 5 are permitted to be members of any block. These two individuals, whom White, Boorman, and Breiger call "floaters," also play an ambivalent role in the block model. They can be assigned to any of the blocks without disturbing the null blocks. Except for this ambiguity, the two postulated block models have unique solutions (in the sense of partitioning the population) and so deserve some confidence as a reflection of some aspect of social reality.[5]

Another application of the block model was aimed at revealing the gross sociometric structure of a group of scientists working in a specialized area of biomedical research (Breiger, 1976). A list of scientists was compiled from authors of papers published in that area. Each was sent the same list and asked to indicate his "closeness" of association with each individual on the list, ranging from "close collaborator" to "unaware of the man or his work." Three binary relations were used to construct block models, "mutual contact," "unreciprocated unawareness" (aRb, if a is unaware of b's work, but b is aware of a's), and "reciprocated unawareness."

The BLOCKER algorithm was used to test intuitively plausible block models, shown in Matrices 15.7, 15.8, and 15.9 for the three relations mentioned above.

	B_1	B_2	B_3	B_4
B_1	1	1	1	0
B_2	1	1	1	0
B_3	1	1	0	0
B_4	0	0	0	0

Matrix 15.7

	B_1	B_2	B_3	B_4
B_1	0	1	1	1
B_2	0	0	1	1
B_3	0	1	1	1
B_4	0	1	1	1

Matrix 15.8

	B_1	B_2	B_3	B_4
B_1	0	0	1	1
B_2	0	0	1	1
B_3	1	1	1	1
B_4	1	1	1	1

Matrix 15.9

Each block model was fully confirmed for a random sample of 28 scientists. The four blocks shown in Matrices 15.7, 15.8, and 15.9 were interpreted by White, Boorman, and Breigner (1976) in status terms. Note that the two bottom blocks are not connected either internally or with each other on the symmetric "mutual contact" relation. The very lowest block has no connections to any other, including itself.

Turning our attention to the top block, we see that *no* block has an symmetric unawareness connection with it (see Matrix 15.8). In other words, it is not true of any scientist that he/she is unaware of any scientist in the top block while the latter is aware of him/her. We note further (see Matrix 15.9) that there is no "mutual unawareness" among the members of the two top blocks. On the contrary, as we see in Matrix 15.7, there is mutual awareness among these scientists and also some between these and block 3, but none *within* block 3. The status differences between these blocks becomes quite apparent.

Application of the CONCOR algorithm (with no *a priori* hypothesized structure) yielded a very similar picture, which was replicated in another sample of scientists.

White, Boorman, and Breiger remark that neither these blocks nor the global pattern of relations over the network could have been brought out by the earlier sociometric methods, such as measuring the "popularity" rating of each scientist (as by the frequency with which he is cited) or by conventional clique analysis.

NOTES

[1] In large sociograms—for example, with $n = 900$ (see Rapoport and Horvath, 1961)—this distribution is well approximated by a negative binomial reflecting heterogeneity embodied in a "popularity bias" (see "accident proneness," discussed in Chapter 8).

[2] If the population were infinite, a sociogram with out-degree 2 and complete reciprocity could also be represented by an infinite chain in which each individual chose his or her two neighbors and was, in turn, one of each of these neighbors' choices. In a finite population, however, the individuals at the end of the chain would have only one choice each.

[3] In a sociogram, it is usually assumed that no one names self as friend. If we adopt the opposite convention that every one names self as friend, the Luce-Perry cliques would be represented by principal submatrices in which all the entries are "1."

[4] A completely connected graph represents a complete binary relation (see p. 265).

[5] Unfortunately, the numbers assigned to individuals by White, Boorman, and Breiger (1976) do not correspond to those assigned by Newcomb (1961). For this reason, we cannot connect the block models with the sociograms representing the high attractiveness units (see Figures 15.2, 15.3, and 15.4).

CHAPTER SIXTEEN

Spatial Models

So far we have thought of structure as a finite set of binary relations defined on a finite set of elements. The structure of a geometrical space can be conceived as an infinite set of special relations defined on an infinite set of elements. Consider a plane and a point singled out on it called the origin. Assume that we know what we mean by the distance between two points. Next, consider the set of points P_i that are at a distance r from 0, the origin. If by distance we mean ordinary (Euclidean) distance, these points all lie on a circle around the origin with radius r. Form the Cartesian product set $R^{(2)} \times \{0\}$, where $R^{(2)}$ is the set of all the points in the plane and $\{0\}$ is the single set consisting only of the origin. Now define the (symmetric) binary relation $D_r \in R^{(2)} \times \{0\}$ as follows: $P_i D_r 0$ if and only if $d(P_i, 0) = r$, where $d(P_i, 0)$ denotes the distance between P_i and 0. Clearly, this relation defines the same circle around the origin with radius r. Since r can be any real number, the set of all circles with all possible radii r ($0 \leqslant r < \infty$) comprises all the points of the plane. By defining these points in terms of a particular family of relations, we have imposed a *structure* on our plane. That is, we have conceptualized the plane in a particular way; namely, as a set of concentric circles.

Note that our conceptualization was based on a particular definition of "distance" between two points; namely, the Euclidean distance, whereby the distance from the origin of any point (x, y) in the plane was defined as $\sqrt{x^2 + y^2}$. Distances can be defined in other ways. For instance, the distance between two locations in a city laid out in a grid pattern (as most North American cities are) appears *in practice* (for example, in terms of taxi fares) as the sum of the absolute differences of their corresponding coordinates because one can travel only along streets. Here the distance of a point (x, y) from the origin must be defined as $|x| + |y|$. The set of all points at a distance r from the origin will no longer define a circle but a diamond-shaped square around the origin. In terms of this distance, the structure of our space will be conceived as the totality of concentric diamond-shaped squares.

There are many other possible definitions of "distance." However, to preserve some intuitively required properties of what we conceive as "distance," we will want to impose certain requirements on such definitions. The following axioms represent such requirements.

M_1. $d(x, y) \geqq 0$. We ask that the distance between any two points be nonnegative. (We do not want to conceive distance as a directed or a signed quantity. That is, we want to think of a distance *between* two points, not from one point to another.)

M_2. $d(x, y) = d(y, x)$. This symmetric requirement again reflects our conception of distance as a relation *between* two points without regard to order.

M_3. $d(x, x) = 0$; $d(x, y) > 0$ if $x \neq y$. The distance from any point to itself is zero; but the distance from any point to any other point is positive.

M_4. $d(x, y) + d(y, z) \geqq d(x, z)$. This axiom asserts the so-called *triangular inequality*. If one goes from x to z "directly," the distance traversed should be no greater than if one goes through any intervening point y. The axiom corresponds to the axiom of Euclidean geometry which states that the straight line is the shortest path between two points.

Any function $d(x, y)$ satisfying M_1–M_4 is called a *metric*. It can easily be verified that ordinary Euclidean distance is a metric. There are, however, other metrics; that is, definitions of distance that satisfy the four requirements. The "taxi meter distance" mentioned above is an example. More generally, a metric is defined by any function

$$d(x, y) = \left\{ \sum_{i=1}^{n} |x_i - y_i|^p \right\}^{1/p}, \tag{16.1}$$

where x_i and y_i are the ith coordinates of two points in a space with n dimensions and p is any real number equal to or greater than one, or else infinite. Ordinary Euclidean distance in n-dimensional space appears as a special case with $p = 2$. In the "taxi meter distance," $p = 1$. Also of some interest is the case where $p = \infty$. Here the distance between two points turns out to be the largest of the absolute values of the differences of the corresponding coordinates.[1] In terms of this definition of distance, a plane is conceptualized as a family of squares with sides parallel to the coordinate axes with the origin at their common center.

Thus a geometric space can be described in terms of two categories: the number of dimensions and a metric. For example, the surface of a sphere is a space of two dimensions because any point on it can be represented by two real numbers, say a "latitude" and a "longitude." The metric of this space is not Euclidean since the distance between two points determined *on the surface* is not the length of a straight line but that of the shorter arc of the great circle defined by them.

The fundamental problem in constructing a *spatial model* of some situation is the following. Suppose we are given a set of n elements and some information about "distances" between pairs of these elements. We ask whether it is possible to represent each of the elements as a point in a k-dimensional space in such a way that the distances among pairs of elements in that space, as defined by some metric, will be consistent with the information we have about those distances. If the answer is yes, we ask: "What is the smallest number of dimensions of a space that will accommodate the points in the above sense?"

As an example, let the n elements be n individuals. Can we assign to each individual a position in some space, preferably with very few dimensions, and a metric to that space such that the geometric distances between pairs of individuals so defined will be consistent with the a priori given information? If so, we shall have a spatial model of a "social structure." Different social structures can then be compared with each other. Or a social structure can be followed in time, suggesting, perhaps, a dynamic theory.

Whether it is possible to construct a spatial model on the basis of information about distances between elements depends on the specificity of that information. If this information is entirely specific (that is, if all of the $n(n-1)/2$ distances as well as a metric are exactly specified), it may not be possible to "imbed" this set of n points in a space with any number of dimensions. For example, let the set of points be $\{x, y, z, w\}$, let the metric be Euclidean, and let the six distances be given by

$$d(x, y) = d(y, z) = d(z, x) = 1 \tag{16.2}$$

$$d(x, w) = d(y, w) = d(z, w) = 1/2. \tag{16.3}$$

The first three prescribed distances require that x, y, z be situated at the vertices of an equilateral triangle. The last three prescribed distances require that w be equidistant from x, y, and z. Now if w is situated at the center of the equilateral triangle determined by x, y, and z, its distance from each of these points will be $\sqrt{3}/3 > 1/2$. To preserve the equality of the three distances, w must be situated on a line perpendicular to the plane of the triangle passing through its center. But if w is anywhere on that line, its distance from x, y, and z will be no smaller than $\sqrt{3}/3$. Therefore the prescribed conditions cannot be satisfied.

If information about distances were less complete, the conditions might be satisfied. For instance, if we require only that w be equidistant from x, y, and z, while the distances among the latter are all 1, we can imbed the four points in three dimensions whereby x, y, and z will form an equilateral triangle and w will be situated anywhere on the line through its center and perpendicular to its plane.[2]

Spatial models of social and psychological situations are usually possible to construct because information about distances between pairs of elements is typically less than complete. For example, these distances may be given only on an ordinal scale. Or else structural information may be given not about distances between pairs of points, but about angles between the lines joining the points to the origin. Factor analysis is based on this sort of information.

Literature on factor analysis and its applications in the behavioral sciences is very extensive. Here we will present only a brief outline of it to show how it fits into the scheme of spatial models.

The method has its roots in the processing of data by *analysis of variance*. Consider a psychological experiment in which *k* groups of subjects are subjected to *k* different "treatments" (for example, *k* different experimental conditions) and produce quantifiable responses to stimuli. For example, the treatments may be different presentations of material to be memorized, and the responses, being reproductions of the material, are quantified according to the amount retained in the memory. A question of interest is whether the treatments have a differential effect on the amount retained.

One way of comparing the results of the treatments is by comparing the means of the amounts retained in the several groups of subjects. In general, the means will be different, but this does not by itself constitute sufficient evidence that the treatments have differential effects because the differences may reflect only the sampling errors due to the individual differences among the subjects or other extraneous factors. The method of analysis of variance enables the investigator to separate the two sources of variation; that is, the variation *within* the groups of subjects (due to individual differences and, possibly, extraneous effects) and the variation *among* the groups that can be ascribed to the different treatments. The investigator then applies statistical tests to decide whether the amount of variation among the groups is sufficiently larger than the amount of variation within the groups to warrant the rejection of the "null hypothesis"; namely, that the treatments produce no differential effects.

The method is readily extendable to situations where several "factors" may have an effect on the observations. Passing to a sociological context, suppose we are interested in ascertaining the possible effects of (1) educational level, (2) ethnic origin, and (3) religious affiliation on earning capacity. We can gather data on the dependent variable of interest associated with every possible combination of the factors. For example, in North America, levels of educational background may be elementary, secondary, and higher; ethnic origins may be southern European, eastern European, northwestern European, Asian, Latin American, or African; religious affiliations may be Catholic, Protestant, Jewish, Buddhist, and so on. The total variation of incomes can be broken up into components generated by each of the different factors, those generated by the interaction of factors, and those generated by within-group variances. In consequence, the effects of the different factors and of their interactions can be assessed as significant or insignificant. From here it is only a step to comparing the relative magnitudes of the effects reflected in the proportions of the total variance contributed by each to the total variance.

The method of factor analysis was the next development along these lines. Returning to the psychological context, suppose we have performance scores of a large number of individuals on some composite test, say a test that purports to assess "intelligence," quantified as an I.Q. score. The test has several components, some involving formal reasoning, some the scope of vocabulary, some memory, some spatial perception, and so on. Now, if "intelligence" were some faculty measurable on a one-dimensional scale, and if that faculty were equally relevant to performance on each of the components of the test, we would expect high correlations among the partial scores attained by the subjects on the separate components. Those who scored high on one component would score high on all the components; those who scored low on one would score low on all. "Intelligence" could be measured by the score on *any one* of the components. If, on the other hand, "intelligence" involved a number of different independent faculties such as reasoning ability, spatial perception, memory, and so on, the partial scores would not necessarily be correlated. That is, a subject might score high on memory but low on reasoning ability, or vice versa. In the intermediate case, performance on some of the tests might be closely correlated with that on some other tests but very weakly with the performance on still other tests. Thus we might find that subjects who scored high on formal reasoning also scored high on mathematical problems but not necessarily on scope of vocabulary. The aim of factor analysis is to single out *as few factors as possible* in terms of which to describe the scores attained. In this way, a subject's overall score on the test would be describable as a weighted sum of the magnitudes of each of the factors.

The relation of this method to the construction of a spatial structural model is clear. We mentioned several supposed faculties that are thought to comprise "intelligence." Those singled out in the construction of a test reflect intuitive notions about the structure of intelligence. These notions, however, may be mistaken; or we may wish to start without any preconceived notions about such factors. The aim of factor analysis is to *reveal* the factors which, on the basis of a particular method of data processing, appear to be relevant to overall performance and are relatively independent or, to use the terminology of factor analysis, are *orthogonal* to each other. If a small number k of these factors can be singled out to account for a sufficiently large proportion of the total variance, each score can be imbedded in a space of k dimensions such that the coordinate on each dimension represents the partial score on each of the factors revealed. The end product of this analysis is a spatial model of the "structure of intelligence."

Factor analysis can be interpreted as a spatial model in the following way. As we have seen, the raw data processed by factor analysis are correlations between scores on pairs of tests across a population of subjects. A correlation, being a number between -1 and $+1$, can represent the cosine of an angle. A correlation coefficient of $+1$ corresponds to an angle of $0°$, a correlation coefficient of 0 to $90°$, and -1 to $180°$. Thus if scores on two tests are perfectly correlated, the tests can be represented by two collinear vectors in a geometric space. A pair of tests with completely uncorrelated scores can be represented by a pair of orthogonal vectors, and so on.

Now, given the entire set of correlations between all pairs of scores, we want to know the minimum number of dimensions that a geometric space must have to accommodate the corresponding vectors. Clearly, two sets can always be accommodated in two dimensions by simply making the cosine of the angle between the vectors representing the tests correspond to the correlation between them. It may not be possible to accommodate three sets in two dimensions because in two dimensions, two of the angles will determine the third. But a third dimension provides the additional degree of freedom required to accommodate three tests. In fact, n tests can always be accommodated in n dimensions. The object of factor analysis is to see whether n tests can be accommodated in *fewer* than n dimensions. In general, the fewer the dimensions that turn up, the easier the theoretical interpretation of these dimensions.

Being a straightforward technique, factor analysis has been applied in a large number of empirical investigations, sometimes justifiably, sometimes with questionable justification. To take a situation relevant to behaviorally oriented political science, consider a questionnaire administered to a random sample of respondents in the United States. The questionnaire consists of a large number of statements, which the respondent is asked to mark on a 7-point scale ranging from "strongly agree" to "strongly disagree." Samples of such statements might be

1. Labor unions should be prohibited.
2. The United States should disarm unilaterally.
3. Racial integration of schools should be rigidly enforced by bussing, if necessary.
4. A landlord should have the right to refuse to rent premises to an applicant at his discretion.
5. The Soviet Union presents a continued threat to the United States.
6. There should be no legal restrictions to abortion.

Each respondent will have a "score" on each of the statements ranging from, say, -3 (strongly disagree) to $+3$ (strongly agree). It is to be expected that some of the scores will be strongly correlated across the respondents. For example, those strongly agreeing with statement 5 will very likely strongly disagree with statement 2, and vice versa, thus providing a large negative correlation between these two scores.

Intuitively, we feel that degrees of agreement or disagreement with the statements will be generated by strengths of feeling on certain basic issues. People may range in their attitudes along the "hawk-dove" axis from a strong militarist position to pacifism. They may range on the racial issue from integrationist to segregationist attitudes. They may range on the issue of "sexism" and on other widely discussed issues. Factor analysis may single out these issues, including some that may have eluded our attention. In this way the field of political attitudes could be represented by a spatial structural model.

In some cases, we may not have any idea of what basic factors may underlie certain kinds of attitudes. Some years ago, a cross-cultural study was made on attitudes of people relating to a "philosophy of life" (Morris, 1942). Factor analysis revealed components that could be interpreted as a "mysticism-rationalism" scale, an "active-passive" scale, and an "individualism-collectivism" scale.

Another series of studies (Osgood, Luci, and Tannenbaum, 1957) consistently brought out a decomposition of affect-laden connotations of words along a "good-bad" dimension, a "strong-weak" dimension, and an "active-passive" dimension. Thus each of a set of stimulus words selected for their usually strong affective connotations (for example, myself, spouse, love, work, death, and so on) could be assigned a position in the subject's "semantic space" on the basis of his/her ratings of the word on each of the three dimensions. For example, on a scale ranging from -3 to $+3$, the subject might rate "myself" as $+2$ on the good-bad scale, -1 on the active-passive scale, and -3 on the strong-weak scale. Then the stimulus word "myself" would be plotted as the point $(2, -1, -3)$ in this subject's "semantic space." The spatial configuration of the set of stimulus words so obtained could then be examined visually for any cues that it might provide about the subject's personality or about his/her current state of mind. In particular, configurations produced by different subjects or by the same subject at different times might be compared.

This approach was used in a clinical study of a young woman who was said to pass from one to another of three "identities" completely separated in her consciousness (Osgood et al., 1957).

Needless to say, the validity of this method purporting to reveal a subject's "semantic space" is extremely difficult to evaluate. Indeed, the genuineness of so-called split personality cases has been impugned in view of the possibility of ascribing them either to hoaxes, autosuggestion, or hypnotic effects generated by a therapist. The "semantic differential," as the method of constructing a connotative space has been called, can be regarded as an attempt to relate almost entirely intuitive clinical practices to an objective procedure.

"Objective procedures" such as factor analysis and the semantic differential tend to become extremely popular. Whatever mathematical or psychological insights were involved in developing these tools, their application has frequently been reduced to routines. Much pedestrian research in the behavioral sciences can be attributed to the circumstance that such standard techniques are available. Misapplication of these tools and misinterpretations of the results have been frequent.

As an example, we may cite a study in a political context. During the 1956 presidential election campaign in the United States, the candidates in primary elections included Adlai Stevenson (a Democrat), Dwight Eisenhower, and Robert Taft (Republicans). The names of these candidates as well as some affect-laden political terms like "socialism" were used as stimulus words on subjects differentiated by declared preference for the candidates. It turned out that in the "semantic space" of both Eisenhower and Stevenson supporters, "Taft" appeared close to "socialism." The result seems anomalous because the strongly conservative views of Taft were highly publicized and must be assumed to have been generally known. It is not hard to see that the result was simply an artifact of the instrument. In rural Illinois, where the study was conducted, "socialism" evoked negative affect even among "liberal" voters. So did Taft. This brought the positions of the two stimuli "Taft" and "socialism" close together, at least on the "good-bad" dimension. It should be clear that the structure of a person's "semantic space" reflects at most the emotional connotations of words evoked in that person, not their semantic content. The structure of a denotative (as contrasted with a connotative) semantic space would be interesting to examine. It is highly unlikely, however, that the denotative space can be reduced to a small number of dimensions.[3]

Applications of structure-analytic procedures based on factor analysis are predicated on two assumptions. First, the quantified data (for example, scores, evaluations on preassigned scales) must be given on at least an interval scale. Second, in calculating the proportion of variance accounted for by factors, the distributions of these quantities in the populations of subjects are assumed to be normal. In practice, either of these assumptions may not be justified, which limits the range of application of factor analysis or else distorts the results if the method is applied indiscriminately. Other types of spatial models do not presuppose either an interval scale for the data or normal distributions, and thus can be applied more widely. We will mention two such approaches, *multidimensional scaling* and *unfolding models*.

MULTIDIMENSIONAL SCALING

Data subjected to multidimensional scaling are typically "distances" between pairs of points. These distances may be either subjectively estimated or defined *ad hoc*. For example, in a psychological experiment, suppose the stimuli are colored discs varying in hue, brightness, and saturation. The stimuli may be presented to the subject in triples or quadruples. If a triple (x, y, z) is presented, the subject is asked whether y is "closer" to x than to z, or vice versa. If a quadruple is presented, the subject is asked whether x and y or z and w are "closer" to each other. If the subject's responses are sufficiently consistent, he will have ranked the distances between pairs on an ordinal scale. In another context, let the objects of interest be corporations. Let the "distance" between two corporations be defined on an ordinal scale in terms of the number of directors shared by the two, so that the larger this number, the "closer" the corporations are to each other. Here "distances" were defined objectively; that is, in accord with hard data, but also *ad hoc*; that is, in a way thought to be suitable to the particular context.

The question to be answered by multidimensional scaling is the following. What is the smallest number of dimensions in which the stimuli (or objects) can be imbedded in a way that preserves the given rank ordering of the distances between pairs? Note that this analysis is analogous to the one posed in factor analysis except that the "angles" in the spatial model represented by factor analysis have been replaced by "distances" in multidimensional scaling.

Multidimensional scaling begins with a configuration of the "points" representing the stimuli or objects in which all the distances are equal. If there are n points, they can always be placed in this manner in $n - 1$ dimensions. For instance, three points can always be placed on a plane as the vertices of an equilateral triangle. Four equidistant points can be the vertices of a regular tetrahedron in three-dimensional space, and so on.

Now, each point can be very slightly displaced so as to reproduce the rank order of distances given in the data. We are interested in whether we can reduce the number of dimensions without disturbing the rank order of the distances. To visualize the process, suppose we had four points. Initially, they were placed at the vertices of a regular tetrahedron. Then each point was slightly displaced as required to reproduce the rank order of the six distances. We still have a tetrahedron. Now we want to know what would happen if we "flattened" this tetrahedron so that as a result, the four points would lie in a plane. If the rank order of the distances were not changed by this "flattening," we would have succeeded in reducing the number of dimensions from three to two while preserving the agreement between our spatial model and the data.

Let us see what happens in the process of "flattening" a configuration. Imagine a sphere with some points on the surface, and consider what happens when the sphere is flattened into a two-dimensional region. As a consequence, the *variance* of the distances will be increased: the points that are farthest apart will be pulled out to become even farther apart. This suggests a way of "flattening" our initial configuration. Namely, increase the distances between points that are far apart and decrease the distances between points that are close together. If this procedure is done by very small steps, the "correct" rank order of the distances may be preserved for a while. Eventually, however, the process may introduce distortions in the form of reversals of the rank order of distances. When a violation of this sort is observed, an opposite "corrective" displacement is performed. If the distance between two points is larger than prescribed (by rank order), these two points are pulled closer together; if smaller, they are pulled further apart. Alternating between the "flattening" and the "corrective" procedures, we finally arrive at a stage when no further flattening is possible because if it is attempted, order is violated, and if order is restored, the flattening is "neutralized."

We thus arrive at a maximally flattened space. However, the cordinates of the points are still components of $(n-1)$-dimensional vectors. The problem now is to rotate the axes of our space so as to eliminate the "extra" dimensions. To illustrate, consider three points in two dimensions with coordinates $(0, 0)$, $(1, 1)$, and $(2, 2)$. Although each point is designated by two coordinates, it is clear that the three points lie on a straight line. Rotating the axes will put the three points on a principal axis, say the X-axis; so that their new coordinates will be $(0, 0)$, $(\sqrt{2}, 0)$ and $(\sqrt{8}, 0)$. Now the Y coordinate is superfluous, and we have displayed our three points in a single dimension. Rotation of axes in many-dimensional space is analogous.

The procedure yields a "theoretical dividend." We started with our data described only on an ordinal scale; namely, by a rank order of distances between pairs of points. After we have "forced" our points into a space with a minimum number of dimensions, we have some *metric* information about these distances, for now the positions of the points are designated (within some margin of tolerance) by cardinal coordinates. We thus recover more than we put in, as it were; that is, we have recovered some information about the relative magnitudes of the distances between the points not only with regard to which are larger, but also to some extent with regard to how much larger some are than others. An interpretation of this finding may be of some theoretical interest.

Recall the sociogram (see p. 286). To subject it to multidimensional scaling we simply rank order the "distances" between pairs of persons according to the number of links separating them. We do not prejudge the metric of this distance. After transforming the data by multidimensional scaling, we may get a configuration in a few dimensions, say two or three. These dimensions may have a suggestive interpretation. For example, distance between persons (note that this is a "social" distance) may be determined by the disparity of their incomes, their social status, and their attitudinal sets. If so, each person will be represented by a point with coordinates that can be interpreted as magnitudes of those variables. Moreover, we will have some information about how cardinal distance varies with the number of links separating the persons; for instance, whether the difference between two and three links is larger as a "social distance" than between three and four links.

If the data are perceived as "distances" between stimuli, multidimensional scaling sheds some light on the fundamental problem of psychophysics—that of "mapping" physical magnitudes on subjectively perceived magnitudes. For many kinds of physical stimuli, it is difficult to obtain subjective judgments of distances on a scale stronger than a difference-ordinal scale.[4] For instance, a subject may be able to say that the "distance" between disc x and disc y, which differ in hue and saturation, is larger than the "distance" between disc y and disc z, but not by how much. The rank ordering of differences suffices for multidimensional scaling. Suppose the procedure recovers the two dimensions— hue and saturation. Together with this we also obtain metric information on each of the dimensions, thus some indication about how the physical measure of hue (light frequency) and the physical measure of saturation are "mapped" upon the subjective perception of these quantities.

The "power" of multidimensional scaling compared to earlier methods of constructing spatial models was demonstrated in the analysis of data on paired comparisons of hues. In a study by Ekman (1954), subjects were asked to rate "qualitative similarity" of each pair of 14 colors on a five-step scale. The mean ratings were the elements of a 14×14 matrix. When normalized on the interval [0, 1], these ratings were treated as correlation coefficients and subjected to factor analysis. The analysis yielded five factors interpreted as violet, blue, green, yellow, and red. The result is somewhat surprising because perception of hue is usually modeled by the so-called color circle to account for the fact that although violet and red are farthest apart on the spectrum, they are perceived to be more similar to each other than, say, green and red. Clearly, only two dimensions (not five) are needed to accommodate the color circle. On the other hand, when the transformed similarities as given by Ekman were taken directly as proximity measures and subjected to multidimensional scaling, the familiar "color circle" was recovered as shown in Figure 16.1.

Since Shepard's pioneering work on multidimensional scaling, (see Shepard 1962a, 1962b), several alternative models have been developed. Of these, the INDSCAL model has proved to be useful since it determines the weights that a particular subject assigns to the various dimensions of his perceptive space. Thus for subject *i*, the perceived distance between stimuli is a "weighted" Euclidean distance:

$$d_{jk}^{(i)} = \left[\sum_t w_{it}(x_{jt} - x_{kt})^2 \right]^{1/2}, \tag{16.4}$$

where $x_{jt} - x_{kt}$ are respectively the coordinates of the two stimuli on dimension *t*.

P. E. Green and V. R. Rao (1972) have described in detail several such alternative models and have compared the results of corresponding analysis of a single set of data.

These were obtained in an experiment where subjects were asked to judge 15 foods (all kinds of bread or pastry eaten with breakfast or with snacks). This study provides a good overview of the various models and of the associated algorithms. It is hardly necessary to point out that availability of computers has been a powerful stimulus to the proliferation of models and associated algorithms of multidimensional scaling.

Mechanization of data processing has also made it practical to elicit considerably more information from the subjects, with the view of constructing spatial models of different aspects of their perceptions. For instance, the subjects

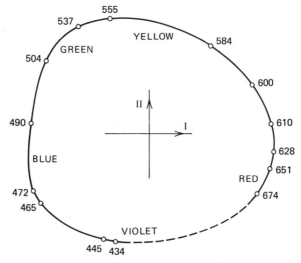

Figure 16.1. (Adapted from Shepard, 1962b). Multidimensional scaling model representation of color perception in two dimensions.

in the food comparison experiment were asked not only to rate dissimilarities between pairs of foods, but also to give ratings to each food on 10 bipolar scales using 7-point equal interval scales; for example, "easy to prepare/hard to prepare," "high calories/low calories," "expensive/inexpensive," and so on. In addition, they were asked to give preference orderings of the 15 foods in different contexts; for example, "when I'm having a breakfast consisting of juice, bacon and eggs, and beverages"; "at snack time with beverage only"; and so on. Finally, personal backgrounds were collected; for example, sex, age, habitual breakfast or snack, beverage, whether overweight, and so on. Computerized data processing permits aggregation and disaggregation of data in many different ways. Thus pictures emerge of the perceptual space from various perspectives, or filtered through different "lenses," as it were.

Multidimensional scaling amounts to extending to several dimensions the fundamental problem of quantitative psychology—the measurement of subjective magnitudes. As we have seen in Chapters 6 and 12, the problem presents itself in two different situations. In one, there exists a scale of physical magnitudes, and the problem is to find the relation between this scale and a corresponding subjective scale.

In the other situation, there are no physical magnitudes that can be directly associated with the stimuli, but there is reason to suppose that the subjects' perceptions can be described in the form of a perceptive space. Such is the case, for example, in comparisons of stimuli according to their aesthetic appeal or of facial expressions according to emotional context.

There are also intermediate and mixed situations. For instance, economic levels of countries can be operationally defined by gross national product, by mean or median income, or whatever. Political complexions of countries cannot be as easily defined by objective scales, but some consensus (a sort of substitute for objectivity) may exist in rating them on a "totalitarian–pluralistic" scale, on a "capitalism–socialism" scale, or whatever. Where such objective or quasi-objective scales exist, spatial models based on subjects' perceptions (in fact, on perceptions of subjects with different backgrounds or political orientations) can be compared with maps constructed on the basis of the objective scales or on the basis of consensus.

An experiment on perceptions of nations (Wish, Deutsch, and Biener, 1972) exemplifies the approach. Subjects were asked to estimate degrees of similarity between pairs of nations from a set of 15; to rate these 15 countries on 16 bipolar scales (for example, "I dislike/I like," "internally divided/internally united," and so on); and on political alignment in the international arena (East-West rivalry). In addition, the subjects' attitudes with regard to U.S. involvement in Vietnam was elicited. (The study was conducted during that involvement.) Application of a modified INDSCAL program to the data on similarities yielded four dimensions, interpreted as political alignment, economic development, geography and population, and culture and race. A projection of the four-dimensional perceptive space in two dimensions, political alignment and economic development, is shown in Figure 16.2. The figure appears to be a fairly

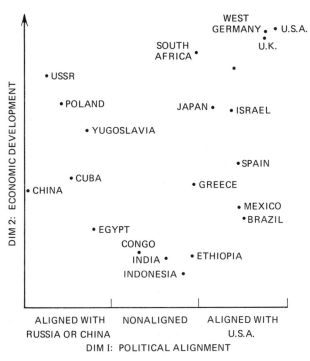

Figure 16.2. (Adapted from Wish, Deutsch, and Biener, 1972). Four-dimensional perceptive space of nations projected in two dimensions (political alignment and economic development).

accurate reproduction of the generally accepted economic-political picture in 1970.

Ratings on the bipolar scales provided further information on the subjects' perceptions, such as correlations of these ratings with the coordinates on the dimensions singled out by the multidimensional scaling and the weights assigned by the subjects of different nationalities and different political orientations to these dimensions in judging the degree of similarity. It is interesting to observe, for instance, that American and British subjects weighed the economic dimension most heavily, whereas Thai subjects assigned the smallest weight to this dimension and the largest to "culture and race." Similar (mostly expected) differences were observed between "hawkish" and "dovish" subjects.

THE UNFOLDING MODEL

Data processed by an unfolding model consists of two sets. In a psychological experiment, these are usually a set of subjects and a set of objects. Each subject orders the set of objects according to some criterion, say preference. Thus we obtain an ordinal scale for each subject. These scales are called *I*-scales. As in multidimensional scaling, the question to be answered is the following: What is the smallest number of dimensions in which *both* the subjects and the objects can be accommodated with the distances from each object to each subject corresponding to the assigned ranks of preference, the most preferred object being nearest?

Let us look at some cases. Suppose we have two subjects and three objects. Label the subjects 1 and 2 and the objects x, y, and z. Since the labeling is arbitrary, we will label the objects in such a way that subject 1 prefers them in the order (xyz). Then there are six possible preference orders that subject 2 may have, corresponding to the six permutations of the set $\{x, y, z\}$. Observe that in every one of these cases we can arrange the two subjects and the three objects on a single straight line in such a way that the distances between each subject and the three objects will reflect the preferences. The arrangements are shown in Table 16.1.

Each arrangement is called a *J*-scale. In general, a *J*-scale represents an amalgam of all the given *I*-scales. In the above example, each *J*-scale is an amalgam of two *I*-scales imbedded in a one-dimensional space.

In the following example, a one-dimensional *J*-scale does not exist. Let there be three subjects and three objects. Let the preference orders of the three subjects be (xyz), (zyx), and (zxy). It is easy to verify that no arrangements of subjects and objects on a single line can reflect these preference orders as distances between the subjects and the objects. On the other hand, the configuration *can* be represented in a *two*-dimensional space. For example, we can place x at the origin $(0, 0)$, y at $(1, 0)$, z at $(0, 3)$, subject 1 at $(0, -1)$, subject 2 at $(1, 3)$, and subject 3 at $(0, 2)$. Then the distance between 1 and x will be 1; between him and y, $\sqrt{2}$; and between him and z, 4, reflecting his preference order (xyz). The distance between subject 2 and the objects will be $\sqrt{10}$, 3, and 1 respectively, reflecting (zyx). The distances between subject 3 and the objects will be 2, $\sqrt{5}$, and 1 respectively, reflecting (zxy).

Table 16.1. J–scales That Reflect one Subject's Preference Order (xyz) Coupled with Each of the Other Subject's Possible Preference Orders

Preference Order of Subject 2	J-Scale
xyz	1 2 *x* *y z*
yzx	1 *x* *y* 2 *z*
zxy	*y x* 1 *z* 2
zyx	1 *x* *y* *z* 2
yxz	*z* *x* 1 *y* 2
xzy	*y* 1 *x* 2 *z*

The question naturally arises as to the necessary and sufficient conditions on the set of preference orders (*I*-scales) that permit the construction of a *J*-scale of a given number of dimensions. This question leads the mathematical psychologist into purely mathematical investigations. As the number of prescribed dimensions increases, the solution of this problem becomes progressively more difficult. To aid practical work, computer programs have been developed which provide *J*-scales of minimum numbers of dimensions that can accommodate the data[5]. The use of the method is illustrated in the following example.

The unfolding model was applied by J. H. Levine (1972) in a study of interlocking directorates of several American banks and industrial concerns. Specifically, 14 banks and 70 corporations were examined. Of the latter, each shared one or more directors with one or more banks. A "distance" on an ordinal scale was defined between a bank and a corporation according to the number of shared directors. Thus the concern with which a bank shared the largest number of directors was assumed to be nearest and the concern that shared no director with the bank was interpreted as the farthest from it.

If the banks represent "subjects," the corporations "objects," and the distances "degrees of preference," we have an *I*-scale for each bank. The problem is that of constructing a *J*-scale; that is, a spatial model in which both the banks and the corporations would appear as points such that the distances between each bank and each of the corporations would correspond ordinally to the distances defined by the numbers of shared directors.

It turned out that such a *J*-scale could be represented in a three-dimensional space. Moreover, the banks and the corporations could be distributed on the surfaces of two concentric spheres—the corporations on the outer one, the banks on the inner one. In this way, although raw data consisted only of distances on an ordinal scale, the unfolding procedure produced some metric information about these distances; in particular, information about distances *between* banks and *between* corporations, which was not given by the raw data directly. The raw data had initially been represented by a proximity matrix with 70 rows and 14 columns with entries showing the number of shared directors between each of the banks and each of the corporations. The matrix reveals no clear patterns to the "naked eye." The spatial model, on the other hand, presents a clearly perceptible pattern. Clusters of both banks and corporations appeared on their respective sphere surfaces. One such cluster comprised the First National Bank of Chicago, Northern Trust, American National, and Continental Illinois. All of these are Chicago banks. Thus the cluster recovered from the unfolding reproduces a geographical cluster. But the banks were not identified by geographic location either in the raw data or in the computer program that performed the unfolding. The program was supposed to reveal only "social" clusterings. The fact that the social clusterings so revealed correspond to the geographic clusterings (this was the case also with other cities) lends credibility to the assumption that the model represents an aspect of "reality," for we would expect *corporations* to be linked most closely to banks in their geographic vicinity, and hence the geographic vicinity of corporations (and through them, of banks) to also reflect the "social" vicinity of both categories.

So far the unfolding revealed only what was expected on intuitive grounds. However, once our confidence in the model has found support, we can examine the emerging pattern for more information; for instance, for metric (in addition to ordinal) information about distances, from which "spheres of influence" and "sectors" associated with the banks can be deduced. It is amusing to note, as Levine points out, that these terms, which had been widely used in their metaphorical sense, assume a "literal" (that is, geometric) meaning in the context of the model.

The close correspondence between geographic and "social" proximity revealed in this study need not be the case in general. In our age of almost unlimited mobility and instantaneous communication, geographic proximity has lost much of its importance as a determinant of social bonds. It becomes correspondingly more important to obtain pictures of "social maps" from which interdependencies generated by all kinds of relationships can be deduced. The design of spatial models of social structures has been guided in great measure by this need.

NOTES

[1] As p tends to infinity, we have

$$\lim_{p \to \infty} \left[\sum_{i=1}^{n} |x_i - y_i|^p \right]^{1/p} = \max_i (|x_i - y_i|).$$

[2] Actually, two dimensions suffice, since w can be placed at the center of the triangle xyz. If more information is given—for instance, $d(w, x) = d(w, y) = d(w, z) > d(x, y)$—three dimensions are required.

[3] An attempt at constructing a denotative semantic space was made by An. Rapoport, Am. Rapoport, and W. P. Livant (1966).

[4] An ordinal difference scale fixes the order of magnitudes of differences between magnitudes. It is stronger than an ordinal scale but weaker than an interval scale.

[5] A detailed exposition of unfolding models is given in Coombs (1965).

CHAPTER SEVENTEEN

An Overview of Decision Theory

In its normative aspect, decision theory is concerned with problems of optimization—finding a course of action that leads to the "best" of a set of situations or, at least, to situations that are more acceptable than others. As in all contexts, the use of mathematical analysis involves absolute logical rigor in definitions and in deductive reasoning. Therefore, before a problem of optimization can be attacked by mathematical methods, it must be formulated in mathematically acceptable terms.

Specifically, the set of possible courses of action must be specified and criteria of value established for judging the relative worth of outcomes of actions. Next, the sort of data must be specified on the basis of which "optimal" actions can be singled out. In particular, if these data are to be quantified, the corresponding measurement procedures and the associated scales must be specified since these determine the legitimacy of mathematical operations on the data. Finally, if the solution of the optimization problem is a prescription, the actor or the set of actors to whom the prescription is addressed must be specified. (As we shall see, this requirement is often lost sight of.)

It follows that a substantial portion of formal decision theory must be devoted to structural analysis of decision problems. The goal of this analysis is the *formulation* of problems or classes of problems. Once this task is accomplished, the actual solution of the problem is a matter of applying appropriate mathematical procedures. These procedures, however, are quite independent of the subject matter of behavioral sciences. Therefore, a discussion of those aspects of decision theory that *can* be properly regarded as relevant to behavioral science must be centered primarily around analytic-descriptive theories. We will approach decision theory in this spirit. In this chapter, we will present a taxonomy of decision problems.

The first fundamental dichotomy of this taxonomy is between decision situations involving only one actor or decision maker and those involving more than one actor. An *actor* is specified not by his ontological status but by a specific set of interests. He or she may be an individual, a group of individuals, an institution, or a state; any entity, in fact, to which recognizable actions can be ascribed and which can be assumed to be governed by aims, goals, preferences, or the like.

A *rational actor* is one who uses available information in attempting to relate his or her actions to resulting outcomes; that is, one who guides his or her actions by comparing their envisaged consequences. It follows that a rational actor imposes a relation on the set of consequences—an asymmetric preference relation. Included in the concept of rationality is usually an assumption that this preference relation be at least a suborder (see p. 268), that is, have no cycles. As a rule, stronger ordering relations are assumed.

If there is only one rational actor, we can suppose that his or her preference ordering of the outcomes induces in some way a preference ordering on the actions. The solution of a decision problem then amounts to a selection of an action (or a set of actions) to which no other action is preferred. The simplicity of this definition of a solution stems from the absence of conflicts of interest *among* actors and justifies the above-mentioned dichotomy.

Within the class of decision problems involving a single actor, further taxonomic subdivisions can be made. Specifically, three types of decision problems are distinguished: decision under certainty, decision under uncertainty, and decision under risk.

In decision under certainty, a one-to-one correspondence can be established between actions and outcomes. The solution of the decision problem is then to choose the action that leads to an outcome to which no other is preferred.

From the standpoint of decision theory, this solution is trivial. Of course, there may be formidable problems associated with *finding* the action that leads to a most preferred outcome, but methods of solving these problems are developed in other branches of applied mathematics such as linear and nonlinear programming, control theory, and so on. They have no bearing on structural decision theory as such.

In decision under uncertainty, structural decision theory comes into its own. The first task is to represent the problem. If the number of alternative courses of action is finite, the courses of action can be represented by the rows of a matrix. The columns of that matrix are the so-called states of the world (here assumed to be discrete). The model represents decision under uncertainty if the actor is totally ignorant about which of these states of the world actually obtains or will obtain when he takes the action. The ijth entry in the matrix represents the outcome that obtains if the actor takes action i and the state of the world is j.

The commonplace decision problem, "Should I take the umbrella or not?" illustrates the situation. The actor must choose between taking the umbrella or leaving it at home. Two relevant (future) states of the world are "rain" and "shine." The four outcomes are shown in Matrix 17.1.

	R (Rain)	S (Shine)
U: Take umbrella	Relatively dry	Dry, but encumbered by umbrella
Ū: Leave it home	Wet	Dry and unemcumbered

Matrix 17.1

Assume that the actor prefers the outcomes in the following order: dry without umbrella >dry with umbrella >relatively dry >wet. Without knowing the impending state of the world, it is not possible to assign preferences to actions without ambivalence, because if it rains, U is preferable to $\bar{U}$; but if it does not, $\bar{U}$ is preferable to U. However, it is possible to state a *principle* of decision that can be defended by a rationale; for example, the *maximin* principle. This is a conservative or a pessimistic principle of action. It is based on the assumption that the actual state of the world will be the most unfavorable one with respect to the action taken. The maximin principle guarantees the "best" of all the "worst" outcomes associated with each action. Since the worse outcome associated with U (dry, encumbered) is preferable to the worse outcome associated with $\bar{U}$ (wet), the maximin principle prescribes U (take umbrella) in this case.

The pessimistic assumption embodied in the maximin principle lays it open to objections since it can be argued that "always expecting the worst" does not capture the essence of rationality. But the maximin principle is not the only one that has been proposed for decision under uncertainty. The so-called principle of *minimax regret* proposed by L. J. Savage (1951) aims at minimizing the maximum "regret" engendered by retrospective knowledge. Once an action has been chosen and taken, an outcome results which depends on the particular state of the world that obtains. Had the actor known that the particular state of the world would accompany his action, he would have chosen the action that would have maximized his utility, given that state of the world. If the utilities of the outcomes are given numerically, the "regret" associated with an outcome can be defined as the difference between the utility of the "best" outcome in that column and that of the outcome actually obtained. In symbols,

$$r_{ij} = \operatorname*{Max}_i(i_{ij}) - u_{ij}, \tag{17.1}$$

where r_{ij} is the regret and u_{ij} is the utility of the ijth outcome. The matrix (r_{ij}) is the regret matrix. The minimax regret principle prescribes the action that contains the smallest maximal regret.

To illustrate the difference between the maximin and the minimax regret principles, consider the decision problem represented by Matrix 17.2, where numerical utilities have been assigned to the outcomes.
The maximin choice is A_2.

Matrix 17.3 is the regret matrix derived from Matrix 17.2.
Since the minimum of the row maxima in this matrix is 4, the minimax regret principle prescribes A_1.

	S_1	S_2	S_3	S_4
A_1	1	-3	3	3
A_2	3	1	-2	3
A_3	5	0	3	-3

Matrix 17.2

	S_1	S_2	S_3	S_4
A_1	4	4	0	0
A_2	2	0	5	0
A_3	0	1	0	6

Matrix 17.3

In contrast to the maximin principle, the *maximax* principle prescribes the action that contains the most preferred outcome. Accordingly, in the above decision problem this principle prescribes A_3. Obviously, this principle is extremely "optimistic." A compromise between the maximin and the maximax is embodied in the so-called Hurwicz-α. One chooses a number α $(0 \leqslant \alpha \leqslant 1)$ and computes $\alpha \min_j(u_{ij}) + (1 - \alpha) \max_j(u_{ij})$ for each row i, then chooses the action that maximizes this quantity. The choice of α characterizes the actor's degree of pessimism (or optimism) since when $\alpha = 1$, the Hurwicz-α principle reduces to the maximin; when $\alpha = 0$, it reduces to the maximax. In the above problem, an actor with $\alpha = \frac{1}{2}$ would choose A_3; one with $\alpha = 3/4$ would choose A_2.

Finally, the so-called principle of insufficient reason proposed by Laplace is based on the idea that in the absence of any reason to believe that any of the states of the world is more likely to occur than any other, one must assume that all the states of the world are equiprobable and choose so as to maximize expected utility. Such an actor would be indifferent between A_2 and A_3.

The above analysis suggests that there is no single criterion of "rational choice" in decisions under uncertainty. Preference for one or another principle can be engendered by an actor's inclinations; for example, toward pessimism or optimism. There are, however, other more formal considerations. Note that either the maximin or the maximax principle can be applied if the utilities of outcomes are given only on the ordinal scale because the property of being "most preferred" or "least preferred" is invariant under order-preserving transformations of the utilities (see p. 24). The same cannot be said of the other principles. For example, the minimax regret can be applied only if it makes sense to calculate *differences* of utilities or at least to order these differences by their magnitudes. This operation necessitates a scale stronger than the ordinal but not as strong as the interval scale. Both the Laplace and the Hurwicz-α principles necessitate at least an interval scale, invariant under positive linear transformations (see p. 21). It appears, therefore, that the choice of decision principle in decisions under uncertainty is narrowed down if one wishes to apply such a principle in situations where only weak scales can be established for utilities. *Mutatis mutandis*, the choice of some principles involves a requirement that the scale on which the outcomes are given be of a certain strength.

Besides these requirements, there may be others that one might wish to impose on a principle of decision under uncertainty. A mathematically rigorous formulation of such requirements constitutes an axiomatic approach to the formal theory of decision under uncertainty.[1]

The third category of decision situations with a single actor comprises *decisions under risk*. A crucial aspect of these situations is that the probabilities associated with the states of the world are assumed to be known. Therefore, if utilities are given on an interval scale, it is possible to calculate the expected utility of each action, and a natural principle of choice suggests itself; namely, the choice of action that maximizes expected utility. (This choice is invariant under positive linear transformations of utilities.)

Decision under risk problems have given rise to numerous explorations in operations research having to do with evaluating the utility of information. This direction remains outside the scope of this book. The interested reader is referred to Raiffa and Schlaifer (1961) for a detailed treatment of these methods.

We turn to the other branch of the first dichotomy—decision situations involving more than one actor and therefore, in general, conflicts of interests.

The next important dichotomy can be made between situations involving exactly two actors and those with more than two. The importance of the two-actor situation is that it constitutes the point of departure for the theory of games, mathematically the most developed and, in some ways, the most sophisticated branch of formal decision theory.

Continuous games involve infinite sets of possible decisions available to each player. Examples are *games of timing*, where a player must decide on a moment of time to perform an action. Other examples are *differential games*, generalizations of problems of control (see Chapter 5), where strategies are trajectories, usually functions of time.[2]

A two-person game in which each player has a finite number of available strategies can be represented by a matrix where the rows designate the actions (strategies) available to one player ("Row") and the columns those available to the other ("Column"). A choice of a strategy by each player determines the *outcome* of the game. The corresponding entry in the game matrix is a pair of payoffs (utilities), one to each player.

An important distinction is made between two-person constant-sum games and two-person nonconstant-sum games. In the former, the sum of the payoffs in each cell of the game matrix is the same. It follows that the larger the payoff to one of the players, the smaller the payoff to the other; so that the interests of the players are diametrically opposed. In nonconstant-sum games, this is generally not the case. Since the payoffs are generally assumed to be given on an interval scale, the constant payoff sum in a constant-sum game can without loss of generality be taken as zero. For this reason, constant-sum games are often called zero-sum games. The two concepts are equivalent.

The normative theory of the two-person constant-sum game can be regarded as complete in the sense that in each such game, it is possible to prescribe an optimal strategy independently to each player, and algorithms exist for calculating these optimal strategies.

The simplest class of two-person constant-sum games are those with *saddle points*. A saddle point is a cell in the matrix where the payoff to Row is minimal in its row and maximal in its column; or, equivalently, where the payoff to Column is minimal in its column and maximal in its row. If both players choose a strategy that contains a saddle point in a zero-sum game, the outcome is always a saddle point (this is not generally true of nonconstant-sum games.) If the players choose in this way, each can *guarantee* himself a certain minimal payoff and, since the game is constant-sum, can prevent the other player from getting more than a certain maximal payoff. In this sense, the choice of strategy that contains a saddle point is regarded as "rational" in the context of a two-person zero-sum game with a saddle point. It is easily seen that this choice of strategy is prescribed by the maximin principle (see p. 323). "Expecting the worst" is justified on the assumption that the opponent will "do her best."

In two-person games without saddle points, each player can guarantee himself a minimal *expected* payoff and at the same time prevent the other from getting more than a maximal expected payoff (see Von Neumann, 1928). Thus the corresponding strategies can also be regarded as optimal. However, these optimal strategies in games without saddle points are *mixed*. That is, they are chosen probabilistically with the probabilities corresponding to the several available strategies determined by the payoff structure of the game matrix.

Rational outcomes of two-person zero-sum games are *equilibria* in the sense that neither player can do better than choose a strategy ("pure" or mixed) that contains an equilibrium outcome, if the other player does the same. Prescriptions to choose equilibrium-containing strategies can be made unequivocably and independently to each player for two reasons. First, even if the game matrix has several equilibria, two equilibrium-containing strategies always intersect at an equilibrium. Second, the payoff pairs in all equilibrium outcomes are the same. Equilibria having the first property are called *interchangeable*; those having the second property are called *equivalent*. Thus all equilibria in two-person zero-sum games are equivalent and interchangeable.

The concept of equilibrium applies also to nonconstant-sum games, but if such games have more than one equilibrium, they are not necessarily either equivalent or interchangeable. An example is shown in Matrix 17.4, representing a game nicknamed "Chicken."

	S_2	T_2
S_1	1, 1	$-10, 10$
T_1	$10, -10$	$-100, -100$

Matrix 17.4

Note that in this game, outcomes $T_1 S_2$ and $S_1 T_2$ are both equilibria in the sense that neither player can "shift away" from either outcome without impairing his payoff if the other does not shift. Nevertheless, if Row chooses T_1 and Column chooses T_2, outcome $T_1 T_2$ results, which is not an equilibrium and, moreover, is the worst outcome for *both* players.

Noninterchangeable and nonequivalent equilibria are characteristic of many nonconstant-sum games. For this reason, the prescription of a rational strategy to each player in nonconstant-sum games presents problems. J. C. Harsanyi (1962) provided a rationale for the solution of these problems and thus extended the concept of rational decision to non constant-sum noncooperative games. To do this, however, he was obliged to introduce further complications into the notion of individual rationality.

The problem of noninterchangeable or nonequivalent equilibria does not arise if a nonconstant-sum game has only one equilibrium. An example of such a game, nicknamed "Prisoner's Dilemma," is shown in Matrix 17.5.

	C_2	D_2
C_1	1, 1	$-10, 10$
D_1	$10, -10$	$-1, -1$

Matrix 17.5

The only equilibrium in this game is the outcome $D_1 D_2$. Moreover, the choice of D is prescribed to both players by the so-called *sure-thing principle* because D awards a larger payoff to a player *regardless* of how the other chooses. Nevertheless, the outcome $D_1 D_2$ must be regarded as unsatisfactory since $C_1 C_2$ is preferred by *both* players to that outcome. It can be said that outcome $D_1 D_2$ in Matrix 17.5, although prescribed by *individual rationality*, violates *collective rationality*. Outcome $C_1 C_2$ is collectively rational, but its realization necessitates some sort of *enforceable agreement* between the players.

Introducing the concept of an enforceable agreement generates another dichotomy between *noncooperative* and *cooperative* games. So far, we have discussed noncooperative games, in which strategies are chosen independently by each player. In a cooperative game, the players have the opportunity to *coordinate* their choices of strategy and to effect enforceable agreements about these choices.

Solutions of cooperative games are derived from sets of axioms which stipulate "desirable properties" of a solution. Several different solutions have been proposed. The interested reader is referred to Nash (1953), Raiffa (1953), and Braithwaite (1955).

Noncooperative *n*-person games have been used as models in a normative theory of voting (see Farquharson, 1959). The bulk of game theory concerned with *n*-person games ($n > 2$) deals with cooperative games, in which subsets of players can form coalitions in pursuit of their collective interests. That is to say, the members of a coalition can coordinate their strategies and make binding agreements to carry them out. In most formulations, members of a coalition can also make *side payments* to each other; that is, can apportion their joint payoffs themselves. This requires a conception of utility that is *transferable* (like money).

The usual formulation of an *n*-person cooperative game is in *characteristic function form*. The characteristic function indicates a minimal guaranteed payoff to each potential coalition of players. An outcome of a game is represented as an apportionment of payoffs among all the players. If the sum of the payoffs equals the amount that the *grand coalition* (of all *n* players) can get by coordinating their strategies, and if each individual payoff is no smaller than what the player can guarantee himself if he plays alone (a coalition of one) against everyone else, the outcome reflects both the individual rationality of each player and the collective rationality of all players (though not necessarily the collective rationality of every subset of players). Such an outcome is called an *imputation*.

Several solution concepts have been proposed (see Von Neumann and Morgenstern, 1947; Shapley, 1953; and Aumann and Maschler, 1964). Each solution concept is based on some rationale; that is, a set of considerations involving the individual rationality of each player and either the collective rationality of all players (as when solutions are imputations) or the collective rationality of subsets of players in coalitions. In addition, since the solutions of n-person cooperative games amount to instances of conflict resolution, certain considerations based (explicitly or implicitly) on concepts of equity or fairness are also involved. It is noteworthy that in the theory of *n*-person cooperative games, the originally envisaged principal problem of game theory—that of singling out strategically optimal decisions in conflict situations—has been lost sight of. The principal problem became that of selecting a *collective* decision which satisfies certain criteria stated in advance.

The same problem is central in the other principal branches of decision theory involving several autonomous actors; namely, the theory of social choice. Here the autonomy of the actors is no longer characterized by an ability to choose strategies or courses of action, but solely by the ability to present to some arbitrating body a preference ordering on a set of alternatives. The arbitrating body, usually called society, then faces the problem of imposing a preference ordering on the same set of alternatives according to some rule (the social choice function) that satisfies some "desirable" criteria.

Again, an important dichotomy suggests itself between situations involving only two alternatives and those involving several alternatives. With two alternatives, several rules of social choice can be designed to satisfy prescribed intuitively acceptable criteria. In fact, the multiplicity of these rules induces a taxonomy. One can investigate the properties of the simple majority rule (where abstainers or absentees are not counted), the strict majority rule, or rules governing a quorum, weighted majority rules, the consequences of conferring a veto power on specified actors, the structure of representative systems, and so on.

When more than two alternatives are involved, the theory of social choice is constricted by the so-called Impossibility Theorem. This theorem is, in a way, an antithesis of the Fundamental Theorem of Game Theory. The latter states that every finite two-person zero-sum game has a "solution" that satisfies certain criteria of individual rationality. It has served as a point of departure for the subsequent development of game theory. The Impossibility Theorem in the theory of social choice asserts a contrary proposition; namely, that there does *not* exist a social choice rule that satisfies a certain set of intuitively desirable criteria if the set of alternatives contains more than two elements. Nevertheless, the Impossibility Theorem has also served as a point of departure in the development of the theory of social choice. It has instigated the examination of the structural characteristics of several types of social choice rules that do not

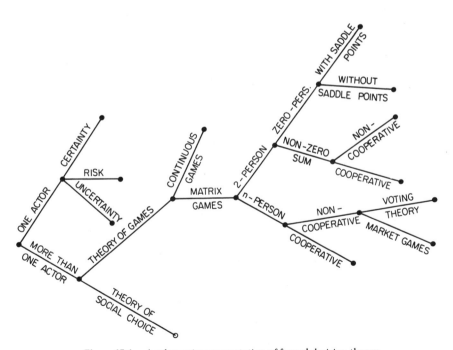

Figure 17.1. A schematic representation of formal decision theory.

satisfy all the criteria (which indeed they cannot), but which nevertheless seem "reasonable." Clearly, *some* social choice rule is inherent in every formalized procedure of collective decision, in particular in every procedure deemed "democratic"; that is, one in which the preferences of the members of a constituency somehow determine the decisions made by society.

The outline of decision theory presented here is schematized in Figure 17.1. It goes without saying that this outline can be amplified by further refinements, which, however, are likely to be of interest only to the specialist. In what follows, we will examine somewhat more closely the theory of social choice with more than two alternatives (Chapter 18), applications of game-theoretic concepts in political science (Chapter 19), and applications of these concepts in experimental social psychology (Chapter 20).

NOTES

[1] An axiomatization of decision principles under uncertainty is given in Luce and Raiffa (1957, Chapter 13) and in Milnor, 1954.

[2] The interested reader will find a thorough exposition of continuous games in Karlin (1959) and of differential games in Isaacs (1956).

CHAPTER EIGHTEEN

Theory of Social Choice

Any form of social organization obliges individuals to abide by certain decisions even if these decisions do not coincide with their interests, inclinations, or wishes. In autocratic forms of organization, decisions binding on all are made by the autocrat. In all other forms, some process of collective decision must take place. Explicit rules governing this process were doubtless designed with the view of avoiding costly or disruptive protractions of controversies, paralyzing dead-locks, and struggles for influence and power, which would otherwise accompany divergence of views or interests. In fact, explicit rules of collective decision become practically mandatory when large numbers of individuals, who may be strangers to each other, participate in the decision process. For this reason, formal constitutions, by laws, and the like are almost always incorporated in nonautocratic forms of organization. These are essentially agreements made in an abstract (and therefore neutral) context on how disagreements in concrete (and therefore partisan) contexts are to be resolved.

"Majority rule" is commonly viewed as a characteristic of democratic decision making. The process was already in use in decisions made by enfranchised populations or the ruling bodies of Greek city states and of the Roman republic. The principle survived even under the Empire, at least in the Senate in matters subject to its jurisdiction. It is therefore interesting to observe that as early as the second century, there was an awareness of problems generated by the principle of majority rule.

The reference is to a remarkable letter by Senator Pliny the Younger to his friend, Titus Aristo, apparently an expert in juridical matters, complaining of the voting procedure that decided a case before the Senate.[1]

It seems that a consul, Africanus Dexter, was found dead, and his freedmen faced trial. There were three possible verdicts: (1) suicide, in which case acquittal was called for; (2) killed by his freedmen at his own request, in which case the freedmen were to be banished; (3) murder, in which case the accused were to be put to death.

It appears from Pliny's letter that the initial motion to acquit was defeated, whereupon the Senate voted on the punishment, and banishment was the final verdict. In Pliny's opinion, the voting procedure was not fair because in the first vote, the proponents of the death penalty together with the proponents of banishment formed a majority in spite of the fact, as Pliny put it, that their views were "further apart" (because of the irreversibility of the death penalty) than the views of the banishers and the acquitters. At any rate, the acquitters lost, even though they were the most numerous. Evidently, Pliny favored a decision by *plurality*, for he writes: "I desired that the three different opinions should be numbered; and that the two parties who had made a momentary truce, should be separated . . ."

But if the acquitters had won, someone might have pointed out that such an outcome would also be less than fair because the majority was *against* acquittal. In fact, in any three-choice situation where none of the alternatives is favored by a majority, it can happen that the alternative favored by the fewest voters can win in a two-stage voting procedure. Problems of this sort (and others) are bound to arise whenever collective decisions involve choices among more than two alternatives.

Structural-analytic approaches to problems associated with collective decisions were undertaken in the last decades of the eighteenth century, when ideas about democracy were in the ascendance. An implicit (at times explicit) aim of this analysis was to construct a "fair" procedure of collective decision; that is, essentially to operationalize the concept of "the greatest good for the greatest number." Some of this analysis, as we shall see, involved not only considerations of how many people favored a given alternative, but also how strongly they preferred it to other alternatives. Note that Pliny also raised this question when he argued that the position of the banishers was "closer" to that of the acquitters than to that of the proponents of the death penalty. He writes: "What agreement can be framed between the sentence for death and the sentence for banishment? No more indeed than between the sentence for banishment and for acquittal. The two latter are however a little nearer than the two former. In both the last cases life is spared; by the former it is taken away."

To this day, we have a number of rather complex voting procedures, such as the Hare system, the Australian ballot, and so on, some of which reflect attempts to incorporate strengths of preferences as well as numbers of proponents as "weights" in arriving at collective decisions.

A landmark in the development of a formal theory of collective decision was the so-called Impossibility Theorem proved by K. Arrow (1951). We will deal with it and its ideational "spin-offs" below, after we have laid the conceptual groundwork for a mathematically rigorous theory of social choice.

THE SOCIAL CHOICE FUNCTION

The problem of social choice can be formulated as follows. There is a finite set $N = \{1, 2, \ldots, n\}$ of *voters* and a finite set $X = \{x, y, \ldots, z\}$ of *alternatives*. Each voter is associated with a certain asymmetric binary relation on the set of alternatives. Let each voter *i*'s relation, designated by D_i, denote "is preferred to." We will assume that each voter is "rational," at least to the extent that D_i is a suborder (see p. 268); that is, contains no cycles. Thus we will not allow an individual voter to prefer x to y and also y to z and z to x. (We might also demand that D_i be stronger than a suborder; for instance, that it be transitive, which would make it a strict partial order; or that it induce a transitive indifference relation, which would make it a weak order; or even that it be a linear order.)

To arrive at a social choice among the given alternatives, society asks each voter *i* to submit his D_i, and from this list of D_i ($i = 1, 2, \ldots, n$), called a *preference profile*, society selects some subset of the alternatives in accordance with a rule of selection previously agreed upon. This subset is called the *social choice*. It may, of course, consist of a single alternative, but need not.

It will be readily recognized that this general formulation encompasses some well-known special rules of choice. Consider an election with two candidates. Here X consists of two elements: $X = \{x, y\}$, where x and y represent the candidates. Each voter is asked to submit his D_i on the set $\{x, y\}$. Now the ordered pairs that form the elements of $\{x, y\}$ are (x, x), (y, x), (x, y), and (y, y). There are 16 subsets of this set of four pairs. But since D_i is asymmetric, it can consist only of the following singlet subsets: $\{(x, y)\}$, $\{(y, x)\}$, or $\emptyset$. If voter *i* submits $D_i = \{(x, y)\}$, he has voted for x; if he submits $D_i = \{(y, x)\}$, he has voted for y; if he submits $D_i = \emptyset$, he has abstained.

One way of deciding the election (that is, a particular selection *rule*), is to declare x the winner if more voters submitted (x, y) than (y, x), and to declare y the winner in the opposite case, perhaps with some provisions for breaking ties. In this method, abstaining voters are ignored. This rule is called *simple majority*. Another rule might to be declare a candidate winner only if a majority of *all* voters submitted (x, y). There are many other possible rules. For instance, the voters might be given different "weights," so that one voter's D_i is counted more times than another's. There might even be a rule that declares x the winner *regardless* of how the voters have voted. A rule that specifies a social choice need not be "democratic" or "fair." All that is demanded of such a rule is that it specifies a non-null subset of the alternatives once all the D_i submitted by the voters are known.

Now we have assumed that initially each voter's preference is expressed as an asymmetric relation on the entire set of alternatives X. In an actual instance of social decision (for example, an election), only a subset Y of X may be presented to the voters, a so-called *feasible* subset of alternatives. A social choice *function* is defined in such a manner that, given a full set of preference relations on X and *any* nonempty feasible set of alternatives $Y \subset X$, the function determines a nonempty subset of Y as the social choice. The formal definition involves two other sets besides X, Y, and N; namely,

    (i)   The set $\mathscr{X}$ of nonempty subsets of X. Thus if $Y \subset X$, $Y \neq \emptyset$, then $Y \in \mathscr{X}$. Usually $\mathscr{X}$ is taken as $2^X - \emptyset$.

    (ii)   A set $\mathscr{D}$ of ordered *n*-tuples $(D_1, D_2, \ldots, D_n)$.

Usually $\mathscr{D}$ comprises the entire set of these n-tuples. Thus if D is an n-tuple $(D_1, D_2, \ldots, D_n)$, then $D \in \mathscr{D}$.

A social choice function can now be defined formally as a mapping F: $\mathscr{D} \times \mathscr{X} \to \mathscr{X}$, such that $F(D, Y) \subset Y$, and $F(D, Y) \neq \emptyset$.

Note that the domain of F is a Cartesian product whose elements are the ordered pairs (D, Y), with $D \in \mathscr{D}$, $Y \in \mathscr{X}$. The elements of its codomain are the subsets of X. Given a pair (D, Y) (that is, given a particular set of preferences of the voters and a feasible subset of the set of alternatives), the function determines the social choice in the form of a nonempty subset of the feasible set.

This general definition implies no properties of a social choice function that one might wish to ascribe to it on the basis of notions of "fairness," "democratic procedure," or even consistency. We may well have a social choice function that, on the basis of a given preference profile on $X = \{x, y, z\}$, chooses x whenever $Y = \{x, z\}$ and x whenever $Y = \{x, y\}$, but y whenever $\{x, y, z\}$. Or we may have a social choice function that, on the basis of some D, selects x from $Y = \{x, y\}$, y from $\{y, z\}$, and z from $\{x, z\}$, thus exhibiting an "intransitivity of preference." Indeed, this can very well happen if the social choice function is majority rule in paired presentations of alternatives.

Consider the Dexter case discussed above, and suppose for simplicity that the Roman Senate consists of just three senators, Primus, Secundus, and Tertius. Each submits a linear order on the three alternatives, a ("acquit"), b ("banish"), and c ("condemn to death"). Primus' preference order is (abc). That is, he wants acquittal, but if he cannot get an acquittal, he prefers banishment to the death penalty. Secundus' preference order is (bca). Tertius votes (cab). Tertius' preference order may seen strange but can well be imagined. Tertius believes the accused to be guilty and deserving the death penalty, but if they are not condemned to death, he would rather see them acquitted than banished because he is strongly opposed to applying any punishment other than the death penalty to murderers of patricians.

Suppose now that the Senate reaches its decisions by majority rule. In other words, the Senate prefers each pair of alternatives in the same order as the majority of the senators. We see that Primus and Tertius (a majority) prefer a to b; Primus and Secundus (a majority) prefer b to c; Secundus and Tertius (also a majority) prefer c to a. In this case, majority rule induces a social preference relation that is not a suborder (is cyclic).

This "paradox" of voting is known as the Condorcet Paradox.[2] It can arise in any situation where more than two alternatives are involved in a problem of social choice.

We will now examine the situation in a more general context. Since each D_i is a binary relation on X, D_i is a subset of the Cartesian product of X with itself. Now if $Y \subset X$, then $Y \times Y$ is also a subset of $X \times X$. The intersection $D_i \cap (Y \times Y)$ is called the *restriction* of D_i on Y, and the profile of these restrictions is called the restriction of D on Y.

Now let F be a social choice function, D a profile, and Y a pair of alternatives $\{x, y\}$. Since by definition of social choice function, the restriction of D on Y

must determine a nonempty subset of Y as the choice set, this choice set must be either $\{x\}$, $\{y\}$, or $\{x, y\}$. We can interpret this result in terms of an asymmetric binary relation *induced* by D on $\{x, y\}$. Namely, if the choice set is $\{x\}$, this relation is given by xPy (society prefers x to y); if $\{y\}$, then yPx; if $\{x, y\}$, then $x\mathcal{P}y$ and $y\mathcal{P}x$ (society is indifferent between x and y.)

Thus we can say that a social choice function associates with every permissible D an asymmetric binary relation on X. If this relation is to represent an internally consistent preference relation, it should be some sort of order.

Now in the interest of clear-cut social decisions, it would be desirable if P would determine the strongest possible order on X; namely, a linear order, for in that case, society could select the "best" alternative on X. Moreover, if that "best" alternative could not for some reason be actualized, society would be justified in substituting the "second best" alternative for the social choice and so on.

Of course, a binary asymmetric relation need not determine a linear order. The next best thing, then, would be a weak order; if not that, then a strict partial order. At any rate, one would like P to be at least a suborder because, as we have seen, any "consistent" preference relation should be at least noncyclic.

By our example above, we see that D under majority rule may fail to induce even a suborder on a set of three alternatives—the case of "intransitive majorities."

We need not insist on a majority rule, however. Are there, perhaps, other social choice functions that can be shown to induce at least a suborder on society's preference, given any permissible profile D? This property would be a desirable property of a social choice function. Having brought up the subject of desirable properties, we are moved to list other such properties that we might expect a "good" social choice function to have. We will attempt to draw up a "minimal" list of desirable properties of a social choice function. Some may feel that the list represents the "least one can expect" of a social choice function that purports to be democratic.

The method pursued here is that of an axiomatically formulated model (see p. 25). The list of properties "advertises," so to say, for a function that can satisfy the requirements embodied in the axioms. Before we deduce the consequences of the axioms. let us see what the result might be. We are looking for social choice functions that satisfy the axioms. There are three possibilities. There may be just one such function. There might be a class of such functions comprising more than one. Or there may be no function that satisfies all our requirements. From one point of view, a uniquely determined social choice function would be the most desirable result, for then we would know how to design a "constitution" (as a social choice function could be interpreted) that satisfies the "minimal" requirements of democracy, and we would be sure that no other "constitution" does so. From another point of view, a class of social choice functions determined by the axioms would be the most desirable result, for this would indicate that several varieties of democratic constitution are possible. Or else the requirements could be strengthened to include more of the desirable properties and so narrow down the class of acceptable social choice functions. If we value democratic principles of social decision, we would be disappointed if the set of social choice functions satisfying our minimal requirements turned out to be empty. This result might be interpreted to mean that "democracy is impossible." On the other hand, the vacuous result might move us to look more deeply into what could or should be understood under "democratic decision." In other words, the "disappointing" result might turn out to have some theoretical leverage.

THE IMPOSSIBILITY THEOREM[3]

We will now assume that each voter i ($i = 1, 2, \ldots, n$) presents a weak order on X and turn our attention to the set of axioms purporting to characterize a democratic social choice function.

A_1.   (i)   The number of alternatives in X exceeds two.

(ii)   The number of voters exceeds one.

(iii)   All profiles $D \in \mathcal{D}$ are permissible and each induces a social preference relation P, which is at least a weak order.

Comments: It is hardly necessary to justify (ii). If there is only one "voter," the problem of *social* choice does not arise. Robinson Crusoe did not have to deal with that problem until Friday joined him. As for (i), it is introduced because if there are only two alternatives, a great many social choice rules can be designed that are deemed "good"; for example, several types of majority rule. The *problem* of designing a "good" social choice function would not have arisen if situations with more than two alternatives to choose from did not arise. Recall that Pliny the Younger raised the problem in the context of three alternatives. The Condorcet Paradox (see p. 334) also arose in that context. As for (iii), it reflects the desideratum that the rule be sufficiently general so that it can prescribe a social ordering of alternatives *whatever* profile of preference is produced by the voters. Another way of viewing (iii) is that it reflects a complete freedom of choice enjoyed by the voters; and moreover, that the individual preference orderings are independent, as guaranteed by the secret ballot.

A_2.   If in a social ordering, x is preferred to y in consequence of a given profile D, then this preference should remain unchanged if D is modified as follows:

(i)   In individual orderings, preferences involving alternatives other than x are not changed.

(ii)   In individual orderings, preferences involving x are either unchanged or are changed in x's favor.[4]

Comment: In the changes envisaged, x's "stock" either goes up in someone's estimation or remains the same. It never goes down. Under these conditions,

x's status in the social ordering should not decline with regard to some other alternative.

A_3.   Let $Y \subset X$, and let a profile D be modified in such manner that the restriction of D on Y remains the same. Then the restriction of P on Y should remain the same.

Comment: A_3 expresses the so-called principle of *independence from irrelevant alternatives.* To see how the principle works in a concrete situation, let $Y = \{x, y\}$. Let the ordering produced by some profile D be such that xPy. Now let D be changed in any manner whatsoever, except that whoever preferred x to y under D still prefers x to y under the new ordering D'. Also, whoever preferred y to x under D still prefers y to x, and whoever was indifferent between x and y is still indifferent between these two alternatives. Then in the ordering produced by D', xPy must also hold.

Now when D is replaced by another profile D', the "distance" between two alternatives may be changed in individual orderings without reversing the preference between them. By the "distance" between two alternatives in an individual ordering we mean the number of alternatives that separate them in that ordering. For example, in the ordering $(xyzw)$, x and y are adjacent, but in the ordering $(xzwy)$, they are separated, so that the "distance" between them is larger. Nevertheless, by transitivity of D_i, xD_iy in both orderings. According to A_3, a modification of D that induces only changes of "distance" between two alternatives but does not reverse the preference between them in any individual ordering should not reverse the preference between them in the social ordering.

It would seem that A_3 is not as innocuous as it appears to be at first sight. It might happen that under one profile, y was the least preferred alternative for all voters, while under another it moved to second place for several voters. This change of "status" should not change the preference order between x and y in the social ordering, according to A_3, as long as the preference between x and y remained the same for all voters.

If the "distance" between two alternatives is interpreted as the "degree of preference difference" between them, then A_3 in effect asserts that this "degree of preference" should not be taken into account as long as the stated conditions are satisfied. Some arguments have been put forward impugning the reasonableness of this axiom, and it has also been vigourously defended, for example, by Fishburn (1973).[5] At this time, we will not take sides in this matter.

A_4.   For each pair of alternatives x, y, there is some profile of individual orderings that leads to a social preference of x over y.

Comment: This axiom has been called "citizens' sovereignty." If A_4 is violated, then it may happen that even a *unanimous* preference of x over y in the individual orderings results in a preference of y over x in the social ordering (or indifference between them). In that case, "the will of the people" is ignored, something naturally regarded as a violation of democratic procedure. A_4 declares that the voters can "force" society *in some way* (for example, by unanimous vote) to prefer any alternative x to any alternative y.

We now proceed to draw some consequences from axioms A_1–A_4. Let a certain social choice function satisfy these four axioms.

Consider an ordered pair of alternatives (x, y) and a set of voters $V \subset N$ such that whenever all the voters in V prefer x to y, so does society, according to that social choice function, regardless of how the voters in the complementary set $N - V$ order these alternatives. Then V is called *decisive* for the ordered pair (x, y).

For example, let there be a provision in the constitution that no individual may be deprived of his life without his consent. Then if x_i stands for "i is allowed to live" and y_i for "i shall be killed," the singlet set $\{i\}$ is decisive for (x_i, y_i). Of course, $\{i\}$ is not decisive for any other pair (x_j, y_j), where x_j stands for "j is allowed to live" and y_j for "j shall be killed," if $j \neq i$. Note also that $\{i\}$ is not necessarily decisive for (y_i, x_i). That an individual cannot be deprived of his life without his consent does not mean that he has the right to commit suicide or that his command that he be killed must be obeyed if everyone is against his death.

More generally, a set V has absolute veto power if it is decisive for all (x, y), where x stands for "status quo" and y for any other decision. Absolute veto power is not dictaorial power. V would have dictatorial power (could be called an "oligarchy"), if it were decisive for all ordered pairs (x, y).

A set V is called *minimal decisive* for an ordered pair (x, y) if it is decisive for that pair and if none of its proper subsets is decisive for *any* pair. We assert that there must be some pair (x, y) and some nonempty set V which is minimal decisive for it.

To see this, note that the null set cannot be decisive for *any* pair because if it were, then the entire set of voters N would not be decisive for that pair, whereas axioms A_1, A_2, and A_4 imply that N is decisive for every pair. Now add a voter to the null set. If this singlet set is minimal decisive for some ordered pair, we have proved our assertion because its only proper subset is the null set, which is not decisive for any pair. If the singlet set is still not decisive for any pair, add another voter, and so on. Eventually, a set must be reached that is minimal decisive for some pair, otherwise N would not be decisive for any pair, which is impossible. Therefore there must be some nonempty set V which is decisive for *some* ordered pair (x, y) and is minimal decisive for that pair.

We fix our attention on the pair (x, y) so determined and on the set V minimal decisive for it. Being nonempty, V must contain at least one voter. Call him j. Let $W = V - \{j\}$, $U = N - V$. Since all profiles of weak orderings are allowed by A_1(iii), and since, in view of A_1(ii), there are at least three different alternatives

x, y, z, imagine the following profile:

j	W	U
x	z	y
y	x	z
z	y	x

That is to say, j's preference ordering is (xyz), everyone in W submits (zxy), and everyone else submits (yzx). Note that although W may be empty, W and U cannot both be empty, otherwise our "society" would consist of a single indivi-dual, j, contrary to A_1 (ii).

Now since everyone in $V = \{j\} \cup W$ prefers x to y, and since V has been assumed to be decisive for (x, y), it follows that society must prefer x to y.

Next, we show that society must not prefer z to y, where z is any alternative different from x or y, for assuming that society prefers z to y would imply that W is decisive for (z, y), contradicting the construction of V as the *minimal* decisive set. Now if P is a weak ordering, xPy and zPy imply xPz; so $\{j\}$ is decisive for (x, z). It follows that $\{j\}$ cannot be a proper subset of V (again because V is minimal decisive), and so $\{j\} = V$. Since by hypothesis V is decisive for (x, y), $\{j\}$ is decisive for (x, y). And we have also shown that $\{j\}$ is decisive for (x, z), where z is any alternative different from x and y.

Now suppose w is an arbitrary alternative different from x, and imagine the following profile:

j	U
w	z
x	w
z	x

We have $\{j\} \cup U = N$ because W was shown to be empty. Therefore, everyone prefers w to x, and by the unanimity principle (N is decisive for every pair), society must also prefer w to x. Thus wPx and, since $\{j\}$ has been shown to be decisive for (x, z), xPz, and by transitivity, wPz. But j is the only voter who prefers w to z. Therefore, $\{j\}$ is decisive for (w, z), and so for any pair of which x is not a member.

Finally, imagine the profile

j	U
w	z
z	x
x	w

Since $\{j\}$ is decisive for $\{w, z\}$, we must have wPz. By unanimity, zPx. Therefore, by transitivity, wPx, and $\{j\}$ is decisive for (w, x). But the alternatives z and w

were chosen arbitrarily. Therefore, $\{j\}$ is decisive for any ordered pair of which x is the second member. Since we have also shown that $\{j\}$ is decisive for any pair of which x is the first member—that is, for (x, y) and for (x, z), where $z \neq x$—we have shown that $\{j\}$ is decisive for every pair. Therefore, we can call j a *dictator*. (A dictator is defined as an individual in a society who has his way in any social decision, regardless of the preferences of all other members of the society.)

We conclude that the only kind of social decision rule that simultaneously satisfies axioms A_1–A_4 is one that designates some individual as a dictator. Originally, the formulation of the impossibility theorem comprised a fifth axiom:

A_5.   There is no individual $j \in N$ such that xPy if and only if xD_jy.

The impossibility theorem derives its name from the fact that it is impossible to construct a social choice function that satisfies A_1–A_5.

The importance of the Impossibility Theorem is obviously not in that it shows that "democracy is impossible" or anything of the sort. There is a large gap between formal, logical, and absolutely precise definitions of "democracy" as embodied, for example, in the above axioms, and what people intuitively feel to be "democratic procedures." And after all, the value of "democracy" is not that it is logically and absolutely consistent with some rules but that it is felt by people who espouse the idea to be somehow fair or just. Clearly, there *are* procedures of social choice that large majorities in some societies subscribe to as "fair" or "just." Here we invoke Kenneth Boulding's famous dictum, "Anything that exists is possible." The value of analysis lies elsewhere; namely, in revealing the gap between logically rigorous conceptions and intuitive ones and so inculcating the habit of rigorous analysis when conflicts or contradictions arise.

RAMIFICATIONS OF THE THEORY OF SOCIAL CHOICE

The formal theory of social choice has been developed in two directions. Following one of them, one can start with the Impossibility Theorem and ask how its underlying axioms can be weakened so as to make them compatible with each other. Following the other direction, one can examine some specific classes of social choice functions to single out their desirable and undesirable properties. Obviously, none of these functions can satisfy all the axioms A_1–A_5, but in examining their properties, one can form an idea of what is being "sacrificed" in each type of social choice function. In this way, our analysis will be linked to our values, which, in the opinion of this writer, is not to be avoided but, on the contrary, encouraged, provided we are aware of the linkage.

Examining the list of requirements A_1–A_5, we find that we cannot very well drop either A_2, A_4, or A_5 if we want society to be even minimally responsive to "the will of the people." Further, if we drop A_1 (i), we shall be evading the issue, as has already been pointed out (see p. 336). If we drop A_1 (ii), the whole concept of social choice becomes vacuous. There remain only A_1 (iii) and A_3.

One way of relaxing A_1 (iii) is by restricting $\mathscr{D}$, the set of "permissible" profiles D. Such a restriction may be interpreted as a restriction of the freedom of choice of the voters, but it need not be so interpreted in concrete contexts because the profiles D actually occurring in specific situations may be "naturally" restricted to certain types.

As an example of such a situation, imagine N, the set of voters forming a committee that is to decide on the maximum penalty for some crime, say armed robbery. To fix ideas, suppose that the possible alternatives are terms of imprisonment measured in integral numbers of years. Some members of the committee feel that three years is the most appropriate maximum penalty, some prefer five years, some eight, and so on. There are also some members of the committee who believe that the prison system should be abolished altogether; consequently, their most preferred term of imprisonment is zero years. (Penalties other than imprisonment are not considered in this phase of deliberation.)

Now consider a member of this committee whose most preferred alternative is five years. We may suppose that she considers four years as too short and six years as too long. If her degree of preference decreases monotonically in either direction away from five years, we say her preference ordering is *single-peaked*.

We can also suppose that the opponent of imprisonment will have a single-peaked preference ordering with a peak of zero if his degree of preference decreases monotonically with the number of years. The same can be said of the proponent of the longest feasible term, say 20 years, if his degree of preference increases monotonically with the number of years.

A single-peaked preference ordering can also have one "plateau," provided no alternative is preferred to any of the alternatives on the plateau. Thus our three-year proponent may be indifferent between two, three, and four years, as shown in Figure 18.1.

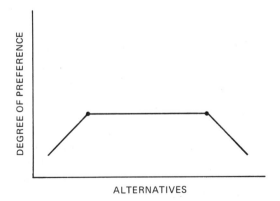

Figure 18.1. A single-peaked preference relation with a plateau.

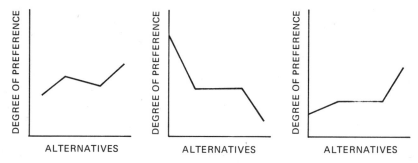

Figure 18.2.   Preference relations that are not single-peaked.

Examples of preference orderings that are not single-peaked are shown in Figure 18.2.

It has been shown that if $\mathscr{D}$ consists only of single-peaked preference orderings, then a social choice function *can* be found that satisfies A_1-A_5. For instance, in our example, let the social choice be the *median* of the underlying scale; that is, one half of the voters have their peaks above that number of years, and the remaining voters have their peaks below. This rule satisfies all five axioms, if all the preference orderings are single-peaked.

How frequently single-peaked preference orderings occur in real political contexts is of interest in political science. They can be expected to occur if some one-dimensional scale is perceived by the voters to underlie the alternatives. In our example, this was a time scale. There may be other examples. Some political alternatives or candidates for office may be perceived to occupy positions on a "left-right" scale. (In fact, such a scale will be assumed in some mathematical models of coalition formation to be discussed in Chapter 19.) Foreign policy decisions of some states may be perceived to occupy positions on a "hawk-dove" scale, and so on.

The finding that the restriction of $\mathscr{D}$ to single-peaked preference orderings guarantees the existence of "democratic" social choice functions reveals a connection between the political-ideational structure of a society and the possibility of designing a *general* rule for collective decisions that satisfies a given set of requirements. However, the finding establishes only the fact that a "one-dimensional" political-ideational structure is *sufficient* to guarantee the possibility of designing such a rule. A mathematician, true to the traditions and values of his profession, naturally wants to know whether such a structure is also *necessary*. Pursuit of an answer to this question leads into richly ramifying mathematical investigations that may or may not be relevant to the original substantive problem posed.

Mathematical investigations have a way of "taking off," driven by the investigators' commitment to completeness, rigor, and generality. Quite often, the problems that had provided the original impetus for the research are completely lost sight of. In view of the often dramatic role of serendipity in science, one hesitates to prejudge these departures as irrelevant formalistic exercises. Besides, mathematically interesting findings can be justified in their own right if mathematics, as such, is valued as a buoyant exercise of what is, perhaps, the most developed of the most uniquely human faculties. On the other hand, someone concerned with a substantive content-oriented field of inquiry (for instance, political science) can justifiably ask the mathematician how her findings can help him to better understand the problems arising in his field.

Thresholds of perceived relevance differ. The completely pragmatically oriented may dismiss as useless any knowledge that gives no hint about how to proceed toward a chosen goal. The strongly empirically oriented may be well-disposed toward "pure science"; but they recognize as "genuine" knowledge only what is empirically verifiable. They will not demand of the mathematician "how to do it" applications, but they will demand empirically testable models. Considerably wider is the range of interest of those who seek understanding of the essential features of a class of phenomena, which are often revealed by structural analysis that is not connected (nor needs to be) to concrete observations. The above analysis of the logical structure of social choice was an example.

Nevertheless, abstract as this analysis is, the fundamental concepts are still idealizations or refinements of concepts that pervade political thought; for example, democracy, dictatorship, freedom of preference, the political-ideational spectrum, and so on. It is only when mathematical analysis leaves even these idealizations behind that all contact with behavioral science is lost.

Examples of this breach are readily found in the ramifications of formal decision theory, both in the theory of social choice and in many developments of the mathematical theory of games. We will give one example.

As has been pointed out, if X contains just two alternatives, there are many social choice functions that satisfy all the axioms (except A_1 (i), of course). A task of analytic-descriptive theory is to classify these functions. One class comprises so-called *representative systems*. Politically, a representative system consists of two or more layers of voting bodies organized hierarchically. Results of voting in a body at a lower level determines a vote for the one or the other alternative on the next higher level, and so on. The voters in the various voting bodies can also be regarded as voters in a single body. Now starting with this single body, one asks whether it is possible to design a social choice function for it such that the decisions will always coincide with the decisions made by a representative system composed of the same individuals. To put it in another way, what are the necessary and sufficient conditions on a social choice function that makes it equivalent to some representative system? It turns out that sufficient conditions are easy to state and easy to interpret in terms of intuitively evident political concepts. Not so with necessary and sufficient conditions. These can be stated only in terms of exceedingly abstruse set-theoretical concepts and suggest no intuitively graspable political interpretations. Nevertheless, researchers in formal decision theory have gone to great lengths to find these conditions and to state them.[6] Possibly it is a point of honor.

My intention has been not to venture into those regions beyond the horizon of concepts that at least have some resemblance to notions related to behavioral science. But I have approached those regions, as the reader may have noticed. It is most difficult to draw the line between mathematical methods in the behavioral sciences and mathematics.

OPTIMAL SOCIAL CHOICE

The idea of an optimal social choice goes back at least to Jeremy Bentham (1823), who advanced the much-discussed principle of "the greatest good for the greatest number." As stated, the principle is hardly an adequate guide to social choice. Determining the "greatest good" apparently refers to a maximization of some quantity, but quantity of what? Many situations involving social choice involve a *distribution* of some commodity or of a number of commodities. Many commodities or their surrogates (for example, money) are in limited supply, otherwise the problem of distribution would not arise. How does one combine "the greatest good" with "the greatest number" in these situations? If a commodity is distributed among more people (a greater number), each gets on the average a smaller share. Perhaps some quantity is to be maximized that is related to the way it is distributed. Let us pursue this idea.

To sharpen the meaning of "the greatest good for the greatest number," assume that the possession of some quantity of some good is associated with a "utility" afforded to the possessor. If the utilities of all the members of a society could be meaningfully added, we could obtain the total (social) utility determined by a particular distribution of that good. Perhaps the distribution that maximizes this social utility could be interpreted as "the greatest good for the greatest number."

For definiteness, assume that the "good" is a pile of coconuts gathered by a party of shipwrecked sailors on a desert island. The problem of social choice is how to divide the coconuts among the sailors. Egalitarians urge equal division. Proponents of the principle "to each according to his work" insist that the number of coconuts received by each should be somehow related to the number he has gathered. Still others maintain that seniority or state of health should be a consideration. What can "the greatest good for the greatest number" mean in this context? We are not prejudging any rule of division. We are only asking that some such rule be unambiguously defined and somehow justified.

The problem of dividing the coconuts is a drastically simplified version of a problem that has occupied a central position in politics, wherever politics has been a public concern—the problem of distribution, whether of wordly goods, of power, or of opportunities.

To simplify the problem still further, assume that the number of sailors is two. Suppose that for each of them, the number of coconuts received has a certain utility. The simplest assumption is that this utility is proportional to the number of coconuts. We will assume, however, that each sailor is characterized by a different proportionality constant. That is, a coconut is worth a units of utility to sailor A and b units to sailor B. Then if A gets x of the n coconuts available, he gets $u_A(x) = ax$ units of utility, and B gets $u_B(x) = b(n - x)$ units. If we assume that social utility of a distribution, $u(x)$, is the sum of the two utilities, we have

$$u(x) = u_A(x) + u_B(x) = ax + b(n - x) = (a - b)x + bn. \qquad (18.1)$$

Then if $a > b$, social utility is maximized if we set $x = n$. In this case, sailor A gets all the coconuts. If $a < b$, u is maximized if we set $x = 0$, whereby sailor B gets all the coconuts. If $a = b$, u will remain constant regardless of the way the coconuts are divided. None of these possible solutions is attractive.

We could go on to other models. Introducing a Fechnerian "diminishing returns" function for utility, let $u_A(x) = a \log_e x$, $u_B(x) = b \log_e(n - x)$. Again assuming additivity, we have

$$u(x) = a \log_e x + b \log_e(n - x). \qquad (18.2)$$

To maximize u, we set its derivative with respect to x equal to zero. Then

$$\frac{a}{x} - \frac{b}{n - x} = 0 \qquad (18.3)$$

$$an - x(n + b) = 0 \qquad (18.4)$$

$$x = \frac{an}{a + b} \; ; \; n - x = \frac{bn}{a + b}. \qquad (18.5)$$

If $a = b$, $n = n - x = n/2$. If $a \neq b$, the sailor to whom each coconut is "worth more" gets more coconuts.

This solution is, perhaps, intuitively somewhat more satisfactory. We must keep in mind, however, that it was derived from very strong assumptions. We have assumed that utilities are represented by numbers but have not indicated how these numbers can be determined in a real situation. Preference orderings of alternatives can frequently be obtained without much difficulty, especially if quantities of goods are compared of which one can never have too much. (There is some evidence that money is widely regarded as a good of this kind). But an ordering of preference establishes utility only on an ordinal scale. It is not meaningful to add ranks of alternatives given by different persons because quite different sets of numbers can represent the same rankings. As we have seen in the Introduction (see p. 21), in some circumstances utilities can be determined on a utility scale stronger than ordinal. But even on that scale, utilities of different persons for the same alternative cannot be meaningfully compared, let alone added.

Nevertheless, even ordinal scales can tell us something about strengths of preferences of voters with respect to a given set of alternatives. As we shall see, some social choice functions take these strengths of preferences into account.

AN EXAMPLE[7]

A host wanting to decide what to serve submits a list of beverages to his five guests and asks each of them to rank order the beverages by preference. He gets the following results.

Preference ordering of three guests	Preference ordering of two guests
Chocolate	Tea
Milk	Chocolate
Coffee	Soft drink
Tea	Milk
Soft drink	Water
Water	Coffee

Now the host was not really serious about serving water. Besides, he found out after the vote was taken that he was out of everything except tea and coffee. These two beverages then become the feasible alternatives. If the host wants to apply majority rule, he must serve coffee because a majority of his guests prefer coffee to tea. But should a thoughtful host apply the majority rule in this case? The two guests in the minority put tea at the top of the list and coffee at the bottom. They hate coffee. They would rather have water than coffee. The three guests in the majority seem not to feel very strongly about their preference for coffee over tea, both of which are in the middle of their lists. Even though coffee precedes tea in their orderings, their strengths of preference may not be large. Wouldn't it be more fair in this case to concede to the minority and to serve tea?

The above argument is, of course, far from rigorous. Its main point, however, is incorporated in the so-called Borda Method of social choice.[8] As originally formulated, Borda's Method is not a completely specified social choice function because it fails to specify a choice set for every subset of the complete set of alternatives. However, social choice functions that "agree" with Borda's Method where it applies can be constructed.[9]

Borda's Method is frequently used in social decisions. Academic search committees entrusted with the task of recommending a new appointment usually discuss a list of applicants for the job. They may end their deliberations by having each member submit a rank ordering of the candidates. If there are n candidates, each gets $n - 1$ points for every time he appears first in a preference ordering, $n - 2$ points for every time he receives second choice, and so on. Adding the points received by each candidate produces a collective preference ordering. Thus a choice set is determined; namely, the set of candidates that have received the largest numbers of points. To make a unique selection, some tie-breaking procedure may be required.

In this way, Borda's Method takes into account both the number of voters who favor a candidate and their "strengths of preference." For example, if the host in our example used Borda's Method, he would serve tea, which would have received 16 points, rather than coffee, which would have received only 9 points.

CONDORCET FUNCTIONS

As can be seen from the example, Borda's Method may violate the principle of majority rule. Marquis de Condorcet was a strong proponent of majority rule, although he was aware that its application may lead to anomalies, as exemplified in the Condorcet Paradox (see p. 334). Structural analysis leads to refinements of the concept of majority rule, to which we now turn our attention. In addition to the sets defined above (see p. 332f), we need to define two additional sets.

> $P(Y, D)$: The set of alternatives in Y that beat (by simple majority) every other alternative in Y under the profile D. Clearly, $P(Y, D)$ must be either a singlet set $\{x\}$ (since no more than one alternative in a set can beat every alternative in that set) or else $P(Y, D) = \emptyset$.

> $R(Y, D)$: The set of alternatives in Y that are unbeaten by any other alternative in Y by simple majority. Unlike $P(Y, D)$, $R(Y, D)$ may contain more than one alternative. It may also be empty.

A social choice function F is said to satisfy the *weak Condorcet condition* if and only if for all (Y, D), $F(Y, D) = (P(Y, D)$ whenever $P(Y, D) \neq \emptyset$.

In words: Whenever in every feasible subset Y there is an alternative that beats every other in that subset by a simple majority, that alternative should be the social choice among the alternatives in the feasible set Y.

> A social choice function is said to satisfy the *Condorcet condition* if and only if $F(Y, D) \subset R(Y, D)$ whenever $R(Y, D) \neq \emptyset$.

In words: Whenever in every feasible subset Y of X there is a set of alternatives unbeaten by any other alternative in Y, the set of alternatives that constitute the choice set should be among these unbeaten ones.

> A social choice function is said to satisfy the *strong Condorcet condition* if and only if for all (Y, D), $F(Y, D) = R(Y, D)$ whenever $R(Y, D) \neq \emptyset$.

In words: Whenever in every feasible subset Y there is a set of alternatives unbeaten by any other alternative in Y, the set of alternatives that constitute the social choice should consist of that entire set of unbeaten alternatives.

The conditions are labeled in the order of increasing strength because the stronger one always implies the weaker one. Note that these conditions say nothing about what the choice set should be if $P(Y, D)$ or $R(Y, D)$ is empty. Since this can easily happen (see the Condorcet Paradox), a social choice function must also specify choice sets in these contingencies.

A social choice function is called a *Condorcet function* if it agrees with the simple majority rule and satisfies any of the above conditions, regardless of the provisions it makes for situations where feasible subsets contain no unbeaten alternatives. These functions were named after Condorcet because majority rule is firmly incorporated in them. In fact, it is difficult to raise objections, at least against the weak Condorcet condition, if one believes (as Condorcet did) in majority rule as a mainstay of democratic decisions, for if an alternative x is preferred to every other alternative by a majority (even though not necessarily by the same majority) when x is matched with different alternatives, it seems natural to declare x the "winner." But is a Condorcet function really unchallengeable? Consider two situations with five alternatives: $X = \{x, y, a, b, c\}$; and five voters: $N = \{1, 2, 3, 4, 5\}$.[10]

Situation 1: For some D, the induced social preference relation turns out to be a linear order, specifically, $(xyabc)$.

Situation 2: Profile D' is presented, and it turns out that x has two first-place votes, one second-place vote, one fourth-place vote, and one fifth-place vote. Alternative y has two first-place votes, two second-place votes, and one third-place vote. Observe that in this situation, the "best" configuration of positions for some third alternative is one first-place vote (because four are already occupied by x and y), two seconds, and two thirds. Comparing the positions of x, y, and a possible third, we have in situation 2,

> y: 2 (1st), 2 (2nd), 1 (3rd).
> x: 2 (1st), 1 (2nd), 1 (4th), 1 (5th).
> Best other: 1 (1st), 2 (2nd), 2 (3rd).

In situation 1, we may feel intuitively that x should be the winner. In the second situation, it is difficult to deny victory to y, who has as many first choices as x, one more second choice, and one more third choice. Moreover, x is rated "worst" or "next to worst" by two voters, while y is not rated in this way by anyone.

The results would not be surprising if they were obtained from two different profiles D and D'. Actually, however, they were obtained from the same profile; namely,

$$D_1 = (xyabc), D_2 = (yacbx), D_3 = (cxyab), D_4 = (xybca), D_5 = (ybaxc).$$

As we have seen, the weak Condorcet condition is satisfied by any F that chooses x under D. A social choice function that agrees with Borda's Method chooses y. By this method, x receives 12 points, while y receives 16 points. No other alternative receives more than 12 points.

Condorcet used this example to "prove" that Borda's Method was "wrong."

But of course his proof was based on the assumption that majority decisions ought to take precedence over "strengths of preferences."

To bring out more specific differences between Borda's and Condorcet's views, let us examine the following condition, which is in the "spirit" of Condorcet.

The Reduction Condition. For all (Y, D), $F(Y, D) = F(Y - \{y\}, D)$ whenever $y \in Y$ and $x \gg_D y$ for some $x \in Y$.

Here $x \gg_D y$ means that under the profile D *everyone* prefers x to y. The reduction condition demands in that case that y should not be in the choice set $F(Y, D)$. But it says even more: not only should y not be in the choice set $F(Y, D)$, but the choice set should be in no way affected if the dominated alternative y is removed from the set of feasible alternatives.

Now we state the *principle of independence from infeasible alternatives,* closely related to the principle of independence from irrelevant alternatives (see p. 00): Whenever the restriction of one profile (D) on Y equals the restriction of another profile (D') on Y, then $F(Y, D) = F(Y, D')$. In words: No matter how voters vote on *other* alternatives, if they vote the same way on alternatives in Y in both profiles, then the choice sets determined by the two profiles in Y should be the same.

When the reduction condition and independence from infeasible alternatives are both in force, they assert that a *dominated* alternative (one to which another is unanimously preferred) should be treated in the same way as an infeasible alternative.

Note that the reduction condition is compatible with the weak Condorcet condition. This does not mean that any F that satisfies the weak Condorcet condition must satisfy the reduction condition or vice versa; but it does say that for any X and N, there are choice functions that satisfy both conditions. Borda's Method, on the other hand, does not satisfy the reduction condition in the above example. By Borda's Method, $F(X, D) = y$. Now everyone prefers y to a and also y to b. The reduction condition says that a and b can be eliminated. But then in the "run-off election," we have the following profile, assuming that the preference orderings of the remaining "candidates" remain the same:

$$D_1 = (xyc), D_2 = (ycx), D_3 = (cxy), D_4 = (xyc), D_5 = (yxc),$$

whereby x gets $2 + 1 + 2 + 1 = 6$ points, y gets $1 + 2 + 1 + 2 = 6$ points, and $F(\{x, y, c\}, D) = \{x, y\} \neq y$.

The mathematician C. L. Dodgson, better known to the English reading public as Lewis Carroll,[11] offered the following example with four alternatives and 11 voters:

> 3 voters declare $(bacd)$
> 3 voters declare $(badc)$
> 3 voters declare $(acdb)$
> 2 voters declare $(adcb)$

Counting points, a has $(6 \times 2) + (5 \times 3) = 27$ points, while b has $6 \times 3 = 18$ points. By Borda's Method, a outweighs b by far and ought to win. Observe, however, that an *absolute majority* (6 voters) name b as their *first choice*. Should not the majority prevail in the opinion on what alternative is "best"?[12]

We see the reason for the discrepancy here between "absolute majority" rule and Borda's Method. The majority principle looks only at how many voters *like* a candidate better than other candidates. Borda's Method takes into account the views of voters who *dislike* a candidate. By that principle, b lost because he was put *last* by more voters than a.

It is interesting to note that Dodgson in his later writings changed his mind and abandoned Borda's Method in favor of the weak Condorcet condition.

In sum, Borda's Method focuses on "degrees of preference," whereas Condorcet functions focus on majorities. In the former, how strongly people feel about alternatives is important; in the latter, only how many people prefer one alternative to another. Borda's Method can be said to emphasize psychological facets, whereas the Condorcet functions emphasize sociological ones.

A salient feature of the Condorcet conditions is that they say nothing about choice sets when $P(Y, D) = \emptyset$ or when $R(Y, D) = \emptyset$. It follows that the Condorcet functions (those that satisfy any of the Condorcet conditions) can be constructed with arbitrary provisions for profiles that leave $P(Y, D)$ or $R(Y, D)$ empty. The idea of combining the Condorcet conditions with Borda's Method naturally suggests itself. A social choice function proposed by D. Black (1958) does just that. Black's function satisfies the weak Condorcet condition and resorts to Borda's Method when $P(Y, D) = \emptyset$.

Example. Consider the following profile with four alternatives and five voters:

$$D_1 = (xyzw), D_2 = (wxyz), D_3 = (wxyz), D_4 = (yzxw), D_5 = (yzxw).$$

This profile D induces the linear order $(xyzw)$, and every $F(Y, D)$ in Black's function is determined by the weak Condorcet condition.

But now let D' be obtained from D by changing D_2 to $(wzxy)$. Again the weak Condorcet condition determines $P(Y, D')$ for all subsets Y except the entire set X and the set $\{x, y, z\}$, where $P(Y, D') = \emptyset$. Resorting to Borda's Method, we get $F(X, D') = F(\{x, y, z\}, D') = y$. Note, however, that the change from D to D' neither reversed the relative positions of x and y anywhere nor changed their adjacency. Thus Black's function violates A_3.

Another species of Condorcet function was proposed by A. H. Copeland (1961). Let $s(x, Y, D)$ be the number of alternatives in Y for which xPy (by simple majority) minus the number of alternatives in Y for which yPx. Thus given Y, each alternative $x \in Y$ is assigned a score. Then the choice set for Y consists of the alternatives with the highest s scores. Copeland's function satisfies the weak Condorcet condition but not the stronger ones.

The final social choice function we will examine was proposed by Dodgson. Let D_1 and D_2 be two linear orders on X. In comparing D_1 and D_2, an *inversion* is counted whenever an alternative x precedes y in D_1 but is preceded by y in D_2.

The total number of inversions in going from D_1 to D_2 is the total number of ordered pairs that become inverted. For example, let $D_1 = (abcxy)$ and $D_2 = (axbcy)$. Then in going from D_1 to D_2, two pairs are inverted, (c, x) and (b, x).

Given (Y, D), let $t(x, Y, D)$ be the fewest number of inversions in D to obtain D' for which $P(Y, D') = x$. Thus $t(x, Y, D)$ is a score assigned to each x. Given (Y, D), the Dodgson function selects the xs with the smallest scores. In the example used to illustrate Copeland's function, Dodgson selects y in agreement with the Borda method but in disagreement with Copeland.

The three social choice functions discussed last, Black's, Copeland's, and Dodgson's, are all Condorcet functions in the sense that they agree with some Condorcet condition. Each specifies another method of determining the choice set when $P(Y, D) = \emptyset$. In doing so, they can arrive at different choice sets, given the same profile. Fishburn (1973) illustrates this by a hypothetical case of three board commissioners charged with selecting one of nine land-use plans for a certain area. Of the nine alternatives, x represents park land, y an airport, and z a residential area. Let the profile be

$$D_1 = (azcyxbfed), \quad D_2 = (xdbaefyzc), \quad D_3 = (yzbxcaedf).$$

The reader is invited to verify that Black's function selects the park land proposal, Copeland's the airport, and Dodgson's the residential area.

In view of the Impossibility Theorem, we know with certainty that as long as preferences of individuals are given only on an ordinal scale, it is impossible to design a rule of social choice which would in all cases satisfy what can easily be accepted as the minimal requirements of a democratic procedure. Therefore, all social choice functions must be "defective" in some sense. The fact that social choice functions (that is, rules of collective decision) do exist and for many people apparently satisfy the requirements of a democratic procedure implies that in the minds of those people, some of the criteria proposed by Arrow, from which the Impossibility Theorem was derived, are not of overriding importance. Or else preferences are regarded as being given on a scale stronger than the ordinal, stronger than the interval scale even, if comparison of interpersonal utilities is implied in the procedure. One purpose of the analyses exemplified in this chapter is to lay bare these implicit assumptions.

NOTES

[1] An English translation of excerpts from this latter is given in Farquharson (1969).

[2] Named after Marquis de Condorcet (1743–1794), a French mathematician, philosopher, and revolutionist who analyzed the consequences of majority rule in collective decisions.

[3] The original formulation of the Impossibility Theorem is given in Arrow (1951). We essentially follow the presentation of Luce and Raiffa (1957).

[4] "Changes in x's favor" mean the following: If in the original profile xD_iy holds, then the same holds in the modified profile; if in the original profile $x \sim_i y$ or yD_ix holds, then in the modified profile $x \sim_i y$ or xD_iy.

[5] Fishburn (1973, p. 7) writes, "If in fact the social choice can depend on infeasibles, which infeasibles should be used? For with one set of infeasibles, feasible x might be the social choice, whereas feasible $y \neq x$ might be the social choice if some other infeasible set were adjoiced to Y. Hence, the idea of allowing infeasible alternatives to influence the social choice introduces a potential ambiguity into the choice process that can at least be alleviated if not removed by insisting on the independence condition."

[6] See the treatment of this problem in Fishburn (1973, Chapter 3).

[7] Example given in Luce and Raiffa (1957).

[8] Named after J. C. Borda (1733–1799), French mathematician.

[8] See Fishburn (1973, p. 163ff).

[10] This and the following examples are taken from Fishburn (1973).

[11] The author of *Alice in Wonderland*.

[12] If this were an ordinary election (each voter voting for one candidate), b would certainly have won since he or she received an absolute majority of the votes cast.

CHAPTER NINETEEN

Game-theoretic Models: Coalitions and Consensus Formation

In Chapter 17, we classified the theory of games as the branch of decision theory that deals with situations involving two or more actors whose interests (that is, preferences for the outcomes of decisions) do not coincide. The impetus to the theory of games, as its name implies, was given by the strategic analysis of games of strategy, the so-called parlor games (chess, bridge, and so on). Accordingly, the theory was originally developed along the lines of a normative or prescriptive theory, where the central problem was that of singling out optimal strategies for making decisions involving conflicts of interest. The clearest examples of situations of this sort are two-person constant-sum games (see p. 326) involving exactly two players with diametrically opposed interests.

The fundamental theorem of game theory has established the existence of optimal strategies in two-person constant-sum matrix games. As we have seen (cf. p. 327), the definition of "optimality" (hence also of "rationality") presents difficulties in the context of noncooperative nonconstant-sum games. Consequently, in subsequent developments of the theory of nonconstant-sum games, attention shifted away from the problem of finding optimal strategies to that of *defining individual rationality*. This problem is central in Harsanyi's theory of equilibrium solutions of noncooperative games (see Harsanyi, 1977).

In cooperative games, the concept of *collective rationality* becomes prominent, and the erstwhile central problem of finding optimal strategies is lost sight of altogether. Attention is focused on the final outcome; that is, on the *solution* of the game played by players who are both individually and collectively rational. In the so-called characteristic function format of the *n*-person cooperative game, game theory ceases to be a theory of optimal strategic decisions and becomes a theory of *outcomes of conflict resolution* that can be defended as optimal in some sense. It is this conception of game theory that has played the most prominent part in applications to political science.

THE *n*-PERSON GAME IN CHARACTERISTIC FUNCTION FORM

An *n*-person cooperative game in characteristic function form is specified by a set of players N and a function $v: 2^N \rightarrow \mathbb{R}$ (real numbers), which assigns to each subset S of N a *value v*. Thus we denote such a game G by the pair $\langle N, v \rangle$.

The value $v(S)$ associated with the subset S represents the guaranteed minimal joint gain that the members of S can obtain in an outcome of the game if they properly coordinate their strategies. This definition implies that the individual payoffs of the players can be meaningfully added; and consequently, that the payoffs (or utilities) are given on a scale stronger than the usual interval scale (see p. 345). In what follows, we will assume that the payoffs are expressed in some transferable and conservative commodity like money.

The meaning of "minimal guaranteed payoff" must be elucidated. Suppose the players in S, when they form a coalition, assume the "worst"; namely, that the members of the complementary set $N - S$ will form a countercoalition and will coordinate their strategies so as to keep the joint payoff to S to its minimum. If this happens, the *n*-person game becomes, in the eyes of S, essentially a two-person antagonistic game between the two coalitions. The Fundamental Theorem of Game Theory guarantees the existence of an optimal strategy by means of which S can get at least a certain minimal amount which is the value of the game to S. This is $v(S)$, the characteristic function of the game $\langle N, v \rangle$.

Any function $v: 2^N \rightarrow \mathbb{R}$ can serve as a characteristic function of an *n*-person game, provided it satisfies the following two conditions:

(i) $v(\emptyset) = 0$.
(ii) $v(S \cup T) \geq v(S) + v(T)$, for all $S, T \subset N, S \cap T = \emptyset$.

The first condition states simply that the empty coalition gets no payoff, positive or negative, regardless of the outcome of the game. The second states that disjoint sets of players joining in a single coalition ($S \cup T$) can get at least as much jointly as they would get if they remained in two separate coalitions S and T. This follows from the assumption that whatever the two coalitions can do without coordinating their strategies, they can do if they coordinate their strategies. Note that the costs of forming a coalition or possible restrictions on what coalitions can be formed are not taken into consideration in this assumption.

As a normative model (that is, assuming the players to be rational), the characteristic function formulation might be expected to answer the following questions.

1.   Which coalitions ought to form?
2.   How ought the payoffs be distributed in the final outcome?

In view of condition (ii) above, the *n* players joined in a *grand coalition* can get jointly at least as much as they can get if they do not join in a single coalition.

Therefore, the formation of the grand coalition is at least consistent with collective rationality of the n-players. If $v(N)$ is actually larger than the joint payoff accruing to players partitioned into more than one coalition, then collective rationality prescribes the formation of the grand coalition. For the time being, we by-pass the question of what coalition is "rational" if the grand coalition does not actually confer a larger payoff on its members than some smaller coalition. We will assume that the grand coalition will eventually form. The question that now remains is how the joint payoff $v(N)$ is to be apportioned among the players.

Consider the set of vectors

$$\left\{(x_1, x_2, \ldots, x_n) : x_i \geq v(i), i = 1, 2, \ldots, n, \sum_{i=1}^{n} x_i = v(N)\right\}.$$

This is the set of payoff apportionments in which each player i receives x_i, which is at least as much as what i would get if he played as a "coalition of one" against everyone else; and, moreover, the sum of these payoffs x_i adds up to $v(N)$, the most that the players can get jointly in this game. Such apportionments are called *imputations*.

We see that imputations as final payoff apportionments do not violate individual rationality in the sense that each player's payoff in an imputation is at least as large as he could guarantee himself if he were in a coalition only with himself. Imputations also satisfy collective rationality of all n players because they are given jointly as much as they can get in this game. The question now arises as to whether an imputation satisfies the collective rationality of a proper subset of N.[1]

Consider such a subset S and the joint payoff that accrues to the members in the imputation $x = (x_1, x_2, \ldots, x_n)$; namely, $\sum_{i \in S} x_i$. If the members of S left the grand coalition and formed their own coalition, they could get at least $v(S)$, by definition of $v(S)$. Now if $v(S) > \sum_{i \in S} x_i$, collective rationality of the players in S prescribes that they do just that: leave the grand coalition and form their own. Taking such a possibility into account, we can now define *domination* as a relation on the set of imputations.

Imputation $y = (y_1, y_2, \ldots, y_n)$ is said to *dominate* imputation $x = (x_1, x_2, \ldots, x_n)$ via S if every member of S gets more in y than he does in x and, moreover, if S can actually get jointly the amount that accrues to them in y. In symbols,

$$y \succ_S x \Leftrightarrow \left[i_i \in S, \Rightarrow y_i > x_i \quad \text{and} \quad \sum_{i \in S} y_i \leq v(S)\right]. \tag{19.1}$$

Consider the three-person game $\langle N, v \rangle$ with $N = \{a, b, c\}$ and

$$v(a) = v(b) = v(c) = 0; \; v(ab) = v(bc) = 100; \; v(abc) = 100. \tag{19.2}$$

The game can be interpreted as follows. Three individuals a, b, and c are to divide 100 units of utility among themselves. The apportionment is to be decided by majority vote. Then no single individual can guarantee himself more than 0. Each pair, on the other hand, being a majority, can guarantee themselves 100. And, of course, all three can also get the 100 units of utility.

Next, consider two imputations: $x = (30, 40, 30)$ and $y = (40, 50, 10)$. We see that y dominates x via the set $\{a, b\}$ because both a and b get more in y than in x and, moreover, their joint payoff in y is within the range guaranteed to them by the characteristic function since $v(ab) = 100$. We can say that both a and b prefer y to x and that their preference is "realistic" since they can get even more than what accrues to them in y by forming a coalition from which c is excluded.

An imputation y is said to *dominate* imputation x if there exists a set $S \subset N$ such that y dominates x via S. In symbols,

$$y \succ x \Rightarrow \exists S \subset N, y \succ_S x. \tag{19.3}$$

We can now picture a bargaining process in which the players participate. Suppose the players agree it is in their common interest to form the grand coalition (so as to get the largest possible joint payoff). Someone proposes an imputation x, according to which this joint payoff is to be apportioned. If this imputation is dominated by another imputation y via some subset S, this subset demands to get jointly more than in x and backs up its demand by a threat to leave the grand coalition and to form its own. The threat is credible because the fact that x is dominated via S by y implies that the members of S can get jointly at least as much as they get in y and, moreover, that *every member* of S prefers y to x. So the members of S propose y instead of x, backing their proposal by a threat to form a coalition of their own if the proposal is not accepted. At this point, another subset T (which may or may not overlap with S) may point out that z dominates y (via T) and may make similar demands and threats. Conceivably, the bargaining might come to an end if some imputation could be found that was not dominated by any other imputation. Then no subset of N could make any credible threats to form a coalition of its own if its demand is not met, and agreement might be reached to apportion the payoffs according to the undominated imputation.

A normative theory could then prescribe any one of such undominated imputations as the "solution" of the n-person game on the grounds that the corresponding apportionment would be consistent not only with individual rationality and with the collective rationality of the entire set of players (by definition of imputation), but also with the collective rationality of every subset of players (because it is undominated).

The set of undominated imputations of an n-person game is called the *core* of the game. Unfortunately, in many n-person games, including all constant-sum games, the core is empty. That is, every imputation in such a game is dominated by some other imputation via some set of players. It follows that the core can be advanced as a "rational solution" only for some n-person games; namely, for those that have nonempty cores. For games with empty cores, other concepts of rational solution must be defined. A large portion of n-person game theory concerns the development of these concepts. We will briefly discuss only three of these besides the core; namely, the Von Neumann-Morgenstern

(V-M) solution, the Shapley value, and the nucleolus. Then we will pass to some applications of game-theoretic descriptions of conflict situations in some branches of political science.

THE VON NEUMANN-MORGENSTERN SOLUTION

The V-M solution (Von Neumann and Morgenstern, 1947) was the first of the several types of solution proposed for the n-person game. It is based on the dominance relation defined above. Consider the game $G = \langle N, v \rangle$ and the set of imputations I_0 that satisfies the following two conditions:

(i)   No imputation in I_0 dominates any other imputation in I_0.
(ii) For every imputation not in I_0, there is an imputation in I_0 that dominates it via some $S \subset N$.

In symbols,

(i) $x, y, \in I_0 \Rightarrow x \nsucc y$.
(ii) $x \notin I_0 \Rightarrow \exists y \in I_0, y \succ x$.

We note that a V-M solution singles out a *set* of imputations (namely, I_0), which in general contains more than one imputation. Moreover, we shall see in a moment that there may be several such (not necessarily disjoint) sets, all of which are solutions.

Consider once again our illustrative three-person game. It is easy to see that the set of three imputations

$$I_0 = \{(50, 50, 0), (50, 0, 50), (0, 50, 50)\}$$

constitutes a V-M solution. Condition (i) is obviously satisfied. To test condition (ii), take any imputation $x = (x_1, x_2, x_3)$ not in I_0. Then for some pair of components we must have $x_i < 50$, $x_j < 50$; otherwise $x \in I_0$. Then the imputation in I_0 where $x_i = x_j = 50$ dominates x.

I_0 might be regarded as an intuitively acceptable normative solution of the game. Since any pair of players can appropriate the "prize" (100) and since the "bargaining leverage" of the three players is the same, it seems reasonable to prescribe the equal division of the prize among the pair that appropriates it. As for *which* pair should appropriate the prize, the V-M solution makes no prescription, as one would expect in view of the symmetric positions of the players.

One can raise the question whether this apparently normative solution can properly be called "prescriptive" since it is not clear *to whom* the prescription is addressed. There is no difficulty, however, in regarding this solution as normative since it implies that an equal division of the prize among just two of the players is *expected* if all three players are rational. Each of the two winners is expected to resist tempting offers by the loser because accepting such an offer makes him vulnerable to a coalition of the other two against him. As for the loser, he can do nothing to improve his share if the two winners stick to their agreement to divide the prize equally. Admitting that the identity of the two winners remains an open question or, perhaps, is determined by chance, the set I_0 can be regarded to be characterized by a sort of "stability."

It turns out, however, that the set I_0 is not the only V-M solution of the game. Consider the set of imputations $J_c = (c, x_2, x_3)$, where c is a constant ($0 \leqslant c < 50$) and $x_2 + x_3 = 100 - c$. Clearly, for all x, $y \in J_c$ $x \not\succ y$ because no *two* players can get more in y than in x. (If $y_2 > x_2$, then $y_3 < x_3$, while c remains constant.) On the other hand, consider an imputation $y \notin J_c$, which implies that $y_1 \neq c$. Let $y_1 < c$. Note that we cannot have both $y_2 \geqq 100 - c$ and $y_3 \geqq 100 - c$ since both inequalities would imply $y_1 + y_2 \geqq 200 - 2c > 100$ (since $c < 50$). Therefore, either $y_2 < 100 - c$ or $y_3 < 100 - c$. In the first case, $(c, 100 - c, 0)$ dominates y; in the second case, $(c, 0, 100 - c)$ dominates y. If $y_1 > c$, then $y_2 + y_3 < 100 - c$. Since $x_2 + x_3 = 100 - c$, we can choose $x_2 > y_2$ and $x_3 > y_3$ so that (c, x_2, x_3) dominates y via players 2 and 3.

The set J_c contains an infinity of imputations since x_2 and x_3 range over all nonnegative values which satisfy $x_2 + x_3 = 100 - c$. Also, c can range over a continuum of values in the interval $[0, 50)$. Moreover, the constant payoff c can be assigned to any of the three players. In fact, the set of imputations that is the union of all the V-M solutions of this game is identical with the entire set of imputations, so that *any* imputation is in at least one V-M solution. Consequently, the set of all V-M solutions of this game does not separate "rational" imputations from others and at least in this context cannot serve as a prescription of a normative theory.

In the general case, the V-M solution does single out proper subsets of imputations. The determination of these solutions in any but the simplest games involves rather sophisticated mathematical techniques. This makes the associated problems interesting to mathematicians but raises doubts about the applicability of the theory in decision situations.

THE SHAPLEY VALUE

Another form of solution of an *n*-person cooperative game, called the Shapley value, is conceptually much simpler than the V-M solution and has the advantage of being sharply testable since it singles out just one imputation as a "prescribed" apportionment of $v(N)$. Note that the address of the prescription is quite definite in this context: it is the entire set of players. Therefore the Shapley value is clearly in the spirit of "conflict resolution."

Consider a game $G = \langle N, v \rangle$ and suppose a coalition $S \subset N$ has just formed. We suppose that all formations of coalitions are tentative. Their purpose is to allow the players to assess their "bargaining leverage" in the game. It is assumed that after these bargaining leverages have been assessed, the grand coalition will form and $v(N)$ will be apportioned, taking the differential bargaining leverages into account.

Suppose a player i contemplates joining with the players in S who have just formed a tentative coalition. The characteristic function makes known the amount $v(S)$ that the players in S can guarantee for themselves. It also makes known $v(S \cup \{i\})$; that is, the value of the game to the coalition that forms when i joins with S. Consequently, $v(S \cup \{i\}) - v(S)$ represents the value to the players in S of having i join them. To be sure, they will have to make it worth while for i to join them, and i can "reasonably" demand *up to* the amount he "brings into the coalition" by joining it. This maximum "justifiable" demand averaged over all possible ordered subsets of N that i could join is his payoff in the Shapley value of G.

As an example, consider the three-person game with $N = \{a, b, c\}$ defined by the following characteristic function:

$$v(a) = v(b) = v(c) = 0;\ v(ab) = 40;\ v(ac) = 50;\ v(bc) = 60;\ v(abc) = 100. \qquad (19.4)$$

The Shapley value can be calculated as follows. Imagine that the grand coalition forms by recruitment of individual players. There are six possible orders of recruitment of the three players. These are shown in the columns of Table 19.1. Below each order the "contributions" of a, b, and c respectively are shown.
The Shapley value vector is $(170/6, 200/6, 230/6)$. Its components are the payoffs to a, b, and c, respectively. Note that the sum of the components is $100 = v(abc)$.

The components reflect the relative "bargaining leverages" of the players. Thus a is the "weakest" of the players because he is the least valuable as a partner in a pair-coalition, whereas c is the most valuable partner, as can be seen from the characteristic function. In a way, therefore, the Shapley value can be regarded as a distribution of "power" among the parties in a conflict situation. This becomes even more apparent in a political context.

Consider a legislative body, say a parliament, with several political parties, each with a given number of seats. Since normally the support of a majority in such a body is required in order for a government to function, coalitions of two

Table 19.1.   The Components of Shapley Value are the Means of Rows a, b, and c.

	a	b	c	c	b	a
	b	c	a	b	a	c
	c	a	b	a	c	b
a	0	40	50	40	40	0
b	40	0	50	60	0	50
c	60	60	0	0	60	50

or more parties are formed in support of a government if no single party commands a majority.

The situation can be modeled by an n-person game in characteristic function form. The players are the parties. Every subset of N which collectively commands a majority is called a *winning coalition*. The other subsets are called *losing coalitions*. The characteristic function is given by

$$v(S) = 1, \text{ if } S \text{ is a winning coalition}$$
$$= 0 \text{ otherwise.} \qquad (19.6)$$

Games of this sort where v takes on only two values are called *simple games*. From the point of view of structural analysis, the actual numerical values of the game to winning and losing coalitions are of no consequence as long as the former is larger than the latter.

In the political context just described, the coalitions are clearly visible, and the winning coalitions are clearly distinguishable from losing ones. What is less clear is the apportionment of the "prize," represented by "1" in the characteristic function. Certainly the parties in the coalition that forms a government derive benefits; for instance, in the form of cabinet posts distributed among their members and opportunities for carrying out their programs, at least in part. But there is no clear way of attaching numerical utilities to the cabinet posts, much less to legislative measures as they reflect party "ideologies." Therefore, although the components of Shapley value can be calculated directly from the characteristic function (which specifies all winning coalitions), there is no way of prescribing this imputation in terms of the distribution of benefits nor of comparing it to the actual distributions. For this reason, the testing of a game theoretic model of coalition formations (when it is regarded as a predictive model) consists of examining not imputations, but rather the winning coalitions that actually form.

A hypothesis that naturally suggests itself is that of the winning coalitions defined by the characteristic function, the one that will actually form will be in some sense "minimal." For if the prize is the same regardless of which winning coalition forms, it stands to reason that it is advantageous to the members of the coalition to have to divide the prize among as few members as possible. The question is, in what sense is "minimal" to be understood? There are at least three interpretations. A winning coalition may be minimal in the sense of containing the fewest political parties (among all the winning coalitions). It may also be minimal in the sense of containing the smallest number of individual delegates. Finally, a winning coalition may be minimal in the sense that the sum of its Shapley value components is smallest.

When a normative theory singles out several *a priori* justifiable prescriptions, it can hardly be regarded as a prescriptive theory. On the other hand, the possibility of "pitting" the normative solutions against each other suggests tests of the theory which, it will be recalled, provide more theoretical leverage than a test of a single model. This was, in fact, the approach to a theory of political coalitions taken by A. De Swaan (1973).

TESTING SEVERAL MODELS OF POLITICAL COALITION FORMATION

De Swaan's data were 90 instances of coalition cabinets in nine multiparty parliamentary systems (eight Western European and Israel). He proposed 12 different models to account for the observed coalitions, among which the core (see p. 356) and a model based on Shapley value were included. Of these, the core model is the most closely related to ideas derived from the theory of games. We will therefore examine it in some detail.

Since the core of a game in characteristic function form is defined as the set of undominated imputations, and the latter are defined as payoff apportionments, an application of the core model necessitates a definition of the payoffs of the game. These payoffs will be defined in terms of distances between "policy positions" of the players (or actors), who in this context will be the political parties.

The parties are supposed to lie on a political "spectrum" which can be regarded as stretching from the political "left" to the political "right." In most contemporary parliamentary systems, there is usually good agreement about the relative positions of the parties on this spectrum. The problem now is to define the "distance" between two policy positions or, equivalently, the distance between two actors respectively associated with the positions. We will exemplify our definitions by the following concrete example.

Assume there are four political parties with positions (from "left" to "right") and numbers of seats in parliament as given in Table 19.2.

Table 19.2. *Hypothetical Distributions of Seats Among four Political Parties*

Political party	A	B	C	D
Position on political spectrum	1	2	3	4
Number of seats	32	23	30	15

If positions are defined only on an ordinal scale, distances cannot be quantitatively compared, but they can be ordered. For esample, in the system shown in Table 19.2, *D* is farther from *B* than from *C*, but we cannot say whether *C* is closer to *B* than to *D* or vice versa. If, on the other hand, we assume (arbitrarily) that the positions of the parties on the political spectrum are equally spaced, we can define the distance between two parties on a ratio scale. Naturally, an assumption of this sort is quite strong and entirely *ad hoc*, and there is no way to check it against reality. In defense of it, one can only point out that a "political position" is not "objective reality" anyway. If there is a "reality" behind it, it exists only in the minds of political actors. Therefore, if these actors *believe* that parties are equally spaced on the political spectrum, this belief may itself relate the assumption to reality. At any rate, we will be investigating the *consequences* of a particular assumption; namely, that the *delegates* are equally spaced on the political spectrum. The *a priori* correspondence of this assumption to "reality" is not the issue.

A basic assumption of the political distance theory, which is involved in the core model, is that an actor choosing between joining a coalition *S* and coalition *T* will prefer to join a coalition whose "expected policy position" is closer to his most preferred position. Further, it is assumed that an actor's preferred policy position is closer to an expected policy of a coalition (which includes him) if he is a *pivotal member* of that coalition than if he is not.

A pivotal member of a coalition is the one that contains its "center of mass." To put it in another way, a member of a coalition is pivotal if the absolute difference between the number of votes "to the left" of him and the number "to the right" of him does not exceed his own voting strength; that is, if he can "swing" the vote either way.

The algebraic difference of the votes of the members to the left and to the right of a pivotal member is called the *excess* of the coalition. Of two coalitions, the coalition with the larger excess will have an expected policy to the left of the pivotal member's preferred policy.

The next assumption is that of the two coalitions in which an actor is a pivotal member, he will prefer the one with the smaller absolute value of the excess.

Note that the pivotal actor as a one-actor coalition has excess zero. Thus his expected policy in that case coincides with his own preferred policy, as should be intuitively evident.

As a numerical example, consider four actors *a*, *b*, *c*, *d*, shown in Table 19.2. Table 19.3 shows the relevant features of all winning coalitions.

Table 19.3.   Calculation of Excess Associated with the Pivotal Actor of Each of the Winning Coalitions Determined by the Distribution in Table 19.2

Winning Coalitions	Total Weight	Pivotal Actor	Excess
(*ab*)	55	*a*	$0 - 23 = -23$
(*ac*)	62	*a*	$0 - 30 = -30$
(*bc*)	53	*c*	$23 - 0 = 23$
(*abc*)	85	*b*	$32 - 30 = 2$
(*abd*)	70	*b*	$32 - 15 = 17$
(*acd*)	77	*c*	$32 - 15 = 17$
(*bcd*)	68	*c*	$23 - 15 = 8$
(*abcd*)	100	*b* .	$32 - 45 = -13$

Source: Adapted from De Swaan (1973).

It should be noted that we have so far not introduced any cardinal utilities. We have confined ourselves to ordinal preferences of players for the different coalitions. The introduction of cardinal utilities would necessitate much stronger assumptions than those listed above. Aside from assuring a numerical distance between expected policy positions, we would have to postulate a real-valued function from these distances to an actor's utilities. Nevertheless, even from our assumptions about ordinal preferences, some conclusions can be drawn. We can order each actor's preferences for the various coalitions, leaving ambiguous the preference positions of coalitions not comparable on the ordinal scale.

As an example, let us look at b's preferences. Recall that according to our assumptions, b prefers to be a member of a winning coalition in which he is pivotal to being a member of a coalition in which he is not. Among the winning coalitions, b is pivotal only in (abc), $(abcd)$, and (abd), so he prefers any of these to any of the other coalitions. Moreover, the prefers the above three coalitions in that order because, as we see from Table 19.3, (abc) has the smallest absolute excess and (abd) has the largest.

Comparing the other three coalitions of which b is a member but not a pivotal member, we see that b prefers (bc) to (bcd) since the expected position of (bc) on the political spectrum must be closer to his own that that of (bcd). As for (ab), it is not comparable to either (bc) or (bcd) from b's point of view because if expected positions are evaluated on an ordinal scale, the "weight" of voters to the left of b cannot be compared to the weight on his right.

Thus we have b's preference ordering of the six winning coalitions of which he is a member. The numbers in parentheses are the ordinal "values" assigned by b to the several coalitions, 6 being the largest:

$$abc(6) \succ abcd(5) \succ adb(4) \succ ab(1, 2, \text{ or } 3) \sim bc(2 \text{ or } 3) \sim bcd(1 \text{ or } 2)$$

A similar preference ordering can be constructed for each of the actors.

We can now construct the preference *matrix*, using the ordinal preferences of the various actors for the various winning coalitions. The preference matrix is shown in Table 19.4. By way of explanation, consider the observation that coalition (ac) is dominated by $\{bcd\}$ and by $\{bc\}$. This is so because b can "lure" c out of c's coalition with a (for which c has an ordinal preference of only 1) to join in a coalition with b, for which c has an ordinal preference of 4. Of course, b also profits from this shift since his ordinal preference increases from 0 to 2 or 3. However, a and d together can "lure" b away from this coalition to join with them because b has an ordinal preference of 4 for $\{abd\}$; that is, larger than 2 or 3. Naturally, a and d will also gain from this shift. But then (abd) is, in turn, dominated by $\{ac\}$. We might expect the process $ac \rightarrow bc \rightarrow abd \rightarrow ac$ to go on forever.

The illustration shows that the relation of dominance in this context is not a transitive relation. On the other hand, consider the coalition $\{abc\}$. There is no enticement that d can offer either to a, b, or c to lure them out of this coalition, as can be seen by examining the winning coalitions of which d is a member. The grand coalition $\{abcd\}$ is likewise undominated since no subset of its members can by breaking away form a coalition where each will "get more" than in the grand coalition. Thus the coalition $\{abc\}$ and the grand coalition constitute the core of this game. On the basis of the policy distance theory, we might suppose that either $\{abc\}$ or $\{abcd\}$ will form. If we further add the requirement that of all the coalitions in the core, the minimal winning coalition will form, the two requirements together predict the formation of $\{abc\}$.

Table 19.4. Dominance Structure of Winning Coalitions

Coalitions	Actors[a]				Pivot	Remarks
	a	*b*	*c*	*d*		
(*ab*)	6	(123)	0	0	*a*	*b*'s preferences indeterminate; dominated by (*bc*) or (*bcd*)?
(*ac*)	5	0	1	0	*a*	Dominated by (*bc*) and by (*bcd*)
(*bc*)	0	(23)	4	0	*c*	Dominated by (*abd*)
(*abc*)	3	6	2	0	*b*	Undominated
(*abd*)	4	4	0	1	*b*	Dominated by (*ac*)
(*acd*)	1	0	5	3	*c*	Dominated by (*ab*), (*bcd*)
(*bcd*)	0	(12)	6	4	*c*	*b*'s preference indeterminate; dominated by (*ab*)?
(*abcd*)	2	5	3	2	*b*	Undominated

Source: Adapted from De Swaan (1973).

[a]Columns 2–5 show the corresponding actors' ordinal preferences for the coalitions in Column 1. Parentheses indicate indeterminate preferences. For example, (123) in row 1 indicates that *b* could assign ordinal value 1, 2, or 3 to coalition (*ab*).

We will now illustrate the application of this approach to a historical example; namely, the situation in Norway in 1965. There were five actors:

SOCD   (Social Democrats)
LIB   (Liberals)
CHPP   (Christian People's Party)
CENT   (Center Party)
CONS   (Conservatives)

There is general agreement that the ordering is from "left" to "right," except possibly for the Liberals and Christians, who may be regarded to "tie" for the position on the political spectrum.

The preference matrix is shown in Table 19.5.

There are 16 winning coalitions. These are numbered 1–16 in the left-hand column. The composition of these coalitions can be deduced by noting the party or parties whose preferences for that coalition are zero and who, therefore, are not members of it. For instance, coalition 7 consists of Social Democrats, Christians, and Conservatives (with Liberals and Center left out).

The policy distance theory singles out three of the sixteen coalitions that are undominated. They constitute the core of the *n*-person game. The policy distance theory predicts that the coalition that actually forms will be one of these three; namely, 1, 2, or 15. The coalition that actually formed was 2, the "all-bourgeois" coalition. Thus the Social Democrats, after being in power for 20 years, were excluded from the government.

Table 19.5. Dominance Structure of Possible Coalitions in the Norwegian Parliament of 1965

Actors[a]	1	2	3	4	5					
Weights	68	18	13	18	31					

Coalitions[b]		Ordinal preferences				S^c	L^d	R^e	M^f	Remarks
1	1	8	7	7	6	148	68	49	2	Undominated
2	0	5	5	8	7	80	31	31	4	Undominated
3	3	0	6	5	4	130	0	62	1	Dominated by 16
4	2	7	0	6	5	135	0	67	1	Dominated by 15
5	4	0	0	4	3	117	0	49	1	Dominated by 2
6	3	6	6	0	4	130	0	62	1	Dominated by 13
7	5	0	3	0	2	112	0	44	1	Dominated by 12
8	4	4	0	0	3	117	0	49	1	Dominated by 11
9	7	0	0	0	1	99	0	31	1	Dominated by 2
10	4	4	4	4	0	117	0	49	1	Dominated by 9
11	7	0	2	2	0	99	0	31	1	Dominated by 16
12	6	3	0	3	0	104	0	36	1	Dominated by 9
13	8	0	0	1	0	96	0	18	1	Dominated by 2
14	7	2	2	0	0	99	0	31	1	Dominated by 13
15	9	0	1	0	0	81	0	13	1	Undominated
16	8	1	0	0	0	86	0	18	1	Dominated by 15

Source: Adapted from De Swann (1973).

[a] Actors: 1—SOCD, 2—LIB, 3—CHPP, 4—CENT, 5—CONS.

[b] The coalitions can be inferred by deleting the actors whose preference for the coalition in question is 0.

[c] S: Number of seats possessed by the coalition.

[d] L: Number of seats "to the left" of the pivot party.

[e] R: Number of seats "to the right" of the pivot party.

[f] M: Pivotal member of the coalition.

It would indeed be remarkable if the policy distance model were uniformly successful in predicting parliamentary coalitions. But of course it is not. In fact, of the 12 models proposed by De Swaan, it is one of the least successful. None of the models gives uniformly good predictions, as one would expect in view of the very different political situations in different countries. The most that can be extracted from the effort is a comparison of the various models across the entire set of cases, perhaps disaggregated by countries, by the number of parties in each system, or by some other categories.

The selection of a criterion of comparison presents a methodological problem. Recall that the "success" of a model must be evaluated not only with reference to the frequency of its successful predictions, but also with reference to the a priori improbability of these predictions. For details as to how this is done in the present instance, the interested reader is referred to De Swaan, 1973.

On the basis of De Swaan's criterion, the most successful model was the so-called *closed minimum range* model. A *closed* coalition is one that includes only parties that are adjacent on the political spectrum. A *minimal range* (winning) coalition is one that has the fewest actors (parties) in it. The finding that this model is the best predictor of government coalitions is not particularly surprising. The principle of "closure" seems to be dictated by ideological or programmatic considerations; the principle of minimum range by a tendency to exclude redundant members.

Still, some theoretical leverage can be extracted from this model by turning attention not to its successes but to its *failures*. The model makes a very poor showing in two instances: in the case of France and in the case of Israel. This raises questions about possible political peculiarities of these two countries during the period under consideration.

At this point, the experienced observer of political life might point out that she knew all along that France and Israel have political features that are "different" from those of other parliamentary systems. If so, the model builder can retort that this confirms the validity of her "purely objective" analysis. If the intuitively guided political scientist denies that those two systems are somehow apart from the others, the model builder can invite him to "look again," in case her analysis has pointed to something that the political scientist had not been aware of. Thus the model builder makes a point either way.

In De Swaan's game-theoretic approach to political coalitions, the question posed was which coalitions are likely to form rather than which imputations are likely to be accepted, which has been the central question in the theory of co-operative n-person games. The difficulty in defining imputations in a political context stems from the circumstance that utilities of political payoffs (patronage, appointments to ministerial posts, and the like) are usually hard to assess. In conflicts of economic interest, on the other hand, payoffs are easily identified and can be reasonably quantified. Resolutions of such conflicts in the sense of acceptable distributions of the payoffs can be regarded as a political component of the conflicts, provided "politics" is conceived in terms of equitable distributions instead of, as is more usual, in terms of strategic struggles for power. Be this as it may, let us turn to the central problem of n-person game theory, the search for acceptable distributions of some "good" determined by a solution of such a game.

In the context of a prescriptive theory, the uniqueness of such a solution is a desideratum. As we have seen, the V-M solution does not, in general, have this property; the Shapley value does. But uniqueness is not the only desirable property of a solution. Its "stability" is also an important consideration. A solution can be regarded as stable if it is consistent with both the individual rationality and the collective rationality of all the players. As we have seen, all the imputations of a game are consistent with individual rationality and with the collective rationality of the *whole set* of players. An imputation is consistent with the collective rationality of all the *subsets* of players only if it is in the core of the game. But we have also seen that some games do not have cores. If the core is empty, then the Shapley value cannot be "stable" in the sense defined. If a game does have a core, the Shapley value may or may not be in it. Moreover, the core may contain several imputations, and the problem of finding a unique solution remains unsolved.

The *nucleolus* of an *n*-person game is a unique solution. If a core exists, the nucleolus is an imputation in it. Otherwise, the nucleolus can be regarded as a "closest approximation" to a stable solution of a game without a core.

Suppose that a game $\langle N, v \rangle$ has no core. Thus any imputation is subjected to a "centrifugal pressure" in the sense that it is in the collective interest of some proper subsets of players to leave the grand coalition and to form one of their own whereby they can jointly get more than is afforded them in the grand coalition.

Players can be discouraged from doing this if every possible coalition except the grand coalition is "taxed." Suppose a uniform tax of this sort is imposed. Then if for some $S \subset N \sum_{i \in S} x_i < v(S)$ (an inducement for the members of S to leave the grand coalition), coalition S can be discouraged if $\sum_{i \in S} x_i \geq v(S) - \varepsilon$. The question posed now is what is the smallest ε that will make the formation of any coalition except the grand coalition unprofitable; that is, will change the game $\langle N, v \rangle$ into a game with a core.

An answer to this question is found by solving the following problem:

Find minimum ε for which $\displaystyle\sum_{i \in S} x_i \geq v(S) - \varepsilon$ for all $S \subset N$ and $\sum x_i = v(N)$

$$(19.6)$$

has a solution in the form of a vector $x = (x_1, x_2, \ldots, x_n)$.

Since Equation 19.6 must be satisfied by singlet subsets $\{x_i\}$, x will clearly be an imputation. The set of imputations satisfying Equation 19.6 is called the *least core* of the game $\langle N, v \rangle$.

If there are several imputations in the least core, the problem arises of reducing this set to a single imputation. This is done as follows. In the original game define the *excess* of a coalition S with respect to an imputation x as $v(S) - \sum_{i \in S} x_i$. Call the largest excess (over all S) $e_1(x)$, the next largest excess $e_2(x)$, and so on. Then the set of imputations X_1 which minimize $e_1(x)$ is the least core. Determine X_2, the subset of X_1 of imputations that also minimize $e_2(x)$. Continuing in this way, we eventually obtain X_k which contains a single imputation. This imputation is called the *nucleolus* of the game $\langle N, v \rangle$. Because it is determined by the smallest tax that creates a game with a core, the nucleolus, although strictly speaking unstable, "comes closest" to stability.

Now consider a game that already has a core. The problem now is to "shrink" the core so as to reduce it to a single imputation. This is done by "encouraging" coalitions; for example, by "subsidies" (that is, "negative taxes"). Again the least core can be obtained by solving Equation 19.6, whereby negative values of ε are admissible. If the least core still contains several imputations, the nucleolus is obtained by the same method.

A variant of the nucleolus called the *proportional nucleolus* is found by first finding the *proportional least core*. This is done by imposing on every coalition S a tax (or granting a subsidy) proportional to $v(S)$. The problem to be solved now is the following:

$$\text{Find minimum } t \text{ for which } \sum_{i \in S} x_i \geq (1 - t)v(S) \qquad \text{for all } S \subset N$$

$$\text{and} \qquad \sum x_i = v(N) \tag{19.7}$$

has a solution x.

The nucleolus is calculated as before, except that the excess of S with respect to x is now taken as $[v(S) - \sum_{i \in S} x_i]/v(S)$.

AN APPLICATION

The Shapley value and the nucleolus served to shed more light on the allocation problem that recently arose in Skånen, Sweden. A number of communities considered the possibility of creating a common water supply. This venture would be economically feasible if a sufficient number of communities would join in the enterprise. The attractiveness of joining in turn depended on the foreseen costs of supplying the water allotted to a community. Clearly, if the cost exceeded what the community was paying for water from its own sources, it would not join. Moreover, communities could join in smaller combines to create a joint water supply. If by doing so they stood to gain more than by joining the grand project, they would rather do so. (Young, Okada and Hashimoto, 1980).

Let the present cost of water of community i be $c(i)$ and the foreseen cost to a coalition of communities S be $c(S)$. The saving effected by coalition S would then be

$$v(S) = \sum_{i \in S} c_i - c(S). \tag{19.8}$$

The function $v(S)$ can represent the characteristic function of an n-person game $\langle N, v \rangle$.

There are several traditional methods of allocating costs of communal projects. In the present case, costs could be allocated in proportion to the populations of the participating communities, in proportion to the demand for water, so as to produce equal per capita savings, and so on. An allocation of savings associated with some particular distribution of costs may or may not be an imputation in the game $\langle N, v \rangle$. It will be an imputation if no community increases its cost by joining the project, but not otherwise. If an allocation is an imputation, it may or may not be stable. It will be stable if it is in the core of the game (provided, of course, the game has a core). Thus any particular allocation can be evaluated by such criteria, and since each *method* of distributing costs produces a particular allocation of savings in the case at hand, each method can be evaluated.

Besides the criteria mentioned, there are others. One is *monotonicity*. Suppose the costs rise. If some method of cost distribution is used, a new allocation will result. It is reasonable to expect that no participating community will profit; that is, will pay less as a result of rising costs. As a consequence of some of the distribution methods (including game-theoretic solutions), this might nevertheless happen. Conversely, suppose the costs decrease. One should expect that no participating community should be penalized thereby; that is, pay more in the new distribution of costs. In the problem discussed, still other criteria of evaluating cost distribution methods have been proposed.

The cost distribution in Skånen was computed by several methods. On the basis of several different criteria, the proportional nucleolus produced the most satisfactory result.

The question naturally arises as to what extent solutions of this sort can serve in determining "fair" allocations of costs or resources. It is generally accepted, at least among those concerned with the role of science in human affairs, that questions about what is "fair" (or "just" or "good") are different from those about what is "true." At least in the context of the natural sciences, criteria of truth based on an evaluation of empirical evidence are regarded as sufficiently clear to resolve disagreements about what is true when enough evidence accumulates in favor or against different opinions. That is to say, the "objective" nature of scientific truth is generally recognized. On the other hand, agreements on what is "fair" or "just" are based on commonly held values, usually culturally determined. There is a widespread opinion that science provides no criteria by which to test the "validity" of values and that attempts to establish them on a "scientific" basis are misguided. At this time, I will not take a position on this matter, except to point out that habits of thought induced by scientific analysis and practice often influence the formation of a value system. Because the axiomatic bases of game-theoretic solutions of decision problems and of various social choice functions are logically explicit, they make reexamination of various value systems possible and forestall fixation on the emotive connotations of concepts as well as circular reasoning.

For instance, "equality before the law" sounds like a good slogan. Examination of the axioms from which this principle can be derived shows why it is attractive. It says essentially that in deciding an issue involving a conflict of interest, the issue should be decided on its merits rather than the identities of the contending parties. Formally, this means that if the parties were to exchange roles, the decision should be the same.

Of prime importance in evaluating the fairness of a decision (for instance, a distribution of costs or benefits) is an agreement on what constitutes a fair distribution *in principle*; that is, regardless of specific circumstances except to the extent that these are taken into account *in advance* of particular conflicts of interest. The formal models of collective decisions, as these have been developed in the theory of social choice or in the theory of cooperative *n*-person games, represent attempts to do just this. The abstract formulation ensures "objectivity."

Imparting a general understanding of the reasoning underlying theories of collective decisions remains a problem because much of this reasoning is often quite abstruse. But so is the reasoning that establishes objective truths about physical reality. That this abstruseness is no longer a hindrance to the pursuit of truth in that realm is a consequence of institutionalized science. The development of "objective" standards of fairness or "justice" depends on the extension of analogous modes of thought to the realm of human affairs.

NOTE

[1] Here we have in mind a "shortsighted" rationality of the members of $S \subset N$ whereby they consider only the immediate prospects opened to them if they leave the grand coalition to form one of their own, without taking into account possible further consequences. For instance, the newly formed coalition may be vulnerable to tempting offers to its members by players outside it. Consider the game with characteristic function $v(abc) = v(ab) = v(ac) = v(bc) = 1$; $v(a) = v(b) = v(c) = 0$. The payoff vector $(1/3, 1/3, 1/3)$ is an imputation. Players a and b may be tempted to leave the grand coalition since they can jointly get 1; that is, 1/2 each instead of 1/3 each. But if they make this agreement, each of them could be tempted by c to desert his partner by an offer of more than 1/2, which c is surely ready to offer since otherwise he gets 0. If c succeeds in luring one of the defectors away from the grand coalition, the other defector is left with noting.

CHAPTER TWENTY

Experimental Games

Game models of conflicts provide an opportunity for studying conflict in the laboratory. Since the controlled experiment has been established as a principal tool of research at least in the natural sciences, it is hardly necessary to emphasize its methodological value. The extension of the experimental method to the behavioral sciences, however, is associated with serious problems, as is the extension of mathematical deductive methods to these areas of research.

Actually, these problems also arose in the biological sciences. The behavior of living matter *in vitro* is often quite unlike its behavior *in vivo*. If one does not wish to succumb to the temptation of resorting to vitalistic explanations of this difference, one must admit that it is often impossible to reproduce a living environment of living tissue in a test tube. But understanding the difficulty does not remove it.

In the social sciences, these difficulties are magnified. In a physiological experiment, it is sometimes possible to recognize or at least to guess what is lacking when living tissue is placed in an artificial environment and so to hope that with further development of experimental techniques, the missing components of the environment can be filled in. But the hope of reproducing the social environment of a subject in a laboratory is indeed dim. Consequently, the generalization of laboratory findings to real-life situations is seldom warranted, even if their internal consistency is well established by replications.

There is a well-known inverse relationship between the degree of "realism" introduced into a laboratory experiment modeled after a real-life situation and its tractability. But it is difficult to estimate this "trade off"—how much "realism" must be sacrificed in return for how much tractability. It seems reasonable, therefore, to forego attempts to imitate "real life" in the laboratory altogether and to extract as much information as possible from laboratory experiments as such.

The value of laboratory experiments is not in answers they can provide to direct questions about determinants of human behavior but rather in the opportunity they provide for constructing a theory of behavior under controlled conditions. This theory, then, can serve as a point of departure for a theory of behavior *in vivo*. In particular, if regularities of behavior can be deduced from a mathematical model, the *parameters* of the model can serve as building blocks of a cumulative theory.

The importance of creating such areas of theoretically organized knowledge cannot be overemphasized, even if they constitute separate "islands" and lie far removed from the problems that originally stimulated the investigations. The entire history of science is a reflection of this process. Generally, a science can give direct, reliable answers to questions generated by "practical needs" only in its mature phase. The social sciences are nowhere near this stage of development. A science matures by following the well-trodden path of all systematically developed sciences. Frankly speaking, this path is often the path of least resistance: one investigates problems suggested by problems already solved, if they, in turn, seem to be solvable. At times, the "practical" problems originally posed lose their importance, sometimes even become meaningless, because new knowledge generates new concepts and with them new *kinds* of questions. The transition from astrology to astronomy and from alchemy to chemistry are frequently cited examples of such changes of perspective which eventually led to much more "useful" knowledge (serendipity) than the knowledge originally sought. Here the emphasis is not so much on the circumstance that "useful" knowledge often comes from unexpected sources (the usual justification of research guided by "pure" curiosity") as on the circumstance that the conception of "useful" knowledge has itself undergone radical and far-reaching changes.

EXPERIMENTAL GAMES

Experimental games can be used in two different ways. One direction comes nearer to the original conception of game theory as a mathematical foundation of strategic science concerned with finding optimal courses of action in conflict situations. If optimality criteria are already defined in game-theoretic models of conflict, the derivation of optimal strategies is carried out exclusively by mathematical duduction. In strategically oriented games, the purpose of studying the behavior of participants is to see how closely their behavior approaches optimal behavior as defined, or the extent to which they learn to behave optimally. Games of this sort are frequently used in teaching; for example, in military or business schools, where competence in military tactics and strategy or in economic competition is presupposed as a necessary condition of professional success (see Shubik, 1975a, 1975b).

The other direction, more relevant to the content of this book, centers on the simplest conceivable games in the design of experiments, especially on games of interest to psychologists, just because they do *not* have unambivalently "correct" solutions. Here behavior is not studied in order to assess the subjects' "competence," but rather with the view of assessing their motivations. It has been shown that motivations (as reflected in behavior) can change radically with the payoff structure of a game and with experimental conditions, and that they vary from subject to subject. In this way, it is possible to relate dependent to independent variables; that is, to lay the foundation of a quantitative experimental method for studying some aspects of human behavior, whereby these aspects are more directly related to "interesting" psychological categories than those traditionally studied in psychological laboratories. Above all, experimental games have been developed as tools of experimental *social* psychology.

The first game-theoretic model that attracted the attention of psychologists was Prisoner's Dilemma, discussed in Chapter 17 (see Matrix 17.5). It is reproduced here with rows and columns reversed.

	S_2	T_2
S_1	−1 / −1	−10 / 10
T_1	10 / −10	1 / 1

Matrix 20.1

The principle of dominance (see p. 327) dictates the choice of the dominant strategy S to both players. Collective rationality, on the other hand, demands the choice of T. Collective rationality, however, rests on the assumption that the coplayer is also guided by collective rationality and will therefore resist the temptation to choose S in order to exploit the first player's collective rationality and so obtain the largest payoff. We see that in addition to "strategic competence," concepts like "exploitation," "cooperation," "suspicion," and the like enter *per force* in the analysis of behavior; they may even displace "strategic competence," which is difficult or even impossible to define in this context. For this reason, behavior patterns in this game must be described by a vocabulary richer than that by which competence in parlor games (chess, bridge, and so on) are described.

Analysis of experimental games requires operational definitions of concepts related to interactions of individuals in terms of patterns of concrete acts (choices of strategies). The question as to what extent concepts so defined reflect "real" psychological meanings remains, for the time being, open, pending the testing of hypotheses suggested by results of experimental games in real-life situations.

Prisoner's Dilemma has been by far the most widely used game in experimental social psychology. Doubtless its use has been spurred by the opportunity it provided to study conflicting pressures toward "cooperation" and "competition" or "exploitation" in the laboratory. The interested reader is referred to the voluminous literature on this subject.[1] Here we will examine some results of experiments with some less thoroughly investigated simple two-person games. We will also examine some results on cooperative games.

THE 2 × 2 GAMES

The simplest two-person games are so-called 2×2 games, where each of two players must choose between two strategies. Suppose the payoffs are given only on an ordinal scale; that is, the players' preference orderings of the four possible outcomes of the game. If both preference relations induce a linear order (that is, preference between every two outcomes is strict and transitive), then the payoffs can be assigned to the four outcomes in $4! \times 4! = 576$ different ways. However, the resulting 576 different matrices do not represent so many different games because interchanging rows, columns, or players does not change the strategic structure of a game. When strategically equivalent matrices are identified as a single game, 78 games remain strategically distinct (Rapoport and Guyer, 1966). If the preferences of the players induce a weak order (that is, if a player may be indifferent between two or more outcomes), the number of strategically distinct games turns out to be 732 (Guyer and Hamburger, 1968).

Strategically different games induce different "motivation pressures" on the players. If both players have a dominating strategy, we can expect that both are strongly motivated to choose it (in accordance with the "sure thing" or dominance principle). In a game where only one player has a dominating strategy, the other is not subjected to this pressure. However, the player may see from the game matrix that the other has a dominating strategy and can be expected to maximize his own payoffs, acting on the assumption that the other will choose his dominating strategy. Not all players, however, are able to "put themselves in the shoes" of the other player. For example, small children are generally unable to do this (see Perner, 1978).

So far, we have discussed only strategic considerations. As we have seen, in some games these do not suffice to determine a choice. For example, in Prisoner's Dilemma, both players have a dominating strategy, but collective rationality (or, if you will, a desire to cooperate, coupled with trust that the coplayer has the same intention) suggests the choice of the dominated, not the dominating strategy.

As another example, consider the following game.

	S_2	T_2
S_1	5 0	0 5
T_1	−1 −2	−2 −1

Matrix 20.2

Both players have a dominating strategy, S_1 or S_2. Individual rationality prescribes this strategy, resulting in the outcome S_1S_2. Collective rationality is not thereby violated since the outcome is *Pareto-optimal* in the sense that no other outcome is preferred to it by *both* players.

This game can be played cooperatively (in case negotiations and agreements to coordinate choices are allowed) or noncooperatively (where there is no opportunity for such coordination). The game can also be played just once or repeated several times.

Consider first an experiment in which the game represented by Matrix 20.2 is played many times in succession by the same pair of players. The payoffs are usually in money. Utilities of small amounts of money can reasonably be supposed to be linear functions of the amounts. If both players are "rational," S_1S_2 will be the outcome of each play. This outcome, however, may seem "unfair" to Row. The question arises what Row can do to improve his situation. Row controls the rows of the payoff matrix, thus the only thing he can do is choose T_1 instead of the "rational" alternative S_1. If Column continues to choose S_2, the outcome will be T_1S_2, which "punishes" Column but also Row. Can Row expect that by choosing T_1, he can get Column to switch to T_2, whereby T_1T_2 results, after which if Column continues with T_2, Row can by switching to S_1 effect his most preferred outcome S_1T_2? This is possible if Column "gets the message," which Row is trying to convey. Namely, by switching to T_1, Row communicates his dissatisfaction with S_1S_2. By switching to T_2, Column can "appease" Row by giving him an opportunity to effect S_1T_2. Interpreted in this way, Row's switch to T_1 can be regarded as a "strike."

Clearly, all these considerations are irrelevant if the game is played only once. In this case, Row's choice of T_1 violates individual rationality without prospect of compensation. (In repeated plays, as we have seen, a "strike" can be justified, especially if after repeated strikes, Column gets the idea that by alternating between S_2 and T_2 and thus sharing the largest payoff with Row, he can forestall future strikes.)

Now the question arises as to how frequently Row must resort to "strikes" to convey his message and how persistent he should be in choosing T_1 if Column refuses to shift to T_2. Next, if Column does alternate between S_2 and T_2, with what relative frequencies should he choose these strategies; that is, what share of the largest payoff should he give Row in repeated plays to forestall strikes? We expect that answers to these questions will depend on the magnitudes of the payoffs (within the constraints determined by the structure of this game), on individual players, on experimental conditions, and so on. To the extent that the answers are replicable (that is, statistically stable), they can lead to interesting social-psychological conjectures and hypotheses.

In iterated plays, a programmed player sometimes replaces a bona fide subject. A programmed player is a confederate of the experimenter who makes his choices in accordance with a prearranged schedule. In particular, a programmed player in the role of Column can adopt an "adamant" strategy, that is, always choose S_2, thus refusing to share under any circumstances. Now Row's behavior can be studied under this condition. By "Row," we understand a "composite" subject in the role of Row. His "behavior" is a distribution of choice patterns.

We can, for example, observe the proportion of subjects who never switch to the "threat strategy" T_1 (that is, the "nonresisters"); the proportion of those who resort to T_1 frequently but retreat to S_1 when this strategy does not affect Column's behavior; or the proportion of those who stubbornly repeat T_1 even though this appears to be futile.

A programmed player in the role of Row can be assigned the choice of S_1 100% of the time; that is, the role of a nonresister. Now we can observe the proportion of subjects in the role of Column who nevertheless share with Row; the proportion who share much (for example, choose T_2, with, say, 50% frequency); the proportion who give a mere pittance; the proportion who "exploit" the nonresister (that is, never switch to T_2); and so on. The reader interested in the results of these experiments is referred to Rapoport, Guyer, and Gordon, 1976, Chapter 19.

The social attitudes of the players can be an important behavioral variable in game situations. In experiments conducted in the United States and Canada, men and women played in both roles in the "threat game" described above. It was found that when a woman played Column (that is, was "top dog"), the frequency of T_1 choices by Row was significantly larger than when a man was top dog. This result was observed regardless of whether a man or a woman was in the underdog role.

Finally, some results on games played once are instructive. First, however, we must point out some purely logistic difficulties associated with single play experiments. Recruiting subjects and instructing them in the rules of the game costs time. Besides, subjects are paid for participating in an experiment. It seems wasteful of time and money to recruit and instruct a pair of subjects in order to get just two units of data, a choice by Row and one by Column. For this reason, it is usual to design single play experiments in such a manner that a pair of subjects plays several games once each. If the outcomes of each play are not announced to the subjects during the experiment, learning effects can be assumed to be excluded. It has turned out, however, that some "contagion" effects remain. For instance, in an experiment where every subject played every one of the 78 nonequivalent games once, over 95% of the subjects chose S_1 in the role of Row and S_2 in the role of Column in the game represented by Matrix 20.2. When, however, that game was one of several games with the same or closely similar structure, the proportion of subjects who chose S_2 was 90%, whereas the proportion who chose S_1 was only 70%. This result suggests that some players were guided by other than the "sure thing" principle in their choices. For instance, Row players may have preferred outcome $T_1 S_2$, where both players suffer a loss, to $S_1 S_2$, where Column gets a positive payoff, while Row gets 0.

A similar result was observed in Prisoner's Dilemma played once. When the game was included in the entire set of 78 games, only 12% of the players chose the dominated (cooperative) strategy. When Prisoner's Dilemma was imbedded in a set of games with the same or similar structure, the cooperative strategy was chosen with a frequency of 50%. The latter result was also observed when pairs of subjects were recruited "from the street" to play Prisoner's Dilemma once and no other game.

The following explanation suggests itself. When the subject's task is to make a long series of choices, and when the structure of the decision problem varies from one to the next, the subject may adopt an "across the board" strategy. If the dominance principle is part of that strategy, dominating strategies will be chosen when they are available. The special peculiarities of games like the Threat Game and Prisoner's Dilemma, where pressures *against* the choice of the dominating strategy may be acting, may be ignored. When, on the other hand, all the games in a set are characterized by the same or similar structure, their peculiarities may be noticed; for instance, the non-Pareto-optimality of the S_1S_2 outcome in Prisoner's Dilemma or the "unfairness" of that outcome in the Threat Game. This may account for the considerably smaller frequency of dominating strategy choices in these games when they are presented with similar games.

Reasonable as this explanation may sound, it is apparently insufficient. In quite a number of games with two dominating strategies, the *dominated* strategy is chosen with considerable frequency, even when the whole set of 78 games is presented. Further analysis has shown that the dominance principle is by no means decisive for certain "types" of players. Indeed, anomalies of this sort have suggested a taxonomy of "archetypes" of players and hypotheses concerning the interrelationship between this taxonomy and the taxonomy of 2×2 games.

Introducing a taxonomy of players requires disaggregation of data. For instance, aggregated data on the iterated threat game indicate that the composite Column player shares about 25% of the positive payoff with a nonresisting Row player. Actually, the distribution is strongly bimodal. About 50% of the Column players do not share at all, but those that share usually share 50%. Aggregated data suggest that subjects playing Prisoner's Dilemma against a programmed player who cooperates 100% of the time cooperate about 50% of the time in iterated play. Disaggregated data show that this distribution is also bimodal. About half the subjects cooperate fully with a cooperating stooge; about half exploit him fully.

Besides disaggregation of players, disaggregation of motivations is important in analyzing the motivational structure of subjects in experimental games. This is not easy, even in experiments with simple 2×2 games. Consider Prisoner's Dilemma. In this game, the opposite motivational pressures (to choose S or T) are built into the structure of the game. The choice of S can be attributed to the dominance principle, to the opportunity this choice provides to get the largest payoff, to a desire to get more than the coplayer (competition), or else to the fear of getting the smallest payoff should the other choose S. The first two of these pressures can be regarded as direct, stemming from considerations of one's own payoffs; the last two as indirect, stemming from considerations of the other's payoffs or motivations.

The motivation to choose T in Prisoner's Dilemma can be also decomposed. The cooperative choice can be attributed to collective rationality; in iterated play, to a desire to communicate "trust" in the coplayer's good intentions; or else to a tit-for-tat strategy which rewards the coplayer's cooperative choices (while punishing the uncooperative choices).

Since all these motivations are interwoven, it is difficult to draw "psychological" conclusions from the behavior patterns of players in many 2×2 games. Nevertheless, games drawn from the complete set of 732 2×2 games can be used in "isolating" motivational components.

Consider the following game.

		S_2 53	T_2 47
S_1	72	5 / 1	5 / 1
T_1	28	1 / 1	1 / 1

Matrix 20.3

If Row contemplates only his own payoffs, he can be assumed to be indifferent between S_1 and T_1. Therefore, a predominant choice of S_1 can be attributed to something other than an attempt to maximize one's own payoff; for instance, to a desire to give Column a larger payoff. In this game, Column, too, can be assumed to be indifferent between his choices, the more so because he cannot affect Row's payoffs by one choice or the other any more than his own.

Thus Game 20.3 provides an opportunity to study "purely benevolent" choices. The numbers on the left of Matrix 20.3 show the percentages of subjects ($n = 70$) who chose the corresponding rows in a single play experiment when this game was included among similar games (Lendenmann and Rapoport, 1979). The numbers above represent the percentages of subjects who chose the corresponding columns. We note the following: whereas the percentages of Column players choosing S_2 and T_2 respectively are not significantly different, the percentages of Row players who chose S_1 and T_1 respectively are quite different. We can assume that the results reflect a tendency to choose "benevolently", when this choice involves no cost. Equally interesting are the results on the following two games.

We note that in both games, Row has a *weakly dominating* strategy; namely, S_1. Nevertheless, it turns out that although 94% of the Row players chose S_1 in Game 20.5, only 56% chose S_1 in Game 20.4.

Note that in Game 20.5, S_1 is prescribed by the dominance principle and is also "benevolent" toward Column. Thus self-interest and benevolence act in the same direction. In Game 20.4, the two pressures act in opposite directions since

$$S_2 \qquad T_2$$
$$91 \qquad 09$$

	S_1 56		

Matrix 20.4

$$S_2 \qquad T_2$$
$$79 \qquad 21$$

Matrix 20.5

Row's benevolent strategy is T_1. It is, therefore, interesting to note that in this game, 44% of Row players acted "benevolently" *against* their self interest.

No less interesting is Column's behavior in the two games. In Game 20.4, the choice of T_2 could be justified only by the expectation that Row would act "benevolently" against his own interest. We could surmise that only 9% of Column players acted on that expectation (although fully 44% of Row players in fact acted "benevolently" against their own interest). In Game 20.5, S_2 is prescribed by the expectation that Row will choose the weakly dominating strategy S_1; that is, will act rationally and/or benevolently. The Maximin Principle prescribes T_2. It is supported by the expectation that Row will act *malevolently* against his own interest! Nevertheless, 21% of Column players chose T_2, providing a measure of "distrust" in the subject population. That this distrust was not fully justified appears from the fact that only 6% of Row players acted in this way.

These examples bring out the structural complexities of even the simplest two-person games.

COOPERATIVE GAMES

A theory of a cooperative two-person game can be regarded as a prescriptive theory in the sense that it prescribes a solution of a game in the form of a probabilistic mixture of *outcomes*. Note the difference between this conception and that of a solution of a two-person noncooperative game, which prescribes to each player a *strategy* (pure or mixed). Mixtures of outcomes are possible only if outcomes can be achieved by coordination of strategies. This is possible only in cooperative games. In this way, the players can achieve outcomes which both prefer to other outcomes. Mixtures of these outcomes can be regarded as compromises since the interests of the players diverge with regard to Pareto-optimal outcomes.

In Chapter 18, we discussed cooperative games with more than two players. In *n*-person theory of cooperative games, it is usually assumed that utility is a transferable, conservative commodity, like money. Thus the principal concept underlying the solution of an *n*-person cooperative game is that of an imputation, essentially a distribution of an amount of utility among the players. In the theory of two-person cooperative games, utility is usually regarded as given only on an interval scale, which means that utilities of the two players cannot be compared, let alone added. Therefore, imputations do not enter this theory.

Nash's solution of a two-person cooperative game is grounded in four postulates (Nash, 1953). These may be regarded as desiderata of a solution analogous to the desiderata of a social choice function listed in formal theories of social choice (see Chapter 17). Nash's axioms are:

N_1.   *Symmetry.* The solution should be independent of the labeling of the players.

N_2.   *Linearity.* The probability mixture of outcomes that constitutes the solution should be independent of positive linear transformations of the payoffs.

N_2.   *Pareto-optimality.* The mixture should involve only Pareto-optimal outcomes.

N_4.   *Independence from irrelevant alternatives.* If the threat point (to be explained below) of a game is unchanged and if some region of the feasible solution space (to be explained below) not including the solution is eliminated, the solution should not be affected thereby.

Remarks: N_1 can be regarded as a principle of fairness. If the solution of a cooperative game serves as a resolution of a conflict, then the same resolution should apply if the players exchange roles. N_2 is required if utilities are given on a scale no stronger than the interval scale. N_3 means that the solution should not violate collective rationality. N_4 is analogous to the corresponding desideratum (independence from irrelevant alternatives) underlying some prescriptive theories of social choice (cf. Chapter 18).

It turns out that barring trivial cases, a unique mixture of outcomes satisfies all four postulates. To illustrate a solution of a 2×2 cooperative game, we plot the pairs of utilities associated with the four outcomes on a Cartesian plane, where the x coordinate represents Row's utilities, the y coordinate Column's.

Next, the four points are enclosed in a *convex hull*; that is, the smallest convex region which contains them either inside or on its boundary. A convex region is one where a straight line connecting any two points of the region lies entirely within it or on its boundary. Each pair of points of the convex hull represents a possible pair of payoffs that can be realized by an appropriate pair of coordinated strategies (pure or mixed) chosen by the players. Thus the convex hull can be called the feasible outcome region of the game.

Figure 20.1 shows the geometric representation of Game 20.2. All possible outcomes determined by pairs of pure or mixed strategies are represented by points within or on the boundary of the quadrilateral (the feasible region). In view of N_3, the solution of the game must lie on the straight line connecting $S_1 S_2$ and $S_1 T_2$, the two Pareto-optimal outcomes determined by pure strategies. The solution is the point (x^*, y^*) which maximizes the quantity $(x - x_0)$ $(y - y_0)$, where $y = y(x)$ is the equation of that straight line and the point (x_0, y_0) is the *threat point* of the game. It is the intersection of the players' optimal *threat strategies.*

A threat strategy is one that a player says he will choose if no agreement is reached on the mixture of Pareto-optimal outcomes as the solution of the game.

The choice of optimal threat strategies is determined by a solution of a certain constantsum game induced by the original game (see Rapoport, 1966, Chapter 8). This constant-sum game represents the conflict of interests of the players with respect to the choice of the mixture of Pareto-optimal outcomes. In Game 20.2, the optimal threat strategies turn out to be T_1 and S_2. They intersect at $T_1 S_2$. The threat point, therefore, is $x_0 = -2$, $y_0 = -1$.

The equation of the line connecting the two Pareto-optimal outcomes is $y = 5 - x$. Therefore, to find the solution, we maximize $(x - 2)(6 - x)$. Differ-

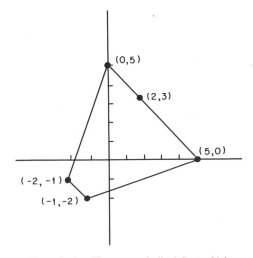

Figure 20.1. The convex hull of Game 20.2.

entiating with respect to x, we obtain

$$6 - x - x - 2 = 0$$
$$x = 2; y = 5 - 2 = 3. \tag{20.1}$$

The mixture that produces this result is $S_1 S_2$ with probability 0.6 and $S_1 T_2$ with probability 0.4. In iterated play, the players can agree to realize $S_1 S_2$ 60% of the time and $S_1 T_2$ 40% of the time. It is easy to verify that although the numerical values of the solution payoffs vary with positive linear transformations, the mixture does not.

Rapoport, Frenkel, and Perner (1977) tested the first three of Nash's axioms experimentally. Matrices 20.6–20.17 represent the games used in that experiment. Each game appeared in three variants, obtained by positive linear transformations of the payoffs to serve as a test of postulate N_2. Postulate N_1 was tested by interchanging the roles of each pair of players. N_3 was tested by assessing the deficiency of average payoffs with respect to Pareto optimality. Postulate N_4 was not tested.

The Nash solutions of the four distinct games expressed as mixtures of the Pareto-optimal outcomes and in terms of corresponding payoffs are shown in Table 20.1.

Table 20.1.

Game	Mixed Outcomes	Solution Mixture	Variant I Row	Variant I Column	Variant II Row	Variant II Column	Variant III Row	Variant III Column
1	AX, AY	3/5, 2/5	2	3	8	3	2	1
2	AX, AY	3/10, 7/10	7	1.8	7	5.4	4	1.8
3	AX, BY	8/15, 7/15	4.33	8.6	4.33	17.2	0.33	8.6
4	AX, BY	5/6, 1/6	4.5	10.5	9.0	10.5	4.5	5.5

The threat outcome in all four games is BX.

The subjects were 40 male students at the University of Toronto. They were randomly paired and assigned to two experimental conditions. Each subject played each of the three variants of each of the four games, once as Row, once as Column. They could communicate and bargain but were not allowed to make or promise side payments. They bargained over the probabilities with which each of the outcomes agreed upon would be realized. When a mixture was agreed upon, the payoffs were determined as the statistically expected amounts.

In the experimental condition called "Chosen Threat," failure to agree resulted in a *confrontation* whereby each player independently made a "final offer" in the form "If you don't agree to the mixture I have proposed, I will choose strategy _____." Thereupon, if no agreement was effected, each chose a strategy independently. However, a player was not obliged to carry out his threat. The threat might be a bluff.

Game 1

	X	Y
A	5 / 0	0 / 5
B	−1 / −2	−2 / −1

Matrix 20.6
Variant I

	X	Y
A	5 / 0	0 / 20
B	−1 / −8	−2 / −4

Matrix 20.7
Variant II

	X	Y
A	3 / 0	−2 / 5
B	−3 / −2	−5 / −1

Matrix 20.8
Variant III

Game 2

	X	Y
A	6 / 0	0 / 10
B	−3 / −1	−4 / 1

Matrix 20.9
Variant I

	X	Y
A	18 / 0	0 / 10
B	−9 / −1	−12 / 1

Matrix 20.10
Variant II

	X	Y
A	6 / −3	0 / 7
B	−3 / −4	−4 / −2

Matrix 20.11
Variant III

Game 3

	X	Y
A	10 / 2	2 / 10
B	3 / −5	7 / 7

Matrix 20.12
Variant I

	X	Y
A	20 / 2	4 / 10
B	6 / −5	14 / 7

Matrix 20.13
Variant II

	X	Y
A	10 / −2	2 / 6
B	3 / −9	7 / 3

Matrix 20.14
Variant III

Game 4

	X	Y
A	12 / 3	−12 / −4
B	−3 / −9	3 / 12

Matrix 20.15
Variant I

	X	Y
A	12 / 6	−12 / −8
B	−3 / −18	3 / 24

Matrix 20.16
Variant II

	X	Y
A	7 / 3	−17 / −4
B	−8 / −9	−2 / 12

Matrix 20.17
Variant III

As an illustration, consider Game 4, Variant II (Matrix 20.16). The outcome most preferred by Row is BY; by Column, AX. The players bargain over a mixture of these two outcomes. They fail to agree. At confrontation, Row threatens to play B, and Column threatens to play X. If both make good their threats, BX results. But either could have been bluffing. For example, Row may not dare play B because if Column does play X, Row suffers a loss of 18. So Row may "retreat" and play A after all, so as to risk only a loss of 8.

In the other experimental condition, called "Imposed Threat," the *experimenter* tells the subjects what will surely occur if they do not agree; namely, the threat outcome BX.

These conditions were introduced into the experiment to test a conjecture. In each game, one player is in a better bargaining situation than the other, as can be seen in Table 20.1. For example, Column is the advantaged player in Game 1 in the sense that the mixture determined by the Nash solution assigns probability 0.6 to Column's preferred outcome and only 0.4 to Row's. In Game 2, on the other hand, Row is the advantaged player because the solution assigns probability 0.7 to his preferred outcome.

The hypothesis tested was the following: In the Imposed Threat condition, the observed mixture agreed upon will be more "egalitarian" (that is, nearer to (0.5, 0.5) than in the Chosen Threat condition. The hypothesis was suggested by the conjecture that when subjects see themselves threatened by an outside authority, they are more likely to develop a feeling of "solidarity" and with it inhibitions against fully exploiting their bargaining advantage vis-a-vis the coplayer.[2]

Table 20.2 shows the main results of the experiment. The entries are averages of mixtures (in percentages) of the final demands made by the players following the negotiation phase of each play. The fact that some of these demands add up to more than 100% indicates that some were incompatible. In this case, there was either a confrontation (in the Chosen Threat condition) or the threat outcome resulted (in the Imposed Threat condition). Cases where demands add up to less than 100% reflect the plays where the players demanded less than they could safely do, presumably to avoid confrontation or the threat outcome. We see from Table 20.2 that our hypothesis was confirmed in 11 out of 12 cases. Expect in Game 3, Variant II, the mixtures were more "egalitarian" in the Imposed Threat condition.

The symmetry postulate states that exchange of roles by the players should not influence the solution. Let r_i be the last demand of player i ($i = 1, 2$) as Row and c_i the last demand of player i as Column. Then the quantity $\frac{1}{2}(|r_i - r_2| + |c_1 - c_2|)$ is a measure of asymmetry. According to the symmetry axiom, this quantity should not be significantly different from zero.

In the Imposed Threat condition, the mean of this quantity (in percent) was 6.51 with standard deviation 5.71; in the Chosen Threat condition, 8.56 with standard deviation 9.75. The distribution of this measure of asymmetry is not known. However, assuming that the 10 pairs of subjects in each condition made their choices independently, we can conclude that the standard deviation of the

Table 20.2. Average Mixtures of Outcomes Preferred by Row and Column, Respectively in the Rapoport–Frenkel–Perne Experiment

Threat condition	Variant I		Variant II		Variant III	
	Row	Column	Row	Column	Row	Column
			Game 1			
Chosen	38.0	62.7	18.7	87.7	41.8	61.0
Imposed	44.5	56.7	28.8	70.7	45.5	56.0
			Game 2			
Chosen	57.0	43.5	75.2	24.5	43.5	57.0
Imposed	56.0	43.7	72.7	27.5	51.3	49.5
			Game 3			
Chosen	25.0	80.8	42.8	60.7	35.7	73.5
Imposed	32.5	67.2	35.5	64.7	42.0	58.0
			Game 4			
Chosen	22.0	78.5	12.8	89.0	26.5	74.5
Imposed	28.0	72.5	20.0	79.7	38.0	62.3

means were respectively $(5.71)/\sqrt{10} = 1.8$ and $(9.75)/\sqrt{10} = 3.1$. Thus in the Imposed Threat condition, the asymmetry measure deviates 3.6 standard deviations from zero; in the Chosen Threat condition, somewhat less than 3.0 standard deviations. If we apply the ultraconservative Tchebyshev inequality, the deviations from zero are near 0.1 level of significance. It is nevertheless likely that the deviation from zero is significant in both cases, even assuming a strongly skewed distribution, and consequently the symmetry postulate appears to be violated. This should not be surprising because different subjects are probably characterized by different bargaining abilities, whereas the symmetry postulate ignores these differences.[3]

Of the three tested postulates, linearity was most clearly violated. We see from Table 20.2 that the mixtures differ sharply from variant to variant of the same game in contradiction to the linearity postulate. The result is significant for a theory of social welfare. The assumption that utilities of different individuals cannot be compared (a consequence of their being given on a scale no stronger than the interval scale) essentially precludes the construction of a social welfare function on the basis of aggregated individual utilities. A decisive experimental discorroboration of the linearity postulate indicates that persons engaged in bargaining (or in resolving conflicts of interest) probably do compare their utilities for the possible outcomes. Once interpersonal comparisons are permitted, social welfare functions can be constructed, and resolutions of conflicts based on maximizing some social good suggest themselves.

As we have seen, the Nash solution of a two-person cooperative game maximizes the product of the differences between the players' utilities at the threat point and those on the Pareto-optimal set. This solution remains invariant under positive linear transformations of the payoffs and therefore can be applied whenever utilities are given on an interval scale. The same principle can be applied in n-person cooperative games where comparisons of interpersonal utilities are not made. The utility-product maximization principle can also be applied when interpersonal utilities are compared (for example, "normalized" on a common scale but not added, as will be shown in the following example).

AN EXPERIMENT IN CONSENSUS FORMATION

An exercise in conflict resolution using maximization of utility products was carried out in connection with a recent space exploration project (Dyer and Miles, 1977). In the late summer of 1977, the United States Aeronautics and Space Administration (NASA) sent two unmanned space ships to pass near the planets Jupiter and Saturn for the purpose of collecting physical data on these planets and their satellites. Several teams of scientists were interested in obtaining different sets of data. For instance, the team representing radio science was interested in obtaining data on the physical properties of the atmospheres and ionospheres of the two planets. The team representing photopolarimetry was interested in chemical data; for example, concentrations of methane, ammonia, molecular hydrogen, and so on. The team representing the study of magnetic fields had its own priorities, and so on.

Obviously, to obtain the clearest and most reliable data on each of these groups of characteristics, some trajectories would be better suited than others, so that no one trajectory would be "best" for all the different tasks. There was thus a "conflict of interest" among the various teams of scientists. Aside from these conflicts of interests, there were certain constraints on the trajectories imposed by technological problems and cost ceilings.

Taking into consideration the constraints and the various requirements of the several teams, 105 trajectories were initially designed that met the criteria of feasibility, more or less. Since two space ships were to be sent on the same mission, the problem was to select the "best" pair from the set of trajectory pairs. By a process of elimination, 32 trajectory pairs were finally selected as the "candidates" from which one pair was to be "elected." This was the "political" content of the project.

Each team attached a numerical utility to each of the 32 trajectory pairs. Note that this involved more than a rank-ordering of the trajectories by the several teams. Utilities were determined on an *interval* scale by the process of lotteries described in the Introduction. Specifically, team i was assumed to attach utility $u^i(t_j)$ to trajectory pair t_j if it was indifferent between getting that trajectory and getting a lottery ticket that entitled it to its most preferred pair t_1 with probability $u^i(t_j)$, or its least preferred pair t_{32} with probability $1 - u^i(t_j)$.

Now the Nash solution in the form of a coordinated "mixed strategy" in this context would amount to a "lottery ticket" on the set of trajectory pairs with probabilities corresponding to the mixture. Clearly, this form of solution would not be appropriate. An "expected utility" has little meaning in a situation that by its nature cannot occur with any appreciable "frequency": space probes are much too expensive! The utility-product maximizing solution that is definitive rather than probabilistic requires a normalization of utilities on a common scale.

To make utilities of the several teams comparable, it suffices to fix the utility of each team's most preferred pair at 1 and to use an additional lottery in order to fix the utility of the least preferred pair. It would not do to fix this latter utility at zero because this would not reflect the possibly very different ranges in various teams between the largest and the smallest utilities. Some teams were relatively indifferent between the various trajectory pairs since the quantity or quality of the data important to them were relatively insensitive to variations in trajectories. Other teams, on the contrary, were very sensitive to these differences.

To fix the zero point of each team's utility scale, a "null trajectory" was introduced, one which yielded no data. With typical American humor, the null trajectory was named the Atlantic Ocean Special, a sardonic allusion to the ill-fated Mariner 8 mission, which aborted and plunged the spacecraft into that ocean. Assigning utility zero to the null trajectory, the utility of the least preferred trajectory pair could be determined by designing a lottery involving the null trajectory and the most preferred pair so that the lottery was indifferent to the least preferred t_{32}. It is interesting to observe that the utilities assigned to the least preferred pair ranged extremely widely; namely, from 0.1 to 0.8. The very high values are explainable by the fact that since this project was of long duration (about 10 years if the processing of the data is included), it represented for many scientists the only opportunity to participate in a space project of this sort. The more reluctant such a scientist was to accept a risk (even a small one) of getting stuck with the null trajectory, the higher the value he would assign to his least preferred trajectory pair (t_{32}). On the other hand, it must be borne in mind that the larger a team's range of utilities, the more influence this team's utilities would have in the final selection. Since no one seriously believed that the null trajectory would actually be used, teams could safely accept a large risk for the null trajectory, thus spreading their scale widely across the $[0, 1]$ interval and increasing their weight in the overall evaluation. Nevertheless, some of the preference scales had narrow ranges.

The utility-product maximizing solution was only one of several used in that exercise. Others were Borda's Method of rank sums, discussed in Chapter 18 (see p. 00); the maximin rule (see p. 00); and weighted additive rules, where the utility of each trajectory pair was calculated as the weighted sum of the utilities assigned to it by the several teams, with the weights determined by the arbitrating authority. Two versions of this rule were used, one with individual utilities calculated relative to the null trajectory as "zero," another with $u(t_{32}) = 0$.

Comparison of collective utilities of the 10 high-ranking trajectory pairs is shown in Table 20.3. As can be seen, the ranks obtained by the four methods are very highly correlated. For instance, the rank-order correlation between the rank-sum (Borda) method and the additive method with null trajectory included is 0.89. The correlation between the multiplicative (Nash) method and additive (null trajectory included) is 0.95.

Table 20.3. Degrees of Collective Preference for Trajectories in the Mariner Jupiter/Saturn Project Obtained by Various Methods of Collective Decision

Trajectory	Rank	Sum	Additive $u(\emptyset) = 0$		Additive $u(t_{32}) = 0$		Multiplicative (Nash) $u(\emptyset) = 0$	
31	1	0.822	2	0.887	1	0.724	1.5	0.877
29	2	0.797	3	0.875	3	0.692	3	0.865
26	3	0.795	1	0.889	2	0.710	1.5	0.877
27	4	0.719	4	0.856	4	0.641	4	0.839
5	5	0.683	6	0.791	6	0.555	6	0.776
25	6	0.678	5	0.822	5	0.597	5	0.804
35	7	0.655	7	0.757	8	0.511	8	0.745
17	8	0.622	10	0.738	11	0.475	10.5	0.725
8	9	0.611	8	0.755	9	0.488	7	0.746
10	10	0.605	12	0.738	7	0.514	14	0.706

Source: Adapted from Dyer and Miles (1976).

Of course, the important thing in arriving at consensus by any of the methods is the degree to which the participants feel that the methods are "fair." Questionnaires filled out by the representatives of the several teams gave rather expected results. Those whose favorite trajectories came out with low priorities had reservations about the methods. Those who were the "winners" in the process had mostly good things to say about the procedure. Clearly, there is no objective way of comparing the "fairness" of mechanisms by which consensus is generated. The important thing is that the participants in conflicts of interest *agree in advance* (that is, without knowing on which side of a conflict they are likely to be) on consensus-generating procedures. Only if such agreement comes readily can one look forward to applying some of the game-theoretic ideas to effecting acceptable compromises in conflicts of interest.

A GROSS VIOLATION OF PARETO-OPTIMALITY

An experiment performed by Ust-Peter Reich (1971) demonstrated a dramatic violation of collective rationality as manifested in the principle of Pareto-optimality.

The participants in the experiment were 31 political scientists, all from the Federal Republic of Germany. They were instructors in political science departments and assistants at research institutes. Teams of them were assigned to represent eight countries at a conference: the Federal Republic of Germany, the German Democratic Republic, and United States, the Soviet Union, France, Britain, Czechoslovakia, and Poland.

In the first session of the experiment, each team was presented with a list of statements, examples of which are given below. It was understood that as the "final product" of the conference, a communiqué would be issued consisting of a selection of statements (which could be modified). Such a communiqué would be issued only if all the delegates agreed to it. That is, every delegation had veto power. The following are examples from the list of statements.

1. The participants of the conference unite in their endeavor for complete general disarmament under international control.

3. The participants declare their readiness to renounce in their mutual relations the application of threat or violence in any form whatsoever.

4. The existing borders in Europe are inviolable; they may be changed only by mutual agreement.

9. The participants recognize each other as equal.

12. West Berlin has a particular status and does not belong to the Federal Republic.

14. The participants welcome and confirm that in Central Europe neither atomic nor biological nor chemical weapons are being produced.

18. On the basis of a divided Germany, lasting peace in Europe is not possible.

24. All foreign troops stationed in any European country shall be withdrawn.

In the first session, each team was to mark each of the statements "+" or "−" to signify whether it wanted the statement to be included in the final communiqué or not.

In the second session, the teams broke up to form four different committees with one delegate per state each. Each committee was to engage in a general discussion, with the statements as issues. The object of this session was not to come to any agreements but simply to become familiar with the points of view of the various governments represented by the teams. In other words, this was a role-playing session. In the third session, the national teams reconvened. This time numerical values (utilities) had to be assigned by each team to each of the statements on the list, ranging from large negative values attached to least acceptable statements, to large positive values attached to most acceptable ones. The value 0 was fixed to represent "status quo"; that is, "no communiqué." Utilities were assume to be additive. That is, the value of a combination of statements was to be the algebraic sum of the individual values. Totally unacceptable statements, those to which a team would decide not to agree under any circumstances, were to be given negative values sufficiently large numerically to outweigh any positive value of any other combination. The scale was arbitrary (it was later normalized). These normalized values attached by the teams to the statements cited above are given in Table 20.4.

Table 20.4.   Numerical Degrees of Preference for Various Position Statements by Members of a Simulated European Security Conference

Statement	FRG	Czech.	GDR	France	Britain	U.S.A	USSR	Poland
1	0.000	0.034	0.100	0.020	0.111	0.005	0.050	0.026
3	0.189	0.086	0.159	0.202	0.139	0.032	0.500	0.257
4	0.038	0.137	0.100	0.071	0.111	0.054	−0.100	−0.257
9	0.095	0.017	0.120	0.071	0.000	0.000	0.100	0.051
12	−2.273	0.017	0.159	−1.212	−0.083	−2.688	1.000	0.103
14	0.019	0.086	0.159	0.202	0.111	0.011	−0.500	0.257
18	0.758	−0.120	−2.191	0.020	0.000	0.161	−5.810	−0.514
24	−2.273	0.068	−0.100	0.505	−1.667	−5.376	0.000	0.180

Source: Adapted from Reich (1977).

If the simulated conference were to be modeled by an *n*-person game in characteristic function form, the function v would have to be defined. The veto power conferred on every player (team) implies $v(S) = 0$ for all proper subsets S of the set of players N. That is to say, in the absence of unanimous agreement, status quo (no communiqué) would be the outcome. As for $v(N)$, this quantity can be defined only if the utilities can be added not only across the statements for each player (as already assumed), but also across the players, which would be a much stronger assumption.

In the theory of *n*-person cooperative games, "side payments" are usually assumed to be possible. In certain political settings they may be. In American political jargon, they are called "log rolling" and refer to behind-the-scenes agreements like "I will vote for your proposal if you vote for mine." Bribes, too, are not unknown. On the basis of such assumptions, $v(N)$ could be defined as the maximal algebraic sum of utilities that can be achieved collectively by the eight teams. Thus all the statements with the exception of 12, 18, and 24 would be included in the communiqué to obtain the maximal joint utility. Even in the absence of side payments and without additivity across players, the inclusion of statements 1, 3, and possibly a slight modification of 4 would have made everyone's payoff larger than that conferred by status quo. That is to say, status quo was certainly not Pareto-optimal in this situation. It is in this sense that the final outcome that actually obtained (no communiqué) appeared to violate collective rationality.

In this connection, the very different results obtained in the simulated European security conference and in the NASA experiment are instructive. To be sure, in the former experiment, the cards were stacked against consensus by the nature of the political situation simulated and by the absence of an arbitrating authority; whereas in the NASA experiment, some solution was guaranteed by the procedure itself. But it is precisely this difference between the two situations that is clearly brought out by structural analysis. The value of the analysis is in its potential for suggesting ways of *structuring* conflict situations so as to make them amenable to collectively rational solutions.

AN OVERVIEW

Game-theoretic models of conflict of interest can be useful tools in experimental social psychology. As often happens during the development of a new approach, there was a "wave" of investigations using experimental games, especially in the 1960s. A picture of this "wave" is shown in Figure 20.2.

It is fair to ask what knowledge was generated by this large experience. The answer will not satisfy the "practically" oriented. Following a firmly established tradition of experimental psychology, most of the experiments were undertaken

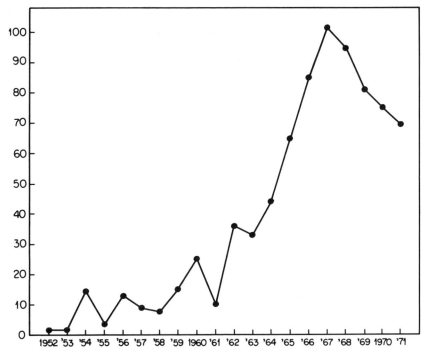

Figure 20.2. Numbers of experimental game papers published yearly during the 1950s and 1960s.

to test specific hypotheses about the behavior of the subjects to be observed in the experiment. Thus every investigation was designed so as to extract "a bit of knowledge" in the hope that a coherent theory could be built with the aid of these bits. That a well-formed theory of conflict has not been generated by game experiments can be attributed to different circumstances. The most important of these are the severely constrained conditions under which laboratory experiments must be performed. They preclude generalizations from experimental results to real life, not only because the laboratory experiment is a drastically simplified model of a conflict situation but also because the subjects are not likely to be a representative sample of the general population. Indeed, the personality of the subject is often regarded as a principal independent variable in game experiments. The large number of independent variables and the divergent interests of the investigators have contributed to confusing the picture.

Another circumstance is related to the sociology of science, to be discussed further in the last chapter. The natural striving to produce publishable results induces researchers to choose hypotheses that seem likely to be experimentally confirmed. Thus experiments often serve to corroborate ideas suggested by common sense, and contributions to knowledge remain slight.

The contribution of game experiments to general knowledge could be considerable, but one should not expect them to answer general questions about human behavior in conflict situations. Rather, the experiments should provide a framework of cumulated knowledge confined to systematically varied experimental situations. Seen in this way, the experiments provide the opportunity of extending the laboratory method to the study of human behavior. Even though the environment in which behavior is studied is severely restricted by the demands of controlled experimentation, nevertheless, game experiments permit investigations of components of behavior that have a distinct psychological flavor As we have seen, motivations reminding of "trust," "suspicion," "cooperation," "solidarity," and so on can be studied by operationalizing these concepts in terms of clearly observed and quantifiable actions. What, if any, relation these simulated motivational pressures have to "real life" can be surmised only in the light of long-systematized experience and critical evaluations of experimental results.

NOTES

[1] A bibliography compiled by Guyer and Perkel (1972) lists over a thousand known experiments. More than half of these were on Prisoner's Dilemma.

[2] There is an alternative explanation. In the chosen threat condition, each player has the opportunity to "retreat" from the confrontation. He has no such opportunity in the imposed threat condition. Consequently, the players in the chosen threat condition can afford to bargain harder, and this may account for the larger differences between the top dog's and the underdog's final offer.

[3] It must nevertheless be stressed that the argument just offered is far from convincing. Since the value of the random variable $(1/2)(|R_1 - R_2| + |C_1 - C_2|)$ cannot be negative, its mean must be positive (as long as its variance is positive), whatever the distribution of this random variable. Therefore, as long as the expected value of this variable under the null (symmetry) hypothesis is not known, we cannot determine the magnitude of the deviation of the observed mean from the expected mean and so have no way of justifying the acceptance or the rejection of the null hypothesis.

PART IV

PROBLEMS OF QUANTIFICATION

CHAPTER TWENTY ONE

Parameters and Indices

In the Introduction, where we sought a way of specifying objectively what we meant by the assertion "this table is large," we constructed an *index*; namely, the length of the table expressed in centimers. In his *World Dynamics*, Forrester singled out an index intended to represent quantitatively the "quality of life," composed of production levels (as positive contributions), measures of crowdedness, and pollution (as negative contributions).

The indices just mentioned are either themselves directly measurable quantities or are composed of such. As their components vary, the indices vary. In a mathematical model they may serve as either independent or dependent variables. Thus in the "If . . . , then . . ." paradigm, they enter the "if" part (if they are regarded as independent variables) or the "then" part (if they are regarded as dependent variables). But they imply in themselves no connection between the "if" and the "then" and therefore are not subject to validating tests, except possibly checks on accuracy of observations.

These *quantification indices* can serve as components of purely descriptive models devoid of predictive content. For instance, the observed time course of the armament budget of a state confined to historical data constitutes a purely descriptive model, where this variable can be regarded as an index of "hostility," of the influence of the military establishment on its body politic, or whatever this variable is assumed to reflect. In a learning experiment, the learning curve in which cumulated errors are recorded as a (smoothed) function of the number of trials generates an index that may be regarded as the "rate of learning"; namely, the negative second derivative of the curve, inasmuch as this derivative can be interpreted as the rate of decrease of the probability of making an error. Here some mathematical reasoning is involved in defining the index. Nevertheless, the index reflects no *theoretical* assumptions about how learning proceeds. It is merely a way of describing what has been observed, even though it is suggested by a quantification of an intuitively grasped theoretical construct—"rate of learning." As such, the quantification cannot be falsified except, perhaps, by discovery of inaccuracies in observations or in the recordings of observations.

Another type of index is represented by a *parameter* of a mathematical model. Recall that a parameter represents a quantity that remains constant in some specific situation but may vary from one situation to another. In our pendulum model in the Introduction, the independent variable was time and the dependent variable was x, the deviation of the pendulum from its equilibrium position. Three other quantities entered the model; namely, x_0, the initial deviation; L, the length of the rod supporting the pendulum; and g, the acceleration of gravity. These were parameters, held constant in each situation. Now we may deliberately vary x_0 and also g, the latter by going to different localities or to the moon. Suppose we perform experiments on the same pendulum. Will L truly remain constant? Of course, we can answer this question directly by measuring L in each instance. In doing so, we shall very likely be satisfied that L does remain constant. There is, however, another way of posing the question concerning the constancy of L, which involves our *theory* of the pendulum. Recall the equation deduced from that theory:

$$x = x_0 \cos(\sqrt{g/L}\, t). \tag{21.1}$$

From Equation 21.1 we deduce

$$\text{arc } \cos(x/x_0) = \sqrt{g/L}\, t \tag{21.2}$$

$$\frac{[\text{arc } \cos(x/x_0)]^2}{t^2} = g/L \tag{21.3}$$

$$L = g\, \frac{t^2}{[\text{arc } \cos(x/x_0)]^2}. \tag{21.4}$$

According to Equation 21.4, L is constant if the right side of that equation is constant. But this is just what our theory implies. Therefore, the observation that the right side of Equation 21.4 remains constant (regardless of how the manipulable parameters x_0 and g are varied and how the dependent variable x varies with the independent variable t in consequence of these manipulations) is a corroboration of our theory. On the other hand, any variation of L in consequence of these manipulations that is not attributable to experimental error will constitute a falsification of our theory.

Now let us imagine a civilization of intelligent extraterrestial beings who cannot measure lengths directly. The meter stick as a measuring instrument was never invented in that civilization. However, those creatures can measure angles and time intervals. They construct an exact theory of the pendulum in which only the angle of deviation appears as the dependent variable. Their model is

$$\frac{d^2}{dt}(L\theta) = g \sin \theta. \tag{21.5}$$

Recall that in the Introduction we used the approximation $L\theta = x$ to get a mathematically simpler approximate solution. Our beings cannot test the simplified model because they cannot measure x; but being good mathematicians, they solve the differential Equation 21.5. They will get a more complicated expression in θ, θ_0, and t, but this expression will still be equated to a constant, L/g. Their theory will be corroborated if that expression remains constant for all values of the manipulated parameter θ_0. (We assume that their acceleration of gravity is constant over the entire surface of their planet.)

As they experiment with *different* pendulums, this constant will vary, but it will still be constant for the same pendulum for all values of θ_0. Therefore, they will regard this constant as a characteristic of a *particular* pendulum, and they will give it some name. When we examine their theory, we will, of course, immediately recognize the significance of that constant. It is simply the length of the pendulum measured in appropriate units (to incorporate the constant g). To them, however, the constant will represent a sophisticated parameter specifying a characteristic of the pendulum and deriving its importance from the fact that it *is* a constant feature of the pendulumn's behavior.

The example illustrates the second type of index—the parameter—one derived from a corroboration of a mathematical model, which asserts that some combination of manipulable and nonmanipulable independent variables and of dependent variables is a constant in a given context. The theoretical leverage of such indices derives from the circumstance that they usually suggest new theoretical constructs in terms of which a substantive theory can be developed. Such indices enrich a theory with quantities that are not directly measurable but which may be of great heuristic importance in the development of the theory. Physics is very rich in such theoretical constructs.

EXAMPLES FROM PHYSICS

Let a block of wood be dragged along a horizontal surface with a small constant velocity. The force required to drag it can be recorded on a spring balance, and so can the weight of the block. Now the weight can be varied; for example, by piling blocks on top of one another. We can verify experimentally that within a certain range of velocities, the force will be relatively independent of the area of contact between the two surfaces and proportional to the weight dragged. Thus if F is the force required to drag a pile of blocks of total weight W at a constant velocity, we will observe

$$\frac{F}{W} = \mu, \text{ a constant.} \tag{21.6}$$

This constant μ is a parameter. It becomes a convenient way to quantify the "amount of friction" per unit force pressing two surfaces together. It characterizes the nature of contact between a particular pair of surfaces.

The operationally defined theoretical constructs of physics can all be regarded as parameters: the electrical resistance per unit length of a wire, the rigidity coefficient of an elastic body, the specific heat of a substance, and so on. All of these appear as "constants" in mathematical models, but they are constant only to the extent that they characterize a specific situation. There are also "universal" constants in physics, like the gravitational constant or Planck's constant. These remain, as far as we know, constant in all physical situations.

EXAMPLES FROM THE BEHAVIORAL SCIENCES

Prospects of discovering "universal constants" in the behavioral sciences are practically nil. The mathematicizing behavioral scientist must content himself with parameters and can consider himself fortunate if he finds any.

In preceding chapters, we have already dealt with both *ad hoc* indices and parameters. For instance, in our discussion of social mobility, we introduced some *ad hoc* indices. They represented no more than operational definitions of social mobility, such as the proportion of father-son pairs in which the son belongs to a different social stratum than the father. We also introduced a stochastic model of social mobility, where the transition probabilities of a Markov chain were assumed to be constant. If that model can be regarded as valid (that is, if the transition probabilities actually appear to be constant), these constants can be regarded as parameters characterizing a given society.

In stochastic models of learning, the operators modifying the state of the learning organism were defined in terms of two parameters, α_1 and α_2 (see p. 248). If the model is corroborated in the sense of successfully predicting a distribution of a population of learning organisms among the various states, the parameter associated with the "success" operator α_1 can be interpreted as an index of learning reinforced by a reward of the correct response. The parameter α_2, associated with the "failure" operator, can be interpreted as an index of learning reinforced by punishment of the wrong response. These parameters characterize a particular organism (usually a particular population of organisms) as well as a particular experimental situation.

The theoretical importance of a parameter is reflected in the range of situations in which it remains constant. Galileo, in his experiments with cannonballs rolling down inclined planes, established the constancy of the ratio s/t^2, where s is the distance transversed in time t. This ratio remained constant for cannonballs of arbitrary weight, but it varied with the angle of inclination of the inclined plane. However, the angle of inclination θ can be incorporated into the model so that the constancy of the expression $s/t^2 \sin(\theta)$ can be established. This expression remains constant for all weights of the cannonballs and for all angles of inclination and is, therefore, of greater theoretical importance. Since this constant involves the acceleration of gravity $(s/t^2)\sin(\theta) = g/2$, it varies with location. The acceleration of gravity on the surface of a planet can be expressed in terms of the geometry and the distribution of mass of the planet and the gravitation constant G. This latter constant is a universal constant and is, therefore, of the greatest theoretical significance.

As has been said, in the behavioral sciences this sort of "final" reference to universal constants is not to be expected. But a mathematical behavioral theory can be said to advance to the extent that the value of parameter indices can be derived from deeper theoretical considerations. This process does not go very far. At best one hopes to establish empirical relations between parameters and variables related to the experimental situation. For instance, in stochastic learning theory one could try to establish relations between the learning parameters α_1 and α_2 and magnitudes of rewards or punishments. The same could be done with regard to parameters of equilibrium distributions deduced from stochastic models. Here a particular interpretation of the parameters can become a point of departure of a particular theory.

As an example, take the negative binomial distribution of the random variable that represents the number of accidents suffered in some stretch of time by an arbitrarily selected individual of a factory. This distribution involves two parameters. As we have seen, these parameters are functions of the intensity of the underlying Poisson process and of the variability of the population with regard to "accident proneness" (if we assume a heterogeneous population). Observing the dependence of these parameters on the milieu (assuming that the form of the distribution is negative binomial in different milieus), we can "disentangle" the two influences and estimate the interaction between them.

To take another example, recall the derivation of a generalized version of Zipf's law from Mandelbrot's entropy-maximizing model (see p. 165ff). The derivation suggests an index characteristic of a language or a language corpus. Mandelbrot (1953) called this index the "temperature" of the language (or of the language corpus). The term seems bizarre, but of course it has nothing to do with physical temperature; it is merely mathematically analogous to it. The relevant interpretation of the index has to do with the "richness" of the language. However, it reflects more than just the size of the vocabulary. Having got hold of such an index, one can study its change in time. Does it decrease or increase monotonically? Does it pass through a maximum or a minimum? How can these observations be related to the history of the language?

As we have seen, the significance of parameter indices depends on the validation of a mathematical model. We do not ordinarily think of analytic-descriptive models as requiring validation since they are usually confined to a compact description of a particular set of data. Nevertheless, the structure revealed by such a model may be validated in other situations. Consider factor analysis applied to an I.Q. test. It reveals a relatively small number of "dimensions" ("factors of the mind," as L. L. Thurstone, the pioneer of factor analysis, called them). The model determines the loadings of the various components of the test on each of the factors. This means that we can use representative components to predict an individual's score on all the components of the test. Comparison of the theoretically calculated score and the observed score is a test of the model.

If the model is sufficiently corroborated, the factors can be "taken seriously" as representing principal dimensions of mental ability. The factor scores obtained from the profile of the I.Q. test score acquire the status of parameter indices, and we can study their variation with age, state of mind or health, population samples, and so on.

In contrast to a parameter which represents a constant in a mathematical model that characterizes a particular situation, an *ad hoc* index need not be constant. The principal use of *ad hoc* indices is that of providing objective bases of comparison, either between systems or between the states of a system in the course of time. For example, all the indices in the Forrester-Meadows global model (see Chapter 4) were *ad hoc* indices. They did not emerge as parameters of dynamic systems, but were defined as certain combinations of variables for the purpose of operationalizing the concepts in terms of which the model was formulated. Once defined, these indices were traced through a historical period, then extrapolated (under assumptions of interactions between them) into the future.

Sometimes an *ad hoc* index exhibits some regularity as it varies, so that its variation can be expressed by a formula. If the constants of that formula can be interpreted in terms related to the situation studied, they become parametric indices.

To take an example, consider a highly simplified model of the longevity of marriages based on the assumption that the incidence of divorce in a population of married couples is a chance event with a constant probability of occurrence in any short period of time. That is to say, the divorces are representable by a Poisson process (see Chapter 8). We fix our attention on a cohort of married couples; that is, a population of couples married at some time $t = 0$. In practice, of course, such a cohort will be defined as the population of couples married during a given year or month, but we are treating time as a continuous variable in our model. Then the proportion of couples still married at time t will be given by

$$P(t) = e^{-at}, \tag{21.7}$$

where a is a constant. In our model, a is a parametric index that characterizes our population.

One way to test the model is by assessing the "goodness of fit" of a curve represented by Equation 21.7 to the observed values of $P(t)$, whereby the constant a is chosen so as to give the "best" fit. Another way to test the model is by examining the "constancy" of a, determined by readings taken at successive times. Differentiating Equation 21.7 with respect to t, we obtain

$$dP(t)/dt = -aP(t) \tag{21.8}$$

or

$$\frac{-1}{P(t)} \frac{dP(t)}{dt} = a.$$

In taking readings, we represent the differentials by finite increments of $P(t)$ and of t. Taking the increments of t as units (say years) so that $dt = 1$, we rewrite Equations 21.8 as

$$\frac{P(t-1) - P(t)}{P(t-1)} = a. \tag{21.9}$$

If the model is accurate, then the ratio of decrements during successive years to the proportion of couples still married at the beginning of each year should be constant during the period under observation.

Suppose this is *not* the case. Then the right side of Equations 21.9 is not a constant but a quantity that depends on t. If we simply record this quantity, it becomes an *ad hoc* index characterizing both our population and each given year. In that case, we no longer have a mathematical model since nothing can be deduced from it. We have only a record of observations.

Suppose now that a, although it varies, can be represented by a reasonably "smooth" function of t; that is, one that can be expressed as a relatively simple formula, say

$$a(t) = a_0 e^{-bt}. \tag{21.10}$$

Here $a_0 = a(0)$, and we can "read off" this value by noting that

$$a(0) = \frac{P(0) - P(1)}{P(0)}. \tag{21.11}$$

Equation 21.10 predicts the values of a that correspond to different values of t. This equation may itself be no more than a compact statement about observed values of a. Or it may have been deduced from some other model. If so, then b plays the part of a parametric index characterizing the period of time examined, and its "constancy" can be tested to corroborate the validity of that model.

If a declines with time, as is implied by Equation 21.10, this trend can be interpreted in various ways. It can be interpreted to mean that the "pressure for divorce," of which a is an index, declines because of some extraneous influence, say because divorce becomes socially less acceptable. Or it can be interpreted to mean that the pressure for divorce decreases as the duration of a marriage increases. Or it can be interpreted in terms of the heterogeneity of our population (some couples being more divorce prone than others). The last interpretation invokes a "natural selection" principle. The most unstable couples break up soon after marriage, leaving the more stable ones in the cohort. If the first explanation is correct, it might be reflected in differential *initial* divorce rates in populations of couples married in successive years. The second and third interpretations are more difficult to "pit against each other," but this can sometimes be done by examining additional information. Each of these interpretations will confer a different meaning on the parametric index b, which now characterizes the situation.

In summary, parametric indices are integral components of *mathematical* models and for this reason are often theoretically suggestive because their constancy in a given circumscribed context points to some stable feature of that context. The very existence of such a constancy is "theoretically pregnant." In contrast, *ad hoc* indices, being merely descriptive, can *always* be constructed if observations can be quantified. They suggest no theory because they cannot be falsified. They are what they are. *Ad hoc* indices serve another purpose: that of formulating economical quantitative descriptions of configurations or of phenomena. Nevertheless, the *choice* of *ad hoc* indices with which to describe observations may be guided by theoretical or even ideological considerations. The choice may reflect an investigator's bias, either his inclination toward a particular theoretical conception or his values. Thus the predominance of economic or technical components in indices of the "standard of living" reflects a culturally conditioned bias. Examples of indices reflecting biases that are possibly introduced deliberately are also encountered. Such may be the numerous gross indices of traffic fatality rates used in different countries. These indices can be calculated in terms of fatalities per capita in a population or fatalities per vehicle, per kilometer of road, per vehicle-kilometer traveled, or per passenger-kilometer traveled. Some of these indices make a country look "good" compared with other countries; some bad. Similarly, "amount of political awareness" in a country may be indexed by the percent of eligible voters showing up at the polls, by the extent of suffrage, or by the social composition of legislative bodies. Each index may give a very different picture. "Internal violence" in a country may be indexed by the number of murders per year per capita, by the frequency of riots, or by the frequency of terrorist acts. The "war proneness" of a nation or of a "community of nations" in a given historical period can be indexed by the frequency of wars, by their mean duration, or by numbers of casualties. Again each index may give a very different impression.

The chapters to follow will be devoted to investigations in which *ad hoc* indices play a central role. Strictly speaking, therefore, some of the formulations that are called "models" by the investigators are not mathematical models as this term has been used in this book because the formulations are predominantly descriptive and do not advance falsifiable hypotheses. These approaches are quantitative without being genuinely mathematical. They were included because quantification is often a precursor of mathematization.

CHAPTER TWENTY TWO

Quantification of Power

The political scientist looking to mathematical models as points of anchorage for a theory faces the problem of selecting some key concepts that are relevant to the content of political theory and can also be quantified in an unambiguous way. The concept of "power" is often singled out by political scientists as a key concept of their discipline. Hence attempts to define this concept operationally in terms of quantities that are in principle measurable have been common. We will examine some such attempts.

Suppose a child stands on a corner in New York and commands all the drivers of cars to drive on the right side of the street. The fact that they do so is certainly not to be taken as evidence that he has power over the drivers. If he seriously insists that he does, we can attribute this to a childish fantasy. The illusory nature of his alleged "power" is easily discovered. Were he to change his command and order the drivers to drive on the left, he would not be obeyed. Also, no one would obey him in London or in Tokyo if he ordered the drivers to drive on the right.

On the other hand, consider a police officer standing on a corner and ordering all the drivers to turn to the right although the road straight ahead is clear and there is no sign directing a compulsory right turn. The fact that the drivers obey his command *is* evidence of the police officer's power in that situation.

The difference between the two situations is inherent in R. A. Dahl's (1957) intuitive conception of power as a relation between two actors. *A* has power over *B* to the extent that *A* can induce *B* to do something *that B would ordinarily not do*. This concept immediately leads to a ramification of questions. If one actor has power over another, we might inquire into (1) *the source* or base of this power; (2) the *means* used in exercising it; (3) its *extent* (amount); and (4) its *scope* (the range of situations where it can be exercised). Dahl exemplifies these concepts by describing the power of the U.S. President over Congress. In exercising this power, the President may *promise* patronage. Other sources of his power are reflected in the circumstance that he may *threaten* to veto a bill, may *appeal* to the electorate by exercising his charisma, and so on. These are the sources of the President's power. The scope of his power is partly defined in the Constitution and partly a function of the specific relationship between him and Congress. The amount of power might be expressed probabilistically; for example, in terms of frequencies of successful attempts in exercising it.

Let A be an *actor*, who supposedly has power over a, called a *respondent*. Dahl introduces the following notation.

(A, w): A does w, where w is some action. For example, the President makes a nationwide appeal on television to increase taxes.

$(A, \bar{w})$: A does not do w.

(a, x): The respondent a does x. For example, Congress votes to increase taxes.

$(a, \bar{x})$: a does not do x.

Next, Dahl introduces the following conditional probabilities:

$P(a, x \mid A, w) = p_1$: the probability that a does x, given that A does w.

$P(a, x \mid A, \bar{w}) = p_2$: the probability that a does x, given that A does not do w.

It is evident that in order for the notion that A has power over a to be intuitively acceptable, three conditions must be satisfied. (1) A's action, designed to elicit compliance from a, must precede a's action identified with compliance. (2) There must be some "connection" between A and a; for instance, a communication channel. (3) The probability that a complies when A "exercises his power" must be larger than the probability that a performs the same act when A did not "exercise his power."

Consider the relation between D (Dahl) and J (Jones), his student. In accordance with the above notation:

(D, w): Dahl threatens to fail Jones if Jones does not read a certain book in a specified time.

$(D, \bar{w})$: no action on Dahl's part.

(J, x): Jones reads the book.

$P(J, x \mid D, w)$: the probability that Jones will read the book if Dahl threatens to fail him otherwise.

$P(J, x \mid D, \bar{w})$: the probability that Jones reads the book if Dahl does not threaten to fail him.

Now the amount of power of Dahl over Jones, given the means w and the action ordered x, can be defined as

$$M(A/a: w, x) = P(a, x \mid A, w) - P(a, x \mid A, \bar{w}) = p_1 - p_2, \qquad (22.1)$$

where Dahl is the actor A and Jones is the respondent a.

Clearly, A's power over a is zero if $p_1 = p_2$. Its maximum value is unity. It can also be negative if A's attempts to induce a to do x result in a *decrease* of the probability that a does x. In principle, negative power could be turned into positive power. All the actor has to do is to try to induce the respondent to do the opposite of what he intends him to do. Therefore, it is more meaningful to relate compliance to the actor's *intent* rather than to the specific means that he uses to effect compliance.

The measure of power expressed by Equation 22.1 is too situation-bound to be of use in political theory. What is wanted is a basis of comparison of the power of actors in more general situations. It was often said that Stalin was the most powerful individual of his time. Many will assent to this statement. But what does it mean concretely? Can we relate it to the definition of power offered?

The concept of scope enters at this point. In assessing the power of actors, we must relate it to the range of respondents and the range of actions that the respondents are induced to perform. A chairman of a meeting can induce a participant to refrain from speaking, but he cannot induce him to leave. In battle, an officer can induce his soldiers to shoot at the enemy or not to shoot, but he cannot induce them to shoot at each other, and he has no power or less power over soldiers not under his command. Most important, the social position of the respondents must be taken into consideration, which raises difficult questions concerning the comparability of power. A professor of political science may be able to induce 20 of her undergraduate students to support a certain piece of legislation. But we do not expect that she can induce 20 senators to support the same piece of legislation. Intuitively, we feel that the professor has less power than the President of the United States, who on occasions *can* induce 20 senators to support the measure. But how is this difference expressed?

Only if a set of actors $\{A, B, C, \ldots\}$, a set of associated respondents $\{a, b, c, \ldots\}$, a set of means $\{w, v, u, \ldots\}$, and a set of acts $\{x, y, z, \ldots\}$ are in some sense comparable is it possible to rank order the actors according to the power they possess over the respective respondents by some proposed measure of power.

It turns out that there is no way of defining "comparability" rigorously. What is comparable and what is not depends on the researcher's assessment. A certain element of subjectivity, therefore, is not removable from assessment of power.

The problem is closely related to that of defining the probability of an event, which in this case is incorporated in the definition of power. The most direct way of defining the probability of an event is in terms of the relative frequency of the event in a set of *comparable* events. In situations where comparability of events appears obvious, the problem is ignored. For instance, few people will object to estimating the probability that a coin comes up heads by the frequency with which it comes up heads in several tosses of the coin. The problem arises when the event in question cannot be regarded as an element of a set of "obviously" comparable events. For example, during the Cuban missile crisis in October 1962, some members of the National Security Council of the United

States and of the Combined Chiefs of Staff offered assessments of the "probability" that a nuclear war would break out between the Soviet Union and the United States. Some assessed it at $\frac{1}{3}$, some at $\frac{1}{2}$, and so on. Moreover, courses of action were advocated on the basis of these assessments. Now a nuclear war is an event that by its nature cannot occur with a "frequency." If, therefore, some connection is made between these assessments and experience, the connection must have been made to events that were *assumed* to be comparable; for example, instances of wars that broke out in "similar" crisis situations. To the objection that nuclear war is not comparable to other kinds of war and that every crisis is different there is no answer.

The example cited is an extreme case of incomparability of events, where, therefore, the concept of probability cannot be applied in any objectively meaningful sense. Between this situation and that of repeated tosses of a coin there is a gradation of situations. In certain institutionalized political processes, it may be justifiable to define a sample space of "comparable" events so that probabilities can be meaningfully assessed. Such a situation was selected by Dahl to assess the relative power of U.S. senators.

To fix ideas, consider a set of "comparable" motions before the Senate. Prior to the roll call vote, as a result of which a motion is either passed or defeated, a particular senator may have done one of three things: (1) work for the motion; (2) work against the motion; (3) nothing. Associated with each course of action is an assessment of the "probability" that the Senate passes the motion; namely, on the basis of the frequency that motions for or against which the senator worked (or did nothing) were actually passed.

We have the following matrix.

Senator

		Works for motion	Works against motion	Does nothing
Senate	Passes motion	p_1	p_2	p_3
	Defeats motion	$1 - p_1$	$1 - p_2$	$1 - p_3$

Matrix 22.1

Now two measures of the senator's power (with respect to the set of motions) can be defined:

$M_1 = p_1 - p_3$: her power when she works for a motion.
$M_2 = p_3 - p_2$: her power when she works against a motion.

A measure of her "power" could be any reasonable combination of the two. The simplest such combination is the sum $M_1 + M_2 = p_1 - p_2 = M$. This index has maximum value unity when the Senate always passes a motion if the senator works for it and always defeats it if the senator opposes it. When she does nothing, the fate of the motion is not related to her power.

The method provides a measure of power of each senator relative to a set of issues. Dahl used a somewhat different method. He constructed for each pair of senators, S_1 and S_2, the following matrix:

$$S_1$$

		Favors the motion	Opposes the motion
S_2	Favors the motion	p_{11}	p_{12}
	Opposes the motion	p_{21}	p_{22}

Matrix 22.2

The entries are the frequencies with which the motion passes, given the senators' positions as determined by the roll call vote. Dahl then constructs two measures of S_1's power relative to that of S_2; namely:

$$M'_1(S_1) = |p_{11} - p_{12}|; \tag{22.2}$$

that is, the absolute value of the change in probability that the motion passes, given that S_2 favors the motion, when S_1 changes his stand from "for" to "against"; and

$$M'_2(S_1) = |p_{21} - p_{22}|; \tag{22.3}$$

that is, the absolute value of the change in probability that the motion passes, given that S_2 opposes the motion, when S_1 changes his position from "for" to "against."

The influence of S_1 is taken to be greater than the influence of S_2 if

$$|p_{11} - p_{12}| > |p_{11} - p_{21}| \text{ and } |p_{21} - p_{22}| > |p_{12} - p_{22}|. \tag{22.4}$$

Now the senators can be rank-ordered in accordance with their influence so defined, which, in this case, is identified with "power."

Note that defining power in terms of absolute values of probability differences makes no distinction between "positive power" and "negative power" (see p. 405). This interpretation might be justified if senators were aware of their "negative power" and used it in the way described above; that is, if they deliberately worked against motions that they favored and vice versa, assuming that their votes in the roll call corresponded to their declared attitudes. I suspect, however, that absolute values were introduced to avoid intransitivites that would otherwise arise in paired comparisons. At any rate, instances of "negative power" turned out to be rare, so that the absolute differences could be taken to be equivalent to algebraic differences. Both inequalities in Equation 22.4 reduce to

$$p_{21} > p_{12}, \tag{22.5}$$

being an indication that S_1 has more influence ("power") than S_2.

Using this measure, Dahl rank-ordered 34 U.S. senators (in the 1950s) according to their power with respect to two sets of issues, foreign policy and tax and economic policy. Classifying the magnitudes of influence into "high," "medium," and "low," he exhibited a table in which senators were identified who were high in influence on both issues, low on both, and high on one while low on the other.

Clearly, the method is open to objections, as Dahl himself points out. The vote of the senator on the roll call was assumed to be identical with his position on the motion previous to the vote. This is, of course, not necessarily the case. Dahl calls this the problem of the "chameleon." In the extreme case, the "chameleon" always guesses the fate of the motion before the vote is taken and votes with the majority. This practice would greatly inflate his "power" as measured above. The other objection concerns the case when a senator always follows the lead of another senator. Thus his power would appear to be equal to that of his mentor. Dahl calls this the problem of the satellite. If one could discover the extent of these perturbations, one could easily take care of them. One could treat chameleon activity as "doing nothing." Since the "doing nothing" column has no bearing on the measure, cases of the chameleon (or satellite) activity could be simply ignored. Conceptually, therefore, these well-known aspects of political life create no difficulties for the construction of the proposed measures. They do, however, pose serious research problems; namely, those of identifying such activities. (Recall the difficulties associated with the possibility of false reporting in the derivation of compromise solutions, as in the trajectory selection problem discussed in Chapter 19.)

The power index proposed by Dahl is an operationalization of a particular concept of power, based on comparing probabilities of events that the actor tries to effect or to prevent. The index is calculated directly from data. A mathematical model of power distribution among a set of actors, on the other hand, leads to construction of indices on the basis of purely theoretical considerations —without recourse to data. These models can be used descriptively to present "pictures" of decision-making bodies; as components of an explanatory theory to explain the behavior of such bodies or of their members; or predictively, to predict such behavior.

We have already examined one such model and an index derived from it; namely, the Shapley value. We will examine two others, defined in the context of *simple n*-person games. These are games in which the characteristic function $v(S)$ (see p. 354) can assume only two values, which without loss of generality can be taken as 0 and 1. Coalitions S with $v(S) = 1$ are called *winning* coalitions; the remaining, *losing* coalitions. In a political context, the winning coalitions are those that are able to effect a decision under the rules governing such decisions.

For instance, let $N = 1, 2, \ldots$ be a set of actors, each with one vote, and let any simple majority be able to effect a decision. Then the set of coalitions $\{S \mid S \subset N, |S| > n/2\}$ is the set of winning coalitions. If members have unequal numbers of votes, then those combinations of members that jointly have more than half the total number of votes are the winning coalitions under the majority rule. Similarly, winning coalitions can be defined under different decision rules; for example, the two-thirds majority rule, rules where certain actors have a tie-breaking right, a veto right, and so on.

In the context of a simple game, the Shapley value is known also as the Shapley-Shubik index. Another measure of power is the Banzhaf index. Consider a set of winning coalitions and an actor i, who is included in all of them. Such an actor is called an *essential* member of a winning coalition if by leaving it he changes the remaining coalition to a losing one. Let n_i be the number of coalitions in which i is essential. Then the Banzhaf power index of actor i is given by

$$\beta_i = \frac{n_i}{\sum_j n_j}. \tag{22.6}$$

Still another index is obtained by considering only the *minimal* winning coalitions. These are the winning coalitions in which every member is essential. It is further assumed that a minimal winning coalition divides the "prize" equally among its members. Then the power index proposed by Deegan and Packel (1979) is

$$\rho_i = \frac{1}{|M|} \sum_{\substack{S \subseteq M \\ i \in S}} \frac{v(S)}{|S|}. \tag{22.7}$$

As has been said, these theoretically constructed indices can be used in two ways. When an index is used descriptively, the associated distribution of power can serve for comparison of different decision-making bodies, of the effects of different decision rules, and so on. For example, the theoretical distribution of power can be compared with the distribution of parliamentary seats among political parties. It should be clear that the distribution of power as defined by the indices can differ widely from the distribution of votes in a decision-making body. For example, in the three-person body with a distribution of votes (50, 49, 1), the Shapley-Shubik index under majority rule induces the power distribution (2/3, 1/6, 1/6); the Banzhaf index (3/5, 1/5, 1/5); and the Deegan-Packel index (1/2, 1/4, 1/4). Next, the sensitivity of the power distribution to changes in the distribution of votes, in the decision rules, or in the composition of the body can be examined. One can ask, for example, how the expansion of the Security Council of the United Nations from 11 to 15 members in 1965 affected the distribution of power in it. Or one could ask how the distribution of power would be affected if two instead of one of the Big Five were required to veto a decision. In legislative bodies of countries with parliamentary systems, parties usually vote in blocks. In the United States, in contrast, party lines are frequently crossed. How does the degree of "looseness" of party discipline affect the distribution of power?

All these implications of theoretically constructed power indices serve in describing and comparing structures of decision-making bodies. They may reveal features of these structures that are not immediately apparent. However, in this role, the indices are not related to the behavior of decision-making bodies or of their members. If a power distribution model of this sort is to be used in an explanatory or predictive theory, observable political *events* must be derived from it. For example, the composition of governments (cabinets) in countries with parliamentary systems depends on the composition of an elected parliament. An empirical test of a theoretical power index could consist, for example, of a comparison between derived and observed frequencies of participation of various political parties in a series of governments. As is well-known, governments in countries with several political parties of comparable size change frequently. Some have had scores of governments within a few decades, permitting statistical evaluation of the comparisons. We will give some examples of each kind of application.

DESCRIPTIVE APPLICATIONS OF THEORETICAL POWER INDICES

R. D. Luce and A. A. Rogow (1956) described the power distribution in the American federal legislature by means of the Shapley-Shubik index. This body consists of three chambers, the Senate, the House of Representatives, and the President. The President belongs, of course, to the executive branch of the government. However, to the extent that he can exercise veto power, he can be regarded as a third chamber of the legislature. To pass a measure, a simple majority of both houses and the signature (or abstention) of the President are required. The President's veto can be overridden by two-third majorities in both houses. Ordinarily, only two parties are represented in the Congress. Partly discipline is "loose" in the sense that party lines are frequently crossed in voting for or against measures. Senators and representatives can be roughly classified as "diehards"—those who always vote with their party—and "mugwumps"—those who at times vote with the other party. Winning coalitions are combinations of senators, representatives, and/or the President, who can pass a measure.

If voting were entirely independent of party affiliation, 1/6 of the total power would be concentrated in the President, according to the Shapley-Shubik index and the above decision rules. However, since voting is partly determined by party affiliation, the distribution of power depends on the proportions of die-hards and mugwumps in the two houses and on whether the President himself is a diehard or mugwump. "To have power" in this context is to have a positive share in the distribution of power. Luce and Rogow have deduced the following results.

1. In most cases, winning coalitions can form, assuming party lines can be crossed. The only exception is when the President is a diehard of the minority party, and the majority party cannot muster a $\frac{2}{3}$ majority even with the defectors of the minority party. The latter part of this result is intuitively obvious, for then the President will veto any bill passed by Congress, and Congress will not be able to override the veto. One might note in passing that American presidents frequently belong to the minority party. Also, two-thirds majorities in both houses are comparatively rare. Thus defectors are a political necessity in the United States: without them, the legislative process would be not infrequently paralyzed.

2. The President is "weak" when the majority party has a $\frac{2}{3}$ majority in both houses, regardless of the party to which the President belongs. That is to say, the President cannot influence legislation one way or another unless he enlists the aid of defectors.

3. When neither party can muster more than a simple majority even with defectors, the President has power (that is, the power of the veto can be fully utilized).

4. The minority party has power only if the President belongs to it and is a diehard.

5. If the defectors from a majority party combined with the minority party are not a majority, then the majority diehards have power. The only other case where they have power is when the President is a majority diehard and the minority can muster only a simple majority together with the majority defectors.

6. Minority diehards have power only when the President is a diehard of that party, the majority party has only a simple majority, and the minority party can muster a majority together with the majority defectors.

Clearly, these results can be deduced by common-sense considerations; for instance, by examining the cases when the President can decide the fate of a bill by exercising his veto or not, the cases when a minority party can push a bill through or block it with the aid of majority defectors, and so on. The results do not even go so far as to analyze specific situations, as is frequently done by seasoned politicians who know by experience how many defectors can be expected when a particular issue comes up, how the President "feels" about a particular bill, and so on. The one advantage of the formal analysis is that the deductive machinery developed in it can be applied to much more complex situations. It is the same with classical mathematics and with symbolic logic. Indices can be of assistance when common-sense reasoning gets entangled in language and puts limits on human attention and memory.

Since, as we have seen, the distribution of power as determined by a theoretical index need not correspond to the distribution of votes in a decision-making body, it may be interesting to compare the distributions of power on the basis of various indices with the underlying distributions of votes. Table 22.1 shows a fictitious distribution of votes and corresponding distributions of power on the basis of three different indices.

Table 22.1.

Actors	A	B	C	D
Votes	50	20	20	10
Power distribution				
Shapley-Shubik	0.75	0.083	0.083	0.083
Banzhaf	0.7	0.1	0.1	0.1
Deegan-Packel	0.625	0.125	0.125	0.125
Power: vote ratio				
Shapley-Shubik	1.5	0.42	0.42	0.83
Banzhaf	1.4	0.5	0.5	1.0
Deegan-Packel	1.25	0.612	0.612	1.25

As can be seen from the table, the voting distribution underestimates A's power and overestimates B's and C's power as measured by all three indices. D's power as measured by the Shapley-Shubik index is overestimated by the voting distribution but his power measured by the Deegan-Packel index is underestimated.

It is also interesting to observe that the use of a power index can lead to a counterintuitive result. For example, given the vote distribution (5, 3, 2, 1, 1, 1), the power distribution deduced from the Deegan-Packel index turns out to be (18/60, 9/60, 11/60, 11/60), whereby the actors with one vote have more power than the actor with two votes.

R. J. Johnston (1978) calculated the Banzhaf power distribution and the corresponding power: vote ratios for nine countries in the European Council of Ministers and the European Parliament. His results are shown in Table 22.2. As can be seen from the table, the distribution of votes reflects the power index of six countries accurately in the Council of Ministers, overestimates that of two countries, and underestimates the power of one (Ireland). In the European Parliament, on the other hand, the power index of the four large countries is overestimated and that of the five small countries, especially of Luxembourg, the smallest, is underestimated. One might conjecture that the Benelux countries have considerably more political leverage in the European Parliament than in the Council of Ministers.

Table 22.2

Country	Council of Ministers		European Parliament	
	Power index	Power:vote ratio	Power index	Power:vote ratio
United Kingdom	0.174	1.01	0.174	0.88
France	0.174	1.01	0.174	0.88
Germany	0.174	1.01	0.174	0.88
Italy	0.174	1.01	0.174	0.88
Belgium	0.087	1.01	0.087	1.49
Netherlands	0.087	1.01	0.087	1.43
Luxembourg	0.043	0.84	0.043	2.97
Denmark	0.043	0.84	0.043	1.11
Ireland	0.043	1.26	0.043	1.19

EMPIRICAL TESTS OF THEORETICAL POWER INDICES

The Shapley-Shubik index was used in an empirical study by W. Riker (1959). Assuming party discipline, Riker examined the power structure of the French National Assembly in the years 1953 and 1954. The events of interest were the "migrations" of deputies from one party to another. In those years, 61 such migrations were observed involving 46 deputies. The question to be answered was whether the migrations tended to increase the power of deputies, as defined by the Shapley-Shubik index, who changed their party affiliation, assuming that the total power of a party was equally distributed among its members. The answer turned out to be no, which may mean either that other considerations took precedence over "increasing one's power," or that power defined in some other sense had greater salience in the perception of the deputies. Obviously, these possible conclusions do not carry the "theory" very far, but at least the construction of an index helps to pose concrete, verifiable hypotheses of political behavior, in contrast to purely verbal "theories," which all too often lead to endless arguments that cannot be settled by evidence one way or another.

The Banzhaf index was used in an empirical study by M. J. Holler (1978). The political structure of Finland is based on a multiparty system. Of her many political parties, 11 were represented in at least one government from 1948 to 1979. In this period, there were nine interelection intervals. The Banzhaf index β_{it} was calculated for each party i in each interelection period t, then weighted by the duration of the interval e_t. Thus the weighted sum

$$p_i = \sum_{t=1}^{9} e_t \beta_{it} \tag{22.8}$$

was taken to represent the average power of party i.

In each interelection interval t, party i could be a member of MWC_{it} potential minimum winning coalitions. This number was also weighted by the relative duration of the interval to obtain another index

$$M_i = \sum_{t=1}^{9} e_t MWC_{it}. \tag{22.9}$$

It should be noted that MWC is not necessarily a monotone function of the number of parliamentary seats assigned to a party. (See the analogous property of the Deegan-Packel index, p. 409). For instance, after the 1951 election, the Democratic Union of the Finnish People had 43 seats and an MWC index of 0.214, while the Finnish Social Democratic Party had 53 seats and an MWC index of 0.179. As in the case of the Deegan-Packel index, this "anomaly" is due to considering only minimal winning coalitions.

During the 30-year period examined, Finland had 62 governments. *Participation* of party i in the government was measured by the index

$$G_i = \sum_{r=1}^{62} t_r m_{ir}, \tag{22.10}$$

where t_r is the duration of government r ($r = 1, 2, \ldots, 62$), and m_{ir} is the relative number of chairs (ministries) which members of party i held in government r.

Finally, the average number of seats held by i in the 30-year period was measured by

$$S_i = \sum_{t=1}^{9} e_t s_{it}, \tag{22.11}$$

where s_{it} is the number of seats held by party i in interval t.

Table 22.3 shows the values of S_i, M_i, P_i, and G_i for the 11 political parties that participated in governments from 1948 to 1979.

Table 22.3

Party (i)	S_i	M_i	P_i	G_i
SDP	0.257	0.180	0.277	0.295
SKDL	0.213	0.171	0.205	0.047
KoK	0.152	0.149	0.103	0.037
Kesk	0.236	0.167	0.243	0.403
RKP	0.064	0.132	0.078	0.080
LKP	0.046	0.102	0.049	0.056
SMP	0.017	0.036	0.019	0.000
SKL	0.007	0.028	0.011	0.000
SKYP	0.000	0.002	0.001	0.000
SPK	0.000	0.002	0.001	0.000
SPSL	0.008	0.027	0.012	0.009

Taking the sums of absolute differences as rough measures of the degree of correspondence between the various indices and participation, we have

$$\sum_{i=1}^{11} |S_i - G_i| = 0.537$$

$$\sum_{i=1}^{11} |M_i - G_i| = 0.771$$

$$\sum_{i=1}^{11} |P_i - G_i| = 0.446.$$

Thus P_i, based on the Banzhaf index, turns out to be the best of the three indices of power of political parties as measured by participation in government; and M_i, based on membership in potential minimal winning coalitions, turns out to be the worst. Table 22.4 also shows that Party Kesk had a considerably larger share of participation in governments than would be surmised from its representation in Parliament or from other indices, whereas SKDL and Kok had a much smaller share. Needless to say, other factors must operate in the political process; for example, ideological considerations, personalities of politicians, and so on. Discrepancies between representation in Parliament and participation in governments can be discerned "with the naked eye." Other indices of power may provide some explanations for these discrepancies, which unlike "personality differences" and the like are general rather than *ad hoc*. Admittedly, the Banzhaf index was not a dramatic improvement in this case, but it may serve as an input into a developing theory of the political process.

CHAPTER TWENTY THREE

Mobilization, Assimilation, Pacification, and so on

For the quantitatively and empirically oriented behavioral scientist, selection and construction of indices is a problem of prime importance. The selection of *ad hoc* indices essentially involves the problem of providing operational definitions for intuited concepts deemed to be of importance in some field of inquiry. The construction of parameteric indices involves, as we have seen, the validation of a mathematical model. Such validations occur only rarely in contemporary quantitative social science. The bulk of quantitative studies entails only a systematized record of observations. Some information can be gained from these displays if trends are discernible in them. Schemata that are often called "models" are typically no more than diagrammatic representations of networks of "influences," showing what influences what and in which direction (by a plus or a minus). These protomodels, as they might more appropriately be called, could serve as points of departure for the construction of genuine mathematical models, in which the magnitudes of the "influences" would then appear as parametric indices.

In some of the following examples, demography and empirically oriented political science meet. The relevance of demography to politics stems from the fact that important political motivations are rooted in people's identification with the categories in which they are placed in a particular political situation. Among the most important sociopolitical problems of our time are those that are generated by such differentiation; for example, ethnic differentiation within a common political system. Serious outbreaks of violence in Nigeria, Malaysia, India, and Pakistan, to name only a few of many instances, appear to be directly related to such differentiation.

MOBILIZATION AND ASSIMILATION

K. W. Deutsch (1967) defines *social mobilization* as "potential politization," which is likely to be along the lines of language and ethnic culture; that is, "nationalism intermingled with and reinforced by elements of rising expectations and frustrations and of social discontent."

Assimilation, on the other hand, is seen as a process "by which individuals come to share common identities usually reinforced by common language, values, and codes of conduct" (Hopkins, 1973).

Typically, assimilation is the slower process, measured by generations. It is integrative. Mobilization is frequently divisive. It seems important, therefore, to study the two processes together.

A model proposed by Deutsch (1966) involves the following population magnitudes:

A: assimilated population
M: mobilized population
D: differentiated population
U: underlying nonmobilized population

The equations of the model are

$$\frac{dA}{dt} = A(a - c) \tag{23.1}$$

$$\frac{dD}{dt} = Dd - Ac \tag{23.2}$$

$$\frac{dM}{dt} = M(b + m) \tag{23.3}$$

$$U(t) = A(t) + D(t) - M(t). \tag{23.4}$$

The constants a, b, and d represent rates of per capita natural increase of A, M, and D respectively; c and m represent rates of per capita net entry of outsiders into A and M as of the initial period examined.

In addition to these rates of change resulting from natural (positive or negative) increments and flows from and to the outside, there are shifts within the population, represented in Figure 23.1. b_i in each cell represents the rates of natural increase. The arrows indicate the assumed directions of shift, and a_{ij} are positive coefficients denoting the proportions of the people who leave the respective subpopulations to move to another subpopulation in a given time period. Thus we have the following difference equations:

$$P_1(t + 1) - P_1(t) = b_1 P_1(t) + a_{21} P_2(t) + a_{31} P_3(t) \tag{23.5}$$

$$P_2(t + 1) - P_2(t) = b_2 P_2(t) + a_{42} P_4(t) - a_{21} P_2(t) \tag{23.6}$$

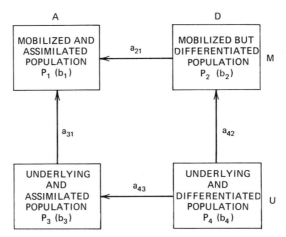

Figure 23.1. (Adapted from Hopkins, 1973). Schematic representation of mobilization and assimilation. A: assimilated population; D: differentiated population; M: mobilized population; U: underlying (nonmobilized) population.

$$P_3(t+1) - P_3(t) = b_3 P_3(t) + a_{43} P_4(t) - a_{31} P_3(t) \tag{23.7}$$

$$P_4(t+1) - P_4(t) = b_4 P_4(t) - a_{42} P_4(t) - a_{43} P_4(t). \tag{23.8}$$

The next step is that of operationalizing "mobilization" and "assimilation" in some specific context so as to make populations P_1, P_2, P_3, and P_4 observable variables. A clear context is provided by Finland, where people can be classified by a double dichotomy: rural and urban, and Swedish and Finnish. Here we can identify "rural" with "underlying" (that is, nonmobilized), "urban" with "mobilized," Swedish with "differentiated," and Finnish with "assimilated." Whether these categories capture the originally intuited meanings of "mobilization" and "assimilation" is a separate question. It crops up more or less severely in all instances of operationalizing intuited concepts. It can never be answered completely satisfactorily and must be sidestepped at some point. We will sidestep it now and will identify the population groups as specified above.

Now we have a mathematical model represented by the difference Equations 23.5–23.8. If the model were validated, the parameters b_1 and a_{ji} would serve as parameteric indices characterizing the population examined. To validate the model, we need estimates of these parameters. The parameters of mobility and of natural increase can be estimated from 1820–1850 data and also by least squares, taking into account the entire process from 1880 to 1950. The estimates are shown in Table 23.1.

Since the estimates were made by "tuning" the parameters to give reasonably good fits to time courses observed in a historical segment, a test of the model must be made by projection. Projections to the year 1960 are shown at the bottom of the table. Clearly, the model is dramatically discorroborated. Using the estimates of parameters from 1820 to 1850, the projected population of urban

Finns in 1960 is over a billion and a half, almost one half of the total world population at that time. At the same time a *negative* (!) population is projected by using the 1880–1950 estimates of the parameters.

Table 23.1. Estimates of Natural Growth and Populations Flow Parameters for Components of the Finnish Population and Projections of These Components on the Basis of the Estimates

Empirical Estimates on the Basis of 1820–1850 Data	Natural Growth Parameter	Least-Square Estimates on the Basis of 1880–1950 Data
1.96	b_1	0.93
3.79	b_2	−0.02
−1.67	b_3	−0.05
10.34	b_4	−0.03

Empirical Estimate on the Basis of 1820–1850 Data	Population Flow Parameter	Least-Square Estimate on the Basis of 1880–1950 Data
3.62	a_{21}	−10.20
−0.18	a_{31}	0.42
−0.02	a_{42}	0.06
10.26	a_{43}	1.02

Population Projected to 1960	Urban		Rural	
	Finns (P_1)	Swedes (P_2)	Finns (P_3)	Swedes (P_4)
On the basis of empirical estimate	1,626,178,000	34,000	3,685,000	569,000
On the basis of least square estimate	−5,987,700	540,486	9,045,710	667,103
Census	1,553,151	148,873	2,557,557	181,665

Source: Adapted from Hopkins (1973).

The failure of a model can conveniently be ascribed to "oversimplification." This serves as a stimulus to add further variables or parameters. For example, one can assume demobilization as well as mobilization and disassimilation as well as assimilation. Cases of both are on record. For example, literacy figures gathered in Malaysia from 1930–1947 censuses suggest that as the population aged from twenties to forties, literacy *declined*, which could be interpreted as demobilization. Cases of disassimilation are also observed. French-speaking residents of Quebec frequently learn English at school or at work. As they age, many forget the acquired language. Nor can assimilation be described by a single criterion. In the United States, for example, many Blacks have in recent decades attained middle class status and some of the concomittant values. At the same time, the feelings of many of these "Black Anglo-Saxons" acquired strong components of differentiation and militancy, a process that is ordinarily thought of as antiassimilationist.

Figure 23.2 shows a more complex conceptual scheme of mobilization and assimilation. Movements between subpopulations are now in both directions with corresponding parameters added. The four additional shift parameters refer to the opposite trends (demobilization, disassimilation). Additional features appear in the scheme. The symbol d is said to represent "social distance," h something designated by "inequality," and m_i ($i = 1, 2$) as something designated "interaction." Supposedly, these factors influence the flow parameters. However, unless these factors are defined with as much operational clarity as the previously specified variables and parameters, the scheme is no longer a mathematical model and cannot serve as an apparatus of deduction. It is only a protomodel.

The original mathematical model represented by Equations 23.5–23.8 led to absurd results, but at least it could be clearly seen that the model was grossly inadequate. In attempting to improve a model, the social scientist frequently loses sight of the requirements of a mathematical model. He turns his attention to what has been "left out" and proceeds to add factors and influences that appear to him to be relevant to the process he intends to study, but which, remaining mathematically undefined, make it impossible to "run" the model. This tendency to encompass the "relevant factors" without regard to their role in a deductive model can be seen in the next scheme shown in Figure 23.3.

Once the variables are defined operationally and the influences indicated in the flow chart are specified as functional relations, a protomodel can be converted into a mathematical model. Clearly, such a model will include a very large number of parameters. If the model is to be incorporated into a predictive theory, the parameters must be estimated. Usually, the simultaneous estimation of all the parameters from the data is out of the question. For this reason, models of this sort are incorporated in computer simulations, a new methodology in the social sciences which was briefly touched upon in the Introduction.

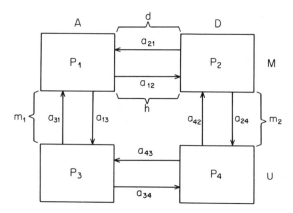

Figure 23.2. (Adapted from Hopkins, 1973).

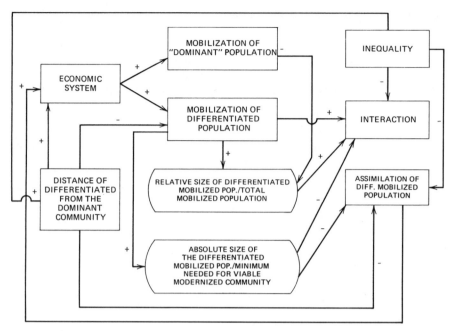

Figure 23.3. (Adapted from Hopkins, 1973). Schematic representations of this sort serve only to identify the factors assumed to be involved in a social process and the directions on influence in interactions among these factors. They sometimes serve as points of departure for simulating complex social processes or global models (see Chapter 4).

Ordinarily, however, the empirically oriented social scientist proceeds to the more modest task of gathering data and perhaps extrapolating them by standard demographic methods. These data comprise the sizes of the four subpopulations defined by some observable criteria. In bilingual or multilingual countries, measures of assimilation suggest themselves in terms of the degree to which the dominant language is adopted. In certain instances, urbanization can serve as a (very rough) measure of mobilization.

The tables below represent some case studies, from which certain conclusions and forecasts are made. Two trends are clearly discernible in Table 23.2: a slow but steady decline in the proportion of the "assimilated" (in this case the unilingual French speakers) and a more rapid increase in the proportion of the "mobilized" (in this case, the urbanized population). Clearly, these trends are consequences of the urbanization of rural, predominantly Flemish-speaking Belgians, who learn French in the process. Hopkins sees this trend as leading to an intensification of social conflict between the subordinate Flemish and the dominant Walloons.

Malaysia is taken as a case study of trends in all four subpopulations. The data are shown in Table 23.3. Here "mobilization" is defined in terms of literacy; assimilation in terms of census records for ethnic identification. Differentiation is between Malays and Chinese.

Table 23.2. **Estimated and Observed Components of the Belgian Population (in Thousands)**

Year	Total Observed	Total Estimated	Assimilated (Only French Speaking) Observed	Assimilated Estimated	%	Mobilized (urban)[a] Observed	Mobilized Estimated	%
1880	5,520	5,520	2,230	2,230	40	2,377	2,377	43
1890	6,069	5,931	2,485	2,365	40	2,895	2,735	46
1900	6,674	6,374	2,575	2,507	39	3,500	3,136	49
1910	7,424	6,851	2,833	2,658	39	4,194	3,471	52
1920	7,406	7,365	2,850	2.818	38	4,260	4,076	55
1930	8,092	7,917	3,039	2,988	38	4,894	4,622	58
1940		8,513		3,168	37		5,222	61
1950	8,512[b]	9,154		3,359	37		5,870	64
1960	9,189[c]	9,844		3,561	36	6,102[c]	6,599	67
1970		10,588		3,775	36		7,380	70
1980		11,389		4,003	35		8,225	72
1990		12,253		4,244	35		9,147	75
2000		13,183		4,499	34		10,104	77

Source: Adapted from Hopkins (1973).

[a]Population in communities over 5,000.
[b]From 1947 census.
[c]Data from 1961.

The trend reflects an increase of the proportion of Malays in the economy of the country. Hopkins notes that the Malays have used legislation to preserve their political dominance. In his opinion, as the position of the Malays becomes more entrenched, the pressure to continue the political inequities may be reduced. Communal hostility, however, might not be reduced unless the distribution of economic rewards becomes more equitable. Rural Malays, Hopkins points out, who constitute the largest population group in Malaysia, have a strong negative image of Chinese. He cites P. J. Wilson (1967), who reports that in one rural village, Malays who have lived among the Chinese in Singapore depicted themselves as being

> ...a minority oppressed and discriminated against, forced to live in the poorest parts of the island and the city, unable to gain access to good housing, welfare, and other benefits, and steadily economically strangled by the Chinese. One [respondent felt that] the only solution ... was either the expulsion or the slaughter of the Chinese, and he personally favoured the latter course ...

Thus increased mobilization, while possibly attenuating legal repressions, may intensify communal strife unless Chinese economic domination is overthrown, which may be likely as Chinese numerical strength declines. On the

Table 23.3. Estimated and Observed Components of the Malaysian Population (in thousands)

Year	Total		Mobilized						Nonmobilized					
			Assimilated			Differentiated			Assimilated			Differentiated		
	Observed	Estimated	Observed	Estimated	%	Observed	Estimated	%	Observed	Estimated	%	Observed	Estimated	%
1931	3,786		324		9	720		19	1,540		41	1,202		31
1947	4,908	5,046	728	763	15	1,196	1,215	24	1,699	1,698	34	1,385	1,370	27
1957	6,256	6,279	1,291	1,303	21	1,649	1,674	27	1,835	1,808	29	1,381	1,494	24
1960		6,705		1,521	23		1,830	27		1,830	27		1,524	23
1970		8,342		2,483	30		2,410	29		1,862	22		1,588	19
1980		10,380		3,905	38		3,057	29		1,825	18		1,594	15
1990		12,917		5,918	46		3,735	29		1,723	13		1,541	12
2000		19,072		8,658	54		4,406	27		1,570	10		1,426	9

Source: Adapted from Hopkins (1973).

Table 23.4. Estimated and Observed Population Components in the Province of Quebec (in thousands)

Year	Total		Mobilized						Nonmobilized					
			Assimilated			Differentiated			Assimilated			Differentiated		
	Observed	Estimated	Observed	Estimated	%	Observed	Estimated	%	Observed	Estimated	%	Observed	Estimated	%
1931	2,875		318		11	1,476		52	78		3	983		34
1941	3,332	3,566	335	389	11	1,774	2,035	57	75	77	2	1,147	1,064	30
1951	4,056	4,422	383	470	11	2,314	2,737	62	80	76	2	1,279	1,139	26
1961	5,259	5,485	532	561	10	3,374	3,644	66	76	74	1	1,276	1,206	22
1971		6,804		664	10		4,803	71		72	1		1,264	19
1981		8,439		779	9		6,277	74		69	1		1,314	16
1991		10,467		907	9		8,139	78		66	1		1,355	13
2001		12,982		1,049	8		10,483	81		62	1		1,383	11

Source: Adapted from Hopkins (1973).

other hand, as the Chinese position becomes shakier, they may offer violent resistance.

As a final result, let us examine an analogous trend in Canada. Table 23.4 shows trends and projections of total, assimilated, and mobilized populations in Quebec from 1931 to 2001 (in thousands). "Mobilization" is defined here in terms of urbanization in towns of 1,000 or more; assimilation is reflected in the exclusive use of English.

The trends suggest that a core of English speakers will remain in Quebec, but that French-speaking Quebec will not be assimilated into a unilingual Canada.

Some theoretical leverage could be obtained even from these very raw data if the situations in the three case studies (Belgium, Malaysia, Quebec) could be compared. At the present stage, however, this cannot be done. "Mobilization" in the industrialized, highly literate countries was defined in terms of urbanization, whereas in Malaysia it was defined in terms of literacy. Assimilation in the former case was defined linguistically, whereas in the latter case it was defined in terms of "ethnic identification." Moreover, if the "full" model as outlined above is to be utilized, concepts like social distance between populations must be operationalized. At best, such operationalization is done *ad hoc*, in terms of whatever observables or indices happen to be suggested. For example, "distance" in Canada was defined in terms of two questions asked in a survey among Canadian youth. One asked respondents to rate how much various juxtaposed groups would agree on Canada's future. There were six possible cleavages: by religion, by birthplace, by wealth, by urbanization, and by language. All groups agreed that the least consensus would be found across the language cleavage. The second question elicited answers that indicated that English Canadians were perceived as closer to Americans than French Canadians. Thus some (ordinal) measure of distance along the various dichotomies could be estimated. However, how these estimates are to be plugged into the "system model" in which distance is a variable remains obscure.

Similar considerations apply to "interaction." It is certainly possible to obtain some "measure of interaction", for example, in terms of intergroup contact frequencies, in language use, residence, school, or personal friends. Again, the question arises as to just how these variables are to be plugged into the system.

One prediction that came from the Quebec study (on the basis of impressions only) is that pressure to assimilate would be toward French in Quebec and toward English in the rest of Canada (Johnstone, 1969). This seems to portend increasing polarization. In 1976, the separatist party in Quebec won an election. The party is committed to the independence of Quebec, legitimized by a plebiscite. To what extent this event constitutes a corroboration of the "model" cannot be estimated without a much more definite formulation of the assumptions and implications of the model. (Assumptions in the form "the more of this, the more of that or the less of that" are wholly inadequate for this purpose because they do not specify "critical values" of the parameters, which if exceeded, lead to qualitative changes.)

In this connection, recall that precise mathematical models such as those of Rashevsky on imitative behavior in massive populations (see Chapter 2) do single out such critical values. These models, however, are also inadequate because of almost total lack of empirical evidence that would serve to corroborate or refute them.

THE SEARCH FOR INDICES TO SERVE AS SYMPTOMS OR GUIDES TO POLICY-MAKING

As we have seen in the previous example, rather vague ideas about social dynamics, thought to be relevant to political dynamics, did not yet produce usable models as components of a predictive theory. The most that could be said of those schema (largely diagrams summarizing the components of a conceptualization and a very rough indication of the interrelations among them) is that they instigated the gathering of data in order to discern trends, on the basis of which conjectures could be made about possible political and social consequences. Such approaches cannot be called mathematical inasmuch as mathematical *deduction* plays hardly any part in them. They are strongly oriented toward gathering large masses of data and have a bearing on possible future mathematical approaches to the extent that those data are largely quantitative.

This orientation predominated in certain circles of the U.S. Establishment during the war in Vietnam. The people who instigated this war were among those who flocked to Washington after Kennedy's election in 1960. The mood in the Establishment was euphoric. The Eisenhower years were regarded as years of stagnation. The change of administration promised a radical change in the style of constructing and conducting policies. The predominant type was the man who was above all *competent*, where competence was associated exclusively with technical competence, and the latter was largely competence in business or in adjoining fields such as corporation law, public relations, and so on; in short, what was traditionally known in America as "man's world."

This was Kennedy's Brain Trust, a throwback to Roosevelt's entourage of educated men, who in the 1930s attempted to cope with the overriding problem of the Great Depression. In the 1960s, the central problem, as the Establishment saw it, was the global struggle for power with the only potential rival, the Soviet Union. Roosevelt's Brain Trust tried to cope with the Depression by infusing policies derived from Keynesian economics, which constituted, as the people of the Brain Trust saw it, an attempt to use a "scientific approach" to the problems of national economy, involving radical departures from established traditions. That was essentially a pragmatic approach, where available knowledge was brought to bear on problems and action was (presumably) guided by evaluating the results of decisions.

Nothing analogous to Keynesian economics was available in political science, but the men who composed Kennedy's Brain Trust did not lack self-confidence. "Models" of global power dynamics were readily constructed by men transplanted from academe into the world of practical affairs. They were spurred by the realization of their fondest ambitions: to put their intellects to work in the "real world."

Many books on global strategy appeared toward the end of the 1950s and in the early 1960s. H. Kissinger's *Nuclear Weapons and Foreign Policy* (1958), H. Kahn's *On Thermonuclear War* (1960), and R. E. Osgood's *Limited War* (1957) are examples.

The seeds of the Vietnam War were planted by the professors turned strategists in Kennedy's entourage. When the war became a full-blown affair, the same "style" of thinking prevailed. Robert McNamara was not a professor; he was a corporate executive. But there was a perfect affinity between the thinking of corporate executives and that of professors who put their "expertise," as they saw it, to work in waging the global power struggle. Hence we have a legacy (or a junk yard?) of innumerable studies on "cost-benefit analysis" of the Vietnam War. The object of this analysis was to direct efforts where they would give maximal "returns." Cost-benefit analysis can conceivably lead to "rational" business policies, where natural quantifications of "effort" and "returns" readily suggest themselves as monetary expenditures and profits respectively. In the context of politics and war, relevant indices of "costs" and "benefits" are less easily definable. Nevertheless, such indices are readily constructed by those who identify "cost-benefit analysis" with "rationality." Habits of thought characteristic of the business mentality become pervasive in a climate where the business community is culturally dominant.

The following is an example of an attempt to reduce the dynamics of the war in Vietnam to quantitative indices.

J. S. Milstein (1973) reports that American policy in Vietnam since the Tet Offensive (1968) had three aims: (1) *Vietnamization* (that is, the taking over of the major military effort by the South Vietnamese government, thus enabling the United States to undertake gradual disengagement); (2) *pacification* (that is, the ability of the Saigon government to "secure the population" from North Vietnamese and Viet Cong attacks); and (3) to engender *confidence* in the population of South Vietnam in the Saigon government.

To undertake an analysis of the interplay of these factors, quantitative indices are needed.

One operational measure of "Vietnamization" might simply be the number of battalion-size or larger ground operations initiated by the Saigon government. Another might be the ratio of South Vietnamese ground operations to U.S. ground operations. Still another, the ratio of South Vietnamese casualties to U.S. casualties.

Similarly, quantitative measures were proposed of anything that could be counted: abductions of civilians by the Viet Cong, helicopter attacks, bomber sorties, defectors from "the other side," everything down to the black market rate of the Saigonese piastre and U.S. public opinion indices—in short, anything that could be regarded as an index of "the way the war was going."

Here is "barefoot empiricism" in its crudest form. Huge masses of data are collected and subjected to "processing." Milstein presents every conceivable regression of one variable on another.

Example.

$$\frac{\text{(s.V. ground operations)}_t}{\text{(U.S. ground operations)}_t} = 12 - (0.004)(\text{Civilians abducted})_{t-1}. \quad (23.9)$$

This is to be read as follows: the ratio of South Vietnamese ground operations to U.S. ground operations (measured in comparable units in month t) when plotted against the number of civilians abducted by the Viet Cong in the previous month $(t-1)$ gives a scatter plot to which a straight line with slope -0.004 and intercept 12 gives the least squares fit.

The correlation of the ratio on the left and the number of abductions turns out to be -0.45. That is to say, if this correlation is significantly different from zero, one could conjecture that the more civilians were abducted, the more U.S. ground operations increased relative to South Vietnamese operations in the following month.

Example.

$$\frac{\text{(S.V. ground operations)}_t}{\text{(U.S. ground operations)}_t} = 24 - (3,000)(\text{Piastre value})_{t-1}. \quad (23.10)$$

Here the correlation (-0.82) turns out to be significant. So one can say that the more the black market value of the piastre fell, the more the South Vietnamese forces engaged in ground operations in comparison with U.S. forces. One could also say, of course, that the more the black market value of the piastre fell, the less the U.S. forces engaged in ground operations in comparison with South Vietnamese forces. Since the value of the piastre was taken as an index of the "degree of confidence" of the South Vietnamese in the Saigon government, one could make conjectures: as this confidence was undermined, more South Vietnamese forces engaged in ground operations relative to U.S. forces, or fewer U.S. forces engaged in ground operations relative to South Vietnamese forces.

Many of these relations belabor the obvious. For instance, the ratio of U.S. casualties to South Vietnamese casualties is positively related to increases of U.S. troops and to the magnitude of U.S. operations. The percentage of U.S. public opinion approval was found to be negatively correlated with the ratio of U.S. troops killed to South Vietnamese troops killed, and so on.

All of these findings are presented in a diagram similar to that shown in Figure 23.3. The diagram is supposed to serve as a guide to a simulation model. That is, various quantities are to be fed into a computer programmed with parameters of increments or decrements, simultaneous or lagged, as indicated by the regression lines exemplified above. The idea is that the simulation would quickly indicate the ultimate effect of changing one or more variables (via the realization of the entire complex net of interrelations, including feedbacks). The "validity" of the simulation is to be tested by "postdictions"; that is, by comparing its predictions with changes in variables already observed in a similar situation in the past. Milstein goes on to say:

> Once such a simulation model proves to make valid predictions, one could exercise the model to see what the likely outcome in a number of dependent variables would be when one changes the values of manipulable independent variables. For example, one could estimate the magnitude of the likely effect on public approval of the president's Vietnam policy if large U.S. ground operations in Vietnam were increased or decreased by given amounts. Or one could find the likely effect to increasing or decreasing the rate of U.S. troop withdrawals from Vietnam on such variables as South Vietnamese political stability, political support for the Viet Cong, or U.S. public opinion . . .
>
> This ability to predict consequences of alternative actions is one of the purposes of scientific and quantitative analysis of international relations. Such analysis strengthens our capability for critical evaluation of existing policies, and potentially could enlighten policy-making so that future tragedies can be avoided (Milstein, 1973, p. 135).

This is, of course, a restatement of the pragmatic rationale of computer simulation. I do not know the extent of its influence on U.S. policy making. The disengagement of the *procedures* (that is, of what goes on inside the computer) from misleading habits of thought, prejudices, vested interests, and so on speaks in its favor. Nevertheless, the choice of indices may be influenced by the same factors and by the ease with which intuited components of causal relations lend themselves to quantification. The range of applicability and the efficacy of computer simulation as a guide to policy making must remain an open question.

CHAPTER TWENTY FOUR

Indices of "International Weather" and Correlates of War

Traditionally, wars have been regarded as the most important historical events. History textbooks, at least in the Euro-American world before 1914, were predominantly accounts of these events accompanied by "causes" (mostly political or strategic) and "effects" (redrawn political maps).

Following the trauma of World War I, another view of war has been in the ascendance, that of a "catastrophe," an event resulting from a "system failure." From this "systemic" point of view, the immediate instigating "causes" of particular wars seem less important than the properties of the "system" that make it war prone. Ambitions of princes, political, economic, and strategic imperatives governing relations among states lose their salience.

Lewis F. Richardson, a pioneer in the global-systemic study of war, ignored these determinants altogether. Being a pacifist, he pictured war only as an outbreak of mass violence and classified wars not according to their supposed causes but simply by magnitude. He defined the magnitude of a war as the logarithm to the base 10 of the number of fatalities engendered by it. Moreover, he lumped war with all other manifestations of lethal violence, so-called deadly quarrels. Thus a murder was recorded as a deadly quarrel of magnitude 0 ($\log 1 = 0$), a small riot with 10 dead as a deadly quarrel of magnitude 1, a large riot with 100 dead as a quarrel of magnitude 2 and so on. Wars fall in the range of magnitudes from 3 to between 7 and 8. A nuclear war is expected to be of a magnitude between 8 and 9. A war of larger magnitude would destroy the human race.

In his book *Statistics of Deadly Quarrels* (Richardson, 1960b), Richardson presents a compilation of data summarized as a frequency distribution of wars according to magnitude. Later he attempted to examine correlations between the incidence of wars and a great variety of indices, but aside from this attempt, his study is predominantly descriptive.

Indeed, one might do well to begin the study of a system with pure description, devoid of theoretical considerations apart from the selection of indices, which is inadvertently influenced by preconceived ideas or commitments. (For example, Richardson's selection of "magnitude" reflects his pacifist view: war is regarded first and foremost as an outburst of lethal violence.)

One can go a step further by introducing the time dimension. A question that naturally suggests itself is whether the total amount of violence engendered by war has increased, decreased, or remained fairly constant in recent history. One need not confine oneself to Richardson's index of violence (number of dead). One could also examine frequencies with which wars were initiated in different historical periods. Severity of wars can be measured by their duration as well as the numbers of dead. Moreover, the number of wars initiated can be taken as absolute or relative to the number of potential instigators of wars; that is, the number of national states comprising the "international system" in the period in question. Numbers of dead and other indices can be similarly relativized.

The following tables present indices of war in absolute and relative terms for a century and a half of recent history. The end points of the periods mark prominent transitions in Euro-American political history. The varying size of the international system and the different lengths of the periods do not distort the indices calculated per nation and/or per year.

One could take the last columns of Tables 24.1 and 24.2 as indices of violence normalized with respect to the size of the system and the lengths of the periods. The index reveals no discernible trend. At most, the last period, 1966–1977 appears to have been the "most peaceful," but since no monotone trend is evident, no inference is justified. The greatest variability of the battle death index (last column of Table 24.2) reflects the two world wars.

Trends in events that are largely determined by chance can be discerened only as a summation of very many minute events. The world wars, however, were of a magnitude far surpassing that of other wars, so that their occurrence over-

Table 24.1.   Measures of War Frequency in the Period 1816–1977

Period	Number of Years	Average Size of System	Number of Wars Begun	Number of Wars Begun per Year	Number of Wars Begun per Year per Nation	Number of War Involvements per Nation per Year
1816–49	34	29	21	0.62	0.021	0.034
1850–70	21	39	19	0.90	0.023	0.062
1871–90	20	34	12	0.60	0.017	0.025
1891–1914	24	42	17	0.71	0.16	0.047
1919–39	21	64	11	0.52	0.008	0.037
1946–65	20	95	11	0.55	0.006	0.025
1966–77	12	135	9	0.75	0.006	0.012

Source: Adapted from Small and Singer (1979).

Table 24.2.   Measures of War Duration in the Period 1816–1977

Period	Number of Years	Average Size of System	Nation Months of War Begun per Nation	Nation Months of War Begun per Year per Nation	Battle Deaths per Year per Nation from Wars Begun
1816–49	34	29	12.37	0.47	359.3
1850–70	21	39	30.45	0.80	998.7
1871–90	20	34	19.59	0.59	564.0
1981–1914	24	42	37.82	0.88	8,525.8
1919–39	21	64	62.30	0.98	12,145.0
1946–65	20	95	67.20	0.71	1,579.0
1966–77	12	135	12.85	0.09	70.1

Source: Adapted from Small and Singer (1979).

Table 24.3.   Measures of War Proneness in the Period 1816–1977

Period	Number of Years	Average Size of System	Number of Confrontations	Number of Confrontations per Year per Nation	Percent of Confrontations Ending in War
1816–49	34	29	29	0.03	21
1850–70	21	39	34	0.04	23
1871–90	20	34	23	0.03	6
1891–1914	24	42	25	0.05	17
1919–39	21	64	51	0.04	10
1946–65	20	95	48	0.02	8
1966–77	12	135	24	0.01	0

Source: Adapted from Small and Singer (1979).

shadowed all other statistical effects. For this reason, no trend can be inferred in the "lethality" of war in the period examined.

Another index examined by Small and Singer was the "morbidity" of military confrontations. A military confrontation is manifested in "threats, displays, or actual uses of military force (by a system member) while engaged in a serious dispute with another member of the system." Some of these have ended in wars; others not. The task of examining all confrontations between all members of the international system is clearly a formidable one. Small and Singer confined themselves to confrontations involving at least one major power. The results are shown in Table 24.3. Again no conspicuous trend is discernible, aside from the relative "peacefulness" of the period 1966–1977. Clearly, in the light of events since 1977, that relative trough in global violence cannot be regarded as a promising symptom.

To look at the international system with somewhat greater resolving power, we turn to the use of indices in describing so-called crises. The following selected studies contain, in addition to pure descriptions, some attempts to find inter-actions among the various indices.

THE 1914 CRISIS

We will first examine an attempt to describe the crisis of 1914 in quantitative terms (Holsti *et al.*, 1968). Naturally, presuppositions are incorporated in any work on data. Holsti and his collaborators start with the assumption that *perception* is involved in any decision-making process. They view the 1914 crisis as a sequence of events resulting from decisions by rulers or policy makers of the nation states involved. In order to respond to a stimulus in a decision-making situation, a person must, first of all, *detect* the stimulus; furthermore, he must *interpret it*. Consequently, they picture the interaction of two states as shown in Figure 24.1.

We note that this feedback loop model resembles that of the Richardsonian arms race (see Chapter 3). The difference is that the stimuli and responses (which themselves become stimuli) are conceived not in terms of "objective" variables (for example, armament levels), but as signals, which in order to serve as stimuli, must be detected and interpreted.

The raw data were distilled from a collection of documents that yielded some 5,000 such cognitive and affective perceptions. The analysis of these data went through several stages. First, only the frequencies of perceptions were recorded; next, the perceptions were scaled by intensity of various attributes; finally, correlational analyses were performed between perceptions and different kinds of "hard" data; that is, overt acts.

The perceptions were abstracted from the documents in terms of the following elements: (1) the perceiving party; (2) the perceived party or parties; (3) the

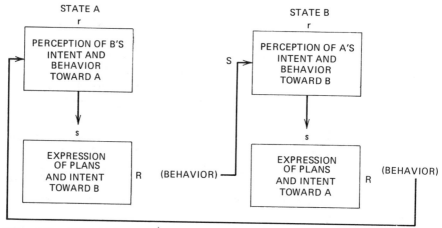

Figure 24.1. (Adapted from Holsti, 1968). Schematic representation of interactions between perceptions, expressions of intentions, and behaviors of two states.

action or attitude perceived; and (4) the target of the action. For instance, an assertion by a Russian decision maker to the effect that "The Austrians hope for the ultimate annihilation of Serbia" is coded thus:

Perceiver	Perceived	Action or Attitude	Target
Russia	Austria	Hope for annihilation	Serbia

Frequency analysis used by D. A. Zinnes, R. C. North, and H. E. Koch (1961) supported a hypothesis directly opposite to a conclusion arrived at by T. Abel (1941). Abel made a survey of decisions to go to war, including the case of 1914, and concluded that "in no case is the decision precipitated by emotional tensions, sentimentality, crowd behavior, or other irrational motivations." Evidence advanced by Zinnes et al. supports the hypothesis that if perceptions of anxiety, fear, threat, or injury are great enough, even the perception of one's own inferior capability will fail to deter a nation from going to war.

Which is closer to the truth? Are strategic or systemic factors dominant? Certainly no definitive conclusion is warranted. The student of international relations is not in a position to conduct a "crucial experiment." Nevertheless, hypotheses "strongly supported" by data that are at variance with conclusions based on looser examination of situations give food for thought.

In a later study, D. A. Zinnes (1963) tested four hypotheses about the relationships between perceptions of hostility and expressions of hostility by key decision makers. She found in the 1914 case that a nation state's tendency to express hostility is positively related to the extent that it perceives itself to be the *target* of another state's hostility. As expected, the hostility is directed against the source of perceived threat.

Intensity of attitudes perceived or expressed were scaled by three judges (presumably independently), who rated perceptions on a 9-point scale. The quantitative results were then aggregated into 12 periods of roughly equal length.

After the items abstracted from the documents were thus recorded and scaled, the hypotheses relating to perceptions of capability and injury were reexamined. It was found that decision makers of each nation strongly felt themselves to be the victims of injury precisely at the time when policy decisions were made of the most crucial nature (Holsti and North, 1965). It was this analysis that led to the conjecture that a feeling of desperation is most conducive to the instigation of a war, typically by the *weaker party*. The Peloponesian Wars, the wars between Spain and England during the sixteenth century, and Japan's attack on the United States in 1941 immediately come to mind. (Of course, counterexamples also come to mind, the most conspicuous being Hitler's attack on the Soviet Union in 1941).

We turn to the summaries of data obtained in various studies of the 1914 crisis. (These were presented in compact form in Holsti et al., 1968).

First, let us look at explicit military actions. Examples of coding are given in the following pages.

Table 24.4. *A Summary of Military Actions During the Crisis of 1914 is Shown in Table 24.4*

Agent	Action	Target
French Chamber	Introduces 3-year military service	General
German fleet	Leaves Norway	General
Austrian army	Bombards	Belgrade
Churchill (Britain)	Orders shadowing	Two German battle cruisers
Germany	Declares war	France

Source: Adapted from Holsti et al. (1968).

Table 24.5. *Table 24.5 Shows Average Intensity Levels of Perceptual and Action Variables by Time Periods*

	Austria	Germany	England	France	Russia	Serbia	All Others	General	Total
Austria	0.00	0.00	0.00	0.00	4.50	6.33	6.00	5.43	5.01
	(0)	(0)	(0)	(0)	(1)	(29)	(1)	(23)	(54)
Germany	0.00	0.00	5.50	6.81	6.00	4.75	6.00	4.62	5.26
	(0)	(0)	(4)	(16)	(11)	(2)	(4)	(57)	(94)
England	0.00	6.25	0.00	0.00	0.00	0.00	7.00	4.38	4.62
	(0)	(4)	(0)	(0)	(0)	(0)	(1)	(36)	(41)
France	0.00	5.00	0.00	0.00	0.00	0.00	0.00	3.84	4.08
	(0)	(13)	(0)	(0)	(0)	(0)	(0)	(51)	(64)
Russia	6.43	6.29	0.00	1.00	0.00	0.00	0.00	5.31	5.52
	(7)	(7)	(0)	(1)	(0)	(0)	(0)	(35)	(50)
Servia	4.64	0.00	0.00	0.00	4.00	0.00	2.50	5.94	5.09
	(7)	(0)	(0)	(0)	(1)	(0)	(1)	(8)	(17)
All others	0.00	0.00	0.00	0.00	0.00	7.00	0.00	4.30	4.38
	(0)	(0)	(0)	(0)	(0)	(1)	(0)	(33)	(34)
Total	5.54	5.58	5.50	6.47	5.73	6.25	5.64	4.60	5.01
	(14)	(24)	(4)	(17)	(13)	(32)	(7)	(243)	(354)

Source: Adapted from Holsti et al. (1968).

Note: Rows: actors; columns: targets. The top number of each entry indicates the average intensity of military actions, as rated by judges. For instance, German fleet leaving Norwegian ports is a military action of relatively low intensity. Bombardment of Serbia by the Austrian army is a military action of the highest intensity. Numbers in parentheses denote frequencies of actions coded for each actor-target relationship.

A summary of military actions during the crisis of 1914 is shown in Table 24.4.
Table 24.5 shows average intensity levels of perceptual and action variables by time periods.

Table 24.6 shows the average intensity of perceptual and behavioral variables of the Dual Alliance (Germany, Austria-Hungary) and Triple Entente (England, France, Russia). Tables 24.7 and 24.8 show interaction variables for the Dual Alliance and the Triple Entente.

Table 24.6. *Average Intensities of Perception and Behavioral Variables in the Course of the 1914 Crisis*

Perception Variables	June 27–July 2	July 2–16	July 17–20	July 21–25	July 26	July 27	July 28	July 29	July 30	July 31	August 1–2	August 3–4
Hostility												
Alliance	3.46	3.63	3.79	4.13	4.54	4.09	4.83	4.99	5.50	5.80	6.89	6.42
Entente	3.67	4.22	4.00	4.25	5.07	4.93	5.61	5.42	5.44	5.58	5.70	6.10
Friendliness												
Alliance	4.79	5.22	4.19	4.61	5.27	5.17	5.60	4.85	5.25	5.95	5.53	4.95
Entene	0.00	6.10	6.00	5.00	4.50	4.10	4.64	4.40	4.77	5.23	4.24	5.46
Frustration												
Alliance	4.93	4.45	3.90	5.33	5.97	4.62	4.49	4.65	5.84	6.22	4.39	6.00
Entente	3.33	4.60	4.33	5.50	4.83	5.46	4.78	5.19	4.78	4.61	4.78	4.42
Satisfaction												
Alliance	2.91	5.83	4.05	2.38	5.33	4.83	3.33	0.00	4.67	5.90	6.00	5.83
Entente	0.00	5.25	5.67	4.22	4.83	4.55	6.17	4.95	5.00	6.00	5.47	6.21
Behavioral Variable												
Violent behavior												
Alliance	4.25	3.00	2.83	5.38	5.37	5.87	6.06	4.64	5.10	6.30	5.58	6.08
Entente	4.38	2.58	2.62	4.28	3.68	4.95	4.68	5.07	4.60	5.50	5.90	6.03

Source: Adapted from Holsti et al. (1968).

Table 24.7. *Action and Perception Variables of Entente*

Period	S^a	r^b	s^c	R^d
June 27–July 2	4.25	2.67	0.00	4.38
July 3–16	4.25	0.00	0.00	2.58
July 17–20	3.00	0.00	3.67	2.62
July 21–25	2.83	0.00	0.00	4.28
July 26	5.38	6.00	0.00	3.68
July 27	5.37	0.00	0.00	4.95
July 28	5.87	0.00	7.33	4.68
July 29	6.06	5.33	3.40	5.07
July 30	4.64	5.33	4.89	4.60
July 31	5.10	6.43	5.00	5.50
August 1–2	6.30	6.19	3.97	5.90
August 3–4	5.88	5.98	6.17	6.03

Source: Adapted from Holsti et al. (1968).

[a]S: Violence of other coalition (that is, response R of Alliance in the preceding period).
[b]r: Perception of hostility of other coalition against self.
[c]s: Perception of own hostility against other coalition.
[d]R: Own violence.

Table 24.8. *Actions and Perception Variables of Alliance*

Period	S	r	s	R
June 27–July 2	4.38	3.98	3.55	4.25
July 3–16	4.38	3.93	3.39	3.00
July 17–20	2.58	4.08	2.92	2.83
July 21–25	2.62	4.45	3.66	5.38
July 26	4.28	4.87	3.89	5.37
July 27	3.68	4.10	3.97	5.87
July 28	4.95	5.16	4.42	6.06
July 29	4.68	4.89	4.79	4.64
July 30	5.07	6.62	4.25	5.10
July 31	4.60	5.48	6.29	6.30
August 1–2	5.50	7.00	7.19	5.88
August 3–4	5.90	6.50	5.70	6.08

Source: Adapted from Holsti et al. (1968).

[a]S: Response R of Entente in preceding period.
[b]r: Perception of hostility of other coalition against self.
[c]s: Perception of own hostility against other coalition.
[d]R: Own violence.

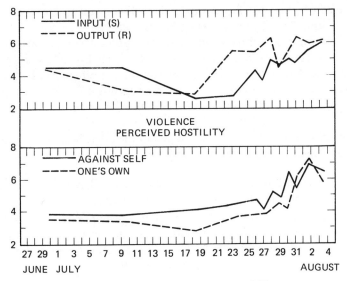

Figure 24.2. (Adapted from Holsti, 1968).

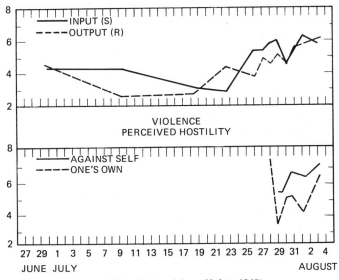

Figure 24.3. (Adapted from Holsti, 1968).

Figures 24.2 and 24.3 show the time courses of violence intensity and perceived hostility of the two sides respectively.

One of the problems posed by the investigators is that of assessing the relative importance of "objective" criteria and "perceptions" as predictors of the behavior of nation states. Results obtained by R. J. Rummel (1964) suggest that in periods of low involvement with external conflict, "objective" criteria are fairly good predictors, but not in periods of high involvement. Now in the period examined, June 27–August 4, 1914 (that is, between the assassination of the Austrian Crown Prince and the outbreak of the general war), it appears that until July 27 (the Austrian ultimatum to Serbia), the Triple Entente was less involved than the Dual Alliance. Possibly the reason for the difference is that until the ultimatum, the conflict appeared to be of local nature, involving Austria (and her German ally). Only after the ultimatum did the crisis assume its "global" character. Thus as Holsti et al. point out, the early period of the crisis concerned a *planned* local war. Only in its last stage did the crisis become systemic with a dynamics of its own. Accordingly, the following hypotheses were proposed:

1. The correlation between input action (S) and policy response will be higher in a situation of low involvement than in one of high involvement.
2. In a situation of low involvement, policy response (R) will tend to be at a lower level of violence than the input action (S), whereas in a high-involvement situation, the policy response (R) will tend to be at a higher level of violence than the input action (S).

Data supporting the impression that the Entente was "less involved" than the Dual Alliance in the early period and that both were highly involved in the late period (July 28–August 4) are those concerning the frequency of perceptions of hostility. During the early period, only 40 perceptions of hostility were manifested by the Entente, compared with 171 by the Alliance. During the later period, the corresponding frequencies were 229 and 270 respectively.

In Table 24.9, $S - R$ denotes the difference between the level of violence in the action of the opposing coalition (S) and the level of violence in the resulting action response (R). Positive values indicate underreaction to the actions of the other coalition; negative values indicate overreaction.

The above hypotheses suggest that the nations of Triple Entente would under-respond to actions from the other side, whereas those of the Dual Alliance would overrespond.

Recall that the present interaction model posits perceptions (that is, the detection and interpretation of stimuli) as intervening between the external stimulus and the output response. The data permit a comparison between stimuli (actions of the opposing side) and the perceptions of those actions; that is, between S and R of Figure 24.1.

Table 24.9 shows these comparisons for the two coalitions.

The hypothesis to be tested is that in the low-involvement situation, r will tend to be at a lower level than S, whereas in the high-involvement situation, r will tend to be at a higher level than S. In other words, the *sensitivity* to stimuli both in detection and interpretation is increased in the high-involvement situation. The data in Table 24.6 support this hypothesis. The Dual Alliance consistently overperceived the level of violence in the actions of the Triple Entente; the latter tended to underperceive the actions for the former.

The same hypothesis can be tested in another way. If, as postulated, the Dual

Table 24.9. *Positive Values of S — R Denote "Underreactions"; Negative Values, Overreaction*

	Alliance		Entente	
Period	$S - R$	Rank	$S - R$	Rank
June 21–July 2	0.13	9.0	−0.13	13.0
July 3–16	1.38	3.0	1.67	2.0
July 17–20	−0.25	16.0	0.38	8.0
July 21–25	−2.76	24.0	−1.45	21.0
July 26	−1.09	19.0	1.70	1.0
July 27	−2.19	23.0	0.42	6.0
July 28	−1.21	20.0	1.19	4.0
July 29	0.04	10.5	0.99	5.0
July 30	−0.03	12.0	0.04	10.5
July 31	−1.70	22.0	−0.40	18.0
August 1–2	−0.38	17.0	0.40	7.0
August 3–4	−0.18	15.0	−0.15	14.0
		$\sum = 190.5 = R_1$		$\sum = 109.5 = R_2$

Source: Adapted from Holsti et al. (1968).

Note: $U = 222 - 190.5 = 31.5$ (Mann-Whitney Test statistic).

$p < 0.025$ (significance).

Alliance was more involved than the Triple Entente in the early phase of the crisis, but equally involved in the final phase, then the difference in the way actions (S) are *perceived* (r) by the nations of the two coalitions should be greatest during the early stages of the crisis. When the data shown in Table 24.6 are reanalyzed in terms of these differences, this hypothesis is also supported. The value of U turns out to be even smaller, yielding a significance value $p = 0.013$ for the earlier period.[1] That is to say, the total overreaction by the Dual Alliance and underreaction by the Triple Entente (in terms of perceptions) is attenuated when these perceptions are examined for the entire period.

Next, we are in a position to examine the difference between r and s. Recall that r denotes perceptions of the other's policy and s the statements of own intent. Following the suggestions of K. E. Boulding (1959) and C. E. Osgood (1962), Holsti et al. propose the following hypothesis:

When there is a difference between perceptions of the other's policy and the statements of own intent, perceptions of hostility in the former will tend to be higher than in the latter in *both* low-involvement and high-involvement situations.

The relevant data are shown in Table 24.10.

From Table 24.10, we see that both parts of the hypothesis are supported. The values of $(r - s)$ are consistently positive throughout the period; moreover, the magnitudes of these differences are not significantly different from each other

Table 24.10. Positive Values of S−r Denote "Undervaluation" of Other Actions; Negative Values, "Overvaluation"

Period	Alliance		Entente	
	$S-r$	Rank	$S-r$	Rank
June 27–July 2	0.40	9.0	1.58	6
July 3–16	0.45	8.0	4.25	3
July 17–20	−1.50	21.5	3.00	4
July 21–25	−1.83	24.0	2.83	5
July 26	−0.59	14.0	−0.62	16
July 27	−0.42	13.0	5.37	2
July 28	−0.21	11.5	5.87	1
July 29	−0.21	11.5	0.73	7
July 30	−1.55	23.0	−0.69	17
July 31	−0.88	18.0	−1.33	20
August 1–2	−1.50	21.5	0.11	10
August 3–4	−0.60	15.0	−1.10	19
		$\sum = \overline{190} = R_1$		$\sum = \overline{110} = R_2$

Source: Adapted from Holsti et al. (1968).

Note: $U = 222 - 190 = 32$ (Mann-Whitney Test statistic). $p < 0.025$ (significance).

for the two coalitions. A notable exception, where $s > r$, is for the Triple Entente on July 28, the day of Austria's declaration of war against Serbia, an indication that the Entente overreacted (in the statements of its intent) to its perception of hostility directed toward *itself* in that declaration of what was initially envisaged as a "local war." On the other hand, the negative values observed on July 31 and August 1–2 for the Dual Alliance are a reflection of Germany's declaration of war against Russia (July 31) and against France (August 1).

The final hypothesis suggested by Holsti et al. is the following:

In the low-involvement situation, s will tend to be larger than R, whereas in the high-involvement situation, the reserve will be the case.

That is to say, in the low-involvement situation, "words will speak louder than acts," and in the high-involvement situation, "actions will speak louder than words." The data shown in Tables 24.11 and 24.12 provide a test of this hypothesis.

From Tables 24.11 and 24.12 we see that the hypothesis is not supported. Most of the values of $(s - R)$ are negative, and one might offer the explanation that in this period of crisis both sides were "highly involved." That would be "cheating," however, since it was originally postulated that the involvement of the Triple Entente, at least in the early stage of the crisis, was "low" compared

Table 24.11. *Positive Values of r − s Denote Perception of More Hostility in Other Than in Self; Negative Values, Perception of More Hostility in Self*

Period	Alliance		Entente	
	$r - s$	Rank	$r - s$	Rank
June 27–July 2	0.43	15	2.67	2
July 3–16	0.54	13	0.00	19
July 17–20	1.16	7	−3.67	23
July 21–25	0.79	11	0.00	19
July 26	0.98	8	6.00	1
July 27	0.13	16	0.00	19
July 28	0.74	12	−7.33	24
July 29	0.10	17	1.93	5
July 30	2.37	3	0.44	14
July 31	−0.81	22	1.43	6
August 1–2	−0.19	21	2.22	4
August 3–4	0.80	10	0.81	9
		$\sum = \overline{155} = R_1$		$\sum = \overline{145} = R_2$

Source: Adapted from Holsti et al. (1968).

Note: $U = 222 - 155 = 67$; not significant (Mann-Whitney Test statistic).

Table 24.12. *Positive Values of s − R Denote "Restrained"; Negative Values, "Overreaction" to Own Perception of Hostility*

Period	Alliance		Entente	
	$s - R$	Rank	$s - R$	Rank
June 27–July 2	−0.70	12	−4.38	23
July 3–16	0.39	4	−2.58	20
July 17–20	0.09	8	1.05	3
July 21–25	−1.72	17	−4.28	22
July 26	−1.48	14	−3.68	21
July 27	−1.90	18	−4.95	24
July 28	−1.64	15	2.65	1
July 29	0.15	6	−1.67	16
July 30	−0.85	13	0.29	5
July 31	−0.01	9	−0.50	11
August 1–2	1.31	2	−1.93	19
August 3–4	−0.38	10	0.14	7
		$\sum = \overline{128} = R_1$		$\sum = \overline{172} = R_2$

Source: Adapted from Holsti et al. (1968).

Note: $U = 222 - 172 = 50$; not significant[1] (Mann-Whitney Test statistic).

to that of the Dual Alliance. Change of hypotheses in midstream is, of course, not permitted.

The summary of findings is cited directly from the article by Holsti et al. (1968):

> The analysis of the 1914 crisis began with an assumption basic to most traditional theories of international politics—that is, the assumption of congruence between input (S) and output (R) action. The data revealed, however, a significant difference between the two coalitions corresponding to the different levels of involvement in the situation. Congruence between (S) and (R) was high for the members of the Triple Entente, which became involved only very late in the crisis. The level of congruence was much lower for the nations of the Dual Alliance, which were engaged for essentially the entire crisis period.

Having failed to account for the escalation from a local incident to a general war with only the action variables, Holsti et al. turned to the perceptual variables r and s. The various links across the model were examined and no significant differences were found between the two coalitions with regard to the $s - R$ step: (R) was higher than (s) in both cases. As predicted, there was little difference between the Triple Entente and the Dual Alliance in the $r - s$ link, both perceiving themselves less hostile than the other coalition. A significant difference did appear at the $S - r$ step, however. The leaders of the Dual Alliance consistently overperceived the actions of the Triple Entente. Thus the $S - r$ link served as a "magnifying" function. The decisionmakers of the Triple Entente, on the other hand, tended to underperceive the actions of the Dual Alliance. This difference in perceiving the environment (the S–r link) is consistent with the pronounced tendency of the Dual Alliance to respond at a higher level of violence than the Triple Entente.

THE BERLIN CRISIS

The next situation we will examine in the light of massive data processing is the so-called Berlin Crisis. Usually, this term is used to designate the period of the airlift to West Berlin in 1948–1949. C. A. McClelland (1968), however, points out that the word "crisis" has become extremely common in discussions of world affairs. When a situation is so labeled by newspapers, it becomes *ipso facto* a "crisis" in people's minds. Thus the characteristics usually associated with a crisis (that is, a rapidly rising intensity of some relevant variables leading to a dramatic denouement) are no longer the crucial criterion. McClelland quotes an unnamed West Berlin official: "What Americans must understand is that there is *always* a Berlin crisis. The Russians see to that." So "crisis" has become practically synonymous with "trouble" in common parlance about international politics. This is a typical example of "semantic degradation," a blurring of distinction between concepts. To restore the distinction between the meaning of "crisis," with its implications of some acute manifestation, in contrast to a chronic condition, one would start with an "operational definition." There are, however, drawbacks associated with this approach inasmuch as operational definitions are to a certain extent arbitrary: they depend on particular criteria that the proposer of the definition is most concerned with or considers most salient for the concept. We have seen how the "operational definition" of "power" varies from study to study.

The outlook characteristic of general systems theory may be of some help here. Recall that the state of a system is defined in terms of the values of a set of variables. Assuming that a set of variables has been singled out that describes the "important" properties of a system, one examines the state so defined over time. Periods during which the state remains approximately constant or changes slowly can be taken to be "crisis-free." Crises can be associated with sudden large changes in the state variables of the system.

Now systems can sometimes be described in terms of other systems that constitute their components. Technological and biological examples immediately come to mind. An automobile, considered as a system, comprises several subsystems—the ignition system, the internal combustion engine, the cooling system, and so on. An organism comprises several functioning subsystems—the digestive, the respiratory, the circulatory, the nervous, and so on. An important difference between an artifact like an automobile and an organism like an animal is that the latter system has regulatory mechanisms that can exert homeostatic influences on its subsystems, which most artifacts do not have, at least not nearly to the same degree. When through exertion oxygen supply becomes depleted, the respiratory system increases its activity and so makes more oxygen available to the muscles. In an automobile, when something goes wrong with the carburetor, the other subsystems are not in a position to restore its normal functioning. This difference suggests the following question about some system under consideration. Is the "supersystem" in a position to influence the functioning of its subsystems or is the functioning of the supersystem no more than a composite of the functioning of its subsystems? Or, to put it another way, do "crises" generated in subsystems add up to a "crisis" of the supersystem, or is the reverse effect more typical? If there were regulating mechanisms in the supersystem, one could expect that "crises" occurring in the subsystems would be, as a rule, "resolved" by the mobilization of these mechanisms. On the other hand, if the supersystem underwent a crisis (that is, if its regulatory mechanisms failed), this would be reflected in rapid changes of states in the subsystems. The latter would undergo crises.

In a political context, consider the global international system as the supersystem and "local interactions" among specific powers or states as the functioning of subsystems. Do crisis in the subsystems generate crises in the supersystem or vice versa? It is not likely that this question can be answered satisfactorily. In fact, it is not even properly put, since in all likelihood "either-or" questions about direction of causality are usually self-defeating. Most likely, feedback operates in all such situations. Nevertheless, the question can stimulate concrete investigations.

McClelland (1961) assumes that the global international system does possess "regulating" mechanisms. This assumption is reflected in the three propositions posed by him.

1. Acute international crises are "short burst" affairs and are marked by an unusual volume and intensity of events. (This is simply a statement of criteria by which to "diagnose" an international crisis.)
2. The general trend in acute international crises will be found to be toward "routinizing" crisis behaviors; toward dealing with the risks, troubles, and dangers involved by means of increasingly "standard" techniques.
3. In the interplay of a crisis, the participants will be reluctant to allow the level of violence to increase beyond the level present at the onset of the crisis.

The last two assumptions reflect the postulation of a regulating mechanism and relate it to the motivations of the decision makers.

The propositions suggest a line of investigations designed to answer the following questions.

1. Can a "change of state" be detected in the activities of a system in the transition from a noncrisis period to a crisis period?
2. Can a designated subsystem that is part of a more general system of action be shown to be responsive to significant disturbances of the general system?
3. Can the three statements about international crisis behavior specified above be confirmed or belied by a study of a body of relevant historical information?

The raw data used in this study consisted of 1,791 events reported in the *New York Times Index*. Here it is appropriate to point out a crucial difference between the method of content analysis and the historiographic method. The historian sees his task as that of reconstructing as faithfully as possible some sequence of events "as they actually happened." To do this, he tries to get hold of all available records pertaining to the events. Then he uses his judgment as to the amount of credence to give to reported incidents and to weigh them with respect to their importance. In contrast, the 1,791 events reported in the *New York Times Index* already represent a selection of incidents, guided by other than historiographic considerations. This body of data is, therefore, quite inadequate from the historian's point of view; but it is not necessarily inadequate from the content analyst's point of view. Content analysis is, for the most part, representative of the systemic approach, and for the content analyst, "the state of the system" may well be reflected in the large corpora generated by the "elite press," of which *The New York Times* is representative.

Next, the content analyst's "extreme empirical orientation" requires that he refrain from prejudging the relative importance of events. If he does assign weights of relative importance (as in the degrees of intensity assigned to actions or statements in the previous study), he does so by using a panel of independent judges, who can themselves be regarded as "instruments" recording the state of the system. In the present study, relative weights were not attached to events. For example, the Soviet order that finally closed the roads, railroads, and canals between West Germany and Berlin on June 24, 1948, was treated as no more and no less weighty than the accusation on July 19, 1953, by the Soviet High Commissioner that American planes were dropping anti-Soviet leaflets on Soviet airfields near Berlin.

Nevertheless, there is no such thing as freedom from preconceptions (the pure empiricist's ideal). The very motivation for an empirical investigation already involves preconceptions. McClelland selected the theme "Access to Berlin" as an example of a "chronic" crisis, which at times exhibited "acute" stages. He pictures the situation as a continuing struggle between the Soviet Union and the West over a concrete pair of incompatible objectives. The West's objective has been that of preserving the status of four-partite occupation of Berlin. The Soviet objective has been to end the occupation status of Berlin and to incorporate the city into East Germany as the capital of a sovereign state. Both sides, however, have been unwilling to have this confrontation escalate into a war. Thus there was a "threshold" that neither side was willing to cross, even though at times they "pushed" against this threshold. The problem that suggests itself for research is that of identifying this "threshold" in some objective terms and of describing the flow and ebb of events in terms of approaches and recessions from it.

Content analysis typically begins with some coding procedure; that is, the construction of indices. In this case, the reported incidents were coded according to occurrence of different categories of actions reported. The names of the categories were assigned to approximate synonyms of the designations of the actions in the reports. The code is shown below.

It will be observed that this code roughly represents a spectrum from "compliance" at one end to overt, violent conflict at the other. In this study, however, this gradation was not used. Analysis was confined to overall frequencies (by years, from 1948 to 1963) of overall activity related to Berlin. The only processing that took account of the distribution of the categories was in the calculation of the measure of "uncertainty." Maximum uncertainty (about 4.1 bits) would be associated with an equiprobable distribution of the 18 categories. (Some are omitted from the above list.) Uncertainty approaching zero would result in a concentration on very few categories; that is, a very "peaked" distribution.

It is not altogether clear how this uncertainty measure is to be related to the state of the system. On the one hand, one might argue that an acute stage of the

Code Term	As Synonym for
Accede	Agree, give consent, approve, permit, . . . , apologize
Withdraw	Release, relent, retreat, avoid contact
Request	Ask, petition, query
Propose	Suggest, urge
Bargain	Make a contingent offer
-	-
Protest	Complain, object
Reject	Turn down, spurn, ridicule
-	-
Accuse	Censure, indict
Demand	Issue statement calling on other party to respond in "must form"
Threaten	State a warning in the form "unless . . . then . . ."
Force	Seize, arrest, execute rule, decree, or policy in some physical manner, take territory (with no physical resistance of opposing group)
Attack	Exert force violently against resistance of other, kill, injure, destroy

crisis would be associated with low uncertainty if, for example, the actions were strongly concentrated at the "conflict end of the spectrum." With equal justification, however, one could associate low uncertainty with the relatively placid stages, when actions become predominantly "compliant."

One could argue, perhaps, that "high uncertainty" could be regarded as reflecting a harbinger of an impending acute stage of the "chronic crisis," when the parties keep shifting among the categories, utilizing the entire range of "options." I suspect, however, that the "uncertainty" index was introduced simply because it was an available index; in other words, in the course of a "fishing expedition" to see what picture this index would yield. Recall that for a pure empiricist there is no such thing as a negative or a disconfirming finding, since he examines the data (processed in any way that may suggest itself) for what they may or may not yield.

Table 24.13 shows the "volumes" of activity by West and East in the 16 years examined in terms of the recorded number of instances as coded. The Berlin Crisis years, 1948 and 1949, are clearly reflected in these data in peaks of "activity," as reported in the *New York Times Index*. In itself, this congruence between the intuitive perception of the situation (that "crises" occurred in those two years) is of little or no theoretical significance because intensification of activity is exactly what one would expect under the circumstances. The value of compiling and examining these data is merely in the confirmation that the "volume of activity" does reflect the situations intuitively perceived as "crises."

The index of "uncertainty," being a less obvious presumed indicator of crises, is more interesting. Values of this index in the same 16 years are shown in Table 24.14. The uncertainty measure recorded in Table 24.14 is relative uncertainty; that is, the ratio of actual uncertainty to the maximum possible uncertainty (4.12 bits). We see from the table that the "crisis" year 1948 shows a peak of relative uncertainty in the reported behavior of both West and East. The other "crisis" year, 1961 (the year the Wall was erected), is almost a peak year, although uncertainty is somewhat larger in both adjacent years in the reported behavior of the West.

It appears, therefore, that both the "intensity" of activity and the "uncertainty" reflect *something* about crises behavior. The correlation between intensity and crises is, of course, expected. That of "uncertainty" and crises is less so. In fact, as already pointed out, one could have expected the opposite: in crises, increased *stereotyped* behavior could be expected to decrease uncertainty. It is therefore interesting to see whether the observed result can be seen elsewhere. Table 24.15 shows analogous results related to the situation in the Taiwan Straits. The underlined months have generally been regarded as corresponding to the acute phase of the crisis. The higher levels of uncertainty in those months are apparent.

We thus have two indices of crisis: frequency of incidents and the "uncertainty" of the crisis. The latter index, not being related to usual notions, appears to have more theoretical leverage. However, the two indices can be expected to be correlated because when the number of incidents falls below a certain level, by chance alone some of the categories will not be represented, which reduces the level of uncertainty. Since increase of frequency is strongly expected on a priori grounds, so should increase of uncertainty. Thus the concordance of the "more interesting" index with intuitive evaluation of crisis phases is not much more informative than the concordance of frequency with these phases.

Nevertheless, certain aspects of the data are of some interest. From Tables 24.13 and 24.14, we see that whereas frequencies of incidents attributed to the East are considerably greater than those attributed to the West, the uncertainty measures are, for the most part, larger in the behavior of the West. If by chance alone uncertainty should be positively correlated with frequency, there is evidence that the responses of the West were inherently more "uncertain" than those of the East. This may be evidence that the West is more "flexible" in its responses; that is, utilizes more varied options, or that it is more "confused."

Of course, it must be constantly kept in mind that the data do not necessarily represent "objective reality" (whatever that may be), since this "reality" has already been filtered through the perceptions of the staff of *The New York Times*. It would then be especially interesting to examine the whole period as filtered through, say, the Soviet press and compare the indices so obtained. Such a comparison would not necessarily put us in closer contact with "objective reality," but may be informative about differences between the perceptions of the East and those of the West.

Another finding is of some interest. The "general understanding" of the Berlin situation identifies three "crises." Besides the two named (the Blockade and the

Table 24.13. Volumes of Activity by West and East With Reference to the Berlin Conflict from 1948 to 1963

	1948	1949	1950	1951	1952	1953	1954	1955	1956	1957	1958	1959	1960	1961	1962	1963
West	144	44	57	39	69	36	16	27	7	7	7	22	33	135	63	23
East	210	81	87	61	128	58	22	38	10	11	14	23	43	149	88	39
Total	354	125	144	100	197	94	38	65	17	18	21	45	76	284	151	68

Source: Adapted from McClelland (1968).

Table 24.14. Index of Uncertainty Calculated for Actions of the West and East with Reference to the Berlin Conflict

	1948	1949	1950	1951	1952	1953	1954	1955	1956	1957	1958	1959	1960	1961	1962	1963
West	0.927	0.869	0.764	0.899	0.792	0.812	0.628	0.734	0.540	0.278	0.540	0.657	0.782	0.781	0.829	0.658
East	0.873	0.740	0.649	0.736	0.658	0.795	0.670	0.694	0.527	0.452	0.501	0.712	0.746	0.812	0.812	0.668
Difference	+0.054	+0.129	+0.115	+0.163	+0.134	+0.017	-0.042	+0.040	+0.013	-0.174	+0.039	-0.055	+0.036	-0.031	+0.017	-0.010

Source: Adapted from McClelland (1968).

448

Table 24.15.   "Index of Uncertainty" Calculated for Actions in the Taiwan Straits
During Presumed Crisis Periods

Jan.	Feb.	Mar.	Apr.	May	Jun.	Jul.	Aug.	Sep.	Oct.	Nov.	Dec.
					1954						
—	—	0.333	0.307	0.380	0.240	0.601	0.703	0.630	0.706	0.706	0.705
H (rel.)											
					1955						
0.807	0.740	0.734	0.814	0.751	0.618	0.732	0.506	0.786	0.532	0.240	0.573
					1958						
—	—	—	0.454	0.333	0.000	0.747	0.556	0.749	0.834	0.742	0.452
H (rel.)											
					1959						
0.555	0.597	0.640	0.333	0.253	0.289	—	—	—	—	—	—

Source: Adapted from McClelland (1968).

Wall crises of 1961), there was also supposedly the "Deadline Crisis." This one is related to Khrushchev's announcement on November 27, 1958, that unless specified changes were made in the status of Berlin within six months, the Soviet Union would conclude its own settlement with East Germany, which was interpreted to mean that East Germany would unilaterally end the occupation. Examination of the data reveals nothing that would identify those six months with an acute stage. This might mean that the indices considered here do not reflect acute stages in all cases or that the so-called Deadline Crisis was not really an acute stage of the systemic process.

CORRELATES OF WAR

We will next examine the application of the "uncertainty" measure to derive a relationship between the number of alliances in which a state has participated and the number of wars in which it was engaged. The period examined is 1815–1945 (Midlarsky, 1970).

The basis of the argument is that each alliance contributes to the "uncertainty" experienced by an actor in the international system since it increases his responsibility to intervene militarily should an ally be involved in a war. Assuming equiprobability, the uncertainty associated with N alliances is $\log(N)$. Moreover, the length of time during which an actor participates in an alliance also contributes to uncertainty. Assuming a uniform frequency distribution over the period of an alliance, the logarithm of the period is also a measure of uncertainty and is assumed to be a contributing factor. Finally, a distinction is made between explicitly defensive alliances and others. Thus for each actor, three independent variables are singled out: (1) total number of alliances in which the actor participated in the 130-year period; (2) number of defensive alliances; and (3) number of years of participation in alliances. For example, Germany (including Prussia up to 1871) participated in 22 alliances, of which 10 were defensive, during 111 years of the 130-year period, whereas Iran participated in 4 alliances, none defensive, during 14 years.

The dependent variable is the number of wars in which each actor participated during the 130-year period. For instance, Germany participated in 7 wars, Italy in 11, Brasil in 2, and so on. Other indices related to wars, such as "magnitude" (measured by duration) or "severity" (measured by the number of casualties), are not considered in this model. Midlarsky points out that alliances are relevant to the incidence of wars but not to their duration or severity, which are presumably determined by other factors, to be discussed below.

The three independent variables and the dependent variable were calculated for each of some 80 countries that were considered to be "actors" in the international system during 1815–1945. The plots of the number of wars against the logarithm of each of the three independent variables (measures of maximum "uncertainty" associated with each of the variables) turned out to be roughly linear. The plot of the number of wars against the logarithm of the total number of alliances is shown in Figure 24.4.

The correlations between the numbers of wars and the three measures of "uncertainty" turn out to be 0.58, 0.70, and 0.59 (all significant) *after* the linear component of the correlations has been factored out, which shows that the

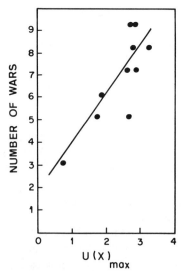

Figure 24.4. (Adapted from Midlarsky, 1975). Abscissa: "maximum uncertainty," $U(x)_{max}$, is measured by the logarithm of the total number of alliances in the system.

logarithmic measure is more appropriate for the independent variables than the simple linear measured advanced, for example, by Singer and Small (1968).

Correlations by themselves do not indicate direction of causality. Thus one could offer two possible explanations for the observed correlations: (1) "Uncertainty" is an intervening variable between alliances and war; that is to say, alliances generate "uncertainty," which contributes to the likelihood of war; or (2) alliances are the intervening variable between "uncertainty" and war; that is, "uncertainty" exists prior to the formation of an additional alliance, and the latter contributes to the likelihood of war. To resolve the issue, a technique known as causal inference analysis can be employed. The results of the analysis support the first formulation against the second with respect to all three independent variables.

The same "uncertainty" measure is applicable in deriving a relationship between the number of borders of a country and the number of wars in which it participated. The corresponding plot is shown in Figure 24.5.

Finally, Midlarsky examines the relationship of the frequency of wars and a measure of "polarity" of the international system. Intuitively, polarity is associated with the extent to which alliances partition the international system into two hostile camps. Thus extreme polarity would characterize a system in which all actors of each camp are allied with each other and regard each actor of the other camp as a potential opponent in a war.

The construction of a quantitative measure of polarity is associated with some difficulties. Intuitively, one might want to identify "complete polarization" with a model of the international system represented by a completely balanced graph

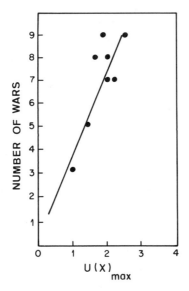

Figure 24.5. (Adapted from Midlarsky, 1975). Abscissa: "maximum uncertainty," $U(x)_{max}$, is measured by the logarithm of the number of borders of a country with its neighbors.

(see p. 282). However, a graph representing an international system in which everyone is allied with everyone is also balanced and certainly cannot be taken to represent a "completely polarized" system. Therefore, one might want to introduce an additional measure of polarization related to the near-equality of the two hostile blocs. But this measure can be used only if the system consists of only two camps. One is tempted to turn once again to the formal measure of "uncertainty," which attains its maximum value in equipartition, but it is not easy to justify such a measure on intuitive grounds.

Nevertheless, Midlarsky, following Rosencrance (1963) and Hopkins and Mansbach (1973), examines the incidence of wars in relation to the "number of poles" in the international system, that is, the number of major foci of alliance systems, which varies from 2 to 5, taking, as usual, the logarithm of this number as a measure of "uncertainty." Comparison of observed and expected frequencies of war is shown in Table 24.16.

Midlarsky distinguishes three classes of indices: those that characterize the international system as a whole, those that characterize the boundary between the actor and the international system, and those that characterize the individual actors. All three cases just considered relate, according to Midlarsky, to the first category. This is reasonable in the case of the index of polarity. However, the number of alliances in which an actor participates and especially the number of borders of a country seem to be more appropriately classified in the second or third category. This discrepancy is of minor importance. A more serious criticism can be leveled at Midlarsky's "uncertainty" models; namely, that they are too "top heavy." When the models are put to empirical test, all that remains of the predicted relations is that the incidence of wars is fairly well described as a linear function of the logarithm of the number of alliances, the number of borders, or the number of poles in the international system, as the case may be. But the characterizing feature of the logarithmic function is that it is monotone increasing with a negative second derivative, exhibiting so-called diminishing returns.

Table 24.16. Frequency of Wars Related to Number of Poles in the International System

Number of Poles (N)	Observed Frequency of Wars[a]		Expected $10 \log_e N$
	Rosencrance	Hopkins-Mansbach	
1.0	2.0	2.0	0.0
1.5[b]	5.0	—[b]	4.05
2.0	7.5	6.5	6.93
5.0	12.0	17.0	16.09

Source: Adapted from Midlarsky (1975).

[a]Expected means in each time period.

[b]Hopkins and Mansbach did not consider a "quasipolar" system, as did Rosencrance.

That the frequency of wars is monotonically related to the above mentioned variables is, of course, not surprising. As for the "diminishing returns" effect, it is observed in a great many monotone relations, and certainly the data are neither numerous enough nor precise enough to support the logarithmic function against many other functions whose graphs are concave downward. There remains only the "rationale" for the logarithmic function, derived from its role as a measure of "uncertainty." However, the relevance of this concept in the contexts discussed is anything but convincing.

STATUS INCONSISTENCY

We turn to the next set of independent variables, which Midlarsky classifies as characterizing the boundary between the actor and the international system. These have to do with so-called status inconsistency.

The notion of status as applied to actors in the international system is of early origin. Already in 1504, Pope Julius II rank-ordered the Christian princes of Europe, beginning with the Emperor of the Holy Roman Empire through the kings (Rex Romanorum, Rex Franciae, Rex Hispaniae, and so on) through the dukes (Dux Burgundiae, Dux Bavariae, Dux Saxoniae, and so on).

In our time, no such authoritative ranking is available. Nevertheless, indices of status can be constructed. For instance, when Stalin asked at the Teheran Conference in 1944, "How many divisions has the Vatican?" he was presumably being sarcastic about the status of the Holy See in international affairs. Crude as this measure (number of divisions) may be, there is no question that indices of importance attached to actors in the international arena play a part in international affairs.

The concept of status inconsistency involves two types of status indices: indices of "achievement" and indices of "ascribed status." The former are strongly weighted by the degree of "modernization" of states and are, in turn, partitioned into two categories: *centralization* and *capability*. Centralization has to do with the facility with which a nation can be organized for some collective action. This depends on its transportation facilities, of which railroad mileage may be a suitable index (at least in nineteenth century Europe). Further, communication facilities are reflected in the telegraph and telephone systems and in mail flow.

Finally, urbanization is another important component of centralization. Capability is reflected in the gross national product and in the total population.

Ascribed status has to do with the "amount of recognition" rendered to the state in question. One way of quantifying this component is by the number and rank of diplomats received (suggested by Singer and Small, 1966). Other measures might be the number of international conferences held in the nation's capital. The last mentioned, however, although it may have been appropriate in the nineteenth century, does not seem to be appropriate today. Favorite sites of international conferences in our day are the neutral countries which are, as a rule, small. For instance, Geneva has certainly had more than its share of international conferences, and this hardly implies a high status assigned to Switzerland.

Another possible index of ascribed status might be the number of international organizations to which a country belongs. This index, too, has lost its significance. Although at one time international organizations were rather selective in their membership, they are wide open today.

Midlarsky uses diplomatic representation as an index of ascribed status. He uses two measures of achieved status, one averaged over the components of centralization, the other averaged over the components of capability. His measure of status inconsistency, however, is not the difference between achieved and ascribed status but between the rates of change of achieved and ascribed status in the time period 1860–1940. All the indices are standardized with mean zero and standard deviation unity. The resulting status inconsistency scores with respect to centralization and capability are shown in Table 24.17.

Positive entries indicate that the corresponding rates of change of achievement were larger than the rates of change of ascribed status. For example, the United States has high positive inconsistency scores with respect to both achievement indices. This means that its rate of centralization and growth of capability in the period 1860–1940 were much larger than the growth of diplomatic recognition. (This is hardly surprising, because diplomatic recognition of the United States was already high in 1860.) Finland and Poland, on the other hand, have negative inconsistency scores. This is also not surprising, because both countries became independent only after World War I and achieved diplomatic recognition at a rapid rate thereafter.

From the data of Table 24.18 we can construct a categorization of countries falling into extreme ranges of inconsistency. From Table 24.18 we see that the

Table 24.17. Indices of Centralization and Potential of Various States, 1860 1940

State	Centralization	Potential
U.S.A.	4.895	3.664
USSR (Russia)	2.006	3.490
Japan	1.175	1.567
Germany (Prussia)	1.270	1.079
England	1.260	0.585
France	0.993	−0.030
Austria (Austria-Hungary)	0.238	0.058
Belgium	−0.235	−0.410
Bulgaria	−0.567	−0.625
Finland	−1.225	−1.399
Czechoslovakia	−3.564	−4.093

Source: Adapted from Midlarsky (1975).

Table 24.18. Countries With Large Positive Inconsistency and Large Negative Inconsistency Between Status and Achievement

Over 1.000 (positive inconsistency)	Less than −1.000 (negative inconsistency)
Centralization	
England	Czechoslovakia
Germany	Finland
Japan	Luxembourg
Russia	Poland
U.S.A.	
Potential	
Brazil	Czechoslovakia
Germany	Finland
Japan	Luxembourg
Russia	Poland
U.S.A.	

Source: Adapted from Midlarksy (1975).

countries with large positive inconsistency scores are large countries that underwent the most rapid development during 1860–1940. Since they are among the most "important" countries, their diplomatic status was already high at the beginning of the period and so could not be increased sufficiently rapidly to keep pace with their development. Equally clear is the presence of Czechoslovakia, Poland, and Finland in the second column for reasons already mentioned. Thus the categorization reveals little that is not already intuited on common sense grounds. Let us now see whether a more detailed statistical analysis sheds more light on the matter.

Midlarsky specifies five independent variables (the five components of status inconsistency) and three dependent variables: frequency of wars, magnitude (duration) and severity (battle deaths). Midlarsky argues that whereas alliances, borders and polarity could be expected to influence only the incidence of wars, status inconsistency could be expected to influence their magnitude and severity. The argument is based on the conjecture that the propensity to wage long and severe wars is enhanced by a determination of an actor to reduce his status inconsistency; that is, to win a "place in the sun" consistent with his "achievement." The idea is somewhat related to J. Galtung's theory of structural violence (Galtung, 1969), according to which revolutionary ferment is generated by "rising expectations." The most aggressive classes, ethnic groups, or, in this context, nations, are not those that are merely "underdogs" (in Galtung's terminology), but rather underdogs already attaining some measure of equality.

It is assumed that the appetite for equality (or "recognition") outstrips the rate at which it is being attained. The applicability of this idea in the present context may be questioned inasmuch as the nations with the largest status inconsistency are certainly not the "underdogs" of the international system (see Table 24.18). It is, of course, possible to attribute the aggressiveness of Germany and Japan during the first half of this century to a determination to attain a "place in the sun" commensurate with their "achievements"; but if so, some measure of status other than diplomatic recognition would be more relevant.

Be this as it may, the empirical orientation requires the investigator to abandon his intuited notions and to push through with the formal analysis based entirely on the data gathered. Assuming a moderate degree of statistical independence among the independent variables, multiple regression analysis is an appropriate procedure. Its purpose is threefold: (1) to reveal the degree of statistical *prediction* afforded by each of the independent variables; (2) to estimate the extent to which *explanation* is afforded by the statistically independent effect of each variable; and (3) *specification* of the predictors that bear the strongest relationship to the criterion. The last mentioned provides the theoretical leverage of the model. It points to the relative importance of the selected indices.

The partial correlations and the values of the F statistic reflecting the significance of the correlations are shown in Table 24.19. From the table we see that achievement alone accounts for less of the variance than inconsistency (except with respect to years in war). We thus have a certain degree of corroboration of the relevance of the inconsistency hypothesis.

Turning to the problem of comparing the explanatory power of the various independent variables, we examine the proportion of variance contributed by the *interaction* of achieved and ascribed status over and above the additive contributions of the variables themselves. L. Broom and F. L. Jones (1970)

Table 24.19. Frequency, Duration, and Intensity of Wars Related to Inconsistency and to Achievement

	Years of War	Number of Wars	Casualties
	Inconsistency		
R	0.76	0.91	0.92
F	10.03[a]	13.20[a]	15.19[a]
	Achievement		
R	0.89	0.71	0.87
F	12.83[a]	3.19[b]	10.33[b]

Source: Adapted from Midlarsky (1975).
Note: R: Correlation. F: F statistic.
[a]$p < 0.01$
[b]$p < 0.05$

faced the same problem with their analysis of voting behavior. They write:

> For the purpose of assessing the status consistency thesis . . . the crucial
> question is not how much of the total variation can be explained, but whether
> a regression equation including terms of status inconsistency explains sig-
> nificantly more of the total variance in voting behavior than one restricted to
> terms for the status variables themselves.

The increased percentage of variance explained over and above additive effects
of the status variables is shown in Table 24.20.

Specification of the most important component among the independent
variables is complicated by the multicoollineality of the components. Cluster
analysis is a technique designed to get around this problem. R. C. Tryon and
D. E. Bailey (1970) describe the aim of cluster analysis as that of "discovering a
minimal number of composites among a collection of variables or objects
without loss of generality, in the sense that the reduced set will reproduce the
intercorrelation among the full array."

Cluster analysis requires less stringent conditions to be satisfied by the data
than factor analysis (see p. 308), and the factors singled out by it need not be
orthogonal. In the present case, cluster analysis singles out three factors. The
first clearly involves all the achievement variables, the second ascribed status,
whereas the heaviest loading is status inconsistency with reference to centralization. The next step is multiple regression analysis involving the factor scores
on these three factors. The result points to centralization inconsistency as the
most relevant and the most reliable predictor of the various components of war

Table 24.20

Criteria	Economic Development	Population	Transportation	Urbanization	Communication
			Inconsistency		
Years of wars	1.34	—	−1.36	−0.36	1.09
Number of wars	7.02	−4.04	−1.23	−2.28	0.87
Casualties	0.68	−0.29	−0.06	0.87	−0.67
			Achievement		
Years of wars	2.48	−1.39	−0.35	0.29	−0.81
Number of wars	2.69	−1.08	−0.52	−0.35	−0.52
Casualties	0.28	0.11	−0.04	1.29	−1.20

Source: Adapted from Midlarsky (1975).

involvement. In view of this finding, Midlarsky advances his conjecture:

> Decision makers acting for their countries internalize the status inconsistencies of their respective nation states. If the nation has a high rate of achievement but a concomittant attributed importance does not follow from this achievement, then the decision makers may behave as frustrated individuals or experience uncertainties as to the precise position or status of the countries they represent. These ambiguities may then lead to international violence as an effort to resolve once and for all the anomalous state generated by the status inconsistencies.

One might next inquire why status inconsistencies with regard to centralization are more relevant than status inconsistencies with regard to capabilities. An *ex post facto* explanation suggests itself in that the capability variables are less directly related to qualitative societal changes than the centralization variables. For instance, the gross national product includes components other than industrial production, and population growth is not entirely due to "modernization," whereas the centralization variables are more directly related to this process. Urbanization (a centralization component) may also have been an important factor in the growth of modern nationalism, which is generally assumed to have been a stimulant of political violence.

We turn to the purely internal factors characterizing individual states and contributing to the incidence, magnitude, and severity of wars.

As usual, the first step is that of selecting indicators and designing some way of quantifying them. This framework is taken from a work by S. N. Eisenstadt (1953), who has listed 65 historical political systems and has coded 88 descriptive variables on which they can be compared. The next step is the application of cluster analysis in order to single out representative variables for each cluster. An example of such a cluster analysis is shown in Table 24.21. Clusters of variables having the highest loadings on the factors are them combined into these

Table 24.21.   Correlation Between Degrees of Development of Various Components of Social Organization

	1	2	3	4	5	6	7
1. Development							
2. Gentry	0.21						
3. Religion	0.21	0.19					
4. Bureaucracy	0.20	−0.09	−0.24				
5. Legal	0.52	−0.11	0.14	−0.18			
6. Military	0.20	0.28	−0.13	0.42	−0.09		
7. Peasantry	0.44	0.18	0.32	−0.05	0.29	0.14	

Source: Adapted from Eisenstadt (1963).

representative variables: (1) development, (2) gentry, (3) religious, (4) bureaucratic, (5) legal, (6) military, and (7) peasantry.

Correlations among these seven turn out to be for the most part weak, indicating approximate orthogonality of the factors.

Factor scores were obtained for a subset of the political systems listed by Eisenstadt; namely, those on which war data are obtainable from a study by P. Sorokin (1962). These are:

Rome, 27 B.C. to 96 A.D.

Rome, 96–193 (the so-called era of "enlightened emperors")

Rome, 193–350 (from military autocracy until the approximate end of the importance of the Western Empire)

Spanish Empire, 1520–1580 (from the conquests to the middle of Philip II's reign)

Austria, 1740–1790 (Maria Theresa to Joseph II)

Spain, 1580–1621 (height of absolutism)

Russia, 1682–1725 (Peter the Great)

Russia, 1725–1761 (decline of absolutism and instability)

Russia, 1762–1796 (Catherine II, "enlightened absolutism")

Prussia, 1640–1740 (Great Elector to Frederick William I)

Prussia, 1740–1792 (Frederick the Great, "enlightened absolutism")

France, 1589–1660 (Henry IV to the personal rule of Louis XIV)

France, 1660–1715 (Louis XIV)

France, 1715–1789 (Louis XV to the Revolution)

England, 1509–1640 (absolutist rule of Tudors and early Stuarts)

England, 1660–1688 (restoration of the Stuarts)

England, 1689–1783 (the "Glorious Revolution" to the loss of American colonies)

Table 24.22 shows the multiple regression analyses of the three characteristics of war. The entries are beta weights. Three specific predictors appear to have significant effect: the military dimension in the case of years of war, and the religious and bureaucratic dimensions in the case of casualties.

Midlarsky points out that the interpretation of the findings is relatively straightforward. The military may be influential in prolonging wars even if they are going badly; hence the positive effect of that factor on the duration of wars. The religious dimension may contribute to battle casualties through intensity of beliefs, while the bureaucracy might be willing to suffer casualties (among the military, naturally—A.R.) to further specific political interests. It should be kept in mind, of course, that all these explanations are *ex post facto*.

Another way of comparing the relative importance of the indicators is to examine those with the largest beta weights associated with each dependent

Table 24.22. Multiple Regression Coefficients of Three Aspects of War Related to Various Components of Social Organization

Criteria	Development	Gentry	Religion	Bureaucracy	Jurisprudence	Military	Peasantry	R	F
Number of wars	−0.13	0.15	0.38	0.25			0.48	0.61	1.44
Years of wars			−0.26	−0.54	0.20	0.69^a		0.70	2.30
Casualties	0.31	−0.35	0.53^a	0.64^a	0.14		0.35	0.78	3.74^a

Source: Adapted from Midlarsky (1975).

$^a p < 0.05$

variable. We note that associated with the numbers of wars, the largest beta weight is given to the peasantry; associated with duration, to the military; associated with battle casualties, to the bureaucracy. We note, further, that the peasantry enters as the second largest beta weight in the regression equation for duration. Midlarsky speculates that the importance of the peasantry may reside in the effects of mass movements on the frequency and duration of war. "The mass population may anger more quickly than their statesmen, given similar provocation, and the desire for victory may prolong a war begun by mass-oriented political authorities" (Midlarsky, 1975). In contrast, the regression equation for battle deaths does not contain the peasantry component. Midlarsky conjectures that the casualties suffered mainly by large groups such as the peasantry may even contribute a weak negative effect.

Of some interest is the apparently anomalous feature of the analysis. We note that the bureaucracy has a strong positive effect on battle casualties but a considerable negative effect on duration. This may be understood in terms of a dual role of bureaucracy. A well-developed bureaucracy may be instrumental in effecting the mobilization of large masses, thus contributing to battle deaths. (This is corroborated to a certain extent by the moderate positive effect of development on battle casualties.) On the other hand, bureaucracy functions in maintaining domestic services and in providing some internal stability. Thus it may be in the interest of the bureaucracy to resist extreme prolongation of a war.

Finally, we observe the *absence* of any statistically significant effects of development on any of the three features of war.

CRITIQUE

Some of the limitations inherent in correlational analysis are well known and understood by its practitioners. To begin with, the direction of causality is not revealed by a correlation. Even if further analysis reveals that one variable lags behind the other, the conclusion that the latter is a "cause" and the former an "effect" may be a case of the *post hoc propter hoc* fallacy. If a train arrives regularly at 10:15, we cannot conclude that the position of the hands on the clock at 10:00 causes the arrival of the train 15 minutes later. The only way to establish a causal relation is by controlled experiments, which are unfortunately (or perhaps fortunately) not possible in the context of international relations.

Aside from these methodological difficulties, however, which are generally acknowledged in appropriate disclaimers, there are others that are, as a rule, ignored by quantitatively oriented social scientists. These are related to the logical foundations of the statistical method.

Consider an elementary problem of statistical inference. It is desired to ascertain whether the means of variables characterizing two populations are significantly different; for instance, the incomes of two distinguishable occupational groups. If the income of every individual in each group is ascertainable, the question can be answered by direct computation of the averages. Statistical inference is irrelevant in this case. In general, however, it is impractical to make all the relevant observations. The statistician resorts to an inference based on examination of samples drawn from the two populations. This method prescribes certain procedures (for example, random selection of units of observation) and is based on certain assumptions (for example, regarding the underlying distributions of the variable of interest). If these conditions are fulfilled, the statistician is justified in drawing a conclusion; for instance, "the difference in the means is significant with $p \leqslant 0.05$." This conclusion is *probabilistic*. It asserts that with probability not exceeding 0.05, a difference at least as large as the one observed would be observed even if the actual means of the incomes of the two populations were equal.

Now to be meaningful in an empirical context, a probability must be translated into a frequency. In our example, the probability 0.05 refers to the expected frequency of observing a difference "at least as large" in a large number of comparisons between pairs of samples taken from the two populations with equal average incomes. In short, the probabilistic statement is empirically meaningful only if observations are made on *samples*, not on the entire populations. If the observations were made on the entire populations, probability (and therefore statistical inference) would not enter the statement of the finding. The finding would be certain.

Similar considerations apply to other statistical inferences, in particular to inferences about correlations. The "significance" of a correlation is a probability and refers to repeated observations on independent samples drawn from a population, which is assumed to be "infinite" (that is, much larger than the samples drawn).

Now in the correlates of war studies discussed in this chapter, the object of investigation is the entire population of wars (for example, from 1815 to 1945) or of countries (for example, those that comprised the international system under consideration). Therefore, the statistical inferences drawn from those observations are devoid of meaning from a strict operational point of view (which is embodied in any strictly empirical approach) and cannot be used to support or refute hypotheses.

Statisticians have frequently pointed to this methodological shortcoming in routine applications of correlational techniques in the social sciences. In my opinion, the approach is not entirely invalidated if one is willing to relax somewhat the demands posed by the logic of statistical inference. For example, the populations of wars or countries examined (although they comprise the entire populations of interest examined in the studies) could be imagined as "samples" from similar populations "in all possible worlds" or "all possible replays of history" or something of the sort. Such a conception is admittedly a philosophical fiction invented for the express purpose of justifying the procedures, but fictions of this sort have at times been indispensable in the construction of theories. At any rate, bad methods are often better than none, provided one is aware of the ways in which they can be misleading.

At times, correlational analysis serves as a sort of microscope by pointing to *possible* relations among variables not discernible by the "naked eye." For instance, the possible differential influences of different social strata on the incidence, duration, and severity of wars would be a most interesting finding if it could be supported by more evidence. The validity of the finding cannot be established by correlation analysis alone, but the fact that the issue of its validity is raised at all is of value in that it suggests further inquiry.

The most serious weakness of correlational analysis in the study of war stems, in my opinion, from two sources: the unavoidable cultural bias of the investigators and the rapidly shifting structure of the international system. Speculations about the role of "rising expectations" on political violence stem clearly from experiences of the last few decades, such as the social unrest among the "underdogs" in industrialized and urbanized societies. Speculations about the influence of different social strata on the components of war may have been suggested by the politics of pressure groups, characteristic especially of American society. The relevance of these forces in Bourbon France or in Russia of Catherine II is, to say the least, questionable. The role of "centralization" in mobilizing a population for war may have been of importance in the two world wars of recent history, but considerably less so, if at all, when wars were fought with small professional or mercenary armies.

Questions can also be raised about the applicability of the traditional conception of the international system (as a "population" of virtually autonomous actors) to the presently emerging system dominated by two or three superpowers. One might question the importance of the "number of borders" of a state. This may have been a factor when states fought predominantly with their neighbors, but hardly in the present age of ICBMs and air-lifted divisions.

These questions appear especially troublesome when investigations of the correlates of war are regarded as contributions to "peace research" in the expectation that a greater understanding of the "causes of wars" will help prevent wars. Generals are sometimes accused of planning to fight the previous war. "Peace researchers" could be reproached for attempting to prevent previous wars.

Thus the hopes pinned on positivist approaches as extensions of natural science methods to the social sciences in the expectation of vastly increased predictive power must be largely discounted. The principal value of the quantitative approach, which in the social sciences is almost always bound up with statistical inference, is that it provides *some* anchorage in evidence for theoretical speculation about the determinants of social events. At least the negative findings of correlational analysis may help to dispel many a cherished traditionbound notion for which no hard evidence has ever been found.

NOTE

[1]In the earlier period (June 27–July 26), $R_1 = 18$, $R_2 = 37$, $U = 40 - 37 = 3$, $p < 0.013$. In the later period (July 27–August 4). $R_1 = 46$, $R_2 = 60$, $U = 77 - 60 = 17$; not significant.

PART V

CONCLUDING REMARKS

CHAPTER TWENTY FIVE

Social Antecedents
and Consequences
of Mathematization

The aim of this book has been that of presenting an overview of mathematical approaches to the behavioral sciences. Needless to say, the total volume of literature on the subject exceeds by more than one order of magnitude the volume of our sample. Some remarks on how the studies were selected for presentation and discussion and, in some cases, for criticism will serve to summarize the principal orientation and theses of this book.

It will be noted that the bulk of selected work was published in the United States. This bias stems partly from the author's background, but only partly. The intellectual climate in the United States has produced the most favorable conditions for the work subsumed under mathematical methods in the behavioral sciences. Developments since World War II contributed much to these conditions. Partly as a gesture of largesse and partly to forestall massive unemployment, the U.S. Congress passed the so-called "G.I. Bill of Rights," which provided for substantial assistance to men and women returning from military service for furthering their education. As a result, both the student bodies and the faculties of American colleges and universities were vastly expanded. The structure of these institutions has always been much looser than that of traditional European universities. In addition to the usual faculties of arts and sciences, American colleges and universities include a large number of extremely diverse professional schools, not only the old established ones like schools of law and medicine, but many others providing training in almost any white collar occupation. In fact, the American educational establishment in its swollen state has come to be called "the knowledge industry." Some use this term approvingly for its connotation of massive production of competent and informed citizens; others use it pejoratively for its connotation of standardization, bigness-worship, and hegemony of the business mentality.

At any rate, what is called academe in America has become a white collar profession comparable to other such professions, not only in size, but also in career requirements. These include certain more or less established levels of competence, but no special dedication or outstanding talent. The scientific establishment, which is very largely incorporated into the educational system, has shared in this "democratization" in the sense of openness to a large sector of the population.

The expansion of science as a profession was, in a way, a by-product of the growing "knowledge industry"; but it was also stimulated by rising expectations with regard to science. Technology and professions associated with it have always enjoyed high prestige in the United States. However, most dramatic innovations of technology (the automobile, airplane, radio, cinema) were associated in the popular mind with "invention" rather than with scientific theory. Edison and Ford were the folk heroes in the early decades of the century. It would be inaccurate to say that in August 1945, Einstein was suddenly promoted to an American "folk hero." He was not "folsky" like Ford or Edison and not even American, but he became a hero to the American people. Since the word "theory" was firmly linked to his name (Einstein's Theory of Relativity) and his name to the atomic bomb, by association, "scientific theory" became established in the public mind as a source of power. This mentality received another stimulus in October 1957, when the Soviet Union ushered in the Space Age by launching the first artificial earth satellite. A flurry of "crash programs" in scientific education of the young followed.

In Chapter 4, I mentioned the growing feeling of ambivalence toward science, which came to be regarded as an incubator of calamities as well as a producer of abundance. Many social scientists in the post-war years were quick to point out that science as the "problem-solving" mode of human activity could show a way out of the dilemma. Namely, social science was advanced as a source of knowledge and consequently of constructive control over social forces with the aim of forestalling or relieving the strains supposedly generated by the gap between man's power over the forces of nature and his helplessness before his own collective irrationality or depravity. Thus the rising expectations were directed also to social science.

Now the social sciences, or more generally, the behavioral sciences, were represented in American universities by departments of psychology, sociology, political science, anthropology, and economics. The rising expectations generated a pressure for adopting a "scientific orientation" in these departments with consequent emphasis on empirically oriented research and positivistically oriented theorizing. This pressure was reinforced by the ubiquitous human appetite for prestige and recognition. In the academic setting, prestige and recognition manifest themselves in legitimation of research efforts, in grants, in the establishment of special areas of study, and so on. In short, most of the representatives of the behavioral disciplines longed for these benefits bestowed upon bona fide members of scientific enterprise. I am not prejudging this aspiration or its effects. In fact, in my opinion, the salubrious effects outweigh the dubious ones. Nevertheless, a sober look at the latter is called for.

The "democratization" of academe added science to the list of "ordinary" professional careers. By an "ordinary" professional career I mean one in which, under ordinary circumstances, there is room, if not for all or even for most, at least for a substantial portion of those aspiring to it. The career of a concert artist, a chess grandmaster, or a statesman is not an ordinary career in this sense. Until recently (historically speaking), the career of a scientist was not an ordinary career. It has become one now. This means that to join the "scientific community," one needs little more than to fulfill some minimal requirements of competence. By "joining the scientific community" I mean making a living by what has come to be regarded as "scientific work." Evidence of this work is publication in scientific journals. In fact, a certificate of competence in this work, at least in North America (and in many European countries as well), is now the Ph.D. degree or its equivalent, which is awarded in return for a piece of research recognized as competent and as a "contribution to knowledge" by a committee whose members have been certified in the same manner.

The so-called science explosion, manifested in an exponential growth of publication volume, attests to a positive feedback effect. Members of the "scientific community" are expected to do publishable research. As their numbers grow, so does the number of pages submitted for publication. This exerts pressure on the publication facilities to expand. As these expand, more pages can be accommodated, and so on.

Now let us look at criteria by which the "publishability" of a piece of research can be judged. When research takes on aspects of mass production, as it must because of sheer volume, these criteria must be routinized. Editors and referees who select materials to be published cannot always apply measures of "profundity" or "long-term significance," again because the sheer volume of submissions and publications schedules do not permit this, especially because editing and refereeing are usually extra activities of academics, not full-time jobs. Besides, editors and referees are members of the same community as the contributors and the pressure to publish applies equally to them. They cannot apply criteria in evaluating other's work different from those they apply to their own. By and large these are criteria of competence.

In empirically oriented, quantitative behavioral science, competence is evidenced by carefully performed experiments or field observations (use of proper controls, and so on) and by correct use of statistical machinery in evaluating the results and in inferring conclusions. With accumulated experience, these criteria can be routinized. In mathematical studies, competence is evidenced by the validity of the mathematical reasoning. Here the criterion of competence is even easier to apply: mathematically deduced results are either valid or invalid.

Thus the work goes on. Not infrequently, "scientifically oriented" behavioral science becomes the target of ascerbic criticism. The principal condemning verdict is "irrelevance," coupled at times with charges of venality; that is, serving the interests of the powers-that-be by directing attention away from important social problems and iniquities and thereby helping to preserve the status quo. Convincing evidence for accusations of this sort is hard to find. At any rate, there is no reason to think that the contemporary "positivist" social scientists defend the "status quo" more consistently or more intensively than the "essay writing" ones. As for the charge of "irrelevance," it seems to echo the charge of "impracticality" frequently directed against intellectual activity by men of affairs, from whom the champions of "relevance" emphatically dissociate themselves.

I believe that the routinely invoked defense of "pure science" on the grounds of its "ultimate," as yet unforseen, applicability is misdirected. In a defense of "pure science," the point of departure ought to be the value of science *as a whole* and as a human *activity*. If this value is denied, further arguments are futile. If it is accepted, then one ought to examine first a *direction* in science for the contributions it makes or purports to make to science as a whole. If a positive contribution of a direction is perceived, then one can examine particular approaches or methods for contributions they make to that direction.

There is admittedly one difficulty with this defense. Since, as has been pointed out, science has become an "ordinary profession," a defense of "science as a whole" can be interpreted as a defense of the interests of that profession and of all the rationalizations that the defense of the special interests of any social group generates. The validity of this interpretation cannot be refuted. In fact, it ought to be admitted. The only reply is that science as a human activity cannot exist without practitioners; so a defense of science cannot be separated from a defense of the profession and from the defense of at least those of its interests that have to do with the continued existence of the profession.

The specific area of concern in this book has been mathematicized behavioral science. This direction is pursued by persons oriented and trained in specific ways. We will regard them as a subgroup of the scientific community. Being human, they are subjected to pressures, both external and internal. The external pressures are those to which all the members of the scientific community are subjected. These are pressures that require a justification of activity on grounds of "relevance," as this is understood in their social environment, and pressures related to advancement in the career. The internal pressures are of a different sort, and these are for the most part not realized by people outside the scientific community, nor even by people of that community outside the subgroup with which we are concerned. I will speak of these internal pressures below.

We will consider first the most crass form of external pressure: the demand for "practical applicability," backed by power to dispense research funds. In the early stages of the Cold War, when the American military establishment dispensed these funds promiscuously and indiscriminately, abuses were rampant. I would hesitate to attribute such abuses to outright charlatanry, but severe self-delusion certainly appears to have been involved. I will cite one extreme example to illustrate the sort of euphoria that was sometimes generated by the rising expectations with regard to hard, mathematicized social science in the immediate post-war years.

In Chapter 15 I described a "tracing procedure" used to generate parameters characteristic of a social network, and pointed out the mathematical analogy between this procedure and a contagion process. In fact, I first developed this procedure in connection with a mathematical model of the "spread of rumors." At one time the model was tested in an experiment with school children (Rapoport, 1956). Soon afterwards, much to my embarrassment, a well-known scientist, author of a very ambitious but largely misguided work on mathematical sociology, sold a research project to the U.S. Air Force purporting to apply this simple model in a situation of military interest. The question to be answered by the model and by experiments suggested by it was how information should be expected to spread through a population by contact. The project's code name, "Project Revere," was a reference to the midnight ride of an American patriot at the outbreak of the American Revolution warning the citizens of Massachusetts of the movement of British troops.

An experiment purporting to test the "contagion model" of information spread was designed on a grand scale in a "real life" setting. A town of appropriate size and in an appropriate location was selected to be bombarded by a leaflet drop. Observers were placed in the airplane on a mountain near the town and in cruising cars to watch the "physical diffusion" of the information, presumably to be factored out in determining the "social diffusion" by contact. A questionnaire was prepared in which respondents were asked whether they had seen a leaflet, picked one up, received one, passed one on, discussed its contents, and so on and so forth. Replies were to be the data to be used in "testing a mathematical model of information spread."

The number 24 has stuck in my memory, but I do not recall whether this was the number of respondents who turned in the questionnaire or the number of people who knew something about the contents of the leaflet. At any rate, the town was divided into a number of regions, and the distribution of the respondents (or the "knowers") among these regions was compared with the random distribution to assess the significance of any deviation. This was the extent of the mathematical analysis.

This fiasco illustrates what I have called "euphoria"; specifically, a euphoria generated by "scientific ritual" in which the trappings or the paraphernalia associated with "science" (operationalization, quantification, mathematization, apparatus, computer programs, and so on) are confused with science as a mode of cognition. This mode involves more than procedures. It presupposes reasonable estimates about the sort and amount of information that can be expected from the application of given instruments of observation and from given techniques of induction and deduction.

At times, completely unjustified expectations can be traced to simple ignorance of facts or to inadequate theory. Galileo is said to have attempted to determine the speed of light. He stationed himself at night on one hill and another observer on another hill a mile or so away. Each was equipped with a lantern. Galileo was to send a light signal by removing the cover of his lantern and his partner was to return the signal as soon as he saw the flash of Galileo's light. Twice the distance separating the two hills divided by the time elapsed between the moment Galileo uncovered his lantern and the moment he saw the other light would then give the speed of light in appropriate units.

Galileo cannot be blamed for not realizing that this procedure was absurd.

He had absolutely nothing to go by. In contrast, a minimum of sober reflection should have made it apparent to anyone that the design of the "spread of information" experiment and the associated expectations were ludicrous. Yet even otherwise-competent investigators when carried away by euphoria generated by scientific ritual may go to ridiculous lengths in their wishful thinking, especially when stimulated by prospects of lavish support.

Scientific method requires that the design of an experiment be guided by a theoretical framework. Scientific ritual suggests such a framework in the form of a multitude of carefully worded definitions. Thus the "theoretical framework" of Project Revere included distinctions between "physical" and "social" diffusion; between first-hand, second-hand, and nth hand information; between "active" and "passive" knowers, and so on. Scientific ritual is served by providing a multitude of observers. A mathematical model puts an experiment in a distinct theoretical light. The mere skeleton of a mathematical contagion model was displayed as the underlying "theory" because it was available. It simply did not occur to the principal investigator that not one of these props would be of any use in his experiment; nor that the experiment would not answer any of the questions posed. Brutally speaking, the experiment was performed because there was a customer ready to buy it, and the bizarre elaborations served to impress him.

A caricature of scientific procedure was presented to illustrate a product of the crassest form of external pressure coupled with a total loss of perspective. Needless to say, it represents an extreme case. The mathematical model builder is generally immune to delusions of the sort described because he is seldom required or expected to demonstrate the "practicality" of his models. He is, to be sure, subjected to the pressure to publish. However, since, as we have seen, competence in the mathematical domain is evidenced by the validity of deductions, the model builder can, in fact must, remain within the bounds of scientific respectability. He is, nevertheless, subjected to internal pressures characteristic of mathematical activity.

The business of the pure mathematician is to prove theorems. Each new theorem can justifiably be regarded as a contribution to knowledge. Normally, accretions to knowledge are generated by steps from something known to something unknown linked to it. A theorem is a new mathematical relationship derived from relationships proved previously. A *direction* in mathematics is often guided by generalization. One starts with a known theorem, then drops or weakens one or more of its assumptions. If another theorem can be proved starting from weaker assumptions, it constitutes a generalization of the preceding one. In fact, the history of mathematics can be regarded as a steady process of progressive generalization.

The business of the applied mathematician is to solve problems. But he need not confine his interests to problems submitted to him by others. He can formulate his own problems. Here, too, there is a straightforward way of generating new knowledge by starting with a solved problem, then changing or complicating the conditions to get another one. Complicating the conditions is tantamount to generalization, since it involves dropping or weakening the simplifying assumptions under which the simpler problem was solved.

There is thus a routinized way of posing new mathematical problems, both in pure and applied mathematics. This supplies the majority of both pure and applied mathematicians with opportunities to do steady work, a necessity in an "ordinary" profession.

The mathematical model builder occupies a position intermediate between the pure and the applied mathematician. Since his models are models of "something," he does not usually assume the stance of the pure mathematician, whose point of departure may be a set of primitive terms and abstractly formulated axioms. On the other hand, since he need not be directly concerned with the testability of his models, he feels free to generate problems that are suggested by the model itself rather than by the reality from which it was presumably abstracted.

In this activity of creating problems to be solved, the model builder, depending on his background and inclinations, may lean either toward the "pure" or toward the "applied" side. Examples of both of these directions were included in this book. Here we will take a second look at some of these examples.

As an example of "application-oriented" model building, let us examine the normative models of "arms control" (Gillespie and Zinnes, 1975) discussed in Chapter 5. The source of the problems is real in the sense that "arms control" is a conspicuous issue on the agenda of world politics. The difficulty of formulating mathematically solvable problems in this area is that policy makers often state issues in vaguely general language rather than in precise terms. The first task of the model builder in this area, therefore, is somehow to "fit" a precisely formulated problem to something that the policy maker will accept as at least a rough representation of his concerns.

Now the model builder already has a repertoire of model types that have been investigated by him or by others. It is from this repertoire that he will select a specific model, hoping to fit it to the policy maker's verbal description of the problem.

Let us imagine a conversation between the builder of a normative model of arms control and an "enlightened" policy maker. The aim of the conversation is to translate the problem as the policy maker sees it into a problem that the model builder can deal with.

MODEL BUILDER   Why are you interested in arms control?

POLICY MAKER   Uncontrolled arms races are dangerous and economically burdensome.

M: Why are they dangerous?

P: If one side gets a preponderance of military potential, it may be motivated to attack the other. What we need is to avoid war.

M: What sort of relation between the war potentials of two potential enemies would be least conducive to the outbreak of a war?

P: Well, of course, a general complete disarmament would be a good thing, provided it could be enforced. But this is a utopian dream. Each side must feel secure against the other. We need a military potential as a deterrent; and, of course, they feel the same way. So if we could achieve a balance of power and stabilize the two military potentials with this balance in mind, this would, I am afraid, be the most one could expect in the immediate future.

M: By balance of power do you mean equal levels of military potential?

P: Not necessarily. We have a weapons system of type U. Our potential enemies have a system of type X. Somehow we must solve the problem of calibrating one type of weapons system to correspond to some proportion of the other to achieve parity.

M: We must defer the concrete solution of that problem. This is something for military specialists to work out. Let us assume that problem has been solved. I will call your side U and the other side X. Assume that parity obtains when u, the military potential of U, equals rx, where x is the potential of X and r a constant representing a proportion.

P (dubiously): Well, this still seems terribly oversimplified to me, but for the sake of hearing more about your idea of getting a mathematical solution of the arms control problem, I will go along with your assumption for the time being.

M: Then if rx got to be much larger than u, you would feel threatened?

P: Assuming everything said so far, yes.

M: How about if u got to be much larger than rx?

P: Well now, I am sufficiently enlightened to realize that X would feel threatened. We should not allow this to happen. As I said, a balance of power is what we are after.

M: Would you say, then, that you would like the difference $u - rx$ to be as small numerically as possible?

P: Put it that way.

M: Then what we need is to minimize $(u - rx)^2$. A deviation from zero in either direction would be interpreted as a "cost."

P: I follow you.

M: But if so, why not simply set your own level, u, which you control, equal to rx and keep it there? Whatever level rx is reached by the other side, you match with u. This will keep the difference $(u - rx)$ at zero.

P: I guess so.

M: But will this stop the arms race? Suppose X keeps increasing x. You would have to keep increasing u to keep up.

P: That would be bad.

M: So evidently you are concerned not just with $(u - rx)^2$ but also with the combined armaments levels of X and U. Is this so?

P: I said at the outset that uncontrolled arms races, besides being dangerous, are also economically burdensome for both sides.

M: Then we will include the combined levels in our representation of "cost." Would you say the quantity $(u - rx)^2 + c(x + u)$ is a fair representation of the "costs" of armaments?

P: Where does the "c" come in?

M: It's a weighting factor. It represents the magnitude of your concern about the combined armaments levels relative to your concern for the "balance of power."

P: As I said, the problem is much more involved than the way you represent it. But I am curious as to what you are driving at.

M: Simplification is unavoidable in any mathematical attack on a problem. This is the price you pay for being allowed to use mathematical reasoning. Let's solve the problem as it is formulated. This will give us a "beachhead" from which we may be able to advance later and eventually include more "real life" features.

P: Fair enough.

M: Now, our representation of cost is really cost per unit time. You can see this clearly if you think of x and u as armament budgets which are expressed in money units per year. So with time the total cost will accumulate. Your problem is to minimize total cost over some time span. Call it your *time horizon*. This could be 10 years or 50 years, or anything you wish. We will just call your time horizon T to get a formal solution of our problem. If you want to translate this solution into policy, you will have to choose some definite value for T. You will also have to assign a value to r, which represents your estimate of how the armament levels should be calibrated for parity. And you will have to assign a value to c, the relative magnitude of your concern about combined levels of armaments. It is not up to me to assign these values. You are the policy maker. My job is to provide you with a general format of a solution which will become a concrete prescription (about how to control u, your own armament level, in order to minimize cost as you have defined it) only after you have chosen values for r, c, and T.

P: Is this, then, all the information you want from me?

M: For the time being, yes. I will now work on the problem. Then we will discuss the solution to see what it implies in the way of policy. It would be foolhardy to promise that the solution will give you a concrete "optimal policy." But if you are to utilize the power of mathematics in solving policy problems, we have to start somewhere. We now have a place to start.

The purpose of this interrogation (with some overtones of a Socratic dialogue) was to get an objective function. To formulate a control problem, our model builder needs a description of a dynamic system. Empirical descriptions of arms races are available.[2] But none of the proposed *models* of the underlying system dynamics are reliable. However, the model builder has to start *somewhere*. So he chooses the simplest model of an arms race, namely Richardson's (see Chapter 3). He can now formulate the control problem discussed in Chapter 5.

$$\text{Minimize } J = \int_0^T [(u - rx)^2 + c(u + x)]dt \tag{25.1}$$

$$\text{Subject to } \dot{x} = -mx + au + g, \tag{25.2}$$

where a, m, and g have the same meaning as in Equation 3.21 of Chapter 3, while r, c, and T are the Policy Maker's parameters defined above.

The form of the problem has only a very rough resemblance (if any) to "reality." It was much more compellingly shaped by the need for mathematical tractability. In fact, the type of problems represented by Equations 25.1 and 25.2 belongs to a well-known class involving a *quadratic objective function* and *linear constraints*. "Quadratic" refers to the integrand in Equation 25.1; "linear" refers to the linearity of the differential Equation 25.2. The problem is solvable by classical analytic methods. The need for mathematical tractability is a powerful input in the construction of mathematical models. To paraphrase Marshall McLuhan's much discussed remark, "The medium in the message," we might well say, "The tool is the theory."

Note further that in the context of a normative model, the question of empirical verification does not arise with reference to the deduced prescription. It arises only with reference to the underlying dynamic system, represented by Equation 25.2. The validity of the prescription stands or falls with the adequacy of that equation. We have already seen that it is next to impossible to "validate" Richardson's arms race theory (isolated instances of "fit" do not constitute validation). Therefore, it is next to impossible to estimate the parameters with any "reasonable" degree of precision. But the very stability of the system depends on the parameters and is, in certain ranges, extremely sensitive to them. In this case, for example, the system is stable or unstable depending on whether m is greater or less than ar. Hence there can be no meaningful talk about applying the normative model to determine an arms control policy, even given a most "enlightened" and sympathetic policy maker.

Useless as the model is for "application," it is quite productive in other ways already mentioned. A solved problem generates others. As mentioned in Chapter 5, the "balance of power" (or "deterrence") model was followed by an "expected first strike" model. Also, the single actor model was followed by a dual control model, equivalent to a differential game.

Needless to say, none of these models is "applicable" in any concrete case. Their proliferation is driven by *their own reproduction capacity* through modification and generalization. This is what we mean by "productivity" of the model in this context.

Quite similar observations apply to classical predictive models. In Chapter 2 we presented the simplest of Rashevsky's contagion models of mass behavior.

Subsequently, this model was elaborated in several ways. This development did not follow the textbook paradigm of the deductive-inductive cycle, where a simple model remains provisionally validated until systematic deviations appear, which are subsequently accounted for by a more complex or a more general model, and so on. In a "self-reproducing" model, the problems are simply posed and solved one after the other *because the machinery for solving problems of this sort exists.* The tool is the theory.

Even when initially predictive models are constructed with empirical validation in mind, the proliferation of problems arising through complication and generalization not infrequently "take over." Recall the development of the stochastic models of social mobility discussed in Chapter 10.

The frequent charge of "irrelevance" leveled at mathematical models in the behavioral sciences usually invokes the remoteness of the content of the models from "substantive social problems." A defense against the charge is usually conducted in terms of a defense of "pure science," often coupled with references to future unforseen applications, to serendipidy, and so on. In other words, the defense stretches the concept of applicability to include any theory that sheds light on some aspect of reality. However, nontestable models (of which we have given several examples) cannot be accommodated under this defense umbrella because, being without connections to empirical reality, they cannot be said to "shed light" on any aspect of reality. The most uncomfortable feature of these nontestable models is their self-reproductive capacity. It suggests the conjecture that model building of this sort serves mainly, if not exclusively, to provide work for the profession.

We will defer the answer to this charge. For the time being, we turn to the pure mathematical orientation in model building.

Investigators with this orientation usually have a considerably more solid background in mathematics than the application-oriented. Frequently, they are mathematicians rather than behavioral scientists. They are attracted to some area of behavioral science for the opportunity it provides for pursuing essentially mathematical research, which means proving theorems—discovering what implies what. Two classes of problems frequently suggest themselves to the working mathematician "of their own accord," as it were. One is "proving the converse"; the other is "proving an existence theorem." Every theorem, of course, is in assertion in the form "p implies q," where p and q are propositions about some mathematical objects or relations. To prove the converse is to show also that "q implies p." To prove a converse of a theorem is sometimes trivially easy, in which case the converse is included in the statement of the theorem. Sometimes it is quite difficult to prove a converse, in which case the converse rates the title of a theorem in its own right. Sometimes the converse of a theorem is not valid, which is also a "finding" to be added to the mathematician's trophies.

A theorem and its converse together constitute "necessary and sufficient conditions." Namely, if $p \rightarrow q$, p is sufficient for q. If also $q \rightarrow p$, then both p and q are necessary and sufficient for each other. The establishment of a necessary and sufficient condition has a flavor of "finality" about it. It settles a question once and for all. For this reason, mathematicians are happy to be able to prove necessary and sufficient conditions, especially when the proof is difficult or involved. Often, however, theorems of this sort, even though their antecedents are rooted in interpretable models, are not themselves interpretable in terms of those models. We mentioned one such situation in Chapter 18 (see p. 343); namely, the establishment of a necessary and sufficient condition for a social choice function to be a "representative system."

An existence theorem carries an aura of "fundamentality." For instance, the theorem that establishes the existence of a complex root of any polynomial with complex coefficients is called the *Fundamental Theorem of Algebra*. In the same spirit, the title of *Fundamental Theorem of Game Theory* was conferred on the result proved by Von Neumann (1928) that established the existence of "optimal" strategies in any finite two-person constant-sum game.

In developing the concept of "solution" for the *n*-person game, Von Neumann hoped to prove a fundamental theorem for such games which would guarantee the existence of a *V-M* solution (see p. 357) in all *n*-person games in characteristic function form. In 1965, W. Lucas showed that this could not be done: he exhibited an example of an *n*-person game in which the set of *V-M* solutions was empty. The result was hailed with enthusiasm in game theory circles because it "settled a question" once and for all. Its "practical" significance derives from the fact that it saves game theoreticians from expending fruitless efforts to prove the existence theorem conjectured by Von Neumann. However, the interpretation of the theorem in the original context of game theory as a theory of strategic conflict (or, for that matter, of conflict resolution) is, to say the least, problematic. Lucas' example is a 10-person game with a nonempty core (see p. 356). This property appears extremely strange to game-theoreticians because when a game does have a *V-M* solution, its core, if it has one, must be contained in that solution. An empty *core* presents no problem because the null set is regarded as a subset of any set (see p. 263). But what is the significance of a nonempty core (which one would expect to be a subset of a nonempty superset) if that superset does not exist?

Of course, Lucas' counterexample is a challenge to game theoreticians. Namely, it poses the problem of finding necessary and sufficient conditions for the existence of a *V-M* solution. I am certain that as I write this, ambitious game theoreticians are working on that problem. Furthermore, I am certain that when and if that problem is solved, the result will be hailed as a milestone in game theory. I doubt, however, that the nature of the difference between games with and without *V-M* solutions can be interpreted in terms of social situations which served as models for the *n*-person cooperative game to begin with. Just as in some predictive models the connection between model and empirical test is often severed as the problems proliferate, so in the case of structural axiomatically oriented models (like the game-theoretical), the connection between model and interpretation often fades away as the theorems proliferate.

The strivings of the model builders that carry them beyond the range of "practical application," even beyond the range of empirical testability and even at times beyond the range of structural interpretation, are inseparable from the very process of mathematical model building. Attempts to stem this activity would amount to cutting off the intellectual nourishment of the researchers. The problem of justifying at least some of this activity entails the problem of justifying the existence of a *profession* and with it the needs of the profession. If such justification can be found, the misgivings mentioned above (that most of the work in mathematical approaches to the behavioral sciences is generated by self-serving interests of a profession) can be at least partially dissipated.

Does a "civilized society" need a profession, the business of whose practitioners it is to think mathematically about human affairs? The answer might be "Yes, if the profession contributes to 'practical knowledge'." Here "practical knowledge" is most often understood as knowledge that increases the power of prediction and control. If so, then major directions of research concerned with the mathematization of the behavioral sciences cannot honestly be justified. Nor can these directions be justified by the well-known appeals to "future applications"—the appeal for more time. For eventually, the day of reckoning must come, and vast amounts of research will surely be shown to have led to no "practical results." Disappointments generate a "backlash" and undermine confidence. Vague promises about future "returns on investments" only undermine the profession.

The answer might be "Yes, if the profession contributes to knowledge about the real world." This condition is less stringent. It is not predicated on an expectation of "practical results" in the vulgar sense. Proponents of this position feel comfortable about social support of work on the "black holes" in the cosmos regardless of whether it contributes to the technology of space travel. They feel comfortable about social support of research on dead languages or in descriptive biology with its discovery of millions of species of insects. They value "knowledge for knowledge's sake." But they conceive of knowledge as something that relates to something "out there" in the real world. If support of mathematically oriented behavioral science is predicated on that conception of knowledge, much of the research described in this book can be justified, but by no means all, perhaps not even most.

The answer I give to the question posed is the following: "Yes, civilized society needs a profession, the business of whose practitioners it is to think mathematically about human affairs because mathematical thinking is the most disciplined form of thinking, and civilized society needs a *pool* of men and women who have mastered techniques of disciplined thought *especially* in areas that have *some* (even if a tenuous) bearing on human affairs."

Actually, this answer is meant to be an implicit definition of civilized society. Science must be regarded as a respected and nurtured activity in a civilized society, not only, not even primarily because of its contributions to "prediction and control" but because it is the only sphere of human activity which undermines superstition, shakes the foundations of dogmas, and extends horizons of outlooks beyond parochial limits. These potentialities of science coincide with those of a "civilized society" as I define this term.

Scientific thinking, of which mathematical thinking is the "purest" form, embodies a remarkable synthesis of maximum freedom and maximum discipline, something extremely difficult to combine in human affairs, where "freedom" and "discipline" almost always appear to be in opposition. Scientific analysis confers freedom from encrusted thinking habits, above all freedom from the "tyranny of words," which forces people to think in terms of culturally inherited or politically imposed verbal categories that need not be either internally consistent or related to anything in the real world. At the same time, the scientific mode of cognition imposes a discipline of its own, which, somewhat paradoxically, enhances freedom rather than inhibits it. Tyranny thrives on the canonization of nonsense and on the perpetuation of falsehood. Scientific thinking is a powerful antidote to tyranny because it separates sense from nonsense and truth from falsehood. No tyranny can survive without stifling the search for truth at least in some areas of cognition and preventing the exposure of nonsense in ritualistic verbiage.

Of these three features of scientific thinking, precision, generality, and objectivity, the first two characterize mathematical thinking in the highest measure. In achieving complete precision and the highest degree of generality, mathematics in its historical development has paid a price: it has severed the connection between the objects of its contemplation and the "real" (that is, observable) world. For this reason, the criterion of objectivity does not apply to mathematical thinking as such if we ascribe the usual meaning to objectivity; namely, agreement between independent *observers* about "what is the case." However, since in mathematical models of real phenomena, the connections between the deductions of the models and the observable world are frequently at least partially established, mathematics also contributes to this feature of scientific thinking.

Therein lies the potential of science, especially of quantified or mathematicized science in establishing a basis for the community of man. A fundamental, although mostly implicit, assumption underlying the scientific conception of truth is that our senses provide us with a basis of agreeing about what has been observed. The mere existence of this basis is not yet sufficient to establish a universal criterion of "truth" because the primacy of observation as the basis of knowledge of "what is the case" is by no means taken for granted in all cultures or world outlooks. In fact, Plato explicitly denied the primacy or even the relevance of observations in arriving at truth. Even Plato, however, laid stress on the importance of independent *reasoning*, as evidenced in a scene from *Meno*.[1]

The scientific conception of truth emphasizes both the primacy of independent observations and the primacy of independent logical deduction. That a basis of agreement on the truth of assertions about the world and on the validity of conclusions deduced from assumptions exists for human beings seems to be the case. Reality testing by the use of the senses and rudiments of valid logical deductions are found in all cultures, at least on the level of everyday affairs directly related to problems of survival. One might assume that without these faculties, man, with his weak instinctual repertoire and far from adequate bodily adaptation to his physical environment, could not survive. Reality testing and rigorous logical reasoning become rare in areas of thought where man exercises his imagination and where he has established rationales for practices, rules of behavior, or forms of social organization. It is in those areas that the farthest departure from the principles of scientific cognition have occurred. Thus the scientific outlook includes not only a faith that a common ground for a criterion of truth exists in the human sensorium and in his thinking capacity. It involves also a value judgment; namely, that this common ground *ought* to be expanded beyond the sphere of everyday, survival-oriented behavior to the higher forms of mental activity involving abstraction, imagination, and generalization.

There is ample evidence that this extension broadens the basis for establishing a community of man. In a sense, a global scientific community already exists, not in the sense of common values in every aspect of human life (scientists are human and are still bound to their parochial cultures or loyalties in many ways), but in the sense of the most complete communality ever achieved with respect to the conception of objective truth and logical rigor. Nowhere is this communality more complete than in mathematics. Directions in content-oriented scientific research may still be influenced by value systems prevailing in different societies, and specialization in different content areas may create communication barriers. Mathematics, on the other hand, is the most completely unified field of cognition. It is all of one piece, as it were. Its concepts developed in some sectors often facilitate deep insights in others. Mathematics generates aesthetic ideals shared by mathematicians more completely than any other aesthetic ideals shared by human beings. All mathematicians speak the same language, not only in the sense of the same grammatical structure and the same lexicon, but also in the sense of the same conceptual content. This communality stems from the independence of mathematical concepts from empirical content, which is necessarily influenced by cultural heritage and social milieu.

Despotic regimes are well aware of the potential of science as a source of power. They are also aware (in varying degree) of the potential of scientific thinking as a source of challenges to the hegemony of power. Science policies of those regimes reflect both of these concerns. Allocation of support is heavily biased in favor of investigations with immediately perceived or expected potential of technological, especially military, applications. Attempts to mobilize or at least neutralize the ideological spin-offs of scientific thinking are reflected in the imposition of an orthodox cognitive framework to which scientific thinking is supposed to be subordinated.

At times, these impositions have spawned pseudosciences like the racist "theories" in Nazi Germany or Lysenko's "theory" of heredity in the Soviet Union. In other instances, whole areas were removed altogether from the domain of scientific investigation; for example, some sectors of history or sociology. It must be noted, however, that *all* content-oriented science rests on some cognitive framework, which may be inadequate or altogether false. No content-oriented science rests on a foundation of absolute truth. Ptolemy's cosmology and Newton's corpuscular theory of light were both false but nonetheless scientific. Agassiz could reject the theory of evolution and yet be an outstanding biologist. In contrast, a mathematically valid result cannot be invalidated except by a discovery of a demonstrable error. Nor can a mathematical contradiction be tolerated regardless of the prevailing philosophical climate. Mathematics is incorruptible. It can be prohibited, but its ideas cannot be perverted to serve the ends of power or ideology. This is why, although the areas of investigation, directions, and even findings in content-oriented sciences may vary in various cultures or political milieus, mathematics wherever it is nurtured is everywhere the same. It is the lingua franca of disciplined thought par excellence.

Of course, this privileged position of mathematics stems from its contentlessness. For this reason, the applied mathematician, who is blessed with certainty regarding the internal validity of his findings, must cultivate extreme scepticism concerning the implications of these findings with regard to the real world. It is said that when a victorious Roman general honored by a triumphal procession drove his chariot past cheering crowds, an officer was stationed behind him in the chariot whose duty it was to whisper alternately in the general's ears, "Remember, thou art only a man."

The investigator immersed in data on human behavior can justifiably assume the role of this officer with regard to the mathematical model builder. The latter, with his preoccupation with the certainties of rigorous deduction, the universality of the mathematical language, and the incorruptibility of mathematics, may not have sufficient appreciation of the formidable difficulties of obtaining data on human behavior relevant to his model and how erratic and unreliable these data can be.

Thus the proper stance to be taken by the builder of mathematical models of human psychology, human behavior, social systems, and the like is one of confidence in the deductive powers of his models coupled with scepticism concerning the range of applicability. To achieve this stance, the mathematically oriented behavioral scientist must practice his trade. If civilized society needs people with this outlook on the problem of extending the scientific method to the analysis of human affairs, then it must tolerate the "exercises" that serve to train such people and contribute to their scientific maturation.

In short, one of the principal values of developing mathematical methods in the behavioral sciences lies in their effect on the intellectual climate. Facility with quantitative and mathematical methods inculcates certain thought habits which, in my opinion, ought to be cultivated in a civilized society. The habit of thinking "operationally" is especially important. It provides protection against the tyranny of words, whether the tyranny is perpetuated through encrusted traditions, imposed by a despotic regime, or inculcated by professional habits.

Consider the deep-seated value judgments implicit in comparing class structures of different societies. These value judgments, coupled with parochial loyalties, often becloud controversial issues. "Equality of opportunity" is usually regarded as a desideratum, being an aspect of "democracy." But on the face of it, it is only a slogan. In contrast, indices of social mobility can be subjected to objective comparison. The question of which society is more mobile is by no means settled thereby, because, as we have seen, the term "social mobility" can be operationalized in many different ways, and comparison of different indices may give different results. But the very ambivalence of the concept of "social mobility," revealed by the multiplicity of operational definitions, revealed by the multiplicity of operational definitions, is in itself a value. It steers thinking away from slogans toward analysis.

We have already seen in the context of another type of analysis (namely, in the axiomatic approach) what intricacies are involved in attempts to rigorously define the concept of "democratic social choice." Mathematical analysis helps to clarify the ambivalences, contradictions, and paradoxes involved in intuitive verbal definitions. In this way, the mathematical analyst distances himself from the antiscientific heckler, who also calls attention to the enormous gap between model and reality but only with the view of dismissing mathematization of behavioral science as futile or "irrelevant."

We have seen how mathematical analysis clarifies the vaguely stated problem of relating physical magnitudes of stimuli to the corresponding subjective perception of these magnitudes. This is, of course, the ancient metaphysical problem of the relation of "matter" to "mind." Posed in a psychophysical context, the problem is drastically narrowed down and loses its metaphysical grandeur, but it is made manageable thereby.[2]

We have seen how the concept of "rational decision in conflict situations" dissolves into ambiguities and assumes different meanings in different situations when examined in the merciless light of mathematical analysis. There may be no direct way of "applying" these insights to the formulation of policies because they cannot be translated into prescriptions to individual independent actors. They can be translated only into prescriptions to collectivities of cooperating actors, who do not exist (at least in the international arena). But the insights may contribute to the formation of a new intellectual climate in which the "realism" of power politics is viewed with more scepticism.

We have seen how attempts to forecast "global futures" raise a whole host of new methodological problems (see Chapter 4). These may never be solved in a way that will allow man to predict the future reliably, much less to control it. But the proliferation of problems induces certain mental sets in thinking about man's future—another effect of the mathematical approach on the intellectual climate.

It has been argued that "thinking quantitatively" can be misleading in two ways. It fixates attention on minutiae and inhibits the perception of organismic "wholes" indispensable for understanding living systems, the human psyche, social organization, historical processes, and the like. Qualitative categories, differences, and changes, it is said, do not yield to quantitative analysis. Second, preoccupation with what is countable or measurable is said to distort appreciation of values which depend on qualitative rather than quantitative aspects of things, conditions, or actions.

In answer to the first warning, it can be pointed out that mathematization is not coextensive with quantification. Quantities are, to be sure, the principal objects of study in the mathematics most familiar to the nonmathematician. But they are by no means the only entities subjected to mathematical analysis and manipulation. As we have seen, real numbers and operations on them play only a minor role in structural mathematics, which *is* concerned with holistic concepts and qualitative relations. Mathematization presupposes only rigor, not reduction of all categories to quantities. Early applications of quantitative methods in linguistics focused on statistical properties of large verbal outputs (see Chapter 9). These can be interesting in their own right, but they do not reveal the essential features of language as a carrier of *meaning* (semantics) or even language as a structured system of signs (grammar and syntax). However, the application of structural mathematics (for example, automaton theory) laid the foundations of mathematical (as distinguished from statistical) linguistics, where models of language structure (rather than of sequences of probabilistically determined events) could be developed. The fact that structural mathematics proved to be a useful tool of syntactic analysis demonstrates the applicability of mathematical methods to relations other than quantitative.

The second warning must be taken more seriously. Compulsions to reduce values to measurable quantities can be observed in societies dominated by striving for material gains and by intense competition. The newspaper habit of quoting market prices of great paintings whenever these are in the news, earnings of celebrities, and so on can be regarded as symptoms of vulgarization of values. Indices of popularity of political figures and of television programs encourage simplistic habits of evaluation. George F. Babbit, the archetype "Spitzbürger" in Sinclair Lewis's novel, considers one building more beautiful than another because it is four stories taller.

It is, however, noteworthy that quantification of value is unavoidable whenever an objective rationale must be provided for a value-based *decision*. The use of a drug is most frequently justified on the basis of statistical evidence of its effectiveness in curing or controlling a disease, and it is difficult to find another objective basis for justifying its adoption in therapy. One design of a road system is preferred to another on the basis of estimates of traffic flows. Such rationales are often deplored because the indices on which evaluations are based do not include other considerations that are deemed by some to be more important. The drug may have horrendous side effects. A system of roads, most efficient with respect to traffic flow capacity, may destroy a landscape or a community, or it may increase pollution beyond bearable limits. But effective corrective action against bad decisions of this sort does not consist in decrying the hegemony of quantitative thinking. A cogent critique should be explicit. For instance, it should call attention to the factors excluded from the indices and suggest a different basis of evaluation. This may involve more quantification instead of less; for instance, quantification of undesirable side effects of the drug or quantification of pollution together with weights assigned to them so as to weigh the scales against the decisions.

At any rate, the quality of decisions can be improved only if arguments for or against decisions are clear and explicit. Here quantification, by providing clear and explicit criteria, can be of great help. To measure the degree of national security by the destructive potential of the nation's military machine is, in my opinion, deplorable. But in arguing this position, I must point out that the indices are worthless not because they are "numbers devoid of human feeling," but because they are concocted by military specialists whose professional interests are far removed from concerns that ordinary people associate with security. But the very irrelevance of destructive power to security as it applies to ordinary people can be demonstrated convincingly only by some sort of analysis of historical events, by projection of probabilities of future events, or by whatever appeal to *evidence*. Again, the objective evaluation of such evidence is often aided by quantitative or structural analysis.

Therefore, if the inculcation of scientific habits of thought in all areas, including human affairs, is a mark of a civilized society (as I believe it is), mathematical approaches in the development of behavioral sciences ought to be encouraged and nurtured.

NOTES

[1]By guiding a young slave through a proof of a special case of the Pythagorean theorem, Socrates demonstrates that even a humble untutored human being is capable of arriving at truth by reasoning.
[2]See Smoker, 1965; Yearbook, 1969–1970; Taagepera et al., 1975, O'Neill, 1970.

References

Abel, T. (1941) The element of decision in the pattern of war. *American Sociological Review*, 6: 853–859.

Andrzejewski, S. (1973) *Social Sciences as Sorcery*. New York: Martin's Press.

Arrow, K. J. (1951) *Social Choice and Individual Values*. New York: Wiley.

Aumann, R. J. and Maschler, M. (1964) The bargaining set for cooperative games. In *Advances in Game Theory* (M. Dreher, L. S. Shapley, and A. W. Tucker, eds.). *Annals of Mathematics Studies*, 52. Princeton: Princeton University Press.

Bartholomew, D. J. (1963) An approximate solution of the integral equation of renewal theory. *Journal of the Royal Statistical Society*, B25: 432–441.

Bartholomew, D. J. (1967) *Stochastic Models for Social Processes*. New York: Wiley.

Bennet, J. P. and Alker, H. R. (1977) When national security policies bred collective insecurity. In *Problems of World Modeling* (K. W. Deutsch, B. Fritsch, H. Jaguaribe, and A. S. Markovits, eds.). Cambridge, Mass.: Ballinger.

Bentham, J. (1780) *An Introduction to the Principles of Morals and Legislation*. London: Pickering.

Bernoulli, D. (1730–1731) Specimen theoriae novae de mensura sortis. *Commentarii academiae scientiarum Petropolitanae*, 5: 175–182.

Bertalanffy, L. von (1951) Metabolic types and growth types. *The American Naturalist*, 85: 111–117.

Black, D. (1958) *The Theory of Committees and Elections*. Cambridge: Cambridge University Press.

Blau, P. and Duncan, O. D. (1967) *The American Occupational Structure*. New York: Wiley.

Block, H. D. and Marschak, J. (1960) Random orderings and stochastic theories of response. In *Contributions to Probability and Statistics* (I. Olkin, S. Ghuyre, W. Hoeffling, W. Madow, and H. Mann, eds.). Standford: Stanford University Press.

Blumen, I., Kogan, M., and McCarthy, P. J. (1955) *The Industrial Mobility of Labor as a Probability Process*. Ithaca: Cornell Studies of Industrial and Labor Relations, Vol. 6.

Boole, G. (1854) *An Investigation of the Laws of Thought, in Which Are Founded the Mathematical Theories of Logic and Probabilities*. London: Walton and Maberly.

Boudon, R. (1973) *Mathematical Structures of Social Mobility*. Amsterdam: Elsevier.

Boulding, K. E. (1959) National images and international systems. *Journal of Conflict Resolutions*, 3: 120–131.

Bourne, L. W. and Restle, F. (1959) Mathematical theory of concept identification. *Psychological Review*, 66: 278–296.

Bower, G. (1961) Application of a model to paired associate learning. *Psychometrika*, 26: 255–280.

Bower, G. (1962) An association model for response and training variables in paired associate learning. *Psychological Review*, 69: 34–53.

Braithwaite, R. B. (1955) *Theory of Games as a Tool for the Moral Philosopher.* Cambridge: Cambridge University Press.

Breiger, R. L. (1976) Career attributes and network structure: A blockmodel study of biochemical research specialists. *American Sociological Review,* 41: 117–135.

Broom, L. and Jones, F. L. (1970) Status inconsistency and political preference: the Australian case. *American Sociological Review,* 35: 989–1001.

Coale, A. J. (1956) The effects of changes in mortality and fertility rates on age composition. *Milbank Memorial Fund Quarterly,* 34: 79–114.

Coale, A. J. (1972) The *Growth and Structure of Populations.* Princeton: Princeton University Press.

Coleman, J. S. (1964) *Introduction to Mathematical Sociology.* New York: The Free Press of Glencoe.

Comte, A. (1830–1842) *Cours de philosophie positive.* Paris: Barillière.

Coombs, C. (1964) *A Theory of Data.* New York: Wiley.

Copeland, A. H. (1951) A "reasonable" social welfare function. University of Michigan Seminar on Applications of Mathematics in the Social Sciences (mimeographed).

Dahl, R. A. (1957) The concept of power. *Behavioral Science,* 2: 201–215.

Deegan, J. Jr. and Packel, E. W. (1979) A new index of power for simple *n*-person games. *International Journal of Game Theory,* 2: 113–123.

De Swaan, A. (1973) *Coalition Theories and Cabinet Formation.* Amsterdam, Elsevier, 1973.

Deutsch, K. W. (1966) *Nationalism and Social Communication.* Cambridge, Mass.: M.I.T. Press.

Deutsch, K. W. (1967) Nation and world. In *Contemporary Political Science* (I. D. Pool, ed.). New York: McGraw–Hill.

Dyer, J. S. and Miles, R. F. (1976) An actual application of collective choice theory in the selection of trajectories for the Mariner Jupiter/Saturn 1977 Project. *Operations Research,* 24: 220–224.

Eisenstadt, S. N. (1963) *The Political Systems of Empires.* New York: Free Press.

Ekman, G. (1954) Dimensions of color vision. *Journal of Psychology,* 38: 467–474.

Fararo, T. J. (1973) *Mathematical Sociology.* New York: Wiley.

Farquharson, R. (1969) *Theory of Voting.* New Haven: Yale University Press.

Fechner, G. T. (1860) *Elemente der Psychophysik.* Leipzig: Breitkopf und Haertel.

Feller, W. (1966) *An Introduction to Probability Theory and Its Applications,* Vol. 2. New York: Wiley.

Fishburn, P. C. (1973) *The Theory of Social Choice.* Princeton: Princeton University Press.

Fisher, G. H. (1967) Preparation of ambiguous stimulus materials. *Perception and Psychophysics,* 2: 421–422.

Flament, C. (1963) *Applications of Graph Theory to Group Structure.* Englewood Cliffs: Prentice Hall.

Forrester, J. W. (1971) *World Dynamics.* Cambridge, Mass.: Wright-Allen Press.

Frobenius, G. G. (1912) Über Matrizen aus nicht negativen Elementen. *Sitzungsberichte der königlichen Preussischen Akademie der Wissenschaften, Berlin:* 456–477.

Galtung, J. (1969) Violence, peace, and peace research. *Journal of Peace Research,* 6: 167–191.

Gillespie, T. V. and Zinnes, D. A. (1975) Progressions in mathematical models of international conflict. *Synthese,* 31: 289–321.

Gillespie, T. V., Zinnes, D. A., and Tahim, G. S. (1973). Foreign military assistance and the armament race. A differential game with control. *Peace Science Society (International) Papers,* 25: 35–51.

Glass, D. V. (1954) *Social Mobility in Britain.* London: Routledge and Kegan Paul.

Goodman, L. A. (1952) Population growth of the sexes. *Biometrics,* 8: 212–225.

Green, P. E. and Rao, V. R. (1972) *Applied Multidimensional Scaling. A Comparison of Approaches and Algorithms.* Hinsdale, Ill.: Dryden Press.

Guilliksen, H. (1934) A rational equation of the learning curve based on Thorndike's Law of Effect. *Journal of General Psychology,* 11: 395–434.

Guyer, M. and Hamburger, H. (1968) An enumeration of all 2×2 games. *General Systems*, 13: 205–208.

Guyer, M. and Perkel, B. (1972) *Experimental Games: A Bibliography*. Ann Arbor: Mental Health Research Institute, University of Michigan.

Harary, F., Norman, R. Z., and Cartwright, D. (1965) *Structural Models: An Introduction to the Theory of Directed Graphs*. New York: Wiley.

Harsanyi, J. C. (1962) Rationality postulates for bargaining solutions in cooperative and non-cooperative games. *Management Science*, 9: 141–153.

Harsanyi, J. C. (1977) *Rational Behavior and Bargaining Equilibrium in Games and Social Situations*. Cambridge: Cambridge University Press.

Hill, J. M. M. and Trist, E. L. (1953) A consideration of industrial accidents as a means of withdrawal from the work situation. *Human Relations*, 6: 357–380.

Holler, M. J. (1978) Party power and government formation: A case study. *Munich Social Science Review*, 4: 25–41.

Holsti, O. R. and North, R. C. (1965) Perceptions of hostility and economic variables. In *Comparing Nations* (R. L. Merritt, ed.). New Haven: Yale University Press.

Holsti, O. R., North, R. C., and Brody, R. A. (1968) Perception and action in the 1914 crisis. In *Quantitative International Politics: Insights and Evidence* (J. D. Singer, ed.). New York: Free Press.

Holt, R. T., Job, B. L., and Markus, L. (1978) Catastrophe theory and the study of war. *Journal of Conflict Resolution*, 22: 171–208.

Homans, G. C. (1950) *The Human Group*. New York: Harcourt, Brace, and World.

Hopkins, R. F. (1973) Mathematical modeling of mobilization and assimilation. In *Mathematical Approaches to Politics* (H. R. Alker, K. W. Deutsch, and A. H. Stoezel, eds.). Amsterdam: Elsevier.

Hopkins, R. F. and Mansbach, R. W. (1973) *Structure and Process in International Politics*. New York: Harper and Row.

Horvath, W. J. and Foster, C. C. (1963) Stochastic models of war alliances. *Journal of Conflict Resolution*, 7: 110–116.

Hughes, D. and Wierzbicki, A. (1980) *DRAM: A Model of Health Care Resource Allocation*. Laxenburg, Austria: International Institute of Applied Systems Analysis.

Isaacs, R. (1965) *Differential Games*. New York: Wiley.

James, J. (1953) The distribution of free-forming small group size. *American Sociological Review*, 18: 569–581.

Johnson, R. J. (1978) Political geography and political power. *Munich Social Science Review*, 3: 5–31.

Johnstone, J. C. (1969) *Young People's Images of Canadian Society*, Studies of the Royal Commission on Bilingualism and Biculturalism. Ottawa: Queen's Printer.

Kahn, H. (1960) *On Thermonuclear War*. Princeton: Princeton University Press.

Kalecki, M. (1945) On the Gibrat distribution. *Econometrica*, 13: 161–170.

Karlin, S. (1959) *Mathematical Methods and Theory in Games. Programming, and Economics*. Reading, Mass.: Addison-Wesley.

Kemeny, J. G. and Snell, J. L. (1962) *Mathematical Models in the Social Sciences*. Boston: Ginn & Co.

Kermack, W. O. and McKendrick, A. G. (1927) A contribution to the mathematical theory of epidemics. *Proceedings of the Royal Society* (A), 115: 700–721.

Kissinger, H. A. (1958) *Nuclear Weapons and Foreign Policy*. New York: Doubleday.

Krantz, D. M. (1964) The scaling of small and large color differences (doctoral dissertation). Ann Arbor, Michigan: University Microfilm No. 65–5777.

Land, K. C. (1969) Duration of residence and prospective migration: Further evidence. *Demography*, 6: 133–140.

Land, K. C. (1971) Some exhaustible Poisson process models of divorce by marriage cohorts. *Journal of Mathematical Sociology*, 1: 213–231.

Landahl, H. D. (1941) Studies in the mathematical biophysics of discrimination and conditioning. *Bulletin of Mathematical Biophysics*, 3: 13–26.

Landau, H. G. (1952) On some problems of random nets. *Bulletin of Mathematical Biophysics*, 14: 203–212.

Lendenmann, K. W. and Rapoport, A. (1980) Decision pressures in 2 × 2 games. *Behavioral Science*, 25: 107–119.

Levine, J. H. (1972) The sphere of influence. *American Sociological Review*, 37; 14–27.

Levi-Strauss, C. (1969) *The Elementary Structure of Kinship*. London: Eyre and Spottiswoode.

Lippset, S. M. and Bendix, R. (1960) *Social Mobility in Industrial Societies*. Berkeley: University of California Press.

Lopez, A. (1962) *Some Problems in Stable Population Theory*. Princeton: Office of Population Research.

Lotka, A. J. (1939) A contribution to the theory of self-renewing aggregates with special reference to industrial replacement. *Annals of Mathematical Statistics*, 10: 1–25.

Luce, R. D. (1959a) *Individual Choice Behavior*. New York: Wiley.

Luce, R. D. (1959b) On the possible psychophysical laws. *Psychological Review*, 66: 81–95.

Luce, R. D., Bush, R. R., and Galanter, E. (eds.) (1963–1965) *Handbook of Mathematical Psychology*. New York: Wiley.

Luce, R. D. and Galanter, E. (1963) Psychophysical scaling. In *Handbook of Mathematical Psychology*, Vol. I (R. D. Luce, R. R. Bush, and E. Galanter, eds.). New York: Wiley.

Luce, R. D. and Perry, A. D. (1949) A method of matrix analysis of group structure. *Psychometrika*, 14: 95–116.

Luce, R. D. and Raiffa, H. (1957 *Games and Decisions*. New York: Wiley.

Luce, R. D. and Rogow, A. A. (1956) A game-theoretic analysis of congressional power distribution for a stable two-party system. *Behavioral Science*, 1: 83–95.

Luce, R. D. and Suppes, P. (1965) Preference utility and subjective probability. In *Handbook of Mathematical Psychology*, Vol. III (R. D. Luce, R. R. Bush, and E. Galanter, eds.). New York: Wiley.

Mallman, C. (1977) The Bariloche model. In *Problems of World Modeling* (K. W. Deutsch, B. Fritsch., H. Jaguaribe, and A. S. Markovits, eds.). Cambridge, Mass.: Ballinger.

Malthus, T. R. (1798) *An Essay on the Principle of Population as It Affects the Future Improvement of Society*. London: J. Johnson.

Mandelbrot, B. (1953) An informational theory of statistical structure of language. In *Communication Theory* (W. Jackson, ed.). London: Butterworths.

Mandelbrot, B. (1959) A note on a class of skew distribution functions: Analysis and critique of a paper by H. A. Simon. *Information and Control*, 2: 90–99.

Mandelbrot, B. (1961a) Final note on a class of skew distribution functions: Analysis and critique of a model due to H. A. Simon. *Information and Control*, 4: 198–216.

Mandelbrot, B. (1961b) Postscriptum to "Final Note." *Information and Control*, 4: 224–228.

Marchetti, C. and Nakicenovic, N. (1980) *The Dynamics of Energy Systems and the Logistic Substitution Model*. Laxenburg, Austria: International Institute for Applied Systems Analysis.

Mayer, T. F. and Arney, W. B. (1973–1974) Spectral analysis and the study of social change. In *Sociological Methodology* (H. L. Costner, ed.). San Francisco: Jorsey-Bass.

McClelland, C. A. (1968) Access to Berlin: The quantity and variety of events 1948–1963. In *Quantitative International Politics* (J. D. Singer, ed.). New York: Free Press.

McGinnis, R. (1968) A statistical model of social mobility. *American Sociological Review*, 33: 712–722.

Midlarsky, M. I. (1975) *On War: Political Violence in the International Arena*. New York: Free Press.

Milnor, J. W. (1954) Games against nature. In *Decision Processes* (R. M. Thrall, C. R. Coombs, and R. L. Davis, eds.). New York: Wiley.

Milstein, J. B. (1973) The Vietnam war from 1968 Tet Offensive to the 1970 Cambodian invasion: A quantitative analysis. In *Mathematical Approaches to Politics* (H. R. Alker, K. W. Deutsch, and A. H. Stoezel, eds.). Amsterdam: Elsevier.

Morris, C. (1942) *Paths of Life.* New York: Harper and Bros.

Morrison, P. A. (1967) Duration of residence and prospective migration: The evaluation of a stochastic model. *Demography*, 4: 553–561.

Nash, J. F. (1953) Two-person cooperative games. *Econometrica*, 21: 128–140.

Necker, L. A. (1832) Observations on some remarkable phenomena seen in Switzerland and an optical phenomenon which occurs in viewing of a crystal or geometric solid. *Philosophical Magazine*, 3rd series: 329–343.

Newcomb, T. M. (1961) *The Acquaintance Process.* New York: Rinehart and Winston.

Nordie, P. G. (1958) A longitudinal study of interpersonal interaction in a natural group setting (doctoral dissertation). Ann Arbor: University of Michigan.

O'Neill, B. (1970) The pattern of instability among nations: A test of Richardson's theory. *General Systems*, 15: 175–181.

Osgood, C. E. (1962) *An Alternative to War or Surrender.* Urbana: University of Illinois Press.

Osgood, C. E., Suci, G. J., and Tannenbaum, P. H. (1957) *The Measurement of Meaning.* Urbana: University of Illinois Press.

Osgood, R. E. (1957) *Limited War. The Challenge to American Strategy.* Chicago: University of Chicago Press.

Pareto, V. (1896–1897). *Cours d'economie politique.* Lausanne: F. Rouge.

Parzen, E. (1962) *Stochastic Processes.* San Francisco: Holden-Day.

Perner, J. (1978) The development of children's understanding of principles concerning decisions under risk and uncertainty (doctoral dissertation). Toronto: University of Toronto.

Perron, O. (1907) Zur Theorie der Matrizen. *Mathematische Annalen*, 64: 246–263.

Poston, T. and Stewart, I. (1978) Nonlinear modeling of multistable perception. *Behavioral Science*, 23: 318–334.

Prais, S. I. (1955) Measuring social mobility. *Journal of the Royal Statistical Association*, A, 118: 56–66.

Raiffa, H. (1953) Arbitration schemes for generalized two-person games. In *Contributions to the Theory of Games II* (H. W. Kuhn and A. W. Tucker, eds.). *Annals of Mathematical Studies*, 28. Princeton: Princeton University Press.

Raiffa, H. and Schlaifer, R. (1961) *Applied Statistical Decision Theory.* Boston: Graduate School of Business Administration, Harvard University.

Rapoport, A. (1956) The diffusion problem in mass behavior. *General Systems*, 1: 1–11.

Rapoport, A. (1958) Nets with reciprocity bias. *Bulletin of Mathematical Biophysics*, 20: 191–201.

Rapoport, A. (1966) *Two-person Game Theory.* Ann Arbor: University of Michigan Press.

Rapoport, A., Frenkel, O., and Perner, J. (1977) Experiments with cooperative 2 × 2 games. *Theory and Decision*, 8: 67–92.

Rapoport, A. and Guyer, M. (1966) A taxonomy of 2 × 2 games. *General Systems*, 11: 203–214.

Rapoport, A., Guyer, M., and Gordon, D. (1976) *The 2 × 2 Game.* Ann Arbor: University of Michigan Press.

Rapoport, A. and Horvath, W. J. (1961) A study of a large sociogram. *Behavioral Science*, 6: 279–291.

Rapoport, An., Rapoport, Am., and Livant, W. P. (1966) A study of lexical graphs. *Foundations of Language*, 2: 338–376.

Rashevsky, N. (1938) *Mathematical Biophysics.* Chicago: University of Chicago Press.

Rashevsky, N. (1951) *Mathematical Biology of Social Behavior*. Chicago: University of Chicago Press.

Reich, U.-P. (1972) Possible conflict structure of the European Security Conference. *International Journal of Game Theory*, 1: 131–145.

Rice, A. K., Hill, J. M. M., and Trist, E. L. (1950) The representation of labor turnover as a social process. *Human Relations*, 3: 349–381.

Richardson, L. F. (1948) War moods, I. *Psychometrika*, 13: 147–174.

Richardson, L. F. (1960a) *Statistics of Deadly Quarrels*. Chicago: Quadrangle Books.

Richardson, L. F. (1960b) *Arms and Insecurity*. Chicago: Quadrangle Books.

Riker, W. H. (1959) A test of the adequacy of the power index. *Behavioral Science*, 4: 120–131.

Rogers, A. (1965) *An Analysis of Interregional Migration in California*. Berkeley: University of California Press.

Rogers, A. (1968) *A Matrix Analysis of Interregional Population Growth and Distribution*. Berkeley: University of California Press.

Rosencrance, R. N. (1963) *Action and Reaction in World Politics. International System in Perspective*. Boston: Little Brown.

Rosencrance, R. N. (1966) Bipolarity, multipolarity, and the future. *Journal of Conflict Resolution*, 10: 314–327.

Rummel, R. J. (1964) Testing some possible predictors of conflict behavior within and between nations. *Peace Research Papers*, 1: 79–111.

Schelling, T. C. (1971) Dynamic models of segregation. *Journal of Mathematical Sociology*, 1: 143–186.

Schinnar, A. P. and Stewman, S. (1978) A class of Markov models of social mobility with duration memory patterns. *Journal of Mathematical Sociology*, 6: 61–86.

Shapley, L. S. (1953) A value for *n*-person games. In *Contributions to the Theory of Games*, II (H. W. Kuhn and A. W. Tucker, eds.). *Annals of Mathematics Studies*, 28. Princeton: Princeton University Press.

Shepard, R. N. (1962a) The analysis of proximities: multidimensional scaling with an unknown distance function. I. *Psychometrika*, 27: 125–140.

Shepard, R. N. (1962b) The analysis of proximities: multidimensional scaling with an unknown distance function. II. *Psychometrika*, 27: 219–246.

Shubik, M. (1975a) *The Uses and Methods of Gaming*. New York: Elsevier.

Shubik, M. (1975b) *Games for Society, Business, and War. Toward a Theory of Gaming*. New York: Elsevier.

Simon, H. A. (1955) On a class of skew distribution functions. *Biometrika*, 42: 426–439.

Simon, H. A. (1960) Some further notes on a class of skew distribution functions. *Information and Control*, 3: 80–88.

Simon, H. A. (1961a) Reply to "Final Note" by Benoit Mandelbrot. *Information and Control*, 4: 217–223.

Simon, H. A. (1961b) Reply to Dr. Mandelbrot's Post Scriptum. *Information and Control*, 4: 305–308.

Small, M. and Singer, J. D. (1979) Conflict in the international system, 1816–1977: Historical trends and policy futures. In *Challenges to America: U.S. Foreign Policy in the 1980's* (C. W. Kegley, Jr. and P. J. McGowan, eds.). Beverly Hills: Sage.

Smoker, P. (1965) Trade, defense, and the Richardson theory of arms races: A seven nation study. *Journal of Peace Research*, 2: 161–176.

Solomon, R. L. and Wynne, L. C. (1953) Traumatic avoidance learning in normal dogs. *Psychological Monograph* 67 (4).

Sorokin, P. (1927) *Social and Cultural Mobility.* Glencoe, Ill.: Free Press of Glencoe.

Steindl, J. (1965) *Random Processes and the Growth of Firms.* London: Griffin.

Stevens, S. S. (1959) Cross-modality validation of subjective scales for loudness, vibration and electric shock. *Journal of Experimental Psychology,* 57: 201–209.

Stevens, S. S. (1961a) To honor Fechner and to repeal his law. *Science,* 133: 80–86.

Stevens, S. S. (1961b) The psychophysics of sensory function. In *Sensory Communication* (W. A. Rosenblith, ed.). New York: Wiley.

Stewart, J. Q. (1948) Demographic gravitation; evidence and applications. *Sociometry,* 11: 31–58.

Taagepera, R., Shiffler, G. M., Perkins, R. T., and Wagner, D. L. (1975) Soviet-American and Israeli-Arab arms races and the Richardson model. *General Systems,* 20: 151–158.

Tryon, R. C. and Bailey, D. E. (1970) *Cluster Analysis.* New York: McGraw-Hill.

Tversky, A. (1972) Elimination by aspects. *Psychological Review,* 79: 281–299.

Von Neumann, J. (1928) Zur Theorie der Gesellschaftsspiele. *Mathematische Annalen,* 100: 295–320.

Von Neumann, J. and Morgenstern, O. (1947) *Theory of Games and Economic Behavior.* Princeton: University Press.

Weber, E. H. (1846) Der Tastsinn und das Gemeingefühl. In *Handwörterbuch der Physiologie* (R. Wagner, ed.). Braunschweig: Vieweg.

White, H. C. (1963) *An Anatomy of Kinship.* Englewood Cliffs: Prentice Hall.

White, H. (1970a) *Chains of Opportunity: System Model of Mobility in Organizations.* Cambridge, Mass.: Harvard University Press.

White, H. (1970b) Stayers and movers. *American Journal of Sociology,* 76: 307–314.

White, H. C., Boorman, S. A., and Breiger, R. L. (1976) Social structure from multiple networks, I. Block models of roles and positions. *American Journal of Sociology,* 81: 730–780.

Wilson, P. J. (1967) *A Malay Village and Malaysia: Social Values and Rural Development.* New Haven, Conn.: HRAF Press.

Wish, M., Deutsch, M., and Biener, L. (1972) Differences in perceived similarity of nations. In *Multidimensional Scaling, Theory and Applications in the Behavioral Sciences* (R. Kimholl, R. N. Shepard, and S. B. Neslove, eds.). Vol. II, New York: Seminar Press.

Yasuda, S. (1964) A methodological inquiry into social mobility. *American Sociological Review,* 29: 16–23.

Yearbook of World Armaments and Disarmament 1969–1970. Stockholm International Peace Research Institute. New York: Humanities Press, 1970–1973.

Young, H. P., Okada, N., and Hashimoto, T. (1980) *Cost Allocation in Water Resources Development —A Case Study of Sweden.* Laxenburg, Austria: Institute for Applied Systems Analysis.

Zeeman, E. C. (1976) Catastrophe theory. *Scientific American,* April, 1976: 65–83.

Zinnes, D. A. (1963) Expression and perception of hostility in inter-state relations (doctoral dissertation). Stanford University.

Zinnes, D. A., North, R. C., and Koch, H. E. (1961) Capability, threat, and the outbreak of war. In *International Politics and Foreign Policy.* (J. M. Rosenau, ed.). New York: Free Press.

Zipf, G. K. (1949) *Human Behavior and the Principle of Least Effort.* Cambridge, Mass.: Addison-Wesley.

Author Index

Subject Index

accident(s), 147f, 150f, 155, 161, 191f
  proneness, 148, 150, 304, 399
actor, 322, 328, 353, 364, 405
  pivotal coalition member, 362ff
  power of, 405
adaptive mutations, 85
addiction effect, 201
affiliation, 176f
age distribution, 40ff, 44ff, 49ff, 157, 220
aggregation/disaggregation ratio, 181
aging of a population, 49, 51
aims, 322, 325 (see also "goals")
alchemy, 372
allergy model, 161 (see also "contagion
  effect")
alliances, 77, 133ff, 284
  Anglo-French accord, 135
  Anglo-Russian agreement, 135
  Dual Alliance, 434, 437ff, 442
  size distribution, 177ff
  tightness (rigidity) of alliance structure,
    132ff
  Triple Alliance, 135
  Triple Entente, 135, 434ff, 442
allocation(s)
  "fair", 369
  problems, 103
almost zero blocks, 302
anabolism, 41
analysis of variance, 308
analytic-descriptive
  approach, 325
  model(s), 14ff, 25, 132, 140, 239
anthropology, 14
anthropomorphism, 40
antibiotics, 85
anti-war demonstrations, 62
arithmetic, 3
  clock, 5
  of rotations, 5

armanent(s)
  budgets, costs, levels, expenditures, 75ff, 80f,
    82, 106ff, 117, 126, 136, 240, 475
  policies, 117
arms
  control, 106ff, 117, 473ff
  nuclear, 81
  race(s), 19, 62, 68, 71ff, 77ff, 81ff, 108, 117,
    129, 136, 240, 432, 473ff
aspirations
  level of, 132f
  incompatible, 133f (see also incompatible
    goals, aims)
assimilation, 416ff
  operationalizing of, 418
astrology, 372
astronomy, 372
atomic bomb, 468
attraction unit, 296
attractiveness, 295
Australian ballot, 332
axiomatic approach (formulation), 24f, 325
axioms
  Choice Axiom, 222ff
  existence of utility scale, 22f
  Impossibility Theorem, 336ff
  metric, 306
  physical laws as, 24
  prescribed marriage system, 274ff
  solution of two-person cooperative game,
    380
balance
  of power, 109, 136, 475f
  of terror, 83
balanced graph, 282ff
barefoot empiricism, 426f
bargaining, 356, 384
  leverage (advantage), 357f. 359, 384
Bariloche model (global), 115f
benevolence, 378

496